DICKENS: THE CRITICAL HERITAGE

THE CRITICAL HERITAGE SERIES

GENERAL EDITOR: B. C. SOUTHAM, M.A., B.LITT. (OXON.)

Formerly Department of English, Westfield College, University of London

Volumes in the series include

JANE AUSTEN	B. C. Southam
BROWNING	Boyd Litzinger and Donald Smalley
BYRON	Andrew Rutherford
COLERIDGE	J. R. de J. Jackson
DICKENS	Philip Collins
DRYDEN	James and Helen Kinsley
HENRY FIELDING	Ronald Paulson and Thomas Lockwood
THOMAS HARDY	R. G. Cox
HAWTHORNE	J. Donald Crowley
HENRY JAMES	Roger Gard
JAMES JOYCE (2 vols.)	Robert H. Deming
KIPLING	Roger Lancelyn Green
D. H. LAWRENCE	R. P. Draper
MILTON	John T. Shawcross
SCOTT	John O. Hayden
SPENSER	R. N. Cummings
SWIFT	Kathleen Williams
SWINBURNE	Clyde K. Hyder
TENNYSON	J. D. Jump
THACKERAY	Geoffrey Tillotson and Donald Hawes
TROLLOPE	Donald Smalley
OSCAR WILDE	Karl Beckson

DICKENS

THE CRITICAL HERITAGE

Edited by
PHILIP COLLINS
Professor of English Literature
University of Leicester

NEW YORK
BARNES & NOBLE, INC.

First Published in Great Britain 1971

Published in the United States of America 1971
by Barnes & Noble Inc., New York, N.Y.

© *Philip Collins 1971*

SBN 389 04060 6

Printed in Great Britain

General Editor's Preface

The reception given to a writer by his contemporaries and near-contemporaries is evidence of considerable value to the student of literature. On one side we learn a great deal about the state of criticism at large and in particular about the development of critical attitudes towards a single writer; at the same time, through private comments in letters, journals, or marginalia, we gain an insight upon the tastes and literary thought of individual readers of the period. Evidence of this kind helps us to understand the writer's historical situation, the nature of his immediate reading-public, and his response to these pressures.

The separate volumes in the *Critical Heritage Series* present a record of this early criticism. Clearly, for many of the highly productive and lengthily reviewed nineteenth- and twentieth-century writers, there exists an enormous body of material; and in these cases the volume editors have made a selection of the most important views, significant for their intrinsic critical worth or for their representative quality—perhaps even registering incomprehension!

For earlier writers, notably pre-eighteenth century, the materials are much scarcer and the historical period has been extended, sometimes far beyond the writer's lifetime, in order to show the inception and growth of critical views which were initially slow to appear.

In each volume the documents are headed by an Introduction, discussing the material assembled and relating the early stages of the author's reception to what we have come to identify as the critical tradition. The volumes will make available much material which would otherwise be difficult of access and it is hoped that the modern reader will be thereby helped towards an informed understanding of the ways in which literature has been read and judged.

B.C.S.

Contents

CONTENTS

CONTENTS

CONTENTS

Preface

Most of the 168 items reprinted here are reviews or essays from periodicals, published during Dickens's lifetime and in the decade or so after his death, and most of them have been abbreviated, often drastically. This was a period when a review of a single book could extend over ten thousand words (the *Quarterly Review* devoted about 17 000 words to *Pickwick* and *Sketches by Boz*, in October 1837), and a substantial assessment of an author's work might go well beyond that length. I have preferred to represent a wide range of response to all Dickens's fictional works, and a few others, rather than reprint entire a handful of the most intelligent, or representative, reviews: but I realize that my cuts, like my selection of items, are necessarily a very personal choice, and that another editor, as well-qualified as myself, would have plied his scissors quite differently. Inevitably, the full argument being developed by a critic has sometimes been ill-represented when so much of his evidence has been omitted; and sometimes I have selected from a long item one or two minor points, rather than the author's main argument (which may be of less interest, or may have been fully represented in other items). The reader should, therefore, remember that my aim has been to show a wide range of contemporary responses to Dickens, rather than always to give adequate evidence for an assessment of his critics' qualities. These qualities will, of course, often enough be apparent, but any reader who wants to be sure of being fair to, say, Mrs Oliphant as a critic should consult her items in their original fullness rather than rely on the selections which my special purposes have led me to make.

I have also included some less formal reactions to Dickens, from letters, diaries, and reports of the conversations of his contemporaries. Particularly I have thus tried to show how he struck various people illustrious in literary and public life.

The materials available for such a collection are overwhelmingly numerous, and I am far from having examined them all. The task of doing so may be gauged from what is doubtless the most complete published list of reviews of one novel—Professor Kathleen Tillotson's, in an Appendix to her Clarendon edition of *Oliver Twist* (1966). She lists 109 reviews of *Oliver Twist*, published while it was still being serialized, 19 of the three-volume edition, and (very selectively) a further 21 discussions in other articles about Dickens and contemporary fiction up to 1846—a total of 149 items, from 42 periodicals. I have consulted 25 of these 42, though not in all cases for their discussions of *Oliver Twist*; and, as Professor Tillotson's list reminds us, a single periodical might have a number of reviews of one novel as it had appeared serially. To cite an example: Dickens's letter of thanks to the Editor of the *Sun* (14 April 1848) for its perceptive reviews of *Dombey and Son* sent me—or, to be more precise, my long-suffering wife—to the files of that newspaper. The review which had pleased Dickens (*Sun*, 13 April 1848) had, it was discovered, been preceded by thirteen others, many quite substantial, of the earlier serial parts. The *Spectator* (24 November 1838) noted how Dickens's popularity was promoted by serialization, and the possibility of a book's thus getting twenty notices instead of one (see No. 10). This fact obviously increases an editor's task in collecting, and selecting, his materials. Moreover, the number of periodicals being published increased enormously during Dickens's lifetime—about three-fold between the period of *Pickwick* and *Oliver*, and 1870 when *Edwin Drood* appeared and Dickens died—so, although (as my impression is) the practice of reviewing every serial number became less common, the number of reviews tended to increase. And Professor Tillotson's list excluded provincial newspapers and foreign periodicals—but already, in 1838, John Forster was able to rejoice that 'all England, America, and the literati of France and Germany' concurred in hailing Dickens as a genius (*Examiner*, 25 November 1838, 740), and he could have added Russia and probably several other European nations.

Periodicals are not, of course, the only sources for my collection, though they are much the most important, and I have consulted over a hundred and fifty of them. Nor is the choice restricted to reviews, numerous enough from Dickens's long and prolific career. There are general assessments, controversial exchanges, obituary tributes, and much else, both in periodicals and in books, pamphlets, lectures, sermons, speeches, letters, diaries—most of which forms of response to him I have tried to represent, however inadequately. The world's darling for a third of a century, and in an age of publicity, Dickens is incomparably well-documented. Almost everybody whose letters and biography have come down to us has something to say about Dickens:

they read him, they attended his public readings, they heard him speechifying, or they met him. A short essay could even be written about Victorian Prime Ministers and Dickens: Melbourne rejecting 'that low debasing style', Russell weeping with his wife over *David Copperfield*, Gladstone too responding to Dickens's pathos but noting that in *Nicholas Nickleby* there was 'No church . . ., and the motives are not those of religion', Disraeli sure that Dickens had written himself out by the sixties but much taking to him personally when they met a few weeks before his death.

I have worked, on and off, at this project for four years, and could draw on the accumulations of some years' previous study of Dickens; but manifestly, to master all this material, I could well soldier on for forty. My deadline is passed, however; other duties call, and my wife and family would like to see me again. I have, I hope, consulted all the obvious sources, and some of the less obvious ones. Least adequate, as I well realize, is my coverage of newspapers, of which I have consulted only a few. If the best review of *Our Mutual Friend* appeared in the *West Hartlepool Bi-weekly Echo*, I not unwillingly leave to some future researcher the triumph of rediscovering it. Nor have I made any systematic attempt to survey, or represent by extracts, non-British reviews. This is a large omission (and a large admission), but time, and my learning, are limited. I have included a few American items, and one French, but do not claim that these are the best or the most representative; they are ones I happen to know and find interesting.

'Few are perhaps aware that Mr Dickens once wrote an opera,' wrote R. H. Horne in 1844; 'not very many perhaps know that he wrote a farce for the theatre, which was acted; and the great majority of his readers do not at all care to remember that he wrote a *Life of Grimaldi*, in two volumes' (*The New Spirit of the Age*, i, 46). I have not disturbed the ashes of these dead works by reprinting reviews of them or of other minor items, unless the contemporary reaction was important in the history of Dickens's reception (as was the case over the travel books and some of the now-forgotten Christmas writings). With much greater reluctance, I have saved space by excluding accounts and assessments of his extra-literary activities—his appearances as a notability at banquets, meetings and other such functions, his performances in plays and, above all, his public readings from his works. He was a great public figure, as well as a creative artist, and for his contemporaries these public activities mattered a good deal. My collection is the weaker for not being able to represent them.

The arrangement of the book is chronological, but items devoted to a particular novel have been grouped together, whether they were immediate reviews or later comments. To help readers consulting this book for the reception of one novel, I have headed these groups with a summary of the novel's place in the development of Dickens's reputation. The selections end—apart from an *envoi* by Henry James —at the time of the publication of the *Letters* (1880-2).

Acknowledgments

Many friends, colleagues and students, and many strangers, have helped me by answering enquiries, lending me rare pamphlets, etc., checking details, or suggesting inclusions. To specify all their kindnesses would take pages, and might suggest that I myself did no work at all: so I record their names and repeat to them the warm gratitude I have offered them privately. I thank Mrs Madeline House, of the *Pilgrim Letters*; Mr Leslie Staples and Dr Michael Slater, past and present editors of the *Dickensian*; the late Noel C. Peyrouton, founder-editor of *Dickens Studies*; Professors Sylvère Monod, K. J. Fielding, Harry Stone, and Edgar Rosenberg; Dr Isobel Armstrong, Madame Anny Sadrin, Dr Gunther Hamel, Mr William J. Carlton, Mr Arnold U. Ziegler, Mr John W. Gibson, Mr Eric Trudgill, Mr Mick Rodger, Dr William Oddie, and Mr Dennis Wright. My colleague Mr J. L. Madden, Bibliographer of the Victorian Studies Centre, has given me much useful advice about Victorian periodicals (in which the Centre is specially interested), and Mr Patrick Scott has helped in the sad business of reducing my original draft to a more publishable length. Dr Michael Slater and Dr J. R. Harvey kindly allowed me to use material from their unpublished theses, respectively '*The Chimes*': *its Materials, Making, and Public Reception* (D.Phil., Oxford, 1965), and *The Concern of Serial Novelists with the Illustration of their Work in the Nineteenth Century* (Ph.D., Cambridge, 1969). In an Appendix, I thank various people who have helped me to identify the authors of anonymous items, notably Professor Walter E. Houghton of the *Wellesley Index to Victorian Periodicals*. I have looked for advice often, and never in vain, to the General Editor of this series, Mr B. C. Southam.

The Research Board of the University of Leicester gave a generous grant towards the cost of photo-copying materials, and the University Library staff have been most helpful in tracing and obtaining obscure items. Three typists have struggled bravely and successfully with my handwriting: Mrs Win Abell, Miss Sylvia Gurney, and Miss Anne Sowter.

My sympathies go, posthumously, to my predecessors in tasks such as this, who had to copy out in long-hand the extracts they needed, and they may almost be forgiven their errors of transcription, which were usually numerous. My heartfelt thanks go to Mr Xerox, or whoever it was that invented photo-copying. The universities of the world should shower honorary degrees upon this notable benefactor of all academics, and the present series, like many other such, might well be dedicated to him.

I wish, however, to dedicate the present volume to my dear wife Joyce, who, even without the advantage of being a dedicated Dickensian, toiled uncomplainingly among the bookstacks, helped with the scissors and paste, rescued our infant son from his experiments with these delectable toys, bore with the bad temper that overcomes me whenever I am writing, inspirited me when tired, and doubled my pleasures by sharing them.

Philip Collins

Notes on the Text

Typographical errors in the originals have been silently corrected, but mis-spellings of proper names have been left uncorrected; these are never puzzling or misleading, and the error may indicate the author's degree of familiarity with his subject. One convention has been standardized, except in quotations from manuscripts (letters, etc.): the titles of books have been italicized, to help the skipping eye on the look-out for references to a particular book. Most quotations from Dickens's novels have been omitted, but these and other omissions have been indicated.

When citing Dickens's letters, I have generally followed the convention used by the *Pilgrim Edition* of the *Letters of Charles Dickens* (Oxford, 1965), e.g., *To* T. N. Talfourd, 30 August 1837. As the *Pilgrim Edition* is replacing the former standard edition (the 'Nonesuch' *Letters of Charles Dickens*, ed. Walter Dexter, 3 vols, 1938), references to *Nonesuch* will soon be out-dated, and have always been inconvenient, since only 877 copies of that edition were printed. Letters are from *Pilgrim* (up to 1841) and *Nonesuch* after that, except that letters to Miss Coutts are cited from *Letters from Charles Dickens to Angela Burdett-Coutts 1841–1865*, ed. Edgar Johnson (1953). Any other exceptions are mentioned in the text. These volumes are cited by the abbreviations *Pilgrim*, *Nonesuch* and *Coutts*. Other short-titles are:

Life   John Forster, *The Life of Charles Dickens* (1872–4), ed. J. W. T. Ley (1928).

Dickens Critics   *The Dickens Critics*, ed. George H. Ford and Lauriat Lane, Jr. (Ithaca, New York, 1961).

Ford   George H. Ford, *Dickens and his Readers: Aspects of Novel-Criticism since 1836* (Princeton, 1955).

Introduction

No one thinks first of Mr Dickens as a writer. He is at once, through his books, a friend. He belongs among the intimates of every pleasant-tempered and large-hearted person. He is not so much the guest as the inmate of our homes. He keeps holidays with us, he helps us to celebrate Christmas with heartier cheer, he shares at every New Year in our good wishes: for, indeed, it is not in his purely literary character that he has done most for us, it is as a man of the largest humanity, who has simply used literature as the means by which to bring himself into relation with his fellow-men, and to inspire them with something of his own sweetness, kindness, charity, and good-will. He is the great magician of our time. His wand is a book, but his power is in his own heart. It is a rare piece of good fortune for us that we are the contemporaries of this benevolent genius. . . .[1]

These are the words, not of a bookloving Miss Cosyhearts, but of the great American scholar Charles Eliot Norton, respected friend of artists and writers on both sides of the Atlantic: and these specially 'friendly' feelings were, of course, evoked by Dickens's characters as well as by his whole artistic and public personality. 'All his characters are my personal friends'—and, again, this is not quoted from a book-man of the *Essays of Elia* school, but from Tolstoy, who continued: 'I am constantly comparing them with living persons, and living persons with them, and what a spirit there was in all he wrote.'[2] Dickens was not deceiving himself nor exaggerating, though he may have been sipping at a sweet that contained some poison for him, when he spoke of 'that particular relation (personally affectionate and like no other man's) which subsists between me and the public'.[3]

It seems useful to start from this peculiarity, indeed uniqueness, of Dickens's standing in the minds and hearts of his countrymen, and of readers throughout the world in his own day and since. It does not of itself lead to anything which, by the least exacting of definitions, can be classed as 'criticism'—Norton's 'No one thinks first of Mr. Dickens as a writer' is an inauspicious start for critical discussion— but few who wrote about Dickens in his time, whether participating in this affection or reacting against it, could altogether escape from this 'particular relation' between him and his public. And affection was not the only complicating emotion. 'He is less the author of *Pickwick*, of *Copper-field*, of *Bleak House*, than he is Charles Dickens,' wrote Mrs Oliphant in 1855; 'and we confess that we cannot regard him with the same affection or the same indulgence in the latter character as in the former' (No. 96). For, as she explains, 'he has assumed a leader's place not only in literature, but in the world, in morals, in philanthropy, in questions of social interest.' This offended Mrs Oliphant, both on artistic and political grounds, but for many readers it was a major ingredient in their affectionate respect for him. But whether readers thought of him as a friend, or as the phenomenon 'Charles Dickens' rather than a mere author, he was to this extent accorded a supra-literary status quite unlike that which any other English writer has ever enjoyed; for how-ever one regarded his benevolence and his views on questions of social interest, it was common ground among his admirers and detractors that he was, at least, a considerable author, and no one could deny his enormous and widespread popularity. 'A writer like our author,' wrote a reviewer in 1844, 'with all his benevolence and good intention, disarms criticism of half its point'[4] and many such reviews had, a few months earlier, greeted *A Christmas Carol*, the extra-literary institu-tional Dickens work *par excellence*. 'Most men would as soon think of dissecting a first cousin as of criticizing Charles Dickens,' said *Fraser's* in 1850 (No. 72). The point was put, with more asperity and indigna-tion, by another reviewer a week or so before Dickens's death in 1870: 'he never, by any chance, encounters genuine criticism, and as, if he were to write the most arrant nonsense in the world (which we fear he now not unoften does), nobody would have the candour to say so in print, we may, perhaps, venture to observe'—and criticisms follow, with George Eliot brought in to demonstrate, by contrast, Dickens's deficiencies.[5] Two years later, when her *Middlemarch* was appearing in parts, the *Daily Telegraph* commented that they were causing a stir comparable to what Dickens's monthly 'green leaves' had excited: 'his current story was really a topic of the day; it seemed something almost akin to politics and news—as if it belonged not so much to literature but to events.'[6] Dickens's novels, throughout his career, were a more widespread 'event' than George Eliot's: the *Middlemarch* parts were selling about 5 000, his had ranged between 20 000 and 50 000 for shilling-part serials, and well over 100 000 for the novels in the cheaper weekly forms. Even Lord Acton, who so ad-mired her work, had to confess: 'I am ashamed to think how much more often I return to Dickens than to George Eliot'—Dickens was 'worth anything to busy men, because his fun is so hearty and so easy, and he arouses the emotions by such direct and simple methods.'[8] Not the highest of tributes to Dickens's art and significance; but Victorian readers, even such sophisticated ones as Acton, were less inhibited than we are in acknowledging that hearty fun is a precious literary achievement, and other critics will demonstrate that, highly as Dickens's fun was valued, other qualities were recognized and discussed too.

By the 1870s many critics found George Eliot more impressive (if daunting), and indeed from the late forties many had preferred Thackeray. As the actor W. C. Macready commented in 1849, *Vanity Fair* was, 'as far as style goes, rather to be preferred to my friend Dickens's. There is more mark of the educated man in the freedom of the language'; Thackeray's novel was 'second to none of the present day, which is an admission I make almost grudgingly for Dickens's sake; but the truth is the truth'.[9] The point was argued, more fully and less reluctantly, in scores of reviews and essays in the next decade or so. The comparison became as much one of the set-pieces of Victorian journalism as, in the seventeenth century, had been the comparison between Shakespeare and Jonson—and on very similar lines, with Jonson and Thackeray figuring as 'the educated man' (and, partly for this reason, winning the preference of many educated critics), and Shakespeare and Dickens being credited with the distinction of greater 'genius' (or was it a consolation prize? for one is often reminded of D. H. Lawrence's experience: 'In the early days they were always telling me I had got genius, as if to console me for not having their own incomparable advantages'[10]). The most famous of the Shakespeare/Jonson set-pieces, and the one which did most to confirm Shakespeare as the supreme dramatist, was Dryden's in the dialogue on *Dramatic Poets* (1668); much of Neander's panegyric of Shakespeare can be adapted to describe Dickens, and the climax of his comparison (after acknowledging that Jonson was 'the more correct poet') fits the Thackeray/Dickens comparison: 'I admire him, but I love Shakespeare.' Many Victorian critics more admired Thackeray or George Eliot, but nobody (I think) expressed for them the love which Dickens so widely inspired. As Cornelius C. Felton (another Harvard professor, like Norton) had commented back in 1843, when Dickens was only thirty, this remarkable new writer had 'started into a celebrity, which, for its extraordinary influence upon social feelings and even political institutions, and for the strength of favourable regard and even warm personal attachment by which it has been accompanied all over the

3

world, we believe is without a parallel in the history of letters.'[11] And
many reminiscences by later Victorians comment on this incomparable
status of Dickens in his times—Henry James, for instance (No. 168),
or Justin McCarthy recalling the 1850s: 'No one born in the younger
generation can easily understand, from any illustration that later
years can give him, the immensity of the popular homage which
Dickens then enjoyed.'[12] And, as several of my quotations have
indicated, his popularity was not confined to Britain nor to the
Anglo-Saxon world. America, where prices could be low because
overseas authors enjoyed no copyright protection, quickly printed far
more copies of Dickens than circulated in Britain, and even during the
1830s he was being translated into several European languages. R. H.
Horne was able to report, in 1844, that his works were as popular in
Germany as in Britain, were available in French, Italian, and Dutch,
and 'some of his works are, we believe, translated into Russian'
(No. 58). Horne's information was correct: and, as Professor Henry
Gifford has remarked: 'no foreign writer of that time (or since) ever
became so thoroughly domiciled in the Russian imagination' (see
Bibliography). When Dickens died, not only did the poor as well as the
rich and the articulate present their homage, but also the mourning was
international. It is a remarkable feature of English literature that it has
given to the world, in Shakespeare and Dickens, the two supremely
popular classic authors, in comparison with whom even the greatest of
writers, ancient and modern—Homer, Sophocles, Dante, Molière,
Goethe, the great novelists of France, Russia, and America—are
minority tastes outside, or even inside, their own countries. This of
course does not prove, nor do I assert, that Dickens is necessarily a
greater novelist than Balzac, Tolstoy, Dostoyevsky, or (to come home)
George Eliot: only to recognize that Dickens's qualities are more
readily and widely relished, and have better survived translation into
other languages and presentation to other cultures.

II

THE INITIAL RECEPTION

The extraordinary rapidity of Dickens's success—and not merely
widespread popularity, but critical esteem—has often been described,
and is a reiterated topic in many of the early reviews and later retrospective assessments. 'PICKWICK TRIUMPHANT', Dickens was

soon able to report; a novel he had undertaken as a job in February 1836 ('The work will be no joke, but the emolument is too tempting to resist,' he told his fiancée) was, inside nine months, a candidate for immortality: 'If I were to live a hundred years, and write three novels in each,' he told his publishers, 'I should never be so proud of any of them, as I am of Pickwick, feeling as I do, that it has made its own way, and hoping, as I must own I hope, that long after my hand is withered as the pens it held, Pickwick will be found on many a dusty shelf with many a better book'.[13] A few years later, Thackeray (who had so much longer to wait for recognition and acclaim) wrote about the 'envious critics' of the day: 'How eager they are to predict a man's fall, how unwilling to acknowledge his rise! If a man write a popular work, he is sure to be snarled at; if a literary man rise to eminence out of his profession, all his old comrades are against him. They can't pardon his success ...'[14] This was not Dickens's experience, though he was to hear various snarls and dire predictions. He not only became the rage with the public, but was also widely and enthusiastically reviewed. The heavy quarterlies were all soon paying him lengthy and respectful attention. *Sketches by Boz* (1st series) had appeared in February 1836, and the serialization of *Pickwick* began in April 1836; substantial assessments appeared in the *London and Westminster* in July 1837, the *Quarterly* in October 1837 and June 1839, and the *Edinburgh* in October 1838—the last of these representing 'the "*imprimatur*" of what may properly be regarded as the highest critical tribunal'.[15]

H. G. Wells, discussing his début as a novelist in the 1890s, mentioned the 'odd conventions' of literary criticism in those days: 'Anybody fresh who turned up was treated as an aspirant Dalai Lama is treated, and scrutinized for evidence of his predecessor's soul. . . . In the course of two or three years I was welcomed as a second Dickens, a second Bulwer Lytton and a second Jules Verne.'[16] Plenty of this soul-searching greeted Dickens's early work. 'The Soul of Hogarth has migrated into the Body of Mr Dickens,'[17] Sydney Smith pronounced in September 1837, before the journalists began what became a routine comparison with this artist (see Nos. 19, 58). A novelist so visually graphic was often compared with artists—he was 'the Cruikshank of writers' (*Spectator*, December 1836), 'the literary Teniers of the metropolis' (No. 15), 'in literature very much what Prout is in art' (No. 27), he was in prose 'What Crabbe was in poetry, and Wilkie in painting' (No. 48), he was in various respects like Landseer, Leech, Wilkie, the Dutch painters, Maclise and Frank Stone (No. 73), he was 'the

Constable of Fiction' (*Athenæum*, December 1855, 1392), he was unselectively Pre-Raphælite (No. 86). These comparisons have taken us beyond his forebears; and by the Pre-Raphælite times he was being compared—as indeed he compared himself—to a taker of daguerreotypes, sun-pictures, photographs (Nos. 56, 81, 83, 98, 100), a frequent image in Victorian novel-criticism, the aesthetic bearings of which have still (I think) to be adequately explored. Meanwhile, of course, Dickens's literary ancestry, indebtednesses and analogues had been discussed by the critics. The *Athenæum* reviewer's analysis of *Pickwick* is well-known: 'two pounds of Smollett, three ounces of Sterne, a handful of Hook, a dash of a grammatical Pierce Egan' (No.3). It became a conversational cliché to argue that 'Boz is a perfect Smollett; others [will tell you] that he is a Sterne; and others again that he can be a Fielding when he chooses'—though in fact, as this rather unenthusiastic reviewer acknowledged, he 'really deserves to be ranked as an originalist' (*Monthly Review*, February 1837, i, 153).

Reviewers of the early works (notably John Forster) explored more fully Dickens's relation to these and other great eighteenth-century predecessors—Addison, Defoe, Goldsmith—and tried to assess his stature by comparisons with them, with Scott and even with Shakespeare. He was soon recognized as standing above the ruck of the metropolitan 'wags' of the 1820s and 1830s, Egan, Hook, Poole, Hood, though the analogy with Egan was still invoked by reviewers who remembered how the furore for his *Life in London* had come and gone, and who guessed that the 'Boz-mania' might similarly subside, with Dickens writing himself out through haste, greed, and carelessness (Nos. 18, 23, 25). Washington Irving was another contemporary figure often invoked (Nos. 15, 16, 19), but this comparison, like that with Cervantes (Nos. 2, 19), proved unilluminating beyond the special case of parts of *Pickwick*. Dickens's concern with the humble and the young led to comparisons with Crabbe and Wordsworth, his delight in the quaint and idiosyncratic called up Lamb and Leigh Hunt as analogues (cf. *Pilgrim*, i, 137, 414; *To* Fitzgerald, 2 February 1866). Some of his early experiments in the horrific were compared with, or alleged to derive from, Victor Hugo's (*Morning Chronicle*, 11 February 1836, 3, on 'A Visit to Newgate'). Caroline Fox, reading *Master Humphrey's Clock*, wrote in her journal (18 February 1841):

That man [Boz] is carrying out Carlyle's work more emphatically than any; he forces the sympathies of all into unwonted channels, and teaches us that Punch and Judy men, beggar children, and daft old men are also of our species, and are not, more than ourselves, removed from the sphere of the heroic. He is doing a world of good in a very healthy way.[18]

Not what we now think of as a Carlylean programme: but this is one of the earliest attempts to see Dickens in relation to Carlyle. Some later commentators mention this, but few discuss it at any length; it is indeed surprising that this intellectual relationship, later acknowledged by Dickens in his dedication to *Hard Times* and his Preface to *A Tale of Two Cities* (and more fully in letters unknown to his reviewers), received so little attention—and none, I think, that much clarifies the issue. Few other literary analogues or influences were much discussed.

He was early proclaimed 'the Living Shakespeare'[19]—or was it, as Edward Fitzgerald suggested, 'a little Shakespeare—a Cockney Shakespeare, if you will'?[20]—but few critics took this suggestive comparison much further than brief assertions that Dickens rivalled him in the number of memorable characters created (e.g., Nos. 22, 95), that they were both great imaginative, rather than realistic, authors (Nos. 73, 148), and that the novel was to the Victorian period what the drama had been to the Elizabethan (e.g., *North British Review*, February 1863, xxxviii, 169). Dickens's close friend John Forster suggested a more promising approach. In his review of *Our Mutual Friend*, where he reiterates the argument that Dickens's novels are unified works of art, not a series of happy dips, he develops a notion of the 'true unity so perfectly shown . . . in the literature of England', notably in Shakespeare. (Forster is implicitly rebuking Hippolyte Taine, whose recently-published history of English literature greatly riled him: see No. 97.)

Latinized races accuse English writers of a disregard of unity in works of art, and yet . . . although we recognize even more thoroughly than our neighbours the demand for unity of action, what we mean by that is not outward simplicity and singleness of plot, but a well-harmonized relation of all parts to one central thought. . . . [Forster illustrates this by discussing *Love's Labour's Lost*, *The Merchant of Venice*, *King Lear*, *Julius Caesar*, and *Tom Jones*, before proceeding to *Our Mutual Friend*.] Mr Dickens invariably fulfils in his novels this condition of deep-seated unity which has been always recognized in English art. All readers can feel that he does so. . . .[21]

As I have argued elsewhere (see Bibliography), Forster's reviews of Dickens are of special interest, for often they represent, at least in their general drift, Dickens's own opinions. Forster had unique opportunities for knowing what Dickens was trying to do, and, aware too how sensitive he was to unfavourable or misguided criticism, was un-likely to print, for him to see, anything he would have disliked. I have, therefore, reprinted a number of Forster's reviews, but not his criti-ques in the *Life*, a book which all readers of this collection are likely to have at hand.

One other form of comparison between Dickens and his fellow-authors may be mentioned: his association with current genres of the novel. After he—so quickly—strode clear of the metropolitan humor-ists with whom some early reviewers aligned him, he was not much afflicted with such attempts to categorize him. But *Oliver Twist* (1837–9), following close upon Bulwer Lytton's *Paul Clifford* (1830) and *Eugene Aram* (1832), and seen in juxtaposition to Harrison Ainsworth's *Rookwood* (1833) and *Jack Sheppard* (1838–9), led to his being included in the 'Newgate School' of novelists, which was being fiercely assailed (often for personal reasons) in *Fraser's Magazine* and elsewhere. Dickens was indignant about this, and did his best to reply to the 'jolter-headed enemies' who had made this allegation, in the 1841 Preface to *Oliver Twist* (see No. 12). Dickens's Prefaces, it may here be noted, mostly consist of replies to his critics (usually unnamed); he defends his characters and incidents as more credible, his institutional pictures as more representative, his ideas as more just and salutary, than they have recognized. Again, as these Prefaces are so easily available, I have not reprinted them here.

Dickens did not continue, after *Oliver Twist*, with further studies in the criminal underworld, and nothing that he wrote for some years associated him much with a group (except with his imitators in, for instance, the writing of Christmas stories). Near the end of his career, however, another moralistic critical protest was made, against the new 'Sensation School'.[22] One of its leading figures, Wilkie Collins, was much associated with Dickens and his weekly magazines, and certainly Dickens's novels contained 'sensational' elements, so some reviewers included his novels in articles on this new phenomenon of popular literature. But this attempt to place him in a group was not sustained, nor did he find it as vexatious as the 'Newgate' taunts. He was not writing much at this period—only *Great Expectations* (1860–1) and *Our Mutual Friend* (1864–5)—and neither these nor his other recent novels contained the characteristic ingredients of the main 'Sensation Novels', bigamy, beautiful wicked women, guilty secrets, and so on.

A reason why his work was sometimes associated in the public, or the critic's, mind with inferior popular literature was that his novels were familiarized to a large and often unsophisticated public through dramatizations (over which, in the current state of copyright, he had no control). 'In estimating the probable effects of these writings of Mr Dickens,' wrote a reviewer in 1845, 'we must remember that, in the shape of plays, they have been represented at most of the theatres in the country. In this process of transmutation, the better and more sober parts necessarily disappear . . .' (No. 56). The popularity of these plays from Dickens was unbounded ('Boz furnishes subjects to play-wrights and farce-writers') and lasting ('What', asked a critic in 1871, 'will become of the English stage when the public has grown weary, if it ever does grow weary, of dramatic versions of the stories of the late Mr Dickens?').[23] Henry James, looking back on his childhood in the forties and fifties, recalls the imaginative potency of these drama-tizations, as also of the Phiz and Cruikshank illustrations, and he hints at the degree to which these renderings did Dickens a critical disservice by displacing the novels, in one's memory, by crude simplications or distortions (No. 168).

III

THE ROCKET AND THE STICK

Like many authors, Dickens sometimes claimed that he did not read or regard reviews, but of course he did and he minded. As I have re-marked, his Prefaces are largely devoted to answering criticisms that had appeared during the novels' serialization. Professor Ford lists, in an Appendix to *Dickens and his Readers*, much of the available evidence for his awareness of reviews, and some of my headnotes give instances of it. Not all the reviews he read were complimentary. The reviewers I quoted earlier, who maintained that 'most men would as soon think of dissecting a first cousin as of criticizing Charles Dickens', and that he was a national sacred cow who could write twaddle and none would dare to protest, were of course much exaggerating his immunity to criticism, as my selections will show. Though, as I have indicated, he was immediately greeted in 1836–7 with widespread and respectful critical attention, his 'faults' (of exaggeration, inability to construct a plot, etc.) were also noted at this time, and the durability of his talent and popular appeal was soon in question. Abraham Hayward, who ended his review-article in the *Quarterly* (October

1837: see No. 16) with the famous prophecy that, unless Dickens mended his ways, he who had 'risen like a rocket' would 'come down like the stick', had detected already a falling-off in *Pickwick*: 'the last three or four numbers are certainly much inferior to the former ones' (lix, 514). Throughout his career, the fatal decline of Dickens's talent was confidently proclaimed, though these reports of his literary demise were later discovered to have been greatly exaggerated. The first few numbers of *Master Humphrey's Clock* showed that his 'creative faculty ... was already on the decline', as subsequent publications confirmed (*The Times*, 27 December 1845, 6). By 1845, he had 'written himself out', and by now relied on self-plagiarizing (No. 48). His reputation was 'some time since on the decline' (*Oxford and Cambridge Review*, January 1846, ii, 43), from *Pickwick* he had declined to *Chuzzlewit* (No. 53). Ten years later he was still 'hourly going down in reputation [said Charles Lever] but his sales continue so "*Il se moque de ses critiques*"'.[24] By this time it was evident, at least to the *Saturday Review*, that a generation had been wrong about Dickens: 'our grandchildren will wonder what their ancestors could have meant by putting Mr. Dickens at the head of the novelists of his day' (No. 108). Many other such passages, noting Dickens's decline, prophesying his imminent collapse into nullity, and denying his literary immortality, will be found in my selections: and, when reading the tributes paid to him in 1870, one might also notice what the *London Quarterly Review* printed the next year: 'We have never met a single man of high cultivation who regarded Dickens in the light of an artist at all, or looked upon his books as greatly worth the attention of persons capable of appreciating better things' (No. 154). This reviewer had indeed been unfortunate in his acquaintance with cultivated persons, for Dickens's critical reputation certainly stood higher than this statement implies, whatever reservations his commentators felt about his art, but at least the Editor of the *London Quarterly* (a solid respectable journal) did not think this too absurd a judgment to print.

But, as Lever said, Dickens could afford—at least financially—to ignore his critics. From the beginning, critics who found him faulty had felt powerless to persuade either him or his public that he was so. 'Boz has got the Town by the ear,' reported a reviewer in December 1836, 'and he is not so thorough-bred as we imagine, if he lets go his hold in deference to the critics'—so it would be idle 'to repeat ... our old objections'.[25] And the British public 'stood by him with a piteous fidelity to the last', as Mrs Oliphant tartly recorded in 1871 (No. 155).

For Anthony Trollope, who also disliked much in Dickens's art, such a loud and sustained *vox populi* was a fact that should give critics pause: 'When the masses of English readers . . . have agreed to love the writings of any writer, their verdict will be stronger than that of any one judge, let that judge be ever so learned and ever so thoughtful. . . . It is fatuous to condemn that as deficient in art which has been so full of art as to captivate all men' (No. 95 b). Trollope made a few gestures towards explaining this art, but did not advance the argument far; and, a few years later, he doubtless spoke for many cultivated persons when he said that 'Of Dickens's style it is impossible to speak in praise' (No. 95 c).

IV

THE DEVELOPMENT OF DICKENS'S REPUTATION
IN HIS LIFETIME

My introductory notes to the various sections of this anthology describe the critical reputations of individual novels, and of larger areas of Dickens's work, and they indicate the emergence of some of the main topics debated by his critics. A brief summary may, however, be useful here. The immediate popularity and critical attention which *Pickwick* and the other early works enjoyed have already been described; this extraordinary impetus was maintained through to the writing of *Master Humphrey's Clock* (1840–1), after which he at last took a year off from fiction. In November 1842, however, he published *American Notes*, his first attempt at book-length non-fictional writing. The critics attacked in force, particularly those from the heavyweight journals. It was indeed an unremarkable, as well as uncharacteristic, book; and it gave an opportunity for critics who resented his popularity to point out the deficiencies of this young upstart—Radicalish as well as having small Latin and less Greek.

A Christmas Carol (1843) occasioned a truce in all critical battles; Forster was expressing a general view when he wrote that 'Literary criticism is here a second-rate thing' (*Life*, 318); but *The Chimes* (1844) effectively started up the debate, which was to recur during the rest of Dickens's life and beyond, as to whether social 'purpose' was a valuable or a distorting element in his work, and how intelligent and worthy his 'purpose' was. Much reviewing in this period was, of course, undisguisedly political, and the response of various journals to *The*

Chimes and later stories in which 'purpose' was specially evident was generally predictable. Similarly, journals of a denominational allegiance were apt to criticize him on doctrinal grounds, though some found an occasion here to exercise Christian charity: 'We firmly believe Mr Dickens knows as much of the ways and manners of religious people as a Hottentot (a gentle critic reminded us, when we said so, that "we love him so much we wish he knew more").'[26]

In extenuation of some of the harsher judgments and direr prophecies made by his contemporaries, it should be remembered that they were likely to read, or review, minor works on which, as was only apparent later, Dickens's reputation would not depend. For instance, take the scarifying reviewer in *The Times*, June 1846, urging him not to be too eager to write another novel (he, of course, could not know what qualities *Dombey and Son*, which began four months later, would possess): 'He has . . . to repair the mischief which we assure him has been done by his latest publications. . . . What you have written in an hour, [Mr Dickens], may die in an hour' (No. 37). The reviewer is not thinking (though he should more have done) of Dickens's last novel, *Martin Chuzzlewit* (1843–4), but of *The Cricket on the Hearth* (1845) and *Pictures from Italy* (1846), books for which Dickens's greatest admirers would not claim much. At least most journals continued to pay serious attention to him, though even here there are curious lapses. Professor Michael Wolff, in his suggestive essay 'Victorian Reviewers and Cultural Responsibility' (see Bibliography), has examined the amount and quality of attention given to some of the notable books of 1859, and has found good reason to praise the general standard of priorities adopted by reviewers in that year. Dickens's offering in 1859 was *A Tale of Two Cities*—scarcely noticed by the reviewers, Professor Wolff reports, 'but, where noticed, almost universally scorned'. Lucky the culture which can afford to neglect, and scorn, Dickens's *Tale:* lucky too the *œuvre* which can carry this novel as a make-weight, far from the centre of the author's achievement. *The Times* was one of the journals which ignored it: but what can be said of the 'cultural responsibility' of the leading newspaper of the day, which had also ignored *Bleak House, Hard Times,* and *Little Dorrit*? Similarly the *Edinburgh Review*, having discussed 'Dickens's Tales' in October 1838 (No. 19) and reviewed *American Notes* in 1843 (No. 34), accepted Forster's urgent offer of a review of *The Chimes* in January 1845 (No. 46), and then only once again noticed him during his lifetime—in July 1857, when James Fitzjames Stephen was allowed to continue in its

pages the bitter denunciation of Dickens and other purveyors of 'Light
Literature' begun in the *Saturday Review* (No. 104). Evidently, from its
almost unbroken silence about Dickens the novelist, from 1838 until
after his death, the *Edinburgh Review* had long classed him as belonging
to a Light Literature unworthy of serious discussion. The *Quarterly
Review* does no better. The *Westminster*, with notices of *Chuzzlewit*,
Dombey, *Hard Times*, and *Our Mutual Friend* (see Nos. 66, 91, 132) after
initiating the general rush of long assessments in the 1830s (No. 15), does
best among the quarterlies, but this is still not an impressive recognition
of the greatest author of the age. Far from exercising cultural responsibility, the quarterlies displayed cultural frivolity when, with unique
unanimity, they all reviewed at great length *American Notes* (non-
fiction, and therefore 'serious').

The *Times* in the later 1840s had published a series of sharply dis-
missive reviews (again showing an odd sense of critical proportion
by reviewing all the Christmas books but ignoring the novels), but
it was not until the 1850s that Dickens began to receive sustained
critical rejection, from some quarters. The reasons for this onslaught
were several: the emergence of Thackeray presented a rival of some
stature, such as had been conspicuously absent during Dickens's first
decade as a writer; he had, moreover, now been generally adulated
for so long that he must have seemed, to some, as intolerable as
Aristeides; the sense of social 'purpose' was increasingly insistent in
the novels from *Bleak House* onwards, while the humour was less
abundant and genial, and many critics resented the loss of the latter and
found the new 'darkness' gloomy and the political implications
pernicious. Much the most vociferous and (despite some wilful blind-
ness) the most intelligent of the organs ranged against him at this time
was the *Saturday Review*, established in 1855. It is always a pleasure and
a stimulus to read it, infuriating though its arguments and tone often
are, and I have included several of its pieces on Dickens (most of them,
probably, written by James Fitzjames Stephen). On literary matters,
the tone was a blend of undergraduate iconoclasm, patrician contempt
for the masses, and mandarin defence of cultural tradition against the
inroads of commercial barbarians. Even Charles Kingsley, often a
victim of its reviewers, had to accommodate himself to the institutional
tone when he wrote for it himself. As he explained to Tom Hughes, he
had written for it 'a sufficiently stupid & bald review' of *Tom Brown's
School Days*, because he had 'especial orders "not to lay it on too strong"
—the cantankerous critters hate being genial, & fancy they show their

superior critical powers by picking & paring & balancing & snubbing.'[27]
The leaders of Light Literature, Dickens and Jerrold, came in for the
Saturday Review's bitterest taunts, but astringency and carping superiority were evident in its dealings with most contemporary authors.
'The *Saturday Review*,' complained the publisher Blackwood in 1859,
'has the inconceivable folly to speak of men like Bulwer, Dickens,
Thackeray, etc., in a tone of happy superiority that would not be
justifiable to the humblest literary aspirant.'[28] Some of the controversies raised by the *Saturday Review* may be followed in Nos. 99,
104–6, 108–9, and its influence is evident in such later pieces as Justin
McCarthy's in the *Westminster*, 1864 (No. 126). Mrs Oliphant was
raising some of the same objections in her reviews of Dickens in *Blackwood's* from 1855 onwards (Nos. 96, 124, 155).

Another influential essay from this period was Walter Bagehot's
in 1858 (No. 110), which surveys many of the topics that inevitably
recurred in critiques of Dickens: the question of his 'reality' (were his
characters really caricatures, his accounts of institutions a farcical
travesty?), his use and presentation of London, the wholeness or
scrappiness of his novels (the effects of serialization were often discussed
in this context), the validity of his pathos, the acceptability of his
heroines, the quality and the artistic relevance of his moral and social
values, the decency of his language, the influence of his work on the
popular mind and on contemporary literature. An outside view on many
of these questions is provided by Hippolyte Taine's essay of 1856
(No. 97) which, together with G. H. Lewes's of 1872 (No. 158)
evidently struck John Forster as, by the 1870s, the most formidable
attacks on Dickens that it was his duty to refute. By then, the *Saturday
Review* had lost some of its pristine vigour and influence, and had
ceased attacking Dickens so strongly: its obituary appreciation of him
(No. 140) had been magnanimously generous, though when the
quality of his pathos was under discussion the simplest way of referring
to its depreciators was to identify them as 'essayists of the *Saturday
Review* type of mind'.[29]

Little Dorrit (1855–7) more than any other novel had borne the brunt
of these later attacks on Dickens: my headnotes to it, and to other
novels of the fifties, offer further explanation of this critical reaction,
which had begun over *Bleak House*. Dickens took up some points from
his reviewers, and disputed them in articles or prefaces, but another
kind of reply appears at the end of his Preface to the first edition of
Little Dorrit:

In the Preface to *Bleak House* I remarked that I had never had so many readers. In the Preface to its next successor, *Little Dorrit*, I have still to repeat the same words. Deeply sensible of the affection and confidence that have grown up between us, I add to this Preface, as I added to that, May we meet again!³⁰

The rivalry of Thackeray and George Eliot, and the growing coolness of the more sophisticated critics, made little difference to his popularity, his 'affectionate' relationship with his public, or his institutional status.

An extraordinary demonstration of his standing in British, indeed international, life was the Farewell Banquet given to him in London before his departure on the American tour of 1867. Nearly 450 notabilities assembled in his honour; others, unable to attend, allowed their names to appear on the list of 'stewards' as a mark of their respect. Lord Lytton was in the Chair, and the speakers included the Lord Mayor of London, the Lord Chief Justice, the President of the Royal Academy, Sir Charles Wentworth Dilke, Anthony Trollope, and (from the theatre) Benjamin Webster and J. B. Buckstone. Among those supporting the dinner were Lord John Russell, Gladstone, the Lord Chief Baron, Earl Stanhope, the Duke of Argyll, Lord Shaftesbury, Lord Houghton, Sir Frederick Pollock; artists—Frith, Maclise, Millais, Ward, Tenniel, both Landseers; actors—Macready and Fechter; publishers—Blackwood, Murray, Longman, Smith, Chambers; authors — Tennyson, Arnold, Collins, Reade, Froude, Lewes, Charles Knight, Mark Lemon, Shirley Brooks. Among those who sent commendatory letters, though they could not attend or be associated with the affair, were Carlyle, Ruskin, and Browning. 'Nothing like it has ever occurred in London before,' reported the *New York Tribune* (November 1867). '... The company that assembled to honor Dickens, represented humanity.'³¹ Without going so far as to accept this description of an assemblage of English dignitaries, nor to elevate the dinner (as this reporter did) to the status of 'a high historical event', we may certainly recognize that no such tribute has been paid, or could have been accorded, to any other English author. Lytton, not unreasonably, in his speech as chairman, compared Dickens to royalty: and it was an appropriate gesture that a royal saloon carriage was placed at his disposal for his journey to Liverpool. His visit to America, though a commercial venture in the entertainment industry, 'could in no respect be considered a private event [wrote Charles Kent, the organizer of the Banquet], but, from first to last, was regarded, and reasonably regarded, as a public and almost an international occurrence'.³²

V

THE SALES OF THE NOVELS

Who read Dickens? One might adapt Bagehot's phrase about the scope of his subject-matter: he had depicted English life, said Bagehot, 'from quite the lowest to almost the highest' (No. 110)—and his readers, in England, ranged from quite the highest to almost the lowest. He was the Queen's and the Prince of Wales's favourite novelist, and was also known to some of the readers among those London poor that Henry Mayhew surveyed around 1850. Or, to move from a social to an intellectual hierarchy, he was read by the leading authors, critics, and scholars (though the more high-minded of them such as John Stuart Mill and Matthew Arnold seem not to have felt obliged to read him constantly: see Nos. 77, 87), and even some of the illiterate were familiar with him through theatrical versions or by attending penny readings. His main audience lay of course in that conveniently large group, the middle class (see Mrs Oliphant, No. 96), though he could also be described more demotically, with reference to another vague sociological group, as 'one who is eminently the people's author.'[33] But even the twopence charged for his weekly magazines, and the penny-ha'penny for the 'Cheap Edition' weekly parts of his novels, was quite a sum for the poor, and the shilling for his monthly parts, though it put novel-buying on an instalment-system within the reach of many who could never have afforded the standard guinea-and-a-half for a three-volume novel, was manifestly far beyond the reach of artisans working for ten or fifteen shillings a week. An article published at his death made the interesting observation that:

there have never been in this country anything like those cheap popular editions which have secured to other writers so enormous a sale. For this reason the fame of Dickens is still chiefly confined to the middle and upper classes, while there cannot be any doubt that in the United States, owing to the low price at which his novels have been issued there, they have been read by a far greater number in proportion to population. With us, in fact, Dickens has yet to become, as he inevitably will become, the favourite of the poorer classes. . . . An edition of Thackeray in penny numbers would be certainly a doubtful experiment; but of an edition in that form of Dickens's works . . . what might not be expected? In other countries such editions of valuable copyright works are common enough, even in the author's lifetime. The edition of Victor Hugo's great novel *Les Misérables* in penny numbers, with

Brion's striking illustrations, is a case in point. Of the first issue of this publication it is said that 150,000 copies were sold, probably a greater number than has ever been circulated of the most successful of Mr Dickens's books.[34]

It is more difficult than one might expect to establish whether this essayist's surmise is correct. Forster includes some sales-figures in the *Life*, and Dickens's letters sometimes refer to this topic. Professor Richard D. Altick uses these and other scraps of evidence to devise a useful (if very incomplete) entry on Dickens in the Appendix on 'Best-Sellers' in his book *The English Common Reader 1800–1900* (Chicago University Press, 1957). Altick's comparative figures for other novelists, and his whole discussion of Dickens's place in Victorian publishing history, are of the greatest interest. A much fuller study is now being undertaken by Professor Robert L. Patten, of Rice University, and he has kindly written for me an Appendix on Dickens's sales. Within the short compass of space that could be spared, and writing at a stage when his researches are far from completion, he has managed (I think) to provide, for this volume, the fullest and most accurate account extant of this matter; I am most grateful to him. As he shows, Dickens's sales were substantial but not enormous. A few decades later, they might have been much larger (but, then, a Dickens born and starting work a few decades later would have been very different too). Though his sales were eclipsed, in his day, by one or two cheap novelists like G. W. M. Reynolds, and though an occasional novel such as *Uncle Tom's Cabin* (1852) might surpass his in sales, he was with good reason the envy of the other novelists of repute in his days: see Thackeray's letters *passim*, and the sales-figures in Trollope's *Autobiography* and Professor Haight's edition of George Eliot's letters. 'People who never read any other novels, read Mr Dickens's' (No. 138), and many of the items printed below comment in more detail on the range of his readership and the reasons for this large and sustained popularity.

VI

THE REACTION AGAINST DICKENS

'If literary fame could be safely measured by popularity with the half-educated, Dickens must claim the highest position among English novelists': from this unpromising statement Leslie Stephen began the peroration to his entry on Dickens in the *Dictionary of National Biography*, in 1888, and after a friendly summary of his 'more severe critics' Stephen concluded: 'The decision between these and more eulogistic opinions must be left to a future edition of this dictionary.'[35] Dickens's popularity had not been confined to the half-educated, however much it might suit the Stephen family to think so, but by 1888, though the benighted 'half-educated' persisted in enjoying and admiring him, many of the intelligentsia had found other gods and were reacting against many elements of his art. It soon became easy for even so coarse-grained a writer as Arnold Bennett to dismiss him: 'Of Dickens, dear friend, I know nothing. About a year ago, from idle curiosity, I picked up *The Old Curiosity Shop*, & of all the rotten vulgar un-literary writing . . . ! Worse than George Eliot's. If a novelist can't *write*, where *is* the beggar?'[36] Some of the objections to Dickens current by then are presented (in caricature form) by James Barrie, in a dialogue of 1890, in which the ghosts of Fielding, Smollett, Scott, Dickens, and Thackeray have a disquieting chat with representative modern novelists.

DICKENS—I wrote for a wide public (*Stylist sighs*), whom I loved (*Realist sighs*). I loved my characters, too, (*American sighs*), they seemed so real to me (*Romancist sighs*), and so I liked to leave them happy. I believe I wanted to see the whole world happy (*Elsmerian sighs*). . . .

ELSMERIAN—We have no patience with humour. In these days of anxious thought humour seems a trivial thing. The world has grown sadder since your time, and we novelists of to-day begin where you left off. Were I to write a continuation of *The Pickwick Papers*, I could not treat the subject as Mr Dickens did; I really could not.

STYLIST—Humour is vulgar.

AMERICAN—Humour, sir, has been refined and chastened since the infancy of fiction, and I am certain that were my humorous characters to meet yours mine would be made quite uncomfortable . . .

DICKENS—But if I am not a Realist, nor a Romancist, nor an Elsmerian, not a St–

AMERICAN—Oh, we have placed you. In Boston we could not live without placing everybody, and you are ticketed a caricaturist.

DICKENS (*sighing*)—I liked the old way best, of being simply a novelist.

AMERICAN—That was too barbarous for Boston. We have analysed your methods, and found them puerile. You have no subtle insight into character. . . .[37]

Dickens's humour was indeed quite an offence, or at least a 'placing' characteristic condemning him to a low category, for many serious-minded critics. Professor Ford quotes some happy examples of stiff-necked egg-heads patronizing Dickens for being funny—George Moore wishing that he had learned from the French masters that 'humour is more commercial than literary', Bagehot solemnly re-probating him for the same reason ('You take up the esteemed writers, Thucydides and the *Saturday Review*; after all, they do not make you laugh. It is not the function of really artistic productions to contribute to the mirth of human beings').[38] We have perhaps reformed that indifferently with us, but are far from reforming it altogether: from how many discussions of Dickens in the learned journals would one ever guess that (as Dickens himself thought) humour was his leading quality, his highest faculty,[39] or indeed that he ever indulged in such an unelevated form of writing?

To trace, let alone discuss and account for, the changes in Dickens-criticism from the 1880s to the present day is more than my intro-duction can accommodate or my readers could bear, and the task is the less necessary since Professor Ford's book *Dickens and his Readers* has so recently, and so ably and thoroughly, undertaken just such a survey. Dickens has never been totally neglected or dismissed by the critics, of course. Nothing very striking appeared, after the retrospective assess-ments of the 1870s, until Gissing's study (1898) and Chesterton's (1903), and then nothing much of lasting importance until the 1920s. In 1923, largely on the evidence of appreciative essays by George Santayana and T. S. Eliot, John Middleton Murry was able to announce that there had recently been 'a marked revival of interest and admiration for Dickens among the younger generation', and that now 'the most advanced young man may carry a copy of *Pickwick* in his pocket'. Reasonably, Murry proposed that 'the real test for literary taste was an admiration, not for Jane Austen ... but for Dickens', though he acknowledged that to account for and defend that admiration would much exercise the critical mind:

Dickens is a baffling figure. There are moments when it seems that his chief purpose in writing was to put a spoke in the wheel of our literary aesthetics. We manage to include everybody but him; and we are inclined in our salad days to resent the existence of anybody who refuses to enter the scheme. That is why people tried to get rid of him by declaring that he was not an artist. It was an odd way of predicating non-existence. Now it is going out of fashion, I suppose because it did not have the desired effect of annihilating

Dickens; and also perhaps because simple people asked why the books of a man who was not an artist should have this curious trick of immortality. There was, alas, no answer. So we are beginning to discover that Dickens *was* an artist, but, of course, only in parts. When we have discovered which are the parts we shall breathe again.[40]

How fully that task has been performed in the half-century since Murry wrote, and how confidently we may breathe again after climbing out of the æsthetic impasse of Murry's contemporaries, are not questions I shall now attempt to answer.

VII

DICKENS TODAY, AND DICKENS THEN

We are now the inheritors of thirty years of more substantial work on Dickens, initiated mainly by the essays of Edmund Wilson, George Orwell, and Humphry House, all written around 1940. Belatedly, the universities of the Anglo-Saxon world (and elsewhere) have started devoting a serious, indeed formidable, attention to Dickens criticism and scholarship. I recall that, when I reviewed Professor Ford's book (1955) in *Universities Quarterly*, I commented that on the day when I received his book I read in the *Times Literary Supplement* a review of three books on Milton by American dons—and that I could recall only three books on Dickens, before Professor Ford's, by dons of any kind. I was wrong: the score was eight, three of them not in English: books by Wilhelm Dibelius (1916), Floris Delattre (1927), W. S. Holdsworth (1928), Edward Wagenknecht (1929), E. N. Gummer (1940), Humphry House (1941), Edgar Johnson (1952), and Sylvère Monod (1953). But the quality of academic attention to Dickens has certainly increased markedly in the decade or so since then: a glance along my bookshelves reveals at least forty-three books on him, by dons alone, since Ford's. Now I add to the number, and the Centenary is producing many more.

For much of this new information, and many of these new critical impulses, we must be grateful, haunted though we all must be by Tennyson's lament for the days

> ... Before the Love of Letters, overdone,
> Had swampt the sacred poets with themselves.

What is most noticeable, of course, as one passes from the period covered by the present volume to criticism today, is the shift of emphasis from the early Dickens to the later. Many other differences will occur to the reader, turning to this volume after (most likely) an habituation of current critical writings. Dickens's contemporaries had a keener, simpler relish for 'characters'; they enjoyed the humour and felt little compulsion to explain or justify this delight; many of them responded to the pathos much more uninhibitedly than we do. They were not unaware of his 'imaginative' qualities, but were less concerned with symbolism, allegory, and myth than current critics are. Nor were they so consciously concerned with verbal texture; indeed, most of the comments on his style in the selections below are adverse, though many critics were content to discuss his works with little or no reference to stylistic qualities. Many of my selections, even those showing high critical intelligence, will seem inexact in method, amateurish in approach, by comparison with the modes of criticism now current: on the other hand, few critics then would indulge in the perversities and eccentricities of ingenuity that editors and publishers, and presumably many readers, are now willing to tolerate. What may be learned from these contrasted modes of procedure is rather for the reader to decide than for this editor to pronounce.

VIII

STUDIES OF DICKENS'S RECEPTION AND OF DICKENS–CRITICISM

I salute and thank my predecessors in this area of Dickens-studies, and wish they had been more numerous. I have indeed been amazed to find how little substantial detailed work has been done on the amply-documented reception of an author so great and so central to any cultural debate. But I have been compiling this volume a few years too early: for I notice that there is, just recently, a great vogue for such studies. Every other M.A. or Ph.D. thesis that I examine, and many post-graduate students' essays that I mark, are concerned wholly or partly with the contemporary reception of Victorian authors (and, in reaction against past neglect, students now seem to think that this exercise will solve more critical problems than in fact it ever can). These studies will doubtless soon be achieving publication, and certainly such topics are very suitable for research-students—they are of manageable compass, involve original work, and can be competently undertaken without the critical brilliance and maturity which it would be unreasonable to expect all young post-graduates to have. How much may be done is evident in Dr Slater's thesis on *The Chimes* and other Christmas books, though not all students will be so fortunate, nor so perceptive, as he was.

Pickwick has always been disproportionately popular with non-academic Dickens-students, as with collectors, and its reception has been usefully described and exemplified in books and articles by Walter Dexter, J. W. T. Ley, William Miller, and E. H. Strange. (Details of these, and other items in the next few paragraphs, will be found in the Bibliography.) Professor Keith Hollingsworth has discussed the reaction to *Oliver Twist* in the context of the 'Newgate Novel' controversy, and Dr Walter C. Phillips has seen Dickens alongside Reade and Collins as 'Sensation Novelists'. The headnotes to my selections about *American Notes, Martin Chuzzlewit, Dombey and Son, David Copperfield,* and *A Tale of Two Cities* refer to essays on their reception by Professors K. J. Fielding, Ada C. Nisbet, A. A. Adrian, Heinz Reinhold, and by myself. The reception of a few other items has been surveyed in unpublished theses, mainly American, which I have not examined: but clearly there is a considerable field here for future research. None of the studies known to me, except Dr Slater's, makes any pretension to have covered even the reception in Britain at all comprehensively.

In more general collections, check-lists, and studies, the most useful pioneer is Frederic G. Kitton, notably in his indispensable *Dickensiana* (1886) and in his compilation *Dickens by Pen and Pencil* (with Supplement, 1890). *Poole's Index to Periodical Literature* (vol. i, 1891, and subsequent supplements) contains short and scrappy entries on Dickens; more useful early bibliographies are John P. Anderson's (1887) and Wilhelm Dibelius's (1916). An extensive selection of critical comments is reprinted by J. A. Hammerton (1910), and a smaller collection by Mabell S. C. Smith (also 1910). By far the most comprehensive re-printing of Victorian discussions of Dickens, however, is in the *Dickensian* (1905– continuing). Particularly in its earlier years, this journal has printed hundreds of reviews, tributes, poems to and about Dickens, etc., and many check-lists of discussions of individual novels (*Edwin Drood* being a particular favourite here). Around 1935–6, its editor, Walter Dexter, reprinted as a centenary gesture much contemporary comment on *Pickwick* and other early works. Much the longest list of 'Writings relating to Dickens and his Works' is William Miller's (1946; supplements, 1947, 1953), but unfortunately it has grievous shortcomings, as was pointed out in the devastating review by Philo Calhoun and Howell J. Heaney (1947). My entry on Dickens in the *New Cambridge* bibliography (1969) may be consulted for further items. There have been several recent collections of Dickens-criticism,

most of them—except Ford and Lane's *The Dickens Critics* (1961)—
concentrating almost exclusively on modern essays: those edited by
William R. Clark (Heath's 'Discussions of Literature' series, Boston,
1961), Martin Price (Prentice-Hall's 'Twentieth Century Views',
Englewood Cliffs, 1967), and A. E. Dyson (Macmillan's 'Modern
Judgments', 1968). The introductions to these, particularly Mr
Dyson's, contain useful assessments of recent critical trends, and the
Ford and Lane anthology includes a notably good 'Checklist of Dickens
Criticism, 1840–1960'.

Dr Q. D. Leavis's influential book *Fiction and the Reading Public*
(1932) contained some astringent references to Dickens and his readers.
A fuller and more balanced account appeared in Amy Cruse's *The
Victorians and their Books* (1935), which contained an entertaining and
wide-ranging chapter on Dickens. The first book-length scholarly
survey of Dickens-criticism was by a Finn, Dr Irma Rantavarra (1944).
Published in Helsinki during the war, it is a creditable pioneer effort,
particularly as it was completed in such highly unpropitious conditions.
It is superseded, however, by Professor George H. Ford's study (1955),
based on a much richer scholarship and a finer critical sense. Professor
Ada C. Nisbet's survey (1964) is mainly concerned with recent work,
but is remarkably broad, uniquely covering the study of Dickens all
over the world. Studies of Dickens's reception in France, Germany, and
Russia are mentioned in my Bibliography. There is a perceptive short
survey of books about Dickens in the British Council 'Writers and their
Works' series, by Professor K. J. Fielding. Dickens-criticism, 'past,
present and future directions', was discussed by a distinguished group
of symposiasts at Boston: Professor George H. Ford, Edgar Johnson,
Sylvère Monod, and J. Hillis Miller (ed. Noel C. Peyrouton, 1962).
The studies of Victorian criticism of the novel by Richard Stang (1959)
and Kenneth Graham (1965) contain useful discussions of the responses
to Dickens in the context both of current theories about fiction and of the
response to his major literary contemporaries.

'There is a sense in which James and Conrad can be regarded as being
much closer to the essential nature of Dickens's work than are Bennett
and Wells', though the last two are fuller of 'the obvious Dickensisms',
remarks Professor Ford (*Dickens and his Readers*, 221). Ford made 'the
infinitely complex problem of Dickens's influence' peripheral to his
study (*ibid*, 210), though he threw out some useful hints. No one else
has attempted this daunting task, though this, like a comprehensive
study of Carlyle's influence in his period, stands high among the

desiderata of Victorian scholarship. It remains astounding how little useful work has been done on more modest enquires into Dickens's literary influence upon individual authors of his own time and later. As far the most popular, and generally the most esteemed, novelist of his day, it is clear that he had a profound influence, both at the artistic and the sub-literary commercial levels. We all note this, from time to time, but hardly anyone has undertaken the wide reading and hard thinking necessary to take this beyond the stage of brief asides. The most thorough study of any one aspect is Louis James's of the imitations and plagiarizations of the early Dickens, in his *Fiction for the Working Man 1830–1850* (1963). Dr J. R. Harvey's thesis (see my Preface), which I hope will soon be published, shows convincingly the enormous influence of *Pickwick*, its format and illustrations, upon publishers and authors in the 1830s and 1840s. Another 'infinitely complex problem of Dickens's influence', that of his political and social impact, has received some attention, if with indeterminate results, in Humphry House's *The Dickens World* (1941) and my own *Dickens and Crime* (1962) and *Dickens and Education* (1963); much more remains to be done here, as on many of the topics I have indicated above.

A postscript may be added on such relevant Centenary studies of Dickens-criticism as have come to hand. Outstanding among these is the enlarged Centenary Number of the *Dickensian*, devoted entirely to the development of Dickens's reputation in the century since his death. Most relevant to the present *Critical Heritage* volume is Professor K. J. Fielding's essay '1870–1900: Forster and Reaction'. Dickens's fortunes in the twentieth century are traced by Sylvère Monod, Michael Slater, Philip Collins and George H. Ford. Other useful Centenary studies of Dickens's critical reputation, by Mr E. W. F. Tomlin and Professor Lauriat Lane, are listed in my Bibliography. The December 1969 issue of the French journal *Europe* included essays on Dickens in England, Italy, Bulgaria, Hungary and America. Special Centenary numbers of *Nineteenth Century Fiction*, *Etudes Anglaises* (and doubtless many other journals) are to appear. Professor Ada C. Nisbet is to publish a comprehensive international bibliography of Dickens, which (as her previous work in this field warrants) will be of outstanding thoroughness and interest. One of my students, Dr William Oddie, has completed a thesis, which it is hoped will soon be published, on a topic noted above as of considerable importance: 'Carlyle and Dickens: the question of influence' (Ph.D., Leicester, 1969).

NOTES

1 [Charles Eliot Norton], 'Charles Dickens'. *North American Review*, April 1868, cvi, 671.
2 Quoted by Swinburne, 1903 (*The Swinburne Letters*, ed. Cecil Y. Lang [1962], vi, 171).
3 Letter to Forster, late March 1858 (*Life*, 646).
4 *Monthly Review*, September 1844, n.s. iii, 143, reviewing *Martin Chuzzlewit*.
5 'Our Novels: the Sensational School', *Temple Bar*, June 1870, xxix, 419.
6 June 1872, quoted in *George Eliot and her Readers*, ed. Laurence Lerner and John Holmstrom (1966), 83.
7 For the sales of Dickens's novels, see Appendix I.
8 *Letters of Lord Acton to Mary Gladstone*, ed. Herbert Paul (1913), 26.
9 *Diaries*, ed. William Toynbee (1912), ii, 418.
10 'Autobiographical Sketch', in *Selected Literary Criticism*, ed. Anthony Beal (1955), 3.
11 Review of *American Notes*, *North American Review*, January 1843, lvi, 212.
12 *Reminiscences* (1899), i, 32.
13 *Pilgrim*, i, 147, 129, 189.
14 'Fielding's Works', *Times*, 2 September 1840 (*Critical Papers in Literature* [1904], 207).
15 [John Forster], *Examiner*, 7 October 1838, 628.
16 *Experiment in Autobiography* (1934), ii, 508.
17 Quoted in *Pilgrim*, i, 431 n.
18 *Journals*, ed. Horace N. Pym (1883), 145.
19 *Peter Parley's Penny Library* (1841), quoted in *Dickensian*, xix (1923), 130.
20 *Letters of Edward Fitzgerald*, ed. J. M. Cohen (1960), 232.
21 *Examiner*, 28 October 1865, 681.
22 See No. 135, and Jean Ruer, 'Playdoyer pour la littérature à sensation'. *Bulletin de la Faculté des Lettres de Strasbourg*, Janvier 1969, 233–47; also Walter C. Phillips (in Bibliography).
23 *Quarterly Review*, June 1839, lxiv, 89; *Saturday Review*, 14 January 1871, 50.
24 Charles Lever, letter of 16 April 1857, *Huntington Library Quarterly*, I (1936), 164.
25 *Athenaeum*, 31 December 1836, 916.
26 *Eclectic Review* (a Congregational journal), October 1861, n.s. i, 459.
27 R. B. Martin, *The Dust of Combat* (1960), 217; cf. Kingsley's *Two Years Ago* (1857), ch. vii.

28 *The George Eliot Letters*, ed. Gordon S. Haight (1954-6), iii, 28.

29 See headnote to 'Obituary Tributes, 1870'. For a discussion of the re-action against Dickens's pathos, see my lecture 'The Decline of Pathos: the Victorians and Tears', *English Studies Today*, 5th ser. (Dublin, 1970), and, in shortened form, in *Listener*, 8 May 1969, 635-7.

30 *Little Dorrit* was 'next successor' to *Bleak House* (1852-3) as a twenty-part monthly serial, but it is curious to note Dickens here (like many of his critics and readers) treating *Hard Times* (1854) as a forgettable non-book.

31 Quoted by K. J. Fielding, *Speeches*, 369. For a full account, see *Speeches*, 368-74, and Charles Kent, *The Charles Dickens Dinner*, 1867. My account also draws upon the two-volume album of Kent's correspondence with stewards and guests, now in the Huntington Library, San Marino, California.

32 Charles Kent, *Dickens as a Reader* (1872), 75-6.

33 Wilkie Collins, *Rambles beyond Railways* (1851), 242; cf. Nos. 44, 60.

34 *Graphic*, 13 June 1870, 674.

35 *DNB*, xv, 30.

36 Bennett to George Sturt, 6 February 1898 (*Letters of Arnold Bennett*, ed. James Hepburn (Oxford 1968), ii, 104); Bennett's dots. In other letters Bennett notes that he is put off by Dickens's 'absolute lack of verbal beauty', and that one thing 'you will never get in my fiction, or in any first-rate modern fiction [is] the Dickens or Thackeray grossness' (*ibid*, 157, 175).

37 James Barrie, 'Brought back from Elysium', *Contemporary Review*, June 1890, lvii, 853.

38 Ford, 218 and n. Cf. No. 110.Or did Bagehot have his tongue in his cheek?

39 *Life*, 721.

40 J. M. Murry, *Pencillings* (1923), 31, 35, 40-1. Cf. his essay, 'Seriousness', in the same volume.

THE EARLY WORKS
FROM *PICKWICK* TO *NICKLEBY*

Sketches by Boz
First Series, February 1836
Second Series, December 1836

Pickwick Papers
April 1836–November 1837

Oliver Twist
February 1837–April 1839
(3 vol. edn., November 1838)

Nicholas Nickleby
April 1838–October 1839

During these opening years of his literary career, Dickens, was enormously prolific, often writing and serializing two novels at once. Reviewers sometimes discussed two or more of his books at a time, so it seems more convenient to group these early works together. To these years, too, belong various minor works, no reviews of which have been reprinted here: *Sunday under Three Heads* (June 1836), *The Strange Gentleman* (burletta, produced September 1836, published (?) January 1837), *The Village Coquettes* (comic opera, produced and published December 1836), *Is She his Wife?* (burletta, produced March 1837, published (?) 1837), *Memoirs of Joseph Grimaldi* (February 1837), *Sketches of Young Gentlemen* (February 1838), *Sketches of Young Couples* (January 1840), and short items, such as *The Mudfog Papers* in *Bentley's Miscellany* 1837–9.

According to John Forster, Dickens later much underrated *Sketches by Boz*, but they 'were much more talked about than the first two or three numbers of *Pickwick*' (*Life*, 76). *Chambers's Edinburgh Journal* presciently recommended this 'new writer ... to proceed, for, unless he falls off very miserably in his subsequent efforts, he can scarcely fail to become a successful and popular author' (9 April 1836, v, 83). There were many such cheering prognostications; see No. 1 (*Metropolitan*, March 1836). The review in the *Sun* was typical: 'They evince great powers of observation, and fidelity of description, combined with a humour which, though pushed occasionally to the verge of caricature, is, on the whole, full of promise. But their principal merit is their matter-of-factness, and the strict, literal way in which they adhere to nature' (15 February 1836, 5). Many of the *Sketches* had attracted favourable comment on their first appearance in magazines and newspapers, from December 1833; Forster, who had not yet met Dickens, remarked in his review, 'We were much struck by some of these sketches when we first read them in the publication in which they originally appeared, and a second perusal has strengthened the favourable impression. The author is a good observer. . . .' (*Examiner*, 28 February 1836, 132–3). Walter Dexter has made useful surveys of the reception of *Sketches* (*Dickensian*, xxxi (1935), 105–8; xxxii (1936), 43–50). Later discussions often traced the ways in which 'we see there, already, as it were, the microcosm of the world created by Dickens' (*People's Journal*, 1848, 229, translating Arthur Dudley's essay in *Revue des Deux Mondes*, March 1848).

By August 1836, Dickens was already 'Boz the magnificent' (*Fraser's*, xiv, 242), though the extraordinary rage for *Pickwick* was then only beginning, with the introduction of Sam Weller in ch. x (No. IV, July 1836). Most subsequent reviews remark on this phenomenally rapid and widespread—and soon international—success. Reviewers discussed how far Dickens's comedy and his depiction of London life were original, often through comparisons with Pierce Egan and other recent humorists, while the size of his achievement was soon recognized by comparisons with the eighteenth-century masters and even Shakespeare (see Introduction, p. 7). Other comparisons that soon became current were with *Don Quixote* and Hogarth's engravings. For fuller surveys and extracts from reviews see Walter Dexter, *Dickensian*, xxxii (1936), 216–8, 281–5; *Nineteenth Century*, cxix (1936), 318–29; (with E. H. Strange), *A Centenary Bibliography of the Pickwick Papers* (1936); (with J. W. T. Ley), *The Origin of Pickwick* (1936), ch. v; bibliographies in *Dickensian*, xxvi (1930), 204–6, 273–4. See also George H. Ford, *Dickens and his Readers* (Princeton, 1955), ch. i, 'The Prospering of Pickwick'. *Pickwick* retained its popularity and reputation: *The Times* spoke for many readers, in 1870, when calling it his masterpiece (No. 139).

Reviewers of *Oliver Twist* mostly hailed its greater 'earnestness' and 'purpose', and recognized its advance on *Pickwick* in constructional skill. Some readers were put off by the 'Radicalish tone' (there was of course some argument about whether Dickens was right about the New Poor Law of 1834), or by the lowness of the subject. Henry Fox, for instance, in a letter: 'I know there are such unfortunate beings as pickpockets and street walkers. I am very sorry for it and very much shocked at their mode of life, but I own that I do not much wish to hear what they say to one another' (*Chronicles of Holland House 1820–1900*, ed. Earl of Ilchester (1937), 245). Cf. Lord Melbourne and the young Queen (No. 11). The criminal milieu moved some critics to applaud his ability to touch pitch without defiling himself or his readers, others to doubt his wisdom in familiarizing them with such scenes (see No. 22). Dickens was particularly annoyed by later reviews, which lumped *Oliver Twist* with Ainsworth's *Jack Sheppard* and other 'Newgate novels': see Nos. 12, 58. Keith Hollingsworth surveys this aspect of the novel's reception in his *Newgate Novel* (Detroit, 1963), 125–30. See also Introduction, p. 8. The pathos of Oliver's situation was widely praised, but many critics were doubtful about the characterization of both Oliver and Nancy (Dickens replies to them in his 1841 Preface), and scornful of the Maylie and Brownlow stories. For a full list of reviews see the Clarendon *Oliver Twist*, ed. Kathleen Tillotson (Oxford, 1966), Appendix F.

Nicholas Nickleby seems to have generally pleased, but to have attracted less excited and pointed reviews than its predecessors. Dickens was widely congratulated for the appositeness of his attack on the Yorkshire schools (*Nickleby* was reputed to have caused the closure of many of them). Later there was more dispute about how fair he had been; this became a staple topic in *Notes and Queries* from the 1860s onwards (see Philip Collins, *Dickens and Education* (1963), ch. v). Smike became one of the standard examples of Dickens's pathos, and the Cheerybles of his benevolence. The Crummles episodes, the Mantalinis, and Mrs Nickleby were general favourites; Nicholas himself was not much liked, and Dickens defends his characterization in the 1839 Preface.

1. From an unsigned review of
Sketches by Boz, Metropolitan Magazine

March 1836, xv, 77

We strongly recommend this facetious work to the Americans. It will save them the trouble of reading some hundred dull-written tomes on England, as it is a perfect picture of the morals, manners, habits of a great portion of English society. It is hardly possible to conceive a more pleasantly reading book; delightful from the abundance of its sly humour, and instructive in every chapter. The succession of portraits does not reach higher than of the best of the middle classes, but descends with a startling fidelity to the lowest of the low. Where all is so good, it would be needless for us to particularize any one of these admirable sketches, very many of which would form admirable groundwork for light comedies and farces. We do not know the author, but we should apprehend that he has, from the peculiar turn of his genius, been already successful as a dramatist; if he has not yet, we can safely opine that he may be if he will. Taken altogether, we have rarely met with a work that has pleased us more, and we know that our taste is always that of the public.

2. From unsigned reviews of
Pickwick Papers, Metropolitan Magazine

May 1836 – May 1837

(*a*) (May 1836, xvi, 15, reviewing No. I) '... "Boz" is a rising writer; in his prosperous navigation he has but one shoal to beware of—extravagance. Yet even extravagance may be pardoned in him, when he makes it so laugh-provoking. ...'

(*b*) (July 1836, xvi, 76) 'The third number of this amusing work is well sustained, with the same humour and drollery that have made the preceding parts so popular. . . . We predict that these papers will never be at a discount, though we prophesy that there will always be a great run made upon the publishers of them.' [Then praises the Fat Boy, the cricket-match, and Mr Jingle.]

(*c*) (August 1836, xvi, 110, on No. IV.) '. . . . "Boz" is making for himself a standard fame, and this number is, perhaps, the best that has yet appeared. The wit of these papers is subtle and beneath the surface; their humour is not that of extravagance, but of nature . . .'

(*d*) (September 1836, xvii, 13) 'Boz marches on triumphantly, and has completely taken possession of the ear, and of the heart too, of his countrymen. His fifth number is joyous in the scenes of a contested election . . .'

(*e*) (January 1837, xviii, 6, reviewing No. IX, *not* No. XI as is stated) 'Very good, this number the eleventh [*sic*], indeed. Sam Weller improves upon acquaintance. The world never saw drollery and wit offered to them before in a form so singular. The renowned Mr Pickwick is, himself, the legitimate successor to Don Quixote; indeed, he is the cockney Quixote of the nineteenth century, and instead of armour of iron, he is encased in a good coating of aldermanic fur, and instead of spear and sword, has his own powers of declamation with which to go forth to do fearful battle upon the swindler, the wrong-doer, and the oppressor of the innocent. We wish that the humorous Boz would call to mind that the knight of La Mancha was really the victim of a veritable flame. We should like to see Mr Pickwick confess to the soft impeachment. This gentleman's attendant has the process of mollification already going forward in his heart;—we trust that it will not ascend to his head, but that he will make love with the same effect that hitherto he does everything else. We know of no publication that is productive of more genuine amusement than these Pickwickian papers.'

(*f*) (February 1837, xviii, 46) '[Boz is still going strong in No. X. Christmas at Dingley Dell made us merry.] . . . the inimitable Sam Weller moralizes upon [matrimonial arrangements] in a strain truly philosophical . . .'

(*g*) (March 1837, xviii, 77) '. . . no lack of vigour or originality [in No. XI] . . . We are glad that Boz is getting among the lawyers . .

Boz will be the first person, not a lawyer, who ever made anything by meddling with the law . . .'

(*h*) (April 1837, xviii, 106, reviewing No. XII) '. . . Instead of flagging, they grow more uproarious in their fun, and more rich in their drollery . . .'

(*i*) (May 1837, xix, 16) 'At times, we are almost inclined to wish that the spirit of these papers would flag a little, that we might have a little repose, and thus gain the necessary breathing space to enable us to pick out a few Pickwickian faults. But Boz gives us no such cessation of interest . . .'

3. Unsigned review of *Pickwick Papers* Nos. I – IX, the *Athenaeum*

3 December 1836, 841–3

It has been a fashion of late days, we have observed, to christen a new favourite in the humorous department of literature, after one of the great pleasant fathers; and we have had War-Fieldings and Sea-Fieldings, and Small-Smolletts and Sea-Smolletts, time after time, until we almost get a-weary of the race. True wit, or true humour, ought to provoke no trace of relationship—ought to 'mention no names' —it is, in fact, 'wild wit, invention *ever new*!' or it is not what it assumes to be. A wit or a humourist should remind you of human nature— human nature in its vivid and lustrous colours—and not hunt you back to a foregone work, or a pleasant author-predecessor. The writer of the periodical (for such it is) which is now before us, has great cleverness; but he runs closely upon some leading hounds in the humorous pack, and when he gives tongue (perchance a vulgar tongue,) he reminds you of the baying of several *deep dogs* who have gone before. The *Pickwick Papers*, in fact, are made up of two pounds of Smollett, three ounces of Sterne, a handful of Hook, a dash of a grammatical Pierce Egan —incidents at pleasure, served with an original *sauce piquante*.

Let it not be thought that we dislike *Boz*, we like him, at fit moments, intensely. A relish is a relish, and a *Boz* served up at *the* time carries down the breakfast, or the part of a tea, inimitably. We are of opinion that, if not overdone, the *Papers of the Pickwick Club* will tickle the palates of many of the particular, as well as of many of the deeply voracious. . . .

But we parley too much, and keep our readers too long from the work itself . . . .

[Quotes 'a few racy extracts.']

We have spoken of *Boz* honestly, if plainly; but we earnestly hope and trust nothing we have said will tend to *refine* him. We do not want to be the weekly Hercules to his monthly Antæus, because we are satisfied, that if he were once lifted from the earth he would lose much of his strength:—he is not for the 'cloud-capp'd' towers and gorgeous palaces', for he could not be easy in them or near them.

4. From an unsigned article, 'Some Thoughts on Arch-Waggery, and in especial, on the Genius of "Boz"', *Court Magazine*

April 1837, x, 184–7

. . . Our readers cannot fail to have observed the sudden turn for the comic, which has recently discovered itself in the literary public. Formerly, the maxim was—'You are nothing if not critical;' now it is 'You are nothing if not comical.' The appetite for the jocose, the farcical, the extravagant, is immoderate. It is no longer 'Laughter holding both its sides,' but 'Laughter literally unable to hold its sides.' Accordingly, the magazines have become as funny as it was in their power to become; and, although it is very hard to be funny to order, and fun of that sort is generally very hard, there never was such a quality of obstreperous mirth brought into the market before. . . .

There is no doubt that this sudden taste for crowding upon the sunny side of the road, was originally generated by a facetious gentleman who, for some months, escaped detection under the name of 'Boz.' . . .

Whatever may be said or thought of the style or spirit of 'Boz's' productions, their verisimilitude is undisputable. They reflect the manners to which they are addressed with a felicity that is inseparable from truth. . . . The *vraisemblable* is not 'Boz's' line of art; the *vrai* is with him all in all. What he gives you is literally true, but like a consummate artist, he does not give it to you literally. It is not enough that a portrait should be a good likeness, it must bear a certain air and grace beyond the likeness to constitute excellence—and in this 'Boz' is perfect. His dialogues, without straining for puns or mere surface effects, are excerpta from veritable life, or such as might have been veritable, or would have been so under the circumstances described, heightened of course, to make their full impression. Then his minute details exhibit an almost instinctive knowledge of human character in the classes he depicts, and of the accessories of small and every-day events. For example, his description of the surgeon waiting for the poor woman's hour of release in the workhouse, and 'sitting with his face turned towards the fire, giving the palms of his hands a warm, and a rub, alternately:'—of Sam Weller preparing to write his love-letter, when, 'looking carefully at the pen to see that there were no hairs in it, and dusting down the table, so that there should be no crumbs of bread under the paper, Sam tucked up the cuffs of his coat, squared his elbows, and composed himself to write;'—of the preliminaries to the proceedings of the Temperance Society, when 'the secretary having sneezed in a very impressive manner, and the cough which always seizes an assembly, when any thing particular is going to be done, having been duly performed, the following document was read, &c.;'—and the meeting of the opposite counsel in the court on the morning of Mr Pickwick's trial (the whole of which is inimitable), nodding in a friendly manner to each other, and observing, to the horror of the defendant, that 'it was a fine morning;' are such exact representations of trivial things, as, however inconsequential in themselves, afford at once a test of the author's skill, and a clue to his unprecedented success. The character of Sam Weller is rich in originality, and it is sustained throughout with such likelihood that we never feel as if there was one fraction of his individuality with which we could dispense, or as if there were any thing wanted to complete the delineation. But we need not multiply instances. They are all as familiar to the public as they are intelligible at first sight. The genius of 'Boz' is not dramatic. If it were, it could not be so faithful to actual experience. It is in the intermixture of description and dialogue—of the language and tournure—the modes and costumes of his characters —that his merits and his triumph consist. And it may be observed as a curious and remarkable trait in these whimsical outlines of low and middle life, that while 'Boz' brings before you with a graphic pen, the express image of the poorest and most ignorant orders, he never descends into vulgarity. The ordinary conversations of the loose and ribald multitude are faithfully reported, but by an adroit process of moral alchemy, all their offensive coarseness is imperceptibly extracted. He gives you the spirit, but not the letter of slang; you are never repelled by abasing pruriences, and you are permitted in his pictures to enjoy the broad drollery, released from all its repulsive associations. This is a peculiarity in the writings of 'Boz,' that reflects unbounded credit upon his taste. The subjects are passed through the alembic of his mind, and come, if we may say so, purified before the public.

5. Miss Mary Russell Mitford on *Pickwick Papers*

1837

Extract from a letter, 30 June 1837, to Miss Jephson, an Irish correspondent, *Life of Mary Russell Mitford*, ed. A. G. L'Estrange (1870), iii, 78.
Mary Russell Mitford (1787–1855), author of *Our Village* (1819) and other stories and plays, later became much more critical of Dickens's style and manner: see L'Estrange, iii, 189, 199, 230, 245. Sir Benjamin Brodie, whom she mentions, was a leading surgeon; Lord Denman was Lord Chief Justice. A few weeks earlier, she had commended Dickens to Elizabeth Barrett, for his humour and his 'anti-humbug spirit' (iii, 71).

So you have never heard of the *Pickwick Papers*! Well, they publish a number once a month and print 25,000. The bookseller has made 10,000*l.* by the speculation. It is fun—London life—but without anything unpleasant: a lady might read it all *aloud*; and it is so graphic, so individual, and so true, that you could courtsey to all the people as you met them in the streets. I did think there had not been a place where English is spoken to which 'Boz' had not penetrated. All the boys and girls talk his fun—the boys in the streets; and yet those who are of the highest taste like it the most. Sir Benjamin Brodie takes it to read in his carriage, between patient and patient; and Lord Denman studies *Pickwick* on the bench while the jury are deliberating. Do take some means to borrow the *Pickwick Papers*. It seems like not having heard of Hogarth, whom he resembles greatly, except that he takes a far more cheerful view, a Shakespearian view, of humanity. It is rather fragmentary, except the trial (No. 11 or 12), which is as complete and perfect as any bit of comic writing in the English language. You must read the *Pickwick Papers*. . . .

6. [John Forster], from an unsigned review of *Pickwick Papers*, No. XV, *Examiner*

2 July 1837, 421–2

'. . . how can I thank you for your beautiful notice?' Dickens wrote to Forster on 2 July 1836. '—Can I do so better than by saying that I feel your rich, deep appreciation of my intent and meaning more than the most glowing abstract praise that could possibly be lavished upon me?' For Forster's rewriting of this letter in *Life*, p. 89, see *Pilgrim*, i, 281n.

In [this number, chs. xli–xliii] the author has achieved his masterpiece. We have read it with the deepest interest and admiration. It is devoted chiefly to a delineation of the interior of Fleet prison, of its various inmates, and of the scenes of misery and profligacy that may still, to the shame of our legislature, be witnessed daily within its walls. The exposure, we sincerely trust, will prove as beneficial as it is opportune. The truth and power with which it is made are beyond all praise—so certain, so penetrating, and so deeply-aimed, and yet, at the same time, so obvious and familiar, are the materials employed. Every point tells, and the reality of the whole is wonderful. We place the picture by the side of those of the greatest masters of this style of fiction in our language, and it rises in the comparison.

[Forster describes, with quotations, the scenes in the Fleet prison. 'Over all there is a dreadful restlessness, a terrible and undefined restlessness, which is pictured throughout with the minute reality of a Defoe. . . .']

All of it is real life and human nature. It is not a collection of humorous or pathetic dialogues about people who have no tangible existence in the mind; but it is a succession of actual scenes, the actors of which take up a place in the memory.

We recognise in this fine writer a maturing excellence, which promises, at no distant day, the very greatest accomplishment of that great style in which Fielding—honouring humanity while he exalted literature—achieved those books which are now appealed to as we appeal to truth or nature, and which are indeed among the best evidences of both that we can ever make ourselves acquainted with. We see, in every succeeding work he takes in hand, a superior insight into the general principles of character joining itself to the old and exquisite representations of local peculiarities and humours; and we can rarely now find anything that approaches to caricature or exaggeration without finding also some very shrewd and sound truth concealed beneath it. . . .

The illustrations are, as usual, full of excellent character. The ease and skill with which they are drawn are among the least of their merits; they have an artistical feeling and arrangement, most rare in things of this kind. But it is enough to say of them that they are scarcely unequal to the subjects they illustrate—we feel this to be extraordinary praise.

7. W. M. Thackeray on *Pickwick Papers,* in *The Paris Sketch Book*

1840 (*Works,* Biographical Edition (1898–9), v, 80)

Thackeray (1811–63) did not emerge as Dickens's rival or peer until the publication of *Vanity Fair* (January 1847 – July 1848). A prolific reviewer and miscellaneous contributor to journals in his earlier years, he often commented on Dickens, usually with admiration. When he became a leading novelist he continued to write generously about him, though in private letters he was more candid about what he saw as Dickens's defects, and was constantly measuring himself for size beside the acknowledged king of the profession. He preferred Dickens's humour to his serious characterization or his social reformism. Predicting 'a brilliant future' for him, in July 1840, and noting that he showed no sign of flagging or sense of fatigue, he exclaimed: 'Long mayest thou, O Boz! reign over thy comic kingdom ... Mighty prince! at thy imperial feet, Titmarsh, humblest of thy servants, offers his vows of loyalty and his humble tribute of praise' ('A Pictorial Rhapsody', *Fraser's Magazine,* xxii, 113; *Works,* xiii, 342). See Charles Mauskopf, 'Thackeray's attitude towards Dickens's writings', *Nineteenth-Century Fiction,* xxi (1966), 21–34. See also below, Nos. 12, 40, 74, 101.

... I am sure that a man who, a hundred years hence, should sit down to write the history of our time, would do wrong to put that great contemporary history of *Pickwick* aside as a frivolous work. It contains true character under false names; and, like *Roderick Random,* an inferior work, and *Tom Jones* (one that is immeasurably superior), gives us a better idea of the state and ways of the people than one could gather from any more pompous or authentic histories.

8. C. S. Calverley, from
'An Examination Paper:
The Posthumous Papers of the Pickwick Club'

Fly Leaves (Cambridge, 1872), 121–4

Calverley (1831–84), poet and parodist, was at Christ's College, Cambridge, when he set this examination paper at Christmas 1857; the prizewinners were W. W. Skeat (later Professor of Anglo-Saxon at Cambridge) and Walter Besant (later a popular novelist). Besant recalls the literary tastes of his generation at Cambridge in the late 1850s: 'Tennyson, Kingsley and Carlyle were in everybody's hands, with Dickens of course as the first favourite' (*Autobiography* (1902), 91). Calverley helpfully provides a 'Key' to the examination paper (pp. 125–9). *Pickwick* was, clearly, already a cult-book: and swopping arcane Dickens tags was something of an undergraduate fashion (William Morris was one who indulged in it). At least this is preferable to *Pooh* games, not unknown, it is ignominious to report, in British universities in the 1960s.

1. Mention any occasions on which it is specified that the Fat Boy was *not* asleep; and that (1) Mr Pickwick and (2) Mr Weller, senr., ran. Deduce from expressions used on one occasion Mr Pickwick's maximum speed.
2. Translate into coherent English, adding a note wherever a word, a construction, or an allusion, requires it:
'Go on, Jemmy—like black-eyed Susan—all in the Downs'—
'Smart chap that cabman—handled his fives well—but if I'd been your friend in the green jemmy—punch his head—pig's whisper—pieman, too.'
Elucidate the expression, 'the Spanish Traveller,' and the 'narcotic bedstead.' . . .
4. What operation was performed on Tom Smart's chair? Who little thinks that in which pocket, of what garment, in where, he has

39

left what, entreating him to return to whom, with how many what, and all how big?

5. Give, approximately, the height of Mr Dubbley; and, accurately, the Christian names of Mr Grummer, Mrs Raddle, and the fat Boy; also the surname of the Zephyr. . . .

10. State the component parts of dog's nose; and simplify the expression 'taking a grinder.'

11. On finding his principal in the pound, Mr Weller and the town-beadle varied directly. Show that the latter was ultimately eliminated, and state the number of rounds in the square which is not described. . . .

18. How did the old lady make a memorandum, and of what, at whist? Show that there were at least three times as many fiddles as harps in Muggleton at the time of the ball at Manor Farm.

19. What is a red-faced Nixon? . . .

28. Deduce from a remark of Mr Weller, junior, the price per mile of cabs at the period. . . .

9. Arthur Locker, from 'Charles Dickens', *Graphic*

18 June 1870, 687

Locker (1828–1893), novelist and journalist, was editor of the *Graphic*. Though not as 'elderly' as he editorially claims to be, his nostalgia for the good old *Pickwick* days happily expresses an important element in the charm of *Pickwick* for many readers then. Reviewers who kept regretting that Dickens did not write another *Pickwick* were (in part) lamenting that they were no longer young. Cf. No. 152, and [John Forster], *Examiner*, 20 July 1861, 452.

The young have a great admiration for Dickens, but I am inclined to think that we elderly folks, whose heads are grizzling whose locks are thinning, have the most right to love him. We are old enough to recollect the freshness and the intensity of delight with which we wel-

comed the appearance of the *Pickwick Papers*. But *Pickwick* came upon
me as a new revelation. Being from my earliest childhood a lover of
humorous literature, I had already read Mr Poole's *Little Pedlington*,
which may be regarded as a humble precursor of Boz's creations; but
as soon as I got possession of *Pickwick*, I laid *Little Pedlington* aside....

Again, apart from its humour, *Pickwick* must be to the young almost
an antiquarian book, containing descriptions of bygone manners and
customs, of which they have no personal knowledge. Young people
know nothing about the Fleet Prison; they never saw—except in
Mexico or Australia—a genuine stage coachman; they do not associate
a commercial traveller with a gig, but rather regard him as a gentleman
who passes his days and nights in railway trains, and who possesses a
complete acquaintance with the mysteries of *Bradshaw*. But to us
oldsters *Pickwick*, quite independent of its fun, recalls the England and
the London of our youth, and thus conjures up a host of delightful
recollections. As for Mr Weller the elder, I have sat by his side many
a time a-top of the old Rocket or Regulator coach bound for Ports-
mouth. I have seen him exchange the mystical salutation of the whip
with Tom Smart with his fast trotting mare; I have actually beheld
Tom Smart imbibing rum and milk at a little inn in Petersfield, and,
being a modest schoolboy, thought him very impertinent when he
chucked the barmaid under the chin. All that jolly, old-fashioned,
simple sort of life, described in the pages of *Pickwick* has gone by for
ever. We have Crystal Palaces, and Volunteering, and Athletic Sports,
and mammoth hotels, and all kinds of improvements, but somehow
England is not such a nice place as it seemed in the thirties. Is there any
other elderly lady or gentleman who echoes my complaint?

10. From an unsigned review of *Oliver Twist* in the *Spectator*

24 November 1838, xi, 1114–6

[*Oliver Twist* is 'exceedingly readable, though not enchaining'. Its improbabilities and structural defects are pointed out.]

The numerous readers who have been moved to laughter or to sadness, led to grave reflection, or excited to horror, by some of the passages in *Oliver Twist*, may naturally ask why they and criticism so differ? The answer will be, that they have been moved by *parts*: we are speaking of the work considered as *a whole*, and testing it by a reference to time, and those models of enduring art with which certain over-zealous *clacqueurs* have challenged comparison. Quitting these larger views, we will go a long way with Boz's admiring readers, and endeavour to point out the sources of their admiration, and the reasons of their idol's success. . . . That this author exhibits genius in embodying London character, and very remarkable skill in making use of peculiarities of expression, even to the current phrase of the day, is undoubtedly true; but he has higher merits, and other elements of success. His powers of pathos, sadly touching rather than tearful, are great; he has a hearty sympathy with humanity, however degraded by vice or disguised by circumstances, and a quick perception to detect the existence of the good, however overlaid; his truth and nature in dialogue are conspicuous to all; he has the great art of bringing his actors and incidents before the reader by a few effective strokes; though deficient in *narrative*, his *description* is sometimes nicely true, and often powerful; and his command of language considerable, without his style ever appearing forced. In addition to these qualities, he has a manly self-reliance—above all pretence, and all conventional servilities of classes and coteries; nor does he ever, with a sickly vanity, obtrude *himself* upon the reader's attention. Above all, he has genius to vivify his observation. Three novelists of the present day have, more or less, chosen somewhat similiar subjects; and it is only necessary to compare Boz with his competitors to see at once his preeminence. The personages of HOOK are ill-natured and farcical exaggerations of some prevalent weakness, often mere general abstractions without marks of individuality: the

42

robbers of AINSWORTH are dashing, roystering, high-spirited blades, with sufficient coarseness, but are drawn rather from imagination and the poetry of the 'road' than actual life—they are the romance of thievery: BULWER's 'family men' in *Pelham* and *Paul Clifford* are only disguised dandies, with sentiments drawn from fancy and words from the flash dictionary. But the thieves, their comates, and the Londoners of Boz, are flesh and blood—living creatures.

Besides the extrinsic circumstances which we pointed out formerly[1] as contributing to the immediate success of this writer, a few others may be named. Appearing in parts, each of which contained something striking and readable for all ranks, his works were the very thing for 'the press' to fasten upon, as furnishing a ready means of filling up blank space, without any trouble on the part of the journalist, beyond a hearty panegyric on the writer who had occupied the 'abhorred vacuum;' so that his production really gets a score of 'notices,' where others, however *taking*, only receive one. Boz also very skilfully avails himself of any temporary interest to give piquancy to his pages. When his matter is not sufficiently attractive in itself, he has no objection to paint up to the flaring tastes of the vulgar great and small; nor does he scruple to avail himself of any current prejudice, whether popular or *fee*losophical, without much regard to critical exactness. Thus, Mr Fang, the Police Magistrate, was a hit at LAING of Hatton Gardens, whilst that functionary's pranks were full in the public mind. The earlier workhouse scenes in *Oliver Twist*, with the hard-hearted indifference of the parochial authorities, the scanty allowance of the paupers, and the brutal insolence of office in the beadle, were intended to chime in with the popular clamour against the New Poor-law: but Boz has combined the severity of the new system with the individual tyranny of the old,—forgetting that responsibility amongst subordinate parish-officers and regularity of management came in with the Commissioners. The scenes of pauper misery, whilst Oliver is on liking with the parish undertaker, appear to have been suggested by some inquests: and there are points thrown out by the Jew to flatter the opponents of capital punishment,—although the tendency of the work is to show that nature and habit cannot be eradicated by a sentimentality which contents itself with substituting a penitentiary for a gallows. These things tell with many readers, but they must detract from the permanence of the writer who freely uses them. . . .

[1] *Spectator*, 31 March 1838, xi, 304 (see No. 18).

11. Queen Victoria, from her diaries

1838-9

(*a*) (23 December 1838) 'Read in *Eugene Aram* for some time while my hair was doing, and finished it . . . I am glad I have finished it, for I never feel quite at ease or at home when reading a Novel' (*The Girlhood of Queen Victoria: a Selection from her Diaries 1832–40*, ed. Viscount Esher (1912), ii, 83).

(*b*) (30 December 1838) 'Talked of *Oliver Twist*, which I must say is excessively interesting . . . .' (ii, 86)

(*c*) (1 January 1839) 'Talked to [Lord Melbourne] of my getting on with *Oliver Twist;* of the description of "squalid vice" in it; of the accounts of starvation in the Workhouses and Schools, Mr Dickens gives in his books. Lord M. says, in many schools they give children the worst things to eat, and bad beer, to save expense; told him Mamma admonished me for reading light books.' (ii, 89) [Two days later, she persuaded Lord Melbourne to read *Oliver Twist*.]

(*d*) (7 April 1839) 'Lord M. was talking of some dish or other, and alluded to something in *Oliver Twist:* he read half of the 1st vol. at Panshanger. "It's all among Workhouses, and Coffin Makers, and Pickpockets," he said; "I don't like *The Beggar's Opera;* I shouldn't think it would tend to raise morals; I don't like that low debasing view of mankind." We defended *Oliver* very much, but in vain. "I don't *like* those things; I wish to avoid them; I don't like them in *reality*, and therefore I don't wish them represented," he continued; that everything one read should be pure and elevating. Schiller and Goethe would have been shocked at such things, he said. Lehzen said they would not have disliked reading them. . . .' (ii, 144)

12. [W. M. Thackeray], from 'Going to see a man hanged', *Fraser's Magazine*

August 1840, xxii, 154–5 (*Works*, iii, 436–7)

Thackeray had already attacked *Oliver Twist* in *Fraser's* for failing to present criminal life adequately, in 'Horae Catnachianae' (*Fraser's*, April 1839, xix, 408–9: not in *Works*, but see Hollingsworth, *The Newgate Novel*, 150–1), and *Catherine: a Story*, ch. iii and final paragraphs (*ibid*, June 1839, xix, 701; February 1840, xxi, 211–2). Dickens was rattled by this and other such attacks, and by finding *Oliver Twist* classified as a 'Newgate' novel. 'I am by some jolter-headed enemies most unjustly and untruly charged with having written a book after Mr Ainsworth's fashion. To these jolter-heads and their intensely concentrated humbug I shall take an early opportunity of temperately replying'—so far as he could without being disloyal to his friend Ainsworth (*To* R. H. Horne, ? 8 February 1840). The opportunity came with the publication of a Third Edition of *Oliver Twist*, for which he provided a Preface, dated April 1841. See Introduction, p. 8.

[Thackeray describes the rough crowd assembling to watch an execution. Well to the fore are young blackguards, aged sixteen or seventeen.]

There were a considerable number of girls, too, of the same age: one that Cruikshank and Boz might have taken as a study for Nancy. The girl was a young thief's mistress evidently; if attacked, ready to reply without a particle of modesty; could give as good ribaldry as she got; made no secret (and there were several inquiries) as to her profession and means of livelihood. But with all this, there was something good about the girl; a sort of devil-may-care candour and simplicity that one could not fail to see. Her answers to some of the coarse questions put to her, were very ready and good-humoured. She had a friend with her of the same age and class, of whom she seemed to be very fond, and who looked up to her for protection. Both of these women had beautiful eyes. Devil-may-care's were extraordinarily bright and blue, an admirably fair complexion, and a large red mouth full of white teeth. *Au reste*, ugly, stunted, thick-limbed, and by no means a beauty. Her friend could not be more than fifteen. They were not in rags, but had greasy cotton shawls, and old faded rag-shop bonnets. I was curious to look at them, having, in late fashionable novels, read many accounts of such personages. Bah! what figments these novelists tell us! Boz, who knows life well, knows that his Miss Nancy is the most unreal fantastical personage possible; no more like a thief's mistress than one of Gesner's shepherdesses resembles a real country wench. He dare not tell the truth concerning such young ladies. They have, no doubt, virtues like other human creatures; nay, their position engenders virtues that are not called into exercise among other women. But on these an honest painter of human nature has no right to dwell; not being able to paint the whole portrait, he has no right to present one or two favourable points as characterising the whole; and therefore, in fact, had better leave the picture alone altogether. . . .

13. From an unsigned article, 'Literary Recipes', *Punch*

7 August 1841, i, 39

A STARTLING ROMANCE

Take a small boy, charity, factory, carpenter's apprentice, or otherwise, as occasion may serve—stew him well down in vice—garnish largely with oaths and flash songs—boil him in a cauldron of crime and improbabilities. Season equally with good and bad qualities—infuse petty larceny, affection, benevolence, and burglary, honour and house-breaking, amiability and arson—boil all gently. Stew down a mad mother—a gang of robbers—several pistols—a bloody knife. Serve up with a couple of murders—and season with a hanging-match.

N.B. Alter the ingredients to a beadle and a workhouse—the scenes may be the same, but the whole flavour of vice will be lost, and the boy will turn out a perfect pattern.—Strongly recommended for weak stomachs.

14. [John Forster], from an unsigned review of *Nicholas Nickleby*, *Examiner*

27 October 1839, 677–8

Forster did Dickens proud in the *Examiner*, with nine notices of *Nickleby*. In No. 1 he detected all the old *Pickwick* virtues, 'with the addition of even better promise on the score of well-laid design, and of greater truth and precision of character' (1 April 1838, 195). Nos. V–VI showed that '*Nickleby* is much superior to *Pickwick* . . . in the force and precision of its characters—and already includes a gallery of faces familiar to us as our own' (23 September 1838, 595). The death of Ralph Nickleby much impressed him: 'we have never quoted anything finer from the writings of Mr Dickens' (6 October 1839, 629). The concluding review, on 27 October, while confirming the claim Forster had often made for this and earlier novels, that Dickens was of classic stature, is more explicit than usual about his faults.

Great success is a thing as little understood in literature now-a-days, as great failure. . . . The sale of the *Pickwick Papers* was very generally held to be in the nature of a bookselling curiosity, and when a career as prosperous was foretold for a new work of the same extent by the same hand, wise people shook their heads and said it was impossible. It has been proved possible, notwithstanding. The sale of *Nicholas Nickleby* is understood, even thus early, to have exceeded by many thousands that of the *Pickwick Papers*. Without entering on the question of how far such a circumstance should be taken as a test of genius or even of talent, it establishes the claim of the work to critical consideration on the highest grounds, and with reference to the best models. We propose in this spirit briefly to examine its pretensions to rank with the enduring fictions of our language.

Since Richardson published in successive portions his famous story of *Clarissa Harlowe*, and enthusiastic damsels, eager for the conversion of Lovelace, besieged and implored the author, as for a living sinner whose future state depended on the decision, to 'save his soul alive,' no

47

characters of an unfinished work of fiction have excited anything like the interest manifested by large classes of persons in all ranks for the fate of the various actors in the tale of *Nicholas Nickleby*. The Cibbers of that day, after 'a delicious meal of Miss Byron' in one volume, were not more anxious for 'another slice of her' in the next, than the Cibbers of our own, after regaling themselves with a Squeers, or a Smike, or a Newman Noggs, or a Vincent Crummles in number six, have been for other slices of them in number seven. This shows us, at the outset, a great secret of the popularity of the author. He seizes the eager attention of his readers by the strong power of reality. He thoroughly individualises what he takes in hand. Our sympathies are never left to wander off, into quarters vague or undefined, from the flesh and blood to which he allies them. And this also is the reason why we cannot associate anything that is vulgar or low with his treatment of subjects that in themselves are avowedly so. In everything of that kind that he presents to us, there is, in his manner of doing it, the manliness and simplicity of nature, or the truth of life as it is. We are never repelled by the abominations of egotism, conceit, or dogmatism. We are never disgusted by misplaced ridicule. If there is good going on, there is a vivid and hearty style to bring out all its beauty; and if there is evil, it runs no chance of being mistaken for good. The quantity of invention, observation, and knowledge of character, observable in the writings of Mr Dickens, is never more apparent than are his kindness of heart and capacity for generous emotion.

Now by all the various readers of this tale of *Nicholas Nickleby*—and they separate themselves into classes most widely apart from each other—these various qualities can be in an almost equal degree appreciated and felt. In this we advance further into the causes of so remarkable a popularity. Thousands read the book because it places them in the midst of scenes and characters with which they are already themselves acquainted; and thousands read it with no less avidity because it introduces them to passages of nature and life of which they before knew nothing, but of the truth of which their own habits and senses suffice to assure them. This is a test which only a man of genius could bear. . . .

These are elements in the wide success and popularity of this remarkable writer, that would probably first suggest themselves in a critical examination of the book before us. Incidentally they embrace many others. His style is for the most part admirable. Bating some faults of occasional exaggeration, which we may presently advert to, it is fresh and racy, and has the surpassing charms of simplicity, earnest-ness, animal spirits, and good humour. A rare virtue in it is, that it is always, whether grave or gay, thoroughly intelligible, and for the most part thoroughly natural. Its sparkling stream of vivacity or humour glides down by the easiest transition into deeper currents of seriousness and pathos. It is as quick, as warm, as comprehensive, as the sym-pathies it is taxed to express. We know of none that can paint more powerfully by an apposite epithet, or illustrate more happily by a choice allusion. Whatever Mr Dickens knows or feels, too, is always at his fingers' ends. There is no beating about the bush for it. It is not carefully deposited, ticketed, labelled, elaborately set apart, to be drawn forth only as formal necessity may suggest, from the various cells of his brain. It is present with him through every passage of his book. It animates old facts with a new life, it breathes into old thoughts a new emotion. Who that has read his description of the various localities of London, as set down in this story of *Nicholas Nickleby*, can ever expect to forget them more? A fresh glow of warmth and light plays over the cheerful and familiar places, a deeper mist of misery and blackness settles on the darker scenes. With him, we pass along misty streets in some cold and foggy morning, while but a few meagre shadows flit to and fro or now and then a heavy outline of coach or cab or cart looms through the dull vapour, yet were it only for the noises he strikes from time to time upon our ears, distantly and indistinctly as though the fog had muffled them, we could not doubt that it was LONDON. We enter with him by night, through long double rows of brightly burning lamps, a noisy, bustling, crowded scene, in which he shows us the rags of the squalid ballad-singer fluttering in the same rich light that shows the goldsmith's glittering treasures, and where one thin sheet of brittle glass is the iron wall by which vast profusions of wealth and food are guarded from starved and pennyless men, and this is the same LONDON as before. At all times, and under every aspect, he gives us to feel and see the great city as it absolutely is. Its interior life is made as familiar to us as its exterior forms. We come to know better the very places we have known best. We observe more smoking and hear more singing in Golden square; the Saracen's Head on Snow hill relaxes into a grim cordiality; the Alphonses of Cadogan place reveal themselves plain Bills to our practised eye; and the sight of even a real butterfly, fluttering among the iron heads of dusty area railings in some retired and noiseless City square, startles us no more.

And with all these masterly requisites for his art, is Mr Dickens a perfect novelist? By no means. He has yet to acquire the faculty of constructing a compact and effective story, without which that rank can never be attained. He has yet to subdue his tendencies of exaggeration, to which, though we observe it infinitely less in this work than in the *Pickwick Papers*, he is still too prone. . . .

The great master in our language of the art of constructing a plot, we need hardly observe, is Fielding. For exquisitest contrivance, for happiest extrication of story, he stands quite unrivalled. In this respect *Tom Jones* is an universally acknowledged masterpiece. Not an incident occurs in it from the first page to the last, which does not more or less tell the story, while it illustrates at the same time the character of the agents by which its results are to be worked out. . . . *Nicholas Nickleby* could not stand such a test for an instant. A want of plan is apparent in it from the first, an absence of design. The plot seems to have grown as the book appeared by numbers, instead of having been mapped out beforehand. The attention is ever and anon diverted from the story by digressions, introduced for the apparent uses of mere contrast and effect, while abrupt and startling recurrences are thus of course rendered necessary to recal us to the main interest and action. Admirable and very plausible reasons might no doubt be urged for all this, yet should none be admitted that contravene the sounder claims and more enduring requisites of high and perfect Art. The consequence of it is in this case, that many characters are altogether dropped as the necessities of the story force themselves on the writer, and that the grander effect of some of his most masterly and powerful writing in the latter chapters is marred by the introduction of matters, needful indeed to a gathering up of the loose or broken threads of an imperfect story, but sounding more like the minute recitals of a lawyer's deed than the natural development of a book of so much originality and genius.

Of the occasional sins against verisimilitude on the side of exaggeration, arising out of one-sided views of a certain sort of life, or the love of pampering a favourite joke to excess, we would instance such things as the Muffin and Crumpet Joint-stock Company in the early part of the work, the characters of Messrs Pyke and Pluck, and some portions of the scenes with Sir Mulberry Hawk and Lord Verisopht. We have now and then as the work proceeded, directed attention to things of this kind. We are not certain even that the more amiable characters of the book are always so amiable as we are desired to suppose them, and we must confess an insuperable aversion to the heroics of Nicholas Nickleby himself, when, as it happens sometimes, they obscure even his strong and gentle mind. . . . We are not sure that even Mr Dickens himself is indisposed to quiz now and then these little foibles of his favourite hero. . . . But when . . . we see him in his tender devotion to poor Smike (an always touching and most beautiful feature in the story; wrought, too, with consummate art), when we are with him in his lonely thoughts of sister and home, all other vagaries are forgotten, and nothing is visible to the moistening eye save the simplicity and sweetness of his nature. We have only to make one exception more. We referred to it when we spoke of some exaggerations in mere style. Mr Dickens occasionally overlays his thoughts with needless epithets, and is over profuse in his use of adjectives. It is only in his reflections we find this—and that rarely—in his descriptions never.

And now, having hastily glanced at objectionable points in the conduct or treatment of this famous story, what a host of beauties crowd on our grateful recollection, to which we have neither opportunity nor space to give even a passing glance. With what pleasant thoughts it has stocked our memory, with what true and tender sentiments enriched our hearts, with what a healthy and manly moral instructed our minds. With how much vivid distinctness each character takes its place before us, how plainly we see the individualities of each, the form of their faces, the accident of their habits, the nicer peculiarity of their minds. These are triumphs which only belong to a first-rate writer. The creative powers of the novelist, when properly directed and well sustained, take rank with history itself. The Æschylus of Parson Adams is not less real than the spectacles of Burke, the trumpet of Sir Joshua, or the snuff box of Gibbon. In reserve for Mr Dickens are still greater triumphs if he has patience and perseverance to prepare himself by study and self-restraint, by the pursuit of art and the pruning of common-place exuberance, for their full and satisfactory achievement. We hope that he will not fail in this. Great is the glory, though the strife be hard, and heartily do we wish him strength to surmount the one and long life to enjoy the other. We see in him, at no distant day, if he does entire justice to his powers, the not unworthy successor of our GOLDSMITHS and FIELDINGS.

15. [Charles Buller], from 'The Works of Dickens', *London and Westminster Review*

July 1837, xxix, 194–215

Reviewing *Sketches by Boz* (both series), *Pickwick* Nos. I–XV, and *Bentley's Miscellany* Nos. I–VI. Buller (1806–48), one of the parliamentary radicals, later became chief Poor Law Commissioner. He was one of Carlyle's pupils, before going to Cambridge.

[Much of Buller's article is yet another attempt to] . . . investigate the foundation of a popularity extraordinary on account of its sudden growth, its vast extent, and the recognition which it has received from persons of the most refined taste, as well as from the great mass of the reading public.

It is not, indeed, difficult to discover or to enumerate the causes of this popularity. The merits of Mr Dickens, though great, are not very varied; and the range of his subjects has not been large. The qualities for which every body reads and admires him are his humour and wit: and it is well known that he has delighted to employ these powers mostly in describing and commenting on the comic peculiarities of the lower orders of Englishmen. Indeed, the class which has been the peculiar object of his attention is even more limited. It is easy to see that his observations have been mainly confined to London; that he has minutely observed and most felicitously caught the peculiarities of every class in this great city and its suburbs, from the tradesman down to the cabman or the cad: that he is intimately acquainted with all those classes whom a resident in London gets acquainted with in travelling by coaches, or at inns: but that, though he has sometimes described country life, and sometimes portrayed members of the higher classes, it is not among either of these that his muse finds its favourite subjects. He is the literary Teniers of the metropolis; and he paints the humours of the lower orders of London with all the exactness and all the comic effect with which his prototype has handed to us the comic peculiarities of the

Dutch boors of his time. Mr Dickens is not the first who has perceived the vast fund afforded for comic description by this large class of human beings. A taste for depicting their manners and humour has long been gaining ground in our lighter literature. Mr Dickens has the merit of having done, on a larger scale, and with far more striking effect, what many before him have laboured to do.

We are not surprised that Mr Dickens has been frequently classed with a writer who has exhibited a good deal of comic power in depicting the same class of persons and circumstances. We mean Mr Theodore Hook,—for by that name, we believe, we may speak of the now almost openly acknowledged author of *Sayings and Doings*. But, beyond the similarity of subjects, and the mere general comic tone, it appears to us, that there is little in common between the two. While we acknowledge the pleasure which we have occasionally derived from Theodore Hook's writings, we cannot place him by any means on a level with 'Boz'. The latter stands to him in the relation of the writer of good comedy to one of broad farce. In his writings there is none of that constant straining after the ludicrous, which wearies us in Mr Hook's writings. Even when they describe the same things, the style of 'Boz' always presents a contrast of remarkable simplicity and truth to nature: the humour is always less broad, and more easy: there is an abundance of wit, of which the other gives no proof: there is an absence of exaggeration, of coarseness, and of effort, and a constant indication of a kindly and refined feeling, which we seek in vain in the writer with whom we are contrasting him.

Our readers will, perhaps, be somewhat surprised when we mention Washington Irving as the writer, to the character of whose mind we find the greatest resemblance in 'Boz'.
[Buller develops this comparison. He praises Dickens's comic and descriptive powers.] In his rural scenes he is rather tame; but he is inimitable in his description of inns, of booking-offices, and of attorneys' chambers.

His excellence appears indeed to lie in describing just what everybody sees every day. Almost the first scene in the *Pickwick Papers* is the taking a cab; and the whole process, from the calling 'cab,' and the waterman's answer of 'Here *you are*, Sir,' and his cry of 'fust cab,' down to the jumping out, and the consequent dispute with the driver, is brought before our eyes with a minute accuracy, which elevates this simple and ordinary process into a matter of interest. There are three journies on the top of coaches, one in a fine summer's day, another at

Christmas, another to Bath in February, so admirably brought before our eyes, that we could almost fancy we had performed each. A pot-boy delivering a message furnishes the materials of another exquisite scene. Perhaps the most interesting of these passages, made out of very common-place materials, is that of the chase in chaises, which Mr Pickwick undertakes in pursuit of Jingle, and the subsequent overturn. . . . [The 'inimitable' Bardell *v* Pickwick trial also displays Dickens's full powers: and] we may almost trust that some good may be done by the hardly exaggerated picture of the choleric and incompetent Mr Justice Stareleigh, and of the vehement absurdity of Sergeant [*sic*] Buzfuz. The bullying of Mr Winkle and the other witnesses, and the consequent perversion of truth and justice, place in a strikingly ludicrous, but, at the same time, in no exaggerated point of view, the absurd and odious effects of the English law of evidence, and its practice. Nor are the subordinate tribunals, and the provincial administration of the laws of England, neglected by our author. The scene at Mr Nupkins's, the mayor of Ipswich, looks somewhat like caricature: but it is, at any rate, but a slight exaggeration of the follies and injustice of the Great Unpaid. . . .

A writer so gifted will probably not exhaust his resources for a considerable time. But Mr Dickens will allow us, as sincere admirers, to hope that his great powers are destined to leave some lasting monuments in our literature. This end, however, he will not attain without study, without labour, and without care. To keep up such a reputation as he has acquired by the *Pickwick Papers*, ought, perhaps, to content many, but should not satisfy him. The renown of Fielding and of Smollett is that to which he should aspire, and labour to emulate, and, if possible, to surpass.

Since the conclusion of the foregoing remarks, we have read another of the works of Mr Dickens, published from month to month in *Bentley's Miscellany*, of which he is the Editor. It is called *Oliver Twist, or the Parish Boy's Progress*: and . . . is indeed remarkable as a specimen of a style rather more serious and pathetic than any other of the author's longer works; and it confirms the impression which we previously had of his powers in this style. His capacity of pathetic description is wonderfully great, and his taste in the selection of his objects seems to be constantly improving. Still the work has, though in a diminished degree, the same fault as we have noticed in the pathetic portions of his writings. They are monotonous. The accumulation of little details of misery and discomfort positively pains, and at last harasses the reader.

THE CRITICAL HERITAGE

We must advise the author, in continuing the work, to put in some touches not merely of comedy, which is by no means deficient, but of something descriptive of a little more comfort and happiness. The very accuracy of all these minute details of human wretchedness makes their effect more distressing, and renders such a variation necessary to relieve our feelings.

We extract two passages, which appear to us very admirable, and remind us of the simple pathos, which is Sterne's beautiful characteristic wherever he is not guilty of affectation. The first is the description of the death of Oliver Twist's mother in the workhouse, immediately after his birth.

[Ch. I; the second is Oliver's farewell to Dick, ch. VII.]

16. [Abraham Hayward ?], from an unsigned review of *Pickwick*, Nos. I–XVII, and *Sketches by Boz*, in the *Quarterly Review*

October 1837, lix, 484–518

Hayward (1801–84), essayist, translator, and barrister, contributed to the *Quarterly, Edinburgh, Fraser's*, etc. Dickens wrote to T. N. Talfourd, on 4 October 1837:

Murray [publisher of the *Quarterly*], supposing I presume that any notice in the *Quarterly* must drive so young a man as myself nearly distracted with delight, sent me the *Quarterly* yesterday. I think Hayward has *rather* visited upon me his recollection of my declining his intimate acquaintance, but as the Notice contains a great deal that I know to be true, and much more which may be, but of which I am no impartial judge, I find little fault with it. I hope I may truly say that no writer ever had less vanity than I have; and that my only anxiety to stand well with the world in that capacity, originates in authorship being unhappily my trade, as it is happily my pleasure.

Hayward's 'rocket and stick' prophecy (p. 62) rankled with Dickens (see *Pilgrim*, i, 325, 328), but, at a dinner in April 1837, attended by Sydney Smith and other literary men eager to 'cry down' this new comic writer 'Boz', Hayward had been the only guest who supported Tom Moore in praising him (*Diary of Thomas Moore*, ed. Lord John Russell (1856), vii, 174). See No. 17 for G. H. Lewes's arguments against this review.

The popularity of this writer is one of the most remarkable literary phenomena of recent times, for it has been fairly earned without resorting to any of the means by which most other writers have succeeded in attracting the attention of their contemporaries. He has flattered no popular prejudice and profited by no passing folly: he has attempted no caricature sketches of the manners or conversation of the aristocracy; and there are very few political or personal allusions in his works. Moreover, his class of subjects are such as to expose him at the outset to the fatal objection of vulgarity; and, with the exception of occasional extracts in the newspapers, he received little or no assistance from the press. Yet, in less than six months from the appearance of the first number of the *Pickwick Papers*, the whole reading public were talking about them—the names of Winkle, Wardell, Weller, Snod-grass, Dodson and Fogg, had become familiar in our mouths as house-hold terms; and Mr Dickens was the grand object of interest to the whole tribe of 'Leo-hunters,' male and female, of the metropolis. Nay, Pickwick chintzes figured in linendrapers' windows, and Weller corduroys in breeches-makers' advertisements; Boz cabs might be seen rattling through the streets, and the portrait of the author of *Pelham* [Bulwer-Lytton] or *Crichton* [Ainsworth] was scraped down or pasted over to make room for that of the new popular favourite in the omni-busses. This is only to be accounted for on the supposition that a fresh vein of humour had been opened; that a new and decidedly original genius had sprung up; and the most cursory reference to preceding English writers of the comic order will show, that, in his own peculiar walk, Mr Dickens is not simply the most distinguished, but the first.

Admirers and detractors will be equally ready to admit that he has little, if anything, in common with the novelists and essayists of the last century. Of Fielding's intuitive perception of the springs of action, and skill in the construction of the prose epic—or Smollett's dash, vivacity, wild spirit of adventure and rich poetic imagination—he has none: still less can he make pretensions to the exquisite delicacy, fine finish, and perfect keeping of Steele's and Addison's pet characters. . . .

. . . The only writer who appears to have exercised any marked in-fluence on his style is Mr Washington Irving, whom he undoubtedly has imitated in parts; but these (with one exception, the 'Bagman's Story,' a palpable plagiarism from the *Adventures of my Grandfather*) are far from being the most applauded; and the observation applies more to the *Sketches* than to the *Posthumous Papers of the Pickwick Club*, generally regarded as his *magnum opus*, by which (if ever) the names of Boz and Dickens are to descend to posterity. The plan, however, is so altogether anomalous, that it is no easy matter to determine in what class of composition to place them, or in what their peculiar excellence consists. The opening chapter introduces us to a learned society, whose proceedings bear so close a resemblance to those of sundry learned societies founded for the avowed purpose of enlightening mankind as to the date, formation, composition, monstrosities, probable duration, &c. &c. of the globe, that, at the first view, we were led to anticipate a prolonged quiz upon the whole race of scientific charlatans who, by the aid of meetings and associations, have contrived to fussify themselves into a notoriety which passes current amongst the uninitiated for fame. The subsequent chapters speedily undeceived us, and we were not long in finding out that the title of 'corresponding member of the Pickwick Club' was merely conferred as a travelling name; that no satire was intended against F.R.S.'s, F.Z.S.'s, F.G.S.'s, or any other of the distinguished personages who have purchased the privilege of appending forty or fifty letters to their designations, at (according to Mr Babbage) the moderate rate of ten pounds ten shillings per letter—and that the adventures, rather than the researches, of the Pickwickians were intended to constitute the leading feature of their history. But their adventures, though the transitions are remarkably easy and natural, are still too disconnected, and interspersed with too many episodes, to admit of that concentration of interest which forms the grand merit of a narrative. The only part of the plot calculated to keep the reader in suspense, the great cause of Bardell and Pickwick, does not commence till the eleventh number, and the final result is declared in the seventeenth—most of the intervening space being occupied with extraneous topics—so that it can hardly be as a story that the book before us has attained its popularity.

Our next proposition, that Mr Dickens does not strikingly excel in his sketches of character or descriptions, is, we feel, open to dispute, and it is far from our intention to deny that he has considerable merit in both respects, but certainly not enough to found a reputation, or account for a tithe of his popularity. Incomparably the best sustained of the characters is that of Mr Pickwick, whose every action seems influenced by the same untiring and enlightened spirit of philanthropy throughout. As Mr Southey said of Charles Lamb—'Others might possess the milk of human kindness, but *he* had monopolized the cream.' But Mr Pickwick is endowed with too much good sense to have been a founder or corresponding member of such a club; there is little or nothing in his conversation or conduct to remind us of the author of 'Observations on the Theory of Tittlebats,' and the only weakness that can be charged against him springs not from the overweening vanity or undirected enthusiasm of a would-be discoverer—(a Professor Muff or Nogo)—but from an overflowing goodness of heart, from an excess of *bonhomie* that forbids him to think ill of anybody. A still stronger objection lies against the Wellers, father and son. They both talk a language and employ allusions utterly irreconcileable with their habits and station. . . . Surely hits at book making are as much out of place in old Weller's mouth, as references to Sterne's *Sentimental Journey*, or allusions to Latin law-terms and the discovery of perpetual motion, in his son's. 'Tell me if Congreve's fools be fools indeed,' says Pope. Tell us if these be stage-coachmen and exboot-cleaners indeed, say we.

In description, again, he is sometimes very happy;—nothing, for example, can well be better than the sketch of Mr Pickwick sliding.

[Quotes from ch. xxx.]

This scene, with all its bearings, is brought fully home to the mind's eye without the aid of Phiz's illustrative sketch; but the success of many other passages is due in a great measure to the skill of that artist in embodying them. Indeed, only a faint notion could be formed of the outward man of the great Pickwick himself from the scattered hints afforded in the letter-press; namely that he wore *tights*, gaiters, and spectacles. It is the pencil, not the pen, which completes the vivid conception we undoubtedly possess of his personal appearance; and how tame, without that, would be such situations as those in which he is detected holding Mrs Bardell in his arms, or represented peeping through the bed-curtains at the unknown lady at the inn. A still graver objection even than want of distinctness and individuality, lies against Mr Dickens as a describer and portrait painter: he too frequently condescends to be a copyist, and almost always on such occasions betrays a marked inferiority to his prototypes. In proof of this charge we shall first quote an admirable passage from the *Sketch Book*. [Does so; then quotes comparable descriptions of Tony Weller's appearance (ch. xxiii) and of a coach-journey (ch. xvi).]

The analogy between these passages is too striking to be accidental, and we cannot compliment Mr Dickens on having improved upon the original: 'A broad, full face, curiously mottled with red, as if the blood had been forced by hard feeding into every vessel of the skin,' is ill replaced by a complexion exhibiting 'that peculiarly mottled combination of colours which is only to be seen in gentlemen of his profession, and underdone roast beef;' which exhibits no mottled combination of colours at all. The fact is, the old race of coachmen were going out when Mr Washington Irving first visited England, and were altogether gone before Mr Dickens's time. The modern race are more addicted to tea than beer; the cumbrous many-caped great-coat is rapidly giving way to the Mackintosh; and, with the change of habits and the increase of numbers, they have been doomed to see their authority over stable-boys and their awe-inspiring influence over country people pass away; thus sharing the fate of the other privileged orders, who have been gradually declining in authority from the time that titles might be had for the asking, and the distinctive style of dress was laid aside. Mr Dickens failed therefore, because he had never seen what he pretended to describe.

What, then, it may fairly be asked,—if he is super-excellent neither in descriptive narrative nor character—what is the talent or quality that has procured him so unprecedented a share of popularity? In our opinion he has obtained and well merited it by being the first to turn to account the rich and varied stores of wit and humour discoverable amongst the lower classes of the metropolis, whose language has been hitherto condemned as a poor, bald, disjointed, unadorned, and nearly unintelligible *slang*, utterly destitute of feeling, fancy or force, . . .

The primary cause, then, of this author's success, we take to be his felicity in working up the genuine mother-wit and unadulterated vernacular idioms of the lower classes of London—for he grows comparatively common-place and tame the moment his foot is off the stones, and betrays infallible symptoms of Cockneyism in all his aspirations at rurality. As for game and game-keepers he appears to possess about the same amount of general knowledge concerning them, that Winkly and Tupman display during the shooting excursion; and Wardle's Manor House, with its merry doings at Christmas-time, is neither more nor less than Bracebridge Hall at second-hand. Indeed, one throughout distinguishes at a glance the scenes drawn from actual observation from those copied, imitated, or imagined. Thus, we much doubt whether Mr Dickens was ever present at one of Mrs Leo Hunter's *déjeuners*; but we feel quite sure that he was acquainted with Mr Bob Sawyer, and accompanied Mr Pickwick to the supper party given by that young gentleman to his associates. . . .

He is by no means equally happy in delineating the rival profession of the law and its dependants. Little Perker, the bustling, dapper man of business, is well enough but his clerk Lowten, at his orgies, was evidently suggested by Paulus Pleydell's at High Jinks[1] and Mr Pickwick's preliminary interview with Serjeant Stubbins is improbable, as well as dull—at least, the only probable thing in it is the Serjeant's

[1] In Scott's *Guy Mannering*.

eagerness to get rid of a client who seemed to have no definite object in coming to him, beyond that of delivering a round-about and unnecessary address. It is generally believed that the counsel in *Bardell versus Pickwick* are portraits, but we have tried in vain to discover more than a very faint resemblance in either of them, and Serjeant Buzfuz's speech is certainly not in the manner of the gentleman supposed to be intended under the name.[1] It is simply a clever quiz on a style of oratory which was finally quizzed out of fashion by Lord Brougham many years ago, on an occasion which our professional readers will readily recall. Mr Justice Stareleigh, however, is an admirable likeness of an ex-judge,[2] who, with many valuable qualities of head and heart, had made himself a legitimate object of ridicule by his ludicrous explosions of irritability on the bench. . . .

Having made up our minds as to the origin of Mr Dickens's popularity, it remains to add a word or two as to its durability, of which many warm admirers are already beginning to doubt—not, it must be owned, without reason; for the last three or four numbers are certainly much inferior to the former ones, and indications are not wanting that the particular vein of humour which has hitherto yielded so much attractive metal, is worked out. This, indeed, from its very nature, must have been anticipated by any clear-sighted and calculating observer from the first, and we fear that the quantity of alloy mixed up with the genuine ore to fit it for immediate use, will materially impair its lustre when the polish of novelty has worn off. . . .

[The reviewer turns to *Sketches by Boz*, to test Dickens's range. These sketches contain] much of the same nicety of observation and quaint perception of the ludicrous as in the *Pickwick Papers*; but the essays distinguished by these qualities bear a small proportion to those in which the laboured, the common-place, or the imitative style predominates.

[But some effective passages are quoted.]

Notwithstanding the merit of these and some other passages, we are under the sorrowful necessity of admitting that these *Sketches* are by no means calculated to dissipate the apprehensions which the decline visible in the later numbers of the *Pickwick Papers* has pretty generally diffused, and, in our opinion, the memoirs of *Oliver Twist*, now in a course of publication in a new magazine edited (as stated in the advertisements) by 'Boz,' afford much higher promise of that gentleman's

---

[1] Mr Serjeant Bompas.　　　　　　　　　[2] Mr Justice Gazelee.

ability to sustain himself in the position he has won; for—(speaking simply of effect, and without reference to the tendency, which is most commonly to foster a prejudice)—there is a sustained power, a range of observation, and a continuity of interest in this series which we seek in vain in any other of his works. The fact is, Mr Dickens writes too often and too fast; on the principle, we presume, of making hay whilst the sun shines, he seems to have accepted at once all engagements that were offered to him, and the consequence is, that in too many instances he has been compelled to 'forestall the blighted harvest of the brain,' and put forth, in their crude, unfinished, undigested state, thoughts, feelings, observations, and plans which it required time and study to mature—or supply the allotted number of pages with original matter of the most common-place description, or hints caught from others and diluted to make them pass for his own. If he persists much longer in this course, it requires no gift of prophecy to foretell his fate —he has risen like a rocket, and he will come down like the stick; but let him give his capacity fair play, and it is rich, vigorous, and versatile enough to insure him a high and enduring reputation.

17. [G. H. Lewes?], from a review of *Sketches, Pickwick,* and *Oliver Twist,* in the *National Magazine and Monthly Critic*

December 1837, i, 445–9

Attributed to Lewes by the *Pilgrim Letters* editors (i, 403n, and by Kathleen Tillotson (*Oliver Twist*, Clarendon edn. (Oxford, 1966), 309). Years later, Lewes recalled how 'something I had written on [*Pickwick*] pleased him [Dickens], and caused him to ask me to call on him' (*Fortnightly Review*, 1872, xvii, 152). The *National Magazine* was one of the series of journals with which this 'Prince of Journalists' (as Carlyle called him) was associated. Lewes (1817–78) was one of the most accomplished critics of the novel during the mid-century; see also Nos. 80, 158. Dickens wrote to him, probably in June 1838, an unusually self-exploratory letter. The *Pilgrim* editors (i, 403n) suggest, doubtless rightly, that Lewes, who was much interested in mental phenomena, had been enquiring about the passage in *Oliver Twist*, ch. xxxiv, about the state of mind between sleeping and waking. Dickens wrote:

With reference to that question of yours concerning Oliver Twist I scarcely know what answer I can give you. I suppose like most authors I look over what I write with exceeding pleasure and think (to use the words of the elder Mr Weller) 'in my innocence that it's all wery capital'. I thought that passage a good one *when* I wrote it, certainly, and I felt it strongly (as I do almost every word I put on paper) *while* I wrote it, but how it came I can't tell. It came like all my other ideas, such as they are, ready made to the point of the pen—and down it went. Draw your own conclusion and hug the theory closely.

I strongly object to printing anything in italics but a word here and there which requires particular emphasis, and that not often. It is framing and glazing an idea and desiring the ladies and gentleman [*sic*] to walk up and admire it. The truth is, that I am a very modest man, and furthermore that if readers cannot detect the point of a passage without having their attention called to it by the writer, I would much rather they lost it and looked out for something else.

... People always like to have a *reason* for their likings or dislikings; and it becomes a fit subject of inquiry, whether Charles Dickens (Boz) has attained his astonishing and extensive popularity from the caprice of the moment, the patronage of the great, the puffing of booksellers, or from his own intrinsic merit; whether, in short, people have any reason (beyond the momentary impulse notoriety always creates) for their delight in perusing his works; and whether he has written that which catches the attention of the 'fleeting hour,' or that which the 'world will not willingly let die.' Two of the Quarterlies have taken up the subject, but not in our opinion with sufficient analytic power to settle the question, or to prevent our offering a few remarks. The *London and Westminster's* was immeasurably superior to the *Quarterly's*, (a blundering article, which made Boz's reputation to arise from his having 'struck out a new vein' in the common language of the Londoners! an assertion as false as it is ridiculous,) but, as it seemed to us, very unequal in its criticism. Let us not be supposed to attempt supplying the deficiencies of these articles; all we would endeavour here is to examine some of the more prominent features in Mr Dickens's genius.

'Boz' has perhaps a wider popularity than any man has enjoyed for many years. Nor alone are his delightful works confined to the young and old, the grave and gay, the witty, the intellectual, the moralist, and the thoughtless of both sexes in the reading circles, from the peer and judge to the merchant's clerk; but even the common people, both in town and country, are equally intense in their admiration. Frequently have we seen the butcher-boy, with his tray on his shoulder, reading with the greatest avidity the last *Pickwick;* the footman, (whose fopperies are so inimitably laid bare,) the maid servant, the chimney-sweep, all classes, in fact, read '*Boz*.' And how has this surprising popularity been attained? Not a puff—with the exception of an occasional extract in the newspapers, hardly a notice —no patronage heralded his fame. He chose, perhaps, the worst possible medium for making his *entrée*—the columns of a newspaper! Yet such was the delicacy of touch, the fineness of observation, and the original, quiet humour of these papers, that he was induced to collect and publish them in two volumes. When the *Sketches* came out, 'Have you read Boz?' was the eternal question. We have traced his popularity upwards, and have, in our limited way, done not a little to make all we knew acquainted with them; but we own that we were fairly astonished at the rapidly increasing popularity of his name.

Byron used to say, that he awoke one morning and found himself celebrated: Boz may say the same; for never was a more rapid, more deserved a reputation made.

The *Sketches*, though distinguished by the same nicety of observation that startles us with its fidelity, and a great fund of humour and sympathy, are more evidently the first efforts of a strong genius, and stand, in comparison with the *Pickwick Papers*, and *Oliver Twist*, rather in the shade. In them he certainly did approach nearer to Washington Irving than any living writer; but we think he now transcends his model. In his two last and most celebrated works, we find qualities combined which no other writer ever had; to compare him to Theodore Hook, (who, with a certain talent of a certain sort, has never written any thing that will live,) is absurd. Theodore Hook is all extravagance and affectation—writing like a man who wishes to be thought a gentleman, and considers that a profound contempt for the *canaille* and Bloomsbury Square are the requisite characteristics. 'Boz' should be compared to no one since no one has ever written like him— no one has ever combined the nicety of observation, the fineness of tact, the exquisite humour, the wit, heartiness, sympathy with all things good and beautiful in human nature, the perception of character, the pathos, and accuracy of description, with the same force that he has done. His works are volumes of human nature, that have a deep and subtle philosophy in them, which those who read only to laugh may not discover; but an attentive reading (and we have read some of the numbers three or four times) will convince any one that in nothing he has written has amusement been his only aim.

Boz has been accused of not giving individuality to his characters— an accusation, we think, particularly unsound. We would beg the reader to bear in mind that a character may be hit off by a master hand in a few lines, and yet retain so perfect an individuality as never to be confounded. Again, a character may be left to develope itself in the action of the work—a method Scott always preferred; or, thirdly, it may be described at length, and with great accuracy of detail. The two first methods have been adopted by Boz; the latter (which we conceive as the worst, but which we think his reviewers have mistaken for the only one) he has not attempted. We would ask, are Jingle, Pickwick, the two Wellers, Solomon Pell, the Medical Students, Old Wardle, Job Trotter, not individuals in the truest sense of the word? That they partake of generality is admitted; and they partake of it from the very fidelity to nature with which they are drawn; for, however different individuals may be, there are always certain generalities running through every class;—*if there were not, how should we class them?*—and of these generalities alone do Boz's more prominent characters partake. The fat boy we admit to be a caricature, yet it gives variety to the work, and is too palpable to admit of cause to criticise; he is very laughable, and his peculiarities, however exaggerated, in many situations give great drollery to the scenes. But what we have more to notice regarding him, is that which has been entirely overlooked by the critics. On a former occasion (p. 277), we pointed out a canon, which we think must be always applied to works of imagination, *viz.*, extravagance is *inconsistent imagination;* poetry is *consistent imagination,* i.e. *constant with itself.* Thus, when Ovid, by a beautiful prosopopœia, creates Echo, he so *sustains* the creation throughout, that, though absurd in point of nature, it is true to poetry. Let this be applied to the 'fat boy.' The creation of this character is not true to nature, (and it is immediately seen not to be,) but it is consistent with itself throughout. It has also been said that no man ever uttered broken sentences like Jingle; this we deny, for we ourselves knew a man, who, long before the *Pickwick* came out, always spoke in that way. 'Glorious day, my dear sir—fished—caught plenty—dined—capital wine—good fellow,' and so forth.

If asked by what peculiar talent is Boz characterised, we find ourselves at a dead fault—if we feel inclined to say, startling fidelity of observation, his wit and humour rise before us, and compel us to pause; and we are obliged to answer that we cannot fairly say what we think he is greatest in, but that it is a combination of those qualities (before enumerated) that characterises him. Look, for instance, at the trial scene, the 'Swarry' at Bath, the Medical Students' supper, the scene with Editor Pott and his Wife, (with her throwing herself on the rug, and asking why she was born), the scene in the Fleet, the Christmas Party, the Review, the Sliding and Skating, (with Tupman screaming '*Fire*' when his leader fell into the water), the Election, Nupkins Mayor, the Temperance Meeting, the Madman's Manuscript, and the Stroller's Tale, or any of the admirable situations in this book, and then ask yourself to which quality do you give the preference? There is one thing worthy of notice, because it speaks the kindliness of his heart and the sympathy of his nature; and that is the charm which he throws over every nature, making you love it in spite of yourself. As for Pickwick, he is the incorporation of benevolence, with a dash of the infirmities of humanity; the two Wellers gain every one's good word; so does Wardle; and even Jingle, scamp though he be, shows many of the better points of our nature, and we like him in spite of ourselves. There is also another thing which is remarkable. Although he takes us into scenes of the lowest description, (more particularly in *Oliver Twist*,) and although he gives us the language of vagabond, thief, footman, ostler, and gentleman, catching their several idioms with the most surprising felicity, yet there is not a single coarse word, or one allusion that could call a blush into the cheek of the most fastidious; and it is this circumstance which has not unfrequently raised our bile, to hear affected, mincing girls (who would come admirably under Swift's definition of a *nice* man, 'one with *nasty* ideas,') who utter all their indelicate words in *French*, say they cannot read 'Boz,' he is *so low*! This disgusting affectation alarms some people from mentioning 'Boz' (without exception the purest writer of the day) before them. . . .

'Boz's' satire is the finest that we ever read, because it is generally satire by *implication*, not personality—we do not say that it cuts so deep as Voltaire or Swift, or that it crushes like Hobbes—but it is pointed enough for its purpose, and has none of the bitter, withering tincture which forms so large a portion of satire in general; and it is done in that style that one might easily suppose an individual under the lash laughing at it himself, and feeling its deep truth at the same time—an effect very different to the satire of the great writers above-mentioned. And this satire is also more powerful, for when a man makes us writhe, we are more apt, with roused feelings, to attack him than to think of reforming ourselves, as was the case with Cobbett; he shocked the prejudices of people too abruptly—told them they were fools in too plain a manner, to make them feel so. The meeting of the 'Pickwickians,' and the speeches on the occasion, the Lion Hunting, Mrs Leo Hunter, the Election, the Two Editors, and the Discussion of the Seventeen Foreign Learned Societies and the Seventeen Home Learned Societies on the stone, bearing 'Bill Stumps, his mark,' are playful touches of satire, yet one or two of them containing startling truths.

One of the peculiar merits of 'Boz' is that of bringing before us things which we have all noticed hundreds of times, yet which we never thought of committing to paper, and they are written with such unaffected ease, that we feel convinced he has witnessed every thing of the kind, and laughed at them. Then, too, his language, even on the most trivial points, has, from a peculiar collocation of the words, or some happy expression, a drollery which is spoiled by repeating or reading loud, because this drollery arises from so fine an association of idea that the sound of the voice destroys it. We cannot help remarking, however, in this respect, a continual straining after humorous things, and this straining gives a laboured air to the work, besides which, it gives a want of light and shade, which fatigues the mind, if reading much at a time. While we are finding fault, an ungrateful task, and one which we feel rather reluctant about, when it is with one from whom we have derived so much gratification—we would notice the incongruity (the more remarkable in one so true to nature) of which he has been guilty in the character of Oliver Twist. To say nothing of the language which this uneducated workhouse-boy ordinarily uses, there are many phrases which amount to positive absurdities in one of his standing, among which is his reply to Mr Bumble (when about five or six years old), that he feels as if the blood was rushing from his heart, or some such metaphor, to express his grief. These are sad blots in this otherwise surpassing work—a work pregnant with philosophy and feeling, such as a metaphysician would be proud to have developed, with the same nicety and fidelity of observation, the same admirable delineation of character, and the same wit and humour as the Pickwick. What characters are the artful Dodger, Grimwig, Nancy, and Mr Bumble! We feel we must conclude, although we have not said one half of what we wished, or what we ought to have said. We have, we hope, fulfilled in some measure our purpose, *viz.*, to shew that Boz has hit fame, not popularity, or in other words, that the admiration with which he is almost universally regarded, is well founded.

18. From an unsigned review, 'Boz and his *Nicholas Nickleby*', *Spectator*

31 March 1838, xi, 304

'We can of course say little' about *Nicholas Nickleby*, the reviewer admits: he is noticing No. 1, and reprints specimens to enable the reader to judge Dickens's present performance. Tom and Jerry were the young men-about-town in Pierce Egan's *Life in London* (1820–1).

The popularity of Boz . . . is one of the literary wonders of the day; not indeed altogether inexplicable, but made up of so many elements, that it is difficult to discover them all, and still more difficult to assign to each its exact effect upon the result. The first quality is, no doubt, his perfect plainness, the common-life character of his subjects, and the art with which he imparts vitality to the literal and whatsoever lies on the surface. He calls upon his reader for no exertion—requires from him no mental elevation: he who runs may read Boz—'he is plain to the meanest capacity.' In addition to this, he has a kind of conventional Cockney humour, best described by a phrase from its own dialect, '*werry funny*.' But, mingled with such qualifications for mob-pleasing, are powers of a higher order. He has much of the most electric spirit for operating upon the vulgar, where no appeal can be made to their interests or their prejudices— the real spirit of humanity, which spoke in Terence's '*Homo sum; nil humanum a me alienum puto*.'[1] Boz has also touches of pathos, and of tragic sadness: he sometimes utters, sometimes suggests, penetrating reflections; and he has often points of universal truth. These things have not only contributed to give Boz part of his popularity, but have redeemed his literalness from the meanness and dryness of the inventorial style, and raised his productions above the mere ephemera of the day; whilst the quaint and homely manner in

---

[1] 'I am a man, I count nothing human indifferent to me' (*Heauton Timorumenos*, I, i, 25

which his best thoughts are mostly expressed, add to his present popularity, whatever may be their future effect.

The very faults of this writer increase his immediate circulation; for they appeal to the every-day experience and social prejudices of his readers. The Cockney pronunciation, the cant words, the slang expressions interwoven in his pages, will lose their zest as soon as they are superseded by other; but as long as they are current, they produce an effect, even upon those who can analyze their nature and detect their worthlessness. Much the same may be said of his incidental topics introduced to satirize the times: they resemble the passing hits of a pantomime — side-splitting at first, decreasing in effect at each repetition, and vapid or unintelligible by the end of the season. This temporary attraction, but permanent defect, extends in a measure to the characters; many of whom, though representing an existing class, belong to a fortuitous and temporary species, the product of a peculiar and local state of society congregated in great towns. Hence we suspect that the circulation of Boz takes certain channels, beyond which he is not greatly relished or read. It would be curious, were it attainable, to know respectively the demand for his publications in the metropolis, in large provincial towns, and in the country. In the latter we suspect it would be small, of course supposing the district removed beyond town impulses.

A proportion, too, of the popular circulation of Boz is attributable to mechanical circumstances. The cuts, and the payment by monthly instalments, do something. The publication in numbers, not only enables the writer to render incidents, persons, and, in short, all *forms*, subservient to his convenience or caprice, but gives just enough to serve as a meal to the mob of readers; and this quantity, or a little more, is perhaps as much of him as can be well borne at a time. Had the *Pickwick* been first published in a volume, it is questionable whether its circulation would have reached one-fifth of its actual extent, or whether the work would have been read through by the multitude. It is a significant fact, that the *Sketches* of this writer, collected into volumes, have a far less extensive demand, although they are more adapted for connected publications.

After all, something must be allowed for inappreciable influences. The air induces an epidemic, we know not why; and the mind is similarly affected. Readers not very old can remember the 'Tom and Jerry' mania. So, Boz is wise to make his hay while the sunshine lasts. . . .

19. [Thomas Henry Lister], from a review of *Sketches* (1st and 2nd Series), *Pickwick, Nickleby,* and *Oliver Twist, Edinburgh Review*

October 1838, lxviii, 75–97

Lister (1800–42), a minor novelist, dramatist and historian, held various official appointments, and was, from 1836, Registrar-General. Dickens was delighted by this review: 'It is all even I could wish, and what more can I say!' (*Pilgrim*, i, 438). Irma Ranta-vaara comments that it was a reaction against the criticisms in the *Quarterly* (see No. 16), and that Lister was the first critic to suggest the comparison between Dickens and Hogarth, which became very popular (*Dickens in the Light of English Criticism* (Helsinki, 1944), 92).

Mr. Charles Dickens, the author of the above works, is the most popular writer of his day. Since the publication of the poems and novels of Sir Walter Scott, there has been no work the circulation of which has approached that of the *Pickwick Papers*. Thirty thousand copies of it are said to have been sold. It has been dramatized by several hands, and played in sundry London theatres. A continuation of it by another writer, has been undertaken as a profitable speculation: and no sooner has its genuine successor, *Nicholas Nickleby*, by the same author, made its appearance in monthly numbers, than it is published on the continent, translated into German. Great popularity is doubtless to be accepted as presumptive evidence of merit—and should at least induce us to regard with attention the qualities of one who can exhibit so many suffrages in his favour. But even a cursory glance over literary history will teach its insufficiency as a *proof* of merit. We shall, therefore, regard it merely as a claim to notice—and treat Mr Dickens with no more favour than if he could count only hundreds instead of myriads, among his readers. His reputation as a writer of fiction rests at present upon the above four works. . . . In all these productions the author has called in the aid of the pencil, and has been contented to share his success with the caricaturist.

He has put them forth in a form attractive, it is true, to that vast majority, the *idle* readers—but one not indicative of high literary pretensions, or calculated to inspire a belief of probable permanence of reputation. They seem, at first sight, to be among the most evanescent of the literary *ephemeræ* of their day—mere humorous specimens of the lightest kind of light reading, expressly calculated to be much sought and soon forgotten—fit companions for the portfolio of caricatures—'good nonsense,'—and nothing more. This is the view which many persons will take of Mr Dickens's writings — but this is not our deliberate view of them. We think him a very original writer—well entitled to his popularity—and not likely to lose it—and the truest and most spirited delineator of English life, amongst the middle and lower classes, since the days of Smollett and Fielding. He has remarkable powers of observation, and great skill in communicating what he has observed—a keen sense of the ludicrous—exuberant humour—and that mastery in the pathetic which, though it seems opposed to the gift of humour, is often found in conjunction with it. Add to these qualities, an unaffected style, fluent, easy, spirited, and terse—a good deal of dramatic power—and great truthfulness and ability in description. We know no other English writer to whom he bears a marked resemblance. He sometimes imitates other writers, such as Fielding in his introductions, and Washington Irving in his detached tales, and thus exhibits his skill as a parodist. But his own manner is very distinct — and comparison with any other would not serve to illustrate and describe it. We would compare him rather with the painter Hogarth. What was in painting, such very nearly is Mr Dickens in prose fiction. The same turn of mind —the same species of power displays itself strongly in each. Like Hogarth he takes a keen and practical view of life—is an able satirist— very successful in depicting the ludicrous side of human nature, and rendering its follies more apparent by humorous exaggeration— peculiarly skilful in his management of details, throwing in circumstances which serve not only to complete the picture before us, but to suggest indirectly antecedent events which cannot be brought before our eyes. Hogarth's cobweb over the poor-box, and the plan for paying off the national debt, hanging from the pocket of a prisoner in the Fleet, are strokes of satire very similar to some in the writings of Mr Dickens. It is fair, in making this comparison, to add, that it does not hold good throughout; and that Mr Dickens is exempt from two of Hogarth's least agreeable qualities—his cynicism and his coarseness. There is no misanthropy in his satire, and no coarseness in his descriptions—a merit enhanced by the nature of his subjects. His works are chiefly pictures of humble life—frequently of the humblest. The reader is led through scenes of poverty and crime, and all the characters are made to discourse in the appropriate language of their respective classes—and yet we recollect no passage which ought to cause pain to the most sensitive delicacy, if read aloud in female society.

We have said that his satire was not misanthropic. This is eminently true. One of the qualities we the most admire in him is his comprehensive spirit of humanity. The tendency of his writings is to make us practically benevolent—to excite our sympathy in behalf of the aggrieved and suffering in all classes; and especially in those who are most removed from observation. He especially directs our attention to the helpless victims of untoward circumstances, or a vicious system—to the imprisoned debtor—the orphan pauper—the parish apprentice—the juvenile criminal— and to the tyranny, which, under the combination of parental neglect, with the mercenary brutality of a pedagogue, may be exercised with impunity in schools. His humanity is plain, practical, and manly. It is quite untainted with sentimentality. There is no mawkish wailing for ideal distresses—no morbid exaggeration of the evils incident to our lot—no disposition to excite unavailing discontent, or to turn our attention from remediable grievances to those which do not admit a remedy. Though he appeals much to our feelings, we can detect no instance in which he has employed the verbiage of spurious philanthropy. . . .

Good feeling and sound sense are shown in his application of ridicule. It is never levelled at poverty or misfortune; or at circumstances which can be rendered ludicrous only by their deviation from artificial forms; or by regarding them through the medium of a conventional standard. Residence in the regions of Bloomsbury, ill-dressed dinners, and ill-made liveries, are crimes which he suffers to go unlashed; but follies or abuses, such as would be admitted alike in every sphere of society to be fit objects for his satire, are hit with remarkable vigour and precision. Nor does he confine himself to such as are obvious; but elicits and illustrates absurdities, which, though at once acknowledged when displayed, are plausible, and comparatively unobserved. . . .

[Lister quotes and praises the 'Pickwickian sense' episode (ch. i), the election canvassing scene (ch. xiii) and the 'Chinese metaphysics' joke (ch. li).]

... But Mr Dickens is a satirist of a sterner kind than the preceding extracts tend to show; and makes his lash fall smartly upon abuses of a graver character. The whole story of the action against Pickwick for breach of promise of marriage, from its ludicrous origin, to Pickwick's eventual release from prison, where he has been immured for refusal to pay the damages, is one of the most acute and pointed satires upon the state and administration of English law that ever appeared in the light and lively dress of fiction. The account of the trial is particularly good. ...

... The imprisonment of Pickwick affords an opportunity of depicting the interior of a debtor's prison, and the manifold evils of that system, towards the abolition of which much, we trust, will have been effected by a statute of the past session ...

[Quotes the death of the Chancery prisoner, ch. xliv.]

t is useless to hope that this tragical fiction may be unsupported by truth, or be founded only on events which happened long ago. A London newspaper of August 25, 1838, tells us that on the preceding day an inquest having been held at the Queen's Bench prison, on the body of a female debtor who had been a prisoner there *more than sixteen years*, through a Chancery suit, the jury returned the following verdict—'*Died of nervous fever brought on through long confinement and excited feelings.*'

Mr Dickens is very successful as a delineator of those manners, habits, and peculiarities which are illustrative of particular classes and callings. He exhibits amusingly the peculiar turn of thought which belongs to each; and, as if he had been admitted behind the scenes, brings to light those artifices which members of a fraternity are careful to conceal from the world at large. For example, a medical practitioner in the country thus describes his arts of rising.

Quotes Bob Sawyer, ch. xxxviii.]

Mr Dickens's characters are sketched with a spirit and distinctness which rarely fail to convey immediately a clear impression of the person intended. They are, however, not complete and finished delineations, but rather outlines, very clearly and sharply traced, which the reader may fill up for himself; and they are calculated not so much to represent the actual truth as to suggest it. Analyses of disposition, and explanations of motives will not be found, and, we may add, will be little required. His plan is, not to describe his personages, but to make them speak and act,—and it is not easy to misunderstand them. These remarks are not applicable to *all* his characters. Some are too shadowy and undefined,—some not sufficiently true to nature; in some the representations consist of traits too trivial or too few; and some are spoiled by exaggeration and caricature. Pickwick's companions, Winkle, Snodgrass, and Tupman, are very uninteresting personages,— having peculiarities rather than characters—useless incumbrances, which the author seems to have admitted hastily among his *dramatis personæ* without well knowing what to do with them. The swindler Jingle and his companion want reality; and the former talks a disjointed jargon, to which some likeness may be found in farces, but certainly none in actual life. The young ladies in the *Pickwick Papers* are nonentities. The blustering Dowler, and the Master of the Ceremonies at Bath, are mere caricatures. The medical students are coarsely and disagreeably drawn. Wardle, though a tolerably good country squire, is hardly a modern one; and it may be doubted if Mr Weller, senior, can be accepted as the representative of any thing more recent than the last generation of stage-coachmen.

On the other hand, there are many characters truly excellent. First stand Pickwick and his man Weller,—the modern Quixote and Sancho of Cockaigne. Pickwick is a most amiable and eccentric combination of irritability, benevolence, simplicity, shrewdness, folly, and good sense—frequently ridiculous, but never contemptible, and always inspiring a certain degree of respect even when placed in the most ludicrous situations, playing the part of butt and dupe. Weller is a character which we do not remember to have seen attempted before. He is a favourable, yet, in many respects, faithful representative of the Londoner of humble life,—rich in native humour, full of the confidence, and address, and knowledge of the world, which is given by circumstances to a dweller in cities, combined with many of the most attractive qualities of the English character,—such as writers love to show in the brave, frank, honest, light-hearted sailor. His legal characters, Sergeant Snubbin, Perker, Dodson, Fogg, and Pell, are touched, though slightly, yet all with spirit, and a strong appearance of truth. Greater skill in drawing characters is shown in *Oliver Twist* and *Nicholas Nickleby* than in *Pickwick*. His Ralph Nickleby, and Mrs Nickleby, deserve to be noticed as peculiarly successful.

But Mr Dickens's forte perhaps lies less in drawing characters than in describing incidents. He seizes with great skill those circumstances which are capable of being graphically set before us; and makes his passing scenes distinctly present to the reader's mind. Ludicrous circumstances are those which he touches most happily; of which the *Pickwick Papers* afford many examples; such as the equestrian distresses of Pickwick and his companions, the pursuit of Jingle, and Pickwick's night adventures in the boarding-school garden,—incidents richly comic and worthy of Smollett; and which are narrated with Smollett's spirit, without his coarseness. His descriptions of scenery are also good, though in a minor degree; and among these the aspect of the town is perhaps better delineated than that of the country; and scenes which are of an unattractive kind with more force and effect than those which are susceptible of poetical embellishment.

Hitherto we have dwelt on the characteristics of the author rather than on the merits or demerits of any one of his works. The examination of them is of secondary importance, because the most popular among them owed its success, certainly not to its merits as a whole, but to the attractiveness of detached passages. The *Pickwick Papers* are, as the author admits in his preface, defective in plan, and want throughout that powerful aid which fiction derives from an interesting and well constructed plot. *Nicholas Nickleby* appears to be commenced with more attention to this important requisite in novel-writing; and if the author will relieve the painful sombreness of his scenes with a sufficient portion of sunshine, it will deserve to exceed the popularity of *Pickwick*. But *Oliver Twist*, a tale not yet completed, is calculated to give a more favourable impression of Mr Dickens's powers as a writer of fiction than any thing else which he has yet produced. There is more interest in the story, a plot better arranged, characters more skilfully and carefully drawn, without any diminution of spirit, and without that tone of humorous exaggeration which, however amusing, sometimes detracts too much from the truthfulness of many portions of the *Pickwick Papers*. . . .

[Summarizes the story, with lengthy quotations.]

We have given the foregoing faint outline chiefly for the purpose of making our extracts more intelligible—but it can afford very little idea of the interest of a story of which the merit lies chiefly in the details; and in which, moreover, there are sundry incidents which it is not necessary to mention here, which seem to point to the possible discovery of Oliver's parentage, and invest it with much of that mysterious interest which is always a useful ingredient in fiction. The author, however, must beware lest he converts a certain Mr Monks who figures in the latter chapters, into a mere melo-dramatic villain of romance. There is such perfect truthfulness in the generality of his characters, that deviations from nature are less tolerable than when found in other works. Unfinished as this tale still is, it is the best example which Mr Dickens has yet afforded of his power to produce a good novel; but it cannot be considered a conclusive one. The difficulties to which he is exposed in his present periodical mode of writing are, in some respects, greater than if he allowed himself a wider field, and gave his whole work to the public at once. But he would be subjected to a severer criticism if his fiction could be read continuedly—if his power of maintaining a sustained interest could be tested—if his work could be viewed as a connected whole, and its object, plan, consistency, and arrangement brought to the notice of the reader at once. This ordeal cannot be passed triumphantly without the aid of other qualities than necessarily belong to the most brilliant sketcher of detached scenes. We do not, however, mean to express a doubt that Mr Dickens can write with judgment as well as with spirit. His powers of observation and description are qualities rarer, and less capable of being acquired, than those which would enable him to combine the scattered portions of a tale into one consistent and harmonious whole. If he will endeavour to supply whatever may be effected by care and study—avoid imitation of other writers—keep nature steadily before his eyes—and check all disposition to exaggerate—we know no writer who seems likely to attain higher success in that rich and useful department of fiction which is founded on faithful representations of human character, as exemplified in the aspects of English life.

20. Unsigned notice, 'Loose Thoughts', *Fraser's Magazine*

October 1838, xviii, 500

It was remarked by an acute and well-judging member of the House of Commons, the other day, that a vast proportion of nonsense which was formerly prevalent in that assembly, under the head of personal altercations had been cut down by a single stroke of CHARLES DICKENS's pen. He observed that since the appearance of the first number of the *Pickwick Papers* in which the angry discussion between the linen-draper and the founder of the club takes place, we had not been treated with a single scene of this kind, formerly so common, in which honourable Members, after accusing each other of falsehood, swindling, or some other little irregularities of a similar kind, ended the affair amicably, at last, by declaring that these terms were only meant to apply 'in a *parliamentary* sense'.

This is something for a man to have done, and that by a simple dash of the pen. But still it is much to be regretted, that one possessed of such extraordinary powers, and having such a hold on the public mind as C.D. has now obtained, should turn his vast opportunities to so slender an account. No one who reads his papers can doubt the excellence of his disposition. The very choice of his later subjects proves his desire to do good. The orphan in the workhouse—the exiled child at a Yorkshire school—the poor milliner's slave,—all show the bent of his mind; and, in a measure, each of these exhibitions will do good. The worst of it is, that after all our sympathy, little can we, the million who read his sketches, do to reform *these* evils. But there is a public crime more vast than either of these, and capable, from its peculiar character, of being put down, in whole or in part by legislative enactment. I mean, the *working little boys and girls to death in the factories.* There is another mischief, too, of great and increasing amount,—the demoralization of our agricultural labourers in the beer-shops of our hamlets, the seminaries of poaching, smuggling and all manner of licentiousnesss.

In these matters, and in some others which might be named, Mr Dickens might, without diverging into the thorny path of politics, be of incalculable service to his fellowmen.

21. From an unsigned review of *Oliver Twist*, *Literary Gazette*

24 November 1838, 741

... we will neither enter upon a review of the author's general merits, not attempt to illustrate this particular work by quotations. The former would require a wide scope (wider than we deem advisable at present, when Mr Dickens occupies us under so many shapes, and in so many places); and the latter could only be a repetition of that with which almost every body has already become familiar. We cannot, however, pass over this production so very briefly; and we would advert to one quality which Mr Dickens has displayed to an extent altogether unequalled, if we except, perhaps, the mighty names of Shakspere and Scott. We allude to the creation of individual character: to the raising up and embodying of a number of original human beings in so substantial a form, and endowed with such living feelings and passions, and acting in so real and natural a manner, that they immediately become visibly, personally, and intimately known to us; and we no more doubt of their existence than if we had seen them in the flesh, conversed with them, and observed their conduct. This was made curiously manifest on the appearance of the characters at the Adelphi and Surrey theatres. All classes instantly recognised them; and boxes, pit, and gallery, exclaimed 'That's such a one, and that's such another,' through the whole of the *dramatis personæ* of *Oliver Twist* and *Nicholas Nickleby*. This is true fame; and let us offer a few remarks on its cause.

To speak of the mightiest. Shakspere exhausted worlds, and then imagined new. Scott revelled in the invention of Meg Merrilies, Dominie Sampson, Cuddie Headrigg, Dandie Dinmont, Serjeant Bothwell, Dugald Dalgetty, Bailie Nicol Jarvie, Rob Roy, and a host of others. But coming to others, and to names celebrated in our literature, we find that the creation of a single character, or of two, three, or four, has been deemed sufficient to exalt the reputation of a writer. Robinson Crusoe and Friday glorify the name of De Foe; Uncle Toby and Corporal Trim, Mr Shandy and Dr Slop, are enough for Sterne; John Gilpin, for Cowper; Tam O'Shanter and his comrades, for Burns; and we might enumerate a hundred similar instances. Then look at Dickens—a young man, and not above two or three years before the public. Already has he peopled the regions of imagination with a crowd of new creatures. It would require a page to record them, from Pickwick and Weller to Squeers, Ralph Nickleby, Smike and Newman Noggs—all very original, and all true to the life. At the close of a long career, Richardson, Fielding, Smollett, our brightest lights in fiction, had done no more than he has achieved within this wonderfully short space.

What felicity and acuteness of observation does this single feature in his literary course proclaim! And it is, after all, but a single feature. He has dug deep into the human mind; and he has nobly directed his energies to the exposure of evils—the workhouse, the starving school, the factory system, and many other things, at which blessed nature shudders and recoils. As a moralist and reformer of cruel abuses, we have the warmer thanks of the community to offer him. . . .

22. [Richard Ford], from an unsigned review, *Quarterly Review*

June 1839, lxiv, 83–102

'But we are getting tedious,' writes Ford after eighteen pages, justly and with unaccustomed brevity. A few of his more relevant remarks are here excerpted. Ford (1796–1858) was a contributor to the quarterlies and an author, notably about Spain.

. . . Like Byron, [Boz] awoke one morning and found himself famous, and for a similar reason: for, however dissimilar the men and their works, both were originals, and introduced a new style of writing. They were not, however, causes, but the effects of predisposing causes, like laws which give a form of authority to usages previously decreed by opinion. They both launched on the neap tide; both touched a string which vibrated with another pitched to the same key in their readers' hearts. . . .

[After a long excursion, Ford begins offering an explanation: 'Boz is a truly national author—English to the backbone,' and is catering for the contemporary taste for low life. The 'strange habits' of 'her Majesty's lower orders . . . excite a curiosity in the higher, their antipodes.']

Life in London, as revealed in the pages of Boz, opens a new world to thousands bred and born in the same city, whose palaces overshadow their cellars—for the one half of mankind lives without knowing how the other half dies: in fact, the regions about Saffron Hill are less known to our great world than the Oxford Tracts, the inhabitants are still less; they are as human, at least to all appearances, as are the Esquimaux or the Russians, and probably (though the Zoological Society will not vouch for it) endowed with souls; but, whether souled or not souled, they are too far beneath the higher classes to endanger any loss of caste or contamination in the inquiry. Secure in their own position, these really enjoy Boz. . . .

. . . Boz, like Byron has his imitators: since the increasing demand for the *Nickleby* article, Boz, not being protected by patent like

Mackintosh,[1] has been pirated; cuckoos lay their eggs in his nest; countless are the Factory-Boys which Mrs Trollope has turned loose.[2] ... Whatever may be the merit of these imitations, for which we are not now looking, the strength of Boz consists in his originality, in his observation of character, his humour—on which he never dwells. He leaves a good thing alone, like Curaçoa, and does not dilute it; wit, which is not taught in Gower Street,[3] drops out of his mouth as naturally as pearls and diamonds in the fairy tale; the vein is rich, racy, sparkling, and goodnatured—never savage, sarcastic, malevolent, nor misanthropic; always well placed and directed against the odious, against purse-pride insolence, and the abuse of brief authority. . . . Boz sketches localities, particularly in London, with marvellous effect; he concentrates with the power of a *camera lucida*. Born with an organic bump for distinct observation of men and things, he sees with the eye, and writes with the pen of an artist—we mean with artistical skill, and not as artists write. He translates nature and life. The identical landscape or occurrence, when reduced on one sheet, will interest and astonish those who had before seen with eyes that saw not, and heard with ears that heard not, on whom previously the general incident had produced no definite effect. Boz sets before us in a strong light the water-standing orphan's eye, the condemned prisoner, the iron entering into his soul. This individuality arrests, for our feelings for human suffering in the aggregate are vague, erratic, and undefined. . . The circumstantiality of the murder of Nancy is more harrowing than the bulletin of 50,000 men killed at Borodino. . . .

Boz fails whenever he attempts to write for effect; his descriptions of rural felicity and country scenery, of which he clearly knows much less than of London, where he is quite at home and wide awake, are, except when comical, over-laboured and out of nature. His 'gentle and genteel folks' are unendurable; they are devoid of the grace, repose, and ease of good society; a something between Cheltenham and New York. They and their extreme propriety of ill-bred good-breeding are (at least we hope so) altogether the misconceptions of our author's uninitiated imagination, mystified by the inanities of the kid-glove Novelists. Boz is, nevertheless, never vulgar when treating on subjects

---

[1] Charles Mackintosh patented his invention of waterproof fabrics in 1824. There were many plagiarizations of *Nickleby* and other early works: see Louis James, *Fiction for the Working Man 1830–1850* (1963), ch. iv.

[2] Mrs Frances Trollope's novel *Michael Armstrong, the Factory Boy* was serialized in 20 monthly parts, from February 1839.

[3] Location of the University (College) of London.

which are avowedly vulgar. He deals truly with human nature, which never can degrade; he takes up everything, good, bad, or indifferent, which he works up into a rich alluvial deposit. He is natural, and that never can be ridiculous. He is never guilty of the two common extremes of second-rate authors—the one a pretension of intimate acquaintance with the inner life of Grosvenor Square—the other an affected ignorance of the doings, and a sneering at the bad dinners, of Bloomsbury—he leaves that for people to whom such dinners would be an unusual feast. We are bound to admit that Boz's young ladies are awful— Kate Nickleby is the best of them—but they are all bad enough; but we must also admit that, both in fiction and reality, these bread-and-butter budding beauties are most difficult to deal with, except we are in love with them. They are neither fish, flesh, nor fowl, and, as Falstaff says of Dame Quickly, no man knows where to have them.

Boz is regius professor of slang, that expression of the mother-wit, the low humour of the lower classes, their Sanscrit, their hitherto unknown tongue, which, in the present phasis of society and politics, seems likely to become the idiom of England. Where drabs, house-breakers, and tavern-spouting patriots play the first fiddle, they can only speak the language which expresses their ideas and habits. In order fully to enjoy their force, we must know the conventional value of these symbols of ideas, although we do not understand the lingo like Boz, who has it at his fingers'-ends. We are amused with the comi-cality, in spite of our repugnance that the decent veil over human guilt and infirmities should be withdrawn; we grieve that the deformity of nakedness should not only be exhibited to the rising generation, but rendered agreeable by the undeniable drollery; a coarse transcript would not be tolerated. This is the great objection which we feel to-wards *Oliver Twist*. It deals with the outcasts of humanity, who do their dirty work in work, pot, and watch houses, to finish on the Newgate drop. Alas! for the Horatian precept, '*Virginibus puerisque canto.*'[1] The happy ignorance is disregarded. Our youth should not even suspect the possibility of such hidden depths of guilt, for their tender memories are wax to receive and marble to retain. These infamies feed the innate evil principle, which luxuriates in the super-natural and horrid, the dread and delight of our childhood, which is never shaken off, for no man entirely outlives the nursery. We object to the familiarising our ingenuous youth with 'slang;' it is based in travestie of better things. . . .

[1] 'I sing to maidens and boys' (Horace, *Odes*, III, i, 4).

He appears to propose to himself in all his works some definite abuse to be assailed. Thus Pickwick, the investigator of 'tittlebats,' sallying forth with his disciples on knight-erratic discoveries, conveys a good-humoured satire on the meetings of those peripatetic philosophers who star, sectionise, and eat turtle in the commercial towns, making fools of themselves, throwing a ridicule over science, and unsettling country gentlemen from their legitimate studies of poor, poachers, and turnpikes. Buzfuz and tomata-sauce are a fair exposition of the brow-beating system of our courts of injustice; the verdict does honour to trial by jury. *Nickleby* is aimed, primarily, at those cheap seminaries where starvation is taught gratis, and which we fear were too common throughout England; and we rejoice to hear that the exposure has already put down many infant bastilles. . . .

Oliver Twist, again, is directed against the poor-law and workhouse system, and in our opinion with much unfairness. The abuses which he ridicules are not only exaggerated, but in nineteen cases out of twenty do not at all exist. Boz so rarely mixes up politics, or panders to vulgar prejudices about serious things, that we regret to see him joining an outcry which is partly factious, partly sentimental, partly interested. The besetting sin of 'white-waistcoated' guardians is profusion, not parsimony; and this always must be the case where persons have to be charitable out of funds to which individually they are small contributors. . . .

We shall say very little more about this book, which we presume all our readers have read. The plot, if it be not an abuse of terms to use such an expression, turns on the early misfortunes, persecution, and final prosperity of Mr Oliver Twist. . . .

[Ford describes Oliver's adventures.]

In a word each crime he witnesses is the making of him, and all robbed by his companions of the Clan Fagin are the only people connected with his past history and future fortunes.

The whole tale rivals in improbabilities those stories in which the hero at his birth is cursed by a wicked fairy and protected by a good one; but Oliver himself, to whom all these improbabilities happen, is the most improbable of all. He is represented to be a pattern of modern excellence, guileless himself, and measuring others by his own innocence; delicate and high-minded, affectionate, noble, brave, generous, with the manners of a son of a most distinguished gentleman, not only uncorrupted but incorruptible: less absurd would it be to expect to gather grapes on thorns, to find pearls in dunghills, violets in Drury Lane, or make silk purses of sows' ears. Boz, in his accurate representation of Noah Claypole, shows that he knows how much easier the evil principle is developed than the good. He draws the certain effects of certain causes. Workhouse boys are not born with original virtue; nor was any one except Daniel exposed to wild beasts without being eaten up. We are not afraid that the rational portion of Boz's readers may be misled by examples which they know never did and never can exist in reality, and which they presume were invented in order to exaggerate the pathos, and throw by contrast an additional horror on vice: yet the numerical majority of the young, and of the lower orders—(for whom books in shilling Numbers have the *appearance* of being mainly de-signed)—judge from feelings, and are fascinated by the brilliant fallacies which reach the head through the heart. . . . Our apprehension is that, in spite of honest intentions, he may be found practically a co-operator with those whose aim is to degrade the national mind—well knowing that in a pure and healthy atmosphere of opinion their own gaudy fictions must wither as soon as blown. His *implied* negation of the inevitable results of evil training has a tendency to countenance their studied sentimentalization of the genus *scamp*. But we object *in toto* to the staple of *Oliver Twist*—a series of representations which must familiarize the rising generation with the haunts, deeds, language, and characters of the very dregs of the community; 'where ignorance is bliss, 'tis folly to be wise.' It is a hazardous experiment to exhibit to the young these enormities, even on the Helot principle of inspiring disgust. This perversion of education deadens and extinguishes those pure feelings which form the best guides through life; this early initiation into an acquaintance with the deepest details of crime reverses the order of nature; it strips youth of its happy, confiding credulity— the imputation of no wrong, the heart pure as a pearl. It inspires the caution and distrust which are, alas! natural to age and experience, but out of place and unamiable in the morning of our day.

The certainty, however, of our reaping as we sow is so self-evident, that we may spare our *prose*—and pass on to the heroine, Nancy, a character which all will admit is delineated with great power, however they may differ in regard to its propriety and truth. . . .

The character of Bill Sikes, the housebreaker and murderer, is drawn, we conceive, with equal power and accuracy . . . The account of the behaviour of the murderer after the deed is done is of first-rate excellence: he is traced step by step, where an inferior writer would have generalized. The attempt to drown the dog, and the dialogue while the mail-coach stops, are perfect. Those matter-of-fact, every-day occurrences, which the conscience-haunted outcast applies to self-accusation, heighten the truth of the picture, and evince that close observation of incidents and perception of character and professions so remarkable in our author. . . .

It is hardly fair to conclude an article, however brief and desultory, upon *Oliver Twist*, without making some allusion to the obligations under which author and reader are laid by the graphic running commentary of Mr Cruikshank's etchings. This, we suspect, may be as great an artist in his own way as Boz himself—and it is difficult to say, on laying down the book, how much of the powerful impression we are conscious of may be due, not to the pen, but to the pencil. . . .

23. From an unsigned notice, 'Charles Dickens and his Works,' *Fraser's Magazine*

April 1840, xxi, 381–400

Few writers have risen so rapidly into extensive popularity as Dickens, and that by no mean or unjustifiable panderings to public favour, or the use of low arts of tricking, puffery, or pretence. Four years ago his name was almost unknown, except in some narrow newspaper circles; and his compositions had not extended beyond ephemeral sketches and essays, which, though shrewd, clever, and amusing, would never have been collected as they now are into volumes, but for the speedily acquired and far-diffused fame of *Pickwick*. Before we pass from these sketches, we must say that they contain germs of almost every character Boz has since depicted, as well as of his incidents and stories, and that they display the quaint peculiarities of his style. Some of them, indeed, are, we think, better than any thing which he has written in his more celebrated performances.

They were always liked so far as they were known; and their

success, we suppose, suggested the idea of weaving similar papers into a connected series. Boz was fortunate in meeting with Phiz, and Chapman and Hall fortunate in meeting with both; and Pickwick went on his way rejoicing. The oddity of the hero's appearance in the engravings attracted immediate attention; and the opening paper, though written in a far different style from that which the work assumed in its progress, was, if somewhat commonplace, foolery jocular enough to please.

The machinery of the club was indeed very hackneyed, and it soon became excessively wearisome. Mr Dickens, therefore, was perfectly right in discontinuing it; but, when he informs us [in the Preface to *Pickwick*] that the same objections, which a perusal of his pleasant scenes, when collected, will draw forth, have been made to the works of some of the greatest novelists in the English language, we do not think that he is aware of what the objections to *him* as a novelist really are. No critic worth reading objects to a 'series of adventures in which the scenes are ever changing, and the characters come and go like the men and women we encounter in the real world.' The writer who has the power of so delineating characters has indeed reached at the highest point of dramatic and narrative art. What the critical reader of Boz's novels objects to is, that, whatever we may think of the *come-and-go* characters, that the *standing* characters are *not* like the men and the women of the real world. Dr. Slammer of the 79th, and a great many more of the incidental sketches, are consistent: we have seen such people and their peculiarities are well hit off. But beyond supporting a character consistently through three or four caricature scenes, Mr Dickens's power does not extend.

Let us, for example, take Mr Pickwick himself. His first appearance is that of a vain, old fool, gravely occupied in the serious investigation of frivolous trifles.

[Quotes sample episodes.]

In short Mr Pickwick, as originally designed by Mr Dickens, is a mere butt for caricature, making ridiculous speeches, and getting into ridiculous situations. Such is a tolerably fair and intelligible character, and he is surrounded by fitting companions. . . .

[The reviewer then surveys Mr Pickwick's later development, through to the final chapter's 'Let us leave our old friend . . .']

Mr. Pickwick with a countenance lighted up with smiles which the heart of no man, woman, or child, could resist! Is this the Mr Pickwick of the fight with the cabman,—the hunt after the hat,—the drive to Dingley Dell,—the breakdown in the chase after Jingle,—the tender scene with his landlady,—the hiding in the boarding-school garden,—the wheelbarrow in the pound,—the double-bedded room, with the middle-aged lady,—the top of the sedan-chair,—the Court of King's Bench,—the lodge at the Fleet,—the warden's room,—the encounter with Mrs Bardell,—the remonstrance with Bob Sawyer's mode of travelling,—the contest between the rival editors,—in short, the Mr Pickwick of Phiz from his first plate to the last? To borrow a favourite phrase of Sam Weller's, '*We* ray-ther think *not*.' The fact is, that Phiz is consistent in *his* conception of Mr Pickwick throughout: he is the same idiotic lump of bland blockheadism, unrelieved by thought or feeling, from beginning to end. In the hands of Boz, he commences as a butt and ends as a hero.

In the other characters we have the same inconsistency. Winkle, a poor, unaccomplished, ungentlemanlike poltroon at first, is in the end a delicate and romantic lover, inspiring a handsome and interesting young lady with a refined attachment. Snodgrass, an ass of a poet, not fit to fill half-a-dozen lines of a review in the *Fraser Papers*, turns out to be an honourable and sensible gentleman before the book concludes, and is duly rewarded with the hand of one of its favourite beauties. All this, certainly, is not, as the painters say, in keeping; and Mr Dickens may perhaps now perceive that the objection to the Pickwick papers, as a whole, is not that 'the characters come and go like the men and women we encounter in the real world,' but that they do *not*. He may, perhaps, also find, on reflecting, that this objection never was made to the works of some or any of the greatest novelists in the English language, except by those who do not read them, or cannot understand them.

[The reviewer finds the same defect in *Oliver Twist*: Mr Brownlow and Nancy are inconsistently characterized.]

In *Nicholas Nickleby* the alteration of character is less striking, for the hero himself has no character at all, being but the walking thread-paper to convey the various threads of the story. Kate is no better; and the best-drawn characters in the book, Mantalini and Mrs Nickleby, have only caricature parts to play; and, in preserving them, there is no great difficulty. In the other novels, Jingle and Sam Weller, Bumble and the Dodger, are, for the same reason, consistent throughout; but these are not the characters which people meet in common life. Every one must see that the Smike of the beginning is not the Smike of the end; but, as

Mr Dickens's story met with 'an untoward accident,' which compelled him to alter his original finishing of the character, we shall not say any thing about it. In general we may remark that Boz's good-nature makes him improve his characters as he proceeds. Pickwick the ass becomes Pickwick the wise; Nance the naughty is converted into Nance the noble, and so on. In *Nicholas Nickleby* we have an exception. Squeers and Ralph Nickleby become worse and worse as the story proceeds; and here, too, the end of these worthies is not consistent with the beginning. Squeers at first is nothing more than an ignorant and wretched hound, making a livelihood for himself and his family by starving a miserable group of boys. The man has not intellect for any thing better or worse; and yet we find him at last an adept in disguising himself, in ferreting out hidden documents, in carrying through a difficult and entangled scheme of villany. Ralph Nickleby makes his appearance as a shrewd, selfish, hard-hearted usurer, intent on nothing but making and hoarding money; in the end we find him actuated by some silly feelings of spite or revenge, by which he cannot, under any circumstances, make a farthing, and which he would have looked upon as childish weaknesses that ought not to find their place in the bosom of a man of sense, and knowledge of the world. His committing suicide, and that out of remorse too, is perfectly out of character. There is no need of our going through any of the details of a story so familiarly known to all readers of novels and frequenters of theatres; but it is sufficient to call attention to the fact that Ralph Nickleby has not done any thing that could expose him to legal inconvenience; that he would have held his head in society the day after as he had the day before the discovery of his transactions with Arthur Gride; and that it is quite as probable that he would have been foiled by Lord Verisopht or Smike, as by a couple of such unredeemed and irredeemable idiots as the Brothers Cheeryble. Mr Dickens assures us in his preface that he has drawn these insufferable bores from actual life. It may be so; if it be, we recommend him to abstain from the life academies which furnish no better subjects; for his hand was not intended for drawing such faultless monsters which the world ne'er saw, as these pot-bellied Sir Charles Grandisons of the ledger and day-book. The veritable Cheery-bles may, no doubt, deserve all the compliments with which they are besplattered; but, in the novel, their appearance, or that of their nephew, or of Tim Linkinwater, is quite sufficient to warn the reader to skip the page with the utmost possible activity.

[Among other causes of weakness and carelessness, the reviewer suggests that] . . . the necessity of filling a certain quantity of pages per month imposed upon the writer a great temptation to amplify trifling ingredients, and to swell sentence after sentence with any sort of words that would occupy space. The very spirit of a penny-a-liner, for instance, breaks out in the prolix descriptions of the various walks through the streets of London, every turn in which is enumerated with the accuracy of a cabman. *Oliver Twist* and *Nicholas Nickleby* are stuffed with 'passages that lead to nothing,' merely to fill the necessary room. Now, in the separate monthly essays this was no harm,—on the contrary, it was of positive good to the main objects, viz. the sale; but when we find them collected, they do not improve the sequence of the story, or advance the fame of the writer. In short, the habits of the reporter break out—the copy is to be given in—and what shall we write of but what we know? How fill the paper, but by reports of debates, meetings, societies, police-offices, courts of justice, vestry-rooms, and so forth, spun out as amusingly and as lengthily as possible, all with a view to the foreman's bill at the end?

But this is the only fault of Boz—if fault it can be called, to make hay while the sun shines. We wish him well; but talking of literature in any other light than that of a hack trade, we do not like this novel-writing by scraps against time. He can never do himself or his readers justice. Let him remember the case of Pierce Egan, once quite as popular as Boz is now, and aim at better things. He has one great merit, independent of his undoubted powers of drollery, observation, and caricature,—he has not lent his pen to any thing that can give countenance to vice or degradation; and he has always espoused the cause of the humble, the persecuted, and the oppressed. This of itself would cover far more literary sins than Boz has to answer for; and, indeed, we do not remember any of importance enough to require covering at all. With this we bid not good *speed*, but good moderation of pace; and we trust that, since *Master Humphrey* has set up *a clock*, he will henceforward take *time*.

MASTER HUMPHREY'S CLOCK

4 April 1840 – 27 November 1841

Dickens's original plan to make this weekly a miscellany proved un-
wieldy and unpopular; as Hood remarked, the machinery of Master
Humphrey and his friends was a nuisance (No. 25). For a *Times*
reviewer several years later, the resuscitation of the Wellers, in the early
numbers of the *Clock*, was the first sign of a fact abundantly evident
since, that Dickens's 'creative faculty . . . was already on the decline'
(27 December 1845, 6). The *Clock* was soon turned over to uninterrupted novel-serializing; *The Old Curiosity Shop* appeared in it, 25
April 1840 to 6 February 1841, and *Barnaby Rudge* from 13 February
1841 to the end.

The Old Curiosity Shop was, as a later critic remarked 'more completely *sui generis*' than any of Dickens's novels, its especial charm lying
in 'the mingling of a conception of great poetical beauty with the
events and persons of common life' (*Ecclesiastic and Theologian*, October
1855, xvii, 467). For most readers the novel was essentially the story of
Little Nell; she predominated, as no other hero or heroine in Dickens
had done, and the novel stood or fell according to one's response to her.
The only other character to receive much attention or adulation was
Dick Swiveller. Mrs Oliphant, for instance, who came to loathe 'that
Smike's unceasing drivellings and those everlasting Nells' (*Victorian
Age in Literature* (1892), 269), never ceased to praise Dick (see Nos. 96);
similarly, Thackeray had 'never read the *Nelly* part of the *Old
Curiosity Shop* more than once; whereas I have Dick Swiveller and the
Marchioness by heart' ('Jerome Paturot', *Fraser's Magazine*, September
1843, xxviii, 351). Quilp was praised, but never entered the Dickensian
Pantheon. Little Nell made her mark immediately: Forster was able to
predict for her 'as long a life as any member of the great family of
English fiction can hope to enjoy' (*Examiner*, 4 December 1841, 772).
Comparisons with Cordelia and Imogen were frequent. At a less
literary, more personal, level she could be imagined 'cling[ing] with
a never-ending fondness round our necks, inseparable for ever'
(*Ainsworth's Magazine*, January 1844, v, 88). Many items from later
years, printed below, refer to her. Nor was the international furore

about her restricted to simple unsophisticated readers and arguably ga-ga old men like Landor and Jeffrey. For the austerely intellectual *Westminster Review*, for instance, she was 'the happiest and most perfect of Dickens's sketches . . . a tragedy of the true sort' (1847: see No. 66). For the later fierce reaction against her, see Ford, *Dickens and his Readers*, ch. iv, 'Little Nell: the limits of explanatory criticism', and my lecture, 'The Decline of Pathos', cited on p. 26. For some scepticism about the extent of the grief caused by Little Nell's death, see the Preface to Volume II of the *Pilgrim Letters*, pp. ix–xii. For Landor's enthusiasm, see Forster, *Life*, 145.

Barnaby Rudge seems to have attracted little serious discussion, and not much enthusiasm. Dickens's long-intended historical novel (see John Butt and Kathleen Tillotson, *Dickens at Work* (1957), ch. iv) suffered by comparison both with Scott and with Dickens's own earlier work. For a hostile reviewer in the *North British* (see No. 56), *Barnaby Rudge* proved that Dickens was 'as little at home on the ground of history and philosophical politics, as on that of natural scenery and rustic manners' (May 1845, iii, 70). Even Forster, while hailing the fact that 'The story is told with a purpose: the characteristic of all his later writings', had to acknowledge grave defects in the narrative: 'The interest with which the story commences, has ceased to be the interest before it closes . . .' (*Examiner*, 4 December 1841, 772; cf. *Life*, 169–70). A stupid novel, Ruskin declared: but he, like many others, was charmed by Dolly Varden and Grip the raven, both of whom enjoyed a remarkable vogue (*Ariadne Florentina*, lectures delivered in 1872, *Works* xxii, 447). Gabriel Varden and John Willet were also much relished, and the Maypole Inn stood high among Dickensian taverns. The novel's 'purpose' was not much regarded. As for its mystery elements, see Edgar Ellan Poe (No. 30).

24. From unsigned reviews, *Metropolitan Magazine*

1840–1

(a) That Mr Dickens has created a new era in our popular literature cannot be denied. . . . This author, with a noble disdain, avoiding, or at least merely glancing at the great of the land, and those who sit in high places, has opened the inexhaustible mine of the domestic life of the masses. . . . But great as has been the benefit which he has bestowed on society at large, it has been accompanied by an evil, though of great magnitude, yet in the turpitude of which he in no manner shares—the multiplying around him of a horde of base imitators. He has planted a genuine English rose upon our soil—the rose flourished—and immediately a set of ignorant booksellers, taking advantage of the fertility that Mr Dickens had discovered, immediately fostered into existence a whole forest of noxious weeds and base nettles; hence sprang the felon school, of which *Jack Sheppard* is the type, and a host of other mean periodical productions, that have nothing in common with *Master Humphrey's Clock*, except that they are produced monthly. Mr Dickens's publications are decidedly literature. They have their own species of eloquence—they are natural, humorous, and witty in their general character; and when the occasion calls for it, they rise into pathos, and sometimes, accompanying the immortal soul of man in its loftiest flights, become really sublime. In the series of papers connected together by the horological predilections of Master Humphrey, the principal fault is the want of novelty and of art in introducing them. . . . We feel assured from the highly refined tone of Mr Dickens's mind, that he will gradually incline more and more towards the classical and the elegant (June 1840, xxviii, 51–2).

(b) We shall say but a few words upon the completion of the first volume of this work, and those will be to cheer on the philanthropic and right-minded author. He is now performing most efficaciously the office of a moral teacher. There are even millions who are just emerging from ignorance into what may be called reading classes; all of whom Mr Dickens is educating to honesty, good feeling, and all the finer impulses of humanity. He is the antidote, and a powerful one too, to the writers of the *Jack Sheppard* school. At this period, we wish to warn him against a bias that he has, and which we find is increasing upon him, towards the bombastic. His late description of the manufacturing towns [ch. xxix–xxx, published 17–24 October 1840, not in Vol i] he thinks very fine, or he would not have printed it. It is too turgid even for the atmosphere of the Victoria Theatre. Whatever there may be beneath, there are no such things on the upper crust of the earth as those which he has described (December 1840, xxix, 111).

(c) ... we are sorry ... that happiness, which is so largely at the author's disposal, has not been more generously dealt out by Mr Dickens. The heroine, little Nelly, for whom every reader must have become so deeply interested, demands and deserves a better fate than to die so prematurely. The author should always bear in mind the vast extent of the number of his readers, and think how many of these there be who are, not at all, or only slightly, imbued with religious principles. Moral, mere moral justice would have awarded a happier fate to the poor girl. However, it is all beautifully related, and deeply affecting. . . . (March 1841, xxx, 78)

25. [Thomas Hood], from an unsigned review of *Master Humphrey's Clock,* Vol. I, in the *Athenaeum*

7 November 1840, 887–8

Reprinted in Hood's *Works*, ed. by his son, Tom Hood (1862), v, 353–68.

Hood (1799–1845), poet and wit, was living overseas 1835–40, and first met Dickens about this time. Dickens was much moved by this review: see his 1848 Preface to *The Old Curiosity Shop*, and his letter to Miss Coutts, 18 March 1845. He had written immediately to Hood, who replied:

As to the Review—as in the Grand Reviews at Coblenz—the beauty of the country that was passed over was a sufficient reward. That it was written with a kindly feeling towards you, is true: for books which put us in better humour with the world in general must naturally incline us towards the Author in particular. (So we love Goldsmith for his Vicar of Wakefield)—Add something, for the sympathies of the *Bruderschaft*,—and that I felt you had been unfairly used in a certain Critique—& you will have the whole Animus. Yet I was critical too, & found all the faults I could pick.

My opinion of your Works is a deliberate one:—and in spite of an early prejudice that Boz was all Buzz. Some illchosen extracts when reached me abroad, with the rumour that one of the Prominences was a stage coachman & the other a Boots (what grammar!) led me to think that the Book was only a new strain of Tom-&-Jerryism—which is my aversion. So strong was this notion, that I did not properly enjoy the Work itself on a first perusal, or detect that 'soul of goodness in things evil' the goodness of Pickwickedness. I afterwards read it several times with encreased delight & finally packed off the whole set to a friend, a Prussian Officer, but English by birth & feeling, that he might enjoy its Englishness—to my taste a firstrate merit.

Go on, and prosper!—and I wish it most sincerely, though no man in England has so legitimate a right to envy you, for *my* circulation is so bad that I can hardly keep my hands warm . . .

(Alvin Whitley, 'Hood and Dickens: some new letters', *Huntington Library Quarterly*, xiv, 1951, 392–3). As Dr Harvey (see Preface) has shown, Hood's praise of Samuel Williams's woodcut at the end of ch. 1 ('Look at the Artist's picture . . . it is like an Allegory . . .') led to Dickens's interpolating in the 1841 edition four important paragraphs here, echoing Hood's phraseology. These paragraphs begin, 'I sat down in my easy chair . . .'

. . . The main fault of the work is in its construction. The parts are not well put together; and some of the figures, however ornamental, tend seriously to complicate and embarrass the movements of the machine. We allude to Master Humphrey and his leash of friends. They were never intended, as the author states in his preface, to be active agents in the stories they are supposed to relate; but it was assumed that the Reader would be interested in the interest taken by those shadowy Personages, in the narratives brought forward at their Club-meetings. This was a mistake. In the Arabian Nights, indeed, we take an interest in the interest excited in the Sultan, by each of the Thousand and One Tales; because a yawn from Shahriyar would be the story-teller's death warrant; but the auditors of Master Humphrey possess no such despotic power—his head does not hang by its tale; and accordingly, whilst interested ourselves at first hand,—say by the history of the Old Curiosity Shop and its Inmates,—we think no more of the gentle Hunchback, his friends, and the Old Clock, than of as many printing-house readers and an Editor's Box.

The truth is, the Author is rather too partial to one of the most unmanageable things in life or literature, a Club. The Pickwick began with one, which soon dispersed itself; and the character of its name-father and President was infinitely better for the dissolution. In the present work there are two—the Clock Club above stairs, and the Watch Club below; and between them they lead to so many difficulties and discrepancies, that it becomes necessary to get rid of them by something like a *coup-d'état*. . . .

The revival of some of the Pickwickians supplies its own excuse. It affords us an agreeable glimpse of our old favourites; and moreover, the re-introduction of Old Weller,—the same, but with a difference,—in a new character, and with a title that had long 'laid dormouse in the family,'—is strictly legitimate. His fears of 'inadwertent captivation,' and his wish that he knew how to make himself ugly or disagreeable, are pleasantly characteristic; so is also his graphic description of railway travelling; and who can read his inimitable comparison of the screech of the steam-whistle, without exclaiming with one of our Uneducated Poets,—

> Arn't that ere Boz a tip-top feller!
> Lots writes well, but he writes Weller! . . .

To turn from the old loves to the new, we do not know where we have met, in fiction, with a more striking and picturesque combination of images than is presented by the simple, childish figure of Little Nelly, amidst a chaos of such obsolete, grotesque, old-world commodities as form the stock-in-trade of the Old Curiosity Shop. Look at the Artist's picture of the Child, asleep in her little bed, surrounded, or rather mobbed, by ancient armour and arms, antique furniture, and relics sacred or profane, hideous or grotesque:—it is like an Allegory of the peace and innocence of Childhood in the midst of Violence, Superstition, and all the hateful or hurtful Passions of the world. How sweet and fresh the youthful figure! how much sweeter and fresher for the rusty, musty, fusty atmosphere of such accessories and their associations! How soothing the moral, that Gentleness, Purity, and

Truth, sometimes dormant but never dead, have survived, and will outlive, Fraud and Force, though backed by gold and encased in steel! As a companion picture, we would select the Mending of the Puppets in the Churchyard, with the mocking figure of Punch perched on a gravestone—a touch quite Hogarthian in its satirical significance.

As for Little Nelly herself, we should say that she thinks, speaks, and acts, in a style beyond her years, if we did not know how poverty and misfortune are apt to make advances of worldly knowledge to the young at a most ruinous discount—a painful sacrifice of the very capital of childhood. . . .

In strong contrast to Nelly, we have the Old Man, her grandfather,— so old, that he seems never to have been young. His very vice is one of those which outlive most others. . . .

Of a lighter sort are the vices of Mr Richard Swiveller; the representative of a very numerous class—plenty as weeds, and though not so noxious as some orders, quite as useless and worthless as any of the tribes. There are thousands of Swivellers growing, or grown up, about town; neglected, ill-conditioned profligates, who owe their misconduct not to a bad bringing up but to having had no bringing up at all. Human hulks, cast loose on the world with no more pilotage than belongs to mere brute intelligence—like the abandoned hulls that are found adrift at sea, with only a monkey on board. Such an estray is Dick Swiveller—a fellow of easy virtue and easy vice—lax, lounging, and low, in morals and habits, and living on from day to day by a series of shifts and shabbinesses. Here are some of them topographically described: they read like truths, and suggest quite a new mode of colouring Mogg's Map of London.

[Quotes from ch. viii.]

Still there is more of folly than of absolute vice about Richard Swiveller. For instance, he might have thought of a mistress, and he dreams of a wife; and he might have been a ruffianly Spring-heeled Jack, instead of a 'Perpetual Grand of the Glorious Apollers.' He is rather weak than wicked. . . .

. . . The character of the wharfinger and dwarfinger, Daniel Quilp, is strikingly brought out: not to forget some clever, though rather melodramatic bye-play, such as where he 'eats hard eggs, shells and all; devours gigantic prawns with the heads and tails on: chews tobacco and water-cresses most voraciously at the same time; drinks boiling tea without winking; and bites his fork and spoon till they bend again.'

In fact, he lays himself out for, and is, a 'Little Enormity.' Whether such beings exist in real life, may appear, at first sight, somewhat questionable; but in fairness, before deciding in the negative, one ought to go and view the 'wilderness' assigned as his haunt; and then to ask whether there may not be for such scenery fit actors and appropriate dramas? It has been said that one-half of the world does not know how the other half lives; an ignorance, by the way, which Boz has essentially helped to enlighten: it is quite as certain that one-half of London is not aware of even the topographical existence of the other; and, although remote from our personal experience, there may be such persons as Quilp about the purlieus and back slums of human nature, as surely as there are such places as the Almonry and Rat's Castle.

After senna comes the sugar; and should the malice of the Diabolical Dwarf taste too bitter, let the reader turn to the episode of the Schoolmaster and his beloved Scholar, who wrote so good a hand with such a 'very little one.' The story is simple, touching, and unaffectedly told; one of those stories which can only come from a well-toned head and heart working in harmony with each other; one of those that, whilst they recommend the book, endear the author,—and no writer's personal character seems more identified with his writings than that of Boz. We invariably rise from the perusal of his volumes in better humour with the world; for he gives us a cheerful view of human nature, and paints good people with a relish that proves he has himself a belief in, and sympathy with, their goodness. Moreover he shows them to us (the Garlands, for instance,) shining in clusters, as if he would fain have a Milky Way of them; whereas he puts forward the bad as rarities, or exceptions, and a Quilp as unique. Above all, in distributing the virtues he bestows a full proportion of them amongst a class of our fellow-creatures, who are favoured in Life's Grand State Lotteries, with nothing but the declared blanks, and even in its Little Goes, with but a moderate share of the undrawn tickets. The poor are his especial clients. He delights to show Worth in low places—living up a court, for example, with Kit and the industrious washerwoman, his mother—to exhibit Honesty holding a gentleman's horse, or Poverty bestowing alms. Of this compensating principle there is a striking instance in the Wax-work Woman, Mrs Jarley, a personage who, in many or most hands, would have been a mere mass of tawdry finery and unmitigated vulgarity. . . .

26. W. C. Macready, in his diaries and in a letter to Dickens

1841

Macready (1793–1873), the leader of the English stage since 1819, met Dickens in 1837 and soon became one of his most intimate friends. They much admired each other's work. *Nicholas Nickleby* was dedicated to Macready, and Dickens's second daughter (born 1839) was named after him. Macready's political radicalism chimed with Dickens's. The 'sufferings' which Little Nell's death reawakened were doubtless his grief over the death of his three-year-old daughter Joan, in November 1840. 'Wonderful Dickens,' he exclaimed on reading the final number of the *Clock*, 'which ends very sadly and very sweetly.'

(21 January 1841) 'Called on Dickens . . . Asked Dickens to spare the life of Nell in his story, and observed that he was cruel. He blushed. . . .' (*The Diaries of William Charles Macready 1833–1851*, ed. William Toynbee (1912), ii, 116).

(22 January 1841) 'Found at home . . . [a note] from Dickens with an onward number of *Master Humphrey's Clock*. I saw one print in it of the dear dead child that gave a dead chill through my blood. I dread to read it, but I must get it over. I have read the two numbers; I never read printed words that gave me so much pain. I could not weep for some time. Sensation, sufferings have returned to me, that are terrible to awaken; it is real to me; I cannot criticise it.' (*Ibid.*)

(25 January 1841: letter to Dickens. He is still overwhelmed by this 'beautiful fiction'.) 'Go on, my dear, my excellent friend—make our hearts less selfish and teach us the duty of love to one another . . . I cannot express my own opinion of what you have done in terms too enthusiastic to be sincere.' (*Pilgrim*, ii, 193n)

27. John Ruskin on
The Old Curiosity Shop

1841, 1883

Ruskin (1819–1900) was a warm, if sometimes unpredictably critical, admirer of Dickens. As (*a*) shows, he was not deeply impressed by *The Old Curiosity Shop* when it first appeared. His later comment on Little Nell, in *Fiction, Fair and Foul* (1880) is often quoted: 'Nell, in *The Old Curiosity Shop*, was simply killed for the market, as a butcher kills a lamb (see Forster's *Life*) . . .' (*Works*, ed. E. T. Cook and Alexander Wedderburn (1903), xxxiv, 275n). But, granted the later Ruskin's peculiarities of temperament and experience (he is probably alluding here to Rose La Touche, who had died in 1875), the passage (*b*) from *Fors Clavigera* does more to explain the appeal Little Nell had for many Victorians.

(*a*) Extract from a letter, 6 June 1841, to W. H. Harrison:

'I saw another advertisement of *Barnaby Rudge* the other day, and hope better things from it than we have got out of the *Clock*. Can it be possible that this man is so soon run dry as the strained caricature and laborious imitation of his former self in the last chapters of the *Curiosity Shop* seem almost to prove? It is still what no one else could do; but there is a want of his former clear truth, a diseased extravagance, a violence of delineation, which seem to indicate a sense of failing power in the writer's own mind. It is evident the man is a thorough cockney, from his way of talking about hedgerows, and honeysuckles, and village spires; and in London, and to his present fields of knowledge, he ought strictly to keep for some time. There are subjects enough touched in the *Sketches* which might be worked up into something of real excellence. And when he has exhausted that particular field of London life with which he is familiar, he ought to keep quiet for a long time, and raise his mind as far as in him lies, to a far higher standard, giving up that turn for the picturesque which leads him into perpetual mannerism, and going into the principles out of which that picturesqueness should arise. At present he describes eccentricity much oftener than character; there is a vivid, effective touch, truthful and accurate, but on the surface only; he is in literature very much what Prout is in art.' (*Works*, xxxvi, 25–6)

(*b*) Extract from *Fors Clavigera*, letter 90, May 1883: 'I think the experience of most thoughtful persons will confirm me in saying that extremely good girls (good children, broadly, but especially girls), usually die young. The pathos of their deaths is constantly used in poetry and novels; but the power of the fiction rests, I suppose, on the fact that most persons of affectionate temper have lost their own May Queens or little Nells in their time. For my own part of grief, I have known a little Nell die, and a May Queen die, and a queen of May, and of December also, die;—all of them, in economists' language, as good as gold, and in Christian language, only a little lower than the angels, and crowned with glory and honour. And I could count the like among my best-loved friends, with a rosary of tears.' (*Works*, xxix, 424–5)

28. Henry Crabb Robinson on *Barnaby Rudge* in his diaries

1841

Crabb Robinson (1775–1867), diarist and bookman. A former journalist and barrister, and acquaintance of successive generations of literary men, he records in his diary his serial reading of most of Dickens's novels. But 'I shall read no more of Dickens's things in numbers,' he had decided (14 February 1841), after finishing *The Old Curiosity Shop*. It was a resolution he could rarely keep, though *Barnaby* had been running for six months before he succumbed. See also No. 79.

(*a*) Extract from journal entry, 29 August 1841: 'I began to-day *Barnaby Rudge*, which promises to be one of the most delightful of

Dickens's works. He improves in general style.' (*Henry Crabb Robinson on Books and their Authors*, ed. E. J. Morley (1938), ii, 598).

(*b*) Extracts from journal entry, 1 September: 'I arose very early, but I had so worked myself into the tale of *Barnaby*, the idiot (who thus far is not important), that I would not walk out till I had finished a part before breakfast. Then I took a short walk with *Barnaby Rudge* and the book occupied me all day ... Dickens will lose popularity with the saints, for he too faithfully exposes cant.' (*ibid.*)

(*c*) Extract from journal entry, 4 September: 'The picture of the riots of Lord George Gordon's mob is excellent and has poetical truth whether it be historical or not.' (ii, 599)

(*d*) Extract from journal entry, 5 September: 'Finished all of *Barnaby Rudge* yet published. . . . I will read no more till the story is finished. . . . I will not expose myself to further anxieties.' (*ibid.*)

29. [Thomas Hood], from a review of *Barnaby Rudge*, *Athenaeum*

22 January 1842, 77–9

Reprinted in Hood's *Works*, ed. by his son, Tom Hood, (1862), vi, 115–22.

... In our review of the *Old Curiosity Shop*, we discussed the characteristics of Boz, as an author, and did justice to the amiable tone and moral tendency of his writings. On these points, we have nothing to revoke, whilst, as to workmanship, we consider the present story as better built than any of its predecessors. It is true, that the Great Riots of '80 which professedly served for the foundation, are scarcely hinted at till the thirty-fifth chapter, which abruptly introduces the reader to Lord George Gordon. But this circumstance, instead of being a defect, is to the advantage of the story, and if not artistically contrived for the purpose, serves very happily to heighten the effect of the metropolitan tumults, and to point the moral of the tale. The famous overture to *Der Freyschütz*, with its infernal music, certainly forestals, and therefore, in some degree, impairs the horrors it precedes,—at least, we do not recollect to have been more affected by any of the subsequent *diablerie*, than by that awful and unearthly prelude. The novel, on the contrary, opens with peaceful and pastoral scenery—greenly and serenely, like the calm before a storm. Thus, the first chapter pleasantly plants us, not in Cato Street, but on the borders of Epping Forest, at an ancient ruddy Elizabethan inn, with a Maypole for its sign—an antique porch, quaint chimneys and 'more gable ends than a lazy man would care to count on a sunny day.' The ornamented eaves are haunted by twittering swallows, and the distorted roof is mobbed by clusters of cooing pigeons. Then for its landlord, there is old John Willet, as square and as slow as a tortoise, and for its parlour customers Long Parkes and Tom Cobb, both taciturn, and profound smokers,—and Solomon Daisy, that parochial Argus, studded all down his rusty black coat, and his long flapped waistcoat, with 'little queer buttons, like nothing except his eyes, but so like them, that as they twinkled and glistened in the light of the fire, which shone too in his bright shoe-buckles, he seemed all eyes, from head to foot.' In short, it is an inn for gentle Izaak Walton and his peaceable fraternity to have haunted. And when the Riots do eventually break out,—when Newgate is in flames and Langdale's in a blaze, even these scenes, terrible as they are, scarcely come home to the feelings so impressively as the picture of the quaint hostel, late the abode of Peace and Plenty, with its pastoral Maypole dashed through the window, 'like the bowsprit of a wrecked ship,' and its pinioned proprietor, slow John, staring in a stupor at his staved barrels, shattered punch-bowls, and demolished furniture. For this powerful effect, as an intentional and not accidental contrast, we give Boz credit; seeing how elaborately he has fitted up the Bar—'the very snuggest, coziest, and completest bar that ever the wit of man devised,'—only to give the greater force to the profanation of poor Willet's sanctorum, and the smash of his household gods. . . .

For the loves of Edward Chester and Miss Haredale, honest Joe and free-hearted Dolly Varden, and other serious and comic episodes and interludes, we have no space. We may observe, however, generally, that the flesh and blood interest of the story is to be found in the Locksmith's household, and the bar of the Maypole; honest Gabriel is as good a representative of a genuine Englishman as we should desire, were we called upon by the contemporary novelists of Europe to send forth a home specimen to a congress of national creations;—cheerful, sensible, benevolent, slow but not stupid, bearing with his wife's 'convexities' with burly goodhumoured patience, we feel, so soon as we have made his acquaintance, as if all the parties in whom we take interest were safe in his ample shadow. . . .

We have said that *Barnaby Rudge* is a well-built story; it is also interesting, and particularly well-timed. It is a matter of pride with some of our old citizens, to remember the Great Riots of '80. They delight in recalling how many fires they saw blazing at one time—the activity of the City Horse, the inactivity of the City Mayor—the flitting past of liberated felons with their clanking fetters—the showers of down from ripped feather beds—the volleys of the military, and the shrieks of the victims, while flaming liquor ran down the kennels like an infernal snapdragon, enveloping human wretches instead of raisins— they seem to recall every particular of the tumult, except the causes that led to it. Otherwise, looking round at the present day, they would recognize some of the same elements at work; the same—nay, a worse

fanatical demon abroad, ready to burn, not merely Catholic Chapels
and Distilleries, but Picture Galleries, Museums, Literary Institutions,
Her Majesty's Theatres, and the people's Punch and Judy: who, like
Zeal-of-the-land Busy, cries, everywhere, 'Down with Dagon! Down
with Dagon!' Seriously, there is a growing spirit extant, that is setting
itself against Art, Science, Literature, the Drama, and all public
amusements;—a sect who would preach down the sun, the moon, the
stars, and the gas, so that we might have no shining lights but their
own, wherewith they would make us as cheerful, as pleasant, and as
comfortable, as we are with a set of linkboys in a London fog!

30. Edgar Allan Poe, from a review in *Graham's Magazine*

February 1842, xix, 124–9

Reprinted in Poe's *The Literati* (New York, 1850), 464–82. Poe
(1809–49) had been writing stories since 1833. He was early in
welcoming Boz (*Southern Literary Messenger*, June 1836; see
Dickensian, xxxvi (1940), 163–9), and in 1842 they met. Dickens
tried to find an English publisher for him; see G. G. Grubb's
series of articles on their relationship, *Nineteenth-Century Fiction*,
1950–1. Poe's review of *The Old Curiosity Shop* in *Graham's
Magazine* (May 1841) is reprinted in *The Dickens Critics*, 19–24,
and his review of the early numbers of *Barnaby Rudge* (*Philadelphia
Saturday Evening Post*, 1 May 1841) in *Dickensian*, ix (1913), 274–8.
For discussion of the latter, see William Robertson Nicoll,
Dickens's Own Story (1923), 221–44. *Barnaby Rudge* helped to
inspire his poem 'The Raven' (1844). His review in *Graham's
Magazine*, of which he was literary editor, opens with a summary
of the plot.

We have given, as may well be supposed, but a very meagre outline
of the story, and we have given it in the simple or natural sequence.

That is to say, we have related the events, as nearly as might be, in the order of their occurrence. But this order would by no means have suited the purpose of the novelist, whose design has been to maintain the secret of the murder, and the consequent mystery which encircles Rudge, and the actions of his wife, until the catastrophe of his discovery by Haredale. The *thesis* of the novel may thus be regarded as based upon curiosity. Every point is so arranged as to perplex the reader, and whet his desire for elucidation:—for example, the first appearance of Rudge at the Maypole; his question; his persecution of Mrs Rudge; the ghost seen by the frequenter of the Maypole; and Haredale's impressive conduct in consequence. What *we* have told, in the very beginning of our digest, in regard to the shifting of the gardener's dress, is sedulously kept from the reader's knowledge until he learns it from Rudge's own confession in jail. We say sedulously; for, the intention once known, the traces of the design can be found upon every page. There is an amusing and exceedingly ingenuous instance at page 145, where Solomon Daisy describes his adventure with the ghost.

'It was a ghost—a spirit,' cried Daisy.

'Whose?' they all three asked together.

In the excess of his emotion (for he fell back trembling in his chair and waved his hand as if entreating them to question him no farther) *his answer was lost upon all* but old John Willet, who happened to be seated close beside him.

'Who?'—cried Parkes and Tom Cobb—'Who was it?'

'Gentlemen,' said Mr. Willett, after a long pause, 'you needn't ask. The likeness of a murdered man. This is the nineteenth of March.'

A profound silence ensued. [ch. xxxiii]

The impression here skilfully conveyed is, that the ghost seen is that of Reuben Haredale; and the mind of the not-too-acute reader is at once averted from the true state of the case—from the murderer, Rudge, living in the body.

Now there can be no question that, by such means as these, many points which are comparatively insipid in the natural sequence of our digest, and which would have been comparatively insipid even if given in full detail in a natural sequence, are endued with the interest of mystery; but neither can it be denied that a vast many more points are at the same time deprived of all effect, and become null, through the impossibility of comprehending them without the key. The author, who, cognizant of his plot, writes with this cognizance continually operating upon him, and thus *writes to himself* in spite of himself, does not, of course, feel that much of what is effective to his own informed perception must necessarily be lost upon his uninformed readers; and he himself is never in condition, as regards his own work, to bring the matter to test. But the reader may easily satisfy himself of the validity of our objection. Let him *re-peruse Barnaby Rudge*—and with a pre-comprehension of the mystery, these points of which we speak break out in all directions like stars, and throw quadruple brilliance over the narrative, a brilliance which a correct taste will at once declare unprofitably sacrificed at the shrine of the keenest interest of mere mystery.

The design of mystery, however, being once determined upon by an author, it becomes imperative, first, that no undue or inartistical means be employed to conceal the secret of the plot; and, secondly, that the secret be well kept. Now, when, [at the end of ch. i], we read that 'the body of *poor Mr Rudge, the steward, was found*' months after the outrage, etc., we see that Mr Dickens has been guilty of no misdemeanor against Art in stating what was not the fact; since the falsehood is put in-to the mouth of Solomon Daisy, and given merely as the impression of this individual and of the public. The writer has not asserted it in his own person, but ingeniously conveyed an idea (false in itself, yet a belief in which is necessary for the effect of the tale) by the mouth of one of his characters. The case is different, however, when Mrs Rudge is repeatedly denominated 'the widow.' It is the author who, himself, frequently so terms her. This is disingenuous and inartistical; accident-ally so, of course. We speak of the matter merely by way of illustrat-ing our point, and as an oversight on the part of Mr Dickens.

That the secret be well kept is obviously necessary. A failure to preserve it until the proper moment of *dénouement*, throws all into confusion, so far as regards the effect intended. If the mystery leak out, against the author's will, his purposes are immediately at odds and ends; for he proceeds upon the supposition that certain impressions *do* exists, which do *not* exist, in the mind of his readers. We are not pre-pared to say, so positively as we could wish, whether, by the public at large, the whole mystery of the murder committed by Rudge, with the identity of the Maypole ruffian with Rudge himself, was fathomed at any period previous to the period intended, or, if so, whether at a period so early as materially to interfere with the interest designed; but we are forced, through sheer modesty, to suppose this the case; since, by ourselves individually, the secret was distinctly understood imme-diately upon the perusal of the story of Solomon Daisy, which occurs at the seventh page of this volume of three hundred and twenty-three.

In the number of the Philadelphia *Saturday Evening Post*, for May the first, 1841 (the tale having then only begun) will be found a *prospective notice* of some length, in which we made use of the following words:—

That Barnaby is the son of the murderer may not appear evident to our readers—but we will explain. The person murdered is Mr Rueben Haredale. He was found assassinated in his bed-chamber. His steward (Mr Rudge, senior) and his gardener (name not mentioned) are missing. At first both are suspected. 'Some months afterward'—here we use the words of the story—'the steward's body, scarcely to be recognized but by his clothes and the watch and ring he wore, was found at the bottom of a piece of water in the grounds, with a deep gash in the breast, where he had been stabbed by a knife. He was only partly dressed; and all people agreed that he had been sitting up reading in his own room, where there were many traces of blood, and was suddenly fallen upon and killed, before his master'. [ch. i]

Now, be it observed, it is not the author himself who asserts that *the steward's body was found;* he has put the words in the mouth of one of his characters. His design is to make it appear, in the *dénouement*, that the steward, Rudge, first murdered the gardener, then went to his master's chamber, murdered *him*, was interrupted by his (Rudge's) wife, whom he seized and held *by the wrist*, to prevent her giving the alarm—that he then, after possessing himself of the booty desired, returned to the gardener's room, exchanged clothes with him, put upon the corpse his own watch and ring, and secreted it where it was afterwards discovered at so late a period that the features could not be identified.

The differences between our preconceived ideas, as here stated, and the actual facts of the story, will be found immaterial. The gardener was murdered, not before but after his master; and that Rudge's wife seized *him* by the wrist, instead of his seizing *her*, has so much the air of a mistake on the part of Mr Dickens, that we can scarcely speak of our own version as erroneous. The grasp of a murderer's bloody hand on the wrist of a woman *enceinte*, would have been more likely to produce the effect described (and this every one will allow) than the grasp of the hand of the woman upon the wrist of the assassin. We may therefore say of our supposition as Talleyrand said of some cockney's bad French —*que s'il ne soit pas Français, assurément donc il le doit être*—that if we did not rightly prophesy, yet, at least, our prophecy *should have been* right.

We are informed in the Preface to *Barnaby Rudge* that 'no account of the Gordon Riots having been introduced into any work of fiction, and the subject presenting very extraordinary and remarkable features,' our author 'was led to project this tale.' But for this distinct announcement (for Mr Dickens can scarcely have deceived himself) we should have looked upon the riots as altogether an afterthought. It is evident that they have no necessary connection with the story. In our digest, which carefully includes all *essentials* of the plot, we have dismissed the doings of the mob in a paragraph. The whole event of the drama would have proceeded as well without as with them. They have even the appearance of being *forcibly* introduced. . . .

. . . In fact, the title of the work, the elaborate and pointed manner of the commencement, the impressive description of The Warren, and especially of Mrs Rudge, go far to show that Mr Dickens has really deceived himself—that the soul of the plot, as originally conceived, was the murder of Haredale, with the subsequent discovery of the murderer in Rudge, but that this idea was afterwards abandoned, or rather suffered to be merged in that of the Popish riots. The result has been most unfavorable. That which, of itself, would have proved highly effective, has been rendered nearly null by its situation. In the multitudinous outrage and horror of the Rebellion, the *one* atrocity is utterly whelmed and extinguished.

The reasons of this deflection from the first purpose appear to us self-evident. One of them we have already mentioned. The other is that our author discovered, when too late, that *he had anticipated, and thus rendered valueless, his chief effect.* This will be readily understood. The particulars of the assassination being withheld, the strength of the narrator is put forth, in the beginning of the story, to whet curiosity in respect to these particulars; and, so far, he is but in proper pursuance of his main design. But from this intention he unwittingly passes into the error of *exaggerating anticipation.* And error though it be, it is an error wrought with consummate skill. What, for example, could more vividly enhance our impression of the unknown horror enacted, than the deep and enduring gloom of Haredale—than the idiot's inborn awe of blood—or, especially, than the expression of countenance so imaginatively attributed to Mrs Rudge—'the capacity for expressing terror—something only dimly seen, but never absent for a moment—the shadow of some look to which an instant of intense and most unutterable horror only could have given rise?' But it is a condition of the human fancy that the promises of such words are irredeemable. In the notice before mentioned we thus spoke upon this topic:—

This is a conception admirably adapted to whet curiosity in respect to the character of that event which is hinted at as forming the basis of the story. But this observation should not fail to be made—that the anticipation must surpass the reality; that no matter how terrific be the circumstances which, in the *dénouement*, shall appear to have occasioned the expression of countenance worn habitually by Mrs Rudge, still they will not be able to satisfy the mind of the reader. He will surely be disappointed. The skilful intimation of horror held out by the artist produces an effect which will deprive his conclusion of all. These intimations—these dark hints of some uncertain evil—are often rhetorically praised as effective, but are only justly so praised where there is *no dénouement* whatever—where the reader's imagination is left to clear up the mystery for itself; and this is not the design of Mr Dickens.

And, in fact, our author was not long in seeing his precipitancy. He had placed himself in a dilemma from which even his high genius could not extricate him. He at once shifts the main interest, and in truth we do not see what better he could have done. The reader's attention becomes absorbed in the riots, and he fails to observe that what should have been the true catastrophe of the novel is exceedingly feeble and ineffective.

A few cursory remarks:—Mr Dickens fails peculiarly in *pure* narration. See, for example, page 296, where the connection of Hugh and Chester is detailed by Varden [ch. lxxv]. See also in *The Old Curiosity Shop*, where, when the result is fully known, so many words are occupied in explaining the relationship of the brothers. The effect of the present narrative might have been materially increased by confining the action within the limits of London. The *Notre Dame* of Hugo affords a fine example of the force which can be gained by concentration, or unity of place. The unity of time is also sadly neglected, to no purpose, in *Barnaby Rudge*. That Rudge should so long and so deeply feel the sting of conscience is inconsistent with his brutality. On page 15 [ch. i], the interval elapsing between the murder and Rudge's return is variously stated at twenty-two and twenty-four years. It may be asked why the inmates of The Warren failed to hear the alarm-bell which was heard by Solomon Daisy. The idea of persecution by being tracked, as by bloodhounds, from one spot of quietude to another, is a favorite one with Mr Dickens. Its effect cannot be denied. The stain upon Barnaby's wrist, caused by fright in the mother at so late a period of gestation as one day before mature parturition, is shockingly at war with all medical experience. When Rudge, escaped from prison, unshackled, with money at command, is in agony at his wife's refusal to perjure herself for his salvation—is it not *queer* that he should demand any other salvation than lay in his heels?

Some of the conclusions of chapters—see pages 40 and 100 [ends of chs. vii and xxii]—seem to have been written for the mere purpose of illustrating tail-pieces.

The leading idiosyncrasy of Mr Dickens's remarkable humor, is to be found in his *translating the language of gesture, or action, or tone*. For example—

The cronies nodded to each other, and Mr Parkes remarked in an undertone, shaking his head meanwhile, *as who should say 'let no man contradict me, for I won't believe him,'* that Willet was in amazing force to-night. [ch. i]

From what we have here said—and, perhaps, said without due deliberation—(for, alas! the hurried duties of the journalist preclude it) —there will not be wanting those who will accuse us of a mad design to detract from the pure fame of the novelist. But to such we merely say in the language of heraldry 'ye should wear a plain point sanguine in your arms.' If this be understood, well; if not, well again. There lives no man feeling a deeper reverence for genius than ourself. If we have not dwelt so especially upon the high merits as upon the trivial defects of *Barnaby Rudge* we have already given our reasons for the omission, and these reasons will be sufficiently understood by all whom we care to understand them. The work before us is not, we think, equal to the tale which immediately preceded it; but there are few— very few others to which we consider it inferior. Our chief objection has not, perhaps, been so distinctly stated as we could wish. That this fiction, or indeed that any fiction written by Mr Dickens, should be based in the excitement and maintenance of curiosity, we look upon as a misconception, on the part of the writer, of his own very great yet very peculiar powers. He has done this thing well, to be sure—he would do anything well in comparison with the herd of his contemporaries; but he has not done it so thoroughly well as his high and just reputation would demand. We think that the whole book has been an effort to him, solely through the nature of its design. He has been smitten with an untimely desire for a novel path. The idiosyncrasy of his intellect would lead him, naturally, into the most fluent and simple style of narration. In tales of ordinary sequence he may and will long reign triumphant. He has a *talent* for all things, but no positive *genius* for *adaptation*, and still less for that metaphysical art in which the souls of all *mysteries* lie. *Caleb Williams* is a far less noble work than *The Old Curiosity Shop*; but Mr Dickens could no more have constructed the one than Mr Godwin could have dreamed of the other.

31. Dickens's Reception in America

1842

(a) From Dickens's letter to John Forster, 29 January 1842 (*Life*, 205–6); (b) from Dickens's speech at the banquet in his honour, Boston, 1 February 1842 (*Speeches*, ed K. J. Fielding (Oxford, 1960), 19–21).

Dickens arrived in America, January 1842, and was received with extraordinary fervour—more than royal honours, as many said. Men illustrious in American public and artistic life assembled to honour him at banquets and other public functions, and in the streets and public places he was embarrassingly popular. See William Glyde Wilkins, *Dickens in America* (1911) and Paul B. Davis, 'Dickens and the American Press, 1842', *Dickens Studies*, iv (1968), 32–77. Dr William Ellery Channing, mentioned in (a), was the prominent Unitarian preacher and divine; Dickens met, corresponded with, and much admired him. Dickens's declaration of his literary faith at the Boston banquet (b) echoes his expressions at a similar banquet in Edinburgh, 25 June 1841, another occasion when the novelist—still not thirty years old—received conspicuous public recognition.

(a) What further he had to say of that week's experience, [his first in America], finds its first public utterance here. How can I tell you what has happened since that first day? 'How can I give you the faintest notion of my reception here; of the crowds that pour in and out the whole day; of the people that line the streets when I go out; of the cheering when I went to the theatre; of the copies of verses, letters of congratulation, welcomes of all kinds, balls, dinners, assemblies without end? There is to be a public dinner to me here in Boston, next Tuesday, and great dissatisfaction has been given to the many by the high price (three pounds sterling each) of the tickets. There is to be a ball next Monday week at New York, and 150 names appear on the list of the committee. There is to be dinner in the same place, in the same week, to which I have had an invitation with every known name in America appended to it. But what can I tell you about any of these things which will give you the slightest notion of the enthusiastic greeting they give me, or the cry that runs through the whole country! I have had deputations from the Far West, who have come from more than two thousand miles distance: from the lakes, the rivers, the back-woods, the log-houses, the cities, factories, villages, and towns. Authorities from nearly all the States have written to me. I have heard from the universities, congress, senate, and bodies, public and private, of every sort and kind. "It is no nonsense, and no common feeling," wrote Dr Channing to me yesterday, "It is all heart. There never was, and never will be, such a triumph." And it is good thing, is it not, . . . to find those fancies it has given me and you the greatest satisfaction to think of, at the core of it all? It makes my heart quieter, and me a more retiring, sober, tranquil man to watch the effect of those thoughts in all this noise and hurry, even than if I sat, pen in hand, to put them down for the first time. I feel, in the best aspects of this welcome, something of the presence and influence of that spirit which directs my life, and through a heavy sorrow has pointed upwards with unchanging finger for more than four years past. And if I know my heart, not twenty times this praise would move me to an act of folly. . . . '

(b) It is not easy for a man to speak of his own books. I dare say that few persons have been more interested in mine than I; and if it be a general principal in nature that a lover's love is blind, and that a mother's love is blind, I believe it may be said of an author's attachment to the creatures of his own imagination, that it is a perfect model of constancy and devotion, and is the blindest of all. But the objects and purposes I have in view are very plain and simple, and may easily be told. I have always had, and always shall have, an earnest and true desire to contribute, as far as in me lies, to the common stock of healthful cheerfulness and enjoyment. I have always had, and always shall have, an invincible repugnance to that mole-eyed philosophy which loves the darkness, and winks and scowls in the light. I believe that Virtue shows quite as well in rags and patches as she does in purple and fine linen. I believe that she and every beautiful object in external nature, claim some sympathy in the breast of the poorest man who breaks his scanty loaf of daily bread. I believe that she goes barefoot as well as shod. I believe that she dwells rather oftener in alleys and by-ways than she does in courts and palaces, and that it is good, and pleasant, and profitable to track her out, and follow her. I believe that to lay one's hand upon some one of those rejected ones whom the world has too long forgotten, and too often misused, and to say to the proudest and most thoughtless,—these creatures have the same elements and capacities of goodness as yourselves, they are moulded in the same form, and made of the same clay; and though ten times worse than you, may, in having retained anything of their original nature amidst the trials and distresses of their condition, be really ten times better.—I believe that to do this is to pursue a worthy and not useless avocation. Gentlemen, that you think so too, your fervent greeting assures me. That this feeling is alive in the Old World as well as in the New, no man should know better than I—I, who have found such wide and ready sympathy in my own dear land. That in expressing it we are but treading in the steps of those great master-spirits who have gone before, we know by reference to all the bright examples in our literature, from Shakespeare downward.

There is one other point connected with the labours (if I may call them so) that you hold in such generous esteem, to which I cannot help adverting. I cannot help expressing the delight, the more than happiness it was to me to find so strong an interest awakened on this side of the water, in favour of that little heroine of mine, to whom your President [Josiah Quincy, Jr., President of the State Senate] has made allusion, who died in her youth. I had letters about that child, in England, from the dwellers in log-houses among the morasses, and swamps, and densest forests, and deepest solitudes of the Far West. Many a sturdy hand, hard with the axe and spade, and browned by the summer's sun, has taken up the pen, and written to me a little history of domestic joy or sorrow, always coupled, I am proud to say, with something of interest in that little tale, or some comfort or happiness derived from it; and my correspondent has always addressed me, not as a writer of books for sale, resident some four or five thousand miles away, but as a friend to whom he might freely impart the joys and sorrows of his own fireside. Many a mother—I could reckon them now by dozens, not by units—has done the like, and has told me that she lost such a child at such a time, and where she is buried, and how good she was, and how, in this or that respect, she resembled Nell.

I do assure you that no circumstance of my life has given me one-hundredth part of the gratification I have derived from this source. I was wavering at the time whether or not to wind up my *Clock*, and come and see this country, and this decided me. I felt as if it were a positive duty, as if I were bound to pack up my clothes, and come and see my friends; and even now I have such an odd sensation in connexion with these things, that you have no chance of spoiling me. I feel as though we were agreeing—as indeed we are, if we substitute for fictitious characters the classes from which they are drawn—about third parties, in whom we have a common interest. At every act of kindness on your part, I say to myself 'That's for Oliver; I should not wonder if that were meant for Smike; I have no doubt that is intended for Nell'; and so I become a much happier, certainly, but a more sober and retiring man than ever I was before. . . .

32. From an unsigned article, 'The Reception of Mr Dickens', *United States Magazine and Democratic Review*

April 1842, 315–20

A specimen of popular American eloquence of the time, which might well have gone into *Martin Chuzzlewit*. The comment on the political implications of Dickens's work is extravagant, but registers a part of his appeal for some readers. A more sensible American comment on 'Boz and Democracy' from this period was Walt Whitman's (*Brother Jonathan*, 26 February 1842). As Forster commented, 'The sources of Dickens's popularity in England were in truth multiplied many-fold in America ... [He] was almost universally regarded by them as a kind of embodied protest against what was believed to be worst in the institutions of England, depressing and overshadowing in a social sense, and adverse to purely intellectual influences' (*Life*, 209). Some modern American critics of Dickens (it might be argued) generate a similar enthusiasm for—and misunderstanding of—him by seeing him as an embodied protest against the shortcomings of twentieth-century American life.

Bating our characteristic extravagance in perhaps overdoing the matter, the enthusiasm attending Mr Dickens's welcome to our shores has afforded a spectacle which may justly be regarded, not alone with satisfaction, but even with pride. We see in it an evidence of the quick and warm sympathy with which the popular heart rarely fails to respond to the hand that touches its finer chords, by appealing to its sense of the beautiful, the noble, and the good, its kindly charities and universal human affections. . . .

. . . Who, tell us, is this young stranger, about whose path we crowd with so warm and eager a homage of our hearts—towards whom our souls thus yearn so kindly, as to some dear friend or brother whom we have long loved, though never seen—whom we are so anxious to clasp hand to hand, and to meet in that silent sympathy which passes between men like the transit of the electric spark when their eyes meet —who is he? Is it a soldier, coming crowned with all the crimsoned laurels of wars. . . ? No, no—there is no taint of 'the military' about him, . . . No, no, thank God! . . . [Further rhetorical questions elicit the information that he wields the Pen, not the Sword.] But in our day and generation the Pen is a far more powerful weapon to open the world's oyster than ever was the Sword, and in the position to which it has already elevated this poor and obscure youth, we delight to read an expression of the homage of the age to its divine right and its magic might.

The chief secret of his extraordinary success is to be found in the accordance of the spirit generally pervading his writings with the democratic genius now everywhere rapidly developing itself as the principle of the new civilization, whose dawn is just brightening upon the world. We see that his mind is strongly possessed with a true sense of the unjust suffering, moral and physical, by which the mass of mankind are everywhere pressed down to the dust, and especially in the country to which hitherto the scope of his observation has been confined, with a kindly and brotherly sorrow for the hapless fate of its victims, and a righteous and manly indignation against its causes. This is that deep chord in the mighty lyre of the great popular heart, from which his touch has drawn forth a note at the same time so powerful, and attuned to so fine and sweet a harmony with the spontaneous sympathies of millions. We warn Wellington and Peel, we warn Toryism in general, against this young writer. If they had at their disposal the Bastilles and *lettres-de-cachet* of another day, we would advise their prompt application, as soon as he shall set foot in England again, on his return from his present visit, where his popular tendencies are not likely to be weakened. There is nothing in any of the books he has yet produced of a manifest political character, or of any probable political design. Yet there is that in them all which is calculated to hasten on the great crisis of the English Revolution (speed the hour!) far more effectively than any of the open assaults of Radicalism or Chartism.

AMERICAN NOTES AND PICTURES
FROM ITALY

October 1842, May 1846

American Notes was Dickens's first attempt at a serious and sustained non-fictional work; *Pictures from Italy* (serialized in the *Daily News* earlier in 1846) was a less ambitious attempt in the same kind. He never tried his hand at such a task again, except in *A Child's History of England* (1851–3) where the explicitly juvenile readership would excuse the shortcomings in scholarship and understanding which reviewers of the travel-books had vigorously demonstrated.

'Public expectation will not be disappointed in this book', John Forster hopefully proclaimed at the beginning of a sycophantic two-part review of 'these delightful volumes' of *American Notes* (*Examiner*, 22 and 29 October 1842, 676–9, 692). He could not better have justified the accusations of 'literary *cliquism*' which were often—and often unfairly—thrown at Dickens and himself and the *Examiner* group. For, as was soon evident, *American Notes* got a far worse press than any of his previous books. As a reviewer of the later travel-book recalled, 'Mr Dickens was unfortunate in his book on America. It rashly gave the admiring public the true gauge of his mind' (*Tait's Edinburgh Magazine*, July 1846, xiii, 461). Members of the literary establishment, not unwilling to cut down to size this uneducated and Radicalish young writer of uncertain social origins, found in *American Notes* an excellent opportunity: hence the unique unanimity with which all the heavy quarterlies weighed into this book (none of his subsequent novels was so favoured), though it was criticized less harshly in the *Westminster* and *Dublin* (both in February 1843) than in the reviews selected below. The book was found entertaining and mildly instructive by less exacting organs, such as *Ainsworth's* and the *Monthly*, and by Thomas Hood in the *New Monthly* (all in November 1842), but no one thought Dickens had disclosed new talents or increased his reputation here. In America, injured pride led to some fierce reviewing and dark threats. On the reception, and for further reasons for Dickens's set-back, see the studies by K. J. Fielding and Ada C. Nisbet (headnotes, Nos. 33, 35).

Pictures from Italy aroused much less interest: none of the heavies reviewed it except the *Dublin Review*, which predictably was offended by Dickens's attitude to Roman Catholicism (September 1846, xxi, 184–201; cf. April 1871, No. 153). The main blast came from *The Times* (No. 38). Reviewers found it thin, if agreeable and sometimes lively—'chit-chat . . . but then it is so much better than the chit-chat of common-minded persons' (*Chambers's Edinburgh Journal*, 20 June 1846, n.s. v, 389). Dickens liked it very much (*To* Madame de la Rue, 17 April 1846).

33. [Samuel Warren], from a review in *Blackwood's Magazine*

December 1842, lii, 783–801

Warren (1807–77), barrister and author of the highly successful *Ten Thousand a Year* (1839–41) and other novels, considered himself Dickens's equal or superior, and proposed to John Blackwood a '*fair, prudent,* and *real* review [of *American Notes*]—bearing in mind my own position as a sort of *honourable yet fearless rival* of his'. While acknowledging Dickens's genius in *American Notes,* he detected 'mannerism; *exaggeration*; glaring but unconscious egotism & vanity; glimpses of underbreeding. These last I should touch on in a manly and delicate & generous spirit. Rely on *Sam Warren* . . . Oh what a book I could have written ! ! ! I mean I who have not only observed but *reflected* so much on the characters of the people of England and America' (quoted in K. J. Fielding's '*American Notes* and some English reviewers', *Modern Language Review,* lix (1964), 527–37). Warren offered Dickens some more lofty advice in *Blackwood's,* November 1846, lx, 636–9 (discussing No. 1 of *Dombey*). In the present review, he surveys Dickens's early career and popularity, hints that his 'early education, opportunities, habits, acquirements, and society' were not altogether impressive, and then turns to his book on America.

. . . Alas, how very sad it is to have to own the feelings of chagrin and disappointment with which we have risen from the perusal of these volumes of Mr Dickens, and to express our fears that such will be the result of the perusal of them by the Americans. . . . [There is too little about 'the great men of America with whom he must have frequently come into close contact', too much about the personal *trivia* of his journeys, too much about spitting.]

Again—we do not feel the least desire to accompany Boz in his character of inspector of prisons and visitor of lunatic asylums; to discharge which melancholy duties seems to be his first and anxious object on arriving at any new town. Boz is undoubtedly always eloquent and graphic on these occasions—often painfully so; and his sketch of the system of solitary confinement at Philadelphia, is powerful and harrowing. We did not want the many political or statistical details, nor the minute descriptions of buildings, streets, squares, villages, and towns, which so frequently appear in these volumes. They are neither interesting, valuable, nor new; we expected, at all events, *different* topics from Boz. Whenever he descends from the stilts of political and moral declamation, and walks quietly along on his own ground—the delineation of manners and character, especially among the lower classes—Boz is delightful, and fresh as ever; though displaying, here and there, an evident anxiety to make the most of his materials.—We shall now, however, go rapidly over these volumes, making such observations as occur to us in passing along. Boz must bear with us when we speak a little unpleasant truth—recollecting that *sweet are the wounds of a friend*. Boz is strong enough in his own just consciousness of genius, and in his established reputation, to bear a little rough handling without being either shaken or hurt by it. . . .

[Warren then surveys the book, with ample quotations.]

. . . His description of the Senate and House of Representatives, then sitting, are very meagre and unsatisfactory; and nothing can be more turgid and feeble, than the long paragraph of declamation which follows them; most irritating and offensive in tone to the Americans, however well-founded in fact. Topics of this sort should be handled with great delicacy and sobriety, in order to have a chance of being beneficial in America, or appreciated by persons of judgment here. Here again, too, Boz goes out of his way to indulge in a very foolish and puerile sneer at our Houses of Lords and Commons. Its tone is more that of some wearied reporter for a radical newspaper, than of an intelligent and independent observer; and it affords a strong illustration of a remark we have already made, on the perpetual tendency of Mr Dickens to undervalue and abuse our best institutions. . . .

Now, however, for *Boz at Niagara*.

It was not until I came on Tablerock, and looked—Great Heaven! on what a fall of bright green water!—that it came upon me in its full might and majesty.

Then, when I felt *how near to my Creator I was standing* [!]—*the first effect*, and the enduring one—instant and lasting—of the tremendous spectacle, was PEACE [!] *Peace of mind* [!]—*tranquillity* [!]—*calm recollections of the dead*—

great thoughts of eternal rest and happiness—nothing of gloom or terror. Niagara was
at once stamped on my heart an image of Beauty, to remain there, changeless
and indelible, until its pulses cease to beat.

Boz is a man of unquestionable genius; but this (and there is more
like it) is quite unworthy of him; it is wretched, in most seriously
questionable taste, and gives an utterly improbable and inconceivable
account of the real state of his feelings *at the time*—unless, indeed, his
mind is very oddly constituted. Many observations occur to us on the
foregoing paragraph; but we really love Boz, and shall abstain from
them. . . .

Thus ends Mr Dickens's book on America; and it is so very flimsy a
performance—we must speak the disagreeable and painful truth—
that nothing but our strong feelings of kindliness and respect for a
gentleman of his unquestionable talents, and of gratitude for the
amusement which his better and earlier works have afforded us, could
have induced us to bestow the pains which were requisite to present
so full an account of it as that which we have above given our
readers. . . .

. . . It is again very obvious that Mr Dickens, as he has a perfect right
to be if it so please him, is a man of very 'liberal' opinions in politics.
We are as strong Tories as he is a Whig or Radical; but we earnestly
advise him not to alienate from himself the affections of his readers, by
indulging, in such works as his, in *political* allusions and dogmas. We
greatly doubt whether he has read or thought sufficiently long and
deeply on such matters, to enable him to offer confident opinions on
them. In his own peculiar line, he is original, admirable, and unrivalled
—and that line, too, is one which lies level with the taste of *the million*
of persons of all shades of political opinions. We offer this hint in
unaffected friendship and anxiety for his continued success. We have no
personal knowledge of him beyond having once seen him at dinner;
when we were so much pleased with his manly and unaffected conduct
and demeanour, that we felt a disposition to read what he wrote with
much greater favour than ever. He must, however, take far more time,
and bestow far more care, in his future writings, than he has hitherto
done. The present work is written in a very careless, slipshod style. The
perpetual introduction, for instance, and not only in this but his other
works, of the expressions—*'didn't,' 'shouldn't,' 'don't,'* even when writing
in a grave strain, is annoying as an eyesore. They are mere vulgar
Cockney colloquialisms . . . Many minor blemishes of style, such as—

'*mutual* friend' (p. 31, vol. i.) for '*common* friend,'—and sentences concluded with the word '*though*,' might be pointed out were it worth while.
We would beg to recommend to Mr Dickens's attentive perusal, (if
he be not already familiar with it,) before commencing his next
publication, the essay 'On Simplicity and Refinement in Writing' of
that great master, Hume; in the opening of which there are a few
sentences which Mr Dickens, if we mistake not, will feel specially applicable to himself. If he will, after reading it, turn to pages 1, 2, 4, 7, 12,
19, 24, 25, 30, 31, 146, 173, 184, 187, 280, (we could have cited *at
least* a hundred others,) he will find instances of such strained, and
whimsical, and far-fetched images and comparisons, as very greatly
impair the character and general effect of his composition. Though the
eternal recurrence of such comparisons as that of a bed on shipboard to
'a surgical plaster spread on [a] most inaccessible *shelf*,' (?) p. 1; and of
such illustrations as 'portmanteaus no more capable of being got in at
the door, *than a giraffe could be persuaded or forced into a flower-pot*,' may
provoke a loud laugh from readers of uncultivated taste; to persons of
superior education and refinement they are puerile and tiresome indeed.
Let Mr Dickens but keep a little check upon his wayward fancy—
bestow adequate pains on the working out, both in thought and
language, of his fictions; write at far longer intervals than he has
hitherto allowed himself, (employing these intervals in the judicious
acquisition of new materials, by observation of nature, and the perusal
and study of the best masters,)—let him follow the leadings of his
strong and original genius, rather than goad and flog it into unnatural,
excessive, and exhausting action;—let him do this, and his works will
live, and his name be remembered, after nineteen-twentieths of his
contemporaries shall have passed into eternal oblivion. . . .

. . . Our last word to him we deem of perhaps greater importance
than any: as he values his permanent reputation—as he would cherish his
genius—let him at once and for ever avoid and fly from the blighting,
strangling influence of *petty cliques and coteries*.

34. [James Spedding], from a review in the *Edinburgh Review*

January 1843, lxxxvi, 497–522

Reprinted in Spedding's *Reviews and Discussions* (1879), 240–270, with additional material and discussion, 270–6.

T. B. Macaulay had intended to review *American Notes* in the *Edinburgh* but, finding it 'at once frivolous and dull', and being unwilling to hurt Dickens, he returned it to the editor, Macvey Napier. Both Napier and Macaulay were hoping to enrol Dickens as an occasional contributor to the *Edinburgh*, so Napier was embarrassed when the second man he sent the book to, James Spedding, submitted a very cool review. He deleted or toned down some offensive phrases; Napier restored these when reprinting the essay in 1879, and they have been printed as footnotes in the present collection. Spedding also reprinted part of his correspondence with Napier, and defended his review. Trouble had occurred over a passage (omitted in the present selection) where Spedding, incorrectly but in good faith, alleged that Dickens had gone to America not to study the country but 'as a kind of missionary in the cause of International Copyright' (lxxxvi, 500). Dickens denied this, in a sharp letter to *The Times* (16 January 1843, 5). Spedding's comments on the newspaper press, British and American (also omitted here), occasioned further controversy. See K. J. Fielding's essay (headnote, No. 33).

Spedding (1801–81), best remembered for his edition (1857–9) and biography (1861–74) of Bacon, was educated at Trinity College, Cambridge, where he was an 'Apostle' and became a lifelong friend of Tennyson. He had recently been in America, when he undertook to review *American Notes* at short notice.

... we have looked forward with considerable interest to a work on America by Mr Dickens;—not as a man whose views on such a subject were likely to have any conclusive value, but as one with whom the public is personally acquainted through his former works. We all know 'Boz,' though we may not have seen his face. We know what he thinks about affairs at home, with which we are all conversant—about poor-laws and rich-laws, elections, schools, courts of justice, magistrates, policemen, cab-drivers, and housebreakers—matters which lie round about us, and which we flatter ourselves we understand as well as he. We know, therefore, what to infer from his pictures of society abroad; what weight to attribute to his representations; with what caution and allowance to entertain them. If his book abound in broad pictures of social absurdities and vulgarities, we know that[1] his tendency in that direction is so strong, that, though possessing sources of far finer and deeper humour, he can hardly refrain from indulging it to excess. If he draw bitter pictures of harsh jailers and languishing prisoners, we know that his sympathy for human suffering sometimes betrays him into an unjust antipathy to those whose duty it is to carry into effect the severities of justice.[2] We know, in short, where we may trust his judgment, where we must take it with caution, and where we may neglect it.

Mr Dickens has many qualities which make his testimony, as a passing observer in a strange country, unusually valuable. A truly genial nature; an unweariable spirit of observation, quickened by continual exercise; an intimate acquaintance with the many varieties of life and character which are to be met with in large cities; a clear eye to see through the surface and false disguises of things; a desire to see things truly; a respect for the human soul, and the genuine face and voice of nature, under whatever disadvantages of person, situation, or repute in the world; a mind which, if it be too much to call it original in the highest sense of the word, yet uses always its own eyes, and applies itself to see the object before it takes the impression—to understand the case before it passes judgment; a wide range of sympathy moreover—with sweetness, and a certain steady self-respect, which keeps the spirit clear from perturbations, and free to receive an untroubled image;—a mind, in short, which moves with freedom and pleasure in a wider world than has been thrown open to the generality of men. This happy combination of rare qualities, which Mr Dickens's previous works show that he possesses, would seem to qualify him, in

[1] he commenced his literary career as an illustrator of Seymour's cockney caricatures, and that . . .

[2] If he grow learned on questions of government and politics, we know that his opinions on such matters are not much enquired after at home.

some respects, beyond any English traveller that has yet written about the United States,—if not to discuss the political prospects of that country, or to draw comparisons between monarchical and republican institutions, yet to receive and reproduce, for the information of the British public, a just image of its existing social condition. To balance these, however, it must be confessed that he labours under some considerable disadvantages. His education must have been desultory, and not of a kind likely to train him to habits of grave and solid speculation. A young man, a satirist both by profession and by humour, whose studies have lain almost exclusively among the odd characters in the odd corners of London, who does not appear to have attempted the systematic cultivation of his powers, or indeed to have been aware of them, until they were revealed to him by a sudden blaze of popularity which would have turned a weaker head—who has since been constantly occupied in his own peculiar field of fiction and humour—how can he have acquired the knowledge and the speculative powers necessary for estimating the character of a great people, placed in circumstances not only strange to him, but new in the history of mankind; or the working of institutions which are yet in their infancy, their hour of trial not yet come—in their present state resembling nothing by the analogy of which their tendency and final scope may be guessed at? Should he wander into prophecies or philosophic speculations, it is clear that such a guide must be followed with considerable distrust. How,[1] indeed, can his opinions be taken without abatement and allowance, even in that which belongs more especially to his own province—the aspect and character of society as it exists? As a comic satirist, with a strong tendency to caricature, it has been his business to observe society in its irregularities and incongruities, not in the sum and total result of its operation; a habit which, even in scenes with which we are most familiar, can hardly be indulged without disturbing the judgment; and which, among strange men and manners, may easily mislead the fancy beyond the power of the most vigilant understanding to set it right. . . .

And though Mr Dickens *knows* better, it is too much to expect of him that he should have always acted upon his better knowledge; especially when we consider that he had his character as an amusing writer to keep up. The obligation which he undoubtedly lies under to keep his readers well entertained, (failing which, any book by 'Boz' would be universally denounced as a catchpenny,) must have involved him in

---

[1] 1879 has *Nor* instead of *How*.

many temptations quite foreign to his business as an impartial observer; for any man who would resolutely abstain from seeing things in false lights, must make up his mind to forego half his triumphs as a wit, and *vice versa*. Even his habits as a writer of fiction must have been against him; for such a man will always be tempted to study society, with a view to gather suggestions and materials for his creative faculty to work upon, rather than simply to consider and understand it. The author of *Pickwick* will study the present as our historical novelists study the past—to find not what it is, but what he can make of it.

. . . we cannot say that his book throws any new light on his subject. He has done little more than confide to the public, what should have been a series of Letters for the entertainment of his private friends. Very agreeable and amusing Letters they would have been; and as such, had they been posthumously published, would have been read with interest and pleasure. As it is, in the middle of our amusement at the graphic sketches of life and manners, the ludicrous incidents, the wayside conversations about nothing, so happily told, and the lively remarks with which these *Notes* abound—in the middle of our respect for the tone of good sense and good humour which runs through them —and in spite of a high appreciation of the gentlemanly feeling which has induced him to refrain from all personal allusions and criticisms; and for the modesty which has kept him silent on so many subjects, concerning which most persons in the same situation (not being reminded of the worthlessness of their opinions by the general inattention of mankind to what they say) are betrayed into the delivery of oracles, —in the middle of all this, we cannot help feeling that we should have respected Mr Dickens more if he had kept his book to himself; if he had been so far dissatisfied with these *American Notes* as to shrink from the 'general circulation' of them. . . .

We do not suppose that his conversation has lain much among Professors, or that his thoughts on Universities are entitled to much authority. . . .

[Spedding quotes, however, the account of Harvard from ch. iii. Nor are the 'somewhat meagre notices' of the manners and character of the best society in America very impressive. But public institutions— schools, hospitals, workhouses, prisons—are more in Dickens's line.] Now, in these matters, Mr Dickens's testimony is not only very favourable and very strongly expressed; but is really of great value. Prisons and madhouses have always had strong attractions for him; he went out with the advantage of a very extensive acquaintance with establishments of this kind in England; and, wherever he heard of one in America, he appears to have stayed and seen it. His report leads irresistibly to the conclusion, that in this department New England has, as a people, taken the lead of the civilized world; and that Old England, though beginning to follow, is still a good way behind. And the superiority lies not merely in the practical recognition of the principle, that the care of these things belongs properly to the State; and should not be left, as with us, to the charity and judgment of individuals, however securely that charity may be relied on; but in the excellence of the institutions themselves in respect of arrangement and management. Our limits will not allow us to follow him through his observations and remarks on this subject; which are, however, upon the whole, the most valuable and interesting part of the book. He carefully inspected not less (we think) than ten institutions of this class; and of these he has given minute descriptions. . . .

Upon one doubtful and difficult question, which has of late excited a good deal of controversy in England, Mr Dickens's observations will be read with great interest—we allude to the effects of the *solitary* as contrasted with the *silent* system. Against the solitary system Mr Dickens gives his most emphatic testimony; which will, no doubt, have due weight with the department on which the consideration of this question, with reference to our own prison system, devolves. For our own part, we must confess that, highly as we esteem his opinion in such a matter, and free as we are from any prejudice in favour of the system which he condemns, we are not altogether satisfied. His manner of handling the question does not assure us that he is master of it. His facts, as stated by himself, do not appear to us to fit his theory. If not inconsistent with it, they are certainly not conclusive in favour of it. We sometimes cannot help doubting whether his *judging* faculty is strongly developed, and whether he does not sometimes mistake pictures in his mind for facts in nature. He is evidently proud of his powers of intuition—of his faculty of inferring a whole history from a passing expression. Show him any man's face, and he will immediately tell you his life and adventures. A very pretty and probable story he will make of it; and, provided we do not forget that it is all *fiction*, a very instructive one. But, in discussing disputed points in nature or policy, we cannot admit these works of his imagination as legitimate evidence.

[Spedding quotes extensively from ch. vii, where Dickens tries to picture the state of mind of prisoners arriving at the Philadelphia Penitentiary. Spedding argues that Dickens's confident analyses of the prisoners he describes are affecting literary creations, but unreliable and improbable. He regrets that Dickens has so little to say about other institutions—law courts, churches, education, literature—and offers his own remarks on American newspapers.]

We have now nearly exhausted these volumes of the information which they supply, available for the purpose with which we set out. Of the manners of the mass of the people, Mr Dickens gives many amusing illustrations; most of which have been already quoted in various publications, and have made us all very merry. It is but justice to him, however, to say, that he saw all these things in their true light; and that, while indulging his sense of the ludicrous by a hearty English laugh, he was not betrayed by them into any foolish conclusions, or illiberal (we wish we could add *un-English*) contempt. The following sensible remarks are worth extracting, not because they tell us any thing which is not obvious to any man who thinks; but because so few people trouble themselves with thinking about the matter. The scene is Sandusky, at the south-western extremity of Lake Erie.

[Quotes the description of the inn-keeper, from ch. xiv.]

35. [Cornelius C. Felton], from a review in the *North American Review*

January 1843, lvi, 212–37

'Dickens's Notes', wrote Longfellow in January 1843, 'are scattered
to the four winds by a blast in *Blackwood*—and brought together
again by Felton in the *North American.*' Ada C. Nisbet, quoting
this, remarks that Felton's was the most enthusiastic review of the
ill-received *American Notes* ('The Mystery of *Martin Chuzzlewit*',
Essays . . . presented to Lily B. Campbell (Berkeley & Los Angeles,
1950), 209). It is included here mainly, however, as an eloquent
expression of American enthusiasm for the early Dickens. Felton
(1807–62) was Professor of Greek at Harvard. Dickens had met him
during his American tour and found him 'a delightful fellow';
a warm friendship ensued. Felton's review greatly pleased Dickens.
'You cannot think how much notice it has attracted here,' he told
Felton (2 March 1843); Lord Brougham, Lord Ashburton, and
many others, had written congratulating him upon it. The review
begins with a long account and explanation of his international
popularity (quoted in Introduction, pp. 3–4).

Mr Dickens's wit and humor are so abundant, that most people hardly
think of the more serious aspects of his genius. He has an inexhaustible
vein of the pleasantest exaggeration, which keeps his readers either
roaring with laughter, or getting ready to roar. He is constantly
surprising us with the most unexpected turns, which the solemnity of a
stoic could not stand against. Whimsical peculiarities of scenes or
persons are so constantly presented in an amusing light, that the
grimmest scorner of mirth and frolic cannot choose but surrender at
discretion. A single expression, even a word, is often so charged with
drollery, that, before it is fairly read, the reader and the hearer (if there
be one) are thrown into convulsions. We have known people, who are
utterly overcome by seeing even the covers of *Pickwick*, and could

no more help shouting with laughter, though their very lives depended on preserving silence, than they could make the sun to stand still at a word. This abundant wit is all of the right kind. Puns and unnatural distortions of words are rarely found in his books. Strange but striking comparisons, a sudden bringing together of opposite ideas, exact delineation of comical character, happy narration of comic incident, and pleasant exaggeration, are the materials out of which he has woven ten thousand witty passages, which will be read with delight, as long as wit is understood, as long as men are men. . . .

The very name of Boz suggests a thousand comical traits, and he is generally regarded as chiefly to be praised for wit and humor. This is far enough from being the case. Dickens is an original poet. Many of his characters are drawn with earnestness and enthusiasm. He has sounded the depths of the human heart, as well as skimmed over its surface. The vigilance of his eye, no beauty of nature and no form of human passion escapes. Scattered all over his works, especially his later ones, are the most exquisite delineation of the outward world, in language prosaic in form, but wonderfully poetical in spirit. . . .

The character of Little Nell, is by universal consent placed among the loveliest creations of genius. In some respects it is the pendant of Oliver. The one reminds us of the other. Yet each has a striking individuality; each character has an independent existence; each is a creation of finished and exquisite art. Little Nell is the favorite child of the author's genius. On her he seems to have lavished the richest powers of his mind, and the deepest affections of his heart. Her course, through the trying and agitating scenes of her short and spotless life, he saw from the beginning with certain eye, and traced with unerring hand. He seems to have watched her with real, heartfelt solicitude; he certainly gave to her little adventures, and her mighty sorrows, and her heroic endurance a living reality, which month after month deepened the sympathies, and held at their highest tension the feelings, of the whole reading world. Her death is perhaps the most pathetic scene in the literature of the age. Nothing has so profoundly stirred the world's great heart for many years.

A peculiarity of Dickens's writings, which has often been dwelt upon with praise and pleasure, is their freedom from expressions and allusions which offend a fastidious delicacy. Considering the regions of life where many of his scenes are laid, this is a most remarkable fact. He loses by it nothing that is racy or striking. So sure is the felicitous instinct of his genius, that he presents each scene and circumstance in its happiest aspect; he draws each group, and places every figure, in its most characteristic action and attitude, and never for an instant forgets what is due to the nicest sense of propriety. He gains immeasurably by this delicate dealing with his materials. . . .

Another striking peculiarity of Dickens's works is their practical moral aim. They are not constructed merely upon certain abstract principles of art, with no reference to the condition of men. They are the outpourings of a heart, that feels deeply all that belongs to the race; of a mind, that sees clearly the wrongs and sufferings under which half mankind are bowed down. Dickens sees the right, and, in all his works, holds it steadily in view. Besides the beauty breathed over his more serious writings by an imagination of extraordinary brilliancy and power, we feel they have the more mysterious beauty of a generous and disinterested spirit, which claims kindred with every human heart. They are, to borrow Mr Talfourd's strong expression, 'mortised into the living rock of humanity,'—and greatly has humanity been the gainer. The immediate effects of these works in England, for whose condition they are more especially adapted, are said to be extraordinary. . . . These are great and noble ends for genius to have accomplished. These are worthy of the proudest ambition, the loftiest aspirations after fame. Dickens has thus powerfully cooperated with the great philanthropic movements which mark the present age. . . .

Mr Dickens's English style is one of great originality and power. . . . His command over the English language, in its most native and idiomatic parts, is really marvellous. His style is original, almost beyond that of any writer of English in this age. It is formed, not by the study of classical models, not by consuming the midnight oil in laboriously mastering the learning of books; but it is caught from the lips of men, speaking under the influence of the passions in daily life. It is formed from the commonest materials, selected with an instinctive tact, and used with singular directness and force. It abounds in racy and expressive idioms, and has a strange flexibility in conveying at once to the reader's mind every variety of thought and passion. It may be said to be unstudied, though it must have required long habits of composition to bring it to its present state of completeness. What we mean is, that Mr Dickens is one of those original thinkers, who look directly upon the objects of their thoughts, and express their views, feelings, or conceptions in the first words that come to hand,—those first words being almost always the best. He seems to be under no influence from other minds; he rarely makes an allusion to others' works; his style has none of the purple patches that varied scholarship is so apt to give to language, sometimes to the injury of its point and force; but, with a self-reliance, which rarely disappoints him, he marches forward to his aim; beautiful and brilliant thoughts spring spontaneous and abundant around his rapid pen; the stream of language flows at its own sweet will, and never runs low or threatens to fail; it changes, with a curious and natural felicity, from stirring narrative to witty dialogue; from keen satire, it softens easily to heart-moving pathos; it rises from shrewd observation, to vehement eloquence; and from homely but expressive prose, it ever and anon melts into the sweetest music. He draws his illustrations not from the great book of literature, but from the greater book of human life. His common-places are not taken from the classics, but from the soul of man. His descriptions of men and nature are the records, not of his reading, but of what he has seen in the thronged thoroughfares of the city, or the sweet solitudes of the country. His style, therefore, is strikingly original; original in the sense in which Homer is original, Shakespeare is original, Scott is original.

But, with all its excellences, Dickens's style is marred by several solecisms, which the writers of the last twenty years have admitted into their works, and these he repeats again and again. The use of 'directly' in the sense of 'as soon as,' is an abomination first made popular, though not first used, by Bulwer, and appearing more than a thousand times in Dickens's works. It is an irredeemable cockneyism, and as such never to be tolerated in good society. . . .

[Other such solecisms cited.]

Such are our impressions of the genius of Mr Dickens; and thinking thus, and believing that the majority of American readers had pretty much the same views, we were not surprised at the enthusiasm with which his late arrival was hailed in the United States. Some few individuals,—as is always the case with popular excitements,—were disposed to sneer. But, when we consider the extraordinary influence that this young author had wielded; the beautiful humanity that every-where breathed from his pages; the delicacy from which, in the wildest freaks of fun and frolic, he had never departed; the deep sympathy he had ever shown with the afflicted of his race; the exquisite creations which his genius had so lavishly poured out upon the world, and the years of enjoyment he had brought to every house in the land; we cannot help feeling that the universal enthusiasm with which he was welcomed was perfectly natural, and just what was to be expected from a generous people. True, the spectacle of a young man, without wealth or political influence, receiving such homage, was a novel one. Popular candidates for office, men in high station, presidents and those who hoped to be presidents, had often before, in their progresses through the country, received the plaudits of the multitude; bells had been rung, and vast quantities of villanous saltpetre had been burned to do them honor; and nobody thought these tumultuous proceedings censurable. But here was a youthful foreigner with nothing but God's gifts,—a great genius and a generous heart,—from whom no other benefit had been received or was to be expected, but the delight of reading his books,—and people rushed to receive him with open arms. To our apprehension the scene was beautiful and affecting. It did as much honor to the people as to the distinguished visiter. And, though, many ludicrous incidents marked the popular enthusiasm ... still, on the whole, the reception was highly creditable to the feeling and good sense of the country.

[Felton then refers favourably to Dickens's social demeanour in America and defends his taking a stand over international copyright. Turning at last to the book under review, he assumes that all Americans have now read these *Notes*.] We believe they have been read with general approbation. Certainly they are pleasant reading, and highly characteristic of their author. Persons who expected from Dickens long disquisitions upon what are called American Institutions,—philosophical tirades upon the working of the republican machine of government,—or the future prospects of the world as affected by what we style the great experiment of self-government,—expected what they had no right to look for from the author of *Pickwick*. Mr Dickens had too much good sense to attempt a work for which he was unprepared by previous studies, habits of thought, and intellectual peculiarities; for which, had he possessed every needful prerequisite, his residence in the country was too short, and his opportunities of calm observation too limited and few. But he has a quick eye, from which nothing that comes, within its range escapes; in his rapid passage from place to place, he would seize many characteristic points, and take in at a glance many amusing traits. Little incidents, that others would pass unnoticed, with him would be the germs of entertaining remark.

We had a right, therefore, to expect from him, not a didactic work, but a book full of graphic touches, good feeling, and pleasant observation; and in this expectation we have not been disappointed. Many of his strictures have given offence in various quarters. [—but, Felton argues, unnecessarily. Some judgments in the book are, however, doubtful: and some minor factual matters are wrong.]

The style of this book is, like that of Dickens's other writings, free, graphic, and flowing. It has a rapid movement, as if he wrote as fast as his pen could be driven across the paper. Sometimes, therefore, it is incorrect, and it is frequently disfigured by the two or three solecisms we have mentioned before. It abounds in touches of the poetical and imaginative. Striking expressions, brilliant descriptions, witty turns, and humorous sallies, are scattered in sparkling profusion over its animated pages. The sea-passages have attracted great and deserved admiration. The graver parts of the book,—such as the visit to the Blind Institution at South Boston, the affecting account of Laura Bridgman, and the forcible comments upon the solitary system of prison discipline in Philadelphia,—are written in a deep, earnest, fervent spirit, and come from a heart throbbing with the best sympathies of our nature. The tone of the book, throughout, is frank, honest, and manly. . . .

[Felton ends by praising the description of Niagara, ch. xvi.]

The sublime figure at the close of the passage, is worthy of the greatest poet. It is a conception, that would be admired in the awful genius of Dante.

36. [John Wilson Croker], from an unsigned review, *Quarterly Review*

March 1843, lxxi, 502–28

Croker (1780–1857), Tory politician, essayist, editor and historian, had contributed to the *Quarterly* since its inception in 1809, and was famous for his slashing style.

... It was ... we confess, with no particular pleasure that we heard we were to have a picture of America from the pen of Mr Dickens. Mr Dickens is, as everybody knows, the author of some popular stories published originally in periodical parts—remarkable as clever exhibitions of very low life—treated however, generally speaking, with better taste and less vulgarity[1] than the subjects seem to promise. ... But we must confess that we doubt whether the powers—or perhaps we should say the habits of his mind—are equal to any sustained exertion. His best things, to our taste, are some short tales published under the absurd pseudonyme of BOZ—in which a single anecdote, lively or serious, is told with humour or tenderness as the subject may require, but always with ease and felicity. His longer works owe, we are afraid, much of their popularity to their having been published *in numbers*. There is in them, as in the others, considerable truth, but in the long run somewhat of sameness; and the continuous repetition of scenes of low life—though, as we have said, seldom *vulgarly* treated—becomes at last exceedingly tedious. We at least can say for ourselves that we followed the earlier portions of *Nickleby*, as they were published, with that degree of interest and amusement which serves to while away what the French so apppropriately call '*les moments perdus:*' but it

[1] This, however, must be taken *cum grano salis* [with a pinch of salt]—for Mr Dickens's works afford a double exemplification of the difference between *describing vulgar objects* and *describing vulgarly*. His low-life—his Weller, Noggs, or Mantellini—is never vulgar — it is real; but the vulgarity of his attempts at the aristocracy—his lords and baronets—is woeful [*Croker's footnote*].

happened that we did not see the latter half till the whole had been collected in *a volume*—and then, we must confess that we found some difficulty in getting through, in this concentrated shape, a series of chapters, which we have no doubt we should have read, at the usual intervals, with as much zest as we had done their predecessors. In short, we are inclined to predict of works of this style both in England and France (where the manufacture is flourishing on a very extensive and somewhat profligate scale) that an ephemeral popularity will be followed by early oblivion.

But, however this may be, there is, we think, little doubt that it was Mr Dickens's reputation as a kind of moral caricaturist—a shrewd observer and powerful delineator of ridiculous peculiarities in diction and in manners, that suggested the idea of his undertaking a voyage to America and this consequent publication. . . .

But with whatever intentions—whether serious or comic—Mr Dickens may have undertaken his tour, the result, we think, will equally disappoint those who feared and those who hoped that he would exhibit the interior of American life with the same shrewd perception of the ridiculous, and the same caustic power of describing it, for which he had become so celebrated at home. In fact the work has very little of Mr Dickens's peculiar merit, and still less, we are sorry to say, of any other. It seems to us an entire failure; and yet, paradoxical as it may appear, the failure is probably more creditable to his personal character than a high degree of literary success might have been. [He has been at pains to avoid] . . . as far as possible anything that was likely to give offence. He seems also to have had a delicacy—not very usual amongst modern travellers—as to mentioning *anything* whatsoever about private persons, or even private life. . . .

But this strange and, as we think, ultra-delicate determination that it should not be discoverable from his book that he had ever partaken of one private meal, or even entered one private house (or not more than one), has forced Mr Dickens to eke out his volumes with such common and general topics as we have had over and over again from other travellers, and by most of them, we think, better handled. It would be impossible to exhibit, *by extracts*, the extent to which Mr Dickens pushes the practice of dwelling on certain classes of subjects which, we think, might have been much more succinctly treated, and of slurring over other matters on which we should have been desirous to hear his opinion; but the following synopsis of the topics treated in the first half of his first volume, including his sojourn at

Boston, and of the space allotted by him to each subject, will explain the manner in which the book has been concocted.

His visit to Boston—the city of all America in which he gives us to understand—and we believe justly—that society (including, of course, literature, manners, arts, &c.) is on the best and most satisfactory footing, concludes with the 142nd page—and these 142 pages are thus occupied:—

Topics	Pages	
'Passage out'	53	
Cases of a boy and girl in the Blind Asylum. . .	32	
General observations on prisons, hospitals, and houses of correction	30	
Religion, its various sects and influence—including two pages of a sermon by a sailor turned preacher . .	8	
General description of the city of Boston . . .	6	
Courts of law and administration of justice . . .	5	
Hotels—furniture, attendance, style of living in them .	2	
University of Cambridge—excellence of its professors, and beneficial influence on society	$1\frac{1}{2}$	Lines
'Social customs' and general modes of life . . .	0	17
The ladies, their beauty, education, moral qualities, and amusements	0	14
The theatres	0	4
Appearance and proceedings of the Senate and House of Representatives	0	3
'Tone of Society in Boston' . . . (not quite)	0	2
State of literature	0	0 !
Fine arts	0	0 !!
Material, moral, and political condition, occupations, manners, &c. of the various classes of the people .	0	0 !!!
Trade, commerce, finance, public works, army, navy, professions, dress, equipages, government, &c. &c. &c. .	0	0 !!!!

Of New York, 'the *beautiful metropolis of America*,' as he designates it, his account is still more meagre. . . . again, as at Boston, of private life, of arts or science—literature or politics—law or commerce—public works or individual enterprise—national feelings or social manners—not a word. On all such topics his account of the 'beautiful metropolis' is as barren as if he had been bivouacking for a single night in some embryo village of the western wild . . . indeed the utter inanity of Mr Dickens's pages as to all topics of information, or even rational amusement, is not more to be regretted than the awkward efforts at jocularity with which he endeavours to supply their places.

We might, in return, be very facetious in exposing Mr Dickens's bad taste, but we prefer seriously remonstrating with him on nonsense so deplorable that we are almost ashamed to give one other specimen. We have already stated that of the account of New York a few lines only are given to a general view of society in that city, while several pages are employed on the lowest and most trivial topics; but our readers will hardly be prepared for such stupid puerility as we have now to produce. It seems that the streets of the 'beautiful metropolis' are very much frequented by *pigs*. This gives Mr Dickens the opportunity of dedicating not merely to pigs in general, but to *one individual and selected pig*, three pages of his *American Notes*, being, we calculate, six times more space than he has given to the statesmen, orators, literators, artists, and heroes of America all put together.

[Quotes from ch. vi.]

And so on for three pages! Our readers will, we think, excuse us from producing any further specimens of this species of pleasantry, and will only wonder how any man, with a tithe of Mr Dickens's cleverness and a grain of tact, could publish such trash. . . .

37. From an unsigned review of *Pictures from Italy*, *The Times*

1 June 1846

'It has been too much the habit, following the key-note given by the sneering reviewer in *The Times*, to undervalue Mr. Dickens's book on Italy,' wrote Shelton Mackenzie in his *Life of Dickens* (Philadelphia, [1870], 175). That this review should be thus remembered over twenty years after publication suggests that it indeed had an effect. The reviewer is the man who had been slamming the Christmas books: see No. 43.

. . . There is nothing new in the book from beginning to end. It has no purpose, and attempts to work out no definite idea. Had John

Jones been its author it would never have been heard of. Nay, Jones would have been far too wise to risk his honourable name in such a venture. We miss, for the first time, even the Pickwickian zest with which Mr Dickens has known how to give at least piquancy to the majority of his undertakings. We did not expect learning, but we did look for fun. Investigations, original or otherwise, were out of the question; but life-like illustrations of character, grotesque images of Italian natives,—these we were sure of. . . . We are sadly disappointed. Things are described which have been described a hundred times before, but without spirit, and without conveying accurate or distinct ideas to the reader's mind; a story here and there comes out as old as the hills, and a custom is solemnly adverted to which we remember to have read of in the days of the first form. The book has been written as a task; . . . certainly without love, without inspiration, and without the healthy motives that actuated Mr. Dickens in his earliest achievements.

Mr Dickens, like the majority of men whose experience in early life has been limited and local, forgets, as circumstances enlarge that experience, that new forms and new scenes, striking and wonderful to him, are familiar enough to others, who in youth have enjoyed a wider range of observation than himself. When we read the interesting account of Mr Dickens's sea sickness on board the steamer that carried him to America [*American Notes*, ch. ii], we felt assured not only that his marine experience was confined to Gravesend and shrimps, but that he fully believed the experience of his readers to be equally circumscribed. . . .

We have spoken on a former occasion of the extraordinary style of composition which Mr Dickens is endeavouring to engraft upon the national literature. He does not fail to recommend it again in the present little work. We have already entered our protest against it, but with becoming humility, and with the consciousness of our inability to soar so high as genius would lead us. The style to which we refer may be called, for want of a better term, the *literary ventriloquial*, for it aims at producing in words to the eye precisely the same effects as ventriloquism achieves in sounds in the ear. . . . [Gives examples from *The Cricket*. He also remarks that here, as usual, Dickens] amply avails himself of his license to employ, at any cost or risk, the most exaggerated similes and far-fetched metaphors. . . .

[He cites examples.]

. . . We have only space for one word of advice to Mr Dickens, offered in a spirit of true friendliness, and, he may believe us, with a view solely to his future success. Italy is not his ground; travels and grave essays on men and manners are not his vocation. No one is better aware of the fact than himself. He acknowledges it in the preface to the volume under review, when he frankly states that he is aware of having committed a great mistake when he broke off the old relations between himself and his readers. He is about to resume those relations, 'joyfully' he says, in Switzerland. Let him not, we entreat him, be too eager to resume them. He has not only to sustain his past reputation, but to repair the mischief which we assure him has been done by his latest publications. It may not be useless to consider whether the mere appearance of his books may not be improved. His extraordinary regard for capital letters at certain times and in certain places is unaccountable and foolish; his punctuation would disgrace a schoolboy. The time perhaps may have come for dismissing the crutch hitherto afforded by the painter and caricaturist, and for walking above in the manliness and strength of proud and conscious self-reliance. The time must come, when the good public, sick of illustration, will demand that he shall rely, like his great predecessors, upon his own unaided power. Anticipate that demand, Mr Dickens, and be your own emancipator! Above all things, remember that the tree which endures is that which it has taken generations to bring to maturity. What you have written in an hour may die in an hour. Carry your undoubted genius to subjects that are worthy of it and patiently and carefully address yourself to the understanding and sympathy—not of the petty clique class which toadies you—but of such as shall transmit you with approval and love to the remotest posterity.

38. From an unsigned review, *Gentleman's Magazine*

July 1846, n.s. xxvi, 3-21

... There are in this volume numerous little quaintnesses, obliquities, and oddities of expression, peculiar *locutions*, all Mr Dickens's own, such as we have been used to in his previous works, modes of thinking and writing that have been habitual to him, that he cannot do without; some very amusing, some overstrained, and not to be swallowed without an effort: they are numerous enough to any one who will look after them; as for instance:—

8: 'Queer old towns, draw-bridged, and walled; with odd little towers at the angles, like grotesque faces, as if the wall had put a mask on, and were staring down into the moat. . . extinguisher-topped turrets, and blink-eyed little casements,' &c.—P. 11: 'The *femme de chambre* of the Hotel de l'Ecu d'Or is here, and a gentleman in a glazed cap, with a red beard *like a bosom friend*, who is staying at the Hotel de l'Ecu d'Or', &c.—P. 16: 'The courier cuts a joke. The landlord is affectionate, but not weakly so. He bears it like a man.'—P. 41: 'We sit upon a stone by the door, sometimes, in the evening, like Robinson Crusoe and Friday *reversed;* and he generally relates, towards my conversion, an abridgment of the history of St Peter—chiefly, I believe, from the unspeakable delight he has in his imitation of the cock.' —P. 53: Describing the beggars at Genoa, 'Sometimes they are visited by a man without legs, on a little go-cart, but who has such a fresh-coloured, lively face, and such a respectable, well-conditioned body, that he looks as if he had sunk into the ground up to his middle, or had come but partially up a flight of cellar-steps to speak to somebody.' Speaking of the loungers in the apothecaries' shops, he says, 'They sit so still and quiet that either you don't see them in the darkened shop, or mistake them—as I did one ghostly man in bottlegreen, one day, with a hat like a stopper—for horse medicine.' Sitting in any of the Catholic churches is likened to 'a mild dose of opium.' But what shall we say to the following allusion, speaking of the system of washing so prevalent on the Continent,—'The custom is to lay the wet linen which is being operated upon on a smooth stone, and hammer away at it with a flat wooden mallet. This they do as furiously as if they were revenging themselves on *dress in general for being connected with the Fall of Mankind.*' The wild festoons and vine wreaths, which in Italy extend from tree to tree in so graceful and picturesque a manner, must strike every eye; but it is not any imagination that has described 'the long line of trees all bound and garlanded together, as if they had taken hold of one another, and are coming dancing down the field.' The amphitheatre of Verona has suggested many a picturesque association to the classical traveller, but probably never before that of 'being like the inside of a prodigious hat of plaited straw, with an enormously broad brim and shallow crown.' These are a few of Mr Dickens's odd quaintnesses, humorous touches, and conceits—mannerisms of his own—often exciting a smile— a laugh, as often marking how much his favourite recreations and studies are in his daily thoughts; as, for instance, speaking of the Pope's Swiss Guards: 'They wear a quaint striped surcoat and striped tight legs, and carry halberts like those which are usually shouldered by those theatrical supernumeraries, who never *can* get off the stage fast enough, and who may be generally observed to *linger in the enemy's camp after the open country, held by the opposite forces, has been split up the middle by a convulsion of nature.*' Upon the whole, after our perusal of this volume, admirers as we are to the full of Mr Dickens's genius, in his various works of fiction, we hardly feel that the following sentence of an animated historian, whom we have previously mentioned, describing Goldoni's[1] talents and acquirements, would be unjust towards the character of the writer of *Pictures of Italy*, but without allusion to his other productions:—'His life would seem to be spent among actors and play-writers; his acquaintance was with stage heroes and heroines. He had but rare opportunities of an intimate intercourse with the best classes. Like one of our modern tourists, he travelled through, but had hardly leisure to inspect, the world: he saw it through the glare of the stage-lamps. His heroes too often remind us of the green-room; their faded lineaments are apparent through the varnish of their theatrical paint,' &c.

[1] Carlo Goldoni (1707–93), Italian comic dramatist.

THE CHRISTMAS BOOKS

A Christmas Carol,
December 1843

The Chimes,
December 1844

The Cricket on the Hearth,
December 1845

The Battle of Life,
December 1846

The Haunted Man,
December 1848

'The very name of the author predisposes one to the kindlier feelings', wrote Thomas Hood, welcoming the *Carol* (*Hood's Magazine*, January 1844, i, 68). Though its sales were surprisingly small (about 15 000 by early 1844: see *Life*, 314–5), it rapidly became a national institution, as Thackeray proclaimed (No. 40), a book of extra-literary and supra-critical standing, 'not to be talked about or written of according to ordinary rules' (E. L. Blanchard in *Ainsworth's Magazine*, January 1844, v, 86).

'The popularity of the first two works in the annual [Christmas] series was unrivalled in English literature' (*Tait's Edinburgh Magazine*, January 1849, xvi, 57)—but *The Chimes* aroused much controversy at the time, being 'attacked and defended with a degree of ardour which scarcely any other subject is capable of inspiring' (*Globe*, 31 December 1844, quoted by Michael Slater, 'The Christmas Books', *Dickensian*, lxv (1969), 17). Some reviewers applauded its social message and detected here a substantially new Dickens (e.g., *The Times* and *Economist*, Nos. 43, 47), others deplored the loss of the former comedy and high spirits, disliked the machinery, and held that 'were it not a five-shilling book, and unlikely, therefore, to be read by those whom it professes to school in their interests, we should pronounce it one of the most mischievous ever written' (*Union Magazine*, February 1846, 234). The pathos was found very affecting (as had been the Tiny Tim episodes in the *Carol*). 'Yes,' wrote Lady Blessington to Forster, 'this book will melt hearts and open purse strings. . . . I was embarrassed to meet the eyes of my servants, mine were so red with tears' (*Memoir . . . of the Countess of Blessington*, ed. R. R. Madden (1855), ii, 400). There was a minor controversy over whether Dickens had been fair to Sir Peter Laurie, recognizably lampooned as Alderman Cute.

The *Cricket* was less well received: 'Mr Dickens's reputation as a writer, some time since on the decline, will gain nothing by this book. . . . It is Dickensism diluted' (*Oxford and Cambridge Review*, January 1846, ii, 43). Thackeray made the nice discrimination that it was 'a good *Christmas* book. . . . In quieter day, and out of the holiday hubbub, . . . Mr Dickens will hardly paint so coarsely' (*Review*, *Chronicle*, 24 December 1845). Some reviewers were relieved that this Christmas book was a-political, but there was general disappointment. And *The Times* began its ferocious onslaught on the Christmas books (maybe impelled, at this time, by a desire to discredit the editor of its new rival, the *Daily News*, announced for imminent publication). As *Tait's*, however, pointed out, Dickens's sales increased despite this poor critical reception (No. 52), and next year the same thing happened: as Wilkie Collins noted, everybody abused *The Battle of Life* but everybody read it. It was 'condemned by the critics, pooh-poohed by the public, hissed at the Lyceum, and finally "dead-and-buried" by *The Times*' (*Sharpe's London Magazine*, January 1849, viii, 188). Christmas no longer dominated the story, but some critics were charmed by the love-story and moved by 'the sublimity' of Marian's self-sacrifice (*Working Men's Friend*, 21 August 1852, n.s. ii, 327). J. Westland Marston significantly opened his favourable review in the *Athenaeum*: 'The noblest feature of our current literature is its reverence for the affections' (26 December 1846, 1319). In 1847 there was no Christmas Book. *The Haunted Man* (1848) struck *Sharpe's* as a wonderful recovery from the *Battle* fiasco: 'We should be sorry to call him our friend who does not rise from its perusal a wiser and a better man' (*loc. cit.*, 190). It had good reviews in the *Athenaeum*, *Examiner* and *Literary Gazette* (all 23 December 1848), though confirmed enemies like *The Times* and *The Man in the Moon* remained unmoved. The *Spectator* wrote, in superior tones, about the 'ragged, outcast, beggar boy . . . made to illustrate the blue book conclusions touching education, public health bills, and ragged schools' (23 December 1848, 1236), but the Phantom's speech about him ('There is not a father by whose side . . . these creatures walk . . .', ch. iii) was one of the most widely-quoted passages Dickens ever wrote.

When Dickens began giving paid readings in May 1858, his total repertoire consisted of Christmas books (*Carol*, *Chimes*, and *Cricket*). The *Carol* had been his first public reading, in 1853, and figured in his final farewell performance in 1870; it was his most popular item. See Philip Collins, 'Dickens's Public Readings', *Studies in the Novel*, i (1969), 118–32. Still familiar through dramatized versions, the *Carol* (like the other Christmas Books) has lately received hardly any critical attention. Recent exceptions are John Butt's essay in *Pope, Dickens and Others* (Edinburgh, 1969) and Michael Slater's (cited above). Dr Slater's unpublished thesis on *The Chimes: its Materials, Making and Public Reception* (D.Phil., Oxford, 1965) is masterly. See also Philip Collins, '*Carol* philosophy, cheerful views', *Etudes Anglaises* (Dickens Centenary issue, 1970).

39. Lord Jeffrey on *A Christmas Carol*, in a letter to Dickens

26 December 1843

(Lord Cockburn, *Life of Lord Jeffrey, with a selection from his correspondence* (Edinburgh, 1852), ii, 380–1.)

Francis Jeffrey (1773–1850), Scottish judge and critic, was a founder and former editor of the *Edinburgh Review*. He had met Dickens in 1841, and took a warm interest in his family affairs and his writings: 'You know I am your *Critic Laureate*,' he told him in 1847 (Cockburn, ii, 425). *The Cricket on the Hearth* was dedicated to him and Dickens's third son (born 1844) named after him. His sensitivity to Dickens's pathos is attested, not only by his letters to the author, but also by the well known story of his being found by a house-guest, collapsed in tears over the table in his study. She apologized for having intruded on his grief, asking, 'Is anyone dead?' 'Yes, indeed,' Jeffrey replied, 'I'm a great goose to have given way so; but I couldn't help it. You'll be sorry to hear that little Nelly, Boz's little Nelly, is dead' (J. C. Young, *A Memoir of Charles Mayne Young* (1871), ii, 110–11). See Cockburn, ii, 390–2, for his blessings on Dickens for writing *The Chimes*, and No. 63 for his comments on *Dombey*. He even admired *The Battle of Life* (Forster, *Life*, 435).

Blessings on your kind heart, my dear Dickens! and may it always be as light and full as it is kind, and a fountain of kindness to all within reach of its beatings! We are all charmed with your *Carol*, chiefly, I think, for the genuine *goodness* which breathes all through it, and is the true inspiring angel by which its genius has been awakened. The whole scene of the Cratchetts is like the dream of a beneficent angel in spite of its broad reality, and little *Tiny Tim*, in life and death almost as sweet and as touching as Nelly. And then the schoolday scene, with that large-hearted delicate sister, and her true inheritor, with his gall-lacking liver, and milk of human kindness for blood, and yet all so natural, and so humbly and serenely happy! Well, you should be happy yourself, for you may be sure you have done more good, and not only fastened more kindly feelings, but prompted more positive acts of beneficence, by this little publication, than can be traced to all the pulpits and confessionals in Christendom, since Christmas 1842.

And is not this better than caricaturing American knaveries, or, lavishing your great gifts of fancy and observation on Pecksniffs Dodgers, Baileys, and Moulds. Nor is this a mere crotchet of mine, for nine-tenths of your readers, I am convinced, are of the same opinion; and accordingly, I prophecy that you will sell three times as many of this moral and pathetic *Carol* as of your grotesque and fantastical *Chuzzlewits*. . . .

40. [W. M. Thackeray], from 'A Box of Novels', *Fraser's Magazine*

February 1844, xxix, 166–9

(*Works*, xiii, 416–8) Signed 'M.A.T.', i.e. Michael Angelo Titmarsh. See also Thackeray's reviews of other *Christmas Books*: of *The Cricket on the Hearth* in *Morning Chronicle*, 24 December 1845 (reprinted in *Contributions to the Morning Chronicle*, ed. Gordon N. Ray (Urbana, 1966), 86–93), and of *The Battle of Life* in *Fraser's*, January 1847, xxxv, 111–26. Dickens was 'touched to the quick' by Thackeray's review of the *Carol* (*Letters . . . of Thackeray*, ed. Gordon N. Ray (1945), ii, 165).

As for the *Christmas Carol*, or any other book of a like nature which the public takes upon itself to criticise, the individual critic had quite best hold his peace . . . it is so spread over England by this time, that no sceptic, no *Fraser's Magazine*,—no, not even the god-like and ancient *Quarterly* itself (venerable, Saturnian, big-wigged dynasty!) could

review it down. 'Unhappy people! deluded race!' one hears the
cauliflowered god exclaim, mournfully shaking the powder out of his
ambrosial curls, 'What strange new folly is this? What new deity do ye
worship? Know ye what ye do? Know ye that your new idol hath
little Latin and less Greek? Know ye that he has never tasted the birch
of Eton, not trodden the flags of Carfax, nor paced the academic flats of
Trumpington? Know ye that in mathematics, or logics, this wretched
ignoramus is not fit to hold a candle to a wooden spoon? See ye not
how, from describing low humours, he now, forsooth, will attempt the
sublime? Discern ye not his faults of taste, his deplorable propensity to
write blank verse? Come back to your ancient, venerable, and natural
instructors. Leave this new, low, and intoxicating draught at which ye
rush, and let us lead you back to the old wells of classic lore. Come and
repose with us there. We are your gods; we are the ancient oracles, and
no mistake. Come listen to us once more, and we will sing to you the
mystic numbers of *as in presenti* under the arches of the Pons Asinorum.'
But the children of the present generation hear not; for they reply,
'Rush to the Strand! and purchase five thousand more copies of the
Christmas Carol.'

In fact, one might as well detail the plot of the *Merry Wives of
Windsor*, or *Robinson Crusoe*, as recapitulate here the adventures of
Scrooge the miser, and his Christmas conversion. I am not sure that
the allegory is a very complete one, and protest, with the classics,
against the use of blank verse in prose; but here all objections stop. Who
can listen to objections regarding such a book as this? It seems to me a
national benefit, and to every man or woman who reads it a personal
kindness. The last two people I heard speak of it were women; neither
knew the other, or the author, and both said, by way of criticism, 'God
bless him!' A Scotch philosopher, who nationally does not keep Christmas Day, on reading the book, sent out for a turkey, and asked two
friends to dine—this is a fact![1] Many men were known to sit down after
perusing it, and write off letters to their friends, not about business,
but out of their fulness of heart, and to wish old acquaintances a
happy Christmas. Had the book appeared a fortnight earlier, all the
prize cattle would have been gobbled up in pure love and friendship,
Epping denuded of sausages, and not a turkey left in Norfolk. His royal
highness's fat stock would have fetched unheard of prices, and

[1] Thomas Carlyle: see his wife's, Jane Welsh Carlyle, letter to Jeannie Welsh, 23
December 1843. Carlyle's unwonted access of Christmas feeling overwhelmed her,
especially as she did not know how to stuff a turkey.

Alderman Bannister would have been tired of slaying. But there is a Christmas for 1844, too; the book will be as early then as now, and so let speculators look out.

As for TINY TIM, there is a certain passage in the book regarding that young gentleman, about which a man should hardly venture to speak in print or in public, any more than he would of any other affections of his private heart. There is not a reader in England but that little creature will be a bond of union between the author and him; and he will say of Charles Dickens, as the woman just now, 'GOD BLESS HIM!' What a feeling is this for a writer to be able to inspire, and what a reward to reap!

41. From a review of R. H. Horne's
A New Spirit of the Age,
Westminster Review

June 1844, xliv, 374-7

The review is signed 'N.U.S.' For Horne's book, see No. 58. Several months later, Dickens was answering some criticisms Forster had made of *The Chimes* (while it was still in manuscript), and remarked: 'File away at Filer [the economist in the story], as you please; but bear in mind that the *Westminster Review* considered Scrooge's presentation of the turkey to Bob Cratchit as grossly incompatible with political economy' (*Life*, 355). *The Fool of Quality* (1766-72), mentioned in this extract, was a novel by Henry Brooke, full of liberal sentiments and benevolence.

. . . The secret of Dickens's success doubtless is, that he is a man with a heart in his bosom; and as most men and women—though not all— have hearts, a sympathy is created which predisposes liking. He has also a strong perception of all the commoner class of excitements—the murderous, the malignant, and the ludicrous. A very large portion of the common people are susceptible of the former; people of all classes are susceptible of the latter. With all this, he has the eye of a Dutch and also of an Italian artist for all external effects. A street, a dwelling, a rural scene, and the human beings therein, are so painted to the life, and doubtless from the life, that no one who has ever seen them can doubt the resemblance. And all people like to behold portraits of things and persons familiar to them. ... But Dickens has, beyond this, a strong perception of physical beauty, and also of the beauty of generosity, not merely the hackney-coachman kind of generosity—the shilling giving—but generosity in the large sense—the love of kind, the unselfish attachment of man to man, and of man to men, and also of men to man; the protection of the poor by the rich, of the helpless by the powerful, and of the kindly gratitude thence arising. But with all this, he is not an imaginative writer, he is not a philosophical writer; he pleases the sensation, but he does not satisfy the reason; he pleases and amuses, but he does not instruct; there is a want of base, of breadth, and of truth; and therefore, though he is probably the most widely-popular writer, he is not a great writer. The great elementary truths on which man's physical well-being, and consequently his mental well-being, must depend, he apparently has not mastered; and the pleasure we feel reading his works is akin to the pleasure we feel in reading any other work of fiction—the pleasure of fine description and sympathy with human adventure. The impression which his works leave on the mind is like that with which we rise from the perusal of the *Fool of Quality*— that all social evils are to be redressed by kindness and money given to the poor by the rich. This, doubtless, is something essential; but it is only a small part of the case. The poor require justice, not charity, *i.e.* almsgiving. Charity is a word of large import. The necessity for almsgiving implies previous misery. Destroy the misery by earnest care in the early training of men and women, the disease will be eradicated, and the symptom-soothing process of charity, i.e. almsgiving, will not be needed.

In most of Dickens's works there is to be found some old gentleman with surplus cash going about redressing the evils which some other old or young gentleman goes about perpetrating. It is the principle of the proceedings of Harlequin and Pantaloon. Thus the Brothers Cheeryble are the incarnation of the good principle, and Ralph Nickleby of the evil principle; and the good principle is made to triumph. Nickleby Junior comes to his fortune, which his wicked uncle has kept him out of, and Miss Nickleby is respectably married. Most excellent people are those same mill-owning Brothers Cheeryble; but we cannot help reflecting on the position of the mass of workmen whose labours have accumulated their capital. We do not object to the help given to the Nicklebys, but we think justice is the most essential part of generosity. Justice being done in early training, Ralph Nickleby would not have been enabled to accomplish his evil deeds, and the almsgiving of the Brothers Cheeryble would not have been needed.

So in *Oliver Twist*, Mr Brownlow is the good fairy who thwarts the evil one, and Oliver Twist is finally made happy. Pickwick, too, is a benevolent old gentleman with abundant ready cash, who treats the poor prisoners in the Fleet, as the uncle of Henry Moreland does in the *Fool of Quality*—pays away his surplus cash to palliate the pressing wants of a few amongst a huge class who suffer under the radical evils of bad legislation. A strong contrast to this 'good fairy' system is found in Bulwer's *Paul Clifford*. The unfortunate, ill-trained child, who has grown up to be a highwayman, finds no old gentleman to give him a fortune. By indomitable energy, he escapes from the punishment awarded to his ignorant acts, to a 'great country where shoes are imperfectly polished and opinions are not persecuted' (by the State), and there he makes himself a home by the force of his own powers. He becomes useful to his fellowmen and accumulates wealth, wherewith he repays the owners of the property he had taken with the strong hand in the days of his ignorance, while gaining his living by rapine, and revenging himself on the injustice of society. This is the true perception of eternal justice, at which Dickens has not yet arrived in his writings. Dickens is a Londoner, Bulwer is a cosmopolite.

In the *Christmas Carol*, Scrooge the Miser is so drawn as to leave an impression that he cheats the world of its 'meat, clothes, and fire,' which he buries in his own chests, whereas in truth he only cheats himself. He is the conventional miser of past times; and, when reformed by his dreams, he gives away half-crowns to boys to run quickly to buy turkeys to give away, and pays cabmen to bring them home quickly, to say nothing of giving bowls of punch to clerks. A great part of the enjoyments of life are summed up in eating and drinking at the cost of munificent patrons of the poor; so that we might almost suppose the feudal times were returned. The processes whereby poor men are to be enabled to earn good wages, wherewith to buy turkeys for themselves, does not enter into the account; indeed, it would quite spoil the *dénouement* and all the generosity. Who went without turkey and punch in order that Bob Cratchit might get them—for, unless there were turkey and punch in surplus, some one must go without—is a disagreeable reflection kept wholly out of sight. . . .

With all these defects, which we hope to see amended in future, as well as the caricature pictures of the Americans, which—bating local circumstances and peculiarities—will apply equally well to the English, the books of Dickens are unquestionably humanizers of the people; and the speeches he has made, and the public meetings he has attended in furtherance of general education, are indications of still better things. At present he is the 'form and pressure of the age.' He may become a spirit of the age in time. . . .

42. From an unsigned review of *The Chimes*, *The Mirror of Literature, Amusement, and Instruction*

21 December 1844, n.s. vi, 401–3

The organisation of labour has engaged the attention of more than one mind. The rights and wrongs, the virtues and vices of the poor, have been pourtrayed in vivid and powerful colours by many of the writers of the present day, but to none is the poor man more indebted than to 'Boz.' He it was who struck out a path peculiar to himself; he it was who first drew those admirable portraits of the poor—called lower orders—which have rendered his name so truly dear to every lover of his country. . . .

Criticism is out of the question in regard to a work like this. We must not hint that it is abrupt, or that the slovenly speech of his characters is carelessly or affectedly given into by the narrator of their sayings and doings. It is Mr Dickens who writes; his object we know to be a kindly one; and in such a case, with a less meritorious author, we should prepare to

Take the good the Gods provide us,

without stretching our eager desires beyond what has been prepared for us. We hasten, then, not to examine but to quote—not to give an opinion of its merits, but some of the merits themselves. . . .

Although only a story, a deep moral lesson may be learnt. Its point is truth. Attention of late has been roused to the condition of the labouring classes, and men's minds are becoming alive to the conviction that their fellow creatures should not be worked like machines merely and solely at the call of capital, to increase that which is already great, but that labour should have its limits, and that the suffering poor should be encouraged on their weary pilgrimage, and not be regarded, as heretofore, with indifference and contempt.

43. From an unsigned review of *The Chimes, The Times*

25 December 1844, 6

Misleadingly summarized in *The History of 'The Times'* (1939), ii, 487, as beginning 'a series of queerly savage attacks on Dickens'. The series starts, in fact, a year later, with an indignant two-and-a-half-column review of the *Cricket*: 'We owe it to literature to protest against this last production of Mr Dickens. . . . a twaddling manifestation of silliness almost from the first page to the last . . . the babblings of genius in its premature dotage' (27 December 1845, 6). Over *The Battle of Life* the reviewer felt bound 'to repeat the remonstrance of the past year': even compared with other men's Christmas books, in 'the deluge of trash' which Dickens had initiated, the *Battle* was 'of all the bad Christmas books . . . *the worst . . . the very worst*' (2 January 1847, 6). Dickens wrote about this, to Forster: 'I see that the "good old *Times*" are again at issue with the inimitable B. Another touch of the blunt razor on B.'s nervous system. . . . Dreamed of *Timeses* all night. Disposed to go to New Zealand and start a magazine' (*Life*, 481). Shortly afterwards, Dickens identified the author of these attacks (which

also included a pulverizing review of *Pictures from Italy*: see No. 37)
as Samuel Phillips: see headnote to No. 75. *The Haunted Man*
fared little better in *The Times* (21 December 1848, 8). But, as will
be seen, *The Chimes* had been received with considerable respect.

Externally this appears as a companion to the noted *Christmas Carol*-
insomuch as it is a gaily decorated little book, with fanciful decorations,
such as may lie on the round table at Christmas, and invite the curious
after dinner, when conversation flags, and the sonata becomes an
infliction.

Internally it is unlike any book that Mr Dickens has hitherto published. The author comes forward in a character entirely new; he almost
abandons the notion of pleasing by humour or drollery of description;
he raises his voice with solemnity, he becomes the *serious* advocate of
the humbler classes. Using a machinery similar to that of the *Carol*—
that is to say, making a dream the instrument of conveying his lesson
—he employs it with great potency against all that he deems the
enemy of the poor man. . . .

Some of the scenes are conducted with great power, and in the best
portions the author writes out with an earnestness and an intensity
which distinguish the book from all its predecessors. We are greatly
tempted to extract the scene of the dying Magdalen, which is one of
the most pathetic and heart-stirring that ever were written; but we
refrain, as it is too intimately connected with the rest of the work for
the full measure of its pathos to be conveyed in an isolated shape. Therefore, we give the preference to a speech by a country labourer, who is
looked upon as a kind of *mauvais sujet* by his genteel oppressors, and
which, for simple eloquence and unaffected force, can scarcely be
surpassed.

[Quotes his speech beginning 'Now gentlemen,' from 3rd Quarter.]

The merits of this book are its purpose and its power. But it is not
without its faults. There is not that graphic reality to which Mr Dickens
owes so much of his popularity; the scenes do not stand out with that
pictorial distinctness of which we had such remarkable instances in the
Carol. Nor does the author seem to have had any very clear plan in the
construction of his story. The lesson is given by the *Chimes*, not to one
of the heartless rich, who might have profited thereby like old Scrooge,
but to the simple-hearted Toby Veck, who is too humane and good-

natured a fellow to stand in need of supernatural monitors. One wishes that Alderman Cute or Mr Filer, the economist, had been witnesses of the scenes of woe, and that they had been touched to some purpose. A sort of haziness which is spread over the entire tale, is its grand demerit.

And besides these faults in the book considered as a work of art, there is a fault in its tendency, which will furnish many with a much graver objection. We have commended Mr Dickens's purpose, because we believe it is a pure one—we believe he had no other end than that of legitimately defending the poor man, and exhibiting the wrongs which he suffers under our social system. But his character of advocate has led him too far, and he has—unconsciously, no doubt—been led into that school of writers who make a morbid appeal to the sympathies by representing every rich man as bad, and every poor man as good. Hence, though to a properly constituted mind his book will be harmless, and may even be beneficial, there are some among the working classes who may find in it nourishment for discontent, and hatred of the more fortunate members of society. The uniformity of gloom is to be regretted in so genial a writer as Mr Dickens.

As we do not like to leave off with a qualification when dealing with a book displaying so much genius, let us repeat, that for power and eloquence it is one of the most remarkable of Mr Dickens's productions.

44. From an unsigned article, 'A Christmas Garland', *The Northern Star*

28 December 1844

Reprinted in *An Anthology of Chartist Literature*, ed. Y. V. Kovalev, (Moscow, 1956), 307–8. *The Northern Star*, Feargus O'Connor's organ, published in Leeds, was the most important Chartist newspaper. The previous week, it had belatedly welcomed *A Christmas Carol* and had seen Dickens as taking his stand 'by the side of BURNS . . .: and who could desire a destiny more glorious? . . . Yes, DICKENS *is* the poet of the poor . . .' (21 December 1844).

. . . And now, reader, having traced the story of the *Chimes*—imperfectly, we admit—from its commencement to its close, what think you of this latest of the productions of CHARLES DICKENS? Whatever be that opinion, ours shall be given unreservedly. Several of the critic-craft—they must be bright boys at their business!—have very sagely set about comparing the *Chimes* with the previous works of Mr Dickens! The upshot of their comparisons—not *odious*, but *stupid* —has been that these knowing gentlemen have voted the *Chimes* trash! We opine they have discovered by this time that the public, and themselves, hold opinions directly the reverse of each other. It appears not to have struck these worthies that the *Chimes* is a book widely different to any work heretofore written by Mr DICKENS. True, every work yet written by Mr DICKENS has had for its object the elevation and improvement of mankind, and the enlargement of those kindly sympathies which have so much to do with the existence and promotion of human happiness. But, in the *Chimes*, expressing views of man and society far more comprehensive than he has before put forth, Mr DICKENS enters the public arena, as *the champion of the people! Weller-isms*, however happy, would be out of place in a work of this description. The masses are the victims of undeserved suffering; their cause is a solemn one; and solemnly, with an eloquence that was never excelled;

157

in 'thoughts that breathe the words that burn,' Mr DICKENS pleads that cause against the cruel, canting, unnatural, blaspheming doctrines and actions of the ruling classes of society.

But the parties who denounce the *Chimes* as 'trash,' charge on Mr DICKENS the sins of 'exaggeration' and 'extravagance,' 'inflation' and 'falsehood' and an intent to array 'party against party, and class against class.' We leave it to our readers, too many of whom we fear are not far removed from the suffering condition of the *Will Fern's* and *Meggy Veck's*—to say, whether in describing the wrongs of their class, the condition of the agricultural labourer, and the bitter toil of the sempstress, Mr DICKENS has been guilty of 'exaggeration,' 'extravagance,' 'inflation,' or 'falsehood.' 'Party' *is* 'arrayed against party,' and 'class against class;' they have been long so arrayed; for *that*, the rich and the ruling classes are responsible. The advocates for, and apologists of, the rich, are numerous as corruption's wages can purchase; but the advocates of the poor are, like 'angels' visits, few and far between.' Nobly, therefore, does Mr DICKENS throw the weight of his great name into the scale on poverty's side; and if he seems to join in the strife of 'party against party, and class against class,' it is to help the wronged to justice, and the miserable to a better state of existence; ends which not only sanctify the struggle, but would also, if achieved, put an end to the war of classes and of parties, and establish unity and brotherhood in the place of hostility and hatred.

We do not say that the *Chimes* is in each and every title a superior work. On the contrary, in plot and construction, we think it decidedly inferior to any other production of Mr DICKENS's pen. But viewed in its political character and bearings, *it is decidedly the best work Mr Dickens has produced.* It is the voice of poetry; the voice of thought and feeling, appealing to eternal justice against 'man's inhumanity to man:' a voice, which, while it will cause many an oppressor to shrink before its echo, will impart hope to the oppressed, and strengthen in thousands the cheering, saving belief that a *better future for the many will come,* when the condition of England's sons will be the reverse of that of *Will Fern;* and England's daughters be redeemed from that worse than Egyptian bondage, so truly, sadly pictured in the character of *Meggy Veck.*

45. From an unsigned review of
The Chimes, Christian Remembrancer

January 1845, ix, 301–4

In a lengthy discussion of Dickens ('Modern Novels', December 1842), the *Christian Remembrancer*, a High Church and Tory journal, had objected to his religion ('for the most part ... mere pagan sentimentalism') and his politics: he was 'a radical, probably of the better sort ... The radical attacks appointed bounds and ordinances, ancient usage, and prescriptive rights, which, even when not directly and in the highest sense sacred, would nearly always be found helps instead of hindrances to the end he honestly has in view ... Whenever, then, Mr Dickens comes in contact with any one of the objects against which the popular will is most easily tempted into hostility,—the privileged classes, recognized officials, ancient institutions, the laws and their administration,—it is more or less to disparage them ... a proceeding the unfairness of which is fully equalled by its danger' (iv, 585–96). Maclise's frontispiece, criticized in this review, was found offensive: his frontispiece to *The Cricket* even more so. Both were 'outrageous and not very decent' (*The Times*, 27 December 1845, 6); the *Cricket* frontispiece and title-page were 'scarcely ... appropriate to a story of an English home' (*Illustrated London News*, same date, 406).

... With the avowed object of the present story we cannot but sympathize: viz. the claims of the poor on the merciful sympathies of their fellows. To have always held this moral purpose is one, perhaps the great secret, of this writer's success. In *The Chimes*, we find the inborn claims of the poor man; his beautiful side; his surprising cheerfulness under sorrows, and, what shows Dickens's keen observation of nature, the real cause of his apparent sulkiness and unimpressibility, well sketched off. It is a true lesson, that often the poor man most wants, and most desires, to be let alone. We think 'Boz' decidedly unfair to some with whom we own affinities, if he imagines that *their* earnestness for the poor is confined to the cricket-playing; but bating this, we scorn the growing picturesque view of the poor: we are beginning to treat them as we do torn thatch, ruined groves, and blasted trees, as 'nice bits' in a landscape, as telling contrasts, as subjects for sickly sentimentalities. How far district-visiting in carriages (we have seen it ourselves), maypole-dancing during a lull in the opera season, and soup-kitchens when the frost stops the hunting, may have given *some* occasion to Mr Dickens's most bitter sarcasms, we are not called upon to say: we all know that there is something in it. Anyhow, nothing is more improper than the constant pestering and badgering of the poor, which is getting into vogue—the constant 'See what a poor wretch you are, and see what a good, kind gentleman, or lady, I am'.

For showing up this *sham* (by-the-bye, Boz has taken to Carlyle, though he does not own it), we thank *The Chimes*. And when we can get any book with a circulation of twenty thousand, which will, as the present does, cut clean through the detestable school of economists, Malthus, and the 'coarser kind of food' gentry, the preventive-check heathen, and the 'natural effluxes' people, we will welcome it as heartily as we do the present. We hardly know whether it was worth Dickens's purpose to show up an individual, the most contemptible of his most contemptible class, such as Sir Peter Laurie, the worthy who 'puts down' everything—Puseyism and poverty, because they touch his pocket,—suicide and sorrows, because they disturb the city's propriety and peace. But let this pass: the work is done, and never mind who does it. Alderman Cute is settled, once and for ever.

And with all this, shall we say that we find a great blank somewhere? It is not that *The Chimes* is not a religious story; we shall be, perhaps, not altogether misunderstood, if we say we should have been sorry if it had been: but it is because it is,—and the remark holds with the whole *Pickwick* school,—a *moral* story, ostensibly, avowed, ambitiously *moral*, and nothing more. Not a scrap or spark of religion in it: nothing more than morals: the realm of fact, not of grace; the kingdom of the individual will, not of the Spirit and strength of God. For religious stories we have the most sovereign contempt; but such loathing is, we trust, quite compatible with affection, sole affection, for that spirit in fiction which veils the only realities of the soul. And here is the chief defect of Dickens: he seems to be always on the very point of getting hold of the truth—of the right thing—and yet as invariably he misses it, and clutches the shadow,—a very good counterfeit always, but still only the semblance of that which constantly eludes him. He wants, because he knows that the soul wants, unseen influences and mysterious powers, and he embodies a mixed mockery of German diablerie, and fairies, and Socinianism, because, even while he was not called upon to picture it, he has never realized the Catholic doctrine of the angels; and it is quite wonderful, though significant, how this machinery— to speak according to the card—would have helped him. . . .

As a *literary* work we cannot speak highly of *The Chimes;* the clumsy and threadbare trick of a dream is managed with more than its ordinary maladroitness. The pathetic passages are among the most turgid, (witness p. 92[1],) and absurd which this very clever writer has perpetrated; and remembering his many and various grotesque attempts at fine writing, this is saying not a little. But, above all this, there is scarcely a striking feature which we have not fallen in with before:—the influence of the chimes, and the leading idea of the story, is taken from Schiller's Song of the Bell; the mysterious affection and attraction between the Bells and Toby Veck may be traced to Quasimodo, in Victor Hugo's *Notre Dame de Paris;* a good deal of the diction is a palpable borrowing from Carlyle, and, which it most resembles, the higher portions of *Punch;* the false, yet catching, attempt to combine personal degradation and sin with high moral refinement,— we allude to the fate of Lilian,—from the wicked *Mysteries of Paris;* the goblin spirits of the greater bells from Reztsch; and the multitudinous, swarming, trooping mass of sprites from sources, Irish, German, and others, which will be at once apparent. Boz repeats himself in Will Fern: we have seen it somewhere, but we cannot recall where, in his own works.

Neither can we speak highly of the illustrations; such a monstrous *mélange* of kicking, sprawling, nudities, we never witnessed as Maclise's frontispiece. . . . The world of spirits is with Mr Dickens—we ask his pardon—very much indeed of the cast which we used to witness in the last scene of a pantomime: the tin-foil, wires, and tinsel, are too palpable a vast deal; and to talk nonsense is not the language of the spiritual world. . . .

---

[1] The opening of the 3rd Quarter.

46. [John Forster], from a review of *The Chimes, Edinburgh Review*

January 1845, lxxxi, 181–9

John Forster took the very unusual step of writing to the Editor of the *Edinburgh Review* on 16 November 1844 ('*Very Private*') asking if he might review *The Chimes*, which he has just received in manuscript from Dickens, who was then in Italy and 'does not know that I think of proposing any such thing to you'. Forster thought it 'in some essential points the best of his writings. It will certainly make a strong impression' (B.M. Add. MS. 34, 624 ff., cited *Wellesley Index*, i, 494). The review occasioned some comment: doubtless Forster's authorship became known. In a dialogue by 'Bon Gaultier' [Theodore Martin] in *Tait's Edinburgh Magazine*, April 1845, one character asks: 'did you ever read anything so fulsome as that notice of *The Chimes* in the *Edinburgh Review*?' —'I certainly do not think I ever perused a more pitiable paper', Bon Gaultier replies (xii, 239).

... We do not know the earnestness to compare with his, for the power of its manifestation and its uses. It is delightful to see it in his hands, and observe by what tenure he secures the popularity it has given him. Generous sympathies and kindest thoughts, are the constant renewal of his fame; and in such wise fashion as the little book before us, he does homage for his title and his territory. A noble homage! Filling successive years with merciful charities; and giving to thousands of hearts new and just resolves.

This is the lesson of his *Chimes,* as of his delightful *Carol;* but urged with more intense purpose and a wider scope of application. What was there the individual lapse, is here the social wrong. Questions were handled there, to be settled with happy decision. Questions are here brought to view, which cannot be dismissed when the book is laid aside. Condition of England questions; questions of starving labourer and struggling artizan; duties of the rich and pretences of the worldly;

THE CRITICAL HERITAGE

the cruelty of unequal laws; and the pressure of awful temptations on the unfriended, unassisted poor. Mighty theme for so slight an instrument! but the touch is exquisite, and the tone deeply true.

We write before the reception of the book is known; but the somewhat stern limitation of its sympathies will doubtless provoke remark. Viewed with what seems to be the writer's intention, we cannot object to it. Obtain, for the poor, the primary right of recognition. There cannot, for either rich or poor, be fair play till that is done. Let men be made to think, even day by day, and hour by hour, of the millions of starving wretches, heart-worn, isolated, unrelated, who are yet their fellow-travellers to eternity. We do not know that we should agree with Mr Dickens' system of Political Economy, if he has one; but he teaches what before all economies it is needful to know, and bring all systems to the proof of—the at once solemn and hearty lesson of human brotherhood. It is often talked about, and has lately been much the theme; but in its proper and full significance is little understood. If it were, it would possibly be discovered along with it that life might be made easier, and economies less heartless, than we make them. Such, at any rate, appears to be the notion of Mr Dickens, and, to test its worth, he would make the trial of beginning at the right end. . . .

Could we note a distinction in the tale, from the general character of its author's writings, it would be that the impression of sadness predominates, when all is done. The comedy as well as tragedy seems to subserve that end; yet it must be taken along with the purpose in view. We have a hearty liking for the cheerful side of philosophy, and so it is certain has Mr Dickens: but there are social scenes and experiences, through which only tragedy itself may work out its kinder opposite. Even the poet who named the most mournful and tragic composition in the world a Comedy, could possibly have justified himself by a better than technical reason. Name this little tale what we will, it is a tragedy in effect. Inextricably interwoven, of course, are both pleasure and pain, in all the conditions of life in this world: crossing with not more vivid contrasts the obscure struggle of the weak and lowly, than with fierce alternations of light and dark traversing that little rule, that little sway, which is all the great and mighty have between the cradle and the grave. But whereas, in the former stories of Mr Dickens, even in the death of his little Nell, pleasure won the victory over pain, we may not flatter ourselves that it is so here. There is a gloom in the mind as we shut the book, which the last few happy pages have not

163

cleared away; an uneasy sense of depression and oppression; a pitiful
consciousness of human sin and sorrow; a feeling of some frightful
extent of wrong, which we should somehow try to stay; as strong, but
apparently as helpless, as that of the poor Frenchman at the bar of the
Convention, who demanded of Robespierres and Henriots an immediate arrestment of the knaves and dastards of the world!

But then, says the wise and cheerful novelist to this, there *are*
knaves and dastards of our own world to be arrested by all of us, even
by individual exertion of us all, Henriots and Robespierres notwithstanding. It was for this my story was written. It was written, purposely
to discontent you with what is hourly going on around you. Things so
terrible that they should exist but in dreams, are here presented *in a
dream*; and it is for the good and active heart to contribute to a more
cheerful reality, whatsoever and howsoever it can. For ourselves, we
will hope that this challenge may be taken. . . .

47. From an unsigned review of *The Chimes*, the *Economist*

18 January 1845, 53-4

The *Economist* was established in 1843, its policies being those of
Cobden and Bright: 'free trade, free enterprise, and political
reform at home, . . . peace, commerce and fraternity abroad'
(*The Economist 1843-1943: a Centenary Volume* (Oxford, 1943),
10).

Mr Dickens, in his *Christmas Carol*, published a twelvemonth ago,
impressed on all his readers the loveliness of the kind affections: in his
Chimes he has a solemn purpose—he sets forth the terrible consequences
of social and political injustice. At the conclusion of the work he thus
speaks:—

If it be a dream, oh! Listener, dear to him in all his visions, *try to bear in mind the stern realities from which these shadows come,* and in your sphere, none is too wide and none is too limited for such an end, *endeavour to correct, improve, and soften them.* So may the new year be a happy one to you, happy to many more whose happiness depends on you: so may each year be happier than the last, and *not the meanest of our brethren or sisterhood be debarred their rightful share in what our great Creator formed them to enjoy.*

The *Chimes* is a picture of the condition of England, and an earnest exhortation to all classes to amend it, by giving to the meanest of our brethren their rightful share in the advantages of society. The author has been heretofore merely a novelist—in the *Chimes* he is a political philosopher and a social reformer. His book is a political and social essay of intense interest. This is its true character; and the mere story, which some critics have carped at, is of the least importance. It is but the filmy down which, on the wings of the wind, carries from the ripened plant the seeds of wisdom over the earth.

Nevertheless the *Chimes* has a story; it is a tale, or rather it contains, within the compass of 175 pages, a great many thrilling histories. Each person describes, by deeds or words, an interesting life, and, in the large drama, embracing all ranks. There are no walking gentlemen, or mere confidants introduced, as in a French tragedy, merely to listen to the hero's exploits.

It has been said by way of censure, that the tales are police reports, which is the highest praise. What are they? Accurate representations of everyday events, embracing the lives of all classes; and what but genius can impart to them, trite and vulgar, such interest, while all their truthfulness is preserved, and the story made to read with the extreme interest of a romance? The book is remarkable for impressing on the public, by the commonest events, after the manner of all great moralists, the most valuable lessons. It exactly corresponds to the common definition of History—it is Philosophy teaching by example. . . .

We would fain advert, at some length, to the different characters in the book, each of which is the type of a class, and the voice and practical exponent of some social error, but our space forbids; and we must limit ourselves to briefly illustrating the principle with which Mr Dickens seems himself to be imbued through and through, and which, as it were, oozes out of him in every page. One of the remarkable circumstances of the day is the passion—we call it so designedly—which prevails to improve the condition of the working classes. In fact, that is felt by every thinking and feeling man to be an imperative social necessity. Under the influence of this passion, all the so-called *light* writers, who catch their inspiration from the prevailing events, have turned political philosophers, perhaps without knowing it; and, after having lived for years by the practice of ridiculing all serious thought as a bore, have nearly one and all begun to write long articles, in prose and verse, on the most abstruse questions of social economy. Mr Dickens shares this national feeling; and, sharing it, a cruel injustice is done him by those who believe that he has employed the elaborate imagery of the *Chimes*, and described some heart-rending effects of the most natural affections, for the mere purpose of exciting fictitious emotion. If at the moment when the heart of England is filled to overflowing with intense woe, in spite of 'facts and figures' announcing a flourishing revenue, proving that the interest of men in office is terribly at variance with the interest of the industrious people, Dickens could have touched the national misery and its sources with no other object than to tickle his readers into a forgetfulness of their duty, and to put a few pieces of paltry coin into his own pocket, as has been more unworthily and ignorantly imputed to him—he would have been in our estimation one of the meanest spirits, and one of the most degraded writers, of the day. But he aspires to be a social reformer, to make each year happier than the last, by making all classes better. This is the clue to his book. Read merely as a tale, it may perhaps be regarded as a piece of pathetic and impressive writing—read as a reproof of a wide-spread and debasing error, it is not merely a pathetic tale—it is one of the most philosophical works which has for a long period issued from the public press. Under this aspect the *Economist* meets Dickens as a brother, and hails his work as a real light in our now darkened paths. In briefly stating the principle which Dickens has in view, the *Economist* has only to regret that he cannot do justice to the estimable author; and bring shame on some of his ignorant and carping critics.

What, then, is the principle which Dickens enforces. Here is it described in so many words. 'I have learnt it,' cried the old man, 'Oh, have mercy on me in this hour, if, in my love for her so young and good, I *slandered Nature*, in the breasts of mothers rendered desperate. Pity my *presumption*, *wickedness*, and *ignorance* (in slandering nature), and save her.' 'I know there is a sea of time to rise one day, before which all who wrong us or oppress us will be swept away like leaves. I see it on the flow. I know that we must *trust and hope*, and *neither doubt ourselves*, *nor doubt* the GOOD *in one another*.' The opposite error—the mistrust of one another, the mistrust of ourselves, or of human nature and human affections—the assertion that all men are 'born bad,' and require some anti-natural system of coercion to keep them from destroying themselves and others—the overstrained and debasing humbleness of the many, which is the source of arrogance in the few—of their confidence in one another, and their looking only to gaols and governments for protection and safety; this error is reproved by Dickens from the beginning to the end of the *Chimes*.

Mark, too, with what art it is done. He shows a mother's love—the strongest and most enduring, perhaps, of all affections—the fountain of continued life—overborne and borne down (an everyday occurrence, too) by the mistrust of nature, and the teaching and the results of the 'born-bad' doctrine. He may be right or he may be wrong, but all will admit that the importance of the lesson cannot be overrated. He shows sinewy industry, too, anxiously striving to do well and gain a comfortable subsistence, continually beset in its path by the gaol and its fatherly friends, and continually driven to commit infractions on laws framed on the 'born-bad' system, to keep industry honest and good. How came the working classes into their present condition is a problem we are all now deeply interested in solving; and that problem Dickens has solved in a few words in the passage often quoted, which Dickens puts into the mouth of Jem Read—'The gaol meets them at every turn, till they are made gaol birds' by this philosophy. The *Chimes* is, we think, one of the most remarkable books of the day, and it will mark, if not form, an epoch in the thoughts, creeds, and minds of mankind.

48. From an unsigned article, 'Boz *versus* Dickens', *Parker's London Magazine*

February 1845, i, 122–8

The middle of December saw the reading world on the tiptoe of expectation for Mr Dickens' long-announced book—*The Chimes*. . . . And now the world has read the book, and with only exceptions enough to prove the rule, has pronounced that it is not what it should be. With much of good purpose to redeem it, it is sadly wanting in good taste and in plot, and though Mr Dickens has said somewhere that he never reads a review of any of his works, we fear that the year 1845 will scarcely be to him so happy a new year as its predecessor.

We believe the secret of the failure of this book lies here. Mr Dickens has very much changed, since, as Boz the unknown, he took captive the admiration of all classes of readers, and at once sprung into the high place which it so often takes the painful labour of many long and weary years to attain. His early works are very unlike some of his later ones. Those features which they have in common are, in the latter, the redeeming features. They are found in both, because they are the fruits of his original genius, and show its bent; but there will be seen in his earlier works little that resembles the artificial style of writing, which he has since adopted.

Boz became famous by his inimitable manner of hitting off the peculiarities of vulgar life, and of describing trivial and familiar objects which were daily before our eyes. When people first saw them graphically described, they laughed at the faithfulness of the picture, and wondered that they, or somebody else, had never thought of doing the same thing before.

Here it was that Boz gained his sudden and great fame. The *Sketches*, *Pickwick*, and *Oliver Twist*, are of this class, and they are the only works in which the native force of Mr Dickens' genius has not been weakened by that mixture of the artificial with the natural which, as it has grown upon him, has made his subsequent works to differ from the three just named, and to be in the main and on the whole worse than they. These we will call the works of 'Boz.' By the works of 'Dickens' we mean all those written since *Nicholas Nickleby*, which represents the transition from one style to the other. We would only except among this last class, the *Christmas Carol*, in which Boz appears again most palpably, and hence its merit, and popularity. *The Chimes* was to be like it; no doubt it was meant to be, and the world wished it might be; but the author has relapsed into Dickens again, and the world is disappointed.

What Crabbe was in poetry, and Wilkie in painting, Boz was in prose. *The Borough*, the paintings in the National Gallery, and *Oliver Twist*, will prove this. Crabbe lived to round off some of his hard peculiarities—the picture was not always given from his hand so harsh and rugged as at first, but in the main he continued as he begun, and his descriptions of wickedness, and wretchedness, and suffering, are terrible for their faithfulness, while his dry satire and caricature, when he lights upon some livelier subject, are admirable, from the same cause. So of Wilkie's first paintings. Every face, and posture, is a picture and a study. So too Boz's first efforts in depicting cockney life were most successful. But there is a similarity between Wilkie and Dickens, which Crabbe does not share with them. The artist of the 'Penny Wedding,' and 'Blind Man's Buff,' ended by painting the portrait of Sir Peter Laurie, the civic worthy whom the world has resolved to believe also sat for the picture of Alderman Cute! Wilkie left such scenes as the village alehouse afforded, to paint historical pictures and portraits of Egyptian Viceroys and City Aldermen. Mr Dickens left the workhouse and the yard of the Borough inn, to describe matters further from home, and how little success attended him in detailing domestic incident in somewhat more refined society, let Pyke and Pluck in *Nickleby* tell. He betook himself to other walks of life which presented fewer and slighter characteristics for the exercise of his peculiar powers of satire and description. This being so, he had to *invent* characters, whereas Boz described them as he found them. The men and women of the latter are real, while those of the former are fictitious. More than this, he began to meddle with Biography, History, and Foreign Travel, with what success, let his *Life of Grimaldi, Barnaby Rudge, American Notes*, and *Chuzzlewit* bear witness. In the outset of their career, both Wilkie and Dickens were great and original artists. But Wilkie was then young and unknown, as Mr Dickens was when he wrote his earliest and best works. Both became known, admired, and popular, and then they left the paths they had chosen for themselves, to tread the beaten road. Before, they had stood alone, but now they mixed with the crowd, surrendered their personality, and the character which distinguished their early works was gradually exchanged for another, which, as sustained by them, was a worse.

The field in which Boz gained his celebrity, is one in which to conquer once, is to have conquered for ever—when you have seen once, you have seen all. The three works which we have called those of Boz, are each *sui generis*—the characters are original, the style of writing is natural, and suited to the subject. The work which we call those of Dickens, want freshness: they are not *original*. The *characters* are taken from Boz. Sometimes Mr Dickens makes a complete portrait from one of his predecessor's sketches, and sometimes he reduces a large picture into a meagre outline; but, after all, the plagiarism is undeniable, and there are few characters in his works, of which the originals may not be found in Boz.

In *Martin Chuzzlewit* there is certainly one, but only one, really well-drawn original character, that of Mrs Gamp. It is impossible to say the same of Pecksniff, Tom Pinch, the two Martin Chuzzlewits, Tapley, or Jonas. They are all exaggerated caricatures. But the old nurse is the redeeming feature of a book more deficient in originality than any which Mr Dickens has ever written.

Again, the *style* of Boz is original, while that of Dickens is not. That of the former is plain and homely, suited to the characters who speak, and proper to the thing spoken of. There is no straining after effect—none of the ornaments are fastened on, and fit badly, they arise, if at all, out of the essential structure, and are its proper and becoming adornments. The style of Dickens—that which distinguishes him from Boz—is laboured and artificial, as unlike the easy natural style of the latter as a statue is unlike a living, moving man. It may be reckoned beautiful and faultless of its kind, as a statue may, but the kind of beauty is the same in both—it is a lifeless beauty. We believe that the parentage of this style is due to two eminent writers, whom we suppose to be favourite authors of Mr Dickens. We think it is not difficult to perceive in it the German tone of Carlyle, and the quaintness of Tennyson. Boz too had evidently no idea of goblins, ghosts, and bells usurping that faculty of speech which belongs to man—his speakers were all men, women, and children. Dickens, on the contrary, is remarkable for finding 'tongues in trees,' or any other inanimate things. . . .

[The reviewer then gives instances of 'the creations of Boz, adopted and altered by Dickens': the recurrence of illegitimate orphans (Oliver, Smike, Hugh), of undertakers (Sowerberry, Mould), of misers (Fagin, Quilp, Ralph Nickleby, Scrooge, old Martin Chuzzlewit), of Cockney fellows (Sam Weller, Dick Swiveller, Young Bailey), etc.]

It would seem that Mr Dickens has written too fast, and, to use an expressive phrase, has written himself out. He has had to fall back upon his early works for materials, instead of waiting and seeking in nature's wide and ample field for treasures as rich as those which, in his first works, he displayed in such abundance. But all his works have this great *literary* fault, that they want unity. *Oliver Twist* and the *Christmas Carol* are the least open to censure in this respect. The others have no entireness. To read them is like walking through a picture gallery. One visitor is caught by this beauty, another by that; all are pleased, and the end being gained, people are too good-tempered to quarrel with the means. But when they go again to an exhibition of the same artist, and come away disappointed, they are apt to turn critical.

[The review ends with a discussion of Dickens's religious inadequacy. His confession of sympathy with Unitarianism (*American Notes*, ch. iii) provides 'the clue to the coldness and barrenness of his philosophy'.]

49. 'Bon Gaultier' [Theodore Martin], from 'Nights in the Martello', *Tait's Edinburgh Magazine*

April 1845, xii, 239

Martin (1816–1909), an Edinburgh solicitor at this time, later became a versatile man of letters and man of affairs; knighted 1880, for his official biography of the Prince Consort. His *Bon Gaultier Ballads* (a collection of parodies, written in collaboration with W. E. Aytoun) appeared in 1845. O'Malley's prophecy, in this dialogue, that 'Michael Angelo Titmarsh' could surpass Dickens is a very early shot in what became a prolonged critical battle: Thackeray had not yet published *Vanity Fair*, and still had only a modest reputation. *Tait's* had reviewed *The Chimes* favourably, in January 1845: it 'surpasses its genial and fanciful elder brother [the *Carol*]. It is, beyond doubt, fearfully and even alarmingly radical, if to be radical means cutting to the deepest roots of the evils that are upon the face of the earth . . . We shall say nothing of the genius displayed in this work; our admiration being fixed upon the uses to which, in its pages, fancy and imagination are made the ministers' (xii, 60–3).

O'MALLEY

I think simply this, that *The Chimes* is the poorest production which has yet emanated from his pen. The plot, if there be one, is both meagre and clumsy; the personages gross caricatures; and the sentiments downright clap-trap. . . .

BON GAULTIER

I must own there is a great deal in what you say; still, the kindly feeling—

O'MALLEY

Is just part of his literary system, and very little short of humbug. What say you, Charley?

YOUNG SCOTLAND

I have read all of Dickens' works, and I admire some of them exceedingly. His humour is certainly rich, though I can see no evidences of wit; and he possesses the art of making an effective auxiliary of slang. He is great in the pot-house and theatre; quite a Smollett in the gin-shop; clear, minute, and forcible in his delineations of Saint Giles. I think he has an excellent heart, with some tendency to be maudlin; no high or exalted imagination; and not one spark of chivalry. In his ideas he is essentially plebeian. He cannot portray the character of a gentleman: when he attempts that, he invariably fails. What I like least of all, are the constant, though covert, attacks which he is making against the aristocracy, because I believe his charges to be utterly unfounded; and farther, I think that common gratitude—for Dickens certainly has been *fêted* beyond his deserts—might have mitigated his inveterate hatred of what he can neither understand nor feel—the position of a British gentleman. He was obliged to fight his way upwards, and I must needs say that he fought it manfully: at the same time, no obstacle was thrown in his path. He attained, by the force of his talents, such as they were, an eminence which, in all probability, exceeded his most sanguine expectations. But that very success has spoiled him: he is not comfortable in his new place, and he cannot help showing it.

Bon Gaultier

My estimate of him is higher. He neither is nor will be a Scott or a Shakespeare; for I agree with you that his clay is of a common kind. But then it is wonderfully plastic, and suited for familiar use. His great popularity is a proof of this; though I do not always hold popularity to be an accurate test of merit. Right or wrong, he has discovered the secret of ingratiating himself with the million. Mantalinis and Tupmans yet unborn will read his works with avidity, and Dotheboys Hall has a tolerable chance of surviving the oblivion of a century. As for *The Chimes*, I deliver it over to your tender mercies, merely remarking, gentlemen, that if either of you had written as many books as Dickens,— and one, I believe, is not far behind,—you would have cause to plume yourselves if some of them did not prove comparative failures.

O'Malley

I'll back Michael Angelo Titmarsh against him, in his own line, for a hundred pounds, and post the ready, when called on, at the bar of the Cat and Bagpipes.

Young Scotland

There are some touches of nature in *The Luck of Barry Lyndon* that may compete with any thing in our literature. Titmarsh is not adequately appreciated. . . .

50. From an unsigned review of
The Cricket on the Hearth,
Chambers's Edinburgh Journal

17 January 1846, n.s. v, 44–8

We are happy to find that Mr Dickens, in his annual volume for the
present year, has left the question of social wrongs and rights to the
discussion of those who can consider them in a calmer and less partial
spirit, and turned his attention to a subject of purely moral interest,
more within the scope of his powers, and better suited to his habits of
thought and feeling. The title of his new book indicates a theme of the
domestic kind, embellished with fancy. The contents justify the anticipation thus raised. It is a picture of humble life, contemplated in its
poetic aspects, and at its more romantic crises; and shows its author, in
one sense, ambitious of becoming the Wordsworth of prose fiction.
Deficient in the profundity and stern power of that great master, the
novelist yet has some requisites which the poet wants—a certain wit
and humour, and, above all, an experience of civic life, that the bard of
Rydal has failed to cultivate. Moreover, Mr Dickens succeeds quite as
much by tact as genius.

[Summarizes the plot.]

In the working up of these simple materials, Mr Dickens invests
with life and intelligence the inanimate as well as the living portion.
He opens his story with describing the contest between the Kettle on
the Grate and the Cricket on the Hearth, and does this in a style of
personification which, to say the least of it, is bold. The song of the
Kettle he even gives in rhymed words, which, for the sake of a remark it
suggests, we quote:

[Quotes from 'Chirp the First'.]

Now, our readers will have perceived that this song of the Kettle,
though written as verse, is printed as prose. This is a peculiarity in Mr
Dickens's compositions which has not generally been perceived. It was,
however, pointed out some time ago in *The New Spirit of the Age*[1]; and

[1] By R. H. Horne, 1844. See No. 41.

many passages adduced, written in blank verse, of irregular metres and rhythms, such as that employed by Southey and Shelley, in *Thalaba* and *Queen Mab*. The frequency of its occurrence indicates not only a design on the author's part to elevate his style by such means, but a poetic spirit in him, to which some kind of music is necessary as the natural utterance of its better thoughts. But the charm is a concealed charm; the varied harmony has still the look of uniform prose, and therefore steals unobserved into the reader's mind, who is pleased he knows not why. This is a little trick of style, which it is well, we think, to point out, particularly in such a work as the one under review, the merit of which is almost altogether dependent on style, and the poetic form of treatment which, with more or less success, is adopted. ...

51. From an unsigned review of *The Cricket on the Hearth*, *Macphail's Edinburgh Ecclesiastical Journal*

February 1846, i, 71–5

... It will be seen, we think, that there is not much ingenuity, and no nature in the plot of *The Cricket on the Hearth*. Its merit lies in its sentiment which is yet extremely liable to the charge of being mawkish and maudlin. The attempts at wit, which are numerous in the less serious parts of the story, are exceedingly forced and affected. The reader has perhaps met with a wearisome companion, whose every expression was manifestly intended to convey a bright idea. This is Mr Dickens' wit. A horse stamping with his foot is, in Mr Dickens' style, represented as 'tearing up the road with his impatient autographs.' A person placed in company unsuitable for him, is compared to 'a fresh young salmon on the top of the great pyramid.' Caleb Plummer's house was 'no better than a pimple on the prominent red brick nose of Gruff and Tackleton.' Dot, going about with pattens on her feet, 'worked innumerable impressions of the first proposition in Euclid all about the yard.' When the carrier comes home wet, we are told that there were 'rainbows in his very whiskers.' Of Tackleton we are informed that his selfishness 'peered out of one little corner of one little eye like the concentrated essence of any number of ravens.' All this is truly wretched, and is not merely not wit, but undeniable evidence of the absence of the power of being witty. Any puppy that smokes his cigar, and wears his hat on the side of his head, can weary you to death with stuff of this sort. Mr Dickens has powers in the pathetic—never indeed unmingled with great weakness—but his efforts at the brilliant are deplorable. John Peerybingle, his hero, sometimes came near a joke, but his biographer is never within sight of one.

52. From an unsigned review of *The Battle of Life*, *Tait's Edinburgh Magazine*

January 1847, xiv, 55–60

The Battle of Life is the fourth of Mr Dickens's annual publications. *The Christmas Carol*, the first and the best, has reached only a *tenth* edition. *The Chimes* was said to be inferior to its predecessors, and is up to the twelfth edition. *The Cricket on the Hearth* had the worst character of the three, and has, therefore attained its twenty-second edition. The facts merely show that book-buyers and reviewers do not always entertain similar opinions. The latter class pretty generally asserted that Mr Dickens was living—so far as his Annuals were concerned—on his character—eating into his acquired literary capital, while the former has taken care that he should live upon his edition. No book of the past, or many previous issues, has been so successful as the *Cricket* . . . On the ratio of increase in the previous publications, the *Battle of Life* will run into forty-four editions.

[An unfavourable review follows.]

53. [Coventry Patmore?], from a review, 'Popular Serial Fiction', *North British Review*

May 1847, vii, 114–17

Patmore (1823–96) had published his first volume of poems in 1844, and was now on the staff of the British Museum Library. He later contributed poems to *Household Words*.

... Let us come to Mr Dickens and *The Battle of Life*. First, of the author; then, by a great descent, of his latest completed book. It will be impossible for any future age to speak slightingly of the powers of the author of *The Pickwick Papers*. Apart altogether from the artistic merits of any of his works, he will stand forth to the eye of posterity, as leader of a great literary revolution. Like other leaders, he has perhaps followed as much as determined the direction of the national mind. Still, the fact remains, that from the publication of the *Pickwick Papers* dates the real commencement of the new phases of Fiction. A host of copyists have followed in his wake; and—a yet surer sign of original genius—others who are no copyists have not disdained to borrow the form which he had introduced. Nor is it a mere form, a simple accidental circumstance connected with the mode of publication. Forms in such matters affect the substance, and he who creates a new form of literature, is the founder of a school. Minds of all varying casts may adopt it; but under the individual differences there will be traced the family likeness, sufficient to entitle the founder to claim the honours of paternity.

Such honours a future generation will not be slow to award to Mr Dickens. Though seeing, as we begin to see, that when he struck into this new path, the public was already crowding towards the gateway; though feeling, as we begin to feel, that its direction was truly downwards, despite the many beauties of this lower region; though free, as the present generation can never be, from the prestige of his earlier successes;—they will yet acknowledge that it could be no common man to whose lot it fell to guide a movement so prolific of results. For they whom nations choose to follow, bear upon them the stamp of mental royalty. Here, there can be no usurpation: to be obeyed, is the guarantee for a legitimate title.

Unlike other crowns, however, Mr Dickens' diadem has allowed his head to lie too easily in the lap of Fortune. Piquancy and quaintness have too much subsided into fixed mannerisms; 'the charm dissolves apace;' from *Pickwick* we have descended to *Martin Chuzzlewit*; the series which began with *The Christmas Carol* is closed for the present by the *Battle of Life*.

The Battle of Life! It was a noble title; suggestive of high thoughts. We looked for a picture of some lofty nature sorely tried—placed struggling between temptation and duty, between passion and principle, between the promptings of selfishness and the whispers of self-sacrificing love; and we longed to see a battle such as this fought out in the glowing page, as many such are fought and won, unrecorded, in daily life. Instead of this, what have we? Our pen refuses the task of analysis.

[Briefly outlines the story.]

And this is *The Battle of Life*! This is *A Love Story*! Were ever noble titles worse profaned? Did ever book issue from an eminent writer's pen, more fatal to his claims to the character of a master in his art?

For, be it observed, in reviewing such a plot, improbability is our lightest charge. That such 'battles' are not fought in the 'Life' of man, we are thankful. That 'Love' is not apt to choose such modes of showing itself, we are thankful. But there is a kind of improbability which does no discredit to the poet or the novelist. Shakspere's Miranda is as unearthly a form as even his Caliban or his Ariel. No island ever saw so bright a gem. But she, or any other imaginative creation, is unlike real life, simply because more true than nature to nature's principles. . . . Has Mr Dickens so dealt with his Marion? Indignant Nature answers No! Her love is not the love of woman; her battle not the battle appointed for human life. Were it possible for any one so to act, to wring the affections of father, sister, lover, for a mere fancy of her own —we should judge that some fearful malady had befallen her;—the loss, not of reason, but of something higher, the magnet of a woman's heart, true to the pole of love. If the author really meant to portray a type of high-toned self-devotion, most wofully has he missed his mark. . . .

We were about to ask, whence came this feebleness of touch, and had dipped our pen in critical gall for the reply. But a fair vision crossed our path, and the soft voice of little Paul pleaded for a milder sentence. We cannot resist the appeal. We might indeed, were we so minded, find some flaws in the beautiful sentimentalism of Paul's death-bed scene; some affectations of style, some little mawkishness of feeling, more than a little want of a healthy spirit in contemplating death. We might object to the whole description, its too close resemblance, in touch and colouring, and light and tone, to the well-remembered chapters which told the death of Little Nell. We might say, it is not the sign of strength to reproduce old creations. But we forbear. After all our criticism, the spell of beauty and pathos would remain, and we ourselves, the surly critics, must bow with others to its power.

[Patmore concludes with a discussion of *Dombey and Son*, No. VI.]

54. From an unsigned review of *The Haunted Man*, *Macphail's Edinburgh Ecclesiastical Journal*

January 1849, vi, 423–31

. . . Christmas *was* Christmas . . . many, many centuries before Charles Dickens began to celebrate him in *Carols* and *Chimes*. But, as it is, a Christmas book from him is as regular as a Christmas goose; and the one is not more certain of being devoured than the other is of being read, extensively and with strong relish. The public admire Mr Dickens's humorous and pathetic pictures of life, however extravagantly drawn; and, though it be evident that now—exhausted and emptied—he is but reproducing, with some slight modifications, old sketches, he is still as popular as ever. 'For, wha'll be king but Charlie?' . . .

Mr Dickens commenced his career as a novelist, by aiming chiefly, if not entirely, at the *amusement* of the public. . . . Latterly, however, his immense popularity has inspired him with a confidence which is rather presumptuous; and, for some time back, he has sought to be the solemn teacher, as well as the light-hearted jester, of the age. *Punch* wears a prophet's mantle; and the creator of *Pickwick* sets himself forward as the regenerator of the human race! His Christmas books are his grand moral lessons. The pretty and innocent tales are precious allegories, containing, in his opinion, individual and social ethics of transcendent value. We cannot say that we have a profound respect for his teaching, though he surrounds himself with *ghosts* to make himself look very earnest, and to make us very attentive—even awe-struck. He does not grace the chair of national instruction—he is both too tiny and too playful; and just as we could have wished that the *tub* had been the *bonnet* of Diogenes—so we should like well to see Mr Dickens *under* and not *on* the chair. It would not be more absurd for him, with his abilities and his habits to pretend to be a subtle metaphysician, than it is for him to affect the character of a grave moralist, and an earnest social reformer. . . .

The tale opens in a style of smart and flippant common-place. 'Every body said it,' is the first sentence, followed by a would-be-witty exposure of the adage, that 'what every body says must be true.' Every body said that a Mr Redlaw was 'haunted.'—By the way, Mr Dickens is getting a little more Christian in his choice of names for heroes and heroines. We really have a 'Mr Edmund Denham,' and a 'Mr Longford,' and Mr Redlaw is an equally romantic name. To be sure, we have large families of 'Swidgers,' and 'Tetterbys;' yet we are greatly pleased that we have got at least three tolerable names. Generally, Mr Dickens, as if in revenge for his own queer name, does bestow still queerer ones upon his fictitious creations.

Mr Redlaw is the hero of the tale. And it seems that 'everybody *was* right' in calling him a haunted man. He was a chemist, and lectured on the science in the theatre of an old college. . . . It is amusing to notice Mr Dickens's conscious ignorance of chemistry. He, who is so painfully minute in describing the occupations of his heroes, who points out every pin lying on the floor of their daily life, and who introduces into his sketches each smallest particular, yet dares not give an inventory of Mr Redlaw's laboratory, but simply fills it with 'the *reflection of glass vessels that held liquids!*' He must have felt that he might make a mistake even in mentioning the crucible! Had the hero been a coachman, Mr Dickens would have been at home. . . .

[The reviewer summarizes the story of Redlaw's 'haunting' and salvation.]

We are left in perfect ignorance as to how all the fine results, with which the story closes, were brought about. As one of the greatest boons to man, *do*, Mr Dickens, *do* communicate to the world, the secret which blessed Redlaw, the Swidgers, and the Tetterbys, and you will cause the world to spend a happy Christmas; but pray don't mock us by saying, that the charm was in silly Milly's face. Would that face, think you, stealing into the dreams of Shakespeare's *King Lear*, have cured the 'poor old man,' brooding over sorrow, wrongs, and trouble? Lear had a better angel than *Milly*; he had his own sweet child—Cordelia.

Concerning the style—the execution—of this book, it abounds with the Author's worst mannerisms. We select one or to specimens out of a large heap. Describing Mr Tetterby's eldest boy in the act of taking off his comforter, Mr Dickens says—

He unwound his Torso out of a prismatic comforter, apparently interminable.

Describing Milly's ruddy face, the Author says—

In her smooth cheeks, *the cheerful red of her husband's official waistcoat was very pleasantly repeated.*

Describing a quarrel among the juveniles of the Tetterby family, at breakfast, he says—

The contentions between these Tetterby children, for the milk-and-water jug, common to all, which stood upon the table, presented so lamentable an instance of angry passions risen very high indeed, *that is was an outrage on the memory of Dr. Watts.*

Had it not been for the very handsome exterior and the high price of this new Christmas book of Mr Dickens, it was only worthy of appearing in the window of the small shop of *Tetterby & Co.*, the news-vender, whom it celebrates. Let us have a few more returns of Christmas, and Mr Dickens will have destroyed his reputation as a tale-writer. We earnestly recommend him to quit the *twenty-fifth of December*, and take to the *first of April*.

MARTIN CHUZZLEWIT

January 1843 – July 1844

During its serialization, *Martin Chuzzlewit* sold so badly that Dickens was, for the first time in his career as a novelist, severely jolted and perturbed. Even his extemporized device of sending young Martin to America failed to raise the circulation above 23 000; *Pickwick* and *Nickleby* had sold 40–50 000 and the *Clock* (in cheaper weekly parts) 70 000. But, as Forster recorded: 'Its sale, since, has ranked next after *Pickwick* and *Copperfield*' (*Life*, 302), and it was grouped with these two novels by many critics, who found in this trio Dickens's greatest achievement. *Blackwood's* in 1857 was nostalgic for all the long-lost fun of *Chuzzlewit* (No. 102); the *National Review*, 1861, regarded this as Dickens at his most brilliant (No. 57); the *Dublin Review*, April 1871, thought it his best (n.s. xvi, 345), a view taken also by Leslie Stephen, in 1888 (*DNB*, xv, 24). It has not maintained this standing with later critics, and has indeed received very little distinguished attention in recent revaluations of Dickens, but its place in Dickens's development is crucial. As one contemporary said, Dickens here 'first fully displayed, at once the versatility and the strength of his genius' ('Charles Dickens', *Ecclesiastic and Theologian*, October 1855, xvii, 468). Dickens himself was even more emphatic than usual in claiming that his latest work was his best: 'You know, as well as I', he wrote to Forster while it was being published, 'that I think *Chuzzlewit* in a hundred points immeasurably the best of my stories. That I feel my power now, more than I ever did . . .' (*Life*, 305). His sense of one of its differences from its predecessors was suggested by the line of his own verse he wanted to have on the title-page: 'Your homes the scene, yourselves the actors, here!' (*Life*, 311); and a technical advance was asserted in the 1844 Preface ('I endeavoured . . . to resist the temptation of the current Monthly Number, and to keep a steadier eye upon the general purpose and design').

Forster's chapter on '*Chuzzlewit* Disappointments' (Book 4, ch. ii) is one of his most illuminating. The reasons for the initial failure have been further discussed by Professor Nisbet (see No. 36), who attributes it largely to the public disappointment over *Barnaby Rudge* and the very poor reception of *American Notes* (see also Appendix I). But *Chuzzlewit* itself caused some distaste: the *Westminster*, for instance, reviewing Nos. I–X, complained of being introduced to 'a world of knaves and fools, destitute of any one quality that could command respect. ... It has all the dark shades of Rembrandt without a touch of light; we contemplate human nature in *Martin Chuzzlewit* only under an aspect which inspires loathing ...' (December 1843, xl, 457–8). It was, reported the *Critic* a month later (January 1844), 'just now the rage to decry Dickens, by pronouncing his *Chuzzlewit* a failure'. Dickens was the more grateful to Laman Blanchard for a warm review of it and the *Carol* in *Ainsworth's Magazine*, where Pecksniff was hailed as already proverbial, and Dickens's technical advance was recognized: 'There is more art, more consistency and well-considered aim in working out the object ...' (January 1844, v, 85–6; cf. *To* Blanchard, 4 January 1844). Most of the reviews were, in fact, favourable. Forster rightly comments that 'It was felt generally to be an advance upon his previous stories' (*Life*, 308). Excerpts from his review are printed (No. 55). Tom Pinch was a general favourite and 'friend' ('our dear friend "Pinch" ... moves us to tears of pity', *English Review*, December 1848, x, 268), though later he became a bye-word among critics reacting against Dickens's sentiment. Pecksniff and, even more, Mrs Gamp, remained among the half-dozen 'characters' most often cited as the acme of his art. In 1847 Dickens tried to give Mrs Gamp a new lease of life in a pamphlet (it remained a fragment: see *Life*, Book 6, ch. i.) He did so more effectively in 1858, with his popular *Mrs Gamp* public reading.

55. [John Forster], from an unsigned review, *Examiner*

26 October 1844, 675-7

Why indeed did Forster 'delay so long the notice' of *Chuzzlewit*, the final Number of which had appeared on 1 July ? A similar delay occurred in his reviewing of the next novel, *Dombey*, in the *Examiner*—from 1 April 1848 to 28 October 1848—and again Forster had to make jocular-embarrassed apologies. Was he finding it difficult to devise the review that would satisfy his sensitive friend Dickens, or were they having a tiff? I do not know; but it is a strange couple of lapses. After *Dombey*, Forster was always prompt as well as cheering.

A writer who counts his readers by tens of thousands, has stolen a march upon his critics. They toil after him very vainly. Not like the hound that hunts but one that fills up the cry, they are in the condition of *Roderigo*, and find no enjoyment in the chace. We have a contempt for the weakness, but cannot profess ourselves wholly free from it. Or why delay so long the notice due to such a book as this?

Martin Chuzzlewit is Mr Dickens's best work, taken as a whole. His characters have been more agreeable, but never so full of meaning thoroughly grasped and understood, or brought out with such wonderful force and ease. He has written nothing, we think, nearly so decided or effectual. He has observed as truly, and satirized as keenly, but never sent his knowledge and his wit with such a forthright aim into the core of the vices of the time.

The American episode has called forth an amount of American wrath and indignation, quite without measure or example. Doubtless the picture is uncompromising; and its features of vulgarity, pretension, and half-savage barbarism, sufficiently repulsive. But let our friends on the other side of the Atlantic be of good heart. They have not sounded the base string yet. Pecksniff is all our own. . . . Setting up Mr Pecksniff as a glass through which he [the reader] views the characters grouped around him, he will not the less detest what forms and figures of social vice they assume, because he sees, more plainly than before, that there is but one perfectly hopeless and irremediable form of that particular evil. The Anthony Chuzzlewits are bad enough, but their self-inflicted punishment seldom fails; the Jonases and Montagues are execrable, but the law has its halter and its Botany Bay; the Moulds and Mrs Gamps have a pestiferous breath from which we may hope to be cleared in time by the sanitary wisdom of our Southwood Smiths and Chadwicks: but from the sleek, smiling, crawling abominations of a Pecksniff, there is nothing but self-help to save us. Every man's hand must be against him, for his hand is against every man. It is wonderfully shown in this book in what way the social vices and virtues react upon each other; and what a danger there is in that amiable weakness of putting the best face upon the worst things. There is nothing so common as the mistake of Tom Pinch, and nothing so rare as his excuses.

The art with which this delightful character is placed at Mr Pecksniff's elbow in the opening of the story, and the help he gives to set fairly afloat the falsehood he so innocently believes, contribute to a management of the design more skilful in this than in any former work of Mr Dickens . . .

When we speak of the higher art of this *Martin Chuzzlewit*, we do not only speak of the construction of the story. It seems to us that with no abatement of the power which gives out sharp and bold impressions of reality, we have more of the subtler requisites which satisfy imagination and reflection. We have the knowledge as well as the fact. While we witness the transactions of life immediately in hand, we are made conscious of that higher and more permanent life which still hangs and hovers over all. And nothing is more certain, we suspect, than that the character and incidents chiefly dwelt on in the tale would have wearied or revolted in a management less masterly. But Mr Dickens talks of vice, and his readers can but think of virtue. . . .

But we were about to give some instances of the descriptive painting in the book when Tom Pinch and his sister carried us away. There is the scene with which the story opens; the windy autumn night in the little Wiltshire village, with the mad desperation of the hunted leaves and the roaring mirth of the blazing forge. There is the market-day at Salisbury, the winter walk to that city, and the ship voyage to America. There is the stormy midnight travel that goes before the murder, and the stealthy enterprise and cowardly return of the murderer. These descriptions are all of the first-rate order: original in design, and of an execution most powerful, energetic, and masterly.

We must quote one that we have omitted to name, the night journey of the Salisbury coach to London. The blood runs more freely and heartily as one reads it.

[Forster quotes the 'Yoho' passage from ch. xxxvi.]

56. [Thomas Cleghorn?], from 'Writings of Charles Dickens', *North British Review*

May 1845, iii, 65–87

Probably by Thomas Cleghorn (1818–74), a Scottish advocate, who wrote much in the early volumes of the *North British*. Though mainly a review of *Martin Chuzzlewit*, the article begins with a survey of the earlier novels, and ends with a substantial (and highly critical) assessment of Dickens's achievement and influence.

[The reviewer finds Pecksniff grotesque but amusing, young Martin an interesting study, and the love-scenes between Ruth Pinch and John Westlock charming.]

Tom Pinch teaches us many a quiet and useful lesson of self-denial, cheerfulness, and kind considerateness; but certainly more by his example than by the stilted and scarcely intelligible jargon in which the author sometimes pauses to apostrophize him. Such efforts as the following 'to moralize his tale,' remind us not a little of the 'moral crackers' which he puts into the mouth of his Pecksniff, and teem with every possible fault of composition. . . .

Jonas Chuzzlewit is scarcely worthy even of the pencil that drew Sikes, and Quilp, and Sir Mulberry Hawk. . . . He is too hideous and revolting an incarnation of evil. . . . Nothing could be more clumsy than the plot which leads to the death of this worthy. . . .

Revolting as Jonas is, he is not so offensive and intolerable a personage as Sarah Gamp, a midwife, or 'monthly nurse,' in whom the selfishness and greediness of attendants on the sick are coarsely satirized. Her dialect is doubtless copied very faithfully from nature, but her cue is to entertain the reader with a succession of jests, the point of which always lies in sly allusions to the events and secrets of her particular calling. She seems such a favourite of the author that we meet her at every turn, even in the preface, till we are almost provoked to laugh in spite of our disgust.

The author, as usual, luxuriates in the delineation of vulgar people, and in the imitation of the London dialects and idioms. We have not space to criticize minutely this part of the work; yet we cannot pass without observation, a very uncalled for, and, we will say, unfeeling attack on a respectable class of tradesmen, in the person of Mr Mould the undertaker. He is satirized, not for any individual vices, but for the unavoidable peculiarities of his indispensable craft. . . .

We must also find fault with the American scene, clever and amusing as they are. These chapters are an unaccountable excrescence, and while they add to the bulk, mar the unity and effect of the book as a work of art. They are, in fact, a book of travels dramatized, and not in the best or most candid spirit; they form a new and more pungent edition of the *American Notes*, but with only the harshest censures distilled over and concentrated. They have no connexion with the rest of the story. . . .

There is much clever description throughout the book. . . . It is however in incident and character that Mr Dickens excels; we have just room to insert his portrait of Mr Pecksniff, which is no bad specimen of some of the faults as well as merits of his present style.

[Quotes from ch. ii.]

We said the *faults* of *the present style* of Mr Dickens; and certainly no one can read even a single chapter of *Martin Chuzzlewit* without perceiving a very striking declension from the purity and unassuming excellence which marked his earlier compositions. This is apparent, first, in various impurities of expression, and even some gross offences against the English language. For instance, many words, in themselves good and classical, are used in such a collocation, that to make any sense of them at all, we must suppose that the author has imported some new meaning of them from America during his transatlantic trip. Thus, we have *impracticable* nightcaps, *impossible* tables and *exploded* chests of drawers, *mad* closets, *inscrutable* harpsichords, *undeniable* chins, *highly geological* home-made cakes, *remote suggestions* of tobacco lingering within a spittoon, and the *recesses and vacations* of a toothpick. Then again we have the pages bristling over with various strong words employed in their improper colloquial usage—such as *tremendous, terrible, monstrous, desperate, frightful, awful, horrid, horrible, unearthly, appalling, dreadful, enormous,* 'No doubt a *tremendous* fellow to get through his work.' 'It was a *monstrous* comfortable circumstance.' 'Martin was *monstrous* well-disposed to regard his position in that light,' and so on. It is surely improper for an author of established reputation to give his sanction to this vicious habit of speaking, which naturally leads to an exaggerated way of viewing trivial things; and he ought not to degrade these important words from their appropriate functions to the performance of the meanest services in a light and laughing page. But he goes further, and offends grievously against the rules of grammar; catching the infection from his own actors, he adopts their forms of expression, and offends the shade of Lindley Murray with such barbarisms as 'It had not been painted or papered, hadn't Todgers', past the memory of man.' 'She was the most artless creature, was the youngest Miss Pecksniff.' 'Nature played them off against each other; *they* had no hand in it, the two Miss Pecksniffs.' Indeed Mr Dickens seems often purposely to cast his language into the mould of the vulgar characters he represents, and as it were, to fondle their phrases, idioms, and ideas. He makes occasional use of the interjections 'bless you!' 'heaven knows,' &c. He speaks of a place where 'black beetles got mouldy and *had the shine taken out of their backs* by envious mildew;' of a grimace of Master Bailey as 'an easy, horse-fleshy, turfy, sort of thing to do;' of a boorish action at a Yankee table as having 'a juiciness about it that might have sickened a scavenger,' and thus describes the Miss Pecksniffs' contrast of character:—

To behold each damsel in the very admiration of her sister, setting up in business for herself on an entirely different principle, and announcing no connexion with over the way, and if the quality of goods at that establishment don't please you, you are respectfully invited to favour ME with a call. [ch. iii]

Slang, also, seems to come naturally to his lips, for he founds a cumbrous joke in the first chapter on the words *my uncle*, and gives his readers credit for knowing them to be slang for the pawnbroker; he describes some young ladies as having, 'in the figurative language of the day, a great amount of steam to dispose of;' and Mr Pecksniff as getting a bruise 'on what is called by fancy gentlemen the "bark" on his shin;' and the head of one of his American heroes as 'shaking involuntarily, as if it would have said, in the vulgar tongue, on its own account, No go.' . . .

The deterioration of style is further observable in the descriptions. Mr Dickens was always famed for giving life to inanimate scenes, and catching the little characteristic traits of conduct and character; but he now carries minute description to an excess that sometimes, indeed, degenerates into mere extravagance,—his interiors are often inventories rather than pictures. Here is one:—

The drawing-room at Todgers' was out of the common style; so much so indeed, that you would hardly have taken it to be a drawing-room, unless you were told so by some one who was in the secret. It was floor-clothed all over, and the ceiling, including a great beam in the centre, was papered. Besides the three little windows, with seats in them, commanding the opposite arch-way, there was another window looking point blank, without any compromise at all about it, into Jinkins' bed-room; and high up, all along one side of the wall, was a strip of panes of glass, two deep, giving light to the staircase. There were the oddest closets possible, with little casements in them like eight day clocks, lurking in the wainscot, and taking the shape of the stairs, and the very door itself (which was painted black) had two great glass eyes in its forehead with an inquisitive green pupil in the middle of each. [ch. ix]

Mr Fip's office is portrayed with similar minuteness, and the author especially chronicles—

A great black sprawling splash upon the floor, in one corner, as if some old clerk had cut his throat there years ago, and had let out ink instead of blood. [ch. xxxix]

In another place are pointed out—

Very mountebanks of two-pronged forks, which seemed to be trying how far asunder they could possibly stretch their legs, without converting themselves into double the number of iron tooth-picks. [ch. xxxix]

After the interior of a tavern has been elaborately described, the window is thus disposed of:—

It was a little below the pavement, and abutted close upon it, so that pas-sengers grated on the window-panes with their buttons, and scraped it with their baskets; and fearful boys suddenly coming between a thoughtful guest and the light, derided him, or put out their tongues as if he were a physician, or made white knobs on the end of their noses by flattening the same against the glass, and vanished awfully like spectres. [ch. xxxv]

The frequent recurrence of such ludicrous minuteness in the trivial descriptive details induces us to compare Mr Dickens' style of delineation to a photographic landscape. There, everything within the field of view is copied with unfailing but mechanical fidelity. Not a leaf, or stone, or nail is wanting, or out of place; the very bird is arrested as it flits across the sky. But, then, the imitating agent takes exactly the same pains with the dunghill and the gutter, as with the palace and the forest tree; and it is as busy with the latchet of the shoe, and the pattern of the waistcoat, as with the noble features of the human face. Mr Dickens' pencil is often as faithful, and not more discriminating. He lavishes as much attention on what is trivial or useless as on the more important part of the picture, as if he could not help painting everything with equal exactness. Neglecting the effective outline, the charm of harmonious grouping, and of contrasted light and shade, he crowds his canvass with figures, and notes the very hat, and neckcloth, and coat buttons of each; dwelling upon his city scenes, whether connected or not with the business in hand, till he has enumerated the tables and chairs, and even counted the panes of glass. There is no judicious perspective, and withdrawing from view of disagreeable particulars. We stand as close to the most offensive object, and see its details as nakedly, as if it was the most agreeable. Thus, when Tigg is murdered by Jonas, the author affects not to describe the actual deed of blood, but, in the reflections of the murderer afterwards, he thrusts on us the most revolting details. He paints the criminal

in fancy approaching the dead body, and startling the very flies that were thickly sprinkled all over it, like heaps of dried currants. [ch. li]

Mr Dickens never trusts to a vigorous sketch, or a few characteristic touches; he accomplishes his purpose by minute description and copious dialogue, and leaves no work for the imagination of the reader. This leads us to observe, that the vast popularity of these works may, perhaps, in some degree be owing to the indolence of the reading public, and that the very clever 'illustrations' which accompany them all, may have contributed greatly to their success. No reader need ever task his mind's eye to form a picture corresponding to the full description; he has but to turn the page, and there stands the Pickwick, Pecksniff, or Tom Pinch, embodied to his hand, and kindly saving him the labour of thought. . . .

We must now glance at the moral tendency of these works. Our moral health is dependent on the moral atmosphere we breathe. But novels are just an artificial experience, and the well-drawn character becomes a kind of companion. With whom, then, does Mr Dickens bring us into close and familiar contact? Lackeys, stable-boys, thieves, swindlers, drunkards, gamblers, and murderers: and where is his scene most frequently laid, but in their haunts of vulgar revelry or dens of profligacy and crime? Such scenes and characters he dwells upon, until we are intimate with all the details. It has been attempted as an apology by his admirers, that, besides the ability with which he writes, and the witty humour of his characters, he paints very delicately, and withdraws what is offensive, so that the most sensitive cheek need not blush over his writings. We do not accept this apology. . . .

In estimating the probable effects of these writings of Mr Dickens, we must remember that, in the shape of plays, they have been represented at most of the theatres in the country. In this process of transmutation the better and more sober parts necessarily disappear, and the striking figures, amusing low life, smart vulgar conversation, and broad farce, are naturally preserved with care. It is not therefore surprising to find, in the drama of *Martin Chuzzlewit*, that Master Bailey, with his Cockneyisms, draws the chief attention; and that the tipsy quarrel between Mrs Gamp and Betsy Prig is the most effective scene in the piece. The higher ranks thus laugh publicly at the scenes of most hurtful tendency; and it is these principally which are made widely known to the lower classes. . . .

In the next place, the good characters in Mr Dickens' novels do not seem to have a wholesome moral tendency. The reason is, that many of them—all the author's favourites—exhibit an excellence flowing from constitution and temperament, and not from the influence of moral or religious motive. They act from impulse, not from principle. They present no struggle of contending passions; they are instinctively incapable of evil; they are therefore not constituted like other human beings; and do not feel the force of temptation as it assails our less perfect breasts. It is this that makes them unreal.

Faultless monsters, that the world ne'er saw.

This is the true meaning of 'the simple heart' which Mr Dickens so perpetually eulogizes. Indeed, they often degenerate into simpletons, sometimes into mere idiots. Such characters are uninstructive; for in contemplating them we lose sight of the great fact of the corruption of human nature. . . .

57. From an unsigned article, *National Review*

July 1861, xiii, 134–50

A reprinting of *Martin Chuzzlewit* in the Library Edition offered an opportunity for discussing 'what we venture to think the most brilliant and entertaining of all the works of Mr Dickens ... his most characteristic work ...' The *National Review* was originally a Unitarian periodical; R. H. Hutton and Walter Bagehot were its joint editors.

... The objection that a group of very selfish people, contrasted with another group of very unselfish people, is not at all a true representation of the world, is insuperable. But it is not the object of Mr Dickens to represent the world as it is. The comic characters are only true to life in a remote and exceptional way. The serious part of the story may strike the balance, and set off the comic part, although it is strained and, in a certain sense, unreal. It keeps us on the same platform; and even if we cannot greatly admire it, we should probably think much less of the book if it were not there. The satisfaction with which it fills the author, and the zest which this tribute to his self-respect imparts to his composition generally, is communicated to the reader, and we like ourselves better for enduring that a comic book should venture to be instructive after its fashion.

Much the same is to be said of the sentimental passages. It has evidently been a great pleasure to the author to write them, and a certain emotion of pleasure is awakened by reading them. For example, Mr Dickens thinks it worth while to describe minutely the progress of the coach which bears Tom Pinch to town. 'Yoho! among the gathering shades, making of no account the deep reflections of the trees, but scampering on through light and darkness. Yoho! across the village green ... '[ch. xxxvi] This goes on for several pages, and every object that any one can be supposed to see from the top of a coach, and every fancy to which these supposed objects can be conceived to give rise, are, laboriously and carefully noted down. The effect is, that we lose all notion of a coach and of scenery, and of every thing else, in the wealth of fine writing. We feel more and more anxious that Tom Pinch should get to town, and that this Yohoing would stop. But the story probably gains in our eyes by the interlude. We like our author to enjoy himself; and a flux of poetical description is a very creditable form of enjoyment to those who can pour it forth. The writer makes us feel that he sees something besides the burlesque and the comic, and we comprehend that he and we have earned our fun more honestly and respectably by halting a little to give play to fancy.

Mr Dickens is, however, principally known to the public as a comic writer; and, like inferior comic writers, he sometimes carries comic writing to an unpleasant length. There is a peculiar style which he has introduced into English composition, and which consists in giving what is conventionally accepted as a funny turn to language, without there being any fun whatever in the thought. This has been so widely copied, and has reappeared in the compositions of so many purveyors of hackneyed fun, that we are almost tempted to forget that Mr Dickens invented it. The best parts of his best works are singularly free from it. Directly the story is started, and we get to the principal performers of the piece, the fun lies in what they say and do, and in the connection of this with the supposed bases of their characters. But it is hard to start a story of this kind. There must be an introduction of some sort, and Mr Dickens would probably have disappointed both his readers and himself if he had not written this introduction in a recognisable vein of conventional fun. The effect is what might be expected. The contest between the matter and the style is painfully marked, and the opening chapter of *Martin Chuzzlewit* is one of the very worst things Mr Dickens has written. The reason is because it is entirely away from the story, and is all about nothing. The fun is entirely in the language, and the funny language is as flat as funny language about nothing is apt to be.

[The opening paragraph, and first chapter, provide an instance.]

... The result is worth studying by any one who thinks that Mr Dickens's comic style, which may be easily borrowed, will be any security that a facetious composition will please or amuse any human being, except those who are satisfied to laugh when they are bid, and see in funny writing a perpetual order to be merry.

Mr Dickens has also another piece of comic machinery which is very easily imitated. In order to mark off less prominent characters, he is apt to select one salient external feature in their appearance, to which he makes constant reference, or he introduces them as perpetually making use of some phrase by which they are to be recognized. The same observation of minute details, the same power of seizing hold of the ludicrous, which prompts this, also lie at the bottom of his most successful characters. He therefore only stops short when he gives the rudimentary sketches to which we allude. But it is because he does stop short that the personage thus introduced is utterly unreal and seems invented merely to fill up the canvas, and to make us laugh for the moment. Several of these shadowy comic ladies and gentlemen appear at the meeting of the relations of old Martin Chuzzlewit which is held at Mr Pecksniff's house. 'First,' we read, 'there was Mr Spottletoe, who was so bald and had such big whiskers that he seemed to have stopped his hair, by the sudden application of some powerful remedy, in the very act of falling off his head, and to have fixed it irrevocably on his face. Then there was Mrs Spottletoe, who, being much too slim for her years, and of a poetical constitution, was accustomed to inform her more intimate friends that the said whiskers were the "lodestar of her existence."' [ch. iv] . . . And so it goes on, with character after character sketched in this easy fashion. A little point is taken in the outward look or ordinary talk of a person, and it is magnified into absurdity. The fancy is led to elaborate some little conceit about it, and then the task is over; and the shadow of the shade of a farcical character has flitted away from the stage.

These two mechanical contrivances for producing fun have been readily adopted by the best of those writers who have imitated Mr Dickens. Any one who likes to try will find that the trick is easily learnt; but when imitators try to go further, they find that Mr Dickens is in a region entirely his own. In the best works of Mr Dickens such contrivances do occupy a place, for even the good Homer occasionally nods, but the place they occupy is a very subordinate one. In *Martin Chuzzlewit* more especially there is but little of this imperfect and unfinished work. Most of the meaner characters and slighter scenes are excellent, and one great charm of the book is the even interest, amusement, and graphic life of the whole. Even the love-making is unexpectedly pleasant. Mary and Martin, indeed, fill the first places with the traditional sketchiness of heroines and heroes; but John Westlock and Ruth Pinch are a pair of lovers who engrave themselves on our memory in the pleasantest way. They are out of the ordinary beat, and yet are not exaggerated or ridiculous. The scene where Ruth makes the pudding, the meeting by the fountain in the Temple, and the grand dinner in John's chambers, are all new, original, and delightful. . . .

In all comic writing, or at least in all comic writing in which the collocation of external peculiarities is used as the basis of representing men and things, there are endless gradations of reality and unreality in the product. It may happen that the class of persons spoken of present so many external peculiarities that merely accurate description is comic. All that the writer has to do is to handle his materials with judgment, to give enough and not to give too much. On the other hand, the realisation may be the work of the artist only, and may be on the face of it impossible. To draw a character which is conceived after an impossible pattern, to put into its mouth a series of improbable speeches, and yet to have such control over the elements selected that the whole conception shall be impressed vividly on the reader's mind, seem to him to represent something that he likes to have represented, and supply a general image which he can apply, at will, to a host of particular instances, is a very high triumph of art. This, as it appears to us, Mr Dickens has done in Pecksniff. On the other hand, the comic materials were ready to his hand when he undertook to describe the Americans with whom Martin and Mark came in contact. The whole representation of America may be more ludicrous than America is in reality; but the separate facts are not exaggerations, further than the skill of the artist, which brings out forcibly every point he takes, makes a certain degree of exaggeration inevitable. . . .

[The American scenes are further praised, though some episodes are criticized as leaving satire for incredible caricature.]

But the best thing in the whole description of America, the speech of Elijah Pogram about the merits of Hannibal Chollop, the revolver-bearing ruffian of Eden, is certainly not a caricature. It is better than any thing of the same length that could be found in an American paper, but it is only more wonderful because it is more condensed. The thought and style are the same, only the author has arranged the words with a little more than ordinary art. . . .

Of course these scenes and speeches do not give a perfectly fair view of America and Americans. That there are persons over there of a different make in mind and manners, Mr Dickens has himself intimated by the introduction of the kind, sensible, and mild Mr Bevan. But the defence of comic representations does not rest on their being balanced by serious characters. If it is unfair to give ten pages to Elijah Pogram and

General Choke, it cannot become fair by one page being tacked on in which a modest and amiable American is described. Comic writing must stand on its own ground. Ridicule, so far as it is not an utter misrepresentation, is a powerful weapon on the side of good sense and good manners, and we cannot afford to throw it away. . . .

This defence of comic representations ought, however, in all fairness, to be admitted in behalf of other works of Mr Dickens which have been made the subject of much censure. In *Bleak House* Mr Dickens makes a great part of the story to turn on the droll and yet cruel slowness of the Court of Chancery. In *Little Dorrit* he has his fling at the Circumlocution Office. It is said with great truth that the Court of Chancery has, in spite of its slowness, worked out a great system of equitable jurisprudence, and that, although infected by a little of the spirit of red tape and official pedantry, the administrative government of England is singularly pure, honest, and efficient. Still the Court of Chancery was, until its recent changes, most dismally slow, expensive, and disappointing; and in many public offices nothing was done, and done in a pompous and imposing manner, as if to do nothing was a laudable and gentlemanly thing in a public officer. The comic writer satirised that which was ridiculous and foolish, and left out of sight what was good and commendable in the institutions on which he fixed his attention and that of his readers. The criticism that, if we look at the whole truth, we ought to say that the institutions were substantially good, but with a few striking flaws, does not touch the comic writer. He only affects to address himself to a partial truth; and if he brings that partial truth into a strong light, he has effected his aim. . . .

Mrs Gamp is among the very best creations of Mr Dickens. We should venture to pronounce it the best of all, only that these decrees of the critic are not generally very valuable or acceptable to other people. A good character depends for its success on the author possessing two arts—the art of producing the character by observation and filling up details, and the art of imagining how the character thus produced can be worked out through a series of appropriate incidents, and made to say things at once special, and yet not mere parrot-like repetitions of one funny phrase. The care with which the figure, the habits, and the tastes of Mrs Gamp are brought into strong relief by an accumulation of odd touches of description is wonderful. But this is always the strong point of Mr Dickens. He is one of the greatest observers of all that is superficial and on the outside of men and things that has ever written. He has also contrived many scenes, such as the visit of Sarah to Mr and Mrs Mould, and the famous quarrel with Betsey Prig, which bring out her fine qualities in the happiest way. The more successful novels of Mr Dickens are, however, almost invariably successful in this way. If, for example, we are to concede the existence of Sam Weller, he could not be accommodated with happier incidents than the shooting scene at Mr Wardle's, the pursuit of Jingle and Job, or the footmen's swarry. But harder than the conception of comic characters, and harder than the continuance of comic incidents, is the elaboration of comic speeches, when the character keeps up its individuality at a considerable length, and yet appears tolerably natural. It is in this that Mrs Gamp seems to us to be unrivalled.

The accumulation of minute graphic details, designed to bring a comic character with distinctness before the mind of the reader, is illustrated as well perhaps by the description of the preparation for Betsey Prig's visit as by any other portion of Mrs Gamp's history [ch. xlix]. First of all, the bedstead is described, which was what is poetically called a tent; 'the sacking whereof was low and bulgy, insomuch that Mrs Gamp's box would not go under it, but stopped halfway, in a manner which, while it did violence to the reason, likewise endangered the legs of a stranger.' This is exactly one of the touches that make us think that the object described must really exist somewhere. Then we read that this bed was decorated with a patchwork quilt of great antiquity, while 'some rusty gowns and other articles of Mrs Gamp's wardrobe depended from the posts; and these had so adapted themselves by long usage to her figure, that more than one impatient husband, coming in precipitately at about the time of twilight, had been for an instant stricken dumb by the supposed discovery that Mrs Gamp had hanged herself.' It is in this way fancy lends its aid to observation in the hands of a skilful writer.

[The reviewer continues with further discussion of Mrs Gamp.]

But the sustained speeches of Mrs Gamp are, as we have said, the greatest triumph. To make a monthly nurse talk on for half a page without a break, to make her say something that is peculiarly her own, to make each separate portion of her speech amusing, and yet to make the whole connected and harmonious, is a great feat of art. The imaginary Mrs Harris is the key to Mrs Gamp's success. By means of that invaluable ally Mrs Gamp is able to mix up a fictitious dialogue with her own monologue; and thus we have something dramatic to give life and point to her oration.

58. R. H. Horne, from his
The New Spirit of the Age

1844, i, 1–76

Horne (1803–84), poet and miscellaneous author, was friendly with Dickens and later worked on *Household Words*. Dickens is the subject of the first, and much the longest, chapter in this book about eminent contemporaries (modelled on Hazlitt's *The Spirit of the Age*, 1825). Horne duly includes the distinction Dickens had made to him (see headnote, No. 12) between *Oliver Twist* and 'Newgate' fiction: but the point he makes about Bill Sikes is new, and will remind later readers of Dickens's peculiar attachment to the *Sikes and Nancy* public reading. The essay opens with a protracted comparison between Dickens and Hogarth.

. . . In the [pathetic] more especially, Mr Dickens greatly excels; and two or three of his scenes, and numerous incidental touches, have never been surpassed, if the heart-felt tears of tens of thousands of readers are any test of natural pathos. But although their tragic power is so great, it is curious to observe that neither Hogarth nor Dickens has ever portrayed a tragic character, in the higher or more essential sense of the term. The individual whose bounding emotions and tone of thought are in an habitual state of passionate elevation, and whose aims and objects, if actually attainable, are still, to a great extent, idealized by the glowing atmosphere of his imagination, and a high-charged temperament—such a character, which is always ready to meet a tragic result half-way, if not to produce it, finds no place in the works of either. In their works no one dies for a noble purpose, nor for an abstract passion. There is no . . . great cause at stake. Their tragedy is the constant tragedy of private life—especially with the poorer classes. They choose a man or woman for this purpose, with sufficient strength of body and will, and for the most part vicious and depraved; they place them in just the right sort of desperate circumstances which will ripen their previous character to its disastrous end; and they then leave the practical forces of nature and society to finish the story. Most truly, and fearfully, and morally, is it all done—or rather, it all seems to happen, and we read it as a fac-simile, or a most faithful chronicle. Their heroes are without any tragic principle or purpose in themselves. . . .

Yet again, an objection of another kind—for Mr Dickens has quite enough strength to be dealt with unsparingly. It has been previously said, and the reasons for the opinion have been stated, that *Oliver Twist,* the work which is open to most animadversion, has a beneficial moral tendency, and is full of touches of tenderness, and pathos, and of gener-ous actions and emotions.[1] The objection about to be offered, is on the ground of justice being made vindictive and ferocious, which, be it ever so just, has not a good moral tendency. This is said with reference to the death of a most detestable ruffian—Sykes—and it was important that no sympathy should, by any possibility, be induced towards so brutalized a villain. Such, however, is the case; for the author having taken over-elaborate and extreme pains to prevent it, the 'extremes meet.' After the brutal murder of the poor girl Nancy, the perpetrator hurries away, he knows not whither, and for days and nights wanders and lurks about fields and lanes, pursued by the most horrible phantoms and imagin-ings, amidst exhaustion from hunger and fatigue and a constant terror of discovery. Far from making a morbid hero of him, in any degree, or being guilty of the frequent error of late years, that of endeavouring to surround an atrocious villain with various romantic associations, Mr Dickens has shown the murderer in all his wretchedness, horror, and utter bewilderment consequent on his crime. So far, the moral tendency is perfect. A climax is required; and here the author over-shoots his aim. Perhaps, in reality, no retribution, on earth, could very well be too heavy for such a detestable wretch as Sykes to suffer; but we cannot bear to see so much. The author hunts down the victim, like a wild beast, through mud and mire, and darkness, and squalid ways, with crowds upon crowds, like hell-hounds gnashing and baying at his heels. . . . Hunted with tenfold more ferocity than ever was fox, or boar, or midnight wolf—having scarce a chance of escape—certain to be torn and trampled amidst his mad, delirious struggles, into a miry death, when caught—our sympathies go with the hunted victim in this his last extremity. It is not 'Sykes, the murderer,' of whom we think—it is no longer the 'criminal' in whose fate we are interested—it is for that one worn and haggard man with all the world against him—that one

[1] The author's introductory defences to the third edition we have only seen after finish-ing this essay. It is unanswerable, but ought not to have been needed. [*Horne's footnote*]

hunted human creature, with an infuriate host pursuing him, howling beneath for his blood, and striving to get at him, and tear him limb from limb. All his old friends turn away from him—look mutely at him, and aghast—and down below, all round the hideous house, in hideous torch-light boils up the surging sea of a maddened multitude. His throwing up the window, and menacing the crowd below, had a grandeur in it—it rouses the blood—we menace with him—we would cast off from his plunging horse, that man who 'showed such fury,' and offered money for his blood—from the bridge, that man who incessantly called out that the hunted victim would escape from the back— and we would have silenced the voice from the broken wall, that screamed away the last chance of a desperate man for his life. In truth, we would fairly have had him escape—whether to die in the black moat below, or alone in some dark and far-off field. We are with this hunted-down human being, brought home to our sympathies by the extremity of his distress; and we are *not* with the howling mass of demons outside. The only human beings we recognize are the victim—and his dog.

If the above feeling be at all shared by general readers, it will then appear that Mr Dickens has defeated his own aim, and made the criminal an object of sympathy, owing to the vindictive fury with which he is pursued to his destruction, because the author was so anxious to cut him off from *all* sympathy. The overstrained terror of the intended moral, has thus an immoral tendency....

Amidst the various sets of somewhat elaborate memoranda, notes, and outlines, from which this essay is written, there are few more numerous in references than our slip of paper headed with 'Happy Words and Graphic Phrases.' As when the avaricious dotage of the toothless old miser, Arthur Gride, is cheered with a prospect of success, to which he returns no other answer than 'a *cackle* of great delight;' as when the placards of a company of strolling players, are issued 'with letters afflicted with every possible variety of *spinal deformity*;' as when the watery currents 'toyed and sported' with the drowned body of Quilp, 'now bruising it against the slimy piles, now hiding it in mud or long rank grass, now dragging it heavily over rough stones and gravel, now feigning to yield it to its own element, and in the same action *luring* it away,' &c.; as when a set of coffin-lids standing upright, cast their shadows on the wall 'like high-shouldered ghosts with their hands in their pockets;' and an old harpsichord in a dusty corner, is described by 'its *jingling anatomy*;' as when Mr Pecksniff, overcome with wine, speaks of the vain endeavour to keep down his feelings, 'for the more he

presses the bolster upon them, the more they look round the corner!'
Or, when it is said of one of those wooden figure-heads that adorn
ships' bows, and timber yards, that it was '*thrusting* itself forward with
that excessively *wide-awake* aspect, and air of somewhat obtrusive
politeness by which figure-heads are usually characterized.' All these,
moreover, tend to establish the statement previously made as to the
predominating feature of characterization displayed throughout Mr
Dickens' works, and the consequent difficulty of separating this feature
from almost every other, so inwoven is it into the texture of the whole.
The first two paragraphs of the chapter which opens with the description of the interior of the house of the miser Gride, for graphic truth
and originality, as applied to the endowment of old furniture with the
very avariciousness and personal character of their owner, yet without
the loss of their own identity as old furniture, or any assistance from
preter-natural fancies, are probably without parallel in the literature of
this or any other country. [*Nicholas Nickleby*, ch. li]

Mr Dickens' style is especially the graphic and humorous, by means
of which he continually exhibits the most trifling and common-place
things in a new and amusing light. Owing to the station in life of the
majority of his characters, a colloquial dialect of the respective classes is
almost unavoidable; even his narrative style partakes of the same
familiarity, and is like telling the listener 'all about it;' but no one else
ever had the same power of using an abundance of 'slang' of all kinds,
without offence, and carrying it off, as well as rendering it amusing by
the comedy, or tragic force of the scene, and by its unaffected appro-
priateness to the utterers. Sometimes, however, certain of these
licences are not so fitly taken by the author, where they accidentally
slip out of the dialogue into the narrative; nor can good taste approve of
the title-page of *Martin Chuzzlewit*, which reminds one of some of the
old quack and conjuring treatises, servant-maids' dream-books, or
marvellous tracts of bigotted biography and old-fashioned rhodo-
montade. It is unworthy of the work, which, so far as can be judged
at present, will probably be its author's most highly-finished
production. . . .

Mr Dickens is manifestly the product of his age. He is a genuine
emanation from its aggregate and entire spirit. He is not an imitator of
any one. He mixes extensively in society, and continually. Few public
meetings in a benevolent cause are without him. He speaks effectively—
humorously, at first, and then seriously to the point. His reputation,
and all the works we have discussed, are the extraordinary product of

only eight years. Popularity and success, which injure so many men in head and heart, have improved him in all respects. His influence upon his age is extensive—pleasurable, instructive, healthy, reformatory. If his *Christmas Carol* were printed in letters of gold, there would be no inscriptions which would give a more salutary hint to the gold of a country. As for posterity, let no living man pronounce upon it; but if an opinion may be offered, it would be that the earlier works of Mr Dickens—the *Sketches by Boz*, and some others—will die natural deaths; but that his best productions, such as *Nicholas Nickleby*, the *Old Curiosity Shop*, *Oliver Twist*, and *Martin Chuzzlewit*, will live as long as our literature endures, and take rank with the works of Cervantes, of Hogarth, and De Foe.

Mr Dickens is, in private, very much what might be expected from his works,—by no means an invariable coincidence. He talks much or little according to his sympathies. His conversation is genial. He hates argument; in fact, he is unable to argue—a common case with impulsive characters who see the whole truth, and feel it crowding and struggling at once for immediate utterance. He never talks for effect, but for the truth or for the fun of the thing. He tells a story admirably, and generally with humorous exaggerations. His sympathies are of the broadest, and his literary tastes appreciate all excellence. He is a great admirer of the poetry of Tennyson. Mr Dickens has singular personal activity, and is fond of games of practical skill. He is also a great walker, and very much given to dancing Sir Roger de Coverley. In private, the general impression of him is that of a first-rate practical intellect, with 'no nonsense' about him. Seldom, if ever, has any man been more beloved by contemporary authors, and by the public of his time. . . .

Translations are regularly made in Germany of all Mr Dickens's works. They are quite as popular there as with us. The high reputation of the Germans for their faithfulness and general excellence as translators, is well supported in some of these versions; and in others that reputation is perilled. Bad abbreviations, in which graphic or humorous descriptions are omitted, and the characteristics of dialogue unnecessarily avoided, are far from commendable. No one could expect that the Italian *Oliviero Twist*, of Giambatista Baseggio, published in Milan, would be, in all respects, far better than one of the most popular versions of that work in Leipzig. But such is the fact. Some of the French translations are very good, particularly the *Nicolas Nickleby* of E. de la Bédollierre, which is admirably done. Mr Dickens also 'lives' in Dutch, and some of his works are, we believe, translated into Russian.

59. Thomas Carlyle on Dickens

1844, 1856, 1870, 1880

Carlyle (1795–1881) was a friend of both Dickens and Forster. Dickens much admired his works, especially *The French Revolution*, acknowledged a debt to his ideas, and dedicated *Hard Times* to him. Extracts (*a*) to (*d*) come from letters to John Forster. In (*d*) the phrase cited is of course Johnson's, on the death of Garrick, and 1866 was the date of Mrs Carlyle's death. See also No. 156.

(*a*) (6 June 1844) 'I truly love Dickens; and discern in the inner man of him a tone of real Music, which struggles to express itself as it may, in these bewildered stupefied and indeed very empty and distracted days, —better or worse! This, which makes him in my estimation one of a thousand, I could with great joy and freedom testify to all persons, to himself first of all, in any good way.' (Charles Richard Saunders, 'Carlyle's Letters', *Bulletin of the John Rylands Library*, xxx (1955–6), 199–224).

(*b*) (12 December 1846) 'An Arch-deacon, with his own venerable lips, repeated to me, the other night, a strange profane story: of a solemn Clergyman who had been administering ghostly consolation to a sick person (several years ago); having finished, satisfactorily as he thought, and got out of the room, he heard the sick person ejaculate: "Well, thank God, *Pickwick* will be out in ten days any way!"—This is dreadful.' (*Ibid*, but final sentence from MS)

(*c*) (c. 1856) 'Long life to you, dear F.—and recommend me to Dickens; and thank him a hundred times for the "circumlocution office", which is priceless after its sort! We have laughed loud and long over it here; and laughter is by no means the supreme result in it.—Oh Heaven.' (MS, John Rylands Library)

(*d*) (c. 11 June 1870) 'I am profoundly sorry for *you*, and indeed for myself & for us all. It is an event world-wide; a *unique* of Talents suddenly extinct; and has "eclipsed" (we too may say) "the harmless gaiety of Nations". No death since 1866 has fallen on me with such a stroke; no

Literary Man's hitherto ever did. The good, the gentle, ever friendly noble Dickens,—every inch of him an Honest Man!' (Saunders, *loc. cit.*)

(*e*) 'Dickens, he said, was a good little fellow, and one of the most cheery, innocent natures he had ever encountered. But he lived among a set of admirers who did him no good—Maclise the painter, Douglas Jerrold, John Forster, and the like; and he spent his entire income in their society. He was seldom seen in fashionable drawing-rooms, however, and maintained, one could see, something of his old reporter independence. His theory of life was entirely wrong. He thought men ought to be buttered up, and the world made soft and accommodating for them, and all sorts of fellows have turkey for their Christmas dinner. Commanding and controlling and punishing them he would give up without any misgivings in order to coax and soothe and delude them into doing right. But it was not in this manner the eternal laws operated, but quite otherwise. Dickens had not written anything which would be found of much use in solving the problems of life. But he was worth something; he was worth a penny to read of an evening before going to bed, which was about what a read of him cost you. His last book went on as pleasantly as the rest, and he might produce innumerable such like books in time.

I suggested that the difference between his men and women and Thackeray's seemed to me like the difference between Sinbad the Sailor and Robinson Crusoe.

Yes, he said, Thackeray had more reality in him and would cut up into a dozen Dickenses. . . .' (Charles Gavan Duffy, *Conversations with Carlyle* (1892), 75)

(*f*) (Duffy's diary, 1880) 'Speaking of both after they were dead, Carlyle said of Dickens that his chief faculty was that of a comic actor. He would have made a successful one if he had taken to that sort of life. His public readings, which were a pitiful pursuit after all, were in fact acting, and very good acting too. He had a remarkable faculty for business; he managed his periodical skilfully, and made good bargains with his booksellers. Set him to do any work, and if he undertook it, it was altogether certain that it would be done effectually. Thackeray had far more literary ability, but one could not fail to perceive that he had no convictions, after all, except that a man ought to be a gentleman, and ought not to be a snob. This was about the sum of the belief that was in him.' (*ibid*, 77)

60. William Howitt, from 'Charles Dickens', *The People's Journal*

3 June 1846, i, 8–12

This appreciation, in the opening number of the *People's Journal* (which also contained a favourable notice of *The Cricket*), was in a series 'The People's Portrait Gallery'; Dickens was chosen to open it, as 'the unquestionably most popular man of his day'. Howitt (1792–1879), editor of the *Journal*, was a prolific author and journalist; Dickens was on friendly terms with him and his wife Mary, and later invited them to write for *Household Words*.

. . . Every one feels instantly the keen eye which he has for the ludicrous in every character, and the uncontrollable tendency to have his laugh at it. But every one feels at the same moment, that in that laugh there is no malice; it is the merriment of a genuine heart which, while it laughs, loves and does justice . . . you stand in unconscious admiration of the sound, healthy, moral constitution of the writer.

It is the direct consequence of this fine human constitution which has made Mr Dickens so universal in his influence for good. It is not necessary for a man to be a politician, far less the zealot of a party, in order to advance the interests of even his own country; on the contrary, they who do this narrow their sphere of action; they become the heroes of a sect; they are the idols of a few, and the aversion of many; they think it necessary to act violently, to put out their articles of faith prominently, to love and hate according to their colours. This is to diffuse heat as a kitchen-range does, which half roasts your face while your back freezes; not like the sun which gives a universal glow, or leaves you to the uniform and healthy coolness of night or of winter. No man has dreamed of Mr Dickens' politics, or cared to inquire after his religion; he has stood amongst us belonging to us all; of our creed, of our party, of our way of thinking—let us have been of what creed or party, or peculiarity of ideas, we might—simply because he had no party or prejudices, but treated human interests as they belonged to man and not to classes. By this means, and it has been evidently the simple result of feeling and not of policy, his public has consisted of every rank and grade; he has found entrance into every circle, however tabooed to scores of other writers with not a tenth of his power or his dexterity in sketching people's portraits, while they have thought he was painting their neighbours; and the Lords Verisopht themselves have not felt comfortable without their weekly *Nickleby*, nor the moral Pecksniffs either without their *Chuzzlewit*. Yet what man has hit harder at the vices, laughed harder at the follies, or thundered more genuinely against the oppression of society. But then there has been pity and not spite at the bottom of it; and when all classes have had their visits of mercy or of censure, which of them could venture a plea for offence? We talk of the universality of genius, but which of its qualities are so universal as its human sympathies, and its sense of right? Perhaps the sensitive *Americans* may be inclined to question our award of the quality of strict justice to Mr Dickens; they may regard his strictures as more national than generic; but time heals wounds both of the heart and the eye, and we will wait a while ere we ask America to look at Mr Dickens, or to pronounce her final verdict upon him. . . .

It is to this bold and successful attempt to vindicate the claims of the less fortunate, and as we might think, less virtuous part of our fellowmen to our warmest affection, that the public owes, and will ever owe, the deepest obligations to Mr Dickens. We should owe him much if our debt was only that of enjoyment derived from the affluent list of his admirable literary creations. Pickwick, the Wellers, those two Sawbones, Bob Sawyer and Ben Allen; the Bumbles, the good Brownlow, the warm-hearted Losberne, Squeers, Noggs, the Cheerybles, the Willets, Gabriel Varden, Tom Pinch, Jonas Chuzzlewit, the moral Pecksniff, that inimitable representative of a class; old Scrooge, the Fezziwigs, Trotty Veck, and lastly, Peerybingle, the carrier, and his little wife Dot.

This were of itself a rich title to the thanks of the public; but this is merely the result of Mr Dickens's genius—that of his moral nature is still behind and far higher. His writings are a continual preaching from the text of Burns—

A man's a man for a' that!

While they tend to call forth the best feelings of the wealthier classes, they tend equally to elevate the self-respect and estimation of the people. . . .

61. [W. E. Aytoun], from 'Advice to an Intending Serialist', *Blackwood's Magazine*

November 1846, lx, 590–605

Has been wrongly attributed to Samuel Warren. Aytoun (1813–65), part-author of the '*Bon Gaultier*' *Ballads*, was Professor of Belles-Lettres at Edinburgh. The article purports to be a letter from a practising novelist to an aspirant, 'T. Smith, Esq., Scene-Painter and Tragedian at the Amphitheatre'. Assuming that his first and great purpose will be 'to make money, and to make as much as you can', the writer offers ironical advice on how to achieve this. After discussing fiction of the Charles Lever type, he turns to Newgate novels and attacks such 'dunghill' subjects 'which the imagination shudders at whenever they are forced upon it'. But Smith, being 'a bit of a Radical', is more likely to be tempted into abusing the upper classes 'as tyrants, fools, and systematic grinders of the poor'.

I am the more anxious to caution you against putting any such rubbish into your pages, because I fear you have contracted some sort of intimacy with a knot of utilitarian ninnyhammers. . . . Now, Smith, this will not do. There may be inequalities in this world, and there may also be injustice; but it is a very great mistake to hold that one-half of the population of these islands is living in profligate ease upon the compulsory labour of the other. I am not going to write you a treatise upon political economy; but I ask you to reflect for a moment, and you will see how ludicrous is the charge. This style of thinking, or, what is worse, this style of writing, is positively the most mischievous production of the present day. Disguised under the specious aspect of philanthropy, it fosters self conceit and discontent, robs honest industry of that satisfaction which is its best reward, and, instead of removing, absolutely creates invidious class-distinctions. And I will tell you from what this spirit arises—it is the working of the meanest envy. . . .

This is the lowest sort of quackery; but there are also higher degrees. Our literature, of what ought to be the better sort, has by no means escaped the infection. In former times, men who devoted themselves to the active pursuit of letters, brought to the task not only high talent, but deep and measured thought, and an accumulated fund of acquirement. They studied long before they wrote, and attempted no subject until they had thoroughly and comprehensively mastered its details. But we live under a new system. There is no want of talent, though it be of a rambling and disjointed kind; but we look in vain for marks of the previous study. Our authors deny the necessity or advantage of an apprenticeship, and set up for masters before they have learned the rudiments of their art, and they dispense altogether with reflection. Few men now think before they write. The consequence is, that a great proportion of our modern literature is of the very flimsiest description —vivid, sometimes, and not without sparkles of genuine humour; but so ill constructed as to preclude the possibility of its long existence. No one is entitled to reject models, unless he has studied them, and detected their faults; but this is considered by far too tedious a process for modern ingenuity. We are thus inundated with a host of clever writers, each relying upon his peculiar and native ability, jesting—for that is the humour of the time—against each other, and all of them forsaking nature, and running deplorably into caricature.

These are the men who make the loudest outcry against the social system, and who appear to be imbued with an intense hatred of the aristocracy, and indeed with every one of our time-honoured institutions. This I know has been denied; but, in proof of my assertion, I appeal to their published works. Read any one of them through, and I ask you if you do not rise from it with a sort of conviction, that you must search for the cardinal virtues solely in the habitations of the poor —that the rich are hard, selfish, griping, and tyrannical—and that the nobility are either fools, spendthrifts, or debauchees? Is it so, as a general rule, in actual life? Far from it. I do not need to be told of the virtue and industry which grace the poor man's lot; for we all feel and know it, and God forbid that it should be otherwise. But we know also that there is as great, if not greater temptation in the hovel than in the palace, with fewer counteracting effects from education and principle to withstand it; and it is an insult to our understanding to be told, that fortune and station are in effect but other words for tyranny, callousness, and crime.

The fact is, that most of these authors know nothing whatever of the society which they affect to describe, but which in truth they grossly libel. Their starting-point is usually not a high one. . . .

[Aytoun attributes these authors' bilious hatred of the upper classes to their resentment at not having been invited to mix with them on terms of social equality.]

Take my advice then, and have nothing to say to the earnest and oneness-of-purpose men. They are not only weak but wicked; and they will lead you most lamentably astray. Let us now look a little into your style, which, after all, is a matter of some importance in a serial.

On the whole, I like it. It is nervous, terse, and epigrammatic—a little too high-flown at times; but I was fully prepared for that. What I admire most, however, is your fine feeling of humanity—the instinct, as it were, and dumb life which you manage to extract from inanimate objects as well as from articulately-speaking men. Your very furniture has a kind of automatonic life; you can make an old chest of drawers wink waggishly from the corner, and a boot-jack in your hands becomes a fellow of infinite fancy. This is all very pleasant and delightful; though I think, upon the whole, you give us a little too much of it, for I cannot fancy myself quite comfortable in a room with every article of the furniture maintaining a sort of espionage upon my doings. Then as to your antiquarianism you are perfect. Your description of

the old deserted stable, with the old rusty harness hanging upon the old decayed nails, so honeycombed, as it were, by the tooth of time, that you wondered how they possibly could support the weight; while across the span of an old discoloured stirrup, a great spider had thrown his web, and now lay waiting in the middle of it, a great hairy bag of venom, for the approach of some unlucky fly, like a usurer on the watch for a spendthrift. . . .

—that description, I say, almost brought tears to my eyes. The catalogue, also, which you give us of the decayed curry-combs all clogged with grease, the shankless besoms, the worm-eaten corn-chest, and all the other paraphernalia of the desolate stable, is as finely graphic as any thing which I ever remember to have read.

But your best scene is the opening one, in which you introduce us to the aerial dwelling of Estrella di Canterini, in Lambeth. I do not wish to flatter you, my dear fellow; but I hold it to be a perfect piece of composition, and I cannot resist the temptation of transcribing a very few sentences:—

It was the kitten that began it, and not the cat. It isn't no use saying it was the cat, because I was there, and I saw it and know it; and if I don't know it, how should any body else be able to tell about it, if you please? So I say again it was the kitten that began it, and the way it all happened was this. . . . [etc.]

The child—she was a very little one—burst into a flood of tears.

Now, that is what I call fine writing, and no mistake. There is a breadth—a depth—a sort of *chiaroscuro*, about the picture which betrays the hand of a master, and shows how deeply you have studied in a school which has no equal in modern, and never had a parallel in former times. . . .

. . . Your have, and I think most wisely, undertaken to frame a new code of grammar and of construction for yourself; and the light and airy effect of this happy innovation is conspicuous not only in every page but in almost every sentence of your work. There is no slipslop here— only a fine, manly disregard of syntax, which is infinitely attractive; and I cannot doubt that you are destined to become the founder of a far higher and more enduring school of composition, than that which was approved of and employed by the fathers of our English literature.

Your work will be translated, Smith, into French and German, and other European languages. . . . Your works, therefore, will be received in the saloons of Paris and Vienna—it may be of St Petersburg—as conveying accurate pictures of our everyday English life; and I need hardly remark how much that impression must tend to elevate our national character in the eyes of an intelligent foreigner. Labouring under old and absurd prejudices, he perhaps at present believes that we are a sober, unmercurial people, given to domestic habits, to the accumulation of wealth, and to our own internal improvements. It is reserved for you, Smith, to couch his visionary eye. You will convince him that a great part of our existences is spent about the doors of theatres, in tap-rooms, pot-houses, and other haunts, which I need not stay to particularize. You will prove to him that the British constitution rests upon no sure foundation, and that it is based upon injustice and tyranny. Above all, he will learn from you the true tone which per-vades society, and the altered style of conversation and morals which is universally current among us. In minor things, he will discover, what few authors have taken pains to show, the excessive fondness of our nation for a pure Saxon nomenclature. He will learn that such names as Seymour, and Howard, and Percy—nay, even our old familiars, Jones and Robinson—are altogether proscribed among us, and that a new race has sprung up in their stead, rejoicing in the euphonious appellations of Tox and Wox, Whibble, Toozle, Whopper, Sniggleshaw, Guzzlerit, Gingerthorpe, Mugswitch, Smungle, Yelkins, Fizgig, Parksnap, Grubsby, Shoutowker, Hogswash and Quiltirogus. He will also learn that our magistrates, unlike the starched official dignitaries of France, are not ashamed to partake, in the public streets, of tripe with a common workman—and a hundred other little particulars, which throw a vast light into the chinks and crevices of our social system.

I therefore, Smith, have the highest satisfaction in greeting you, not only as an accomplished author, but as a great national benefactor. Go on, my dear fellow, steadfastly and cheerfully, as you have begun. The glories of our country were all very well in their way, but the subject is a hackneyed one, and it is scarcely worth while to revive it. Be it yours to chronicle the weaknesses and peculiarities of that society which you frequent—no man can do it better. Draw on for ever with the same felicitous pencil. Do not fear to repeat yourself over and over again; to indulge in the same style of one-sided caricature; and to harp upon the same string of pathos so long as it will vibrate pleasantly to the public ear. What we want, after all, is sale, and I am sure that you will not be disappointed. . . .

DOMBEY AND SON

October 1846 – April 1848

'The readers of Mr Dickens must be happy to find him again in his proper walk, and as original and amusing as ever,' wrote a reviewer of No. I. It would 'be readily seen', from the excerpts quoted, that 'the good ship Boz is righted, and once more fairly afloat' (*Chambers's Edinburgh Journal*, 24 October 1846, n.s. vi, 269–70). Coming after the poor critical reception of the *Cricket* (December 1845) and *Pictures from Italy* (May 1846), and the fiasco of the *Daily News* editorship (January–February 1846), the excellence of the opening numbers of *Dombey* restored Dickens to general esteem, and the death of Paul Dombey in No. V (February 1847) 'threw a whole nation into mourning' (*Life*, 477). Even Fitzjames Stephen, in the *Saturday Review*, a decade later, found this the *best* piece of sentimentalism in modern literature (25 December 1858, 643). The pathos of Florence Dombey's situation was also found very moving: Macaulay wept over her as if his heart would break, and so did others. Disappointment set in, however, after No. V; many readers felt that Dickens had shot his bolt too early, and that Dombey, his second wife, and Carker proved a poor substitute for the former interest centring on the children.

Wilkie Collins made a suggestive comment on how much the popularity of Dickens's novels was affected by their immediate predecessors. Dickens had written to Forster, when the sales of the early numbers of *Copperfield* proved disappointing: 'I am not sorry I cannot bring myself to care much for what opinions people may form; and I have a strong belief, that, if any of my books are read years hence, *Dombey* will be remembered as among the best of them: but passing influences are important for the time, and as *Chuzzlewit* with its small sale sent me up, *Dombey's* large sale has tumbled me down' (*Life*, 509). Collins commented on this, in the margin of his copy of the *Life*: 'That *Chuzzlewit* (in some respects the finest novel he ever wrote) delighted his readers, and so led to a large sale of the next book, *Dombey*, I don't doubt. But the latter half of *Dombey* no intelligent person can have read without astonishment at the badness of it, and the disappointment that followed lowered the sale of the next book, *Copperfield*, incomparably superior to *Dombey* as it certainly is' (*Pall Mall Gazette*, 20 January 1890, 3).

Reviewers noticed the railways and other evidences of a deliberate up-to-dateness in *Dombey*. Also its symbolism—though sometimes derisively ('cuckoo-clocks—emblems of the fleeting nature of time': see the *Man in the Moon* lampoon, No. 65), or critically ('full to over-flowing of waves whispering and wandering; of dark rivers rolling to the sea, of winds, and golden ripples, and such like matters, which are sometimes very pretty, generally very untrue, and have become, at all events, excessively stale'—*Parker's London Magazine*, May 1848, 201). The increasing centrality of Dickens's social criticism was less widely noted, though there were interesting comments on this in Arthur Dudley's 'Charles Dickens', *Revue des Deux Mondes*, March 1848, xxi, 901–22, translated in part in the *People's Journal*, 1848, v, 229–31. For a survey of criticism see Philip Collins, '*Dombey and Son*, then and now', *Dickensian*, lxiii (1967), 82–94.

Vanity Fair was being serialized, also in twenty monthly numbers, about the same time (January 1847 – July 1848). With this novel, Thackeray for the first time emerged as a major author. By January 1848 Thackeray was reporting to his mother: 'I am become a sort of great man in my way —all but at the top of the tree: indeed there if the truth were known and having a great fight up there with Dickens' (*Letters and Private Papers*, ii, 333). Reviewers began what became the standard exercise of comparing and contrasting them. Dickens appears to have taken much less interest in the 'great fight' than the challenger did; he could feel secure, both in sales and popular acclamation, and in self-regard.

62. From an unsigned review of No. I,
the *Economist*

10 October 1846, 1324-5

We are glad—right glad—to see the footsteps of Dickens again in that pleasant walk of literature in which he is unrivalled, and which he ought never to have left for the thorny paths and uneasy turmoil of newspapers. Never was there a man so little suited to the wear and tear and vulgar huck-a-buck work of the daily press[1], or more formed to shine in the road in which he strode with such gigantic paces to fame and fortune. This great painter of English manners, distinguished alike by pathos and tenderness—a hearty and healthy naturalness—great shrewdness, and minute and accurate observation, should bid adieu to politics and controversy—should cease to paint pictures of Italy—a land which he does not understand—and confine himself to London and Middlesex, or at least to the fair realm of England.

His first best country ever is at home.

To write on Italy, something more than genius and observation are required. A man should possess deep and varied scholarship, ancient and modern—a knowledge of the language, arts, and literature of the country—and in all these requisites Dickens is deficient; for genius and observation are all the store he possesses. But with the wand of an enchanter he may turn these gifts to gold, if he will but confine himself to that sphere in which he is unapproachable—certainly unapproached.

In the present work . . . the author introduces us at once to that busy world of London, in which there is 'food for contemplation even to madness.'. . .

In passing, through the busy haunts of London, down by noisy Walbrook, wicked Wapping, and ancient St Mary Axe, our readers may have stumbled against a wooden middy, taking an observation on a hackney coach before the door. Here is the identical shop, painted in such colours as no living man but Dickens could paint it. . . .

[1] Dickens's short and unhappy period as Editor of the *Daily News* (in which *Pictures from Italy* appeared) was in January/February 1846.

[Quotes from ch. iv.]

There was urgent need to paint such a man as Dombey. The world of London is filled with cold, pompous, stiff, purse-proud men like this, who think, as DICKENS says, the earth was made for Dombey and Son to trade in, and the sun and moon were made to give them light, and that A.D. has no concern with Anno Domini, but stands for Anno Dombei. We can fancy the female children of men made after this fashion, 'with cheeks of parchment and eyes of stone,' and who only look to propagate male babes who will bear the name of the firm; we can fancy the poor daughters 'glancing keenly at the blue coat and stiff white cravat, which, with a pair of creaking boots and a very [loud] ticking watch, embodies their idea of father.'

It is not alone, however, in describing pompous traders that DICKENS excels. There is an admirable sketch of a great London accoucheur—one Dr PARKER PEPS, 'a man of eminent reputation for assisting at the increase of great families, with a round, deep, sonorous voice, muffled for the occasion, like the knocker.'. . .

DICKENS has an eye open to everything within the bills of mortality. In this age of iron it is necessary he should bring a stoker on the scene, and, accordingly, Mr TOODLE is introduced as the husband of the wet nurse of young Dombey. . . .

Quotes the dialogue between Florence and 'Richards', ch. iii.]

This is admirable, and shows that neither newspaper writing nor newspaper have dried up in Dickens those exquisite sources of pathos and tenderness which have by turns saddened and delighted his readers.

63. Lord Jeffrey,
from letters to Dickens

1846-7

A further letter from Jeffrey to Dickens (apparently not extant) had a notable effect on the novel. Dickens wrote to Forster, on 21 December 1847: 'Note from Jeffrey this morning, who won't believe (positively refuses) that Edith is Carker's mistress. What do you think of a kind of inverted Maid's Tragedy, and a tremendous scene of her undeceiving Carker, and giving him to know that she never meant that?' (*Life*, 484). Jeffrey's hint was taken: a rare example of Dickens's yielding to such advice.

(14 December 1846) My dear, dear Dickens!—and dearer every day, as you every day give me more pleasure and do me more good! You do not wonder at this style? for you know that I have been *in love with you*, ever since Nelly! and I do not care who knows it. . . . The Dombeys, my dear D! how can I thank you enough for them! The truth, and the delicacy, and the softness and depth of the pathos in that opening death-scene, could only come from one hand; and the exquisite taste which spares all details, and breaks off just when the effect is at its height, is wholly yours. But it is Florence on whom my hopes chiefly repose; and in her I see the promise of another Nelly! though reserved, I hope, for a happier fate, and destined to let us see what a *grown-up* female angel is like. I expect great things, too, from Walter, who begins charmingly, and will be still better I fancy than young Nickleby, to whom as yet he bears most resemblance. I have good hopes too of Susan Nipper, who I think has great capabilities, and whom I trust you do not mean to drop. Dombey is rather too hateful, and strikes me as a mitigated Jonas, without his brutal coarseness and ruffian ferocity. I am quite in the dark as to what you mean to make of Paul, but shall watch his development with interest. About Miss Tox, and her Major, and the Chicks, perhaps I do not care enough. But you know I always grudge the exquisite painting you waste on such portraits. I love the

Captain, tho', and his hook, as much as you can wish; and look forward
to the future appearances of Carker Junior, with expectations which I
know will not be disappointed. . . . (Forster, *Life of Dickens*, 480n).

(31 January 1847) Oh, my dear dear Dickens! what a No. 5 [chs. xiv–
xvi] you have now given us! I have so cried and sobbed over it last
night, and again this morning; and felt my heart purified by those
tears, and blessed and loved you for making me shed them; and I never
can bless and love you enough. Since that divine Nelly was found dead
on her humble couch, beneath the snow and the ivy, there has been
nothing like the actual dying of that sweet Paul, in the summer sunshine of that lofty room. And the long vista that leads us so gently and
sadly, and yet so gracefully and winningly, to that plain consummation!
Every trait so true, and so touching—and yet lightened by that fearless
innocence which goes *playfully* to the brink of the grave, and that pure
affection which bears the unstained spirit, on its soft and lambent flash,
at once to its source in eternity. In reading of these delightful children,
how deeply do we feel that 'of such is the kingdom of Heaven;' and
how ashamed of the contaminations which *our* manhood has received
from the contact of earth, and wonder how *you* should have been
admitted into that pure communion, and so 'presumed, an earthly
guest, and drawn Empyrial air,' though for our benefit and instruction.
Well, I did not mean to say all this; but this I must say, and you will
believe it, that of the many thousand hearts that will melt and swell
over these pages, there can be few that will feel their chain so deeply
as mine, and scarcely any so *gratefully*. But after reaching this climax in
the fifth number, what are you to do with the fifteen that are to follow?
—'The wine of life is drawn, and nothing left but the dull dregs for this
poor world to brag of.' So I shall say, and fear for any other adventurer.
But I have unbounded trust in your resources, though I have a feeling
that you will have nothing in the sequel, if indeed in your whole life,
equal to the pathos and poetry, the truth and the tenderness, of the
four last pages of this number, for those, at least, who feel and judge
like me. . . . (Lord Cockburn, *Life of Lord Jeffrey* (Edinburgh, 1852), ii,
406–7).

(5 July 1847) I cannot tell you how much I have been charmed with
your last number [No. X, chs. xxix–xxxi], and what gentle sobs and
delightful tears it has cost me. It is the most finished, perhaps, in diction; and in the delicacy and fineness of its touches, both of pleasantry

and pathos, of any you have ever given us; while it rises to higher and deeper passions; not resting, like most of the former, in sweet thoughtfulness, and thrilling and attractive tenderness, but boldly wielding all the lofty and terrible elements of tragedy, and bringing before us the appalling struggles of a proud, scornful, and repentant spirit. I am proud that you should thus shew us new views of your genius—but I shall always love its gentler magic the most; and never leave Nelly and Paul and Florence for Edith, with whatever potent spells you may invest her; though I am prepared for great things from her. I must thank you, too, for the true and pathetic *poetry* of many passages in this number—Dombey's brief vision in the after dinner table, for instance [ch. xxx], and that grand and solemn progress, so full of fancy and feeling, of dawn and night shadows, over the funeral church [ch. xxxi]. I am prepared too, in some degree, for being softened towards Dombey. . . . (*Ibid.*, ii, 428–9).

(12 September 1847, about No. XII, chs. xxxv–xxxviii) . . . my thanks for all the pleasure it has given, and all the good it has done me. That first chapter, and the scenes with *Florence* and *Edith*, are done with your finest and happiest hand; so soft and so graceful, and with such delicate touches of deep feeling, and passing intimations of coming griefs, and woman's loveliness, and loving nature, shown in such contrasted embodiments of gentle innocence and passionate pride; and yet all brought under the potent spell of one great master, and harmonized by the grace as well as the power of his genius, into a picture in which every one must recognize, not only the truth of each individual figure, but the magic effect of their grouping. You have the force and the nature of Scott in his pathetic parts, without his occasional coarseness and wordiness; and the searching disclosure of inward agonies of Byron, without a trait of his wickedness. . . . (ii, 429).

64. Edward Fitzgerald, in a letter to Thackeray

January 1847

(*Letters and Private Papers of W. M. Thackeray*, ed. Gordon N. Ray, (Cambridge, Mass., 1946), ii, 266)

Fitzgerald (1809–83), translator, and friend of many eminent literary men, criticized but much enjoyed Dickens: 'He always lights one up somehow' (*Letters and Literary Remains* (1902), i, 292). As a footnote to the present letter, Professor Ray fittingly quotes George Hodder's famous anecdote about Thackeray's response to Paul Dombey's death: 'Putting No. 5 [chs. xiv–xvi] of *Dombey and Son* in his pocket, he hastened down to Mr Punch's printing-office, and entering the editor's room, where I chanced to be the only person present except Mr Mark Lemon himself, he dashed it on to the table with startling vehemence, and exclaimed "There's no writing against such power as this—one has no chance! Read that chapter describing young Paul's death: it is unsurpassed—it is stupendous!"' (*Memoirs of my Time* (1870), 277).

What a wretched affair is the *Battle of Life*—scarce even the few touches that generally redeem Dickens—. . . Dickens' last *Dombey* has a very fine account of the overcramming Educator's system; worth whole volumes of Essays on the subject if Bigotry would believe that laughs may tell truth. The boy who talks Greek in his sleep seems to be terrible as Macbeth—

219

65. From an unsigned article, 'Inquest on the late Master Paul Dombey', *The Man in the Moon*

March 1847, i, 155–60

The Man in the Moon had been established in January 1847, as a rival to *Punch*; its editors were Angus B. Reach and (until March 1847) Albert Smith, and its contributors included G. A. Sala and Shirley Brooks. Apart from *Punch* and Dickens, its recurrent victims included Jerrold, Forster and his *Examiner*, Carlyle, and Howitt (see, e.g., v, 111, 177, 242). The attacks on *Dombey and Son* were kept up: 'LOST—Somewhere between the stage door of the St James's Theatre and Miss Burdett Coutts's Ragged Schools, the plot of the story of *Dombey and Son*. No use to any body but the owner, and not much to him' (January 1848, iii, 8). Or, in a cod-almanac—'Read *Vanity Fair*, but avoid comparing it with *Dombey and Son*, or you will never be able to bear the latter again' (*ibid*, 14). In February 1848 there was a lampoon, '*Dombey and Son* Finished. Part the Best and Last' (iii, 59–67). Another cod 'Trial' appeared in January 1849: 'Mr Charles Dickens was placed at the bar, charged with having extorted divers sums of five shillings each for a work [*The Haunted Man*], which, on perusal was found to be entirely unintelligible . . .' (v, 50–2). See Mary Edminson, 'Charles Dickens and *The Man in the Moon*', *Dickensian*, lvi (1960), 50–9, which reprints '*Dombey and Son* Finished'. After this lampoon, which made much of Carker's flashing teeth, 'Carker never dared show his teeth' again, according to Harrison Ainsworth (S. M. Ellis, *William Harrison Ainsworth and his Friends* (1911), i, 166). As Miss Edminson comments, 'This is not, in fact, strictly accurate, but it indicates the opinion of another author on the strength of the satire' (*loc. cit.*, 51).

The jury first proceeded to view the body, which they found to be in a state of premature decay.

On their return, the Coroner, after a few severe observations on the conduct of literary parents in adding to the surplus population of the republic of letters, without sufficiently calculating their means of supporting their offspring, proceeded at once with the enquiry.

The first witness called was:

Miss JANE DICKYBIRD: Has known the deceased, Paul Dombey, from his earliest years—she begged pardon—from his earliest numbers. Deceased was a little dear. Had no hesitation in calling him a duck. He was so pretty, and said such sweet little words; quite darlings of words for a dear tiny mite as he was. Fell in love with deceased. Everybody must have. Was quite shocked at his death. Received the news by the last number. Did not quite understand that he was dead at first, the intimation was in such terribly fine writing. Had to read it three times over before she could make anything of it, and then asked her brother. Thought the author of the dear child's existence very cruel—a nasty, sad, naughty man, for killing such a sweet poppet—of course he killed it. Fie for shame upon him. How could he be so wicked? Thought him an odious man. Has quite hated him ever since.

Mr SCRIBBLEY NIBBS was the next witness. Was an author by trade— he meant profession. Had much experience in the rearing of literary bantlings. Had had scores of his own. Thought a great deal of them. Nobody else did. More shame for them. Believed his were the finest children in the world. They were utterly neglected by the public. Thinks the public an ass. Has seen Paul Dombey—thought him a humbug—quite out of proportion—by no means naturally formed—a monster in fact. Considered his mind (if he had any), as affected. Did not think that he would have been good for anything had he grown up; did not see any useful part he could have filled. Thought he would have been very difficult to rear. Never expected that he would have lived. Had prophesied his death to everybody. . . .

At the suggestion of one of the jury, the parent of the child, Mr Charles Dickens, was here put into the witness box. He was respectably dressed in mourning, but seemed to manifest little emotion.

The examination was continued by the Coroner.

Knew the deceased—rather ought to. Had been instrumental in bringing him into the world. Never had any definite notion of what to do with him. The child was very precocious. Thought precocity a very good thing for getting an effective chapter or two out of. Had once thought of making 'Son' the agent of retribution on 'Dombey.' Abandoned the notion. Did not see his way in working it out.

Considered that he had a right to do what he liked with his own. Took things as they came. Did not know what a chapter or a page might bring forth. When he had no more use for a personage, or did not know what to do with it, killed him off at once. It was very pathetic and very convenient.

Here Miss Dickybird fainted, and was carried out.

Had got his change out of Paul. Had been very much afraid of his growing troublesome on his (witness's) hands. Thought it best, on the whole, to get rid of him. If he was asked to name the disease of which Paul had expired, thought it was an attack of acute 'Don't-know-what-to-do-with-him-phobia.' . . .

The jury retired, and having determined upon their decision by tossing up, returned the following verdict, through their foreman, John Forster, Esq.—'That the deceased had died through want of the common necessaries of life.'

THE FUNERAL

This melancholy ceremonial took place upon an uncertain day last month. The popular demonstrations of grief were striking and general. Passing bells were rung by various respectable artisans, who, from an early hour, perambulated the streets and squares of the metropolis, carrying cuckoo clocks—emblems of the fleeting nature of time—under their arms, and sounding a monotonous peal upon the alarums of these useful household implements; while, upon the line of procession, there was not a bankrupt tradesman whose establishment had not been closed.

The mournful *cortège* started from the publishers', at a reasonable hour, in the following order, having been marshalled by the illustrious Shillebeer.

Detachment of Police
Carrying *Literary Gazettes* to Clear the Way

Literary Undertakers, Warranted to Accomplish the Interment of Every New Work	Circulating Library Keepers Two and Two (Strewing Catalogues on the Ground for Flowers)	Literary Undertakers, Warranted to Accomplish the Interment of Every New Work

Parliamentary Mutes Warranted never to Speak to the Purpose	A Street Band, Playing a Lively Air From one of Macfarren's Operas, as a Dead March	Parliamentary Mutes Warranted never to Speak to the Purpose

THE BODY

Borne by Four Virgins in White Robes, viz.:

Miss Niminy	Miss Piminy
Miss Fiddle	Miss Faddle

Members of the *Examiner* Clique	THE AUTHOR Supported by BRADBURY and EVANS The Celebrated and Talented JOHN FORSTER, Esq., Bearing the Author's Hatband, And kept up by Two Able-bodied Porters	Members of the *Examiner* Clique

Penny a Liners	Literary Friends of the Deceased, Two and Two The Rear brought up by BULWER and SERGEANT LYTTON TALFOURD	Penny a Liners

The whole closed by
A Body of Printer's Devils,
'Hallooing, and Singing of Anthems'

Upon the arrival of the procession at the place of interment, and after the melancholy duties had been paid to Paul (without robbing Peter), the following Requiem was chanted over the grave, by the Circulating Library Keepers—the production having been arranged and altered from the Coronach in the 'Lady of the Lake,' expressly for the occasion, by the celebrated and talented John Forster, Esq.

REQUIEM FOR PAUL DOMBEY

Thou art gone from our counter,
　　Thou art lost to our pocket,
Thou hast fallen, brief mounter,
　　Like stick of a rocket.
New numbers appearing,
　　Fresh interest may borrow;
But we go on 'Oh dearing,
　　For Paul there's no morrow'.
　　　　　　　Tol de rol, &c.

The mind's eye of the peeper
　　Saw thy manhood in glory,
But the wits of one deeper
　　Hath cut short thy story.
A first volume may settle
　　The characters dreariest,
But to keep up thy mettle
　　Was none of the cheeriest.
　　　　　　　Tol de rol, &c.

Sure point in a chapter,
　　Best pupil of Blimber,
Safe card for adapter,
　　How sound is thy slumber.
Like the froth on the porter,
　　The cat's penn'orth of liver,
The bomb from the mortar,
　　Thou art gone, as for ever!
　　　　　　　Tol de rol, &c.

At the conclusion of the most musical, most mournful ceremony, the company returned to the domicile of the enterprising publishers, where, in solemn silence—nobody having anything to say for the deceased—was drunk, 'The Memory of the late Master Paul Dombey; and may his early fate be a warning to parents with precocious children, and authors with unmanageable characters.'

66. From a review
(signed 'H') of Nos. I–VI,
Westminster Review
April 1847, xlvii, 5–11

'H' was possibly William E. Hickson (1803–70), Editor of the *Westminster Review*, 1840–52; he was particularly interested in educational matters.

... The happiest and most perfect of Dickens's sketches is that of 'Little Nell,' in the story of *Humphrey's Clock*. Her death is a tragedy of the true sort, that which softens, and yet strengthens and elevates; and we have its counterpart in the death of 'Little Dombey,' in the new work of this gifted author now issuing in parts through the press.

We rejoice to observe, in *Dombey and Son*, the evidence of improved experience and pains-taking. If we may judge of the work as a whole from the early numbers, it is, to our thinking, the best of the productions of the same pen. The chief interest is tragic, but its material is not crime; and we notice this with satisfaction, as an illustration of our argument. The personages of the tale are every-day men and women, with their every-day faults and virtues. Among them, as yet, there is no great villain. Hobgoblins have been exorcised. The first part describes a dying mother—the fifth a dying child—subjects of the most commonplace obituaries, but here treated by a master. No other writer can approach Dickens in a perfect analysis of the mind of children; and in *Dombey and Son* he has put forth the whole of his power. It was a novel but happy idea to sketch society, and human weaknesses, as seen through the eyes of infant philosophy. The satire is at once playful, delicate, and touching. We allude chiefly to the fourth number, where the reflections of little Dombey upon all that is passing about him at Dr Blimber's, is a study for moralists and metaphysicians. The number following concludes the biography of the sick child....

[Makes a quotation from ch. xvi—'a long one, but its merit lies in the *minutiae* and truthfulness of its details, which will not bear abbreviation'. The quotation ends with the two final paragraphs (or 'passages', as the reviewer says) of the chapter.]

The golden ripple on the wall came back again, and nothing else stirred in the room. The old, old, fashion! The fashion that came in with our first garments, and will last unchanged until our race has run its course, and the wide firmament is rolled up like a scroll. The old, old fashion,—Death!

Oh thank God, all who see it, for that older fashion yet, of Immortality! And look upon us, angels of young children, with regards not quite estranged, when the swift river bears us to the ocean.

A simple but affecting narrative; and well told:—one in which every incident is true to nature, and given without any straining after effect. The only attempt at fine writing is in the last two passages, which are not very intelligible, and should have been omitted. Paul had been called 'old-fashioned,' from the eccentricity of his manners, but the term is not appropriate to death and immortality: and we should never have guessed what came in with our first garments, without the author's explanation at the end of the sentence. This is but a trifling matter, and we are glad that beyond a little exaggeration in the portraiture of the fashionable physician, Sir Parker Peps, no graver defects appear. In the humorous parts of the narrative there is as usual a vein of caricature, but not too extravagant, nor more than is required to render the descriptions graphic.

The rising generation will have reason to be grateful to Mr Dickens, for his temperate but yet severe rebuke of all attempts to overtask a child's intellect. By his quiet satire of a fashionable classical institution, in the present work, not less than for his exposure of vulgar and brutal ignorance in another class of academies, described in *Nicholas Nickleby*, he deserves the thanks of all educational reformers.

67. [Charles Kent], from a review in the *Sun*

13 April 1848

On 14 April 1848, Dickens wrote to the Editor of the *Sun* news-paper expressing 'warmest acknowledgments and thanks' for this review. On learning that the review was written by the Editor himself, Charles Kent, he wrote to him personally (18 April 1848): '... allow me to assure you, as an illustration of my sincerity, that I have never addressed a similar communication to anybody, except on one occasion!' A close friendship developed, and Kent pleased him by other reviews. 'I highly esteem and thank you for your sympathy with my writings,' Dickens told him (24 December 1856). 'I doubt if I have a more genial reader in the world.' Al-luding to *King Lear*, he would call him 'my faithful Kent'. See also No. 117.

Kent (1823–1902), editor of the *Sun* 1845–71, contributed to Dickens's weeklies, and organized the farewell banquet to him (6 November 1867) before his visit to America (see *Speeches*, 368–74). Later he wrote, with Dickens's consent and help, *Charles Dickens as a Reader* (1872), and compiled an anthology, *The Humour and Pathos of Charles Dickens: with Illustrations of his Mastery of the Terrible and the Picturesque* (1884).

This review of Nos. XIX–XX of *Dombey* had been preceded by almost monthly reviews, presumably by Kent, of earlier numbers (*Sun*, 2 October, 4 November, 3 December 1846; 1 March, 2 April, 3 May, 1 June, 1 July, 3 August, 6 September, 4 November, and 2 December 1847; 4 January 1848). Most of these had been enthusiastic, and many of them substantial. Once Kent had detected a falling-off: No. XI [chs. xxix–xxxi] had been 'decidedly the least successful' to date, and Phiz had never devised 'more execrable' etchings (3 August 1847). But happily 'The indifference of the eleventh number is more than compensated by the extraordinary brilliance of the twelfth [chs. xxxii–xxxiv]. Mr Dickens begins to develop his plot, and with an art superior to anything of the kind evinced in his preceding fictions' (6 September 1847).

... An old friend has left us—the voice of a dear favourite is silent—
Dombey and Son is completed. Heartily do we regret this, for this true
English story-book, which has appeared from month to month, with
its chequered incidents, its exquisite and touching pathos, its frequent,
spontaneous, and fantastic merriment, its occasional grotesqueness, its
pervading loyalty to the natural, the true, and the beautiful, its home-
touches, its gleams of satire, its erotic benevolence, its unforced philosophy, and above all its many, strange, original, life-like, and admirable
characters—the true English story, we say, in which all this has been
lavished with the abundance of a fruitful but untutored genius, has
imparted so much zest to every successive interval in the course of its
publication, has scattered, as it were, such sweet flowers upon the dusty
path of life, while Time has been rolling us all onward to Eternity, that
we should be ungrateful were we not to lament its termination. We
do regret it—thoroughly. That Mr Dickens can sympathise in this
feeling we know from his books. Their closing sentences are generally
dictated in a mood of sadness and lamentation. As he himself has
happily expressed it in one of his brief but suggestive introductions, the
author, like a dejected host, is fain to loiter upon the threshold even
when he has dismissed his guests, and bade the last of them farewell. In
Dombey and Son, for example, we are loath to imagine that our acquaintance with the different creations in the volume has terminated. ...

[Kent expresses his affectionate delight in Captain Cuttle, Major
Bagstock, Toodle and his family, Towlinson, Morfin, Mrs Pipchin,
the Blimbers, Carker, Perch, Cousin Feenix, Mrs Macstinger, Bunsby,
Susan Nipper, the Dombey family, and others.]

Those, and there are thousands of them, who have, like ourselves,
devoured the work bit by bit—familiarising themselves by long
association with the every characteristic of the ideal personages depicted
in the narrative—and coming at last to regard with a sort of tenderness
even the green covers of the monthly instalment, as being connected
in some fashion with the joys and sorrows of the story, and by consequence with their own tears and laughter, will comprehend our regret
at the dispersion of this imaginary multitude. It is not the least important or the least remarkable among the numerous peculiarities of Mr
Dickens as a novelist, that he sketches a locality with as much vividness
as a painter, and that he imparts to a fictitious being an absolute and
visible individuality. The actors in his tales are no mere pasteboard
fantoccini, moved by the threads of an ingenious plot, and coloured into

the semblance of life by the lustre of his imagination—they are as actual
as flesh and blood, as true as humanity, as filled with the heat of passion
and as fraught with the vitality of sentiment as the creature modelled
by the hand of Prometheus and warmed into animation by the fire
stolen from the celestial laboratory. If there were nothing worthy of
admiration in *Dombey and Son* beyond the passage descriptive of the
death of Little Paul, it would from that solitary passage have been
worthy of a distinguished place among the classic books of our
national literature. In that exquisite chapter—a chapter stamped with
the golden seal of genius—Mr Dickens altogether surpassed himself,
he surpassed his plaintive sketch of Tiny Tim's death in the *Christmas
Carol*, and even that most beautiful, and, as we had once imagined,
inimitable, incident in the *Old Curiosity Shop*—the death of Little Nell.
We envy not that man who can read for the first time the account of
the death of little Paul Dombey with a heart unmoved and an eye
tearless. We can have no sympathy with each other—we are separated
in disposition by a wall of brass. . . .[1] Like most of the preceding fictions of Mr Dickens, *Dombey and Son* inculcates a great moral infer-
entially, and demonstrates the omnipotence of virtue by the transformation of a temperament. . . . For the enforcement of this beautiful
dogma of meekness, for the eloquent revelations of love which are
associated with every fragment in reference to Florence, for the be-
witching delineation of a child's life and the exquisite picture of a
child's death, in the person of little Paul—*Dombey and Son* is assuredly
the masterpiece of Charles Dickens. There is in it no parallel passage,
it is true, to that most eloquent and even sublime reverie in the tower
of Saint Paul's Cathedral, which may be found in one of the random
and insulated chapters of *Master Humphrey's Clock*. There are no
separate paragraphs inspired with such rhetorical animation as those in
Barnaby Rudge, where the murderer is scared by the ringing of the
alarm-bell in the mansion of Mr Haredale, or where the populace are
casting fresh fuel before the burning doors of Newgate. *Dombey and
Son* has no Dick Swiveller, like the *Old Curiosity Shop*; no Brothers
Cheeryble, like *Nicholas Nickleby*; no Sarey Gamp or Seth Pecksniff,
like *Martin Chuzzlewit*. It is inferior to *Pickwick* in point of sustained
drollery, and to *Oliver Twist* in dramatic passion, and epic completeness.
In the three particulars already specified, however, *Dombey and Son*
surpasses every one of the preceding compositions of Mr Dickens; and
in several of the minor parts it is inimitably felicitous. Boxer [the dog

[1] Kent's dots.

in *The Cricket on the Hearth*] is altogether eclipsed by Diogenes; and the description of railway travelling is one of the happiest sketches of our novelist. Captain Cuttle, moreover, is one of the very best characters ever painted by him—a character which will after this occupy a prominent position in the Boz Gallery. . . .

68. [John Eagles], from 'A Few Words about Novels—a Dialogue', *Blackwood's Magazine*

October 1848, lxiv, 468–9

The Reverend John Eagles (1783–1855), a contributor to *Blackwood's* since 1831, had been educated at Oxford and in Italy, and was an artist, poet, and translator.

AQUILIUS—It is a great fault in a very popular novel writer of the day, that he will not give his readers credit for any imagination at all; every character is in extreme. . . . The inanimate nature must be made equally conspicuous, and every thing exaggerated. And it is often as forced in the expression as it is exaggerated in character. He has great powers, great genius, overflowing with matter, yet as a writer he wants agreeability: his satire is bitter, unnecessarily accumulated, and his choice of odious characters offers too frequently a disgusting picture of life.

CURATE—The worst is, that, with a genius for investing his characters with interest, by the events with which he links them together, in which he has so much art, that he compels persons of most adverse tastes to read him,—he is not a good-natured writer, and he evidently, it might be almost said professedly, writes with a purpose—and that I think a very mischievous one, and one in which he is to a certain extent joined by some other writers of the day—to decry, and bring into contempt as unfeeling, the higher classes. This is a very vulgar as well as evil taste, and is quite unworthy the genius of Mr Dickens. And, what is a great error in a novelist, he gives a very false view of life as it is. There is too much of the police-office reporter in all his works. *Dombey and Son* is, however, his greatest failure, as a whole. You give him credit for a deep plot and mystery, ere you have gone far; but it turns out—nothing. Admirable, indeed, are some things, parts and passages of wonderful power; but the spring that should have attached them has snapped, and they are, and ever will be, admired, only as scenes. The termination is miserable—a poor conclusion, indeed, of such a beginning; every thing is promised, nothing given, in conclusion. Some things are quite out of possibility. The whole conduct of the wife is out of nature. Such a character should have a deep cause for her conduct: she has none but the having married a disagreeable man, out of pique, from whom she runs away with one still more odious to herself and every one, and assumes, not a virtue which she has not, but a vice which she scorns, and glories in the stigma, because it wounds her husband. Such a high and daring mind, and from the commencement so scorning contamination, could not so degrade itself without having a stronger purpose than the given one. The entire change of character in Dombey is out of all nature—it is impossible; nor does the extraordinary affection of the daughter spring from any known principle of humanity. The very goodness of some of the accessory characters becomes wearisome, as the vice of others is disgusting.

AQUILIUS—After all, he is an uncomfortable writer: he puts you out of humour with the world, perhaps with yourself, and certainly with him as a writer. Yet let us acknowledge that he has done much good. He should be immortalised, if only for the putting down the school tyrannies, exposing and crushing school pretensions, and doubtless saving many a fair intellect from withering blight and perversion. He takes in hand fools, dolts, and knaves; but Dickens wants simpletonianism. He gave some promise that way in his *Pickwick Papers*, but it was not fulfilled.

69. [John Forster], from an unsigned review, *Examiner*

28 October 1848, 692–3

This review (much delayed: see headnote to No. 55) opens with Forster on the defensive against the new rage for Thackeray, but he had reviewed *Vanity Fair* generously in the *Examiner*, 22 July 1848 (see *Thackeray: the Critical Heritage*, 53–8). The author of *Two Old Men's Tales* (1834) is Mrs Anne Marsh. On Miss Tox's exclamation at the end of ch. xvi, subsequently deleted by Dickens, see articles by Kathleen Tillotson and D. S. Bland, *Dickensian*, March 1951 and Summer 1956.

There has been a criticism in vogue lately which consists in praising one writer at the expense of some other writer. You are instructed to admire A principally and primarily because you ought not to admire B. We cannot fall in with this fashion. Assuming that we admire A, we should be likely to think the more of B for not resembling him. Why talk of writers in this way, when we apply it to nothing else? The value of a thing consists in its being the thing itself, and not in its being some other thing. . . .

. . . We doubt if any writer that ever lived has inspired such strong feelings of personal attachment, in his impersonal character of author. He counts his readers by tens of thousands, and all of them 'unknown friends' with perhaps few exceptions. The wonderful sense of the real thrown into his ideal creations may sufficiently account for this. There was probably not a family in this country where fictitious literature is read, that did not feel the death of Paul Dombey as something little short of a family sorrow. What was said of it by the author of the *Two Old Men's Tales*, that it flung a nation into mourning, was hardly an exaggeration; and perhaps the extent and depth of the feeling was a surprise to even the author himself. Certainly it raised the interest in the story to a formidable height before the story was well launched, and what was meant but as the key-note to a more solemn after-strain had deepened into a pathos of its own too vivid to play that secondary part. Thus the exclamation which breaks from the weeping Miss Tox at the close of the celebrated chapter of Paul's death ('Dear me, dear me! to think that Dombey and Son should be a Daughter after all'), was felt as a jar at the time, and too light an intrusion on a solemn catastrophe; though it now guides us to what the author's intention really was, and enables us to judge of his design justly, as an entire and proportioned one. . . .

Generally of the book before us, as of most part of the later productions of Mr Dickens, we would say that with no abatement of the life and energy which in his earlier works threw out such forcible impressions of the actual, we have in a far higher degree the subtler requisites which satisfy imagination and reflection. For there is nature, in the common life of what she usually does; and there is nature, in the higher sense of what in given circumstances she might or would do; and from the latter the principal power of this novel is derived. But we are not certain if the appeal thus made is not to deeper sympathies than, in the swift and cursory reading which is one of the effects of serial publication, are always at hand to respond to it. In one of the later passages o eloquent reflection to be found in the book, the author speaks of what is 'most unnatural, and yet most natural in being so;' and this is probably what all his readers have not been able to concede, in the instance of Mr Dombey and his Wife. The past antecedents of both make the truth of the existing picture. . . .

Criticism on a book so extensively known is necessarily at some disadvantage. . . . But in . . . recalling to the reader's recollection the leading features of this remarkable book (which is all we profess to do), we have not found any falling off in that handling of common life with clearness, precision, and consistency of humorous delineation, which marked Mr Dickens' outset in literature. The satire is not less wholesome, the laugh not less hearty, the style not less natural, flexible, and manly. What we occasionally find when we would rather have it absent, is, that what should be, and would formerly have been, a mere instinct shown in the silent action of a character, has here and there come to be too much of a conscious feeling, and receives a too elaborate expression. This occurs in the comic as well as tragic portions. But the fault springs from an abundance of resource, and is perhaps inseparable from a power which is even yet not fully developed in its higher and more ideal tendencies. Much that the ordinary reader may pass carelessly in the book, will seize upon the fancy alive to poetical expression, and accustomed to poetical art. The recurrence of particular thoughts and phrases is an instance of the kind, running like the leading colour through a picture, or the predominant phrase in a piece of music, because subtly connected with the emotion which it is the design of the story to create.

[Forster illustrates this by tracing the 'sea' imagery.]

There is a beauty in these and similar passages which goes deeper than the pathos which all readers are ready to acknowledge; and the spell remains when the emotion is passed away. . . .

[Forster then offers samples of the abundant 'hearty mirth' to be found in the novel, and concludes his review thus:]

Among other characters not noticed in this hasty glance the reader will doubtless call to mind the choleric Indian Major (tough and sly J. B.), the sleek villain Carker, and the shaggy comforter Diogenes. The 'grey junior' and his sister should also have had a word, for they belong to a class of delineations suggesting tolerance and charity that can never be too strongly felt, and which will always endear Mr Dickens's books to the widest class of readers. His popularity in this respect is honourable both to giver and receiver; for in proportion as a man would show greater sympathy with the sufferings, and greater for-bearance towards the vices, of the wretched, we should be prepared to hear that he admires or is indifferent to the writings of the author of *Dombey and Son*.

70. Harriet Martineau on Dickens

1849, 1855

Harriet Martineau (1802–76), novelist, journalist, and popularizer of political economy, contributed to *Household Words* 1850–5. On (*a*), see Humphry House, *The Dickens World* (1941), 74–6. She also attacked Dickens's veracity in her *Special Legislation: the Factory Controversy* (Manchester, 1855), for the 'mis-statements' in *Household Words* and in *Hard Times* about the incidence of industrial accidents—though *Hard Times* was the less likely to do harm (she remarked) because 'the Tale, in its characters, conversations, and incidents, is so unlike life,—so unlike Lancashire and English life,— that it is deprived of its influence. Master and man are as unlike life in England, at present, as Ogre and Tom Thumb: and the result of the choice of subject is simply, that the charm of an ideal creation is gone, while nothing is gained in its stead' (p. 36). Her *Autobiography* was written in 1855, when she was expecting to die. In 1873, discussing Forster's *Life*, she remarked: 'At all times, in all his writings, Dickens opposed and criticized all existing legal plans for the relief of the poor' (*Autobiography* (1877), iii, 416). The *Autobiography* contains a sharp attack on Dickens's conduct of *Household Words*, explaining why she ceased contributing as a matter of principle (ii, 418–21).

(*a*) Last and greatest among the novelists [of the period] comes Charles Dickens—the Boz who rose up in the midst of us like a jin with his magic glass among some eastern people, showing forth what was doing in the regions of darkness, and in odd places where nobody ever thought of going to look. It is scarcely conceivable that any one should, in our age of the world, exert a stronger social influence than Mr Dickens has in his power. His sympathies are on the side of the suffering and the frail; and this makes him the idol of those who suffer, from whatever cause. We may wish that he had a sounder social philosophy, and that he could suggest a loftier moral to sufferers; could lead them to see that 'man does not live by bread alone,' and that his best happiness lies in those parts of his nature which are only animated and exalted by suffering, if it does not proceed too far; could show us something of the necessity and blessedness of homely and incessant self-discipline, and dwell a little less fondly on the grosser indulgences and commoner beneficence which are pleasant enough in their own place, but which can never make a man and society so happy as he desires them to become. We may wish for these things, and we may shrink from the exhibition of human miseries as an artistical study; but, these great drawbacks once admitted, we shall be eager to acknowledge that we have in Charles Dickens a man of a genius which cannot but mark the time, and accelerate or retard its tendencies. In as far as its tendencies are to 'consider the poor', and to strip off the disguises of cant, he is vastly accelerating them. As to whether his delineations are true to broad daylight English life, that may be for some time to come a matter of opinion on which men will differ. That they are, one and all, true to the ideal in the author's mind, is a matter on which none differ; while the inexhaustible humour, the unbounded power of observation, the exquisite occasional pathos, and the geniality of spirit throughout, carry all readers far away from critical thoughts, and give to the author the whole range of influence, from the palace-library to the penny book-club. (*A History of the Thirty Years' Peace 1815–1846*, Book 6, ch. xvi (1849; 1879 edn., iv, 438–9).

(*b*) There may be, and I believe there are, many who go beyond me in admiration of his works,—high and strong as is my delight in some of them. Many can more keenly enjoy his peculiar humour,—delightful as it is to me; and few seem to miss as I do the pure plain daylight in the atmosphere of his scenery. So many fine painters have been mannerists as to atmosphere and colour that it may be unreasonable to object to one more: but the very excellence and diversity of Mr Dickens's powers makes one long that they should exercise their full force under the broad open sky of nature, instead of in the most brilliant palace of art. While he tells us a world of things that are natural and even true, his personages are generally, as I suppose is undeniable, profoundly unreal. It is a curious speculation what effect his universally read works will have on the foreign conception of English character. Washington Irving came here expecting to find the English life of Queen Anne's days, as his *Sketchbook* shows; and very unlike his preconception was the England he found. And thus it must be with Germans, Americans, and French who take Mr Dickens's books to be pictures of our real life.

—Another vexation is his vigorous erroneousness about matters of science, as shown in *Oliver Twist* about the new poor-law (which he confounds with the abrogated old one) and in *Hard Times*, about the controversies of employers. Nobody wants to make Mr Dickens a Political economist; but there are many who wish that he would abstain from a set of difficult subjects, on which all true sentiment must be underlain by a sort of knowledge which he has not. The more fervent and inexhaustible his kindliness (and it is fervent and inexhaustible), the more important it is that it should be well-informed and well-directed, that no errors of his may mislead his readers on the one hand, nor lessen his own genial influence on the other.

The finest thing in Mr Dickens's case is that he, from time to time, proves himself capable of progress,—however vast his preceding achievements had been. In humour, he will hardly surpass *Pickwick*, simply because *Pickwick* is scarcely surpassable in humour: but in several crises, as it were, of his fame, when every body was disappointed, and his faults seemed running his graces down, there has appeared something so prodigiously fine as to make us all joyfully exclaim that Dickens can never permanently fail. It was so with *Copperfield*: and I hope it may be so again with the new work [*Little Dorrit*] which my survivors will soon have in their hands. (*Autobiography* (1877), ii, 378–9).

71. [Edwin P. Whipple], from 'Novels and Novelists: Charles Dickens', *North American Review*

October 1849, lxix, 383–407

Reprinted in Whipple's *Literature and Life* (Chapman's Library for the People, 1851), 20–41.

Whipple (1819–86), American critic and reviewer, was prominent in Boston literary circles. His useful series of essays on Dickens's novels, published in the *Atlantic Monthly* in the 1870s, were collected in *Charles Dickens: the Man and his Work*, with an Introduction by Arlo Bates (2 vols., Boston and New York, 1912). This collection also includes his Prefaces to the New Illustrated Library Edition of Dickens (New York, 1876–7). For other items by Whipple, see Nos. 94, 120, 134.

... Dickens as a novelist and prose poet is to be classed in the front rank of the noble company to which he belongs. He has revived the novel of genuine practical life, as it existed in the works of Fielding, Smollett, and Goldsmith; but at the same time has given to his materials an individual coloring and expression peculiarly his own. His characters, like those of his great exemplars, constitute a world of their own, whose truth to nature every reader instinctively recognizes in connection with their truth to Dickens. ... In painting character, he is troubled by no uneasy sense of himself. When he is busy with Sam Weller or Mrs Nickleby, he forgets Charles Dickens. Not taking his own character as the test of character, but entering with genial warmth into the peculiarities of others, and making their joys and sorrows his own, his perceptions are not bounded by his personality, but continually apprehend and interpret new forms of individual being; and thus his mind, by the readiness with which it genially assimilates other minds, and the constancy with which it is fixed on objects external to itself, grows with every exercise of its powers. ... His fellow-feeling with his race is his genius.

The humanity, the wide-ranging and healthy sympathies, and, especially, the recognition of the virtues which obtain among the poor and humble, so observable in the works of Dickens, are in a great degree characteristic of the age, and without them popularity can hardly be won in imaginative literature. The sentiment of humanity, indeed, or a hypocritical affectation of it, has become infused into almost all literature and speech, from the sermons of Dr Channing to the *feuilletons* of Eugène Sue. It is exceedingly difficult for a man to be as selfish and as narrow as he could have been had he lived a century ago. No matter how bigoted may be the tendencies of his nature, no matter how strong may be his desire to dwell in a sulky isolation from his race, he cannot breathe the atmosphere of his time without feeling occasionally a generous sentiment springing to his lips, without perceiving occasionally a liberal opinion stealing into his understanding. He cannot creep into any nook or corner of seclusion, but that some grand sentiment or noble thought will hunt him out, and surprise his soul with a disinterested emotion. In view of this fact, a bigot, who desires to be a man of the tenth century, who strives conscientiously to narrow his intellect and shut his heart, who mumbles the exploded nonsense of past tyranny and exclusiveness, but is still forced into some accommodation to the spirit of the age in which he lives, is worthy rather of the tender commiseration than the shrewish invective of the philanthropists whom he hates, but imitates.

Now Dickens has an open sense for all the liberal influences of his time, and commonly surveys human nature from the position of charity and love. For the foibles of character he has a sort of laughing toleration; and goodness of heart, no matter how overlaid with ludicrous weaknesses, has received from him its strongest and subtlest manifestations.

... He seems himself to be taken by surprise as his glad and genial fancies throng into his brain, and to laugh and exult with the beings he has called into existence in the spirit of a man observing, not creating. Squeers and Pecksniff, Sim Tappertit and Mark Tapley, Tony Weller and old Joe Willet, although painted with such distinctness that we seem to see them with the bodily eye, we still feel to be somewhat overcharged in the description. They are caricatured more in appearance than reality, and if grotesque in form, are true and natural at heart. Such caricature as this is to character what epigram is to fact,—a mode of conveying truth more distinctly by suggesting it through a brilliant exaggeration. When we say of a man, that he goes for the greatest good of the greatest number, but that the greatest number to him is number one, we express the fact of his selfishness as much as though we said it in a literal way. The mind of the reader unconsciously limits the extravagance into which Dickens sometimes runs, and, indeed, discerns the actual features and lineaments of the character shining the more clearly through it. Such extravagance is commonly a powerful stimulant to accurate perception, especially to readers who lack fineness and readiness of intellect. It is not that caricature which has no foundation but in

> The extravagancy
> And crazy ribaldry of fancy;

but caricature based on the most piercing insight into actual life; so keen, indeed, that the mind finds relief or pleasure in playing with its own conceptions. Shakspeare often condescends to caricature in this way, and so do Cervantes, Hogarth, Smollett, and Scott. Though it hardly approaches our ideal of fine characterization, it has its justification in the almost universal practice of men whose genius for humorous delineation cannot be questioned.

That Dickens is not led into this vein of exaggeration by those qualities of wit and fancy which make the caricaturist, is proved by the solidity with which his works rest on the deeper powers of imagination and humor. A caricaturist rarely presents any thing but a man's peculiarity, but Dickens always presents the man. He so preserves the keeping of character, that every thing said or done by his personages is either on a level with the original conception or develops it. They never go beyond the pitch of thought or feeling by which their personality is limited. Thus, Tony Weller, whose round fat body seems to roll about in a sea of humor, makes us laugh at his sayings as much because he says them, as for any merriment they contain in themselves. His oddities of remark are sufficiently queer to excite laughter, but they receive their peculiar unction from his conception of his own importance and his belief in the unreachable depths of his own wisdom. . . .

Much of the humor of Dickens is identical with his style. In this the affluence of his fancy in suggestive phrases and epithets is finely displayed; and he often flashes the impression of a character or a scene upon the mind by a few graphic verbal combinations. When Ralph Nickleby says 'God bless you,' to his nephew, the words stick in his throat, as if unused to the passage [ch. xix, to Kate, not Nicholas, Nickleby]. When Tigg clasped Mr Pecksniff in the dark, that worthy gentleman 'found himself collared by something which smelt like several damp umbrellas, a barrel of beer, a cask of warm brandy and water, and a small parlor full of tobacco smoke, mixed' [*Chuzzlewit*, ch. iv]. Mrs Todgers, when she desires to make Ruth Pinch know her station, surveys her with a look of 'genteel grimness' [ch. ix]. A widow of a deceased brother of Martin Chuzzlewit is described as one, who, 'being almost supernaturally disagreeable, and having a dreary face, a bony figure, and a masculine voice, was, in right of these qualities, called a strong-minded woman' [ch. iv]. Mr Richard Swiveller no sooner enters a room, than the nostrils of the company are saluted by a strong smell of gin and lemon-peel [*Old Curiosity Shop*. ch. xxxv]. Mr George Chuzzlewit, a person who over-fed himself, is sketched as a gentleman with such an obvious disposition to pimples, that 'the bright spots on his cravat, the rich pattern of his waistcoat, and even his glittering trinkets, seemed to have broken out upon him, and not to have come into existence comfortably' [ch. iv]. Felicities like these Dickens squanders with a prodigality which reduces their relative value, and makes the generality of style-mongers poor indeed.

DAVID COPPERFIELD

May 1849–November 1850

Few reviewers have prognosticated with such decisive erroneousness as the *Spectator's* on *David Copperfield*—'likely to be less popular than many of the previous tales of Mr Dickens, as well as rather more open to unfavourable criticism. . . . The first numbers are slow, not to say prosy; the same may be said of the last' (23 November 1850, xxiii, 119–20). This was of course Dickens's 'favourite child' (1867 Preface), and it immediately became, and remained, a general favourite. Not all admirers were as categorical as Tolstoy: 'If you sift the world's prose literature, Dickens will remain; sift Dickens, *David Copperfield* will remain; sift *David Copperfield*, the description of the storm at sea will remain' (quoted in *Dickensian*, xlv (1949), 144). But there was widespread agreement that *Copperfield* was his masterpiece (many of the 1870 obituary notices repeat this claim), and the storm was the standard example for any critic wanting to maintain that Dickens's gifts included a mastery of the sublime. This storm, it may be added, formed the conclusion to his public reading selected from *David Copperfield* (1861) and his rendering of this passage was generally acclaimed as the grandest moment in his performances.

Many readers, Forster remarks, had 'a suspicion, which though general and vague had sharpened interest not a little, that underneath the fiction lay something of the author's life' (*Life*, 547). The drift of the narrative—David's becoming a novelist, etc.—and the uniquely intimate tone of the Preface, indeed hinted as much, and some reviews mentioned this probability; but none of the reviews known to me pursue the speculation very far.

By coincidence, Thackeray's semi-autobiographical novel *Pendennis*, in which the hero also embarks on a literary career, was being serialized simultaneously (in 24 parts, November 1848–December 1850). Inevitably, many reviewers noticed both novels together: for summaries of other such reviews, see Dudley Flamm, *Thackeray's Critics: an annotated Bibliography of British and American Criticism 1836–1901* (Chapel Hill, 1966). See also A. A. Adrian, '*David Copperfield*: a

Century of critical and popular acclaim', *Modern Language Quarterly*, xi (1950), 325–31, and Jerry Don Vann, *'David Copperfield' and the Reviewers* (Ann Arbor, University Microfilms, 1968).

72. From an unsigned article, 'Charles Dickens and *David Copperfield*', *Fraser's Magazine*

December 1850, xlii, 698–710

Probably there is no single individual who, during the last fourteen years, has occupied so large a space in the thoughts of English folk as Charles Dickens. Not that these years have been by any means deficient in events. This time of profound peace (as it is officially designated) has seen many a contest fought out head to head, horn to horn, in the good old John Bull style. More than one combatant has distinguished himself from the herd, been hailed as veritable hero by all his brethren, *minus* one, and worshipped accordingly. During these fourteen years kings have been tumbled from their thrones and set up again, unless killed by the fall; ministers have been ousted and reinstalled; demagogues have been carried on the popular shoulders, and then trampled under the popular feet; innumerable reputations have flared up and gone out; but the name and fame of Charles Dickens have been exempt from all vicissitude. One might suppose him born to falsify all the common-places about the fickleness of public favour, to give the lie to all the proverbs, to destroy the resemblance of all the similes. In his case this same public favour is a tide that never ebbs, a moon that never wanes; his wheel of fortune has a spoke in it, and his *popularis aura* is a trade wind. Almost on his first appearance his own countrymen unanimously voted him a prophet, and have held by the doctrine with unrivalled devotion ever since. In every other subject men find matter for doubt, discussion, and quarrel. . . .

. . . Dickens only dwells in a little Goshen of his own, away from the shadow of criticism. The very mention of his 'last number' in any social gathering, is sure to be the signal for a chorus of eager admiration. Go where you will, it is the same. There is not a fireside in the kingdom where the cunning fellow has not contrived to secure a corner for himself as one of the dearest, and, by this time, one of the oldest friends of the family. In his company the country squire shakes his jolly sides, the City merchant smoothes his care-wrinkled forehead—as he tells his tale to misses in their teens, mammas, grandmammas, and maiden aunts—God bless them all—their eyes glisten and flow over with the precious diamond-drops of sympathy. We have been told, that when *The Old Curiosity Shop* was drawing to a close, he received heaps of anonymous letters in female hands, imploring him 'not to kill little Nell.' The wretch ungallantly persisted in his murderous design, and those gentle readers only wept and forgave him.

How are we to account for this wide-spread popularity? Not because the author is faultless—he is too human for that; not because his plots are of absorbing interest—neither Shakespeare's nor Scott's are so; but because of his kindly, all-pervading charity, which would cover a multitude of failings, because of his genial humour and exquisite comprehension of the national character and manners, because of his tenderness, because of his purity, and, above all, because of his deep reverence for the household sanctities, his enthusiastic worship of the household gods.

By means of all these blandishments he has nestled close to our hearts, and most men would as soon think of dissecting a first cousin as of criticizing Charles Dickens. Moreover, he is so thoroughly English, and is now part and parcel of that mighty aggregate of national fame which we feel bound to defend on all points against every attack. Upon our every-day language his influence has been immense—for better or worse. We began by using *Wellerisms* and *Gampisms* in fun, till they have got blended insensibly with our stock of conversational phrases; and now in our most serious moments we talk *slang* unwittingly, to the great disgust of the old school, who complain that, instead of seeking the 'well of English undefiled' by Twickenham, we draw at haphazard from the muddy stream that has washed Mile End. . .

[Before the end of 1836], 'Boz' was one of the most famous names in England. The young author had sprung at one bound over the heads of his elder rivals. He had penetrated into the very heart of public opinion, and carried it by storm before the advanced forts of criticism had had time to open their fire upon him. And so, when they did fire, it was only to hail the conqueror with a salvo of applause. For, if possession is nine-tenths of the law, it is all in all of the battle.

But a truce to these warlike metaphors, which cannot without force be applied to one who has done more, we verily believe, for the promotion of peace and goodwill between man and man, class and class, nation and nation, than all the congresses under the sun. One good joke and one general laugh melts reserve into hilarity, and converts the stiffest company into a set of 'jolly good fellows.' Boz, and men like Boz, are the true humanizers, and therefore the true pacificators, of the world. They sweep away the prejudices of class and caste, and disclose the common ground of humanity which lies beneath factitious, social, and national systems. They introduce the peasantry to the peerage, the grinder at the mill to the millionaire who owns the grist. They make John, Jean, and Jonathan, shake hands over the same board—which is not a board of green cloth by any means. Sam Weller, we suppose, made old England more 'merrie' than it had ever been since Falstaff drank, and roared, and punned, at the Globe Theatre. In the interval Britannia had grown haggard and sad, and worn with the double duty of taking care of the pence and providing sops for her lion to keep him couchant; and now, once more, the old lady laughed till the tears ran down her wrinkles. It has done her a world of good. La Belle France, too, who is somewhat chary of her applause, has condescended to pronounce Boz *un gentil enfant*; and Germania has learnt some things from him which were not dreamed of in her philosophy. For his fun is not mere fun. Had it been so we should have tired of it long ago. Deep truths are hidden, scarcely hidden, beneath....

[After a survey of Dickens's earlier works, the reviewer gets to *David Copperfield*.]

This ... is, in our opinion, the best of all the author's fictions. The plot is better contrived, and the interest more sustained, than in any other. Here there is no sickly sentiment, no prolix description, and scarcely a trace of exaggerated passion. The author's taste has become gradually more and more refined; his style has got to be more easy, graceful, and natural. The principal groups are delineated as carefully as ever; but instead of the elaborate Dutch painting to which we had been accustomed in his backgrounds and accessories, we have now a single vigorous touch here and there, which is far more artistic and far more effective. His winds do not howl, nor his seas roar through whole chapters, as formerly; he has become better acquainted with his readers, and ventures to leave more to their imagination. This is the first time that the hero has been made to tell his own story,—a plan which generally ensures something like epic unity for the tale. We have several reasons for suspecting that, here and there, under the name of David Copperfield, we have been favoured with passages from the personal history, adventures, and experience, of Charles Dickens. Indeed, this conclusion is in a manner forced upon us by the peculiar professions selected for the ideal character, who is first a newspaper reporter and then a famous novelist. There is, moreover, an air of reality pervading the whole book, to a degree never attained in any of his previous works, and which cannot be entirely attributed to the mere *form* of narration. We will extract one of the passages which seem most unquestionably autobiographical, and which have, therefore, a double interest for the reader (the 'book,' in all probability, was *Pickwick*).

[Quotes from the opening of ch. xlviii.]

David Copperfield the Younger was born at Blunderstone, near Yarmouth—there is really a village of that name. We do not know whether Charles Dickens was born there too; at all events, the number and minuteness of the local details indicate an intimate knowledge of, and fondness for, Yarmouth and its neighbourhood—which are anything but charming at first sight, or on a slight acquaintance. We have reason, however, to believe that the sons of the land are as honest and true-hearted Englishmen as you will find anywhere. We are indebted to one of them for the information that the local details in *Copperfield* are singularly accurate, only in one place he says 'the *sands*' where he ought, in Yarmouth phrase, to have said 'the *deens*.' Our friend also says that he has detected many Norfolk provincialisms in Dickens; for instance, he talks of '*standing* anything up,' where in current English one says 'setting' or 'placing.' Our author probably uses such phrases wittingly, in order to recommend them for general adoption.

Dickens is always great on the subject of childhood—that sunny time, as it is conventionally called, but which, as Dickens represents it, and as we recollect it, is somewhat showery withal. Little David is quite as successful a portrait as little Paul. . . .

Miss Trotwood, the kind-hearted ogress of an aunt, *fortiter in modo, suaviter in re*, is excellent throughout, though her admiration for Mr Dick passes the bounds of probability. About the husband, too, there is a mystery ending in nothing. The Micawbers, both Mr and Mrs, are glorious, with their long speeches, reckless improvidence, everlasting troubles, and hearty appetites; they must be of Irish extraction, though the author does not say so. We never read anything more deliciously absurd, more exquisitely ludicrous, than the following.

[Quotes the Medway Coal Trade passage from ch. xvii.]

One of the finest passages to be found in this, or indeed any, book, is that description of the storm at Yarmouth, which flings the dead body of the seducer on the shore, to lie amid the wrecks of the home he had desolated. The power of the artist impresses such an air of reality upon it all, that we do not think of questioning the probability of such poetical justice.

We have said that in *David Copperfield* there was *scarcely* a trace of exaggerated passion. But for Rosa Dartle, we should have said there was *no* trace. Her character we must think unnatural, and her conduct melodramatic. . . . Such a character is as incongruous and out of place as one of the tragedy queens from a minor theatre would be parading the Strand in full costume in common daylight. Fortunately Miss Dartle is not one of the most prominent characters, and only parades a back street, not the main thoroughfare, of the story. Mrs Dombey, in the former tale, was a blemish of the same kind, only more conspicuous. We hope the genus is becoming extinct, and that the next fictitious world of our author's creation will contain only the familiar animals, and be free from the visitations of any similar Mastodon. Such creatures are common in the Radcliffian formations. If resuscitated in our era, they can be nothing but galvanized fossils, salient anachronisms, frightful to all men.

This last paragraph of ours, which began in English, has slid somehow into Carlylese; which brings us to the *Latter-Day Pamphlets* in general, and No. II. in particular—that on Model Prisons—which has an immediate connexion with our present subject, inasmuch as our author has consigned his two villains-in-chief, Heep and Littimer, to one of these establishments, with the double purpose of punishing the former and satirizing the latter. Fourteen years ago he exposed (by means of the resolute Pickwick) our system, if system it could be called, of Imprisonment for Debt; now he assails our system, systematized to the last degree, of Imprisonment for Crime. . . .

[Quotes from Carlyle's 'Model Prisons' and from *David Copperfield*, ch. lxi, to show the similarities of judgment.]

The coincidence of opinion between the two authors is the more remarkable, as they are probably divided in opinion upon every other subject, secular or sacred. We even remember a passage in *Dombey and Son* which looks like an overt declaration of war against the great priest of Hero-worship.

However this may be, it is certain that no one has been more instrumental than Dickens in fostering that spirit of kindly charity which impels a man to do what he can, however narrow his sphere of action may be, to relieve the sufferings and to instruct the ignorance of his brethren; while Carlyle, on the other hand, treats all such efforts with lofty disdain, and would call them mere attempts to tap an ocean by gimlet-holes, or some such disparaging metaphor. But that is neither here nor there. What we are concerned with just now is, that we have two men, shrewd observers both, who, starting from the opposite poles of opinion, have for once coincided on a practical question. . . .

73. [David Masson], from 'Pendennis and Copperfield: Thackeray and Dickens', North British Review

May 1851, xv, 57–89

Masson (1822–1907), a young Scotsman, was making a living from writing textbooks; later he became Professor of English at University College, London, and at Edinburgh, author of the *Life of Milton*, and editor of *Macmillan's Magazine*. On Thackeray's and Dickens's reception of this review, see No. 74 and Masson's *Memories of London in the 'Forties* (1908), 243. Some of the material from this review-article was revised and incorporated into his *British Novelists and their Styles* (1859), 233–53 (reprinted in *The Dickens Critics*, ed. G. H. Ford and L. Lane (Ithaca, 1961), 25–37). The 'Critical Heritage' *Thackeray* volume contains (pp. 111–27) a long excerpt from this article, and may be consulted for various passages omitted in the present selection.

THACKERAY and DICKENS, Dickens and Thackeray—the two names now almost necessarily go together. . . . From the printing-house of the same publishers they have simultaneously, during the last few years, sent forth their monthly instalments of amusing fiction—Dickens his *Dombey* and his *Copperfield*, and Thackeray his *Vanity Fair* and his *Pendennis*. Hence the public has learned to think of them in indissoluble connexion as friendly competitors for the prize of light literature. There is, indeed, a third writer often and worthily named along with them— Mr Douglas Jerrold. But though, when viewed in the general as humorists and men of inventive talent, the three do form a triad, so that it is hardly possible to discuss the merits of any one of them without referring to the other two, yet, as the characteristic form of Mr Jerrold's literary activity has not been specially that of the popular novelist, he is not associated with his two eminent contemporaries so closely, in this denomination, as they are associated with each other. As the popular novelists of the day, Dickens and Thackeray, and again, Thackeray and Dickens, divide the public attention. . . .

It is admitted that both writers are as well represented in their last as in any of their previous productions. . . . When we say *Pendennis* and *Copperfield*, therefore, it is really the same as if we said Thackeray and Dickens. And this facility of finding the two authors duly contrasted in the two stories, is increased by the fact that the stories are in some respects very similar. In both we have the life and education of a young man related, from his childhood and school-time to that terminus of all novels, the happy marriage-point; in the one, the life and education of the orphan child of a poor gentleman in Suffolk; in the other, the life and education of the only son of a West of England squire, with a long Cornish pedigree. In both, too, the hero becomes a literary man, so that the author, in following him, finds room for allusions to London literary life. There are even some resemblances of a minuter kind, such as the existence in both stories of a mysterious character of the outlaw species, who appears at intervals to ask money and throw the respectable folks of the drama into consternation; from which one might imagine that the authors, during the progress of their narratives, were not ashamed to take hints from each other. But however that may be, there can be no doubt that the general external similarity that there is between the two stories will serve to throw into relief their essential differences of style and spirit.

These differences are certainly very great. Although following exactly the same literary walk, and both great favourites with the public, there are perhaps no two writers so dissimilar as Mr Dickens and Mr Thackeray. To begin with a matter which, though in the order of strict science it comes last, as involving and depending on all the others,—the matter of style or language: here everybody must recognize a remarkable difference between the two authors. . . . Mr Thackeray is the more terse and idiomatic, and Mr Dickens the more diffuse and luxuriant writer. Both seem to be easy penmen, and to have language very readily at their command; both also seem to convey their meaning as simply as they can, and to be careful, according to their notions of verbal accuracy; but in Mr Dickens's sentences there is a leafiness, a tendency to words and images, for their own sake; whereas in Mr Thackeray's one sees the stem and outline of the thought better. We have no great respect for that canon of style which demands in English writers the use of Saxon in preference to Latin words, thinking that a rule to which there are natural limitations, variable with the writer's aim and with the subject he treats; but we should suppose that critics who do regard the rule would find Mr Thackeray's style the more accordant with it. On the whole, if we had to choose passages at random to be set before young scholars as examples of easy and vigorous English composition, we would take them rather from Thackeray than from Dickens. There is a Horatian strictness, a racy strength, in Mr Thackeray's expressions, even in his more level and tame passages, which we miss in the corresponding passages in Mr Dickens's writings, and in which we seem to recognise the effect of those classical studies through which an accurate and determinate, though somewhat bald, use of words becomes a fixed habit. In the ease, and, at the same time, thorough polish and propriety with which Mr Thackeray can use slang words, we seem especially to detect the University man. . . . In Mr Dickens, of course, we have the same perfect taste and propriety; but in him the result appears to arise, if we may so express ourselves, rather from the keen and feminine sensibility of a fine genius, whose instinct is always for the pure and beautiful, than from the self-possession of a mind correct under any circumstances, by discipline and sure habit. . . .

Regarding the general intellectual calibre, for example, of the two men, viewing that as far as possible without reference to their special function as artistic writers, we should say that the passages we have quoted [the descriptions of the model prison in *Copperfield*, ch. lxi, and of the Inn of Court, *Pendennis*, ch. xxix] represent pretty fairly their average powers of thought; their competence, either by native faculty or acquired culture, to deal intellectually with any subject that might be submitted to them. Now, here again, our impression is, that Thackeray's is the mind of closer and more compact, Dickens's the mind of looser, richer, and freer texture. In the passage we have quoted from Thackeray there is certainly no positive or express display either of thought or of learning, and we would by no means cite it as a specimen of what he could do in the way either of speculation or of erudite allusion; still there is about it a knowingness, an air of general ability and scholarship, that suggests that the man who wrote it could take an influential place, if he chose, either in an assembly of critics, or in a committee of men of business. There is a general force of talent, a wordly shrewdness and sagacity, as well as a certain breadth of culture, latent in it, from which we argue that the writer would in any company make himself felt, if not as a man of energetic activity, at least as a man of quiet brain and vigour. Mr Dickens, too, is of course a man whose intellect would be remarkable anywhere; for no writer could rise to his degree of excellence in any department without much of that general force and fulness of mind which would have enabled him to excel in any other; perhaps, also, his natural versatility is greater than that of Mr Thackeray; still we do not see in him that habitual knowingness, that close-grained solidity of view, that impressive strong sense, which we find in what Thackeray writes. Mr Dickens may be the more pensive and meditative, but Mr Thackeray is the more penetrating and reflective writer. ... Dickens, we should suppose, would be more apt to fall into commonplace than Thackeray; indeed, in the passage on model prisons which we have quoted from *Copperfield*, and which, as it is an important passage, and controversial in its tone, may be regarded as a fair average specimen of Mr Dickens's habits as a thinker, it is only the soundness of the conclusion, and the evident sincerity of the feeling, that redeem the writing from a dangerous resemblance to common talk. Neither, on the one hand, does Mr Dickens deepen and elaborate his thoughts by special effort, which might be deemed unsuitable in a novel; nor, on the other hand, do all his thoughts on their first expression, carry with them that air of native weight which would belong, we imagine, to the opinions of Thackeray. A writer of Mr Dickens's celebrity ought not to devote a whole page to the repetition of what everybody says, in very nearly the same words that everybody uses. He ought, by giving his own reasons as profoundly as possible, to elevate and strengthen the common opinion. Here, of course, however, the same remark is of force that we applied to the matter of Mr Dickens's style. As Mr Dickens's language, though loose and redundant in the tame and level passages, gathers itself up and acquires concentration and melody under the influence of passion or pathos, so his thought, ordinarily lax and unwrought, attains real pith and volume when his feelings are moved. For this, we repeat, is the prerogative of an essentially susceptible and poetic nature, that every part and faculty of it, judgment as well as fancy, does its best when the frenzy is upon it. As a man, therefore, more capable of the poetic excitement than the majority of his literary contemporaries, Mr Dickens might occasionally, we think, strike into a *quæstio vexata* with peculiar effect, and render to the public a positive intellectual service. Still, our impression is, that as regards the possession and habitual practice of a cool, masculine, and decisive judgment, Thackeray's writings shew him to be a man more competent to exert an influence on current affairs. Dickens, when enthusiasm did call upon him to interfere, would act more resistlessly; but Thackeray would be the man of more sound and steady intelligence.

Yet, curiously enough, the two writers seem, in this respect, to have exchanged their parts. Dickens is by far the more opinionative and aggressive, Thackeray by far the more acquiescent and unpolemical, writer. The passage on model prisons quoted above, wherein Mr Dickens attacks the silent system of prison management, is but one instance out of hundreds in which he has, while pursuing his occupation as a novelist, pronounced strong judgments on disputed social questions. To whatever cause the fact is to be attributed—whether to a native combativeness conjoined with great benevolence of disposition, or to external circumstances that have developed in him the habit of taking a side in all current controversies—we should say, without hesitation, that few men, dominated so decidedly by the artistic temperament, have shewn so obvious an inclination as Mr Dickens to step beyond the province of the artist, and exercise the functions of the social and moral critic. . . . By means of pamphlets, public speeches, letters to the newspapers, articles in periodicals, and other such established methods of communicating with his fellow-subjects, he speaks his mind freely on practices or institutions that offend him. It ought, indeed, to be a matter for congratulation, when such a man comes forward to give a practical opinion at all; he ought to be listened to with special deference, and his suggestions ought to be carefully considered. Nor is it a secret that Mr Dickens, following the dictates of a warm and generous heart, has rendered, on various occasions, very zealous and important services to the cause of public morality and benevolence. Recently, indeed, his shrewd observation and brilliant powers of writing, have been employed from week to week in the express task of exposing certain anomalies and abuses in our social arrangements, lying, as it would seem, quite snugly out of sight of official vigilance.[1] In all this he merits only encouragement and success. We cannot, however, assent so easily to his habit of interspersing controversial remarks, and direct passages of social criticism and remonstrance, through his fictions. Clearly as these works belong to the department of artistic writing, there is not one of them that does not contain matter that is purely dogmatic in its import—judgments pronounced promptly and peremptorily by Mr Dickens in his own name on various questions of morals, taste, or legislation. Prison-discipline, the constitution of the ecclesiastical courts, the management of schools, capital punishments;

[1] *Household Words* had started publication on 30 March 1850.

Mr Dickens's opinions on these, and many other such topics of a practical kind, are to be found explicitly affirmed and argued in his novels. Nor is he content with expressing his views merely on practical points. Modes of thinking, doctrines, theological and speculative tendencies, likewise come in for a share of his critical notice. Passages might be quoted from his stories, for example, where he has distinctly attacked and denounced transcendentalism in philosophy, and puritanism in religion. Now, of course, a man must have his views on these subjects, and these views must break out in his works, however artistic their form; but it is a dangerous thing thus openly and professedly to blend the functions of the artist with those of the declaimer. . . . For our respect for the talent a man shews as an artist, ought not, as a matter of course, to extend itself so as to shelter all his dicta as a moralist or practical politician. It may be requisite to adjust our relations to him differently, according as he talks to us in the one capacity or in the other. We may owe one degree of respect for Mr Dickens as the describer of Squeers and Creakle, and quite another degree of respect when he tells us how he would have boys educated. Mr Spenlow may be a capital likeness of a Doctors' Commons lawyer; and yet this would not be the proper ground for concluding Mr Dickens's view of a reform in the ecclesiastical courts to be right. No man has given more picturesque illustrations of criminal life in London than Mr Dickens; yet he might not be equally trustworthy in his notions of prison-discipline. His Dennis the hangman in *Barnaby Rudge* is a powerfully conceived character; yet this is no reason for accepting his opinion on capital punishments. In short, the arguments and opinions of an artist must stand on their own merits, with this additional proviso that, for permitting an artist to argue at all, we require him to argue right-royally, like an Apollo in the robe of a barrister. True, very many of Mr Dickens's judgments on practical matters are sound and excellent—some of those we have alluded to in the number; on some points, however, and especially in those higher regions of speculative doctrine into which we have said that Mr Dickens has not seldom ventured, we believe his sentiments to be defective. . . .

Mr Thackeray, though more competent, according to our view of him, to appear in the character of a general critic or essayist, seems far more of a *pococurante* than Mr Dickens. Whether it is that he is naturally disposed to take the world as he finds it, or that, having at some time or other had very unsatisfactory experience of the trade of trying to mend it, he has taken up *pococurantism* as a theory, we have no means of saying; but certain it is, that in the writings he has given forth since he became known as one of our most distinguished literary men, he has meddled far less with the external arrangements of society than Mr Dickens, and made far fewer appearances as a controversialist or reformer. . . .

. . . The artistic faculty of Dickens is more comprehensive, goes over a wider range of the whole field of art, than that of Thackeray. Take Dickens, for example, in the landscape or background department. Here he is capable of great variety. He can give you a landscape proper —a piece of the rural English earth in its summer or in its winter dress, with a bit of water, and a pretty village spire, in it; he can give you, what painters seldom attempt, a great patch of flat country by night, with the red trail of a railway train traversing the darkness; he can even succeed in a sea-piece; he can describe the crowded quarter of a city, or the main street of a country town, by night or by day; he can paint a garden, sketch the interior of a cathedral, or daguerreotype the interior of a hut or drawing-room with equal ease; he can even be minute in his delineations of single articles of dress or furniture. Take him, again, in the figure department. Here he can be an animal-painter with Landseer when he likes, as witness his dogs, ponies, and ravens; he can be a historical painter, as witness his description of the Gordon riots; he can be a portrait-painter or a caricaturist like Leech; he can give you a bit of village or country life, like Wilkie; he can paint a haggard or squalid scene of low city-life, so as to remind one of some of the Dutch artists, Rembrandt included, or a pleasant family-scene, gay or senti- mental, reminding one of Maclise or Frank Stone; he can body forth romantic conceptions of terror or beauty, that have risen in his own imagination; he can compose a fantastic fairy piece; he can even succeed in a powerful dream or allegory, where the figures are hardly human. The range of Thackeray, on the other hand, is more restricted. . . .

On the whole it may be said that, while there are few things that Mr Thackeray can do in the way of description which Mr Dickens could not also do, there is a large region of objects and appearances familiar to the artistic activity of Mr Dickens, where Mr Thackeray would not find himself at home. And as Mr Dickens's artistic range is thus wider than that of Mr Thackeray, so also his style of art is the more elevated. Thackeray is essentially an artist of the real school; he belongs to what, in painting, would be called the school of low art. All that he portrays —scenes as well as characters—is within the limits, and rigidly true to the features, of real existence. In this lies his particular merit; and, like Wilkie,[1] he would probably fail, if, hankering after a reputation in high art, he were to prove untrue to his special faculty as a delineator of actual life. Dickens, on the other hand, works more in the ideal. It is nonsense to say of his characters generally, intending the observation for praise, that they are life-like. They are nothing of the kind. Not only are his serious or tragic creations—his Old Humphreys, his May-pole Hughs, his little Nells, &c.—persons of romance; but even his comic or satiric portraitures do not come within the strict bounds of the real. There never was a real Mr Pickwick, a real Sam Weller, a real Mrs Nickleby, a real Quilp, a real Micawber, a real Uriah Heep, or a real Toots, in the same accurate sense that there has been or might be a real Major Pendennis, a real Captain Costigan, a real Becky, a real Sir Pitt Crawley, and a real Mr Foker. Nature may, indeed, have furnished hints of Wellers and Pickwicks, may have scattered the germs or indications of such odd fishes abroad; and, having once added such characters to our gallery of fictitious portraits, we cannot move a step in actual life without stumbling upon individuals to whom they will apply most aptly as nicknames—good-humoured bald-headed old gentlemen, who remind us of Pickwick; careless, easy spendthrifts of the Micawber type; fawning rascals of the Heep species; or bashful young gentlemen like Toots. But, at most, those characters are real only thus far, that they are transcendental renderings of certain hints furnished by nature. Seizing the notion of some oddity as seen in the real world, Mr Dickens has run away with it into a kind of outer or ideal region, there to play with it and work it out at leisure as extravagantly as he might choose, without the least impediment from any facts except those of his own story. One result of this method is, that his characters do not present the mixture of good and bad in the same proportions as we find in nature. Some of his characters are thoroughly and ideally perfect; others are thoroughly and ideally detestable; and even in those where he has intended a mingled impression, vice and virtue are blended in a purely ideal manner. It is different with Mr Thackeray. The last words of his *Pendennis* are a petition for the charity of his readers in behalf of the principal personage of the story, on the ground that not having meant to represent him as a hero, but 'only as a man and a brother,' he has exposed his foibles rather too freely. So, also, in almost all his other characters his study seems to be to give the good and the bad together, in very nearly the same proportions that the

[1] Sir David Wilkie (1785–1841), R.A., painter of domestic subjects.

cunning apothecary, Nature herself, uses. Now, while, according to Mr Thackeray's style of art, this is perfectly proper, it does not follow that Mr Dickens's method is wrong. The characters of Shakespeare are not, in any common sense, life-like. They are not portraits of existing men and women, though doubtless there are splendid specimens even of this kind of art among them; they are grand hyperbolic beings created by the breath of the poet himself out of hints taken from all that is most sublime in nature; they are humanity caught, as it were, and kept permanent in its highest and extremest mood, nay carried forth and compelled to think, speak, and act in conditions superior to that mood. As in Greek tragedy, the character that an artist of the higher or poetical school is expected to bring before us, is not, and never was meant to be, a puny 'man and brother,' resembling ourselves in his virtues and his foibles, but an ancestor and a demigod, large, superb, and unapproachable. Art is called Art, says Goethe, precisely because it is *not* Nature; and even such a department of art as the modern novel is entitled to the benefit of this maxim. While, therefore, in Mr Thackeray's style of delineation, the just ground of praise is, as he claims it to be, the verisimilitude of the fictions, it would be no fair ground of blame against Mr Dickens in *his* style of delineation, to say that his fictions are hyperbolic. A truer accusation against him, in this respect, would be that, in the exercise of the right of hyperbole, he does not always preserve harmony; that, in his romantic creations, he some-times falls into the extravagant, and, in his comic creations, sometimes into the grotesque.

But, while Mr Dickens is both more extensive in the range, and more poetic in the style of his art than Mr Thackeray, the latter is, perhaps, within his own range and in his own style, the more careful artist. His stroke is truer and surer, and his attention to finish greater. . . . But, after all, it is by the moral spirit and sentiment of a work of fiction, by that unity of view and aim which pervades it, and which is the result of all the author's natural convictions and endowments, all his experi-ence of life, and all his intellectual conclusions on questions great and little—it is by this that the worth of a work of fiction, and its title to an honourable place in literature, ought ultimately to be tried. Even the consideration of artistic merit will be found ultimately to be involved in this. The characters and scenes of a novelist, and the mode in which he evolves his plot from the commencement to the catastrophe, are but the special means by which, in his particular craft, it is allowed him to explain his beliefs and philosophy. Whether he does so consciously

DICKENS

or unconsciously, whether he boasts of his philosophic purpose, or
scouts the idea of having such a purpose, it is all the same. It remains for
us, therefore, to go somewhat deeper than we have hitherto done, in
our discrimination of the spirit of Thackeray's, as compared with the
spirit of Dickens's writings. Here also *Pendennis* and *Copperfield* shall
form the chief ground of our remarks.

Into this important question, as between the two novelists, the
public has already preceded us. Go into any circle where literary talk
is common, or take up any popular critical periodical, and the same
invariable dictum will meet you—that Dickens is the more genial,
cheerful, kindly, and sentimental, and Thackeray the more harsh, acrid,
pungent, and satirical writer. This is said everywhere. Sometimes the
criticism even takes the form of partizanship. We have known amiable
persons, and especially ladies, express, with many admissions of
Thackeray's talent, a positive dislike to him as a writer—grounding
this dislike on his evident tendency to fasten on the weaknesses and
meannesses, rather than on the stronger and nobler traits, of human
nature. . . . On the other hand, there are persons, and ladies too among
them, who take Thackeray's part, and prefer his unsparing sarcasm,
bracing sense, and keen wit, to what they are pleased to call the sentimentalism of his rival. From what we have observed, however, we
should think that Mr Thackeray's partizans are the fewer in number. . . .

Kindliness is the first principle of Mr Dickens's philosophy, the sum
and substance of his moral system. He does not, of course, exclude such
things as pain and indignation from his catalogue of legitimate existences; indeed, as we have seen, few writers are capable of more honest
bursts of indignation against what is glaringly wrong; still, in what may
be called his speculative ethics, kindliness has the foremost place. His
purely doctrinal protests in favour of this virtue, would, if collected,
fill a little volume. His Christmas Books have been, one and all, fine
fantastic sermons on this text; and, in his larger works, passages abound
enforcing it. Not being able to lay our hands at this moment on any
passage of this kind in *Copperfield*, short, and at the same time characteristic, we avail ourselves of the following from *Barnaby Rudge* [ch.
xxv].

Mr Dickens's Apology for Mirth.—'It is something even to look upon enjoyment, so that it be free and wild, and in the face of nature, though it is but the
enjoyment of an idiot. . . .' [etc.]

This doctrine, we repeat, is diffused through all Mr Dickens's writings, and is affirmed again and again in express and very eloquent passages. Now, certainly, there is a fine and loveable spirit in the doctrine; and a man may be borne up by it in his airy imaginings, as Mr Dickens is, (we might add the name of Mr Leigh Hunt,) so cheerily and beautifully, that it were a barbarity to demur to it at the moment without serious provocation. Who can fail to see that only a benevolent heart, overflowing with faith in this doctrine, could have written the *Christmas Chimes* [*sic*], or conceived those exquisite reminiscences of childhood which delight us in the early pages of *Copperfield*? But when Mr Dickens becomes aggressive in behalf of his doctrine, as he does in the foregoing, and in fifty other passages; when, as Mr Cobden is pugnacious for peace, and as some men are said to be bigots for toleration, so Mr Dickens is harsh in behalf of kindliness—then a word of remonstrance seems really necessary. . . . In short, in his antipathy to Puritanism, Mr Dickens seems to have adopted a principle closely resembling that which pervades the ethical part of Unitarianism, the essence of which is, that it places a facile disposition at the centre of the universe. Now, without here offering any speculative or spiritual discussion, which might be deemed inappropriate, we may venture to say, that any man or artist who shall enter upon his sphere of activity, without in some way or other realizing and holding fast those truths which Puritanism sets such store by, and which it has embodied, according to its own grand phraseology, in the words sin, wrath, and justice, must necessarily take but half the facts of the world along with him, and go through his task too lightly and nimbly. To express our meaning in one word, such a man will miss out that great and noble element in all that is human—the element of *difficulty*. And though Mr Dickens's happy poetic genius suggests to him much that his main ethical doctrine, if it were practically supreme in his mind, would certainly leave out, yet we think we can trace in the peculiar character of his romantic and most merry phantasies something of the want of this element. . . .

74. Thackeray, in a letter to David Masson.

6(?) May 1851

(*Letters and Private Papers*, ii, 772–3), thanking him for his review-article on '*Pendennis* and *Copperfield*' (No. 73).

... I think Mr Dickens has in many things quite a divine genius so to speak, and certain notes in his song are so delightful and admirable, that I should never think of trying to imitate him, only hold my tongue and admire him. I quarrel with his Art in many respects: w^h I don't think represents Nature duly; for instance Micawber appears to me an exaggeration of a man, as his name is of a name. It is delightful and makes me laugh: but it is no more a real man than my friend Punch is: and in so far I protest against him—and against the doctrine quoted by my Reviewer from Goethe too—holding that the Art of Novels *is* to represent Nature: to convey as strongly as possible the sentiment of reality—in a tragedy or a poem or a lofty drama you aim at producing different emotions; the figures moving, and their words sounding, heroically: but in a drawing-room drama a coat is a coat and a poker a poker; and must be nothing else according to my ethics, not an embroidered tunic, nor a great red-hot instrument like the Pantomime weapon. But let what defects you (or rather I), will, be in Dickens's theory—there is no doubt according to my notion that his writing has one admirable quality—it is charming—that answers everything. Another may write the most perfect English have the greatest fund of wit learning & so forth—but I doubt if any novel-writer has that quality, that wonderful sweetness & freshness w^h belongs to Dickens—

75. Samuel Phillips, from 'David Copperfield and Arthur Pendennis', *The Times*

11 June 1851, 8

Reprinted in Phillips's *Second Series of Essays from 'The Times'* (1854), 320–38. A different and longer selection reprinted in *Thackeray: the Critical Heritage*, ed. Geoffrey Tillotson and Donald Hawes (1968), 129–35.

Wrongly attributed to W. H. Stowe, in *The History of 'The Times'* (1939), ii, 487. Phillips (1814–54), on the staff of *The Times* since 1845, was unfavourably disposed towards Thackeray. Dickens had suspected that Phillips was ill-disposed to himself, too: he had identified the author of the earlier attacks on him in *The Times* (see No. 43) as 'a Jew of the name of Phillips', who has volunteered these attacks 'in return for old acts of good nature on my part'. He threatened to break down this kind of anonymous stabbing and 'nail up said Phillips by name on the cover of *Dombey*' (*To Thomas Beard*, 22 March 1847). The review of *Copperfield* is not hostile, however; most of it is a routine comparison between Dickens and Thackeray with lengthy summaries of the plots of their two novels.

In *David Copperfield* [compared with *Pendennis*] there are more contrasts of character, more varieties of intellect, a more diverse scenery, and more picturesqueness of detail. It is the whole world rather than a bit of it which you see before you. There is first the childhood, vividly painted, happy and unsuspicious, with its ideas and feelings not at all overdone; in *Pendennis*, on the contrary, you have rather the fact that he was once a child than childhood described. There are, secondly— and it is an artifice of which Mr Dickens is somewhat too fond,—some people without wits in his tale. With Mr Batley we find no fault, for he is a pendant to Miss Trotwood, who could ill be spared; but Dora is an infliction. . . . The Yarmouth group, again, is no exaggeration, and, while introducing another of Mr Dickens's merits, the power of description gives at once the effect of a general contrast running through the tale, and absorbs as much interest as the central figures by the force and dignity of the delineation; the depth of feeling revealed in Mr Peggotty and in Ham, the energetic patience of one, the passive endurance of the other, not less than Mrs Gummidge's sudden conversion from querulousness to activity and self-forgetfulness, are the evidence at once of knowledge and of imagination. Nor is the mute Mr Barkis's expressive gesture or the leg-rubbing and strong vernacular of the boatmen, less true to the life. What we cannot allow to Mr Dickens is the invariable fidelity which accompanies Mr Thackeray's characters. There are cases where his facts are not so true as his ideas. It might be quite true, for instance, that Miss Dartle would hate Steerforth's victim with all the rancour of jealousy; but it is very unlikely that she should seek her out in order to reproach her with her shame, and gloat over her misery with the fiendish violence ascribed to her. The thing is altogether overstrained. We have already said that Dora is not a fact, and we must extend the censure to a frequent want of truth in language, not that the dialect of Mr Peggotty is less racy than the brogue of Captain Costigan, but that in any passage of sentiment Mr Dickens lets the sentiment run away with him. Who ever heard of one young man saying gravely to another, 'You are always equally loved and cherished in my heart,' [ch. xxix] or of a bride who has just entered the travelling carriage coming out with so Tennysonian a decasyllabic as—

It grows out of the night when Dora died? [ch. lxii]

—a fault this, which grows out of the over-poetical tendencies of the author, tendencies discoverable enough in all his works, and evidenced as much, perhaps, in the characters of Barnaby Rudge and Paul Dombey as in any discursiveness of mere expression.

. . . As in language, so in exterior and manners, Mr Thackeray's people are less marked. He does not wish to individualise. Mr Dickens has a perfect passion for being particular, as if the portrait might be wanted in the *Hue and Cry*. We must suppose either that people in the best society have not their little tricks—tricks of the body, that is—or else that Mr Dickens has an unnatural faculty of detecting them. All the accessory characters in his books gesticulate. They have a hundred little ways of identifying themselves. . . . The effect of all this is that you trace something genuine in Mr Thackeray's figures more easily than you do in Mr Dickens's. You have not such a series of peculiarities to separate before you can regard the nature by itself. . . . Compare the tone of the two books, and one will be found, as a whole, light-hearted and hopeful, the other dolorous and depressing. Both books are comic in much of their expression, for both writers are humorists, but the humour of one is more gloomy than that of the other, as if from a shadow fallen upon a life. While in *David Copperfield* the tragedy is consummated in a single chapter, in *Pendennis* it is spread over the whole surface of the story. In the former case a man is slain; in the latter case human aspirations and complacencies are demolished. Rising from the perusal of Mr Dickens's work, you forget that there is evil in the world, and remember only the good. The distinction drawn between the bad and good is a broad one. Rising from Mr Thackeray's, you are doubtful of yourself and of humanity at large, for nobody is very bad or very good, and everybody seems pretty well contented. The *morale* might almost be summed up into the American's creed, 'There's nothing new, there's nothing true, and it don't signify.' One might almost fancy that Mr Thackeray had reduced his own theory of life to that average which he strikes from the practice of all around him. We are brought into a mess and left there, woman's love and purity being the only light upon our path. Mr Dickens touches a higher key; his villains, Heep and Littimer, stand out as villains; his women—and we may take my Aunt and Agnes as equally faithful pictures,—hold an eminence which women may and do reach in this world, and which mere purity and love do not suffice to attain.

. . . As to actual influence, we should, for the reasons aforesaid, assign the higher place to Mr Dickens, partly because the expressed morality comes forth as something definite, the fruit of personal experience, yet conveyed through a personage of the tale, partly because the highest lessons inculcated, such as those of faith in Mr Peggotty and resignation in Ham, are some of the highest that can be inculcated, and partly, also, because the world which Mr Thackeray experiments on is a world of salamanders, fireproof, inclined to disbelieve that the lesson they can criticise may possibly increase their condemnation. Each rejoices to be what he is. Foker and Major Pendennis rejoice in their portraits, save that the latter don't think he is so 'doosedly' made up after all. You may as well write at them as preach at them; and did not the Major go to church? Perfect as *Pendennis* is, then, in execution, we are bound, when weighing it with *Copperfield*, to adjudge the chief merit where the most universal interest is conciliated and the most exalted teaching hidden beneath the tale. The epic is greater than the satire.

76. From an unsigned review, 'David Copperfield and Pendennis', Prospective Review

July 1851, vii, 157–91

The *Prospective* was 'a Quarterly Journal of Theology and Literature', formerly named *The Christian Teacher*.

. . . The serial tale . . . is probably the lowest artistic form yet invented; that, namely, which affords the greatest excuse for unlimited departures from dignity, propriety, consistency, completeness, and proportion. In it, wealth is too often wasted in reckless and riotous profusion, and poverty is concealed by mere superficial variety, caricature, violence, and confused bustle. Nine-tenths of its readers will never look at it or think of it as a whole. A level number, however necessary to the development of the story, will be thrown aside like a flat article in a newspaper. No fault will be found with the introduction of any character or any incident however extravagant or irrelevant, if it will amuse for an hour the lounger in the coffee-room or the traveller by railway. With whatever success men of genius may be able to turn this form to their highest purposes, they cannot make it a high form of art, nor can their works in that kind ever stand in the first class of the products of the imagination. In very many cases the difficulties attending a mode of writing are no unfair measure of its capabilities; but then they must be difficulties which, when once well overcome, are not merely neutralized and rendered harmless, but actually add strength, richness or refinement to the work in hand. Of this latter class are the difficulties of a subtle metre, a varied plot, the exclusion of inferior aids (as description and disquisition are excluded from dramas), and an elaborate compactness and polish of style. *Lycidas*, the *School for Scandal*, *Hamlet*, and the *Rape of the Lock*, are instances in point. But to achieve completeness *in spite* of a straggling form, or dignity *in spite* of a trifling one, though it may show the power of the author, involves a waste of power and consequent deterioration of art. The waste carries with it its own sure retribution, and thus although we are of opinion that *David Copperfield* is a signal triumph over the disadvantages of a bad form, we do not believe that this will or ought to give to it the rank of a classic, or that those who read it for the first time in a collected shape will bear any appreciable proportion to those who have read it as it was coming out, or that its highest qualities will ever be very widely recognised. No blame to the author for this. He who has the instinct to pour forth such multitudinous and multiform images of man's life, and in such prolific haste as Dickens and Thackeray, must have his veins full to bursting with the life of his own age, for any one otherwise constituted is quickly exhausted; and we think that such a man will take his general forms as the spirit of his time puts them into his hand. The modern epic, the modern Elizabethan play, the modern historical painting, have an academical, imitative look, which stamps their producers as the scholars, not the younger brethren of those who are on all hands admitted to have been born to the manner. . . .

We turn with peculiar pleasure to *David Copperfield*, because we are able to say of it that it affords ample evidence of the undiminished vigour of Mr Dickens's powers. There has been a general opinion, in which we have shared, that his later works have not been entitled to rank with *Oliver Twist* and its predecessors. There has been too much sentimentality (though not of a bad case), too much of the melodramatic and unnatural. If Mr Thackeray gives us an overdose of selfishness, Mr Dickens has heretofore treated us to too much Quixotism; and what the former says of women, that they are always sacrificing themselves or somebody for somebody else's sake, is strictly true of too large a proportion of the characters drawn by the latter. This spirit of gratuitous martyrdom was carried to a pitch of extreme absurdity in the *Battle of Life*, where one of the heroines makes believe to elope with a man whom she does not love, in order to give her sister, who is by no means in a pining condition, the opportunity of marrying the man whom the fair runaway loves, and by whom she is beloved. *Martin Chuzzlewit* is very much the best of the later works preceding *David Copperfield*; but *Dombey and Son* was a sad falling off, and led many to despair of ever reading anything more from Mr Dickens which was not either overcharged or caricatured. He seemed likewise to have had the misfortune to strike into a vein of fine writing, yielding whole pages which might have been read off into rather bombastic blank verse. At the same time he had acquired so strong a hold upon every one's regard that his faults were very gently dealt with, and it is with something like a personal feeling of pleasure that we have read his present fresh, healthy book, marked with easy originality from beginning to end, and almost as free from the chief errors of his later style as the *Pickwick Papers* themselves. . . .

The tendency to Quixotism mentioned above has not wholly disappeared from Mr Dickens's mind. His exclusion of selfishness is over-conscious, and sometimes more far-fetched than Mr Thackeray's introduction of it. We are quite sure that when Mr Peggotty was describing his reunion with his niece, and had said, 'You may believe me, when I heerd her voice as I had heerd at home, so playful, and see her humbled as it might be in the dust our Saviour wrote in with his blessed 'and—I felt a wownd go to my 'art in the midst of all its thankfulness;'—he did not continue thus:—'It warn't for long as I felt that; for she was found; I had only to think as she was found, and it was gone. I don't know why I do so much as mention of it now, I'm sure. I hadn't it in my mind a minute ago, to say a word about myself, but it come up so nat'ral that I yielded to it afore I was aweer.' [ch. li] People like Mr Peggotty happily do yield to such natural feelings, without being 'aware' of it, for the purpose either of suppression or repentance. Of a similar kind is David's scruple which withheld him from putting an end to the torturing conversation between Miss Dartle and Emily, because it was for Mr Peggotty to see her and recover her. Perhaps this is one of the few cases in which it was thought necessary to use a roundabout means for reporting conversation in which the narrator did not take part. But indeed Miss Dartle herself is the chief failure in the work. . . .

We cannot refuse ourselves and our readers the pleasure of quoting one passage, not because it is the finest (for indeed the work is too equable to render quotation easy), but because it is one of those numerous ones which will give to those who have read the whole more pleasure on recurrence than it could at the first reading. It describes the beginning of David Copperfield's holiday visit to Yarmouth in the company of Steerforth, from which the more tragic interest of the tale dates. [A seven-page quotation from ch. xxi.]

77. Matthew Arnold, from 'The Incompatibles', *Nineteenth Century*

June 1881, ix, 1034–42

Reprinted in Arnold's *Irish Essays* (1882), 43–53.
Arnold (1822–88) wrote very little, in his published criticism or
even in his letters, about current English fiction. Nor does he seem
to have read Dickens much: several other novels would have
made his point better than *Copperfield*. In this essay he is writing
about the Irish problem. The Irish, he explains, do not much
come across the English aristocracy: 'What they do come across,
and what gives them their idea of our civilization, and of its
promise, is our middle class.'

... Much as I have published, I do not think it has ever yet happened
to me to comment in print upon any production of Charles Dickens.
What a pleasure to have the opportunity of praising a work so sound,
a work so rich in merit, as *David Copperfield! 'Man lese nicht die
mitstrebende, mitwirkende!'* says Goethe: 'Do not read your fellow-
strivers, your fellow-workers!' Of the contemporary rubbish which is
shot so plentifully all round us, we can, indeed, hardly read too little.
But to contemporary work so good as *David Copperfield* we are in
danger of perhaps not paying respect enough, of reading it (for who
could help reading it?) too hastily, and then putting it aside for something else and forgetting it. What treasures of gaiety, invention, life,
are in that book! what alertness and resource! what a soul of good
nature and kindness governing the whole! Such is the admirable work
which I am now going to call in evidence.

Intimately, indeed, did Dickens know the middle class; he was bone
of its bone and flesh of its flesh. Intimately he knew its bringing up.
With the hand of a master he has drawn for us a type of the teachers
and trainers of its youth, a type of its places of education. Mr Creakle
and Salem House are immortal. The type itself, it is to be hoped, will
perish; but the drawing of it which Dickens has given cannot die.

Mr Creakle, the stout gentleman with a bunch of watch-chain and seals, in an arm-chair, with the fiery face and the thick veins in his forehead; Mr Creakle sitting at his breakfast with the cane, and a newspaper, and the buttered toast before him, will sit on, like Theseus, for ever. For ever will last the recollection of Salem House, and of 'the daily strife and struggle' there. . . .

A man of much knowledge and much intelligence, Mr Baring Gould, published not long ago a book about Germany, in which he adduced testimony which, in a curious manner, proves how true and to the life this picture of Salem House and of Mr Creakle is. The public schools of Germany come to be spoken of in that book, and the training which the whole middle class of Germans gets in them; and Mr Gould mentions what is reported by young Germans trained in their own German schools, who have afterwards served as teachers of foreign languages and ushers in the ordinary private schools for the middle class in England. With one voice they tell us of establishments like Salem House and principals like Mr Creakle. They are astonished, disgusted. They cannot understand how such things can be, and how a great and well-to-do class can be content with such an ignoble bringing up. But so things are, and they report their experience of them, and their experience brings before us, over and over again, Mr Creakle and Salem House.

A critic in the *World* newspaper says, what is very true, that in this country the middle class has no naturally defined limits, that it is difficult to say who properly belong to it and who do not, and that the term, *middle class*, is taken in different senses by different people. This is most true. And therefore, for my part, to prevent ambiguity and confusion, I always have adopted an educational test, and by the middle class I understand those who are brought up at establishments which are more or less like Salem House, and by educators who are more or less like Mr Creakle. . . .

We may even go further still in our use of that charming and instructive book, the *History of David Copperfield*. We may lay our finger there on the very types in adult life which are the natural product of Salem House and of Mr Creakle; the very types of our middle class, nay of Englishmen and the English nature in general, as to the Irish imagination they appear. We have only to recall, on the one hand, Mr Murdstone. Mr Murdstone may be called the natural product of a course of Salem House and of Mr Creakle, acting upon hard, stern, and narrow natures. Let us recall, then, Mr Murdstone; Mr Murdstone with his firmness and severity; with his austere religion and his tremendous visage in church; with his view of the world as 'a place for action, and not for moping and droning in;' his view of young Copperfield's disposition as 'requiring a great deal of correcting, and to which no greater service can be done than to force it to conform to the ways of the working world, and to bend it and break it.' We may recall, too, Miss Murdstone, his sister, with the same religion, the same tremendous visage in church, the same firmness; Miss Murdstone with her 'hard steel purse,' and her 'uncompromising hard black boxes with her initials on the lids in hard black nails;' severe and formidable like her brother, 'whom she greatly resembled in face and voice.' These two people, with their hardness, their narrowness, their want of consideration for other people's feelings, their inability to enter into them, are just the type of the Englishman and his civilisation as he presents himself to the Irish mind by his serious side. His energy, firmness, industry, religion, exhibit themselves with these unpleasant features; his bad qualities exhibit themselves without mitigation or relief. . . .

But in Murdstone we see English middle-class civilisation by its severe and serious side only. That civilisation has undoubtedly also its gayer and lighter side. And this gayer and lighter side, as well as the other, we shall find, wonderful to relate, in that all-containing treasure-house of ours, the *History of David Copperfield*. Mr Quinion, with his gaiety, his chaff, his rough coat, his incessant smoking, his brandy and water, is the jovial, genial man of our middle-class civilisation, prepared by Salem House and Mr Creakle, as Mr Murdstone is its severe man. . . .

. . . Our civilisation, as it looks to outsiders, and in so far as it is a thing broadly communicable, seems to consist very much in the Murdstonian drive in business and the Murdstonian religion, on the one hand, and in the Quinionian joviality and geniality, on the other. Wherever we go, we put forward Murdstone and Quinion, and call their ways civilisation. Our governing class nervously watch the ways and wishes of Murdstone and Quinion, and back up their civilisation all they can. But, do what we will, this civilisation does not prove attractive. . . .

78. From Thomas Powell, *Pictures of the Living Authors of Britain*

1851, 175–82

Powell (1809–87), journalist and hackwriter, had gone to America in 1849 to escape prosecution for forgery; Dickens was incensed with his behaviour at this time and later. A more libellous version of his book had been published in New York (1849) as *The Living Authors of England*. There is a biographical and critical account of Dickens (pp. 153–78, New York version; pp. 88–115, London version), unreliable but informative. The comparison with Jerrold—a critical commonplace of the period—appears in his pages on Jerrold.

... We know many critics of great acumen who prefer Jerrold to Dickens; but while we allow that he is a more caustic, sweeping writer, we miss that broad geniality which renders the other so acceptable to all classes. There are curious resemblances, and still stronger contrasts between Dickens and Jerrold: their hatred of oppression is the same; so are their democratic tendencies; and whenever they can expose conventional humbug, they do it unsparingly; but here the likeness ends. Their manner and method of doing these are so totally distinct as to lead us at times to doubt whether the end they have in view is identical. Jerrold is biting, sarcastic, and fierce; there is no sneering banter, as in Thackeray; all is bold, uncompromising, and savage. On the other hand, Dickens is passionate and vituperative: he assaults fearlessly, and carries on an open war. Jerrold flies at his enemy like a tiger, and never lets go while there is life in him; while Dickens contents himself by giving him a sound drubbing. Jerrold is most in earnest, but Dickens is more effective. There is a candour and fair play about him which we miss in Jerrold; the latter will hear nothing in defence of his foe, and consequently punishes him vindictively. This has been one great cause of Jerrold's tales not having the popularity

THE CRITICAL HERITAGE

they deserve; we allude especially to *St. Giles and St. James*, which is admirably written and full of the deepest lessons of life.

... As a writer, Jerrold will never stand higher than he does at present. He is essentially of the day; his allusions are temporary, his affections local; what he does, he does earnestly, but not comprehensively. There is a vengeful personality about him, which leaves the class untouched, while he annihilates the offender. In reading Dickens, you feel more angry with the class than with the individual; with Jerrold you intense your wrath on the culprit ... There is no humour in Jerrold. It is either wit, sarcasm, or banter. Even the latter is fierce and personal. We miss that raciness which pervades Fielding, Smollett, and Dickens. We feel as we read, that a caustic intellect is in utterance, not human beings in the full play of their natures.

271

BLEAK HOUSE

March 1852–September 1853

Bleak House is a crucial item in the history of Dickens's reputation. For many critics in the 1850s, '60s, and '70s, it began the drear decline of 'the author of *Pickwick, Chuzzlewit* and *Copperfield*'; for many recent critics—anticipated by G. B. Shaw—it opened the greatest phase of his achievement. But the 'dreariness' of *Bleak House* became more apparent after the next two novels had failed to relieve the sense of oppression it had caused: hence the severity of the onslaught on *Little Dorrit*. Retrospective assessments in the '70s often linked *Bleak House* with *Little Dorrit* as the nadir of Dickens's career (*Hard Times* was by then invisible to many readers).

Reviews in 1853 had not been predominantly hostile, however. Various special-interest groups were offended by particular elements in the story: low-churchmen by Chadband (see No. 154, *London Quarterly*, 1871), feminists like J. S. Mill (see No. 87) by Mrs Jellyby, lawyers by the Chancery Courts satire (see Fitzjames Stephen, No. 104). Supporters of both foreign missions and 'the home mission' found much cause for indignation: see, among much else—Lord Denman, '*Uncle Tom's Cabin*', '*Bleak House*', *Slavery and Slave Trade* (1853); Harry Stone, 'Dickens and Harriet Beecher Stowe', *Nineteenth Century Fiction*, xii (1958) 188–202; Dickens *To* 'A Correspondent unknown' [Rev. Henry Christopherson], 9 July 1852; *Ragged School Union Magazine*, 1859 and 1864, quoted in *Dickensian*, lv (1959) 106; 'Sir Nathaniel', 'Mrs Pardiggle typically considered', *New Monthly Magazine*, June 1864, cxxxi, 168–84. There was controversy about the scientific feasibility of the spontaneous combustion episode (see No. 80) and, later, about the fairness of depicting Leigh Hunt as Skimpole. Most discussions of the novel, whether adverse or favourable, remained at this fragmentary level. Criticisms such as George Brimley's, who found 'an absolute want of construction' (No. 83), the reviewer in *Bentley's* who was unable to conceive that Skimpole had any function in the novel (No. 84), received no convincing answer from the novel's admirers who, at best, defended it in terms of cunningness of plot.

One critic, indeed, saw *Bleak House* as a prime example of Dickens's skill in combining 'purpose' with art: 'The whole book bristles with social questions. Education, sanatory reform, the Court of Chancery are all introduced, yet all rise so naturally out of the natural course of the story, that no single allusion to them seems out of place.' The Coodle/Doodle satire was, for this critic, 'one of the few occasions in which any allusion to politics is to be found in these novels' (*Ecclesiastic and Theologian*, October 1855,˙xvii, 472–6). Jo 'made perhaps as deep an impression as anything in Dickens,' said Forster, who quotes Dean Ramsay's verdict that nothing in English fiction surpassed his death (*Life*, 563). For many indeed, Jo was 'the gem' of the book (*Eclectic Review*, December 1853, n.s. vi, 672). This reviewer both approved of the dual-narration—Dickens's experiment in this was little discussed—and praised the whole conception and presentation of Esther Summerson (p. 666). The feminine ideal represented in Esther was widely admired, but many who accepted this felt that Dickens had been clumsy in presenting her. See Forster (No. 85), and Charlotte Brontë writing about No. I, to George Smith, 11 March 1852: 'I liked the Chancery part, but when it passes into the autobiographic form . . . it seems to me too often weak and twaddling; an amiable nature is caricatured, not faithfully rendered, in Miss Esther Summerson' (*The Brontës: their . . . Correspondence*, ed. T. J. Wise and J. A. Symington (Oxford, 1932), iii, 322). Other overall faults often alleged were that there were too many disagreeable characters, and little or no humour. One ingredient pleased most readers: Inspector Bucket. He is often mentioned among the dozen or so of Dickens's most delightful and characteristic creations.

79. Henry Crabb Robinson, in his diaries

1852

(*a*) Extract from journal entry, 19 March 1852: 'I began and read the first number of *Bleak House*. It opens with exaggerated and verbose description. London fog is disagreeable even in description, and on the whole the first number does not promise much, except an exposure of the abuses of Chancery practice. The best thing is the picture of a desolate condition of a natural child, but she is removed out of it before sympathy is much called out.' (*Henry Crabb Robinson on Books and their Authors*, ed. E. J. Morley (1938), ii, 715)

(*b*) Extract from journal entry, 8 April 1852: 'Read No. 2 *Bleak House*. Dickens retains his admirable talent at scene-painting . . . Two delicious characters: that of a benevolent man who won't be thanked—an impersonation of goodness, the good genius of *Bleak House*—and a childlike thoughtless creature who allows young women to pay his debts and thinks he does them a kindness by making them feel they take care of him "who for himself can take no care at all".' (ii, 716)

(*c*) Extract from journal entry, 18 June 1852: 'I read at Bear Wood Nos. 3 and 4 of *Bleak House*. It has an excellent picture of Walter Savage Landor as Mr Boythorn. His fierce tones, tenderness of heart, and exaggeration in all his judgements described with great truth and force.' (ii, 717)

(*d*) Extract from journal entry, 23 November 1852: 'I have renewed *Bleak House*—read No. 5—also without any pleasure. But from Dickens one may expect something good to follow what is insignificant.' (ii, 721)

80. G. H. Lewes, from an open letter in the *Leader*

5 February 1853, 137–8

Lewes had protested in the *Leader* (11 December 1852, 1189) against Dickens's killing off Krook by Spontaneous Combustion (ch. xxxii, in No. X, published that month), and thus giving currency to an unscientific theory. In No. XI, Dickens replied to Lewes, with heavy irony about the 'men of science and philosophy' who held that 'the deceased had no business to die in the alleged manner' (ch. xxxiii). Lewes came back at him in the *Leader* (15 January, 64; 5 February, 137–8; 12 February, 161–3), and there was also an exchange of private letters between him and Dickens, who firmly maintained the scientific feasibility of this cause of death. Dickens reverted to the controversy, unrepentant, in the Preface. See Gordon S. Haight, 'Dickens and Lewes on Spontaneous Combustion', *Nineteenth-Century Fiction*, x (1955), 53–63.

My DEAR DICKENS,—What you write is read wherever the English language is read. This magnificent popularity carries with it a serious responsibility. A vulgar error countenanced by you becomes, thereby, formidable. Therefore am I, in common with many of your admirers, grieved to see that an error exploded from science, but one peculiarly adapted to the avid credulity of unscientific minds, has been seriously taken up by you, and sent all over the world with your *imprimatur*—an act which will tend to perpetuate the error in spite of the labours of a thousand philosophers. No journal but the *Leader* has taken up this matter; but I would fain hope that if the case can be clearly stated, and the error shown, on all sides, to be an error, the press of England will lend its aid towards the disabusing of the public mind, and that you yourself will make some qualifying statement in your Preface.

My object in these two letters will be to show, that the highest scientific authorities of the day distinctly disavow the notion of Spontaneous Combustion; that the evidence in favour of the notion is worthless; that the theories in explanation are absurd; and that, according to all known chemical and physiological laws, Spontaneous Combustion is an *impossibility*. . . .

Let me commence with an apology. When this subject was first briefly noticed in the *Leader*, I very much underrated its seriousness. Believing that it was an error long banished to the region of vulgar errors, and that you had picked it up among the curiosities of your reading, without thinking of verifying it, I fancied a few plain statements of a physiological nature would be sufficient to convince you and others. Herein lay my mistake. I have since become aware of a serious fact,—viz., that the belief is very current among medical men, and has grave authorities to support it. This, while it excuses your adoption of the theory, renders that adoption still more dangerous, for the readers of *Bleak House*, startled at the incident of Krook's death, will turn to their medical adviser for confirmation or disproof. . . .

[Much argument and reference to medical authorities follows. Lewes quotes Dickens's attack on the 'men of science and philosophy', which he finds 'humorous, but not convincing!']

81. [Henry Fothergill Chorley], from a review in the *Athenaeum*

17 September 1853, 1087–8

Chorley (1808–72), musicologist, poet, novelist, and critic, was on the staff of the *Athenaeum* from 1833 until shortly before his death, and reviewed many of Dickens's novels there. He contributed to many other journals, including Dickens's weeklies. From 1854, he was a close friend and devoted admirer of Dickens: see G. G. Grubb, 'Dickens and Chorley', *Dickensian*, lii (1956), 100–9.

. . . There is progress in art to be praised in this book,—and there is progress in exaggeration to be deprecated. At its commencement the impression made is strange. Were its opening pages in anywise accepted as representing the world we live in, the reader might be excused for feeling as though he belonged to some orb where eccentrics, Bedlamites, ill-directed and disproportioned people were the only inhabitants. Esther Summerson, the narrator, is, in her surpassingly sweet way, little less like ordinary persons than are Krook and Skimpole. Her own story was of itself sadly romantic enough—the provident beneficence of Mr Jarndyce to her was sufficiently unlike Fortune's usual dealings with those born as she was—to have sufficed for the marvels of one number. But on her mysterious summons to town to join the delightful wards in Chancery with whom she makes an instant and cordial friendship, she is thrown, on the very moment of arrival, into company with a sharp-witted and coxcombical limb of the law, in Guppy,—with an overweening philanthropist, who lets everything at home go to rack and ruin for the sake of her foreign mission, in Mrs Jellyby,—with an infuriated madman who has a mysterious lodger and a demoniacal cat, in Krook,—and with a ruefully fantastic Chancery victim in poor little Miss Flite. . . . Nay, when she gets to the house of her guardian, he, too, must needs be marked out as a curiosity by his whimsical manner of wreaking his vexation at sin, sorrow and meanness, on the weather,—while his guest happens to be none other than

276

such a rare specimen of the man of imagination as Mr Harold Skimpole.—Here is 'the apple-pie made of quinces' with a vengeance, if there ever was such a thing!—Granting the simple heroine of Mr Dickens to possess the immediate power of the daguerreotype in noting at once the minutest singularities of so many exceptional people—granting her, further, in its fullest extent, the instantaneous influence for good in word and in deed which she exercises over every person with whom she is brought into contact,—it surely befalls few such angels of experience, simplicity and overflowing kindness to enter Life through the gate of usefulness down a highway lined with figures so strange as the above. The excuse of Esther's creator, we suppose, lies in the supposed necessity of catching his public at the outset, by exhibiting a rare set of figures in readiness for the coming harlequinade. But in *Bleak House* they stand in one another's way; and seeing that, as the narrative advances, they are reinforced by such a cast-iron *Lady Bountiful* as Mrs Pardiggle, with her terrible children—such a horrible *Darby* and *Joan* as the two old Smallweeds,—such a greasy, preaching *Mawworm* as Mr Chadband—such a *Boanerges* as Mr Boythorn—such an uxorious admirer of his wife's two former husbands as Mr Bayham Badger,—we must protest against the composition of the company, not merely on the ground of the improbability of such an assemblage, but from the sense of fatigue which the manœuvres of such singular people cannot fail to cause.

This resolution to startle, besides being bad in itself, leads the novelist, even though he have of the richest *cornucopia* of humours at his disposal, into two faults—both of which may be seriously objected against *Bleak House*. First, from noticing mere peculiarities, he is beguiled into a cruel consideration of physical defects,—from the unnatural workings of the mind, the step to the painful agonies of the body is a short one. The hideous palsy of Grandfather Smallweed, and the chattering idiocy of his wife, belong to the coarse devices which are losing their hold on the popular taste even at the minor theatres.—The death of Krook—attacked as an impossible catastrophe, and defended by our novelist on medical testimony—would be false and repugnant in point of Art, even if it were scientifically true. We would not willingly look into fiction for the phenomena of *elephantiasis*, or for the hopeless writhings of those who suffer and perish annually in the slow sharp pains of cancer. Again,—in his determination to exhibit snub minds and pimpled tempers, principles that squint, and motives that walk on club-feet (analogous to the mis-shapen figures which ought not to come too

277

frequently even from the professed caricaturist's pencil)—it is difficult, perhaps, for the novelist to avoid touching on another forbidden ground, to abstain from that sharpness of individual portraiture which shall make certain of his *dramatis personæ* recognizable as reproductions of living people. This is not a remark, like our former one, to be sub-stantiated by instances; we will not spread a sore under pretence of exhibiting it.—But the charge has been laid so widely and so univer-sally against *Bleak House*, that it cannot be wholly ignored by any faithful analyst. We will assume that Mr Dickens may not have desired to inflict personal pain on any one—friend or foe. We will concede that the motion of the hand which sketched in this or the other known person in *Bleak House* may, in the first instance, have been involuntary. —The more need is there of strong, grave, friendly protest against devices of style and manner which may lead kindly-natured men so much further than they would care to go.

Thus much recorded as regards the progress in exaggerations which we conceive *Bleak House* to exhibit,—we now turn to the admirable things which this last tale by Mr Dickens contains.—And first, though he has been thereby led away from his great Chancery case further than may have been his original intention, we must signalize the whole machinery by which Lady Dedlock's private history is gradually brought to day—as admirable in point of fictitious construction,—an important advance on anything that we recollect in our author's previous works. Not a point is missed,—not a person left without part or share in the gradual disclosure—not a pin dropped that is not to be picked up for help or for harm to somebody. The great catastrophe is, after all, determined as much by the distant jealousy of Mrs Snagsby, the fretful law-stationer's wife, as by the more intimate vengeance of the discarded lady's maid. Capital, too,—of an excellence which no contemporary could reach,—is the manner in which Mr Bucket the detective officer is worked into the very centre and core of the mystery, until we become almost agreed with Sir Leicester Dedlock in looking on him as a superior being in right of his cool resource and wondrous knowledge. Nor has Mr Dickens wrought up any scene more highly and less melo-dramatically than those of the night-ride into the country in which the over-perfect Esther is included—and of the despairing, affectionate, hopeless expectation of the deserted husband in the town-house. . . .

In his own particular walk—apart from the exaggerations complained of, and the personalities against which many have protested—Mr

Dickens has rarely, if ever, been happier than in *Bleak House*. Poor miserable Mr Jellyby, with all hope, life, and energy washed out of him by the flow of his wife's incessant zeal—the dancing-school in which the African missionary's daughter finds her mission—the cousins who cluster round Sir Leicester Dedlock, giving an air of habitation to the great house, by filling up its empty corners,—could have been hit off by no one else so well. Then, with all his inanity, pomposity, and prejudice in favour of his order, the Lincolnshire baronet is a true gentleman: —we are not only told this, we are made to feel it. His wife is a comparative failure: a second edition of *Mrs. Dombey*,—with somewhat of real stateliness superadded. Trooper George is new:—and here, again, Mr Dickens is masterly, in preserving (though with some exaggeration) the simplicity, sentimentality, and credulity of the original nature which made the man a roamer,—and which have a strong and real life in many a barrack and in many a ship of war. Mr Snagsby 'puts too fine a point' on his intimations concerning the spectre that destroys his home peace, somewhat too ceaselessly. The queerest catch-word may be used too mercilessly, even for a farce,—much more for a novel.— Perhaps among all the waifs and strays, the beggars and the outcasts, in behalf of whose humanity our author has again and again appealed to a world too apt to forget their existence, he has never produced anything more rueful, more pitiable, more complete than poor Jo. The dying scene, with its terrible morals and impetuous protest, Mr Dickens has nowhere in all his works excelled. The book would live on the strength alone of that one sketch from the swarming life around us. Mr Bucket is a jewel among detectives. . . .

82. From an unsigned review, *Illustrated London News*

24 September 1853, 247

'What do you think of *Bleak House*?' is a question which everybody has heard propounded within the last few weeks, when this serial was drawing towards its conclusion; and which, when the work was actually closed, formed, for its own season, as regular a portion of miscellaneous chat as 'How are you?' One obvious distinction is, that a great number of people who ask you how you do, make a practice of neither waiting for, nor listening to, your reply; they pay no attention to the meaning of their own interrogatory. But, on the contrary, those who inquire for your ideas about *Bleak House*, think of *Bleak House*; and, if they do not really want to know your opinion, want you at least to know theirs. . . .

Charles Dickens has become a very important character since the publication of his *Sketches of the Pickwick Club;* we are quite certain that if the present book were the first of its author's, it would strike the public with astonishment. But, partly because the world is so familiar-ised with his manner that people would recognise it in an anonymous work of his, and suspect it even in a work of his professing to be by somebody else; and partly because the extraordinary character of his early performances made impossibilities be expected in the matured powers and richer years of one whose youth produced wonders; and partly, also (it must be allowed), because, in some respects, even that reasonable amount of improvement which ought to have occurred has not shown itself; for these reasons, we say, the effect or success of *Bleak House* is not what it would indubitably be were *Bleak House* the first startling sample of a new class of fiction, by a young author in a manner the like of which the public had never before seen. . . .

Bleak House has one grand defect, while exhibiting every quality of its author's undoubted genius. People want some story in a work of fiction; and not only is the desire for a story perfectly natural and perfectly reasonable (as we could prove if we had time, and if, indeed, it were necessary), but it is, in an artistic sense, one of the essential elements of all good prose works of this nature. Now, most unfortunately, Mr Dickens fails in the construction of a plot. This is the very point in which he has generally been weakest. No man, we are confident, could tell a story better, if he had but a story to tell. We suspect that he is not at all unconscious of his own deficiency; for, in *Bleak House* especially—and, we might add, in many of his other novels—he resorts to a thousand artifices to excite curiosity; and lo! there is nothing about which we need have been curious—there is no explanation by which, when our curiosity has been excited, it will be gratified or satisfied. . . .

Now, a story-teller professing to offer you a representation of real life, yet unable to construct a good plot, is under a disadvantage which we need not enlarge upon. But this describes Mr Dickens's case only in part. The plot is invariably his great difficulty; and, like other gentlemen similarly circumstanced, having failed to overcome his embarrassments, he strives, by every artifice at least to hide them, for the sake of his credit. He wants the reader to trust him. He has the art of exciting the most lively expectations; he has the art of sustaining them. Renewal upon renewal he obtains for these literary bills, during the whole progress of the story's existence; and, when it dies, there are not assets found to pay half a-crown in twenty shillings. Mr Dickens, the noblest, the most munificent of writers in all other qualities, appealing ever to the best sympathies of his readers—elevating, instructing, and charming them throughout; spending the credit which he enjoys at their hands in the most princely and even royal manner; honoured, beloved, and admired while his story lasts, is, when it is wound up, discovered to have been in one point on which he had required and received unwavering faith, a splendid and delightful pretender—pretender, however, by whom it is pleasant to be taken in. It is some comfort to be even deceived in such a style; and people would sooner be cheated by Mr Dickens than paid in full by many other writers.

Besides, this is but one small part of the account. Mr Dickens fulfils his obligations, were they four times told, in the less mechanical duties of his inspired vocation. *Bleak House*, like so many of his former works —like all, indeed, of the longer kind—has beauty enough, and power enough, and is full of passages which those who read them find reason to be glad they have read; passages which ever exercise a most decisive influence where they are designed to exercise it: and which, while they both warm and delight the unimplicated majority, expose fraud, unmask and brand hypocrisy, put selfishness out of conceit with itself, show the pampered turpitude of cant in all the truth of its revolting deformity, and confirm, by irresistible impressions, whatever feelings tend in our day towards the reconciliation of estranged interests, towards the promotion of healthy sentiment among the public, and towards the practical amelioration of society. In these respects the influence of Charles Dickens is, and has from the beginning been, pure, beneficial, and elevating. . . .

As usual, Mr Dickens has, in this book, given to his readers many intellectual daguerreotypes to carry away. These are at once called up by the mere names of the characters; and with those names they will be identified for evermore. Thus, in society, a person might be at some loss to convey his impressions about an individual, whose dispositions, habits, and peculiarities he wanted to describe—but time and power fail. Now, however, a word bears the significance of half a dozen hours' delineations—you mean that the fellow is a sort of Harold Skimpole. Just so—with the exception: and the exceptions are marked off with ease, leaving one of those vivid ideas of the original, which could never have been conveyed but for the help of a great author—in this the most trivial and insignificant of his collateral uses, and, perhaps, collateral abuses. Very few modern writers have furnished, with respect to vulgar life, more of this stenograph—more of this hiero-glyphical nomenclature—more of this algebra of conversational satire, than Dickens. At present, he has added some new full-lengths to his dreaded gallery (and may the salutary terror of it increase!)—to his dreaded gallery of the Denounced. . . . [Mr Chadband, Mrs Jellyby and Mr Turveydrop provide further instances of this.]

83. George Brimley, from an unsigned review, *Spectator*

24 September 1853, xxvi, 923-5

Reprinted in Brimley's *Essays*, ed. W. G. Clark (Cambridge, 1858), 289-301.

Brimley (1819-57), essayist, was Librarian of Trinity College, Cambridge, and a contributor to the *Spectator* and *Fraser's Magazine*. Wright, Keeley, and so on, whom he mentions, were of course popular character-actors.

Bleak House is, even more than any of its predecessors, chargeable with not simply faults, but absolute want of construction. A novelist may invent an extravagant or an uninteresting plot—may fail to balance his masses, to distribute his light and shade—may prevent his story from marching, by episode and discursion: but Mr Dickens discards plot, while he persists in adopting a form for his thoughts to which plot is essential, and where the absence of a coherent story is fatal to continuous interest. In *Bleak House*, the series of incidents which form the outward life of the actors and talkers has no close and necessary connexion; nor have they that higher interest that attaches to circumstances which powerfully aid in modifying and developing the original elements of human character. The great Chancery suit of Jarndyce and Jarndyce, which serves to introduce a crowd of persons as suitors, lawyers, law-writers, law-stationers, and general spectators of Chancery business, has positively not the smallest influence on the character of any one person concerned; nor has it any interest of itself. Mr Richard Carstone is not made reckless and unsteady by his interest in the great suit, but simply expends his recklessness and unsteadiness on it, as he would on something else if it were non-existent. This great suit is lugged in by the head and shoulders, and kept prominently before the reader, solely to give Mr Dickens the opportunity of indulging in stale and common-

283

place satire upon the length and expense of Chancery proceedings, and exercises absolutely no influence on the characters and destinies of any one person concerned in it. The centre of the arch has nothing to do in keeping the arch together. The series of incidents which answers to what in an ordinary novel is called plot, is that connected with the relationship of the heroine (again analogically speaking) to her mother. . . .

[A summary follows.]

. . . Literally, we have here given the whole of what can by any stretch of the term be called the main plot of *Bleak House*. And not only is this story both meagre and melodramatic, and disagreeably reminiscent of that vilest of modern books, Reynolds' *Mysteries of London*, but it is so unskilfully managed that the daughter is in no way influenced either in character or destiny by her mother's history; and the mother, her husband, the prying solicitor, the French maid, and the whole Dedlock set, might be eliminated from the book without damage to the great Chancery suit, or perceptible effect upon the remaining characters. We should then have less crowd, and no story; and the book might be called 'Bleak House, or the Odd Folks that have to do with a long Chancery Suit'. This would give an exact notion of the contents of a collection of portraits embracing suitors, solicitors, law-writers, law-stationers, money-lenders, law-clerks, articled and not-articled, with their chance friends and visitors, and various members of their respective families. Even then, a comprehensive *etcetera* would be needed for supernumeraries. So crowded is the canvas which Mr Dickens has stretched, and so casual the connexion that gives to his composition whatever unity it has, that a daguerreotype of Fleet Street at noon-day would be the aptest symbol to be found for it; though the daguerreotype would have the advantage in accuracy of representation. . . .

The result of all this is, that *Bleak House* would be a heavy book to read through at once, as a properly constructed novel ought to be read. But we must plead guilty to having found it dull and wearisome as a serial, though certainly not from its want of cleverness or point. On the contrary, almost everybody in the book is excessively funny, that is not very wicked, or very miserable. Wright and Keeley could act many of the characters without alteration of a word; Skimpole must be constructed with an especial eye to the genius of Mr Charles Matthews;

O. Smith will of course choose Krook or the sullen bricklayer, but probably the former, for his effective make-up, and the grand finale by spontaneous combustion,—which, however Nature and Mr Lewes may deride in the pride of intellect, the resources of the Adelphi will unquestionably prove possible: the other characters of the piece would be without difficulty distributed among ladies and gentlemen familiar to the London boards. By all which is implied, that Mr Dickens selects in his portraiture exactly what a farce-writer of equal ability and invention would select,—that which is coarsely marked and apprehended at first sight; that which is purely outward and no way significant of the man, an oddity of feature, a trick of gesture or of phrase, something which an actor can adequately present and in his presentation exhaust the conception. And this tendency to a theatrical method shows itself again in the exaggerated form which his satire assumes, and which even when the satire is well directed robs it of its wholesome effect. . . .

The love of strong effect, and the habit of seizing peculiarities and presenting them instead of characters, pervade Mr Dickens's gravest and most amiable portraits, as well as those expressly intended to be ridiculous and grotesque. His heroine in *Bleak House* is a model of unconscious goodness; . . . her unconsciousness and sweet humility of disposition are so profound that scarcely a page of her autobiography is free from a record of these admirable qualities. . . . Such a girl would not write her own memoirs, and certainly would not bore one with her goodness till a wicked wish arises that she would either do something very 'spicy', or confine herself to superintending the jam-pots at Bleak House. Old Jarndyce himself, too, is so dreadfully amiable and supernaturally benevolent, that it has been a common opinion during the progress of the book, that he would turn out as great a rascal as Skimpole; and the fox on the symbolical cover with his nose turned to the East wind has been conjectured by subtle intellects to be intended for his double. We rejoice to find that those misanthropical anticipations were unfounded; but there must have been something false to general nature in the portrait that suggested them—some observed peculiarity of an individual presented too exclusively, or an abstract conception of gentleness and forbearance worked out to form a sharp contrast to the loud, self-assertive, vehement, but generous and tender Boythorne. This gentleman is one of the most original and happiest conceptions of the book, a humorist study of the highest merit. Mr Tulkinghorn, the Dedlock confidential solicitor, is an admirable study of mere outward characteristics of a class; but his motives and character are quite incomprehensible, and we strongly suspect that Mr Dickens had him shot out of the way as the only possible method of avoiding an enigma of his own setting which he could not solve. . .

. . . Inspector Bucket, of the Detective Force, bears evidence of the careful study of this admirable department of our Police by the editor of *Household Words;* and, as in the case of Kenge and Vholes, the professional capacity is here the object, and we do not require a portraiture of the man and his affections. Poor Joe, the street-sweeping urchin, is drawn with a skill that is never more effectively exercised than when the outcasts of humanity are its subjects; a skill which seems to depart in proportion as the author rises in the scale of society depicted. Dickens has never yet succeeded in catching a tolerable likeness of man or woman whose lot is cast among the high-born and wealthy. . . . Sir Leicester Dedlock, Baronet, with his wife and family circle, are no exceptions.

If Mr Dickens were now for the first time before the public, we hould have found our space fully occupied in drawing attention to his wit, his invention, his eye for common life, for common men and women, for the everyday aspect of streets and houses, his tendency to delineate the affections and the humours rather than the passions of mankind; and his defects would have served but to shade and modify the praises that flow forth willingly at the appearance among us of a true and original genius. And had his genius gone on growing and maturing, clearing itself of extravagance, acquiring art by study and reflection, it would not be easy to limit the admiration and homage he might by this time have won from his countrymen. As it is, he must be content with the praise of amusing the idle hours of the greatest number of readers; not, we may hope, without improvement to their hearts, but certainly without profoundly affecting their intellects or deeply stirring their emotions. Clever he undoubtedly is: many of his portraits excite pity, and suggest the existence of crying social sins; but of almost all we are obliged to say that they border on and frequently reach caricature, of which the essence is to catch a striking likeness by exclusively selecting and exaggerating a peculiarity that marks the man but does not represent him. Dickens belongs in literature to the same class as his illustrator, Hablot Browne, in design, though he far surpasses the illustrator in range and power.

84. Unsigned review,
Bentley's Miscellany

October 1853, xxxiv, 372–4

. . . *Bleak House* is, in some respects, the worst of Mr Dickens' fictions, but, in many more, it is the best.

It is the worst, inasmuch as in no other work is the tendency to disagreeable exaggeration so conspicuous as in this. There are a great number of *dramatis personæ* moving about in this story, some of them exercising no perceptible influence upon its action or in any way contributing to the catastrophe of the piece. They disappear from the scene, give no sign, and when we come to look back upon our transient acquaintance with them, we begin to suspect that the story would have profited more by 'their room than by their company.' Now such characters are only serviceable in fiction, when they represent a class, and something is gained to morality, if nothing to art. When, on the other hand, they are exaggerated exceptions, and represent nothing which we have ever seen, or heard, or dreamt of, we cannot but regard them as mere excrescences which we should like to see pruned away. Of what conceivable use, for example, is such a personage as Mr Harold Skimpole? He does not assist the story, and, apart from the story, he is simply a monstrosity. That there are a great many people in the world who sit lightly under their pecuniary obligations is unhappily a fact, but if Harold Skimpoles are moving about anywhere, we will answer for it that they do not meet, in any known part of this habitable globe, such a number of tolerant and accommodating friends as Mr Dickens' 'child' is represented to have encountered. But, leaving such personages as Mr Skimpole, Mrs Pardiggle, Mr Chadband and others, to advert slightly to those who do exercise some influence upon the development of the plot, we cannot help thinking that Mr Dickens has committed a grave error in bringing together such a number of extraordinary personages, as are to be found huddled *en masse* in this romance, the Smallweeds, the Krooks, the Guppys and others. As for poor Miss Flight, we recognize her presence as a legitimacy, for she is the veritable chorus to the great Chancery tragedy, which is here so terribly sustained, even to the dark catastrophe of the death of the young victim. But is it, we ask, within the rightful domain of true art to make the unnatural in character thus predominate over the natural? In *Bleak House*, for every one natural character we could name half a dozen unnatural ones; for every pleasant personage, half a dozen painful ones. Such characters, for example, as the Smallweeds, in which the extreme of physical infirmity, resulting from constitutional decay, is painted with a sickening minuteness, are simply revolting.

There is nothing, indeed, more remarkable in *Bleak House* than the almost entire absence of humour. In this story the grotesque and the contemptible have taken the place of the humorous. There are some passages in the history of Mr Guppy which raise a smile, but beyond these we really do not remember anything provocative of even a transient feeling of hilarity. It would seem, however, that in proportion as Mr Dickens has ceased to be, what he was once believed to be only, a humorous writer, he has been warmed into a pathetic one. The pathos of *Bleak House* is as superior to that of *David Copperfield*, as *David Copperfield* was, in this respect, superior to any of the author's former productions. There are passages, indeed, in it which nothing can excel.

The chief merit of *Bleak House* lies, indeed, in these detached passages. There are *parts* which, without hesitation, may be pronounced more powerful and more tender than anything that Dickens ever wrote—but the whole is disappointing. We feel that the story has not been carefully constructed, and that the undue elaboration of minor and unimportant characters crowding the canvas, and blocking up the space at the author's command, has compelled such a slurring over of required explanations towards the end of the story, that the reader lays down the last number of the series scarcely believing that he is not to hear anything more. The want of art is apparent, if we look only at the entire work. But there is wonderful art in the working out of some of the details. The narrative of the pursuit of Lady Dedlock may be instanced as one of the most powerful pieces of writing in the English language. There is profound pathos, as there is also high teaching, in the description of the death of the poor outcast, Joe; and very touching too is the sketch of the last moments of Richard Carstairs, done to death by his Chancery suit. Of single characters there are some at least which may be cited as new to Mr Dickens' pages. The trooper, George, is a noble fellow, and we are always right glad to meet him. Caddy Jellaby is another who never comes amiss to us. Mr Bucket is a portrait that stands out from the canvas just like a bit of life. And we cannot help thinking that poor Rick, with his *no*-character, is as truthful a bit of painting as there is in the whole book. Of Mr Jarndyce and Esther Summerson we hardly know what to say. We should like to have substantial faith in the existence of such loveable, self-merging natures, whether belonging to elderly gentlemen or young maidens. But we cannot say that we have. Indeed, the final disposal of Esther, after all that had gone before, is something that so far transcends the limits of our credulity, that we are compelled to pronounce it eminently unreal. We do not know whether most to marvel at him who transfers, or her who is transferred from one to another like a bale of goods. Neither, if we could believe in such an incident, would our belief in any way enhance our admiration of the heroine. A little more strength of character would not be objectionable—even in a wife.

We have instanced these defects,—defects which our reason condemns,—defects spoken of commonly by hundreds and thousands of readers in nowise professing to be critics, mainly with the intent of illustrating the wonderful genius of the writer, whose greatest triumph it is to take the world captive in spite of these accumulated heresies against nature and against art. Everybody reads—everybody admires—everybody is delighted—everybody loves—and yet almost everybody finds something to censure, something to condemn. The secret of all this, or, rather, for it is no secret, the fact is, that almost every page of the book is instinct with genius, and that Charles Dickens writes to the hearts, not to the heads, of his readers. It is easy to say,—as we have said, and not falsely either,—that *Bleak House* is untruthful. If there were not wonderful truthfulness in it, it would not have touched so many hearts. But the truthfulness is in the individual details; it is truthfulness in untruthfulness. There are minute traits of character,—little scraps of incident,—small touches of feeling, strewn everywhere about the book, so truthful and so beautiful, that we are charmed as we read, and grieve when we can read no longer. It is unreasonable to look for perfection anywhere, but if the whole of such a work as *Bleak House* were equal to its parts, what a book it would be!

85. [John Forster], from
an unsigned review, *Examiner*

8 October 1853, 643–5

. . . Some are in raptures over one part, some over another, and some very particular fellows are carping at every part. The judgments on *Bleak House* are, in short, as various as judgments are apt to be upon a man whose failings it is thought a subtle test of criticism to discover, for the very reason that all the world admires and likes him, and his books are bought and read by everybody.

. . . That it has also faults is to say that it is not quite a miracle, even though written by him. Many faults truly may be found with it, and such as properly accompany great qualities. In the whole line of immortals throughout the history of literature, there will be discovered few writers indeed who have produced unexceptionable books. Books become everlasting by the genius that is in them, and by their unquestionable elevation above the products of men having only ordinary power. Their accompanying defects are but tokens of a true humanity, and perhaps scarcely detract from the enjoyment we derive from them. Very hard things may be very correctly said of the *Æneid*, and the most admiring critic of *Paradise Lost* cannot omit to note how Milton failed in those passages which have to do with heaven and the angels. . . . Such comparisons are not impertinent. Novels as Mr Dickens writes them rise to the dignity of poems. In the same spirit Fielding wrote, treating his *Tom Jones* as an epic.

Upon this high ground we must stand if we would properly discuss *Bleak House*. It touches and amuses us, but it is destined to draw tears and smiles also from our children's children. Mr Dickens has a large public in the present, and we do not hesitate to declare our belief that he will have one hardly less large in the future. The world will grow wiser than it is, the abuses attacked by this greatest of humorists and kindliest of satirists will disappear—but the spirit in which he writes, and to which he appeals, is indestructible; and the emotions he awakens are not more fresh and true to us than they will be to future generations.

At the close of his preface Mr Dickens marks incidentally the general character of the tale by the intimation that in it he has purposely dwelt upon the romantic side of familiar things. Marvellous is the skill with which, towards this intention, the great Chancery suit on which the plot hinges, and on incidents connected with which, important or trivial, all the passion and suffering turns, is worked into every part of the book. Whenever the occasion arises, or the art of the story-teller requires, the thick atmosphere of law that rises out of Jarndyce *v.* Jarndyce is made to cling like a fog about the people in the story. It may be more or less, but there it is. Either as a thick cloud or a light mist, it is to be seen everywhere. Lawyers of many grades, law clerks of all kinds, the copyist, the law-stationer, the usurer, suitors of every description, haunters of the law courts and their victims, live and move round about the life of the chief persons in the tale, and exercise almost insensibly, but very certainly, a continual influence upon them. Compare this with what a commonplace writer would have preferred, and a congenial critic recommended, and you will understand what the power of a man of genius really is. . . .

Taking the story piecemeal, as a mere gallery of pictures and persons, we are disposed to think that there are particular groups in *Bleak House* finer than anything that even Mr Dickens has yet produced in the same way. Exquisitely true and tender as are his descriptions of the suffering classes in former writings, we can remember none by which we have been touched so deeply, or that has been graced by so much of the very finest writing, as the entire tale of the street-wandering Joe as it may be gathered from the pages of the book before us. In the trooper George, the Bagnets, and their humble household, we have another of those fine broad, hearty exemplifications of humour in which Mr Dickens delights, in which all the ludicrous features of every object or incident are intensely enjoyed and made prominent, yet with a most genuine and charming sentiment at the same time underlying it all. Nothing is repulsive; everything is large, laughable, and true; and the most homely and ungainly figures become radiant with the spirit of goodness. The character of Esther Summerson has been much elaborated, and the early portions of her narrative are as charming as anything Mr Dickens has ever written—indeed some of the best things in the book may be found throughout it, full as it is of noble fancies, and delicate and graceful thoughts; but we suspect that Mr Dickens undertook more than man could accomplish when he resolved to make her the *naïve* revealer of her own good qualities. We cannot help detecting in some passages an artificial tone, which, if not self-consciousness, is at any rate not such a tone as would be used in her narrative by a person of the character depicted. Yet the graces and virtues of Esther have won so many hearts that we do not care to dwell on our objection to his method of displaying them; and as to the one or two other characters of the book which we might have wished away, these are quite lost in that crowd of fresh and ever real creations that will live while the language continues. [E.g., Mrs Jellyby, Boythorn, Skimpole, Chadband,] . . . to say nothing of poor Miss Flite or the immortal Bucket, and a dozen others, have been added here to the long list of ideal people with whom Mr Dickens has made his countrymen intimately and permanently acquainted.

Mr Dickens's characters, as all the world knows, pass their names into our language, and become types. It is an evidence of his possession of the highest power that the best of them are thus made each to embody some characteristic feature, to personify some main idea, which are ever after found universally applicable. Such has been the aim of the highest class of dramatists and novelists since the beginning of all literature. They know little how much there is in any one man's head or heart, who expect to have every character in a tale laid bare before them as on a psychological dissecting table, and demonstrated minutely. We see nobody minutely in real life. The rough estimates we form of character are on the whole (if we possess any tact) correct; but men touch and interfere with one another by the contact of their extremes, and it is the prominences, the sharp angles, that are most likely to appear in a tale really worth the telling. Hence it is therefore, as well as for other reasons, that the dramatist or novelist is concerned chiefly with the display of salient points in each one of his characters. The rest of the sketch is filled up by the reader or spectator instinctively (and sufficiently) out of his own experience. . . .

. . . Of Mr Dickens it is to be said, if of any one, that his main strength has lain in the ability to concentrate his thoughts on objects external to himself. If his mere personality were at every turn set up as the limit and bound to his perceptions, if it were still his recurring habit to take his own character as the infallible test of all other characters, he would in each fresh essay be always retracing only the old weary ground. But ready and eager at all times, with genial warmth and fulness, to enter in all the peculiarities of others, we have him continually throughout his books apprehending and interpreting new forms of character and truth, and carrying with each new achievement

of his genius new pleasure and delight into thousands of homes—
because his genius is his fellow-feeling with his race. . . .[1]

Our next extract is from one of the descriptions of Chesney Wold
on the eve of the shame that is awaiting its grand possessors [ch. xl].
This and similar descriptions throughout the tale, which have great
beauty in themselves, are so employed as to bear always a subtle and
thoughtful reference to the imaginative and romantic design of the
story.

[1] The concluding phrase is silently borrowed from E. P. Whipple (see above, p. 238),
and is repeated in *Life*, p. 562. Other critics, too, appropriated Whipple's happy phrase.

86. [James Augustine Stothert], from 'Living Novelists', *The Rambler*

January 1854, n.s. i, 41–51

The *Rambler* was a Roman Catholic journal, now a monthly, edited by Richard Simpson; prominent Catholics closely associated with it included J. H. Newman and Lord Acton (see No. 123). Stothert (1817–57?), a Scottish priest, was a convert to Roman Catholicism. The books reviewed with *Bleak House* were Thackeray's *Esmond*, Lytton's *My Life*, Lady Georgiana Fullerton's *Lady Bird*, and Charlotte Brontë's *Villette*.

With tens of thousands of Englishmen and Englishwomen, Dickens is a *hero*. His very name gives a sanction to every thing to which he lends it. He could *do* many things among his fellow-creatures, for no other reason than that he wrote *Pickwick* and *Copperfield*.

Charles Dickens is, in fact, pre-eminently a man of the middle of the nineteenth century. He is at once the creation and the prophet of an age which loves benevolence without religion, the domestic virtues more than the heroic, the farcical more than the comic, and the extravagant more than the tragic. The product of a restlessly observant but shallow era, his great intellectual characteristic is a most unusual power of observing the external peculiarities of men and women, as distinguished from all insight into that hidden nature whence flow the springs of their conduct. And morally there is probably not another living writer, of equal decency of thought, to whom the supernatural and eternal world simply *is not*. He has no claims to be regarded as a writer of comedy; his characters are a congeries of oddities of phrase, manner, gesticulation, dress, countenance, or limb, tacked cleverly upon a common-place substratum of excessive simplicity, amiableness, or villany. Take away the gaiters, buttons, gloves, petticoats, hair, teeth, cant phrases, and habitual postures of his men, women, and children, and what is there left for us to fall back upon? Admirably, indeed, he does his work. Never were there such farces off the stage before. No English writer has ever portrayed with so genial a versatility every thing that is visibly odd and eccentric in human life, without resorting to what is profane, coarse, or indecent, by way of giving *a spice* to his comicalities.

Of wit Dickens has none. The intellectual portion of his nature is not sufficiently refined, keen, or polished to appreciate the delicate subtleties of thought and language which are included in that singular and charming thing, a witty idea or expression. He rarely writes a sentence in his own proper character that imprints itself on the memory, or is worth treasuring in the storehouse of the brain. He is not a man of *thought*.

Of course, with such a writer every thing is in extremes. His good creatures are awfully benevolent; his scoundrels are as black as the devil himself; his people of simplicity are positive noodles. In fact, they are not men and women at all; they are stage-characters transferred from the boards to the page. Pecksniff, Ralph Nickleby, Quilp, Sampson and Sally Brass, Uriah Heep, Tulkinghorn, and the rest, they are all so many varieties of the standard stage 'villain.' Of his variations on the dramatic 'benevolent old gentleman,' his last novel furnishes one of his most characteristic specimens. Old Jarndyce is so soft-hearted and soft-headed a model of ultra-beneficence, that for some time we expected him to turn out a deep rogue in the end. This whole story, in fact, is a failure, and, in our judgment, inferior to any thing Dickens has written before. Plot it has none; and it is impossible to feel the slightest interest in the characters with whom we are meant to sympathise. Jarndyce, Richard, and Ada, are poor to the last degree; and as to Esther Summerson, the angelic, self-forgetting young lady, who notes in her journal every thing that a self-forgetting mind would not note, we have found her a prodigious bore, whom we wish the author had consigned to the store-room the moment she was fairly in possession of her housekeeping keys. The manner in which this lady is made to chronicle her own merits, is a proof how unable Dickens is to enter into the real *depths* of a human mind, and draw a genuine character self-consistent in all its parts.

In his intentionally farcical characters, Dickens reigns supreme. From Pickwick downwards, they are a splendid series; and a host they are in numbers. From the rapidly but charmingly touched *Sketches by Boz* down to Mr Bucket the detective in *Bleak House*, what an innumerable list of oddities they are to have proceeded from the brain of one man!

We suppose, of the whole list, that Mr Pickwick and Sam Weller will be unanimously accounted the most thoroughly amusing and excellent; and of the rest, different readers will choose different objects for their preference. We confess, ourselves, to a peculiar *penchant* for Dick Swiveller and the Marchioness; and we question whether in the whole range of Dickens's happiest scenes any thing is to be found superior to the occasion on which the unfortunate Richard wakes from his fever, and bids the cribbage-playing Marchioness mark 'two for his heels.'

Dickens's pathos is little to our taste, speaking generally, for we admit striking exceptions. As a rule, however, he overdoes it. He describes and describes, and lays on his colours with violent elaboration, till the reader is fatigued rather than affected. And so it is in his general style: he makes a catalogue instead of placing a few salient points before the mind's eye. With true pre-Raphaelite toil, he goes through every thing that can be seen or discovered, till the impression on the reader is weakened by the multiplicity of detail, and weariness takes the place of vivid perception. This is melodrama instead of tragedy, and penny-a-lining (clever though it be) instead of powerful writing.

Another peculiarity in Dickens is his taste for nastiness. We do not mean that he tells dirty stories, or makes dirty jokes. Far from it. He is too much a man of the day to give in to any thing of the kind. Yet he has a marvellous liking for whatever is physically offensive. He gloats over mould, damp, rottenness, and smells. There is not a book of his in which dampness and mouldiness are not repeatedly brought in as characterising some spot or building. We believe he cannot conceive of any thing *old* without being *damp*. In the same way, he loves to dwell on offensive peculiarities in his characters. Thus, in *Bleak House* we have a disgusting lawyer with black gloves always picking the pimples on his face. The same story supplies one of the most unpardonably nauseous descriptions which ever disfigured a work of fiction. The details of the spontaneous combustion of the miser Krook are positively loathsome. Any thing more sickening and revolting we never read.

As we have said, Dickens is a man to whom the supernatural world is not. It is melancholy to see one so amiable, so benevolent in his aspirations, so clear in his estimate of domestic virtues, at the same time *stone-blind* to the existence of any thing which eye cannot see, and to an hereafter whose woe or joy is dependent on man's conduct here. . . . We cannot conceive any thing more utterly Pagan and shocking than the whole treatment of the character of the unfortunate Lady Dedlock in *Bleak House*. The *utter* absence of any trace of those feelings which would have been shown by every woman possessed of the slightest remnants of a conscience, is most painful; and also, little as we are convinced that Mr Dickens would wish such a result, most undoubtedly pernicious.

Thus, ignorant of the very elements of a religious faith, it is natural that Dickens should fail in drawing religious hypocrites. The Chadbands of *Bleak House*, and others of his stories, are perfect failures. The class of men whom he wishes to show up, always get hold of something like Christian phrases, and are, in fact, far more offensively disgusting than Dickens makes them. But the slang of Chadband and his compeers is as unlike religious cant as it is tedious and unmeaning.

Such we hold to be the merits and deficiencies of the author of the *Pickwick Papers*. An unrivalled humorist, and eminently respectable in his morals, his knowledge of human nature is as superficial as it is extensive.

87. John Stuart Mill, from a letter to Harriet Taylor

20 March 1854

Michael St John Packe, *Life of John Stuart Mill* (1954), 311.

Mill (1806–73), whose philosophical and political works were to include *The Subjection of Women* (1869), was one of the London intellectuals whose paths rarely crossed Dickens's. Back in 1837 he had seen him at Macready's and was reminded of Carlyle's description of Camille Desmoulins, 'his face of dingy blackguardism irradiated with genius'.—'Such a phenomenon', Mill remarked, 'does not often appear in a lady's drawing-room' (*Earlier Letters*, ed. F. E. Mineka (1963), i, 343).

... That creature Dickens, whose last story, *Bleak House*, I found accidentally at the London Library the other day and took home and read—much the worst of his things, and the only one of them I altogether dislike—has the vulgar impudence in this thing to ridicule rights of women. It is done in the very vulgarest way—just the style in which vulgar men used to ridicule 'learned ladies' as neglecting their children and household etc. . . .

88. Ruskin on the mortality rate: from 'Fiction, Fair and Foul', *Nineteenth Century*

June 1880, vii, 945

Reprinted in Ruskin's *On the Old Road* (1885), and in *Works*, xxxiv, 271–2.

Ruskin cannot count (on his reckoning, it is ten, not nine deaths), but Miss Flite should be deleted from his list. He might, however, have added to his tally Miss Barbary, Mr Neckett, and Mr Gridley, making it twelve. Unfortunately Mrs Bayham Badger's 'dear first' and 'dear second', Captain Swosser and Professor Dingo, are disqualified, though the account of Dingo's final illness provides a happy moment in the dialogue. Another pleasing computation is James Fitzjames Stephen's: 'A list of the killed, wounded and missing amongst Mr Dickens's novels would read like an *Extraordinary Gazette*. An interesting child runs as much risk there as any of the troops who stormed the Redan' ('The Relation of Novels to Life', in *Cambridge Essays* (1855), 174n).

[Ruskin is arguing that the monotony of urban life produces in the city-dweller] a craving of the human heart for some kind of excitement . . . and the ultimate power of fiction to entertain him is by varying to his fancy the modes, and defining for his dullness the horrors, of Death.

In the single novel of *Bleak House* there are nine deaths (or left for death's, in the drop scene) carefully wrought out of or led up to, either by way of pleasing surprise, as the baby's at the brickmaker's, or finished in their threatenings and sufferings, with as much enjoyment as can be contrived in the anticipation, and as much pathology as can be concentrated in the description. Under the following varieties of method:

One by assassination	Mr Tulkinghorn
One by starvation, with phthisis	Joe
One by chagrin	Richard
One by spontaneous combustion	Mr Krook
One by sorrow	Lady Dedlock's lover
One by remorse	Lady Dedlock
One by insanity	Miss Flite
One by paralysis	Sir Leicester

Besides the baby, by fever, and a lively young French-woman left to be hanged.

And all this observe, not in a tragic, adventurous, or military story, but merely as the further enlivenment of a narrative intended to be amusing; and as a properly representative average of the statistics of civilian mortality in the centre of London.

HARD TIMES

Household Words, 1 April–12 August 1854

F. G. Kitton did not include *Hard Times* in his *Novels of Charles Dickens* (1897) but relegated it to the companion-volume, *The Minor Writings* (1900). This typifies a widely-held estimate of its merits and importance, and some of the reviews had signified this immediately by their un-accustomed brevity. For instance, the *Athenaeum*, which usually gave a Dickens novel four or five columns, despatched *Hard Times* in half a column ('a good idea—but . . . scarcely wrought out with Mr Dickens's usual felicity', 12 August 1854, 992). Inevitably, much discussion centred on the justice of Dickens's 'idea', his account of industrial life, and his judgments on the political economists. See the reviews re-printed below; also Harriet Martineau in *The Factory Controversy* (No. 70), and W. B. Hodgson, 'On Economic Science', in *Lectures on Education delivered at the Royal Institution* (1855), 299–304. Hodgson's criticisms were commended in the *Gentleman's Magazine*, September 1854, n.s. xlii, 277–8. The *Athenaeum* reviewer also raised the question of how such didactic fiction should operate: 'The case of Fancy *versus* Fact is here stated in prose, but without the fairness which belongs to a prose argument. A purely ideal treatment was needed for such a pur-pose' (*loc. cit.*). Forster's review (No. 89) may be taken as the semi-official reply to this and similar criticisms; *Hard Times* was one of the few novels to which Dickens did not write a Preface, in which he might have replied himself.

Macaulay's comment is well-known: 'One excessively touching, heart-breaking passage, and the rest sullen socialism. The evils which he attacks he caricatures grossly, and with little humour' (Journal, 12 August 1854, *Life and Letters of Lord Macaulay*, ed. G. O. Trevelyan (1959 edn.) 614). The 'excessively touching' passage was doubtless concerned with Stephen and Rachel. The pathos centring on them was much admired, even by critics (such as Mrs Oliphant) who came to react strongly against the Little Nell aspect of Dickens.

The novel has been warmly admired, notably by Ruskin and Taine (Nos. 93, 97) and later by G. B. Shaw (Preface to *Hard Times*, 1912) and F. R. Leavis (*The Great Tradition*, 1948). See A. J. A. Waldock, 'The

Status of *Hard Times*', *Southerly*, ix (1948) 33–9, the materials collected in the Norton Critical Edition of *Hard Times*, ed. George Ford and Sylvère Monod (New York, 1966), and *Twentieth Century Interpretations of 'Hard Times*', ed. Paul E. Gray (Englewood Cliffs, N.J., 1969).

89. [John Forster], from an unsigned review, the *Examiner*

9 September 1854, 568–9

Hard Times reads admirably in a volume. The divisions into three parts, headed respectively Sowing—Reaping—Garnering, and the prefixing of a title to each chapter, help to give additional sharpness to the outline of the story, and to make its purpose, and the closeness with which it is followed, more distinct to every reader. . . .

So far as the purpose of *Hard Times* involves the direct raising of any question of political economy, we abstain from comment upon it. In a tale, especially a very short one, clearly and powerfully written, full of incident and living interest, it is difficult to find room for a sufficiently full expression of opinion upon details, in the working of a given principle. The principle emphatically laid down by Mr Dickens in the story before us is one to which every sound heart responds. We cannot train any man properly unless we cultivate his fancy, and allow fair scope to his affections. We may starve the mind upon hard fact as we may starve the body upon meat, if we exclude all lighter diet, and all kinds of condiment. To enforce this truth has been the object of the story of *Hard Times*, and its enforcement is not argumentative, because no thesis can be argued in a novel; but by a warm appeal from one heart, to a hundred thousand hearts quite ready to respond. The story is not meant to do what fiction cannot do—to prove a case; its utmost purpose is to express forcibly a righteous sentiment. To run anywhere into a discussion of detail would have checked the current of a tale, which, as it stands, does not flag for the space even of a page. Wherever in the course of it any playful handling of a notion of the day suited the artist's purpose, the use made of it has been artistic always, never argumentative.

Hard Times, in fact, is not meant to be fought through, prosed over, conned laboriously, Blue Book in hand. Is the heart touched with a lively perception of the true thought which pervades the work from first to last—then the full moral purpose of it is attained. The very journal in which the novel appeared is itself a complete answer to any man, who, treating in a hard-fact spirit all the fanciful allusions of the novelist, should accuse Mr Dickens of attacking this good movement and the other, or of opposing the search after statistical and other information by which only real light can be thrown on social questions. What is *Household Words* but a great magazine of facts? And what one is there, of all those useful matters of detail which the novelist has by some readers been supposed to treat with disrespect, which he has not, as conductor of that journal, carefully and fully urged upon the public notice? In his character of journalist Mr Dickens has from the first especially laboured to cultivate the kindly affections and the fancy at the same time with the intellect, and that is simply what he asks men in 'these times' to do. But because he knows that facts and figures will not be lost sight of by the world, he leaves them, when he speaks as a novelist, to take care of themselves, and writes his tale wholly in the interests of the affections and the fancy.

And with unbroken satisfaction will those finer qualities in its readers fasten upon it. The personal regard which Mr Dickens inspires by his books will here have no abatement. Again he garners for himself the first fruits of the harvest of kindliness sown broadcast in all his writings. It is not necessary to review *Hard Times*. When we have said that the remarkably close texture of the story, the carefulness of its elaboration, and the unsuperfluousness of its details, as well as its whole interest, are far more perceptible now that it can be read as a book, than when it was known only as a series of chapters, we have reported all that calls for report from us. A new sense of its design and beauty in its various particulars is awakened by the reading of it as a whole. The homely grace and tenderness of Rachel appeals with more quiet effect, the unobtrusive pathos of her intercourse with Stephen is deepened, and if possible we are more impressed by what is shown of the working man's wrongs and delusions in connection with the truth and constancy of his nature. . . .

Even as we turn over the pages of the volume we are again led to observe the singular closeness of purpose with which the narrative is carried through a series of incidents of which the sequence has been planned with inimitable tact and skill. We quote no more. The story is one written 'for these times' that will be claimed for future times. Its many beauties blind us, as they will blind other generations, to its few defects.

90. [Richard Simpson], from a review in *The Rambler*

October 1854, n.s. ii, 361–2

Simpson (1820–76), Shakespearean scholar, was editor of the *Rambler* and of its successor, the *Home and Foreign Review*.

[Summarizes the plot.]

This dreary framework is filled in by the loves of Stephen, who, in his youth, married a drunkard, from whom, to his and Mr Dickens' disgust, neither death nor the laws will divorce him; and Rachel, a fellow 'hand' of pattern goodness, who is his guiding star. A star of the same kind is supplied to poor Louisa, in her trouble, by Sissy Jupe, the daughter of a clown in Sleary's horseriding troupe, the latter dividing the comic business of the tale with Mrs Sparsit, a sort of brown-holland edition of Volumnia in our author's *Bleak House*, who acts as house-keeper to Mr Bounderby. Here and there we meet with touches not unworthy of the inventor of *Pickwick*; but, on the whole, the story is stale, flat, and unprofitable; a mere dull melodrama, in which character is caricature, sentiment tinsel, and moral (if any) unsound. It is a thousand pities that Mr Dickens does not confine himself to amusing his readers, instead of wandering out of his depth in trying to instruct them. The one, no man can do better; the other, few men can do worse. With all his quickness of perception, his power of seizing salient points and surface-shadows, he has never shown any ability to pierce the depths of social life, to fathom the wells of social action. He can only paint what he sees, and should plan out his canvas accordingly. No doubt great evils exist in manufacturing towns, and elsewhere; but, nevertheless, steam-engines and power-looms are not the evil principle in material shape, as the folly of a conventional humanitarian slang insists on making them. The disease of Coketown will hardly be stayed by an abstinence from facts and figures; nor a healthy reaction insured by a course of cheap divorce and the poetry of nature. In short, whenever Mr Dickens and his school assume the office of instructors, it is, as Stephen Blackpool says, 'aw a muddle! Fro' first to last, a muddle!'

91. From an unsigned review, *Westminster Review*

October 1854, n.s. vi, 604–8

Perhaps by Mrs Jane Sinnett, who regularly did the *Westminster's* 'Belles Lettres' section at this time. She translated many works, mainly of Roman Catholic interest, and wrote some stories. The 'fearful struggle' she mentions was the great strike in the cotton-trade, centred on Preston, during the winter of 1853–4: see Dickens's article 'On Strike', *Household Words*, 11 February 1854, viii, 553–9.

When it was announced, amid the strikes and consequent derangements of commerce, that Mr Dickens was about to write a tale in *Household Words* to be called *Hard Times*, the general attention was instantly arrested. It was imagined the main topic of the story would be drawn from the fearful struggle which was being then enacted in the north, in which loss of money on the one side and the pangs of hunger on the other, were the weapons at command. The inner life of those great movements would, it was thought, be exhibited, and we should see the results of the wrongs and the delusions of the workman, and the alternations of hope and fear which must from day to day have agitated him at the various crises of the conflict, delineated in many a moving scene. Mr Dickens—if any one—it was considered, could be intrusted with this delicate task, and would give us a true idea of the relations of master and workman, both as they are and as they might be. Some of this is done in the book now before us, only this purpose is subordinated and made incidental to another, which is to exhibit the evil effects of an exclusive education of the intellect, without a due cultivation of the finer feelings of the heart and the fancy. We suppose it is in anticipation of some change of the present educational system for one that shall attempt to kill 'outright the robber Fancy,' that Mr Dickens launches forth his protest, for we are not aware of such a system being in operation anywhere in England. On the contrary, it is the opinion

of various continental professors, very competent to form a judgment
on this subject, that more play is given to the imagination and will by the
English system of instruction than by any other. If we look to our public
schools and universities, we find great part, too great part, we think,
of the period of youth and adolescence devoted to the study of the
mythology, literature, and history of the most poetic people of all
time. . . .

In almost every school in the kingdom, passages of our finest poets
are learned by heart; and Shakespeare and Walter Scott are among the
Penates of every decent family. If there are Gradgrind schools, they are
not sufficiently numerous to be generally known. Now, at the very
commencement of *Hard Times*, we find ourselves introduced to a set
of hard uncouth personages, of whose existence as a class no one is
aware, who are engaged in cutting and paring young souls after their
own ugly pattern, and refusing them all other nourishment but facts
and figures. The unpleasant impression caused by being thus suddenly
introduced into this cold and uncongenial atmosphere, is never effaced
by the subsequent charm of narrative and well-painted characters of
the tale. One can have no more pleasure in being present at this com-
pression and disfigurement than in witnessing the application of the
boot—nor in following these poor souls, thus intellectually halt and
maimed, through life, than in seeing Chinese ladies hobbling through a
race. It is not then with the truth Mr Dickens wishes to enforce, but
with the manner in which it is enforced, that we find fault. It was
possible to have done this in a less forbidding form, with actors whom
we should have recognised as more natural and less repulsive than the
Gradgrinds, Bounderbys, and Crakemchilds; to have placed in contrast persons educated after an ordinary and *practicable* plan, and persons of higher æsthetic training; but, at the same time, the task would
have required a deeper acquaintance with human nature. The most
successful characters in *Hard Times*, as is usual with Mr Dickens, are
those which are the *simplest* and least cultivated. Stephen Blackpool,
Rachel and Sissy, Mr Thleary of the 'horth-riding', and his single-
hearted troupe, all act and talk with such simplicity of heart and nobleness of mind, that their appearance on the stage is a most welcome relief
from the Gradgrinds, Bounderbys, Sparsits, &c., who are all odd
characters portrayed in a quaint style; and we regret that more of the
story is not devoted to objects who are so much more within Mr
Dickens's power of representation. Stephen Blackpool, with his rugged
steadfastness, sturdy truth, upright bearing, and fine Northern English

dialect, smacking strongly of the old Saxon, is a noble addition to the gallery which already contained the bluff John Browdie, the Yarmouth boatmen, and so many other fine portraits. The gentle lowly grace of Rachel, and her undeviating instinct of what is right and good, make her a fit companion to the worn and much-wronged Stephen. The story of their unfulfilled love, and its sad catastrophe, is a truly pathetic episode of humble life. But when Mr Dickens leaves his lowly-born heroes and heroines, and weaves personages of more cultivated natures into his plots, the difference of execution is very marked. In humble life, different occupations, different localities, produce marked and distinct hues of character: these differences are made more apparent by the absence of those equalizing influences which a long-continued and uniform education, and social intercourse subject to invariable rules of etiquette, produce upon the cultivated classes. Original and picturesque characters are therefore much more common among the poorer orders; their actions are simpler, proceeding from simpler motives, and they are principally to be studied from without. On the other hand, the characters of more cultivated persons, though more uniform in appearance, are in reality much more complex and various; and both these circumstances tend to render their study, for the purposes of representation, more difficult. Beneath the apparent uniformity lurk thousand-fold shades of difference, indicative of the mind within. ... The fact that Mr Thackeray has succeeded so well in drawing Rebecca Sharpe and Blanche Amory, the representatives of two classes, so like and yet so different, without exaggerating the peculiarities of either, would alone prove him to have the most intimate acquaintance with human nature of any novel writer of the day. Mr Dickens generally solves the problem in a different way; his characters, even when they are only of the *bourgeois* class, are nearly always furnished with some peculiarity, which, like the weight of a Dutch clock, is their ever-gravitating principle of action. The consequence is, they have, most of them, the appearance of puppets which Mr Dickens has constructed expressly for his present purpose. Mr Bounderby, for example, is a most outrageous character—who can believe in the possibility of such a man? Brought up carefully, and pushed on in the world by a poor and devoted mother, he not only pensions her off on a miserable pittance, and denies her all approach to him in his full-blown prosperity, but he is never introduced on the scene without being made to traduce her character, and that of others of his relatives, and invent lies about the way in which he lived, when he was, as he ever gave out, thrown helpless on the world. He is made to entertain his guests with the flavour of the stewed eels he purchased in the streets at eight years old, and with calculations that he had eaten in his youth at least three horses, under the guise of polonies and saveloys. Such things may excite a laugh, perhaps, in a farce spoken at the Victoria, but will hardly do so with any reader of taste. The whole of the Gradgrind family are unpleasant enough, but especially we might have been spared the melancholy spectacle of Mrs Gradgrind's decease. The death-bed of an inoffensive weak-minded woman should not have been made ridiculous, especially as it does not in any way assist the plot. The principal charm of the story is the style, which, aided by his delicate perception, enables Mr Dickens to take off the fleeting peculiarities of time and place, in the manner which has gained great part of his literary reputation. We doubt, however, whether his descriptions will be so intelligible fifty years hence: it is a language which speaks especially to the present generation. It has, however, frequent extravagances, which are indulged in by Mr Dickens and his followers, to a degree that becomes not unfrequently insupportable. The description of Coketown is good —in Mr Dickens's style.

[Quotes the beginning of Book 1, ch. v.]

But this is most intolerable *galimatias*.

[Quotes the opening paragraph of Book 2, ch. ix.]

92. From 'Hard Times (Refinished)', *Our Miscellany*

(new edn., 1857), 142-56

Ed. E. H. Yates and B. R. Brough.

Our Miscellany (which ought to have come out, but didn't) is a collection of parodies and lampoons; other victims include Ainsworth, G. P. R. James, Macaulay, Tennyson, Tupper, Samuel Warren, Longfellow, Poe, Albert Smith, Douglas Jerrold, and Elizabeth Barrett Browning. 'Hard Times (Refinished)' is signed 'B.' so was presumably written by Robert Brough (1828-60), one of the Brough brothers who singly, or in collaboration, produced many theatrical burlesques and much miscellaneous journalism. E. H. Yates was Edmund Yates (1831-94), a contributor to *Household Words* and soon to become an intimate friend of Dickens's. It is surprising that Dickens, who resented attempts to parody him, apparently forgave Yates for his association with this skit. Brough, too, continued after 1857 as an occasional contributor to *Household Words*.

CHAPTER XXXV[1]

They coovered poor Stephen Blackpool's face!

The crowd from the Old Hell Shaft pressed around him. Mr Gradgrind ran to look at the sufferer's face, but in doing so, he trod on a daisy. He wept: and a hundred and sixty more of his hairs turned gray. He would tread on no more daisies! . . .

'Rachel, beloved lass, art thou by me?'

[1] It would seem that the striking want of poetical justice in the usually-received termination of this otherwise excellent story, wherein none of the good people were made happy, and the wicked were most inadequately punished, had caused the author to tremble for his popularity among the female portion of the community—who, it is well known, will stand no liberties of that description. He has therefore (apparently) rewritten it on more orthodox principles; or (not improbably) got somebody else to rewrite it for him; or (as is barely possible) somebody else has rewritten it for him without asking his leave. . . . EDS. O.M.

'Ay, Stephen; how dost thou feel?'

'Hoomble and happy, lass. I be grateful and thankful. I be obliged to them as have brought charges o' robbery agin me; an' I hope as them as did it will be happy an' enjoy the fruits. I do only look on my being pitched down that theer shaft, and having all my bones broke, as a mercy and a providence, and God bless ev'rybody!'

'Stephen, your head be a wandering.'

'Ay, lass; awlus a muddle.'

'Will you take anything, Stephen?'

'I do hoombly thank thee for a good and trew lass thou hast awlus been to me; and I dunnot care if I do take a little soomut warm—wi' a little sugar.'

The sobered man had still credit at the neighbouring tavern. In two seconds he appeared with a steaming glass of rum-and-water, scarcely stopping to sip it by the way. . . .

Stephen drank it, every drop. Finished. Down to the dregs. No heel-taps.

'I do hoombly thank thee, Rachel, good and trew lass as thou hast been to me; but I do feel much better.'

'Oh, here!' Mr Bounderby blustered forward: 'I'm not going to stand this. If a man suspected of robbing Josiah Bounderby, of Coke-town's Bank, is to feel "much better," I should like to know what's the use of Old Hell Shafts. There's a touch of the gold-spoon game in that; and I'm up to the gold-spoon game—rather! And it wont go down with Josiah Bounderby. Of Coketown. Not exactly. Here! Where's a constable?'

There was none. Of course not. There never is, when wanted.

Mrs Sparsit and Bitzer pressed officiously forward, and volunteered to take Stephen into custody.

'Shame!' cried the populace.

'Oh, I dare say,' said Mr Bounderby; 'I'm a self-made man, and, having made myself, am not likely to be ashamed of anything. There, take him along.'

There was a movement, as if for a rescue. The sobered man had been sober quite long enough without a fight, and tucked up his sleeves.

Stephen prevented this explosion.

'Noa lads,' he said, in his meek broken voice; 'dunnot try to resky me. I be fond o' constables. I like going to prison. As for hard labour, I ha' been used to that long enough. Wi' regard to law—it's awlus a muddle.'. . .

They moved on, towards Coketown. The lights were beginning to
blink through the fog. Like winking. The seven o'clock bells were
ringing. Like one o'clock. Suddenly the tramp of horses and the fierce
barking of a dog were heard. . . .

[Sleary and the circus-folk arrive; Jupes's dog, Merrylegs, seizes Mr
Bounderby.]

'Quite enough, Thquire,' said Sleary. 'I call on everybody in the
Queenth name to athitht me in arethting thith man, Jothiah Bounderby,
for the murder of my clown, Jupe, thickthteen yearth ago.'

Sissy fainted into the Whelp's arms. From that moment the latter
quadruped resolved to lead a virtuous life.

Mrs Sparsit and Bitzer, with the alacrity of timeservers, released
Stephen, and seized on their former patron. Stephen slipped quietly
away in the confusion of the moment, remarking, with a wink of
satisfaction to Rachel, 'Awlus a muddle!'

Merrylegs retained his hold on his victim's throat. Like a vice.

'Murder!' cried Bounderby; 'release me from this dog, or demon,
and I will confess all.'

'Mewwylegth, come here, thir!'

Merrylegs released his victim.

'Well, then,' said the detected miscreant, desperately,—'sixteen years
ago I murdered the man, Jupe, to obtain possession of eighteen-pence,
with which I entered Coketown, and set up in business. And now, do
your worst.'

The crowd recoiled in horror. The sobered man picked up Mr
Bounderby's hat, that had dropped off in the scuffle, and immediately
pawned it.

'Off with him!' cried Sleary, in a tone of theatrical authority,—'to
jail!'

To jail! to jail! to jail!

CHAPTER XXXVI

Towards town. The crowd gathering. Like a snowball. Much dirtier,
though. Rather.

'Bitzer.'

The whisper was so hoarse that the light-porter scarcely recognized
his master's tones.

'Sir?'

[Bitzer is persuaded to buy some strychnine for Bounderby—but Stephen Blackpool's wife seizes the bottle from him and thus becomes 'a squalid loathsome corpse'. Bounderby, foiled in this attempted suicide, hears his pursuers approaching, led by a dog.]

What was to be done?

Give himself up. To justice? To be hanged—by the neck—till he was dead? No! He had raised himself from nothing, and he was not the man to trample on his own origin, if he could help it.

Lights at the end of the street.

'Bow! wow! wow! G-r-r-r-r-r-r!'

The dog again! How he wished the lights were in an edible form, and might choke the infuriated quadruped!

'G-r-r-o-o-o-o-w! Yap!'

'He is gaining on him. Good dog! at him, Merrylegs! S—s—tt! Murderers, boy, murderers!'

'Bow-ow-ow-o-o-o-o-w! Yap!'

There is scarcely an inch between the muzzle of the avenging Merrylegs and the seat of the inexpressibles that were considered, scarce an hour ago, worthy to press the highest judicial seat of Coketown. Another leap, and he has him by the trousers!

A yell of exultation bursts from the infuriated multitude. . . .

CHAPTER XXXVII

His melancholy-mad elephants were at work. They were always at work—day and night. I shouldn't like to be a melancholy-mad elephant, to be always at work—night and day. Should you? Not that I don't now and then sit up all night myself. But on those occasions I am not melancholy. By no means. Nor in the elephantine line. Quite the contrary. Mr Bounderby [who has escaped] entered the engine-room. There was a window at the back, by which he might let himself down into the Warren's Blacking river that supplied the mill, and so swim as far as Liverpool. He was alone,—the night-watchman of course had gone out for the evening. He could hear the crowds battering at the door below. In a few minutes he would be in custody.

The melancholy-mad elephants occupied a good deal of room. As will be the case with ill-tempered asthmatic old gentlemen, the building that contained them seemed insufficient space for them to wheeze and squeeze, and groan and moan, and mutter and splutter in. It required the greatest precaution, on the part of Mr Bounderby, to step over the foaming cylinders, exhausted receivers, cranks, levers, and what not, to reach the desired window in safety.

At length he opened it.

'Bow-ow-ow-ow! Gr-r-r-r!'

The dog again! Jupe's avenging angel! In at the window. Sixteen stories high! But of what is the dog not capable?

Bounderby fell back. Into what? Into the clutches of the melancholy-mad elephants. The fly-wheel caught him. Whirr! Burr! Whiz! Fiz! Round and round he went! He was a self-made man, but he had not made himself of sufficiently strong materials to resist the influence of the melancholy-mad elephants. . . .

     ★   ★   ★   ★   ★

Little remains to be told. Rachel and Stephen were married. The robbery of the bank was fixed upon Mrs Sparsit and Bitzer. As the house of Bounderby, however, had never issued anything but forged notes, the culprits were soon detected in the attempt to pass some of them. Sissy married the reformed Whelp, and reared a large family of puppies. Mr Gradgrind ended his days as a clown to Sleary's troop. He had had a lesson in the futility of facts, and during his engagement could never be prevailed upon to accept wages. He lived by borrowing sixpences of the rest of the company—as a penance. . . .

[The fates of all the other surviving characters are described.]

And now, reader, let us love one another. If you will, I will. I can't say fairer. And so, God bless us all.

93. John Ruskin, in *Unto this Last,* *Cornhill Magazine*

August 1860, ii, 159

Reprinted in book-form, 1862.

The essential value and truth of Dickens's writings have been unwisely lost sight of by many thoughtful persons, merely because he presents his truth with some colour of caricature. Unwisely, because Dickens's caricature, though often gross, is never mistaken. Allowing for his manner of telling them, the things he tells us are always true. I wish that he could think it right to limit his brilliant exaggeration to works written only for public amusement; and when he takes up a subject of high national importance, such as that which he handled in *Hard Times,* that he would use severer and more accurate analysis. The usefulness of that work (to my mind, in several respects the greatest he has written) is with many persons seriously diminished because Mr Bounderby is a dramatic monster, instead of a characteristic example of a worldly master; and Stephen Blackpool a dramatic perfection, instead of a characteristic example of an honest workman. But let us not lose the use of Dickens's wit and insight, because he chooses to speak in a circle of stage fire. He is entirely right in his main drift and purpose in every book he has written; and all of them, but especially *Hard Times,* should be studied with close and earnest care by persons interested in social questions. They will find much that is partial, and, because partial, apparently unjust; but if they examine all the evidence on the other side, which Dickens seems to overlook, it will appear, after all their trouble, that his view was the finally right one, grossly and sharply told.

94. Edwin P. Whipple, from an essay on *Hard Times*, in the *Atlantic Monthly*

March 1877, xxxix, 353–58

Reprinted in Whipple's *Charles Dickens: the Man and his Work* (Boston and New York, 1912), ii, 92–115.

... During the composition of *Hard Times* the author was evidently in an embittered state of mind in respect to social and political questions. He must have felt that he was in some degree warring against the demonstrated laws of the production and distribution of wealth; yet he also felt that he was putting into prominence some laws of the human heart which he supposed political economists had studiously overlooked or ignored. ... Dickens's mind was so deficient in the power of generalization, so inapt to recognize the operation of inexorable law, that whatever offended his instinctive benevolent sentiments he was inclined to assail as untrue. Now there is no law the operation of which so frequently shocks our benevolent sentiments as the law of gravitation; yet no philanthropist, however accustomed he may be to subordinate scientific truth to amiable impulses, ever presumes to doubt the certain operation of that law. The great field for the contest between the head and the heart is the domain of political economy. The demonstrated laws of this science are often particularly offensive to many good men and good women, who wish well for their fellow-creatures, and who are pained by the obstacles which economic maxims present to their diffusive benevolence. The time will come when it will be as intellectually discreditable for an educated person to engage in a crusade against the established laws of political economy as in a crusade against the established laws of the physical universe; but the fact that men like Carlyle, Ruskin, and Dickens can write economic nonsense without losing intellectual caste shows that the science of political economy, before its beneficent truths come to be generally admitted, must go through a long struggle with benevolent sophisms and benevolent passions. . . .

In judging the work, neither Ruskin [see No. 93] nor Macaulay [see p. 300] seems to have made any distinction between Dickens as a creator of character and Dickens as a humorous satirist of what he considers flagrant abuses. As a creator of character he is always tolerant and many sided; as a satirist he is always intolerant and onesided; and the only difference between his satire and that of other satirists consists in the fact that he has a wonderful power in individualizing abuses in persons. Juvenal, Dryden, and Pope, though keen satirists of character, are comparatively ineffective in the art of concealing their didactic purpose under an apparently dramatic form. So strong is Dickens's individualizing faculty, and so weak his faculty of generalization, that as a satirist he simply personifies his personal opinions. These opinions are formed by quick-witted impressions intensified by philanthropic emotions; they spring neither from any deep insight of reason nor from any careful processes of reasoning; and they are therefore contemptuously discarded as fallacies by all thinkers on social problems who are devoted to the investigation of social phenomena and the establishment of economic laws; but they are so vividly impersonated, and the classes satirized are so felicitously hit in some of their external characteristics and weak points, that many readers fail to discover the essential difference between such realities of character as Tony Weller and Mrs Gamp, and such semblances of character as Mr Gradgrind and Mr Bounderby. Whatever Dickens understands he humorously represents; whatever he does not understand he humorously misrepresents; but in either case, whether he conceives or misconceives, he conveys to the general reader an impression that he is as great in those characters in which he personifies his antipathies as in those in which he embodies his sympathies.

The operation of this satirical as contrasted with dramatic genius is apparent in almost every person who appears in *Hard Times*, except Sleary and his companions of the circus combination. Mr Gradgrind and Mr Bounderby are personified abstractions, after the method of Ben Jonson; but the charge that Macaulay brings against them, that they have little of Dickens's humor, must be received with qualifications. Mr Bounderby, for example, as the satirical representative of a class, and not as a person who could have had any real existence,—as a person who gathers into himself all the vices of a horde of English manufacturers, without a ray of light being shed into his internal constitution of heart and mind,—is one of the wittiest and most humorous of Dickens's embodied sarcasms. Bounderby becomes a seeming character by being looked at and individualized from the point of view of imaginative antipathy. So surveyed, he seems real to thousands who observe their employers from the outside, and judge of them, not as they are, but as they appear to their embittered minds and hearts. Still, the artistic objection holds good that when a man resembling Mr Bounderby is brought into the domain of romance or the drama, the great masters of romance and the drama commonly insist that he shall be not only externally represented but internally known. There is no authorized, no accredited way of exhibiting character but this, that the dramatist or novelist shall enter into the soul of the personage represented, shall sympathize with him sufficiently to know him, and shall represent his passions, prejudices, and opinions as springing from some central will and individuality. This sympathy is consistent with the utmost hatred of the person described; but characterization becomes satire the moment that antipathy supersedes insight and the satirist berates the exterior manifestations of an individuality whose interior life he has not diligently explored and interpreted. Bounderby, therefore, is only a magnificent specimen of what satirical genius can do when divorced from the dramatist's idea of justice, and the dramatist's perception of those minute peculiarities of intellect, disposition, and feeling which distinguish one 'bully of humility' from another.

It is ridiculous to assert, as Ruskin asserts, that *Hard Times* is Dickens's greatest work; for it is *the* one of all his works which should be distinguished from the others as specially wanting in that power of real characterization on which his reputation as a vivid delineator of human character and human life depends. The whole effect of the story, though it lacks neither amusing nor pathetic incidents, and though it contains passages of description which rank with his best efforts in combining truth of fact with truth of imagination, is ungenial and unpleasant. Indeed, in this book, he simply intensified popular discontent; he ignored or he was ignorant of those laws the violation of which is at the root of popular discontent; and proclaimed with his favorite ideal workman, Stephen Blackpool, that not only the relation between employers and employed, but the whole constitution of civilized society itself, was a hopeless 'muddle,' beyond the reach of human intelligence or humane feeling to explain and justify. It is to be observed here that all cheering views of the amelioration of the condition of the race come from those hard thinkers whose benevolent impulses push them to the investigation of natural and economic laws. Starting from the position of sentimental benevolence, and meeting unforeseen intellectual obstacles at every step in his progress, Dickens ends 'in a muddle' by the necessity of his method. Had he been intellectually equipped with the knowledge possessed by many men to whom in respect to genius he was immensely superior, he would never have landed in a conclusion so ignominious, and one which the average intellect of well-informed persons of the present day contemptuously rejects. If Dickens had contented himself with using his great powers of observation, sympathy, humor, imagination, and characterization in their appropriate fields, his lack of scientific training in the austere domain of social, legal, and political science would have been hardly perceptible; but after his immense popularity was assured by the success of *The Pickwick Papers*, he was smitten with the ambition to direct the public opinion of Great Britain by embodying, in exquisitely satirical caricatures, rash and hasty judgments on the whole government of Great Britain in all its departments, legislative, executive, and judicial. He overlooked uses, in order to fasten on abuses. His power to excite, at his will, laughter, or tears, or indignation was so great, that the victims of his mirthful wrath were not at first disposed to resent his debatable fallacies while enjoying his delicious fun. His invasion of the domain of political science with the palpable design of substituting benevolent instincts for established laws was carelessly condoned by the statesmen, legists, and economists whom he denounced and amused.

Indeed, the great characteristic of Dickens's early popularity was this, that it was confined to no class, but extended to all classes, rich and poor, noble and plebeian. The queen on the throne read him, and so did Hodge at the plow; and between the sovereign and her poorest subject there was no class which did not sound his praise as a humorist. Still, every student of the real genius of Dickens must be surprised at the judgment pronounced on his various romances by what may be called the higher, the professional, the educated classes, the classes which, both in England and in the United States, hold positions of trust and honor, and are bound, by the practical necessities of their posts, to be on a level with the advancing intelligence of the age in legislative, economic, and judicial science. By these persons *The Pickwick Papers* are, as a general thing, preferred to any other of the works of Dickens. The Lord Chief Justice (afterwards Lord Chancellor) Campbell told Dickens that he would prefer the honor of having written that book to the honors which his professional exertions had obtained for him, that of being a peer of Parliament and the nominal head of the law. All persons who have had a sufficiently large acquaintance with the men of practical ability who have risen to power in the United States, whether as judges, statesmen, or political economists, must have been impressed with the opinion of these men as to the superiority of *The Pickwick Papers* over all the successive publications of Dickens. Yet it is as certain as any question coming before the literary critic can be, that a number of the works that followed *The Pickwick Papers* are superior to that publication, not only in force of sentiment, imagination, and characterization, but in everything which distinguishes the individual genius of Dickens,—a genius which up to the time of *David Copperfield* deepened and enlarged in the orderly process of its development. The secret of this preference for *The Pickwick Papers* is to be found in the fact that the author had, in that book, no favorite theory to push, no grand moral to enforce, no assault on principles about which educated men had made up their minds. These men could laugh heartily at Mr Buzfuz and Mr Justice Stareleigh; but when, as in *Bleak House*, there was a serious attempt to assail equity jurisprudence, they felt that the humorist had ventured on ground where he had nothing but his genius to compensate for his lack of experience and knowledge. Thus it is that a work which, with all its wealth of animal spirits, is comparatively shallow and superficial considered as a full expression of Dickens's powers of humor, pathos, narrative, description, imagination, and characterization, has obtained a preëminence above its successors, not because it contains what is best and deepest in Dickens's genius, but because it omits certain matters relating to social and economical science, with which he was imperfectly acquainted, and on which his benevolence, misleading his genius, still urged him vehemently to dogmatize. His educated readers enjoyed his humor and pathos as before, but they were more or less irritated by the intrusion of social theories which they had long dismissed from their minds as exploded fallacies, and did not see that the wit was more pointed, the humor richer, the faculty of constructing a story more developed, the sentiment of humanity more earnest and profound, than in the inartistic incidents of *The Pickwick Papers*, over which they had laughed until they had cried, and cried until they had laughed again. They desired amusement merely; *The Pickwick Papers* are the most amusing of Dickens's works; and they were correspondingly vexed with an author who deviated from the course of amusing them into that of instructing them, only to emphasize notions which were behind the knowledge of the time, and which interfered with their enjoyment without giving them any intelligent instruction.

Still, allowing for the prepossessions of Dickens in writing *Hard Times*, and forgetting Adam Smith, Ricardo, and John Stuart Mill,—looking at him only as a humorous satirist profoundly disgusted with some prominent evils of his day,—we may warmly praise the book as one of the most perfect of its kind. The bleakness of the whole representation of human life proceeds from the Gradgrind Philosophy of Life, which emphasizes Fact and denounces all cultivation of the sentiments and the imagination. . . .

The relation between Mr James Harthouse and Louisa is one of the best 'situations' in Dickens's novels. Harthouse represents a type of character which was the object of Dickens's special aversion, the younger son of a younger son of family,—'born bored,' as St Simon says of the Duke of Orleans, and passing listlessly through life in a constant dread of boredom, but seeking distractions and stimulants through new experiences,—'a thorough gentleman, made to the model of the time, weary of everything, and putting no more faith in anything than Lucifer.' Contrasted with this jaded man of fashion is Louisa Gradgrind, the wife of Mr Bounderby. Far from being morally and mentally wearied by too large an experience of life, she has had no experience of life at all. Her instincts, feelings, and imagination, as a woman, have been forced back into the interior recesses of her mind by the method of her education, and are therefore ever ready to burst forth, with an impetuosity corresponding to the force used in their repression and restraint. Now Dickens, as an English novelist, was prevented, by his English sense of decorum, from describing in detail those sensuous and passionate elements in her nature which brought her to the point of agreeing to an elopement with her lover. A French novelist would have had no difficulty in this respect. Leaving out of view such romancers as Alexandre Dumas and Frédéric Soulié, with what pleasure would story-tellers of a higher order, like Théophile Gautier, Prosper Mérimée, George Sand, and Charles de Bernard, have recorded their minute analysis of every phase of passion in the breasts of the would-be adulterer and the would-be adulteress! As it is, the reader finds it difficult to understand the frenzy of soul, the terrible tumult of feeling, which rends the heart of Louisa as she flies to her father on the evening she has agreed to elope with her lover. Such madness as she displays in the culmination of passion might have been explained by exhibiting, step by step, the growth of her passion. Instead of this, we are overwhelmed by the sudden passage of ice into fire without any warning of the perilous transformation.

The method of the French novelists is doubtless corrupting in just the degree in which it is interpretative. Whatever may be said of it, it at least accounts, on the logic of passion, for those crimes against the sanctity of the marriage relation which all good people deplore, but which few good people seem to understand.

It is needless to add, in this connection, any remarks on the singular purity of the relation existing between Rachel and Stephen Blackpool. Any reader who can contemplate it without feeling the tears gather in his eyes is hopelessly insensible to the pathos of Dickens in its most touching manifestations.

95. Anthony Trollope on Dickens

1855, 1870, 1875-6

Trollope (1815-82) began his career as a novelist in 1847. *The Warden* is his first 'Barsetshire' novel; in extract (*a*), Mr Bold is reading the first number of *The Almshouse*, a novel by 'Mr Popular Sentiment' (i.e. Dickens) inspired by the current allegations about the misappropriation of ecclesiastical endowments, such as at the almshouse where Mr Harding is Warden. 'It's clear,' Bold hears, 'that Sentiment has been down to Barchester, and got up the whole story there ... it's very well done ... his first numbers always are.' (*b*) comes from *St. Paul's Magazine*, of which Trollope was editor; (*c*) from the chapter 'On English Novelists of the Present Day', in the *Autobiography*, where he opens his survey: 'I do not hesitate to name Thackeray the first' (cf. his *Thackeray* [1879]). See also his 'Novel-reading', a review of Dickens's and Thackeray's *Collected Works* (*Nineteenth Century*, January 1879, v, 24-43; much of it used in *Autobiography*, ch. xii). He there cites a happy anecdote to illustrate Dickens's popularity: tradesmen had recently been making 'free-gift offers' of books with certain purchases, and one tea-dealer had ordered 18 000 volumes of Dickens; when the bookseller suggested some other novelties, the tea-dealer insisted that 'Dickens was what he wanted. He had found that the tea-consuming public preferred their Dickens' (v, 32-3). See Ernest Boll, 'Infusions of Dickens in Trollope', *Trollopian*, i (1946), 11-24.

(*a*) In former times great objects were attained by great work. When evils were to be reformed, reformers set about their heavy task with grave decorum and laborious argument. An age was occupied in proving a grievance, and philosophical researches were printed in folio pages, which it took a life to write, and an eternity to read. We get on now with a lighter step, and quicker: ridicule is found to be more convincing than argument, imaginary agonies touch more than true sorrows, and monthly novels convince, when learned quartos fail to do so. If the world is to be set right, the work will be done by shilling numbers.

Of all such reformers Mr Sentiment is the most powerful. It is incredible the number of evil practices he has put down: it is to be feared he will soon lack subjects, and that when he has made the working classes comfortable, and got bitter beer put into proper-sized pint bottles, there will be nothing further for him left to do. Mr Sentiment is certainly a very powerful man, and perhaps not the less so that his good poor people are so very good; his hard rich people so very hard; and the genuinely honest so very honest. Namby-pamby in these days is not thrown away if it be introduced in the proper quarters. Divine peeresses are no longer interesting, though possessed of every virtue; but a pattern peasant or an immaculate manufacturing hero may talk as much twaddle as one of Mrs Ratcliffe's heroines, and still be listened to. Perhaps, however, Mr Sentiment's great attraction is in his second-rate characters. If his heroes and heroines walk upon stilts, as heroes and heroines, I fear, ever must, their attendant satellites are as natural as though one met them in the street; they walk and talk like men and women, and live among our friends a rattling, lively life; yes, live, and will live till the names of their calling shall be forgotten in their own, and Buckett and Mrs Gamp will be the only words left to us to signify a detective police officer or a monthly nurse. . . .

[A summary of *The Almshouse* follows.]

Bold finished the number; and as he threw it aside, he thought that that at least had no direct appliance to Mr Harding, and that the absurdly strong colouring of the picture would disenable the work from doing either good or harm. He was wrong. The artist who paints for the million must use glaring colours, as no one knew better than Mr Sentiment when he described the inhabitants of his almshouse; and the radical reform which has now swept over such establishments has owed more to the twenty numbers of Mr Sentiment's novel, than to all the true complaints which have escaped from the public for the last half century. (From *The Warden* (1855), ch. xv).

(*b*) Of his novels, the first striking circumstance is their unprecedented popularity. This is not the time for exact criticism; but, even were it so, no critic is justified in putting aside the consideration of that circumstance. When the masses of English readers, in all English-reading countries, have agreed to love the writings of any writer, their verdict

will be stronger than that of any one judge, let that judge be ever
so learned and ever so thoughtful. However the writer may have
achieved his object, he has accomplished that which must be the desire
of every author,—he has spoken to men and women who have opened
their ears to his words, and have listened to them. He has reached the
goal which all authors seek. In this respect Dickens was, probably,
more fortunate during his own life than any writer that ever lived. The
English-speaking public may be counted, perhaps, as a hundred millions, and wherever English is read these books are popular from the
highest to the lowest,—among all classes that read. . . . He could
measure the reading public,—probably taking his measure of it unconsciously,—and knew what the public wanted of him. Consequently
the sale of his books has been hitherto so far from ephemeral,—their
circulation has been so different from that which is expected for ordinary novels,—that it has resembled in its nature the sales of legs of
mutton or of loaves of bread. . . .

And no other writer of English language except Shakespeare has
left so many types of character as Dickens has done,—characters which
are known by their names familiarly as household words, and which
bring to our minds vividly and at once, a certain well-understood set of
ideas, habits, phrases, and costumes, making together a man, or woman,
or child, whom we know at a glance and recognise at a sound,—as we
do our own intimate friends. And it may be doubted whether even
Shakespeare has done this for so wide a circle of acquaintances. . . .
Pickwick and Sam Weller, Mrs Nickleby and Wackford Squeers,
Fagin and Bill Sikes, Micawber, Mrs Gamp, Pecksniff, and Bucket the
Detective, are persons so well known to us that we think that they, who
are in any way of the professions of these worthies, are untrue to themselves if they depart in aught from their recognised and understood
portraits. Pickwick can never be repeated;—*nulli similis aut secundus*[1],
he is among our dearest and nearest, and we expect no one to be like
him. But a 'boots' at an hotel is more of a boots the closer he resembles
Sam Weller. . . .

Most of us have probably heard Dickens's works often criticised,
want of art in the choice of words and want of nature in the creation of
character, having been the faults most frequently attributed to him.
But his words have been so potent, whether they may be right or
wrong according to any fixed rule, that they have justified themselves
by making themselves into a language which is in itself popular; and

[1] 'Neither like nor second to any other.'

his characters, if unnatural, have made a second nature by their own force. It is fatuous to condemn that as deficient in art which has been so full of art as to captivate all men. . . .

It always seemed to me that no man ever devoted himself so entirely as Charles Dickens to things which he understood, and in which he could work with effect. Of other matters he seemed to have a disregard, —and for many things almost a contempt which was marvellous. To literature in all its branches his attachment was deep,—and his belief in it was a thorough conviction. He could speak about it as no other man spoke. He was always enthusiastic in its interests, ready to push on beginners, quick to encourage those who were winning their way to success, sympathetic with his contemporaries, and greatly generous to aid those who were failing. He thoroughly believed in literature; but in politics he seemed to have no belief at all. Men in so-called public life were to him, I will not say insincere men, but so placed as to be by their calling almost beyond the pale of sincerity. To his feeling, all departmental work was the bungled, muddled routine of a Circumlocution Office. Statecraft was odious to him; and though he would probably never have asserted that a country could be maintained without legislative or executive, he seemed to regard such devices as things so prone to evil, that the less of them the better it would be for the country,— and the farther a man kept himself from their immediate influence the better it would be for him. I never heard any man call Dickens a radical; but if any man ever was so, he was a radical at heart,—believing entirely in the people, writing for them, speaking for them, and always desirous to take their part against some undescribed and indiscernible tyrant, who to his mind loomed large as an official rather than as an aristocratic despot. He hardly thought that our parliamentary rulers could be trusted to accomplish ought that was good for us. Good would come gradually,—but it would come by the strength of the people, and in opposition to the blundering of our rulers. . . .

He would attempt nothing,—show no interest in anything,—which he could not do, and which he did not understand. But he was not on that account forced to confine himself to literature. Every one knows how he read. Most readers of these lines, though they may never have seen him act,—as I never did,—still know that his acting was excellent. As an actor he would have been at the top of his profession. And he had another gift,—had it so wonderfully, that it may almost be said that he has left no equal behind him. He spoke so well, that a public dinner became a blessing instead of a curse, if he was in the chair,—had its compensating twenty minutes of pleasure, even if he were called upon to propose a toast, or to thank the company for drinking his health. . . . (from 'Charles Dickens', *St. Paul's Magazine*, July 1870, vi, 370–5).

(*c*) He has now been dead nearly six years, and the sale of his books goes on as it did during his life. . . . There is no withstanding such testimony as this. Such evidence of popular appreciation should go for very much, almost for everything, in criticism on the work of a novelist. The primary object of a novelist is to please; and this man's novels have been found more pleasant than those of any other writer. It might of course be objected to this, that though the books have pleased they have been injurious, that their tendency has been immoral and their teaching vicious; but it is almost needless to say that no such charge has ever been made against Dickens. His teaching has ever been good. From all which, there arises to the critic a question whether, with such evidence against him as to the excellence of this writer, he should not subordinate his own opinion to the collected opinion of the world of readers. To me it almost seems that I must be wrong to place Dickens after Thackeray and George Eliot, knowing as I do that so great a majority put him above those authors. . . .

Of Dickens's style it is impossible to speak in praise. It is jerky, un-grammatical, and created by himself in defiance of rules—almost as completely as that created by Carlyle. To readers who have taught themselves to regard language, it must therefore be unpleasant. But the critic is driven to feel the weakness of his criticism, when he acknow-ledges to himself—as he is compelled in honesty to do—that with this language, such as it is, the writer has satisfied the great mass of the readers of his country. Both these great writers have satisfied the readers of their own pages; but both have done infinite harm by creat-ing a school of imitators. No young novelist should ever dare to imitate the style of Dickens. If such a one wants a model for his language, let him take Thackeray (*Autobiography* (written 1875–6, published 1883), ch. xii).

96. Mrs Oliphant, from 'Charles Dickens', *Blackwood's Magazine*

April 1855, lxxvii, 451–66

Mrs Margaret Oliphant (1828–97), prolific novelist, reviewer, and writer of miscellaneous literature, was a frequent contributor to *Blackwood's*, where she wrote about Dickens several times; see below, Nos. 124, 155. See also her *Victorian Age in Literature* (1892), ch. vi, markedly unsympathetic to Dickens's later work and to his pathos. In the present review, she refers to her knowledge of English dissent; this appears in her novel *Salem Chapel* and others in the *Chronicles of Carlingford* series, 1862–76.

... we cannot but express our conviction that it is to the fact that he represents a class that he owes his speedy elevation to the top of the wave of popular favour. He is a man of very liberal sentiments—an assailer of constituted wrongs and authorities—one of the advocates in the plea of Poor *versus* Rich, to the progress of which he has lent no small aid in his day. But he is, notwithstanding, perhaps more distinctly than any other author of the time, a *class* writer, the historian and representative of one circle in the many ranks of our social scale. Despite their descents into the lowest class, and their occasional flights into the less familiar ground of fashion, it is the air and the breath of middle-class respectability which fills the books of Mr Dickens. His heroes are not the young men of clubs and colleges—not the audacious youngsters of Eton, nor the 'awful swells' in whose steps they follow. Home-bred and sensitive, much impressed by feminine influences, swayed by the motives, the regards, and the laws which were absolute to their childhood, Mr Dickens' heroes are all young for a necessity. Their courage is of the order of courage which belongs to women. They are spotless in their thoughts, their intentions, and wishes. Into those dens of vice, and unknown mysteries, whither the lordly Pelham may penetrate without harm, and which Messrs Pendennis and Warrington frequent, that they may see 'life,' David Copperfield could not enter

327

without pollution. In the very heart and soul of him this young man is *respectable*. He is a great deal more; he is pure, a thoroughly refined and gentle-hearted boy; but his respectability is strong upon him. His comings and goings are within a lesser circle than are those of his contemporaries whose names we have mentioned. He cannot afford to defy the world's laugh, or to scorn it. That he has, moreover, no relish for these excitements and investigations—that his course is clear in the common beaten way—and that he has 'a carnal inclination' to be good and virtuous, are other considerations; but in his sphere he would be instantly branded with the evil mark of dissipation and disreput-ableness, were he seen once in the company which the young man about town of a higher rank may go to see with impunity; as students of natural history go to see the new arrivals of reptiles or beasts of prey. In the society of Mr Dickens' admirable stories, there is no such thing as going to the Haunt of nights and coming from thence uninjured. There is no such thing possible or permissible in the class and society which Mr Dickens draws. When the young man there steps aside into such forbidden ways, he goes irretrievably astray—sinks out of charac-ter and respectability—and becomes a very poor wreck indeed, a warn-ing and beacon to all the David Copperfields. For society down below here, in the third or fourth circle of elevation, is more exacting than that grander and gayer society which calls itself 'the world;' and while the multitude of novel-writers set themselves to illustrate, with or without a due knowledge of it, the life of lords and ladies, and the gay realms of fashion, Mr Dickens contents his genius with the sphere in which we suppose his lot to have been cast by nature, in the largest 'order' of our community—the middle class of England. Having identified himself with this portion of society, and devoted his powers to its illustration, this grateful public carries its novelist in its heart; and without denying in any way his claims to that higher genius which can give life and breath—the truth of nature, if not of conventional correctness—to every impersonation of its fellows, we cannot do justice to Mr Dickens without recognising this, his first and greatest claim to our regard, as the historian of a class—the literary interpreter of those intelligent, sensible, warm-hearted households, which are the strength of our country, and occupy the wide middle ground between the rich and the poor.

This middle class in itself is a realm of infinite gradations, and the term has perhaps a different meaning in the lips of every different indi-vidual who says the words; but we take it in its widest sense. . . . To this vast and struggling mass, the great majority of which—every man for himself—earns his own bread, and wins his own fortune, there are laws more limited, and decorums more strict, in form and use, than the easier and loftier circle above them has need of. There is less daring and more timidity. There is the weaker spirit, which finds in what it doubts and trembles at, an evil and contamination which does not exist to the gay and light heart; and there is neither time nor energy to expend in unnecessary adventures. Knowledge of life must be learned here, not in experimental studies, but in the actual combat; and the day's work and the night's rest limit the ways of every man who would keep his place in the constant march. As a consequence, this class does not abound in picturesque situations, and sometimes the meaner vices grow and flourish where respectability and the strong grasp of appearances keep grosser sins away. But nowhere does the household hearth burn brighter—nowhere is the family love so warm—the natural bonds so strong; and this is the ground which Mr Dickens occupies *par excellence* —the field of his triumphs, from which he may defy all his rivals without fear.

. . . Since [*Pickwick*] the story of his [Mr Dickens's] fortune is one almost uninterrupted triumph. His real and great merits have given him a secure place with the worthier portion of his audience, and his very weaknesses and exaggerations have established him in the favour of others. It is to him we owe that form of serial publication which has added so largely to the number of readers, and the success of individual authors. He has his host of followers, his crowd of admirers, like any other great man; and he has assumed a leader's place not only in literature, but in the world, in morals, in philanthropy, in questions of social interest. Mr Dickens has unveiled himself from that personal obscurity which softens so gracefully the presence of a great writer. He has ceased to speak his strictures or to pronounce his approbation out of that mist of half-disclosed identity which becomes the literary censor. He is less the author of *Pickwick*, of *Copperfield*, of *Bleak House*, than he is Charles Dickens; and we confess that we cannot regard him with the same affection or the same indulgence in the latter character as in the former. The man who is not content with giving to the world many admirable pictures of its own living and breathing progress—who is not satisfied with his power of creating a real man, a real woman, and throwing upon these creations of his genius that ideal purity and generous grace which ought to be the very highest aim of the writer of fiction—this man must do something better than indifferent and doubtful pieces of philanthropy and social reformation, before he can hope to establish for himself—the *man* as separate from the *writer*—a second reputation. From the author who has conferred a great many pleasures upon us—who has added so largely to our acquaintance, and given us so many types of real and individual existence with which to enrich our mind and conversation—we are prepared to receive everything with the respect which he merits; but our relative position is very different when we come to be placed opposite, not the writer, but the man. Mr Dickens is the favourite and spoiled child of the popular heart. There is a long ring of applause echoing after him wherever it pleases him to go; but for the sake of his great and well-deserved reputation, we think it would be well for Mr Dickens to discover on which foundation it is that he stands most secure.

And in this volume before us, the latest work he has given to the world—*Hard Times*—we discover, not the author's full and many-toned conception of human life, its motives and its practices,—not the sweet and graceful fancy rejoicing in her own creations, nor the stronger and graver imagination following the fate of her complete idea, rather as a chronicler than a producer of the events which its natural character and qualities call forth,—but the petulant theory of a man in a world of his own making, where he has no fear of being contradicted, and is absolutely certain of having everything his own way....

[After further criticisms of *Hard Times*, Mrs Oliphant surveys Dickens's career from *Pickwick* to *Bleak House*. A selection of her comments is here reprinted.]

With the publication of *Nicholas Nickleby* the world recovered permanently the author of the *Pickwick Papers*. Mr Dickens has never forgotten his memorable experiment in the tragic vein; with more or less success he returns to the field in almost every subsequent novel, but, we are bound to testify, does it discreetly, without inflicting upon us unnecessary horror. His crowd of odd and quaint and out-of-the-way characters, his careful pictures of eccentric benevolence, his descriptions, which exhaust the landscape, and leave nothing suggestive in it, nothing that you cannot see—have gone on from that time to this, improving in execution without diminishing in vitality and freshness. But it is somewhat singular to remark in these volumes—which are perhaps the most universally read of any books existing at this day, which deal in the common circumstances, the most usual belongings of everyday life—how little of the common and everyday character finds a place in their pages. As a matter of personal experience, we do not find the world abound very greatly in oddities—one or two in the circle of his acquaintance is generally as much as an ordinary member of society is gifted with. But the wonderful thing in these books is, that here are no ordinary members of society—that, save the hero himself, the spectator and chronicler of the whole, every man is an 'original.' If we do 'rub each other's angles down' in the world, we certainly do not find it so in Mr Dickens' novels. . . . Is it necessary, then, before we can interest a kindly and familiar audience in an Englishman of the most respectable middle class, to endow him with some exaggerated peculiarity to make him a 'character?' It may be so; yet the art which works its results by means of common men and women, the ordinary everyday creatures, who are neither odd nor eccentric, is certainly the highest art. . . .

. . . Poor little Nell! who has ever been able to read the last chapter of her history with an even voice or a clear eye? Poor little Nell! how we defied augury, and clung to hope for her—how we refused to believe that Kit and the strange gentleman, when they alighted amid the snow at the cottage door, could not do some miracle for her recovery! Mr Dickens acted cruelly to his youthful readers in this conclusion. Does he not confess to a host of letters begging him to spare the child? Yet there is the less to complain of, because we can see from the first the doom of little Nell.

The hero of the *Old Curiosity Shop* is an indisputable creation: the hardest heart in the world, with the exception of that one which wedded the market-gardener, could not resist the manifold fascinations of Dick Swiveller. We have no fault to find with the good-hearted prodigal—in all his ways and fashions he is perfect, amusing us first, to betray us afterwards into liking and regard for him, scamp as he is; and in no circumstances does he swerve from his character, or disappoint our good opinion of him. Dick is worthy to take his place with Sam Weller, a person as distinct and true, and worthy of universal recognition; and it would be hard to find anything better done than the ludicro-sentimental shade which his singular gift in quotations throws over the conversation of Mr Swiveller, a peculiarity which still never makes him *quite* ridiculous, but preserves with admirable skill its mingled tone—absurd, yet sincere, and serious enough in its way, and always quite genuine and unconscious. For Dick, you will perceive, does not suspect you of laughing at him for his dear gazelle, who marries a market-gardener; nor for his tearful vow to the Marchioness, that 'she shall walk in silk attire, and siller hae to spare.' No, poor fellow; Dick is perfectly in earnest, and is giving only a natural expression to his thoughts.

And where, out of the works of Mr Dickens, could one find such a family as the Garlands?—the little old lady and the little old gentleman, Mr Abel and the pony—so odd, yet so kind and pleasant—so unlike common people, yet so far from being impossible ones; or Kit, good, sturdy, honest fellow; or that remarkable piece of still life, little Jacob? We suppose *Master Humphrey's Clock* to have been by no means the most successful of Mr Dickens' works; and we have very little patience with the mumming of the initial chapters here; but Mr Dickens has never surpassed some of these scenes; and we will not consent to class the *Old Curiosity Shop* with the twin story to which the author has been pleased to couple it, *Barnaby Rudge*.

Nor have we much to say of *Dombey*, which is a very imperfect book, though it has capital individuals in its *dramatis personæ*. Toots and Miss Nipper are above criticism, and quite admirable. . . . The story of Edith's elopement is altogether disagreeable; and the hurried and slovenly manner in which Mr Dickens chooses to thrust his villanous Carker out of the way is extremely unsatisfactory. So unceremonious a dismissal for an important—but at that time rather embarrassing— personage, suggests to the suspicious critic a poverty of means of which we hesitate to accuse Mr Dickens; for these extremely fortunate accidents are out of the legitimate range of fiction. We may notice here, too, a peculiarity of our author in the treatment of his heroines. About the climax of the tale it generally happens that one, or more than one, young lady concerned has an explanation to make to somebody— her father, or her lover, or her husband, as the case may happen—in doing which she is greatly moved and excited, yet very calm, and delivers herself of a number of balanced and measured sentences, no doubt quite to the purpose in every instance, but so singularly like each other in form and cadence, that each recalls its predecessor too distinctly to be agreeable. Florence Dombey, if we mistake not, makes two of these speeches—one to her lover, the other to Mr Dombey; Kate Nickleby does a little in the same way; there is a remarkable instance in Annie, Dr Strong's wife in *Copperfield*; poor Mercy Pecksniff follows the universal example; and even Louisa Gradgrind is not behind her predecessors. It would be worth while for any one curious in such matters to compare these little addresses—they are remarkable enough in their way: either the young lady deprecates interruption, or her interlocutor is perfectly silent, and hears her out, overpowered by her earnestness—and the speech is only broken by the author's description of those fluctuations of voice and colour which evidence the excitement of the speaker. This is quite a marked and noticeable feature in the writings of Mr Dickens. . . .

Next in succession comes what, in our judgment, is Mr Dickens' most able and most perfectly satisfactory work, *David Copperfield*. We heard Mr Thackeray commended lately by a judicious critic for the distinctness with which Clive Newcome *grows* in his present book, and the perfectly clear view we have of his progress from a boy to a man. The remark struck us as a very true and just one—and we apply the same praise to David Copperfield, a strangely dissimilar person, but one whose growth is quite as evident. This young man is one of those creations, so entirely yet so unostentatiously life-like, that the first impulse of the reader is to identify him with the author, and make a real autobiography out of the skilful fiction. All about himself is so quiet, and real, and free from exaggeration, that the simple critic hails the conclusion of the book, in which David appears as an author, as proof positive, and exults in this decisive evidence of his or her superior discernment. Beautifully commenced as it is, this book keeps up its pace more evenly than any of its predecessors; and, to our own liking, no other work of Mr Dickens can compete with this in completeness or in beauty. . . .

In Mr Dickens' last great work (an adjective which cannot apply in any sense to his very last one, *Hard Times*), he makes a beginning as pleasant as in *Copperfield;* but great as are the merits of *Bleak House,* we cannot be persuaded into the same thorough liking for it as we entertain for its predecessor. Here we are again on the perilous standing-ground of social evil. . . .

. . . We have another quarrel with Mr Dickens—one of long standing, dating back to the period of his first work: the 'shepherd' of Mr Weller's widow, the little Bethel of Mrs Nubbles, have effloresced in *Bleak House* into a detestable Mr Chadband, an oft-repeated libel upon the preachers of the poor. This is a very vulgar and common piece of slander, quite unworthy of a true artist. Are we really to believe, then, that only those who are moderately religious are true in their profession?—that it is good to be in earnest in every occupation but one, the most important of all, as it happens? What a miserable assumption is this! Mr Dickens' tender charity does not disdain to embrace a good many equivocal people—why then so persevering an aim at a class which offends few and harms no man? Not very long since, we ourselves, who are no great admirers of English dissent, happened to go into a very humble little meeting-house—perhaps a Bethel—where the preacher, at his beginning, we are ashamed to say, tempted our unaccustomed faculties almost to laughter. Here was quite an opportunity for finding a Chadband, for the little man was round and ruddy, and had a shining face—his grammar was not perfect, moreover, and having occasion to mention a certain Scripture town, he called it Canar of Galilee; but when we had listened for half an hour, we had no longer the slightest inclination to laugh at the humble preacher. This unpretending man reached to the heart of his subject in less time than we have taken to tell of it; gave a bright, clear, individual view of the doctrine he was considering, and urged it on his hearers with homely arguments which were as little ridiculous as can be supposed. Will Mr Dickens permit us to advise him, when he next would draw a 'shepherd,' to study his figure from the life? Let him choose the least little chapel on his way, and take his chance for a successful sitting: we grant him he may find a Chadband, but we promise him he has at least an equal chance of finding an apostle instead. . . .

It is very ungrateful, after all this, and acknowledging to the full how excellently this [Lady Dedlock] portion of *Bleak House* is accomplished, to yield to the temptation given us in the conclusion, and suffer our dissatisfaction with that to overshadow the book with all its admirable qualities; but we are obliged to say that we think Esther a failure, and, when she has only herself to talk about, are glad to be done with the complaisant history. Mr Dickens is evidently ambitious of achieving a heroine—witness his vehement endeavour to make something of Ruth Pinch, his careful elaboration of Dolly Varden, and even the pains he has taken with Dora. It is a laudable ambition, for heroines are a sadly featureless class of well-intentioned young women in these days—but we cannot say that the effort is successful in Esther Summerson. In the ordinary type of heroines—in the Agnes Wickfield, the Ada, the Kate Nickleby—Mr Dickens is very generally successful. These young ladies are pretty enough, amiable enough, generous enough, to fill their necessary places with great credit and propriety, but to produce an individual woman is another and quite a different matter.

. . . In his own sphere, no man living equals Mr Dickens—and perhaps there is no modern writer of whom we can say so confidently that his great excellences are innate, and not acquired. Much as he moves us to laughter, we know that quite as skilfully, and often with great delicacy and tenderness, he can move us to tears. Nor do we fail to find noble sentiments and just views of human nature in these works of genius, which may take their place, as illustrations of our age and daily fashion of existence, on an equal platform with the highest productions of the same class in any period of our history. Mr Dickens has won for himself what is more to the purpose than the approbation of criticism, an affectionate welcome in the households and homes of his country. We are told by the authority of statistics that no books are so much read in our public libraries as these—and the persons of his tales are to us all familiar associates, whom we quote with all the ease of acquaintance-ship. But while we grant all this, we would fain add a word of friendly counsel to the warm admiration we offer. The law of kindness has come to man under the very loftiest sanction, and kindness sublimated into charity, Love, is the pervading spirit of the Gospel;—yet there is such a thing as unwise kindness, injurious love, maudlin charity, a weak suffusion of universal benevolence which is good for nothing but pretty speeches, pretty pictures, pretty sentiments and actions. Mr Dickens' hand does not appear, we confess, where his name does, on the periodi-cal which it has pleased him to call *Household Words*, yet he is in some degree responsible for the very poor platitudes which scarcely could reach any public, one would think, save for that 'conducted by Charles Dickens' on the top of the page. What does Mr Dickens mean by all the caressing condescension with which this powerful organ of his strokes down 'the poor'—by all these small admirable moral histories, these truths and wonders diluted to the meanest capacity?—what by his admiration of the frightful little weedy arbours at Battersea or Green-wich, where his working man carries his family, and improves his Sunday by a pipe and a pint of beer? There is a wonderful natural power of degeneracy in all false arguments;—we are not about to enter into what is called the Sabbath question. The Sabbath, sweet-boon of Heaven, was made for man, and we have no desire to thrust our old-fashioned opinion upon the enlightened liberality of Mr Dickens; but when the best way of spending this day of leisure came to be discussed first, does not everybody remember what beautiful pictures we had of the poor man's Sabbath in the fields—of his meditative walk through the lanes and summer footpaths, where the flowers and the trees preached much better sermons to him than he could hear in the ugly little brick church at home? . . . Alas! the scene has changed. We no longer find it necessary to have fancy pictures of worship in the fields;

we give up the stupid necessity of worship anywhere. 'No,' says Mr Dickens, or at all events the person who ought to be Mr Dickens, writing with all the weight and sanction of his name[1]—John Opus, who has been toiling all the week, does not go into the fields to worship; but he goes to a tea-garden, taking with him all the little Opuses, who are only too happy to share their respectable parent's beer. But, in sober earnest, does Mr Dickens believe in this Greenwich tea-garden?—is it so much more satisfactory than the little Bethels? In this nineteenth century, with all our boasts and our enlightenment, are a pipe and a pint of beer the utmost delights which Mr Dickens can offer, in his day of leisure, to the working man? The waiter, in his white apron, with his tray of glasses—is he a better influence than the poor preacher? And the beer-stains on the table in the arbour, and the long pipes, and the talk—are these things more good, more beautiful, more improving for the little Opuses, than even the miseries of church-going? It is an old, old system to set up pleasure as the only thing which makes life tolerable; but this, at the utmost, is only amusement, not pleasure. And every life has insupportable days in it—slow, tedious, lingering hours, when the cry of Patience, patience, will not content the restless agony? What then?—are we to have nothing but the tea-garden?—nothing but the horse-riding? —nothing but the delights of art, however noble, or imagination, however refined? Let Mr Dickens think better of this grievous yet glorious mystery, this life which craves something more than relaxation. . . .

But to Mr Dickens, in his purer and higher authorship, this censure does not reach; and we have nothing to say to the author of David Copperfield, of Tom Pinch, of a hundred other pleasant creations, but the hearty goodspeed which would drown the ravings of the equinox with its resounding echo, could every individual who joins in the wish, join in the utterance. A kinder audience no man ever had, and it becomes their favourite to use them well.

[1] [G. A. Sala], 'Sunday Tea-gardens,' *Household Words*, 31 September 1854, x, 145–8.

97. Hippolyte Taine, from his 'Charles Dickens: son talent et ses œuvres,' *Revue des deux Mondes*

1 February 1856, 2nde période, i, 618–47

Reprinted in his *Histoire de la Littérature anglaise* (Paris, 1863–4), iv, 3–69; translated by H. Van Laun, *The History of English Literature* (Edinburgh, 1871), iv, 115–64. Van Laun's translation is used here.

Taine (1828–93), leading French critic of literature and art, professor of aesthetics and art history at the Ecole des Beaux Arts, was author also of *Notes sur l'Angleterre* (Paris, 1871; translated by W. F. Rae, 1872). Oxford gave him a D.C.L., 1871; he was elected to the Académie française, 1878. His famous positivistic theory that a writer's character is determined by '*la race, le milieu, le moment*' (heredity, environment, and the historical moment) struck the *Edinburgh Review* as shocking 'many received opinions in regard to religion, morals, and history', and as being, when applied to English character and literature, 'offensive to the national pride and cultivated taste of Englishmen' (cxxi [1865], 292). For a more sympathetic contemporary assessment of Taine, see W. F. Rae's series of articles in the *Westminster Review* (July 1861, April 1864, January 1865, April 1866). John Forster keeps girding at Taine who, being 'without the perception of humour' (*Life*, 324), seems to him entirely disqualified as a critic of Dickens; see especially *Life*, Book 10, ch. i.

. . . The imagination of Dickens is like that of monomaniacs. To plunge oneself into an idea, to be absorbed by it, to see nothing else, to repeat it under a hundred forms, to enlarge it, to carry it, thus enlarged, to the eye of the spectator, to dazzle and overwhelm him with it, to stamp it upon him so firmly and deeply that he can never again tear it from his memory,—these are the great features of this imagination and style. In this, *David Copperfield* is a masterpiece. Never did objects remain more visible and present to the memory of a reader than those which he describes. The old house, the parlour, the kitchen, Peggotty's boat, and above all the school play-ground, are interiors whose relief, energy, and precision are unequalled. Dickens has the passion and patience of the painters of his nation; he reckons his details one by one, notes the various hues of the old tree-trunks; sees the dilapidated cask, the greenish and broken flagstones, the chinks of the damp walls; he distinguishes the strange smells which rise from them; marks the size of the mildewed spots, reads the names of the scholars carved on the door, and dwells on the form of the letters. And this minute description has nothing cold about it: if it is thus detailed, it is because the contemplation was intense; it proves its passion by its exactness. We felt this passion without accounting for it; suddenly we find it at the end of a page; the boldness of the style renders it visible, and the violence of the phrase attests the violence of the impression. Excessive metaphors bring before the mind grotesque fancies. We feel ourselves beset by extravagant visions. Mr Mell takes his flute, and blows on it, says Copperfield, 'until I almost thought he would gradually blow his whole being into the large hole at the top, and ooze away at the keys' [*Copperfield*, ch. v]. Tom Pinch, disabused at last, discovers that his master Pecksniff is a hypocritical rogue. He 'had so long been used to steep the Pecksniff of his fancy in his tea, and spread him out upon his toast, and take him as a relish with his beer, that he made but a poor breakfast on the first morning after his expulsion' [*Chuzzlewit*, ch. xxxvi]. We think of Hoffmann's fantastic tales; we are arrested by a fixed idea, and our head begins to ache. These eccentricities are in the style of sickness rather than of health.

Therefore Dickens is admirable in depicting hallucinations. We see that he feels himself those of his characters, that he is engrossed by their ideas, that he enters into their madness. As an Englishman and a moralist, he has described remorse frequently. Perhaps it may be said that he makes a scarecrow of it, and that an artist is wrong to transform himself into an assistant of the policeman and the preacher.

[Taine instances the 'terrible portrait' of Jonas Chuzzlewit.]

. . . Dickens does not perceive great things; this is the second feature of his imagination. Enthusiasm seizes him in connection with everything, especially in connection with vulgar objects, a curiosity shop, a sign-post, a town-crier. He has vigour, he does not attain beauty. His instrument produces vibrating, but not harmonious sounds. If he is describing a house, he will draw it with geometrical clearness; he will put all its colours in relief, discover a face and thought in the shutters and the spouts; he will make a sort of human being out of the house, grimacing and forcible, which attracts our attention, and which we shall never forget; but he will not see the grandeur of the long monumental lines, the calm majesty of the broad shadows boldly divided by the white plaster; the cheerfulness of the light which covers them, and becomes palpable in the black niches in which it dives as though to rest and to sleep. If he is painting a landscape, he will perceive the haws which dot with their red fruit the leafless hedges, the thin vapour steaming from a distant stream, the motions of an insect in the grass; but the deep poetry which the author of *Valentine* and *André* [George Sand] would have felt, will escape him. He will be lost, like the painters of his country, in the minute and impassioned observation of small things; he will have no love of beautiful forms and fine colours. He will not perceive that the blue and the red, the straight line and the curve, are enough to compose vast concerts, which amidst so many various expressions maintain a grand serenity, and open up in the depths of the soul a spring of health and happiness. Happiness is lacking in him; his inspiration is a feverish rapture, which does not select its objects, which animates promiscuously the ugly, the vulgar, the ridiculous, and which communicating to his creations an indescribable jerkiness and violence, deprives them of the delight and harmony which in other hands they might have retained. . . .

This sensibility can hardly have more than two issues—laughter and tears. There are others, but they are only reached by lofty eloquence; they are the path to sublimity, and we have seen that for Dickens this path is cut off. Yet there is no writer who knows better how to touch and melt; he makes us weep, absolutely shed tears; before reading him we did not know there was so much pity in the heart. The grief of a child, who wishes to be loved by his father, and whom his father does not love; the despairing love and slow death of a poor half-imbecile young man: all these pictures of secret grief leave an ineffaceable impression. The tears which he sheds are genuine, and compassion is their only source. Balzac, George Sand, Stendhal have also recorded human miseries; is it possible to write without recording them? But they do not seek them out, they hit upon them; they do not dream of displaying them to us; they were going elsewhere, and met them on their way. They love art better than men. . . .

This same writer is the most railing, the most comic, the most jocose of English authors. And it is moreover a singular gaiety! It is the only kind which would harmonise with this impassioned sensibility. There is a laughter akin to tears. Satire is the sister of elegy: if the second pleads for the oppressed, the first combats the oppressors. Feeling painfully all the wrongs that are committed, and the vices that are practised, Dickens avenges himself by ridicule. He does not paint, he punishes. Nothing could be more damaging than those long chapters of sustained irony, in which the sarcasm is pressed, line after line, more sanguinary and piercing in the chosen adversary. . . . In reality, Dickens is gloomy, like Hogarth; but, like Hogarth, he makes us burst with laughter by the buffoonery of his invention and the violence of his caricatures. He pushes his characters to absurdity with unwonted boldness. Pecksniff hits off moral phrases and sentimental actions in so grotesque a manner, that they make him extravagant. Never were heard such monstrous oratorical displays. Sheridan had already painted an English hypocrite, Joseph Surface; but he differs from Pecksniff as much as a portrait of the eighteenth century differs from a cartoon of *Punch*. Dickens makes hypocrisy so deformed and monstrous, that his hypocrite ceases to resemble a man; we would call him one of those fantastic figures whose nose is greater than his body. This exaggerated comicality springs from excess of imagination. . . .

Plant this talent on English soil; the literary opinion of the country will direct its growth and explain its fruits. For this public opinion is its private opinion; it does not submit to it as to an external constraint, but feels it inwardly as an inner persuasion; it does not hinder, but develops it, and only repeats aloud what it said to itself in a whisper.

The counsels of this public taste are somewhat like this; the more powerful because they agree with its natural inclination, and urge it upon its special course:—

Be moral. All your novels must be such as may be read by young girls. We are practical minds, and we would not have literature corrupt practical life. We believe in family life, and we would not have literature paint the passions which attack family life. We are Protestants, and we have preserved something of the severity of our fathers against enjoyment and passions. Amongst these, love is the worst. Beware of resembling in this respect the most illustrious of our neighbours. Love is the hero of all George Sand's novels. Married or not, she thinks it beautiful, holy, sublime in itself; and she says so. Don't believe this; and if you do believe it, don't say it. It is a bad example. Love thus

represented makes marriage a secondary matter. . . . George Sand
paints impassioned women; paint you for us good women. George
Sand makes us desire to be in love; do you make us desire to be
married.

This has its disadvantages without doubt; art suffers by it, if the public
gains. Though your characters give the best examples, your works will
be of less value. No matter; you may console yourself with the thought
that you are moral. Your lovers will be uninteresting; for the only
interest natural to their age is the violence of passion, and you cannot
paint passion. . . .

[Taine continues in the same vein. Among other 'counsels of public
taste' is that the novelist must contrive 'only an amusing phantasma-
goria'; the variety of events 'have no connection, they do not form a
system, they are but a heap. You will only write lives, adventures,
memoirs, sketches, collections of scenes, and you will not be able to
compose an action.' A later example of how 'the exigencies of public
morality mar the idea of the book' is the ending of Dombey: 'His
daughter arrives in the nick of time. She entreats him; his feelings get
the better of him, she carries him off; he becomes the best of fathers,
and spoils a fine novel.']

Take away the grotesque characters, who are only introduced to fill
up and to excite laughter, and you will find that all Dickens' characters
belong to two classes—people who have feelings and emotions, and
people who have none. He contrasts the souls which nature creates
with those which society deforms. One of his last novels, Hard Times,
is an abstract of all the rest. He there exalts instinct above reason,
intuition of heart above positive knowledge; he attacks education built
on statistics, figures, and facts; overwhelms the positive and mercantile
spirit with misfortune and ridicule; and campaigns against the pride,
hardheartedness and selfishness of the businessman and the aristocrat;
falls foul of manufacturing towns, combats the pride, harshness, selfishness of the merchant towns of smoke and mud, which fetter the body in
an artificial atmosphere, and the mind in a factitious existence. He seeks
out poor artisans, mountebanks, a foundling, and crushes beneath their
common sense, generosity, delicacy, courage, and gentleness, the false
science, false happiness, and false virtue of the rich and powerful who
despise them. He satirises oppressive society; mourns over oppressed
nature; and his elegiac genius, like his satirical genius, finds ready to his

hand in the English world around him, the sphere which it needs for its development. . . .

Let us look at some different personages. In contrast with these bad and factitious characters, produced by national institutions, we find good creatures such as nature made them; and first, children.

We have none in French literature. Racine's little Joas could only exist in a piece composed for the ladies' college of Saint Cyr; the little child speaks like a prince's son, with noble and acquired phrases, as if repeating his catechism. Now-a-days these portraits are only seen in France in New-year's books, written as models for good children. Dickens painted his with special gratification; he did not think of edifying the public, and he has charmed it. All his children are of extreme sensibility; they love much, and they crave to be loved. To understand this gratification of the painter, and this choice of characters, we must think of their physical type. English children have a colour so fresh, a complexion so delicate, a skin so transparent, eyes so blue and pure, that they are like beautiful flowers. No wonder if a novelist loves them. . .

The working-classes are like children, dependent, not very cultivated, akin to nature, and liable to oppression. And so Dickens extols them. . . .

In reality, the novels of Dickens can all be reduced to one phrase, to wit: Be good, and love; there is genuine joy only in the emotions of the heart; sensibility is the whole man. Leave science to the wise, pride to the nobles, luxury to the rich; have compassion on humble wretchedness; the smallest and most despised being may in himself be worth as much as thousands of the powerful and the proud. Take care not to bruise the delicate souls which flourish in all conditions, under all costumes, in all ages. Believe that humanity, pity, forgiveness, are the finest things in man; believe that intimacy, expansion, tenderness, tears, are the sweetest things in the world. To live is nothing; to be powerful, learned, illustrious, is little; to be useful is not enough. He alone has lived and is a man who has wept at the remembrance of a kind action which he himself has performed or received. . . .

98. [George Eliot], from 'The Natural History of German Life', *Westminster Review*

July 1856, lxvi, 55

Reprinted in George Eliot's *Essays and Leaves from a Notebook* (1884).

George Eliot (1819–80) had not yet begun her career as a novelist: *Scenes of Clerical Life* appeared in 1857, and Dickens was one of the few authors to whom she sent a copy. She was delighted by his enthusiastic letters about it and *Adam Bede* (1859), and a friendly though never close relationship developed between them. Mrs Plornish appears in *Little Dorrit*, then being serialized.

. . . We have one great novelist who is gifted with the utmost power of rendering the external traits of our town population; and if he could give us their psychological character—their conceptions of life, and their emotions—with the same truth as their idiom and manners, his books would be the greatest contribution Art has ever made to the awakening of social sympathies. But while he can copy Mrs Plornish's colloquial style with the delicate accuracy of a sun-picture, while there is the same startling inspiration in his description of the gestures and phrases of 'Boots', as in the speeches of Shakspeare's mobs or numb-skulls, he scarcely ever passes from the humorous and external to the emotional and tragic, without becoming as transcendent in his un-reality as he was a moment before in his artistic truthfulness. But for the precious salt of his humour, which compels him to reproduce external traits that serve, in some degree, as a corrective to his frequently false psychology, his preternaturally virtuous poor children and arti-sans, his melodramatic boatmen and courtezans, would be as noxious as Eugène Sue's idealized proletaries in encouraging the miserable fallacy that high morality and refined sentiment can grow out of harsh social relations, ignorance, and want; or that the working-classes are in a condition to enter at once into a millennial state of *altruism*, where-in everyone is caring for everyone else, and no one for himself.

99. [James Fitzjames Stephen], from 'Mr Dickens as a Politician', *Saturday Review*

3 January 1857, iii, 8–9

Stephen (1829–94), son of the civil servant Sir James Stephen and brother of Leslie Stephen; lawyer, judge (from 1879), authority on legal history; created baronet, 1891. Stephen had attacked Dickens —particularly his pathos—in *Cambridge Essays* (1855), and was a prominent contributor to the *Saturday Review* from its inception (1855: see Introduction, p. 13). Also contributed to the *Edinburgh Review* (see No. 104) and other journals. For the background to his fierce contempt for 'Light Literature', see Leslie Stephen, *Life of Sir James Fitzjames Stephen* (1895), 155–61, 180, 345. For him (Leslie Stephen remarked, p. 155), 'A novel should be a serious attempt by a grave observer to draw a faithful portrait of the actual facts of life. A novelist, therefore, who uses the imaginary facts, like Sterne and Dickens, as mere pegs on which to hang specimens of his own sensibility and facetiousness, becomes disgusting. . . . He, therefore, considers *Robinson Crusoe* to represent the ideal novel.' This aesthetic dogma helps to explain Fitzjames Stephen's reaction to Dickens, but the animosity arises also from his family protective feeling towards the machinery of government and administration, and from the communal *Saturday Review* tone of cantankerous superiority and dismissiveness. The *Saturday Review* campaign against Dickens was (falsely) rumoured to have caused him to collapse into bed, ill.

. . . As every system is said to culminate, and every idea to be embodied, it might have been expected *a priori* that an era of reform would find, sooner or later, its representative man. We do not know whether the restless, discontented, self-sufficient spirit which characterises so large a portion of modern speculation—especially on political and social subjects—could have had a more characteristic Avatar than it has found in Mr Dickens. The nature, the sphere, and the character of his influence, and the foundations upon which it rests, furnish a most curious commentary on a vast mass of phenomena which it is impossible for a serious person to view without profound disquiet. In his preface to a late edition of his earliest novel [*Preface* to the Cheap Edition (1847) of *Pickwick*], Mr Dickens informed the world with satisfaction that, since its publication, a great part of the horrors of imprisonment for debt—the special evil which it denounced—have been removed by legislation; and he expressed a hope that, at the republication of each of his works, he might be able to say the same of the particular abuse against which it was levelled. Now, Mr Dickens is the author of some twelve or fourteen books, each as long as three ordinary novels; and in each of them, in addition to the usual tasks which writers of fiction impose on themselves, he had discharged a self-imposed obligation of attacking some part or other of our rotten institutions. In *Pickwick*, he denounced imprisonment for debt—in *Oliver Twist*, the Poor Laws—in *David Copperfield*, the inefficiency of Parliament—in *Bleak House*, the Court of Chancery—and in *Little Dorrit*, the system of administration. We say nothing at present of the satire which he has directed against the Americans, the aristocracy, the middle classes, charitable societies, and Calvinism. To do his best to persuade his neighbours that the institutions under which they live encourage and permit the grossest cruelties towards debtors and paupers—that their Legislature is a stupid and inefficient debating club, their courts of justice foul haunts of chicanery, pedantry, and fraud, and their system of administration an odious compound of stupidity and corruption—is, perhaps, a sufficient responsibility for one man to assume; yet it is very characteristic that he should consider it so light a matter as to be anxious, in addition, to propagate similar views about almost every element of social life.

Such language may be considered too grave for such a subject. Who, it may be asked, takes Mr Dickens seriously? Is it not as foolish to estimate his melodramatic and sentimental stock-in-trade gravely, as it would be to undertake a refutation of the jokes of the clown in a Christmas pantomime? No doubt this would be true enough if the world were composed entirely or principally of men of sense and cultivation. To such persons Mr Dickens is nothing more than any other public performer—enjoying an extravagantly high reputation, and rewarded for his labours, both in purse and in credit, at an extravagantly high rate. But the vast majority of mankind, unfortunately, think little, and cultivate themselves still less. . . . To these classes such writers as Mr Dickens are something more than an amusement. . . . The production, among such readers, of false impressions of the system of which they form a part—especially if the falsehood tends to render them discontented with and disaffected to the institutions under which they live—cannot but be a serious evil, and must often involve great moral delinquency. Except the relations between men and their Maker, no subjects can be more grave than Legislation, Government, and the Administration of Justice; and we do not know that a man can misuse the trust imposed upon him by the possession of great talents and unbounded popularity more mischievously than by leading people to under-estimate the good, and over-estimate the evil, of the institutions of their country. Looking, therefore, at the sphere of Mr Dickens's influence, we are compelled to think of him seriously. He is not entitled to the protection of insignificance. It may be admitted that he can scarcely attract the attention of the more intelligent classes of the community; but he may, and, as we believe, does exercise a very wide and a very pernicious political and social influence.

Our unfavourable opinion applies equally to the ends which he has in view, and to the means by which he seeks to accomplish them. He is the most prominent and popular of the innumerable preachers of that flattering doctrine, that, by some means or other, the world has been turned topsy-turvy—so that all the folly and stupidity are found in the highest places, and all the good sense, moderation, and ability in the lowest. As German students look upon themselves as the elect, and upon the members of the whole social hierarchy as 'philisters,' an opinion, or rather a sentiment, seems to be gaining ground amongst us—and it is carefully fanned by such writers as Mr Dickens—that success in life is not only no evidence of a man's superiority, but is positive proof of his inferiority to his neighbours. For Parliament Mr Dickens has an unlimited scorn. It is, he says, all talk, 'words, words, nothing but words.' The House of Commons, for him, is a stupid debating club, in which no business is transacted except the enunciation of innumerable platitudes. Nor does the law fare better. The Court of Chancery is an abomination, to be cut down root and branch—a mere den of thieves, in which no man can long retain his honesty. But if our laws are made by fools and administered by rogues, what shall we say of those who manage our public affairs? [They are all Barnacles, in Dickens's view.] . . . Such is the lesson which, month by month, Mr Dickens reads to his fellow-citizens. He is, in the main, a kind-hearted man, and would

perhaps be at a loss for opportunities of exercising his powers of vitu-
peration, unless Providence had kindly created dignities on purpose to
be evil spoken of; but as that arrangement has been made, he is enabled,
with an easy conscience, to devote himself to the task of flattering his
readers into the belief that, but for the intelligence of the middle
classes and the unostentatious virtues of the poor, England would be a
perfect paradise of fools and knaves.

Such is his end; and the means he employs are worthy of it. As there
are reproaches which can be uttered by no one but a woman or a child,
there are accusations which can only be conveyed through a novel. It
would be impossible to make any more serious publication the vehicle
of such calumnies—their grave and quiet statement would be their own
refutation. But just as a foolish gossip in a country-town, who says
what she pleases because all the world knows what her tongue is like,
may babble away the purest character, a popular novelist may produce
more disaffection and discontent than a whole army of pamphleteers
and public orators, because he wears the cap and bells, and laughs in
your face when you contradict him. A novelist has no responsibility.
He can always discover his own meaning. To the world at large,
Jarndyce v. Jarndyce represents the Court of Chancery. To any one who
taxes the writer with unfairness, it is merely, he is told, a playful
exaggeration—pretty Fanny's way; and who can have the heart to be
angry with pretty Fanny? To the thousands of feverish artisans who
read *Little Dorrit*, the Circumlocution Office is a *bona fide* representation
of Downing-street. To any one who remonstrates, it is nothing but a
fair representation of what exists, just exaggerated enough to make the
subject entertaining. In this, no doubt, there is a certain amount of
truth; and so there is in the plea of the old woman who destroys her
neighbour's character over her tea, that she only adds colour enough
to her story to make it piquant. No doubt Mr Dickens does not really
mean much harm. He only wants to sell his books; and by way of
persuading himself that he is of some use in the world, he spices them
with a certain amount of advocacy of social reforms, just as clergymen
sometimes sugar their private letters with texts to make them improving. This is just what we complain of. He exercises considerable
political influence with hardly any political convictions. He introduces
the gravest subjects in a manner which makes it impossible that he
should do them justice. He scatters fire, and says, Am I not in sport?
The two fallacies which pervade all his writings are just those which
nothing but care and education can guard against, and which are,

therefore, particularly dangerous when addressed to uneducated people. One is the fallacy of artistic exaggeration. . . . Mr Dickens makes his intelligent tradesmen high-minded and highly-educated gentlemen, and his officials affected shop-boys, and then asks us whether the officials can bear a comparison with the tradesmen. If you are at liberty to allow some of the staring external marks of a class to stand unaltered, whilst its characteristic defects are exaggerated indefinitely, there can never be any difficulty in making out the world to be as absurd as you please. The other fallacy—that of minute description—is less obvious, but quite as effective. It consists in dwelling upon all the details of an incident till the mind invests it with as much dignity as such an introduction would demand. By the help of this device, nothing would be more easy than to make the operation of pulling out a tooth appear utterly intolerable. . . . In the same way, the inside of a workhouse may be made to look like an absolute torture-chamber; whereas, in fact, neither the pauper nor the dentist's patient feels half the agony which the novelist describes.

The truth of the accusations which Mr Dickens brings against society is on a par with the fairness of the manner in which they are urged. No one can deny that there are great abuses in the world in general, and in this country in particular. There is much that wants reform in Parliament, in the law, and in the administration; but no one can reform wisely unless he knows what he is about; and that these institutions want reform is only half, or perhaps even less than half, of the truth. With all their faults, they have the very highest merits; and a man who represents to his fellow-countrymen only the faults, and none of the merits, fosters one of the worst of our national faults—the inveterate habit of self-depreciation. Whatever else our Parliament is, it is the only popular government in the world which has been able to maintain itself; and whatever Mr Dickens may think, it really has done a very considerable amount of work since he began to denounce it, and will probably continue to do so. . . .

The most wonderful feature in Mr Dickens's influence is the nature of the foundation on which it stands. Who is this man who is so much wiser than the rest of the world that he can pour contempt on all the institutions of his country? He is a man with a very active fancy, great powers of language, much perception of what is grotesque, and a most lachrymose and melodramatic turn of mind—and this is all. He is utterly destitute of any kind of solid acquirements. He has never played any part in any movement more significant than that of the fly—generally a gad-fly—on the wheel. Imprisonment for debt on *mesne* process was doomed, if not abolished, before he wrote *Pickwick*. The Court of Chancery was reformed before he published *Bleak House*. In his attacks on Parliament he certainly relied on his own experience, and was utterly and hopelessly wrong. In his attacks on the administration he only followed the lead of Our Own Correspondent.[1] And yet this man, who knows absolutely nothing of law or politics—who was so ignorant of the one subject that he grumbled at the length of an administration suit (which is like grumbling at the slowness of the lapse of time), and so ignorant of the other that he represented Parliament as a debating club—has elaborated a kind of theory of politics. He would have the pace of legislation quickened by the abolition of vain debates— he would have justice freed from the shackles of law—he would have public affairs conducted by officers of vast powers, unfettered by routine. He does not know his own meaning. He does not see the consequences of his own teaching; and yet he is unconsciously tending to a result logically connected with the whole of it. Freedom, law, established rules, have their difficulties. They are possible only to men who will be patient, quiet, moderate, and tolerant of difference in opinion; and therefore their results are intolerable to a feminine, irritable, noisy mind, which is always clamouring and shrieking for protection and guidance. Mr Dickens's government looks pretty at a distance, but we can tell him how his ideal would look if it were realized. It would result in the purest despotism. There would be no debates to worry effeminate understandings—no laws to prevent judges going at once to the merits of the case according to their own inclination—no forms to prevent officials from dealing with their neighbours as so many parcels of ticketed goods. Whether a Mr Dickens would then be able to point out the fact that arbitrary power is not uniformly wise, that arbitrary judges are sometimes corrupt, and that arbitrary officials are not always patriotic, is a very different question.

[1] William Howard Russell, whose reports on the Crimean War, published in *The Times*, led to much agitation against the inefficiency of the governmental and administrative system.

100. [William Forsyth], from 'Literary Style,' *Fraser's Magazine*

March 1857, lv, 260–3

Reprinted in Forsyth's *Essays, Critical and Narrative* (1874), 182–6.

Forsyth (1812–99), a barrister, was editor of the *Annual Register* 1842–68 and author of several historical, scholarly and critical books.

We turn next to the most popular and also the most prolific author of the day—Mr Dickens—whose style, we suppose, is nearly as familiar to our readers as the alphabet. We think he writes too much and too fast; and unless he takes more care than he seems to think it worth while to do so long as the shilling numbers of any new novel from his pen are sold by thousands, we predict that he will be the destroyer of his own reputation. He has fallen into the habit of repeating himself to a degree which becomes wearisome, and his latter works have proceeded in a descending scale. That which is now issuing from the press, *Little Dorrit*, is decidedly the worst. His tone is melodramatic throughout; and by this we do not mean the melodrame of Mr Harrison Ainsworth, whose favourite heroes are highwaymen, and who makes robbery and housebreaking romantic; but we have in his works neither tragedy nor what used to be called genteel comedy, which really meant ordinary social and domestic life. Mr Dickens delights in the sayings and doings of strange, grotesque, out-of-the-way people, of whom we hardly ever meet the prototypes in flesh and blood; and in every one of his tales he fastens some distinctive oddities upon two or three of his characters, and never allows them to speak without bringing out the peculiarity in the most marked and prominent manner. His portraits are in fact caricatures. He daguerreotypes, so to speak, a particular grimace, and presents it every time that the features come into view. Thus Pecksniff is always sententious and hypocritical; Micawber is always full of maudlin sentiment and emphatic nonsense; Gradgrind is always practical, to a degree that ceases to be human;

THE CRITICAL HERITAGE

Mrs Nickleby is always parenthetical and incoherent; Mark Tapley is
never tired of telling us that he is 'jolly;' Boythorn never opens his lips
without being intensely and boisterously energetic; Major Bagstock
always speaks of himself in the third person, as 'J.B.', 'tough old Joe,'
'Joe is rough and tough, sir!—blunt, sir, blunt, is Joe;' Uriah Heep is
always "'umble,' 'very 'umble;' and Mrs Gamp everlastingly quotes as
her authority Mrs Harris. Mr Dickens has also a passion for personification, and for giving to inanimate objects all the attributes of life. We
may take as an instance a passage at the beginning of *Martin Chuzzlewit*,
where he describes a gusty evening.

[Quotes from ch. iii.]

The two opposite poles between which Mr Dickens constantly
oscillates, are comic humour pushed to buffoonery, and sentiment
carried to maudlin excess. He seems to have no conception of a well-
constructed plot, and the interest in his novels is kept up by a succession
of detached and shifting scenes, and the introduction of an endless
variety of funny persons, while the story is left to drift on without
much guidance, and take care of itself as best as it may. His characters
are all exaggerations. We doubt if there is one which, as he has drawn
it, occurs in real life. The substratum, so to speak, may indeed exist
there, but on this he erects a superstructure so fanciful and fantastic
that nature disowns the resemblance. Our readers have no doubt seen
in the shop windows little grotesque figures in *terra cotta* of celebrated
actors, singers, and musicians, where the head is made monstrously
large in proportion to the rest of the body, and the features are ridicu-
lously exaggerated. These forcibly remind us of Mr Dickens's characters. He has also a marvellous talent for minute description. No Dutch
painter ever depicted an interior with more servile fidelity than Mr
Dickens draws still life with his pen. His marine storeshops, his frouzy
dwellings, his dull November streets, his Jews' alleys, and Jacob's
islands, rival the pictures of Teniers and Ostade. But while we admire
the painter we are apt to grow weary of the writer. The eye of the
spectator can take in the whole of a picture at a glance, but the mind of
the reader must go through the successive points of a description until
it becomes fatigued by the multiplicity of details. A favourite form or
rather trick of expression with this author is circumlocution, whereby
he gives an air of comic originality to the commonest incidents and
most hackneyed sayings. He uses, indeed, a circuitous phraseology as
frequently as any of the Barnacle family in his own Circumlocution

Office. His satire is keen, but so far as we remember, is never ill-natured. He delights in showing up a foible, whether of character or manners; and the instrument he employs for this purpose is good-humoured irony, in which he playfully says the very opposite of his real meaning. But we are now criticising the genius rather than the style of this remarkable writer; and yet they are so intimately connected that it is difficult to separate them.

One other fault we must mention before we quit the subject, and that is his habit of pushing an idea to the extreme. He never lightly touches a subject, and then leaves it to the imagination of the reader to fill up the outline. He hugs the child of his fancy in his arms, fondles it, caresses it, forces it on our attention, and asks us to examine it until we grow tired of the display, and refuse to admire what is so perseveringly obtruded on our notice. No man ever rode a metaphor harder than Mr Dickens. We will give one example from *Little Dorrit*.

[the comparisons between Pancks and a tug]

And so it goes on chapter after chapter. We have the Tug puffing and snorting and coaling and pulling and hauling; until we really forget that all the time it is the description of a person and not of a steamboat.

101. W. M. Thackeray, from his 'Charity and Humour'

Works, vii, 724-5

This lecture was first given in New York in 1853, and repeated occasionally in differing forms. Giving it in London in 1857, in aid of the Douglas Jerrold Fund, he 'boldly, and at the same time delicately, instituted a sort of comparison between himself and Mr Dickens. He referred to the misanthropic sentiments which have been laid to his charge, and honestly confessed that he could only paint truth as he saw it with his own eyes. This brought him to a generous commendation of Dickens, whom he said, to his regret he could not resemble, but whom he regarded as a person commissioned by Divine Providence to correct and instruct his fellowmen' (*The Times*, 23 March 1857). Dickens wrote to him that day, having read this report: 'I am profoundly touched by your generous reference to me. I do not know how to tell you what a glow it spread over my heart. Out of its fulness I do entreat you to believe that I shall never forget your words of commendation. If you could wholly know at once how you have moved me and how you have animated me, you would be the happier, I am certain.'

As for the charities of Mr Dickens, multiplied kindnesses which he has conferred upon us all; upon our children; upon people educated and uneducated; upon the myriads here, and at home, who speak our common tongue,—have not you, have not I, all of us reason to be thankful to this kind friend who soothed and charmed so many hours, brought pleasure and sweet laughter to so many homes; made such multitudes of children happy; endowed us with such a sweet store of gracious thoughts, fair fancies, soft sympathies, hearty enjoyments. There are creations of Mr Dickens's, which seem to me to rank as personal benefits; figures so delightful, that one feels happier and better for knowing them, as one does for being brought into the society of very good men and women. The atmosphere in which these people live is wholesome to breathe in; you feel that to be allowed to speak to them is a personal kindness; you come away better for your contact with them; your hands seem cleaner from having the privilege of shaking theirs. Was there ever a better charity-sermon preached in the world than Dickens's *Christmas Carol*? I believe it occasioned immense hospitality throughout England; was the means of lighting up hundreds of kind fires at Christmas time; caused a wonderful outpouring of Christmas good-feeling; of Christmas punch-brewing; an awful slaughter of Christmas turkeys, and roasting and basting of Christmas beef. As for this man's love of children, that amiable organ at the back of his honest head must be perfectly monstrous. All children ought to love him. I know two that do, and read his books ten times for once that they peruse the dismal preachments of their father. I know one who when she is happy reads *Nicholas Nickleby*; when she is unhappy reads *Nicholas Nickleby*; when she is tired reads *Nicholas Nickleby*; when she is in bed reads *Nicholas Nickleby*; when she has nothing to do reads *Nicholas Nickleby*; and when she has finished the book reads *Nicholas Nickleby* over again. This candid young critic, at ten years of age, said: 'I like Mr Dickens's books much better than your books, Papa;'—and frequently expressed her desire that the latter author should write a book like one of Mr Dickens's books. Who can? Every man must say his own thoughts in his own voice, in his own way; lucky is he who has such a charming gift of nature as this, which brings all the children in the world trooping to him, and being fond of him.

I remember when that famous *Nicholas Nickleby* came out, seeing a letter from a pedagogue in the north of England, which, dismal as it was, was immensely comical. 'Mr Dickens's ill-advised publication,' wrote the poor schoolmaster, 'has passed like a whirlwind over the schools of the north.' He was a proprietor of a cheap school; Dotheboys' Hall was a cheap school. There were many such establishments in the northern counties. Parents were ashamed, that were never ashamed before, until the kind satirist laughed at them; relatives were frightened; scores of little scholars were taken away; poor schoolmasters had to shut their shops up; every pedagogue was voted a Squeers, and many suffered, no doubt unjustly; but afterward schoolboys' backs were not so much caned; schoolboys' meat was less tough and more plentiful; and schoolboys' milk was not so sky-blue. What a kind light of benevolence it is that plays round Crummles and the Phenomenon, and all those poor theatre people in that charming book! What a humour! and what a good-humour! I coincide with the youthful critic, whose opinion has just been mentioned, and own to a family admiration for *Nicholas Nickleby*.

One might go on, though the task would be endless and needless, chronicling the names of kind folks with whom this kind genius has made us familiar. . . .

I may quarrel with Mr Dickens's art a thousand and a thousand times; I delight and wonder at his genius; I recognise in it—I speak with awe and reverence—a commission from that Divine Beneficence, whose blessed task we know it will one day be to wipe every tear from every eye. Thankfully I take my share of the feast of love and kindness, which this gentle, and generous, and charitable soul has contributed to the happiness of the world. I take and enjoy my share and say a Benediction for the meal.

LITTLE DORRIT

December 1855–June 1857

'An Act of Parliament would fail to enforce the serious reading' of *Little Dorrit*, pronounced the *Saturday Review* (4 July 1857, iv, 15: probably by Fitzjames Stephen, who had already taken a savage bite at this cherry in the *Edinburgh*; see No. 104). E. B. Hamley, in *Blackwood's* could not even 'wait for the end of the wilderness of *Little Dorrit*' before recording his 'Remonstrance with Dickens' (April 1857; see No. 102). The month before, *Fraser's* had pronounced this 'decidedly the worst' of his novels (see No. 100). For many critics indeed *Little Dorrit* became a by-word for the bad Dickens. Even his defenders tended to be somewhat apologetic about it—Hollingshead, for instance (No. 106), or William Hepworth Dixon in the *Athenaeum*, 'There is enough of genius in this book to have made a sensation for any other name. To say it is not worthy of Dickens, is to pay him an immense compliment' (6 June 1857, 722). A. W. Ward, looking back in 1882, summarized a common view of Dickens's development from *Little Dorrit* to *Great Expectations*:

I well remember, at the time of its publication in numbers, the general consciousness that *Little Dorrit* was proving unequal to the high-strung expectations which a new work by Dickens then excited in his admirers both young and old. . . . Yet while nothing is more remarkable in the literary career of Dickens than this apparently speedy decline of his power, nothing is more wonderful in it than the degree to which he righted himself again, not, indeed, with his public, for the public never deserted its favourite, but with his genius (*Charles Dickens* (1882), 139–40).

Dickens had indeed ended his Preface (dated May 1857) to the novel with the boast that he had never had so many readers: this, perhaps, was his reply to the 'remonstrances' already being expressed. See the headnote to No. 104 for his reply to another attack.

Hollingshead was certainly correct in seeing the onslaught on *Little Dorrit* as (at least to some extent) politically motivated (No. 106). Two years later, an admirer, David Masson, wrote:

And yet, how much we owe to Mr Dickens for this very opinionativeness!

With his real shrewdness, his thoughtfulness, his courage, what noble hits he has made! The Administrative Reform Association might have worked for ten years without producing half of the effect which Mr Dickens has produced in the same direction, by flinging out the phrase, 'The Circumlocution Office'. He has thrown out a score of such phrases, equally efficacious for social reform; and it matters little that some of them might turn out to be ludicrous exaggerations' (*British Novelists and their Styles* (Cambridge, 1859), 247).

For some readers, however, this did seem to matter: and the beliefs and activities of the Administrative Reform Association (the only political body to which Dickens had ever publicly committed himself) were much resented in some quarters. The attacks on *Little Dorrit* doubtless received some impetus from what Dickens as publicist had done, in speeches and his *Household Words* campaign, in support of the Administrative Reform movement, quite apart from what he had written in the novel itself. Beyond these political considerations, many readers were put off by the general 'darkness' of the novel, and its sad middle-aged unglamorous hero. Little Dorrit herself never became a cult-figure, as her similarly-named predecessor Little Nell had been; perhaps the time had passed for such a figure to appeal so widely, and Dickens had now certainly got past his great juvenile-deathbed phase. So Little Dorrit is not killed off.

102. [E. B. Hamley], from 'Remonstrance with Dickens', *Blackwood's Magazine*

April 1857, lxxxi, 490–503

Hamley (1824–93), soldier, later General Sir Edward Hamley, contributed to *Blackwood's* and *Fraser's*, and wrote novels, military works, etc. His review-article begins with an enthusiastic account of *Pickwick* and other early novels, notably *Chuzzlewit*, and then remonstrates with Dickens for leaving his proper field. Walt Whitman commended this article, about 'the degeneracy so evident' in the later Dickens ('Charles Dickens', Brooklyn *Daily Times*, 6 May 1857).

... All this humour [in *Martin Chuzzlewit*] is Pickwickian—redolent of the days of Weller and Wardle and Winkle, the golden age of Cockaigne. Such a wealth of comic power has never been displayed by any other writer. But in these post-Pickwickian works the author aspires not only to be a humourist, but an artist and a moralist; and in his later productions, which we shall talk of by-and-by, he aims at being, besides artist and moralist, politician, philosopher, and ultra-philanthropist. If we direct attention to his weakness in these latter characters, it is solely because he has for years past evinced more and more his tendency to abandon his strong point as humourist and comic writer, and to base his pretensions on grounds which we consider utterly false and unstable. For as a humourist we prefer Dickens to all living men—as artist, moralist, politician, philosopher, and ultra-philanthropist, we prefer many living men, women, and children to Dickens. It is because we so cordially recognised, and so keenly enjoyed, his genius in his earlier works, that we now protest against the newer phase he chooses to appear in. Formerly, his impulses came from within. What his unerring eye saw, as it glanced round the world, was represented in a medium of the richest humour. But gradually his old characteristics have slipt from him, supplanted by others totally different in origin and result. All his inspiration now seems to come from without. We always imagine him beset, while planning a new book, by critics selected from the most ill-judging of his readers, into whose hands he commits himself, and begins writing to order. One tells him, whatever he does to be sure to be graphic; and accordingly the obedient author paints every scene and every character, no matter of what degree of importance, with a minuteness far surpassing that of the most laborious limner of the Dutch school, till still life has no atom left in natural indistinctness; and as for living beings, you may say even the hairs of their heads are all numbered. A booby who aims at being thought a thinker, then assures him that his great strength lies in 'going to the heart of our deepest social problems;' and straightway Dickens, the genial Dickens, overflowing by nature with the most rampant hearty fun, addresses himself to the melancholy task, setting to work to illustrate some enigma which Thomas Carlyle perhaps, or some such congenial dreary spirit, after discussing it in two volumes octavo, has left rather darker than before. Another luminary tells him that it is the duty of a great popular writer to be a great moral teacher, and straightway a piece of staring morality is embroidered into the motley pattern. Next comes an evil whisper, which we always imagine to proceed from a thin young lady of about five-and-thirty, with a pink nose and a blighted heart, to the effect that she hopes there will be plenty of his beautiful sentiment: and, in compliance with the voice of the charmer, some sparkling bits of tinsel, warranted coppergilt, are woven in the web. Lastly comes the worst tempter of all, in the guise of a kindly, large-hearted detector and extoller of perfection, especially among the lower orders, at whose instigation are elaborated some plebeian specimens of all the virtues which, if they had the slightest touch of nature in them, would go far to upset the old-established belief in human weakness and fallibility. The result of some such guidance as we have imagined here appears in *Bleak House* and *Little Dorrit*, as well as in great part of both *Dombey* and *Copperfield*.

In executing this piebald plan, the old natural, easy, unconscious Pickwickian style has given place to one to which all those epithets are totally inapplicable; and the characteristics of which, always to us unpleasant, are growing more prominent in every successive work. . . .

. . . We trace the first appearance of these weeds of his mind to *Chuzzlewit*; but there such brilliant flowers as the Gampia grandiflora, the Bailey Seedling, the Lupin, and the Transatlantic specimens, might

well make us regardless of the surrounding patches of dockens and
thistles, which have now, however, made head to such an alarming
extent that we can't wait for the end of the wilderness of *Little Dorrit*
before recording our earnest protest and deep lament; for in that
wilderness we sit down and weep when we remember thee, O *Pickwick*!...

[A discouraging account of the plot-mechanics follows. 'But if this is
not a work of art, what is it? Is it a work of humour?' No: 'Alas, alas!
shades of Gamp, Hominy, Swiveller, and all the Pickwickian host!
how are the mighty fallen!' Is it, then, a work of character? An examination of the leading figures produces the answer, No.]

A novel which, besides being destitute of well-considered plot, is not
a novel of incident or character, can scarcely be a great picture of life;
indeed, the number of puppets, dummies, and unnatural creations that
grimace and jerk their way along the scenes, forbid it to be so considered. 'All the world's a stage,' says Shakespeare, 'and all the men and
women merely players.'—'All the world's a puppet-show,' says
Dickens, 'and all the men and women *fantoccini*. See here, ladies and
gentlemen, I take this abstract quality, which is one of the characteristics of the present day, and which you will therefore like to see—I
select this individual trait from the heap you see lying by me—I add
a bit of virtue, because it looks well to detect a soul of goodness in
things evil—I dress the combination in these garments, which I got off
a man in the street. Observe now, when I pull the strings (and I don't
mind letting you see me pulling the strings all through the exhibition—
no deception, ladies and gentlemen, none), how natural the action!
how effective the character!' And all the languid people in the boxes,
and the stupid people in the pit, and the gods in the galleries, clap their
hands, and cry, Bravo! hurrah! But there are many people in the
boxes who are not languid, many in the pit who are not stupid, and
there is good sense even among the gods; and the applause is not
unqualified. . . .

What can be weaker in itself, to say nothing of the total want of art
in connecting it with the story, than the intended satire on the Circumlocution Office? We don't in the least wish to stand up for the Circumlocution Office—curse the Circumlocution Office, say we. We know
well the amount of insolence and ignorance to be found among
Government officials of all departments. But the attempt to show it up
in *Little Dorrit* is as inartificial as if he had cut half-a-dozen leading

articles out of an Opposition newspaper, and stuck them in anyhow, anywhere. Besides, in all his attempts to embody political questions, Dickens has never shown a spark of original thought. He is merely waving, as an oriflamme, a ragged old standard, with a great staring legend on it, stained with beer, and smelling villanously of tobacco, in consequence of long figuring at contested elections. We don't blame him for not being a great politician. It would be almost miraculous if a man with such rare power of individualising as he is endowed with, should possess also the power of habitually considering questions in their most comprehensive and abstract bearing. What we blame him for is, for leaving the circle where none dare walk but him, to elbow his way on a thoroughfare open to tagrag and bobtail. The next time Mr Dickens dines out, the gentlemen on each side of him will probably be just as much entitled to a hearing on a political question as he is. We don't want him to be a politician, of whom there are plenty; we want him to be a humourist, and painter of passion and life, where he stands almost without a peer.

On reading over what we have written, we almost fear we have expressed ourself with a little tinge of severity. But Dickens, dear Dickens, no offence—none! We have spoken to thee not in anger, but in sorrow. . . . We know that you must of necessity be surrounded by admirers of more enthusiasm than discretion. . . . Therefore, dear Dickens, don't listen to your adulators—listen to *us*, your true friend and admirer. We appeal from the author of *Bleak House* and *Little Dorrit* to the author of *Pickwick*, the *Old Curiosity Shop*, and the better parts of *Chuzzlewit*. Not in humour only are you dear to us, but in tragedy also, and in pathos we own your power. Paul Dombey— heaven knows how fond we were of that boy!—whose short life we have never yet been able to read consecutively through, the page always growing dim and blurred long before the little spark is quenched. Sykes, too, and Fagin, in their ends attest your tragic power, though we never knew nor cared under what statute the latter was condemned. And for fancy and humour and pathos combined, there is that entire and perfect chrysolite the *Christmas Carol*, which we read aloud ever on a Christmas eve to an audience that ever still responds with weeping and with laughter. Remembering these benefits, ungrateful should we be beyond all measure of ingratitude, should we now write one word in spirit otherwise than of truest friendship of him who wrote so well in the brave days of old. And if you take our advice, and give your rare powers fair play, laying aside your pen for awhile, collecting fitting materials in your own fields, without wandering into regions strange to you, and, when fully ripe, expressing the results of your marvellous faculty of observation in your old natural, humorous, graphic, pathetic way, we, as we read, gladdest of your readers, that matured evidence of your genius, will bow ourselves before you, and (while secretly exulting in the fruit our words have borne) will humbly crave forgiveness for our bold though honest remonstrance, rejoicing more over your repentance than over ninety and nine respectable writers who have never gone astray. But if you do not take our advice, and mean to go on building streets of Bleak Houses, and creating crowds of Little Dorrits, then we recommend you to inscribe on your next serial, 'A Banter on the British Public. By Charles Dickens. In Twenty Parts.'

103. From an unsigned review, the *Leader*

27 June 1857, 616-7

The completion of one of Mr Dickens's monthly number books is to the critic what the termination of great events is to the politician, or the close of an epoch to the historian. . . . There is such an affluence of life in all Mr Dickens's books—so vast a range of character and observation of the world—so broad a canvas crowded with so many shapes and incidents—that the effect on the mind is not so much that of glancing over a finished story, as that of looking at an epitome of life itself. If this involves some degree of imperfection in the mere matter of story-telling, it also involves the highest eulogy that can be pronounced on a novelist whose especial calling is the portrayal of human nature and human action. Mr Dickens is the most dramatic of the novelists. . . . We do not exaggerate when we say that his genius possesses some points of resemblance to that of Shakspeare—something of the very thing which, more than anything else, makes Shakspeare the greatest of dramatic poets. It is not merely that Dickens is himself a poet, and in nothing so much as in his exquisite sensitiveness to those fine threads of analogy which connect the animate with the inanimate world, so that the still life of his scenes is constantly made to reflect the dominant emotion of the characters, in a manner which may appear extravagant to matter-of-fact minds, but which is wonderfully true to all who have ever felt emotion—it is not merely that many of his characters have in them such a strong and self-existent vitality that they have already become part of our actual experience, and remain there like remembrances of our own life—it is not merely that Dickens has added phrases to the language, which are to be found in almost any column of a newspaper you may take up to read haphazard—it is not simply on these accounts that Dickens shows some affinity with Shakspeare, but much more on account of that feeling of universal sympathy with human nature which breathes through his pages like the 'broad and general' atmosphere. He soars above all considerations of sect, above all narrow isolations of creed; and, though a more deeply religious writer is not to be found, in all those elements of religion which rise eternally from the natural emotions of love and reverence, he is never disputatiously theological or academically dogmatic. Certain University-bred reviewers, whose shrivelled souls cannot understand the fresh, spontaneous efflorescence of genius, and who will accept no gold that does not come to them impressed with the college stamp, may affect to despise the large regard of Dickens; but the world will recognise its great ones whether or not they wear the uniform of cap and gown.

As with his other works, so is it with *Little Dorrit*. The whole picture is quick and warm with life. . . . —everywhere and under all circumstances, the vitality of the conceptions asserts itself with all the supremacy of genius. A complete character will start before you within the compass of a few lines; as in the case of the little Frenchwoman of whom Mr Dorrit purchases the gifts for Mrs General, or in that of the Swiss host whom Mr Dorrit almost annihilates for a fancied slight, or in that of the landlady of the Break of Day at Châlons. But these are the mere overflowings of the cup. The main characters are those to which we must chiefly look. And first of Mr Dorrit. What awful truth and solemn voice of warning is there in that weak, selfish, pompous, insanely proud man!— . . . Mr Dorrit is the very type of flunkeyism; and our time stands in need of a lesson against that sordid vice. But a manly detestation of servility is one of the most prominent elements in this tale. We see it again in the character of Mr Merdle, the swindling speculator. Mr Merdle, it is well known, is a portrait from life; but it may be as well to recollect that he is not merely a reflex of one individual. He is true to a very large, and it is to be feared, an increasing, class; a class of individuals not merely corrupt in themselves, but the cause of corruption in others. What matter that the Merdles of real life, like the Merdle of Mr Dickens's fiction, are poor in heart and brain— mere rattling husks of men, with nothing inside but a few dead conventional ideas and phrases; what matter that they are dull in thought, embarrassed in manner, constantly taking themselves into custody under their coat-cuffs with that intuition of their own villany noted by Mr Dickens; what matter that they tremble before their butlers, and move about their drawing-rooms like icebergs that have preserved all their coldness and lost all their sparkle? They are rich, though by the ruin of others; and Bar and Bishop, Horse-Guards and Treasury, Nobility and Commerce, bow down before them, till, as in the typical instance here portrayed, 'the shining wonder, the new constellation, to be followed by the wise men bringing gifts, stops over certain carrion at the bottom of a bath, and disappears.' . . .

We find the same courageous independence of thought once more exhibited in the scorching satire directed against our 'Circumlocution Offices' and 'Tite Barnacle' legislators. How much truth there is in that satire is shown by the fact of its being at once adopted by the popular mind. . . .

We must confess to some disappointment at the explanation, to- wards the close of the book, of the mystery connected with Mrs Clennam and the old house with its strange noises. It is deficient in clearness, and does not fulfil the expectations of the reader, which have been wound up to a high pitch. Indeed, the woof of the entire story does not hold together with sufficient closeness, a fault perhaps insepar- able from the mode of publication. The writing, however, shows all Mr Dickens's singular union of close observation and rich fancy. A few instances suggest themselves as we write. Of Jeremiah Flintwinch, whose head is always on one side, so that the knotted ends of his cravat dangle under one ear, and who has 'a swollen and suffused look,' we are told that 'he had a weird appearance of having hanged himself at one time or other, and of having gone about ever since halter and all, exactly as some timely hand had cut him down.' The watch worn by the same old man was deposited in a deep pocket, 'and had a tarnished copper key *moored above it, to show where it was sunk.*' The garret bed- room of the old house contains 'a lean set of fire irons like the skeleton of a set deceased,' and 'a bedstead with four bare atomies of posts, each terminating in a spike, *as if for the dismal accommodation of lodgers who might prefer to impale themselves.*' Very poetical, also, is the identification of the pent-up fire in Mrs Clennam's sick-room with the invalid herself. 'The fire shone sullenly all day and sullenly all night. On rare occasions, it flashed up pasionately as she did; but for the most part it was suppressed, like her, and preyed upon itself, evenly and slowly.' The light of this fire throws the shadows of Mrs Clennam, old Flintwinch, and his wife, Mistress Affery, on a gateway opposite, like figures from a magic lantern. 'As the room-ridden invalid settled for the night, these would gradually disappear: Mistress Affery's magnified shadow always flitting about, last, until it finally glided away into the air, as though she were off upon a witch-excursion. Then the solitary light would burn unchangingly, until it burned pale before the dawn, and at last died under the breath of Mistress Affery, as her shadow descended on it from the witch-region of sleep.' This is true poetry; but there are a thousand such touches in the book, as in all Mr Dickens's books, which every reader of cultivated perceptions will perceive for himself. In *Little Dorrit*, Mr Dickens has made another imperishable addition to the literature of his country.

104. [James Fitzjames Stephen], from 'The Licence of Modern Novelists', *Edinburgh Review*

July 1857, cvi, 124–56

Stephen, reviewing *Little Dorrit* with Charles Reade's prison-novel *It is never too late to mend* and Mrs Gaskell's *Life of Charlotte Bronte*, here continues the attacks on Dickens and 'Light Literature' he was mounting in the *Saturday Review* (see No. 99). This review in the *Edinburgh* started much controversy; the *Leader* attacked the reviewer's 'tone of unwarrantable assumption' (11 July 1857, 664); the *Saturday Review*, not surprisingly, found great merit in Stephen's 'powerful and very curious article' (18 July 1857, iv, 57). Dickens himself replied to some of Stephen's comments, particularly his citing Sir Rowland Hill's career as an instance of Governmental willingness to accept cheap and efficient modes of action ('Curious Misprint in the Edinburgh Review', *Household Words*, 1 August 1857, xvi, 97–100). His protest was curtly acknowledged in the *Edinburgh Review* (October 1857, cvi, 594).

Fitzjames Stephen's brother Leslie commented on his motives in this review: 'Dickens's attacks upon the "Circumlocution Office" and its like were not altogether inconsistent with some opinions upon the English system of government to which ... Fitzjames himself gave forcible expression in after years. They started, however, from a very different point of view. ... The assault upon the 'Circumlocution Office' was, I doubt not, especially offensive because 'Barnacle Tite,' and the effete aristocrats who are satirized in *Little Dorrit*, stood for representatives of Sir James Stephen and his best friends. In fact, I think, Dickens took the view natural to the popular mind, which always embodies a grievance in a concrete image of a wicked and contemptible oppressor intending all the evils which result from his office. A more interesting and appropriate topic for art of a serious kind would be the problem presented by a body of men of the highest ability and integrity who are yet doomed to work a cumbrous and inadequate system. But the popular reformer, to whom everything seems easy and obvious, explains all abuses by attributing them to the deliberate intention of particular fools and knaves. This indicates Fitzjames's position at the time. He was fully conscious of the administrative abuses assailed, and was as ardent on law reform as became a disciple of Bentham. But he could not accept the support of men who thought that judicious reform could be suggested by rough caricatures. . . .' (*Life of Sir James Fitzjames Stephen* (1895), 159).

. . . These facts [concerning the wide circulation of novels] furnish an apology, which we feel to be necessary, for devoting some attention to two books which justify the opinion we have formed on the influence exercised by such novels over the moral and political opinions of the young, the ignorant, and the inexperienced. That opinion is, that they tend to beget hasty generalisations and false conclusions. They address themselves almost entirely to the imagination upon subjects which properly belong to the intellect. Their suggestions go so far beyond their assertions that the author's sense of responsibility is greatly weakened, and by suppressing all that is dull, all that does not contribute to dramatic effect, and all that falls beyond a certain conventional circle of feelings, they caricature instead of representing the world. This applies even to those ordinary domestic relations, which are the legitimate province of novels. Love, marriage, friendship, grief, and joy are very different things in a novel from what they are in real life, and the representations of novelists are not only false, but often in the highest degree mischievous when they apply, not to the feelings, but to the facts and business transactions of the world. . . .

Little Dorrit is not one of the most pleasing or interesting of Mr Dickens's novels. The plot is singularly cumbrous and confused—the characters rather uninteresting—and the style often strained to excess. We are not however tempted, by the comparative inferiority of this production of a great novelist, to forget the indisputable merits of Mr Dickens. Even those who dislike a good deal of the society to which he introduces his readers, and who are not accustomed to the language of his personages, must readily acknowledge that he has described modern English low life with infinite humour and fidelity, but without coarseness. He has caught and reproduced that native wit which is heard to perfection in the repartees of an English crowd: and though his

path has often lain through scenes of gloom, and poverty, and wretchedness, and guilt, he leaves behind him a spirit of tenderness and humanity
which does honour to his heart. We wish he had dealt as fairly and
kindly with the upper classes of society as he has with the lower; and
that he had more liberally portrayed those manly, disinterested, and
energetic qualities which make up the character of an English gentleman. Acute observer as he is, it is to be regretted that he should have
mistaken a Lord Decimus for the type of an English statesman, or Mr
Tite Barnacle for a fair specimen of a public servant. But in truth we
cannot recall any single character in his novels, intended to belong to
the higher ranks of English life, who is drawn with the slightest
approach to truth or probability. His injustice to the institutions of
English society is, however, even more flagrant than his animosity to
particular classes in that society. The rich and the great are commonly
held up to ridicule for their folly, or to hatred for their selfishness. But
the institutions of the country, the laws, the administration, in a word
the government under which we live, are regarded and described by
Mr Dickens as all that is most odious and absurd in despotism or in
oligarchy. In every new novel he selects one or two of the popular
cries of the day, to serve as seasoning to the dish which he sets before his
readers. It may be the Poor Laws, or Imprisonment for Debt, or the
Court of Chancery, or the harshness of Mill-owners, or the stupidity of
Parliament, or the inefficiency of the Government, or the insolence of
District Visitors, or the observance of Sunday, or Mammon-worship,
or whatever else you please. He is equally familiar with all these
subjects. If there was a popular cry against the management of a hospital, he would no doubt write a novel on a month's warning about the
ignorance and temerity with which surgical operations are performed;
and if his lot had been cast in the days when it was fashionable to call
the English law the perfection of reason, he would probably have
published monthly denunciations of Lord Mansfield's Judgment in
Perrin v. *Blake*, in blue covers adorned with curious hieroglyphics,
intended to represent springing uses, executory devises, and contingent
remainders. We recommend him to draw the materials of his next
work from Dr Hassall on the Adulteration of Food, or the Report on
Scotch Lunatics. Even the catastrophe in *Little Dorrit* is evidently
borrowed from the recent fall of houses in Tottenham Court Road,
which happens to have appeared in the newspapers at a convenient
moment.[1] . . .

[1] Dickens proved the falsity of that allegation, in his *Household Words* reply.

By examining the justice of Mr Dickens's general charges, and the accuracy of Mr Reade's specific accusations, we shall endeavour to show how much injustice may be done, and how much unfounded discontent may be engendered, by these one-sided and superficial pictures of popular abuses.

It is not a little curious to consider what qualifications a man ought to possess before he could, with any kind of propriety, hold the language Mr Dickens sometimes holds about the various departments of social life. Scott, we all know, was a lawyer and an antiquarian. Sir Edward Lytton has distinguished himself in political life, and his books contain unquestionable evidence of a considerable amount of classical and historical reading. Mr Thackeray hardly ever steps beyond those regions of society and literature which he has carefully explored. But in Mr Dickens's voluminous works, we do not remember to have found many traces of these solid acquirements; and we must be permitted to say, for it is no reflection on any man out of the legal profession, that his notions of law, which occupy so large a space in his books, are precisely those of an attorney's clerk. He knows what arrest for debt is, he knows how affidavits are sworn. He knows the physiognomy of courts of justice, and he has heard that Chancery suits sometimes last forty years; though he seems not to have the remotest notion that there is any difference between suits for the administration of estates and suits for the settlement of disputed rights, and that the delay which is an abuse in the one case, is inevitable in the other. The greatest of our statesmen, lawyers, and philosophers would shrink from delivering any trenchant and unqualified opinion upon so complicated and obscure a subject as the merits of the whole administrative Government of the empire. To Mr Dickens the question presents no such difficulty. He stumbles upon the happy phrase of 'the Circumlocution Office' as an impersonation of the Government; strikes out the brilliant thought, repeated just ten times in twenty-three lines, that whereas ordinary people want to know how to do their business, the whole art of Government lies in discovering 'how not to do it;' and with these somewhat unmeaning phrases he proceeds to describe, in a light and playful tone, the government of his country.

Everybody has read the following chapter of *Little Dorrit*; but we are not equally sure that everybody has asked himself what it really means. It means, if it means anything, that the result of the British constitution, of our boasted freedom, of parliamentary representation, and of all we possess, is to give us the worst government on the face of the earth—the clatter of a mill grinding no corn, the stroke of an engine drawing no water.

[Quotes from Book I, ch. x, 'Containing the whole Science of Government'.]

It is not necessary to discuss the justice of Mr Dickens's charges, but it is so much the fashion of the day to speak with unmeasured contempt both of the honesty and ability of the executive government, that we will lay before our readers a few considerations upon the general character of the public service, and upon the principles which ought to govern discussions as to its merits.

The first question which presents itself is, What is the standard of comparison? It would require a knowledge of the details of the administrative system of other countries, which we do not pretend to possess, to institute a detailed comparison between their governments and our own. But without entering on so vast a subject, we think that any person of ordinary fairness and information may easily satisfy himself that the British Government need not shrink from a comparison, either with the transactions of mercantile men, or with those of great public companies. Mr Dickens, and many other denouncers of the incapacity of the Government, have long indulged in the pleasant habit of looking only at one side of the subject. They read in the newspapers of the failures, the prejudices, and the stupidity of the executive; and it never occurs to them that they do not hear of the cases in which the official mechanism works well. We must have some notion of the magnitude of the operations which the Government has to conduct, before we can duly estimate the immense weight of the testimony in its favour, which is conveyed by the absence of complaint on so many subjects. . . .

[Stephen instances the collection and management of the Revenue, about £60000000; and the administration of the Empire overseas.]

Inefficiency, however, is only one of Mr Dickens's charges against the Government. Neglect of useful inventions and gross corruption are thrown in by way of makeweight. Thus in the following oracular conversation in *Little Dorrit*:—

'What I mean to say is, that however this comes to be the regular way of our government, it is its regular way. Have you ever heard of any proprietor or inventor who failed to find it all but inaccessible, and whom it did not discourage and ill-treat?'

'I cannot say I ever have.'

'Have you ever known it to be beforehand in the adoption of any useful thing? Ever known it to set an example of any useful kind?'

'I am a good deal older than my friend here,' said Mr Meagles, 'and I'll answer that. *Never*.' [Book I, ch. x; Stephen's italics]

This is no isolated ebullition. The Circumlocution Office forms one of the standing decorations of the work in which it is depicted. The cover of the book is adorned by a picture, representing, amongst other things, Britannia in a Bath-chair, drawn by a set of effete idiots, an old woman, a worn-out cripple in a military uniform, and a supercilious young dandy, who buries the head of his cane in his moustaches. The chair is pushed on behind by six men in foolscaps, who are followed by a crowd of all ages and both sexes, intended, we presume, to represent that universal system of jobbing and favouritism, which was introduced into the public service by Sir Charles Trevelyan and Sir Stafford Northcote, shortly before the time when Mr Dickens began his novel. The spirit of the whole book is the same. The Circumlocution Office is constantly introduced as a splendid example of all that is base and stupid. Messrs Tite Barnacle and Stiltstalking are uniformly put forward as the representatives of the twenty or thirty permanent under-secretaries and heads of departments, by whom so large a portion of the public affairs is conducted, and every species of meanness, folly, and vulgarity is laid to their charge.

It is difficult to extract the specific accusations which Mr Dickens means to bring against the Government; but we take the principal counts in his indictment to be, that the business of the country is done very slowly and very ill; that inventors and projectors of improvements are treated with insolent neglect; and that the Government is conducted by, and for the interest of, a few aristocratic families, whose whole public life is a constant career of personal jobs. Most men will consider these rather serious charges.

But the burlesque manner and extravagant language in which they are made are at once Mr Dickens's shield and his sword. 'How can you suppose,' he might say, 'that I mean any harm by such representations as these? I am neither a lawyer nor a politician; but I take a fling at the subjects of the day, just in order to give my writings a little local colour, and a little temporary piquancy.' Probably enough this is the true account of the matter, and it forms the very gravamen of our complaint. Men of the world may laugh at books which represent all who govern as fools, knaves, hypocrites, and dawdling tyrants. They know very well that such language is meant to be understood subject to modifications; but the poor and uneducated take such words in their natural and undiluted strength, and draw from them practical conclusions of corresponding importance; whilst the young and inexperienced are led to think far too meanly of the various careers which the organisation of society places before them, and to waste in premature cynicism and self-satisfied indolence some of the most precious opportunities which life affords.

With respect to the first of these charges, we may mention one or two specific instances of the application of inventive power to the regular objects of administration. What does Mr Dickens think of the whole organisation of the Post Office, and of the system of cheap postage, which was invented in this country, and has been adopted by almost every State on the Continent? Every branch of this establishment shows the greatest power of arrangement and contrivance—even mechanical contrivance. Mr Dickens can never tear a penny stamp from its fellows without having before his eyes an illustration of the watchful ingenuity of this branch of the Circumlocution Office. To take another special illustration: what does Mr Dickens say to the London Police? What he has said on the subject, anyone may see, by referring to *Household Words*, in which he will find the organisation of the force praised in almost hyperbolical language. It is not a little characteristic that Mr Dickens should praise one branch of the Circumlocution Office in one of his organs, and shortly afterwards denounce the whole institution as a mass of clumsy stupidity in another. There can hardly be a more delicate administrative problem than that of protecting the persons and property without endangering the liberties of the public; and we should feel some curiosity to see a statement by Mr Dickens of the comparative value of the solutions arrived at by the French, the Russian, and the English Governments.

As to the personal corruption, and the neglect of talent, which Mr Dickens charges against the Government of the country, we can only say that any careful observer of his method might have predicted with confidence that he would begin a novel on that subject within a very few months after the establishment of a system of competitive examinations for admission into the Civil Service. He seems, as a general rule, to get his first notions of an abuse from the discussions which accompany its removal, and begins to open his trenches and mount his batteries as soon as the place to be attacked has surrendered. This was his course with respect both to imprisonment for debt and to Chancery reform; but in the present instance, he has attacked an abuse which never existed to anything like the extent which he describes. A large proportion of the higher permanent offices of state have always been filled by men of great talent, whose promotion was owing to their talent. . . .

[Stephen names some examples.]

Or, to take a single and well-known example, how does he account for the career of Mr Rowland Hill? A gentleman in a private and not very conspicuous position, writes a pamphlet recommending what amounted to a revolution in a most important department of the Government. Did the Circumlocution Office neglect him, traduce him, break his heart, and ruin his fortune? They adopted his scheme, and gave him the leading share in carrying it out, and yet this is the Government which Mr Dickens declares to be a sworn foe to talent, and a systematic enemy to ingenuity. . . .

It is one of Mr Dickens's favourite themes, to compare the modesty, the patience, and the solid business-like sense of his intelligent mechanic, Mr Doyce, with the blundering inefficiency of the Circumlocution Office. We do not deny the justice of the praise which Mr Dickens lavishes on Mr Doyce and his class. It is no doubt well deserved, but we wish to call attention to the fact, that our faith in their good qualities is based entirely upon broad general results, precisely similar to those which, as we say, prove the general ability and honesty of the Government, although the mercantile and mechanical classes have also to account for a vast number of failures of an infinitely more serious kind than those which called into existence Mr Dickens's extravagant fictions. Look, for example, at any of our great railways. No one who observes the traffic, the organisation, the discipline, and all the various members of those immense establishments, can doubt that a vast deal of skill and energy has been employed in their construction; but if we were disposed to denounce them as utterly corrupt and effete, how superabundant the materials of denunciation would be. Imagine Mr Dickens idealising Redpath, and filling in the intervals of his story with racy descriptions of the opposition between the North-Western, the Great Northern, and the Great Western; sketches of trucks laid across the line for engines to run into . . . [etc]. Such a description of English railways would be, neither in kind nor in degree, one whit more unjust, and would not be in its results one-hundredth part as injurious, as the description given in *Little Dorrit* of the Executive Government of this country.

It is as hard to refute a generality as to answer a sneer, and we therefore feel that in combating such statements as those of Mr Dickens, we expose ourselves to the retort that we are fighting with shadows of our own raising. With respect to Mr Charles Reade, our task is far simpler. . . .

105. Matthew Davenport Hill on Stephen's review

14 August 1857

Letter to Lord Brougham (R. and F. D. Hill, *The Recorder of Birmingham: a Memoir of Matthew Davenport Hill* (1873), 333).

Hill (1792–1872), Recorder of Birmingham from 1839, was a vigorous reformer in many educational, penological and philanthropic spheres; he had been associated with Brougham in founding the Society for the Diffusion of Useful Knowledge. He is referring here to Fitzjames Stephen's review (No. 104). M. D. Hill was the brother of (Sir) Rowland Hill, the inventor of the penny postage.

. . . Dickens is open to censure for rarely, if ever, introducing a member of the upper classes into his works except to hold him up to reproach or contempt; but to inveigh against him for his attack on what he calls the 'Circumlocution Office' is childish. He may have exaggerated; but exaggeration directed against an institution, and exaggeration against an individual, are very different things. All satire teems with exaggeration, and ever has done. Institutions and large bodies can bear it, but individuals cannot. Certainly the reviewer made a bad cast when he hauled up Rowland Hill as an instance of the readiness of Governments to encourage improvements, as none know better than yourself who were always his prompt and most powerful advocate. Indeed if Dickens had known the facts he might have made more of the Circumlocution Office.

106. John Hollingshead, from 'Mr Dickens and his Critics', The Train

August 1857, iv, 76–9

Reprinted in Hollingshead's *Essay and Miscellanies* (1865), ii, 277–83, and his *Miscellanies* (1874), iii, 270–4.

Hollingshead (1827–1904), journalist and later a leading theatrical manager, became a contributor to *Household Words* just after writing this dialogue; Dickens wrote to his assistant-editor W. H. Wills, on 26 September 1857, 'I have ... a pretty little paper ... by one Mr Hollingshead, who addressed me as having tried his hand in *The Train.*' He soon became a member of the staff. *The Train* was a short-lived journal, edited by two more of 'Mr Dickens's young men', Edmund Yates and G. A. Sala. Hollingshead's *My Lifetime* contains some interesting reminiscences and assessments of Dickens: e.g., 'Dickens's principles were sound, but they were not deeply rooted, and he was swayed by every breath of feeling and sentiment. He was a Liberal by impulse, and what the "DRYASDUST" school would have called a "wobbler". ... No man, in his inner mind, felt so sure of Westminster Abbey and immortality, and no man kept his mind more carefully concealed. He lived above and beyond the opinion of his contemporaries. . .' (i, 99–100).

Hylas—There is nothing more unfair in criticism than to judge an author by the standard he has created for himself. The minor plays of

Shakespeare are not only abused, but in some instances their author-ship is discredited because their strength is measured against the gigantic proportions of a *Macbeth* or a *Hamlet*.

Philonous—One need not go to the Elizabethan writers for proofs of this injustice, when we have a case before us in the person of Mr Charles Dickens.

Hylas—You allude to the reception of *Little Dorrit*. Let us suppose that the author of this work had appeared for the first time, and laid this production at the feet of the critical public. How it would have stood out from everything around it. Everyone would have felt that here was a new power developed or developing. . . . But while the divine harmony of the *Old Curiosity Shop* still lingers in the ear, while the incomparable pictures of that most perfect fiction are present to the eye, it is easy to declare any new effort of the old master weak and artificial in comparison; but how largely is such a declaration seasoned with ingratitude, and a forgetfulness of the fount from which the criticism is drawn?

Phil—True. I quite agree in your estimate of the literary value of the *Old Curiosity Shop*. . . .

[They continue with praise of this novel.]

Phil—. . . I fear that I can find you many writers now, of no mean authority, who are trying to prove that the god of our idolatry is nothing but a brazen image.

Hylas—They attempt to pull down the idol more for political than for literary reasons. Mr Dickens, in common with all men of quick sympathies and high imagination, is totally opposed to what he con-siders the hard, dry, unfeeling dogmas of political economy. He looks round upon society, and he sees much injustice, much misery, much poverty, and much crime. Not believing in the great economical doc-trine of 'let alone,' he cries out for more government, and knowing the present government to be bad, he cries out for better government, echoing the old cry of 'red tape,' and adding two new cries in the shape of 'Barnacles' and 'Circumlocution Office.' Now, if there is one principle thoroughly established, it is this, that everything which a government undertakes can be better and more economically per-formed by individuals acting under the stimulus of private gain. . . .

Phil—Mr Dickens flies in the face of political economy, forgetting that its great masters are working to the same end as himself,—the good government of society. . . .

Hylas—The duties of poetry are well defined. They are the refining of the human mind, the education of the emotive sympathies, and the spiritual alleviation of the sufferings of humanity. When poetry leaves this useful sphere of action, and attempts the re-organisation of society, what is the result?—an impracticable socialism. . . .

Phil—His opponents do not add to the force of their remarks upon his political principles, when they endeavour to detract from his wonderful literary merit, by treating him as one of the herd of mere comic writers, the Jan Steen of literature, whose mission it is to make men grin and silly women cry—perhaps the most eminent buffoon of his day.

Hylas—When the turmoil of the present century, with all the virulence of its political debate, and all the petty jealousies of its literature shall have passed away, when those who penned the stinging epigram or the caustic satire shall be weak, or dead, or dying—dying, and anxious to give worlds to cancel many a brilliant injustice which their hasty pens have put upon record, then, and not till then, shall we arrive at a calm estimate of the value of the writings of Charles Dickens. Even now I love to picture him far from the din of the critical Babel, surrounded by those delicate and beautiful creations of his fancy, that ideal family, the children of his pen. There, in the twilight of his study, do I see him sitting with his arm round Nell, the favourite child. Her face seems worn and sad, but when she looks up in his eyes, it then becomes suffused with heavenly light. At his feet rest little Dombey and his sister, hand in hand, and nestling to the father who has called them into birth. Poor Joe is there, the fungus of the streets, crouching like a dog beside the fire, grateful for food and warmth and shelter. I hear the clumping of a little crutch upon the stairs, and in hops Tiny Tim, the crippled child. Above them hover the shadowy forms of other children, children who on earth were poor and suffering drudges, workhouse outcasts that the world had turned adrift, but which are now on high a blessed band of angels. And yet this man, great critics, is only a mere buffoon, and nothing more? Truly a fit companion for that low player of the olden time, who wrote *King Lear*, and acted at the Globe.

107. John Cordy Jeaffreson, from his *Novels and Novelists, from Elizabeth to Victoria*

1858, ii, 273–4, 318–30

Jeaffreson (1831–1901), novelist, biographer, and miscellaneous author, was an Oxford graduate. His *Book of Recollections* (2 vols., 1894) contains much gossip about Thackeray and about the London literary scene. The *Rambler*, reviewing his *Novels and Novelists*, felt obliged to 'protest strongly against the absurd claim entered on [Dickens's] behalf by Mr Jeaffreson, who really carried his admiration almost to profanity. A man who looks on *Pickwick* as inspired, and attributes all the progress of the present era to the attentive perusal of *Nicholas Nickleby, Little Dorrit*, and the rest, is clearly very unfit to sit in judgment on the great men who, as novelists, must be submitted to his critical examination in a work like the one before us' (n.s. x, 207).

. . . Those who are in the habit of admiring the truthfulness of Dickens's descriptions will perhaps be astonished by being informed that he is as deceitful, deceiving, and wittingly dishonest a describer as can be found in the entire range of living authors. The triumph of his art is the perfection of his deceit; his purpose in whatever book, chapter, or scene he writes, is to call certain passions of our mind especially into action, and to effect this he brings into the foreground, and makes use of all those facts of life, the description of which will tend to arouse the required emotions; and all that would excite counteracting feelings he carefully keeps out of sight. What he shows us is admirably drawn, often as exactly and as minutely as any pre-Rafaelite painter would use his brush, but still it is not the whole,—and the result is a deception, because we are induced by the consummate skill of the artist to regard the exaggerated and partial statement as all comprehensive and truthful in detail. His Peggotty is not a Yarmouth fisherman, but only certain features of his character put on the stage as a fisherman; of Dick

Swiveller we get only the mirthful and humorous side; Clennam is nothing as the book goes but a good man,—that is less than the ninth part of one. Dickens's habit of minute description gains him a large credit for scrupulous honesty, and being above artistic *legerdemain*. A man so anxious to show even these little things cannot want to keep anything in the background, say simple readers, and so they fail to perceive that he is an artist who, while professing to appeal to their judgment, is making them the dupe of their passions. . . .

. . . His pen is ever at work illustrating a text and enforcing a moral. To the practical man's question, 'what is it for?' whenever it is applied to any of Dickens's books, a plain direct answer can always be returned. Now he brings into contempt the pride and selfishness that lurk beneath social respectability; at another time he leads us to consider the wants and requirements of the destitute and uneducated; a gigantic system of tyranny is grinding and weighing down the poor and helpless—he exposes it; the abuses and abominations of a court of law demand correction—it is his pen that rouses legislators to the work of reform . . . [*etc.*]

There are those who affect a disdain for this high moral purpose in the novel. It is not uncommon to meet with fluent gentlemen who are never so happy as when pouring a watery ridicule upon it. . . . The voice of society is unquestionably against them, and condemns them as the victims of their own stupidity. The wisest and the best as well as the multitudes of men concur in studying with delight and admiration these works; no other kind of novel is so largely patronized by readers of all classes, pursuits, and degrees of intelligence. Let them think of the novels that, during the last few years have produced a startling impression on the public, and say whether or no they possess the miserable zeal for making the world better, or at least wiser. *Never too late to mend, The Newcomes, Uncle Tom's Cabin, The Heir of Redclyffe, Coningsby, Hawkestone, Alton Locke*, and the universally read works of Dickens; all these make a show of moral purpose of some kind or other; their objects are to combat prejudices, alleviate class oppressions, sweep down obstacles in the way of social regeneration, or lead men to commune with their own hearts and be still. . . .

Indeed, to any one unacquainted with the nature and life of men it would be a fit subject for marvel that unquestionably *popular* and *fascinating* writers should be condemned for being *earnest*, for exercising their exquisite genius for illustration on subjects of vital importance, for being too instructive, for not being frivolous. But the wonder ceases when we examine the constitution of society. It is not every one who can alter with the age, and in advanced years adopt the sentiments and aspirations of a new generation. Is it wonderful, then, that those whose tastes were formed at the close of the last century should be somewhat perplexed by the poetry of the present time? A venerable lady, whose long renowned wit remains to her untarnished in her more than eightieth year, said, a short time since, to the writer of these pages, with infinite frankness and humour, 'It's all well for you young men to praise Tennyson and Carlyle, but I am wearied to death by moral illuminators; give me back my poor Byron and Moore. The world is getting a great deal too good for us old sinners.'. . .

. . . But if we attempted to enumerate in succession, all the items of the enormous debt of gratitude our nation, and all civilized countries, owe him, how impossible we should find it to accomplish the undertaking! His benefits to mankind are as innumerable as the flowers that cover the earth, some of the most beautiful and modest of which they also resemble, in being sheltered from observation. There is not a human heart in these islands, so fruitful of wretchedness and depravity, which Dickens has not at some time or other influenced for the better; not a home, however humble and tenanted with evil passions, that his good genius does not occasionally visit, like a peace angel, garnishing, setting in order, and sanctifying with pleasant words of hope. Amongst us there is not a grinding taskmaster who would not have been more extortionate, there is not a mean nature that would not have been more selfish, and there is not a flippant worldling who would not have been more enamoured of frivolity, had Dickens never lived to write. Was not his influence so invariably for good, that we feel he is powerless to exercise it for wrong, it would be fearful to contemplate it. Directly we examine our relations with him, we are positively alarmed at the sway he has held over us,—how we have been in his hands only plastic clay that he has fashioned—to all the honour it was capable of. We cannot walk without his leading strings, or speak without using his texts, or look out upon the world save through his eyes. Indeed it is not our world, but his, that we gaze upon. If an incident render a morning's walk eventful, we refer to his books for a parallel, or explanation, or comment. The crowds that hurry past us in the public ways we classify in a manner he has taught us, and we christen them with names taken from his fictions. It is the same on the gravest occasions, and the most trivial. In the Houses of Parliament, or the law courts, arguments are illustrated and pointed by an allusion to the Jarndyces and Barnacles, as naturally and with as much effect as if Jarndyce and the chief of the Barnacles were veritable items in the Post-Office Directory. In short we have so adopted, or he has so embued us with, his views of the outer world, that in moments of self introspection we are almost frightened lest we should have been too confiding and unquestioning followers. Such in its magnitude is his influence on each one of us, in regard to the external world he has surrounded us with. But there is another even more important division of his artistic influence to be glanced at, which consists not in the colouring he has given to the non-ego of each of us, or simply in the hold he has taken of our young intelligences as an interpreter of social problems, but is found in that kindly humour which he has infused equally into our heads and hearts, stimulating what is best in both of them to extreme activity, and enabling us to think freely and independently—from the force and virtue imparted to us—not in mere imitation of his movements, or as the mechanical echoes of his words, though truly following him, and in all things doing as we could never have done without his aid. . . .

The fact, that during these last twenty-five years, throughout which the schoolmaster has been so busy in informing the brain, and society has been ever applying stronger and yet stronger stimulants to the ingenuity, we have not fallen into the lowest depths of depravity, but on the contrary have made advances in our national morality not less astounding than those made in our external civilization, is a most encouraging one. And it is mainly to be attributed to our hearts having been watched, cherished, and informed by a divinely instructed writer. We have grown in wisdom and cunning, but have not lost one jot of our love of truth; we have expended a perhaps lavish wealth of energy on the arts of peace, but the old lion, wrapped up like a lady's spaniel, by our Manchester silks, is as wakeful and courageous as ever; we have become richer, and, at the same time, less besotted, less luxurious, less selfish. Whence is this? Take any honest-hearted Englishman, and probe cunningly the depths of his nature to discover why it is that he would scorn to tell a lie, to desert a fallen friend, to reap benefit from a deed of shame? that he is so impatient of shams and pretenders? and would strike to the ground any man who asked him to sell his honour for gold? You will find the answer in his affections, in a chivalric belief in the excellence of woman, and the dignity of honesty, in a strong love for the memory of a mother who first taught him to pray, or for lisping babes of his own just learning to falter out accents of entreaty. Whatever he may be, and however circumstanced, without family ties or with them, whatever the affections may be which his experience of life may have made him hold most dear, in them will be found the keynote of his generosity. But carry the examination yet farther. Draw him out on any subject calculated to make him display his sympathies and antipathies. Get him to unbosom himself. He flashes up, his chest rises, and the thunder of his voice rolls about. But, how is this?—every assertion of a principle is backed by a reference to Dickens, he cannot touch on a social difficulty without an illustration from 'Boz;' he talks Dickens, laughs Dickens—for the time being is Dickens.

A writer may be very successful, and make a great impression on his age, and yet his name may never be heard of beyond a small circle of students. . . . Of Charles Dickens's fame a grand feature is its universality. His name is as much a 'Household Word' in every sequestered hamlet lying between the most extreme points of our *home* islands, as it is in the metropolis; and he is as well known in the United States, Canada, and Australia, as he is in the city round St. Paul's. . . . The writer of these pages knows cottages on bleak wolds, over which the winter's winds scream terribly, and cabins fixed in hollows beside damp lanes, where every evening, odd numbers, black and greasy as an old fustian jacket from being thumbed, of the works of Boz—and even stray leaves, sacredly preserved—are spelt out and sobbed over by the family circle. And when the reading is over, they talk first of the story, and then of its writer; whereupon, some rugged patriarch of the plough, whose voice is respected, though he does not know a letter of the alphabet, and has learnt the sad story of Ham and Emily through the lips of his little grand-daughter (who reads like a scholard), tells out slowly to his attentive audience how Charles Dickens is 'one on 'em, and also was one on 'em, and what's more, always will be one on 'em, and nought can take him from 'em, for his heart is right set,' and to us it has ever seemed far nobler to rule men's minds with words, than to drive their bodies with bayonets.

And in every class and grade of society there is a similar sentiment to this. Universally as the genius of Dickens and the elements of his intellectual greatness are discussed on all sides, we still are more prone to regard his moral qualities. His mental endowments take a second place; and ere we say our critical say about the qualities of his humour, the merit of his satire, or the strength of his imagination, we pay homage to him as the good and true. . . .

108. From an unsigned review of the Library Edition of the *Works*, *Saturday Review*

8 May 1858, v, 474–5

Reprinted in *Notorious Literary Attacks*, ed. Albert Mordell (New York, 1926), 162–70. Almost certainly by James Fitzjames Stephen.

... It is impossible to describe the spirit of a writer of whose best books slang is the soul without speaking his own language. Mr Dickens is the very Avatar of chaff, and bigwigs of every description are his game. The joviality, the animal spirits, and the freshness with which he acted this part in his earliest books are wonderful. We cannot mention any caricature so perfect and so ludicrous as the description of Messrs Dodson and Fogg, and that of the trial of Bardell *v.* Pickwick. The mere skill of his workmanship would have unquestionably secured the success of such a writer; but the harmony between his own temper and that of his audience must be appreciated before we can understand the way in which approbation grew into enthusiasm.

It would, however, be a great mistake to suppose that it was merely to banter that Mr Dickens owed his marvellous success. Mere banter soon grows wearisome; and Mr Dickens was led by nature as much as by art to mix up a very strong dose of sentiment with his caricature. From first to last, he has tried about as much to make his readers cry as to make them laugh; and there is a very large section of the British public—and especially of the younger, weaker, and more ignorant part of it—which considers these two functions as comprising the whole duty of novelists. ... No man can offer to the public so large a stock of death-beds adapted for either sex and for any age from five-and-twenty downwards. There are idiot death-beds, where the patient cries ha, ha! and points wildly at vacancy—pauper death-beds, with unfeeling nurses to match—male and female children's death-beds, where the young ladies or gentlemen sit up in bed, pray to the angels, and see golden water on the walls. In short, there never was a man to whom the King of Terrors was so useful as a lay figure.

This union of banter and sentiment appears to us to form the essence of Mr Dickens's view of life. In the main, it is a very lovely world, a very good and a very happy world, in which we live. We ought all to be particularly fond of each other and infinitely pleased with our position. The only drawback to this charming state of things is that a great number of absurd people have got up a silly set of conventional rules, which the rest of us are foolish enough to submit to. The proper course with them is good natured ridicule and caricature, which cannot fail to make them conscious of the absurdity of their position. . . . We are all dear brothers and sisters in *Bleak House* and *Little Dorrit*, just as we were in *Pickwick* and *Nicholas Nickleby;* but we have reached a time of life in which family quarrels must be expected, and we have learned that good-natured banter, when kept up for a quarter of a century, is apt, with the kindest intentions in the world, to degenerate into serious and angry discussion. It is all very well to cork a man's face after a college supper-party, but if the process were kept up for five-and-twenty years, whenever he took a nap, it might come to be worth his while to require a special and serious justification for such conduct.

We cannot now attempt to trace the history of Mr Dickens's publications, or of the various stages through which his style and his opinions have passed, but we may briefly indicate the literary position to which, in our opinion, he has attained. It does not appear to us certain that his books will live, nor do we think that his place in literary history will be by the side of such men as Defoe and Fielding, the founders of the school to which he belongs. *Pickwick* stands as far below *Tom Jones* as it stands above *Dombey and Son* or *Bleak House*. It is an exquisitely piquant caricature of the everyday life of the middle and lower classes at the time to which it refers; but the general theory of life on which it is based is not only false, but puerile. . . . The mixed characters, the confusion, the incompleteness, which meet us at every step in real life, never occur in his pages. You understand what he means on the first reading far better than on any other. The only characters drawn from real observation belong to one or two classes of life. All the oddities of London he has sketched with inimitable vigour; but class characteristics and local peculiarities are of a very transient nature. Fifty years hence, most of his wit will be harder to understand than the allusions in the *Dunciad;* and our grandchildren will wonder what their ancestors could have meant by putting Mr Dickens at the head of the novelists of his day.

Though, however, we do not believe in the permanence of his reputation, it is impossible to deny that Mr Dickens has exercised an immense influence over contemporary literature, or that his books must always be an extremely curious study on that account. Till our own days, almost every popular writer formed his style on the classical model. Even those who revolted most strongly against the canons of composition current in the eighteenth century—Coleridge, Wordsworth, Southey, Charles Lamb, and their associates—had, almost without an exception, been taught to write. They maintained that the stiffness of the style then dominant arose from a misapprehension of the true principles of the art of literature; but that it was an art they never doubted. The first person of mark who wrote entirely by the light of nature, and without the guidance of any other principle than that of expressing his meaning in the most emphatic language that he could find, was Cobbett. Though no two persons could resemble each other less in character, the position of Mr Dickens with respect to fiction is precisely analogous to that of Cobbett with respect to political discussion. The object of the arguments of the one is to drive his opinion into the dullest understanding—the object of the narrative of the other is to paint a picture which will catch the eye of the most ignorant and least attentive observer. Mr Dickens's writings are the apotheosis of what has been called newspaper English. He makes points everywhere, gives unfamiliar names to the commonest objects, and lavishes a marvellous quantity of language on the most ordinary incidents. Mr William Russell and Mr Charles Dickens have respectively risen to the very top of two closely connected branches of the same occupation. The correspondence from the Crimea is constructed upon exactly the same model as *Pickwick* and *Martin Chuzzlewit*, and there can be no doubt that the triumphs which this style has attained in Mr Dickens's hands have exercised, and will continue to exercise, very considerable influence on the mould into which people will cast their thoughts, and indirectly upon their thoughts themselves. We cannot affect to say that we look upon the growth of this habit with much satisfaction. It appears to us to foster a pert, flippant frame of mind, in which the fancy exerts an amount of influence which does not rightfully belong to it, and in which it is very hard for people to think soberly of others, and almost impossible for them not to think a great deal too much about themselves and the effect which they are producing. There is a sex in minds as well as in bodies, and Mr Dickens's literary progeny seem to us to be for the most part of the feminine gender, and to betray it by most unceasing flirtations, and by a very tiresome irritability of nerve.

109. Francis Jacox attacks the *Saturday Review*, *New Monthly Magazine*

June 1864, cxxxi, 168–77

From 'Mrs Pardiggle: Typically Considered'.

This essay, signed by 'Sir Nathaniel', was followed (pp. 177–84) by 'Bunsby: Typically Considered'. Presumably 'Sir Nathaniel' was the author of the similar 'Typically Considered' essays appearing in *Bentley's Miscellany*: Harold Skimpole (July 1863) and Mr Micawber (March 1864) by 'Monkshood', and Mr Gradgrind (August 1866) by Francis Jacox (1825–97, a clergyman and prolific miscellaneous author). The social and psychological 'typicality' of these characters is demonstrated by numerous contemporary parallels. The present excerpt will not, however, exemplify this, but quotes entirely from an extended footnote aimed at the *Saturday Review*. According to an author in the *St. James's Magazine*, some demonstration that the *Saturday Review*, while attacking Dickens, depended on him almost weekly for proverbial expressions, was so conclusive 'that, in very shame, the *Review* from that day ceased its attacks upon the great man's fame' (August 1870, n.s. v, 696–7). The point had been made, more briefly, in 1860 (Godfrey Turner, 'Mr Dickens and his Reviewers,' *The Welcome Guest*, i, 375–7) and, without specific reference to the *Saturday Review*, by David Masson in 1859:

Take any periodical in which there is a severe criticism of Dickens's last publication; and, ten to one, in the same periodical, and perhaps by the same hand, there will be a leading article, setting out with a quotation from Dickens that flashes on the mind of the reader the thought which the whole article is meant to convey, or containing some allusion to one of Dickens's characters which enriches the text in the middle and floods it an inch round with color and humor (*British Novelists and their Styles*, 252).

The author in the *St. James's* could have meant any of these, and his story is probably apocryphal; but 'Sir Nathaniel's' footnote certainly shows how thoroughly Dickens had permeated the language and mythology of the period. 'Sir Nathaniel' begins his article by quoting a *Saturday Review* essay about domineering philanthropists. This gives him an excuse for his footnote.

Mrs Pardiggle might have been cited as an exaggerated type of this sort of unfeeling philanthropy. Very probably she *is* so cited in some parallel passage of some other essay, in the same periodical. For, as the *Review* in question (if not the Reviewer) is frequent in its sallies against domineering well-doers, and dictatorial goody busybodies, and too patronising philanthropists, of the fussy, inter-meddling sort,—so is it almost curiously addicted (*some* of its contributors at least are) to point a moral or enliven an argument by illustrations drawn from the writings at large of Mr Charles Dickens.

Indeed, it must often have been felt by Mr Dickens as a practical compensation for the *Review*'s strictures on not a few of his writings, that it yet cares to profit so copiously by allusions to stock characters of his creation.

As this is a foot-note, and may the better afford scope and cover for a digressive excursus, let us just put together a few instances of these drafts on Dickens;—merely premising that they are taken, not systematically and exhaustively, but occasionally and at random, from such numbers of the *Review* as happen to be within present reach; and that if the popular author only thinks half as well of the perhaps unpopular (*odit enim profanum vulgus*)[1] but certainly powerful *Review* as this present notetaker and foot-notemaker does, he must be substantially consoled for the hard hits which, first and last, it may have dealt him, by the abundance of material it finds in his pages for passing reference and pungent allusion. There would be no purpose in presenting this συλλογή[2] of illustrations, but that they are taken from a journal which by no means favours Mr Dickens.

[1] 'For it hates the uninitiate mob' (adapted from Horace, *Odes*, III, i, 1).
[2] Collection.

The first volume of that *Review* which happens to be within reach is the fifth. And the first example in it occurs in a reference to the then (1858) Attorney-General (Bethell) lamenting his powerlessness for legal reform, as held in check by Lord Chancellor Campbell—'explains [like Mr Spenlow in *David Copperfield*] that he himself heartily assents [to legal reform], but that he is obliged to consult his senior partner on the woolsack, and that the dreadful Jorkins always says, No.' (*Saturday Review*, vol. v. p. 7.)

So again Commodore Paulding, of the United States Navy, is pitied for not suspecting that his instructions as to Filibustering 'were to be understood only in a Pickwickian sense.' (*Ib.*, p. 56.) Lord Palmerston's shifting policy and plans (1858) receive the comment that 'the political Mr Toots always accompanies even the offer of his heart and hand with the explanation that "it does not in the least signify." ' (*Ib.*, p. 105.) Then, too, Lord Palmerston's new Double Government of India, or rather its curiously constituted Council, was hailed as the New Circumlocution Office—the Councillors to sit round the President, and make remarks which nobody is bound to attend to. 'We are obliged to Mr Dickens for the right word descriptive of the proceeding. It is Circumlocution—Circumlocution exactly. We have always said that Mr Dickens's sketch of a Public Office was a caricature. It was reserved for Lord Palmerston to create a department deliberately modelled, not on the Office, but on the caricature.' (*Ib.*, p. 177.)

On the next page but one (p. 179) Louis Napoleon is called an Imperial Montague Tigg.

Farther on again he figures as an Imperial Pecksniff—reproaching England for her ingratitude. 'Mr. Pecksniff, too, felt that the great aggravation of the final catastrophe in which his head and dignity suffered so much, was that he had been very kind to the irascible old gentleman who caned him at last.' (*Ib.*, p. 260.)

The *Posthumous Papers of the Pickwick Club* are quoted at large in a subsequent article on Palmerston's apparent Ministry of Transition— (p. 305)—the episode of Mr Jingle (as Captain Fitz-Marshall) deluding the Nupkinses, being the theme in use. In a later article in the same number (p. 311) is quoted Mr Potts of the *Eatanswill Gazette*.

An article on the British Empire in India, in the *North American Review* (1858), is said to be about as accurate in its statements of fact as the conversation of the gentlemen with whose company Martin Chuzzlewit was favoured on his road to Eden. (*Sat. Rev.*, vol. vi. p. 99.)

Mr Bernal Osborne, in the character of a disgusted patriot, is likened to Charley Bates after the establishment of Mr Fagin was finally broken up. (*Ib.*, p. 151).

The style of Sir E. B. Lytton's introductory despatch, in sending Mr Gladstone to Corfu, is compared to Mr Swiveller idealising the dingy servant-of-all-work into a Marchioness.—On the same page, Mr Milner Gibson is defined 'the light literary gentleman of politics. Like Miss Mowcher, he seems always to be interspersing his remarks with the inquiry, "Oh, ain't I volatile?"' (*Ib.*, p. 579)

['Sir Nathaniel' continues in this vein for a further 1,500 words.]

110. [Walter Bagehot], from 'Charles Dickens', *National Review*

October 1858, vii, 458–86

Reprinted in Bagehot's *Literary Studies* (1879), ii, 184–220.

Bagehot (1826–77), economist, political thinker and journalist, was joint-editor of the *National Review* from 1855 and editor of the *Economist* from 1861. For these and other journals he wrote a number of literary essays. His essay on Dickens was a review of the Cheap Edition of the *Works* (1857–8).

... There is no contemporary English writer whose works are read so generally through the whole house, who can give pleasure to the servants as well as to the mistress, to the children as well as to the master. Mr Thackeray without doubt exercises a more potent and plastic fascination within his sphere, but that sphere is limited. It is restricted to that part of the middle class which gazes inquisitively at the *Vanity Fair* world. The delicate touches of our great satirist have, for such readers, not only the charm of wit, but likewise the interest of valuable information; he tells them of the topics which they want to know. But below this class there is another and far larger, which is incapable of comprehending the idling world or of appreciating the accuracy of delineations drawn from it, which would not know the difference between a picture of Grosvenor Square by Mr Thackeray and the picture of it in a Minerva-Press novel, which only cares for or knows of its own multifarious, industrial, fig-selling world,—and over these also Mr Dickens has power.

It cannot be amiss to take this opportunity of investigating, even slightly, the causes of so great a popularity. And if, in the course of our article, we may seem to be ready with over-refining criticism, or to be unduly captious with theoretical objection, we hope not to forget that so great and so diffused an influence is a *datum* for literary investigation,—that books which have been thus *tried* upon mankind and have thus succeeded, must be books of immense genius,—and that it is our duty as critics to explain, as far as we can, the nature and the limits of that genius, but never for one moment to deny or question its existence. . . . His genius is essentially irregular and unsymmetrical. Hardly any English writer perhaps is much more so. His style is an example of it. It is descriptive, racy, and flowing; it is instinct with new imagery and singular illustration; but it does not indicate that due proportion of the faculties to one another which is a beauty in itself, and which cannot help diffusing beauty over every happy word and moulded clause. We may choose an illustration at random. The following graphic description will do:

[Quotes from *Barnaby Rudge*, ch. xxxvii, 'If Lord George Gordon had appeared in the eyes of Mr Willet, overnight, a nobleman of somewhat quaint and odd exterior,' and the next three paragraphs.]

No one would think of citing such a passage as this, as exemplifying the proportioned beauty of finished writing; it is not the writing of an evenly developed or of a highly cultured mind; it abounds in jolts and odd turns; it is full of singular twists and needless complexities: but, on the other hand, no one can deny its great and peculiar merit. It is an odd style, and it is very odd how much you read it. It is the overflow of a copious mind, though not the chastened expression of an harmonious one.

The same quality characterises the matter of his works. His range is very varied. He has attempted to describe every kind of scene in English life, from quite the lowest to almost the highest. He has not endeavoured to secure success by confining himself to a single path nor wearied the public with repetitions of the subjects by the delineation of which he originally obtained fame. In his earlier works he never writes long without saying something well, something which no other man would have said; but even in them it is the characteristic of his power that it is apt to fail him at once; from masterly strength we pass without interval to almost infantine weakness,—something like disgust succeeds in a moment to an extreme admiration. Such is the natural fate of an unequal mind employing itself on a vast and various subject. . . . Mr Dickens's novels . . . aim to delineate nearly all that part of our national life which can be delineated,—at least, within the limits which social morality prescribes to social art; but you cannot read his delineation of any part without being struck with its singular incompleteness. An artist once said of the best work of another artist, 'Yes, it is a pretty patch.' If we might venture on the phrase, we should say that Mr Dickens's pictures were graphic scraps; his best books are compilations of them.

The truth is that Mr Dickens wholly wants the two elements which we have spoken of as one or other requisite for a symmetrical genius. He is utterly deficient in the faculty of reasoning. . . . He is often troubled with the idea that he must reflect, and his reflections are perhaps the worst reading in the world. There is a sentimental confusion about them; we never find the consecutive precision of mature theory, or the cold distinctness of clear thought. Vivid facts stand out in his imagination, and a fresh illustrative style brings them home to the imagination of his readers; but his continuous philosophy utterly fails in the attempt to harmonize them,—to educe a theory or elaborate a precept from them. Of his social thinking we shall have a few words to say in detail; his didactic humour is very unfortunate: no writer is less fitted for an excursion to the imperative mood. At present we only say what is so obvious as scarcely to need saying, that his abstract understanding is so far inferior to his picturesque imagination as to give even to his best works the sense of jar and incompleteness, and to deprive them altogether of the crystalline finish which is characteristic of the clear and cultured understanding.

Nor has Mr Dickens the easy and various sagacity which, as has been said, gives a unity to all which it touches. He has, indeed, a quality which is near allied to it in appearance. His shrewdness in some things, especially in traits and small things, is wonderful. His works are full of acute remarks on petty doings, and well exemplify the telling power of minute circumstantiality. But the minor species of perceptive sharpness is so different from diffused sagacity, that the two scarcely ever are to be found in the same mind. . . . [The more sagacious thinkers] show by their treatment of each case that they understand the whole of life; the special delineator of fragments and points shows that he understands them only. In one respect the defect is more striking in Mr Dickens than in any other novelist of the present day. The most remarkable deficiency in modern fiction is its omission of the business of life, of all those countless occupations, pursuits, and callings in which most men live and move, and by which they have their being. In most novels money *grows*. You have no idea of the toil, the patience, and the wearing anxiety by which men of action provide for the day, and lay up for the future, and support those that are given into their care. Mr Dickens is not chargeable with this omission. He perpetually deals with the pecuniary part of life. Almost all his characters have determined occupations, of which he is apt to talk even at too much length. When he rises from the toiling to the luxurious classes, his genius in most cases deserts him. The delicate refinement and discriminating taste of the idling orders are not in his way; he knows the dry arches of London Bridge better than Belgravia. He excels in inventories of poor furniture, and is learned in pawnbrokers' tickets. But, although his creative power lives and works among the middle class and industrial section of English society, he has never painted the highest part of their daily intellectual life. He made, indeed, an attempt to paint specimens of the apt and able man of business in *Nicholas Nickleby*; but the Messrs Cheeryble are among the stupidest of his characters. He forgot that breadth of platitude is rather different from breadth of sagacity. His delineations of middle-class life have in consequence a harshness and meanness which do not belong to that life in reality. He omits the relieving element. He describes the figs which are sold, but not the talent which sells figs well. And it is the same want of the diffused sagacity in his own nature which has made his pictures of life so odd and disjointed, and which has deprived them of symmetry and unity.

The *bizarrerie* of Mr Dickens's genius is rendered more remarkable by the inordinate measure of his special excellences. The first of these is his power of observation in detail. We have heard,—we do not know whether correctly or incorrectly,—that he can go down a crowded street and tell you all that is in it, what each shop was, what the grocer's name was, how many scraps of orange-peel there were on the pavement. His works give you exactly the same idea. The amount of detail which there is in them is something amazing,—to an ordinary writer something incredible. There are pages containing telling *minutiæ* which other people would have thought enough for a volume. Nor is his sensibility to external objects, though omnivorous, insensible to the artistic effect of each. There are scarcely anywhere such pictures of London as he draws. No writer has equally comprehended the artistic material which is given by its extent, its congregation of different elements, its mouldiness, its brilliancy.

Nor does his genius—though from some idiosyncrasy of mind or accident of external situation, it is more especially directed to city life— at all stop at the city-wall. He is especially at home in the picturesque and obvious parts of country life, particularly in the comfortable and (so to say) mouldering portion of it. . . .

Nevertheless, it may be said that Mr Dickens's genius is especially suited to the delineation of city life. London is like a newspaper. Everything is there, and everything is disconnected. There is every kind of person in some houses; but there is no more connection between the houses than between the neighbours in the lists of 'births, marriages, and deaths.' As we change from the broad leader to the squalid police-report, we pass a corner and we are in a changed world. This is advantageous to Mr Dickens's genius. His memory is full of instances of old buildings and curious people, and he does not care to piece them together. On the contrary, each scene, to his mind, is a separate scene,—each street a separate street. He has, too, the peculiar alertness of observation that is observable in those who live by it. He describes London like a special correspondent for posterity.

A second most wonderful special faculty which Mr Dickens possesses is what we may call his *vivification* of character, or rather of characteristics. His marvellous power of observation has been exercised upon men and women even more than upon town or country; and the store of human detail, so to speak, in his books is endless and enormous. The boots at the inn, the pickpockets in the street, the undertaker, the Mrs Gamp, are all of them at his disposal; he knows each trait and incident, and he invests them with a kind of perfection in detail which in reality they do not possess. He has a very peculiar power of taking hold of some particular traits, and making a character out of them. He is especially apt to incarnate particular professions in this way. Many of his people never speak without some allusion to their occupation. You cannot separate them from it. Nor does the writer ever separate them. What would Mr Mould be if not an undertaker? or Mrs Gamp if not a nurse? or Charley Bates if not a pick-pocket? Not only is human nature in them subdued to what it works in, but there seems to be no nature to subdue; the whole character is the idealisation of a trade, and is not in fancy or thought distinguishable from it. Accordingly, of necessity, such delineations become caricatures. We do not in general contrast them with reality; but as soon as we do, are struck with the monstrous exaggerations which they present. You could no more fancy Sam Weller, or Mark Tapley, or the Artful Dodger really existing, walking about among common ordinary men and women, than you can fancy a talking duck or a writing bear. They are utterly beyond the pale of ordinary social intercourse. We suspect, indeed, that Mr Dickens does not conceive his characters to himself as mixing in the society he mixes in. He sees people in the street, doing certain things, talking in a certain way, and his fancy petrifies them in the act. He goes on fancying hundreds of reduplications of that act and that speech; he frames an existence in which there is nothing else but that aspect which attracted his attention. Sam Weller is an example. He is a man-servant who makes a peculiar kind of jokes, and is wonderfully felicitous in certain similes. You see him at his first introduction:

[Quotes from *Pickwick*, ch. x.]

One can fancy Mr Dickens hearing a dialogue of this sort,—not nearly so good, but something like it,—and immediately setting to work to make it better and put it in a book; then changing a little the situation, putting the boots one step up in the scale of service, engaging him as footman to a stout gentleman (but without for a moment losing sight of the peculiar kind of professional conversation and humour which his first dialogue presents), and astonishing all his readers by the marvellous fertility and magical humour with which he maintains that style. Sam Weller's father is even a stronger and simpler instance. He is simply nothing but an old coachman of the stout and extinct sort: you cannot separate him from the idea of that occupation. But how amusing he is! We dare not quote a single word of his talk; because we should go on quoting so long, and everyone knows it so well. Some persons may think that this is not a very high species of delineative art. The idea of personifying traits and trades may seem to them poor and meagre. Anybody, they may fancy, can do that. But how would they do it? Whose fancy would not break down in a page,—in five lines? Who could carry on the vivification with zest and energy and humour for volume after volume? Endless fertility in laughter-causing detail is Mr Dickens's most astonishing peculiarity. It requires a continuous and careful reading of his works to be aware of his enormous wealth. Writers have attained the greatest reputation for wit and humour, whose whole works do not contain so much of either as are to be found in a very few pages of his. . . .

[A survey of *Pickwick* leads to the analysis—]

The humour essentially consists in treating as a moral agent a being who really is not a moral agent. We treat a vivified accident as a man, and we are surprised at the absurd results. We are reading about an acting thing, and we wonder at its scrapes, and laugh at them as if they were those of the man. There is something of this humour in every sort of farce. Everybody knows these are not real beings acting in real life, though they talk as if they were, and want us to believe that they are. Here, as in Mr Dickens's books, we have exaggerations pretending to comport themselves as ordinary beings, caricatures acting as if they were characters. . . .

It perhaps follows from what has been said of the characteristics of Mr Dickens's genius, that he would be little skilled in planning plots for his novels. He certainly is not so skilled. He says in his preface to the *Pickwick Papers*, 'that they were designed for the introduction of diverting characters and incidents; that no ingenuity of plot was attempted, or even at that time considered very feasible by the author in connection with the desultory plan of publication adopted;' and he adds an expression of regret that 'these chapters had not been strung together on a stronger thread of more general interest.' It is extremely fortunate that no such attempt was made. In the cases in which Mr Dickens has attempted to make a long connected story, or to develop into scenes or incidents a plan in any degree elaborate, the result has been a complete failure. A certain consistency of genius seems necessary for the construction of a consecutive plot. An irregular mind naturally shows itself in incoherency of incident and aberration of character. . . .

The defect of plot is heightened by Mr Dickens's great, we might say complete, inability to make a love-story. A pair of lovers is by custom a necessity of narrative fiction, and writers who possess a great general range of mundane knowledge, and but little knowledge of the special sentimental subject, are often in amusing difficulties. The watchful reader observes the transition from the hearty description of well-known scenes, of prosaic streets, or journeys by wood and river, to the pale colours of ill-attempted poetry, to such sights as the novelist wishes he need not try to see. But few writers exhibit the difficulty in so aggravated a form as Mr Dickens. Most men by taking thought can make a lay figure to look not so very unlike a young gentleman, and can compose a telling schedule of ladylike charms. Mr Dickens . . . pours out painful sentiments as if he wished the abundance should make up for the inferior quality. The excruciating writing which is expended on Miss Ruth Pinch passes belief. Mr Dickens is not only unable to make lovers talk, but to describe heroines in mere narrative. As has been said, most men can make a jumble of blue eyes and fair hair and pearly teeth, that does very well for a young lady, at least for a good while; but Mr Dickens will not, probably cannot, attain even to this humble measure of descriptive art. He vitiates the repose by broad humour, or disenchants the delicacy by an unctuous admiration. . . .

Mr Dickens's indisposition to 'make capital' out of the most commonly tempting part of human sentiment is the more remarkable
because he certainly does not show the same indisposition in other
cases. He has naturally great powers of pathos; his imagination is
familiar with the common sorts of human suffering; and his marvellous
conversancy with the detail of existence enables him to describe sick-
beds and death-beds with an excellence very rarely seen in literature. A
nature far more sympathetic than that of most authors has familiarised
him with such subjects. In general, a certain apathy is characteristic of
book-writers, and dulls the efficacy of their pathos. Mr Dickens is
quite exempt from this defect; but, on the other hand, is exceedingly
prone to a very ostentatious exhibition of the opposite excellence. He
dwells on dismal scenes with a kind of fawning fondness; and he seems
unwilling to leave them, long after his readers have had more than
enough of them. He describes Mr Dennis the hangman as having a
professional fondness for his occupation: he has the same sort of fondness apparently for the profession of death-painter. The painful details
he accumulates are a very serious drawback from the agreeableness of
his writings. Dismal 'light literature' is the dismallest of reading. The
reality of the police-reports is sufficiently bad, but a fictitious police-
report would be the most disagreeable of conceivable compositions.
Some portions of Mr Dickens's books are liable to a good many of
the same objections. They are squalid from noisome trivialities, and
horrid with terrifying crime. In his earlier books this is commonly
relieved at frequent intervals by a graphic and original mirth. As—we
will not say age, but maturity, has passed over his powers, this counter-
active element has been lessened; the humour is not so happy as it was,
but the wonderful fertility in painful *minutiæ* still remains.

Mr Dickens's political opinions have subjected him to a good deal
of criticism, and to some ridicule. He has shown, on many occasions,
the desire,—which we see so frequent among able and influential men,
—to start as a political reformer. ... The most instructive political
characteristic of the years from 1825 to 1845 is the growth and influence
of the scheme of opinion which we call radicalism. There are several
species of creeds which are comprehended under this generic name,
but they all evince a marked reaction against the worship of the English
constitution and the affection for the English *status quo*, which were
then the established creed and sentiment. All radicals are anti-Eldonites.
This is equally true of the Benthamite or philosophical radicalism of the
early period, and the Manchester or 'definite-grievance' radicalism,

among the last vestiges of which we are now living. Mr Dickens represents a species different from either. His is what we may call the 'sentimental radicalism;' and if we recur to the history of the time, we shall find that there would not originally have been any opprobrium attaching to such a name. The whole course of the legislation, and still more of the administration, of the first twenty years of the nineteenth century were marked by a harsh unfeelingness which is of all faults the most contrary to any with which we are chargeable now. The world of the 'Six Acts,' of the frequent executions, of the Draconic criminal law, is so far removed from us that we cannot comprehend its having ever existed. It is more easy to understand the recoil which has followed. All the social speculation, and much of the social action of the few years succeeding the Reform Bill bear the most marked traces of the reaction. The spirit which animates Mr Dickens's political reasonings and observations expresses it exactly. The vice of the then existing social authorities and of the then existing public had been the forgetfulness of the pain which their own acts evidently produced,—an unrealising habit which adhered to official rules and established maxims, and which would not be shocked by the evident consequences, by proximate human suffering. The sure result of this habit was the excitement of the habit precisely opposed to it. Mr Carlyle, in his *Chartism*, we think, observes of the poor-law reform: 'It was then, above all things, necessary that outdoor relief should cease. But how? What means did great Nature take for accomplishing that most desirable end? She created a race of men who believed the cessation of outdoor relief to be the one thing needful.' In the same way, and by the same propensity to exaggerated opposition which is inherent in human nature, the unfeeling obtuseness of the early part of this century was to be corrected by an extreme, perhaps an excessive, sensibility to human suffering in the years which have followed. There was most adequate reason for the sentiment in its origin, and it had a great task to perform in ameliorating harsh customs and repealing dreadful penalties; but it has continued to repine at such evils long after they ceased to exist, and when the only facts that at all resemble them are the necessary painfulness of due punishment and the necessary rigidity of established law.

Mr Dickens is an example both of the proper use and of the abuse of the sentiment. His earlier works have many excellent descriptions of the abuses which had descended to the present generation from others whose sympathy with pain was less tender. Nothing can be better

than the description of the poor debtors' gaol in *Pickwick*, or of the
old parochial authorities in *Oliver Twist*. No doubt these descriptions
are caricatures, all his delineations are so. . . . But a beadle is made for
caricature. The slight measure of pomposity that humanises his unfeelingness introduces the requisite comic element; even the turnkeys
of a debtors' prison may by skilful hands be similarly used. The
contrast between the destitute condition of Job Trotter and Mr Jingle
and their former swindling triumph, is made comic by a rarer touch of
unconscious art. Mr Pickwick's warm heart takes so eager an interest
in the misery of his old enemies, that our colder nature is tempted to
smile. We endure the over-intensity, at any rate the unnecessary
aggravation, of the surrounding misery; and we endure it willingly,
because it brings out better than anything else could have done the
half-comic intensity of a sympathetic nature.

It is painful to pass from these happy instances of well-used power
to the glaring abuses of the same faculty in Mr Dickens's later books.
He began by describing really removable evils in a style which would
induce all persons, however insensible, to remove them if they could;
he has ended by describing the natural evils and inevitable pains of the
present state of being in such a manner as must tend to excite discontent
and repining. The result is aggravated, because Mr Dickens never
ceases to hint that these evils are removable, though he does not say
by what means. Nothing is easier than to show the evils of anything.
Mr Dickens has not unfrequently spoken, and what is worse, he has
taught a great number of parrot-like imitators to speak, in what really
is, if they knew it, a tone of objection to the necessary constitution of
human society. . . .

There has been much controversy about Mr Dickens's taste. A
great many cultivated people will scarcely concede that he has any
taste at all; a still larger number of fervent admirers point, on the other
hand, to a hundred felicitous descriptions and delineations which
abound in apt expressions and skilful turns and happy images,—in
which it would be impossible to alter a single word without altering
for the worse; and naturally inquire whether such excellences in what
is written do not indicate good taste in the writer. The truth is that
Mr Dickens has what we may call creative taste; that is to say, the
habit or faculty, whichever we may choose to call it, which at the
critical instance of artistic production offers to the mind the right word,
and the right word only. If he is engaged on a good subject for caricature, there will be no defect of taste to preclude the caricature from

being excellent. But it is only in moments of imaginative production that he has any taste at all. His works nowhere indicate that he possesses in any degree the passive taste which decides what is good in the writings of other people and what is not, and which performs the same critical duty upon a writer's own efforts when the confusing mists of productive imagination have passed away. Nor has Mr Dickens the gentlemanly instinct which in many minds supplies the place of purely critical discernment, and which, by constant association with those who know what is best, acquires a second-hand perception of that which is best. He has no tendency to conventionalism for good or for evil; his merits are far removed from the ordinary path of writers, and it was not probably so much effort to him as to other men to step so far out of that path: he scarcely knew how far it was. For the same reason he cannot tell how faulty his writing will often be thought, for he cannot tell what people will think.

A few pedantic critics have regretted that Mr Dickens had not received what they call a regular education. . . . To men of regular and symmetrical genius . . . such a training will often be beneficial. . . . But the case is very different with men of irregular and anomalous genius, whose excellences consist in the *aggravation* of some special faculty, or at the most of one or two. . . . In the case of Mr Dickens, it would have been absurd to have shut up his observant youth within the wall of a college. They would have taught him nothing about Mrs Gamp there; Sam Weller took no degree. The kind of early life fitted to develop the power of apprehensive observation is a brooding life in stirring scenes. . . .

Perhaps, too, a regular instruction and daily experience of the searching ridicule of critical associates would have detracted from the *pluck* which Mr Dickens shows in all his writings. It requires a great deal of courage to be a humorous writer; you are always afraid that people will laugh at you instead of with you: undoubtedly there is a certain eccentricity about it. You take up the esteemed writers, Thucydides and the *Saturday Review*; after all, they do not make you laugh. It is not the function of really artistic productions to contribute to the mirth of human beings. All sensible men are afraid of it, and it is only with an extreme effort that a printed joke attains to the perusal of the public: the chances are many to one that the anxious producer loses heart in the correction of the press, and that the world never laughs at all. Mr Dickens is quite exempt from this weakness. He has what a Frenchman might call the courage of his faculty. The real daring which is shown in the *Pickwick Papers*, in the whole character of Mr Weller senior, as well as in that of his son, is immense, far surpassing any which has been shown by any other contemporary writer. . . .

We have throughout spoken of Mr Dickens as he was, rather than as he is; or, to use a less discourteous phrase, and we hope a truer, of his early works rather than of those which are more recent. We could not do otherwise consistently with the true code of criticism. A man of great genius, who has written great and enduring works, must be judged mainly by them; and not by the inferior productions which, from the necessities of personal position, a fatal facility of composition, or other cause, he may pour forth at moments less favourable to his powers. Those who are called on to review these inferior productions themselves, must speak of them in the terms they may deserve; but those who have the more pleasant task of estimating as a whole the genius of the writer, may confine their attention almost wholly to those happier efforts which illustrate that genius. We should not like to have to speak in detail of Mr Dickens's later works, and we have not done so. There are, indeed, peculiar reasons why a genius constituted as his is (at least if we are correct in the view which we have taken of it) would not endure without injury during a long life the applause of the many, the temptations of composition, and the general excitement of existence. Even in his earlier works it was impossible not to fancy that there was a weakness of fibre unfavourable to the longevity of excellence. This was the effect of his deficiency in those masculine faculties of which we have said so much,—the reasoning understanding and firm far-seeing sagacity. It is these two component elements which stiffen the mind, and give a consistency to the creed and a coherence to its effects,—which enable it to protect itself from the rush of circumstances. If to a deficiency in these we add an extreme sensibility to circumstances,—a mobility, as Lord Byron used to call it, of emotion, which is easily impressed, and still more easily carried away by impression,—we have the idea of a character peculiarly unfitted to bear the flux of time and chance. A man of very great determination could hardly bear up against them with such slight aids from within and with such peculiar sensibility to temptation. A man of merely ordinary determination would succumb to it; and Mr Dickens has succumbed. . . .

THE WEEKLY PERIODICALS

Household Words

30 March 1850 – 28 May 1859

All the Year Round

30 April 1859 until (and beyond) Dickens's death.

Dickens's periodicals were very popular, with a steady circulation of around 50000 in the 1850s, and of well over 100000 in the 1860s, and their articles on public affairs (especially in earlier years) commanded a good deal of attention. Many outstanding novels were serialized in them: Mrs Gaskell's *Cranford, North and South*, and others, Collins's *Woman in White, No Name*, and *The Moonstone*, novels by Lytton, Charles Reade, and Charles Lever, and of course Dickens's own *Hard Times* (1854), *A Tale of Two Cities* (1859), and *Great Expectations* (1860–1). His other contributions to these periodicals included *A Child's History of England* (1851–3), *The Uncommercial Traveller* (1860, 1863, 1868), and many essays and articles, some of which he collected in *Reprinted Pieces* (1858).

The Christmas Numbers were particularly popular, reaching sales of over 250000. Dickens had discontinued his Christmas Books after 1848; these shorter Christmas Numbers, in which he had help from collaborators, proved easier to produce annually, and his decision to end the series in 1867 was widely lamented. Not much read now, his contributions to these Numbers are very uneven, much the best being the *Mrs. Lirriper* and *Doctor Marigold* stories, 1863–5. Many of his Christmas items were written with a view to their being adapted into public readings: of these, *Doctor Marigold* was the most successful.

On Dickens's involvement as 'Conductor' of his journals, see Harry Stone's long Introduction to his edition, *Charles Dickens' Uncollected Writings from Household Words 1850–1859* (2 vols, Indiana University Press, 1968; London, John Lane, 1969).

111. [Samuel Lucas], from a review of *The Perils of Certain English Prisoners, The Times*

24 December 1857, 4

Lucas (1818–68), an Oxford man and a barrister, was a frequent contributor to *The Times*. He correctly interpreted Dickens's intentions: the emotions aroused by the Indian Mutiny (in which one of his own sons was at risk) provoked him to one of his few fictional expressions of simple patriotic sentiment. See *To Miss Coutts*, 4 October and 25 November 1857, and *To Henry Morley*, 18 October 1857. *The History of 'The Times'* misleadingly summarizes this review as rebuking Dickens for being sentimental (ii, 487). Lucas in fact applauds Dickens's venture into the heroic, though realising that he will probably be faulted in 'the prevalent spirit on criticism' (i.e., the attacks on Dickens in the *Saturday Review* and elsewhere in 1857): but even the *Saturday Review* called a truce in its vendetta with Dickens, to accord to *The Perils* a 'cordial commendation on very high grounds', gladly 'embracing the opportunity' to demonstrate that it could praise Dickens for work such as this (26 December 1857, 579).

As usual at Christmas the extra number of *Household Words* contains a story, the greater part of which is written by Charles Dickens, but which on this occasion is less a festive tribute to the season than a celebration of the great qualities displayed by our race in recent emergencies, Crimean and Indian. The reader may, indeed, object to this description that there is no mention of India or the Crimea in its pages, that its scenery belongs to fable land, and that its characters and incidents are purely imaginary. But the moral elements are the same in either case, in the historical events and the ideal narrative, and there is so far an identity in both series of transactions that the novelist may be charged with a public function and convicted of a patriotic interest in political crises. In the prevalent spirit of criticism we have little doubt

*   403

that Mr Dickens will be put on his trial for this great irregularity. It may be argued that *'the perils of certain English prisoners and their treasure in women, children, silver, and jewels'* are a sort of professional or pre-occupied ground, and that the novelist has no title to seek in public transactions which are passing under his eyes materials for his idealization, or to furnish romantic types of the actual achievements which history will ascribe to the heroism of his countrymen and contemporaries. His readers, on the other hand, may reply to this objection that it is clearly symptomatic of a growing tendency to extend patent rights over the residue of creation, and so may evince their sympathy with the trespasser. At all events, his offence has its phase of utility, and is not insignificant as a part of the dispensation by which national virtues are kept alight, and their splendour lives in familiar observation. From the *Iliad* downwards men of imagination have been foremost to display the qualities of their respective races when roused to heroic heights of emotion and action; they have laboured to bring these into high relief and to range them monumentally for recognition and honour; and in gathering fame themselves out of such endeavours they have rendered no petty service to their compatriots. In these days, when the men of imagination for the most part write novels, or, in other words, when the novelists for the most part do the work of men of imagination, there is no reason that we know of why they should neglect this portion of it. Originally the chief ministrants in this behalf were poets, but the poets of this day have hung their harps upon the willows and taken to celebrate their 'souls' agonies' and personal inconveniences. The writer who would touch a national theme at all must at least have some claim to be considered national himself— national in his fame or national in his sympathies; and we question if any one of his harshest critics will deny that this qualification is possessed by Charles Dickens. . . .

Short and slight as this story is, it enables Mr Dickens to bring out the salient traits so recently displayed by his countrymen and countrywomen amid hardships and dangers which have never been exceeded. Their intrepidity and self-confidence, their habit of grumbling at each other without occasion and of helping each other ungrudgingly when occasion arises, the promptitude with which they accommodate themselves to any emergency and the practical ability with which they surmount every embarrassment, the latent sympathy between gentle and simple, the rude and refined which common hazards stimulate and common sufferings sanctify; in short, the spirit of mutual reliance, of reciprocal service and sacrifice, which they have exhibited in fact Mr Dickens has striven to reproduce in fiction. It was impossible that he should touch this or any theme whatever without infusing into it some of his humour or of the force of his genius. But he has evidently to contend with the very fullness of his subject, which leaves little margin for imaginative decoration. The awful horrors of which we know the literal particulars have been mingled with such spectacles of moral grandeur and heroism that invention can hardly elevate or ingenuity enhance them. . . . Where the reported reality is so astounding it is only the talent of Mr Dickens, employed for a legitimate purpose, which could induce us for a moment to listen to the echo.

112. From an unsigned review of *A House to Let*, *Saturday Review*

25 December 1858, vi, 644

A House to Let was the *Household Words* Extra Christmas Number, 1858. Dickens wrote the second story ('Going into Society', about a dwarf) and collaborated with Wilkie Collins on a brief final episode ('Let at Last') not mentioned by the reviewer. Collins wrote the introductory section (this includes the Dickensian passage about Mr Jarber, quoted by the reviewer, and the character named Trottle), and another story; Mrs Gaskell and Anne Adelaide Procter wrote the rest. As usual, all items were anonymous, and the reviewer may be forgiven for not distinguishing between Mr Dickens and 'his imitators'; few reviewers did, or could. On Dickens's contributions to this Christmas Number, see his *Uncollected Writings from Household Words*, ed. Stone, ii, 595–617, cited on p. 402. This review is probably by James Fitzjames Stephen.

The minor works of Mr Dickens have, in a literary point of view, something of the same sort of interest that the specimens of raw material in museums and exhibitions may claim from a trader or manufacturer. This is the ore by which all the iron-works of Stafford-shire and Warwickshire are kept in work. This is the clay from which we get our finest pottery. This is the cotton upon the plenty of which depends all the prosperity of Manchester and Liverpool. There is something interesting in examining these various products—in weigh-ing the ironstone, handling the clay, testing the fibre of the cotton, and thinking of all the uses to which they are put. Our modern literary arrangements are frequently so contrived that a precisely analogous operation can be performed on the works of a great author. A man writes on and on till he acquires a power of production which to some appears disastrous, and to others miraculous. After fascinating or astonishing a large circle of readers by his earlier performances, he at last reaches a kind of established level, on which he proceeds with hardly any variation. You always know what you are to have for your money. You can estimate with strange precision the kind and degree of satisfaction which you will derive from what is written. . . .

Mr Dickens has long since reached this [exhausted] stage in his career. Most of the gunpowder in the catherine-wheel has exploded, but now that the sparks have gone out, and the cartridge-paper revolves in a somewhat more leisurely manner, we are able to observe more accurately than before the principles on which the firework was con-structed, and the manner in which its startling effects were produced. Mr Dickens's present Christmas story appears to us to illustrate with singular completeness all the peculiarities of his style, whilst it has few of those merits which in his earlier works made it a difficult matter to criticize what he wrote with entire impartiality. His influence over some departments of literature has been so marked, and his imitators are so numerous, that we may be excused for devoting to what is meant to be a very trifling, and is intrinsically a very insignificant performance, what might otherwise be a disproportionate amount of attention. The four stories contained in the *House to Let* are interesting only from the fact that they are samples of an important article of literary commerce.

[The reviewer summarizes them.]

Each of these stories is in itself too trifling to tell. They are mere specimens of a style, the great element of which is simple grotesqueness —the habit of describing the most ordinary and commonplace things in an unexpected manner. For example, the old lady who is to tell the story comes up from Tunbridge Wells to London, and this is made into a point. Her manservant is called Trottle; her superannuated admirer is Mr Jabez Jarber. Mr Jarber wears a cloak which clasps round his neck with a couple of fierce little brass lions, and he is elaborately painted in such words as these:—'He was always a little squeezed man, was Jarber, in little sprigged waistcoats, and he had always little legs, and a little smile, and little roundabout ways.'

This artifice is worth some attention, for it is intimately connected with Mr Dickens's success, and is most characteristic of all the efforts of his imitators. Its commonness is a great misfortune in a literary point of view, for it supplies an easy mode of being amusing and impressive upon almost any and every subject in the world. It is like a highly-flavoured sauce, which will disguise any kind of meat, and it is almost a mechanical trick which any one might be taught to perform who has the most elementary knowledge of composition. The whole art consists in giving an undue prominence to the small grotesque features which exist in every department of life. Most of us probably would notice a sort of odd congruity between the name of Trottle and an old-fashioned self-important manservant accustomed to take liberties with his master, just as we have all known men who from their boy-hood upwards have been called Peter or Charley, although their sponsors never gave them any legal right to those names. To take a mere grotesque fancy of this kind as the germ of a character, and to model the whole man upon it—making him on every occasion act and talk and think as a man with an out-of-the-way name might be expected to act or talk—is a trick of style which might be caught, and with a little practice repeated to any extent, just like Swift's well-known trick of making a monstrously absurd assumption and reasoning upon it with the gravest, most exact, and most symmetrical logic. It was once observed of a certain family, that all its members were distinguished by having straight hair and curly teeth. If this remarkable phrase had occurred to Mr Dickens, he would have deduced the whole character and conduct of the owners of such peculiarities from these two circumstances. There is a whimsicality about the combination which might, and no doubt would, have been worked backwards and forwards in a thousand ways. There are almost an infinite number of situations in which the fact that a man had lank hair would heighten the habitual expression of his face, and there is no limit to the use which might be made of curly teeth at the crisis of a story. In *Dombey and Son*, Mr Carker's teeth are made to shine and glare, and act as eyes which could see in the dark, and go through every sort of wonderful performance. If the infirmity to which we have referred were attributed to the hero of a novel, his teeth would wriggle like a nest of vipers, or sprawl like toads, or curl in contempt over his lips, as if they were making confidential remarks to the straight hair, and would determine the whole course of the story, character, and conduct of their fortunate possessor from one end of the book to the other.

It may seem a fanciful, but we believe it is a perfectly true observation, that there is the closest possible connexion between this habit of making grotesque trifles into the test and the germ of character and the more serious peculiarities of Mr Dickens's modes of thought. By dwelling upon this side of life the mind is carried into a region of which it is not exactly fair to say that it is entirely furnished with trifles, but in which trifles are regarded as the best evidence upon matters of importance.

113. [James Fitzjames Stephen?], from an unsigned review of *The Uncommercial Traveller*, *Saturday Review*

23 February 1861, xi, 194-6

Probably by Fitzjames Stephen, who had a special fondness for *The Uncommercial Traveller* (Leslie Stephen, *Life*, 156) and for the *Pickwick Papers*, the Illustrated Library Edition of which was also under review here. Other passages in the review, omitted in this selection, repeat points Stephen had made elsewhere. If indeed Stephen is the author, it is pleasant to see how warm and intelligent was his regard for some aspects of Dickens. The *Uncommercial Traveller* essays began appearing in *All the Year Round* during 1860; a collection was published in 1861.

Mr Dickens has had so many imitators that we are almost tempted to forget, until we recur to *Pickwick*, how original a writer he is. In the best of his books there are many faults, and *Pickwick* is crude, sketchy, and affected, as compared with the best of his tales; but the life, the variety, and above all the freshness of the book, seem as wonderful on the twentieth as on the first perusal. The *Uncommercial Traveller* is much quieter, for men cannot preserve high spirits during a quarter of a century; but it is in Mr Dickens's good manner. It is pleasant, witty, shrewd, and unhackneyed. It treats of things that we like to read about, and in a manner that is peculiar to the writer, but is not a mere copy of his own former drolleries. It is also interesting as showing how Mr Dickens has come to write the stories that have made him famous, and as illustrating the mode in which his observations are recorded and his style worked out. It gives a key to many well-known passages and well-known characters. We receive with the greatest pleasure a book that does Mr Dickens justice, and in which he is once more entertaining, spirited, and himself. No one can be always awake, and a man whose business it is to write serials year after year must naturally have his periods of feebleness. There is no possibility of pretending that *Bleak House, Little Dorrit,* and *The Two Cities* were not surprisingly bad— melodramatic, pretentious, and, above all, deadly dull. It seemed scarcely conceivable that a writer who had drawn Sam Weller and Mrs Nickleby should really compose the dreary narrative of *Little Dorrit* and her wooden lover. We are delighted to say that the *Little Dorrit* days seem over. It is impossible to praise Mr Dickens's books when they are bad; but a good book from Mr Dickens is far too great a gain not to be gladly acknowledged.

The *Uncommercial Traveller* and *Pickwick* show the limits of thought within which Mr Dickens writes, and observance of which has largely contributed to his popularity. He occupies himself with things that interest a great variety of persons, and has the gift of being able to think about ordinary, commonplace, familiar matters. Few persons are aware how special a gift this is, or, if the power is acquired by practice, how much labour must precede the acquisition. If we go into a railway refreshment room, or call for a casual lunch at an hotel, we most of us notice that we are very uncomfortable and very badly served, and then we dismiss the subject from our thoughts. A person who has the gift of observing and reflecting on daily life finds a thousand points to notice in these wretched entertainments. He examines the things served up and the faces of those who serve them. He scans the accessories of the repast, the fittings of the room, the decorations of the table, the cruets, the salt-cellars, the knives and forks. His fancy keeps working

all the time, if he has any fancy, and he throws his observations together into a picture which is exaggerated perhaps, but which, if a little
highly coloured, strikes us as substantially the very thing with which
we are familiar. The most entertaining chapter in the *Uncommercial
Traveller* describes English places of refreshment with the greatest
accuracy and point. Who, for example, does not recognise the truth
of the following description of a cutlet at a Railway Hotel? 'A sort of
fur has been produced upon its surface by the cook's art, and in a sham
silver vessel staggering on two feet instead of three, is a cutaneous kind
of sauce of brown pimples and pickled cucumbers.' The familiar cutlet
is in a moment before us. We recognise the fur on its outside; we
remember the brown pimples of the sauce. A thing of common life
has been presented to us in a light at once true and new, and we are
pleased. In the same way Mr Dickens sees what is characteristic in
common-place people, and allows his fancy to dwell on it. But good
manners and refined habits prevent any characteristics being presented
which can be easily seized on and reproduced in a popular shape under
the influence of fancy. It is only that portion of society which does
things in a free and uncontrolled manner, or which has the mere
rigidity of conventionalism, that admits of being represented in a funny
way, or of being easily associated with funny characters. Mr Dickens
is successful in proportion as he adheres to this principle . . . he has
never descended to the depths of his imitators. There is an abyss of
comicality into which he has never fallen. And whenever he is at his
best, he always keeps his fun within the bounds which the proper subordination of fun to all that is elevated in life would dictate. *Pickwick*
is a caricature of life, but it is only a caricature of a life that does not
even aspire to be great.

A world where the genteel people live at Pentonville and the un-
genteel people frequent the bars of inns, old chambers, wharfsides,
small shops, and minor theatres, is the true world for Mr Dickens. This
world can be reproduced by sketches which are constructed on the
plan of minutely observing details, letting the fancy run on about them,
and never going beyond the popular and accepted views of things. It is
one great feature of Mr Dickens's writings that they contain no
philosophy. There is no view of life in them peculiar to the author.
There is a vast amount of shrewd remark, there are many expressions
of feeling, there are even free expositions of principle; but all are of the
exact kind at which clever men arrive without thought. So far as the
popular views of men with sound sensible minds who do not reflect

deeply are right, Mr Dickens is right. It is curious to observe how exactly this holds of the *Uncommercial Traveller*, where the topics are drawn from actual circumstances, just as it used to hold of the tales. Mr Dickens is very properly severe on the condition in which the soldiers were sent home in the *Tasmania*. He has got a good case, and he works it well. He shows up the delinquencies of the officials. But no one could act on what Mr Dickens says. He does not even pretend to distinguish between particular officials being in fault and the advisability of entirely reconstructing the machinery of our administration. He assumes the position of a person who has nothing to do with governing, and whose only business is to make fun of the shortcomings of those who do govern. It is quite open for any one to do so. In a free country there must be popular criticism of all institutions in order to keep these institutions in vigour, and Mr Dickens is an excellent popular critic. But he never goes beyond this; he never makes a remark which could help those who have to govern; he never looks at abuses from the point of view in which they must be regarded before they are remedied. In the same way he gives an excellent description of the Sunday Preachings at Theatres. He tells the truth as he saw it. He lets us know that the preacher whom he heard produced no impression on him, and talked a great deal of nonsense. But when he comes to give his view about what preaching ought to be, he at once betrays that he does not care to reflect deeply on the matter. He is content to take up with the modern delusion that Christianity is a scheme for making things pleasant; and this notion runs throughout all his books. It is indeed a true notion within very narrow limits, and it is the only notion perhaps that can harmonize with the facetious view of life. We do not quarrel with it as a popular way of thinking. But that it should satisfy a man of a vigorous mind shows that this mind is only concerned with the superficialities of things. We do not at all hold that authors are bound to go deeply into any philosophy, or to embrace a wide range of life. Mr Dickens's stories are quite true and deep enough to be very pleasant reading ... drollery is natural to the human mind, and an author who can represent it to us may very well leave philosophy alone. The absence of any deeper vein of feeling, and thought prevents Mr Dickens being a great humorist, but in his own line he is unrivalled.

Mr Dickens has raised up even more imitators of his style than of his way of regarding men and manners, and his style in his last book is very like his style in his first. It is the natural result of his method of fanciful observation. When it is at its best, it charms us by the copious detail into which the observation is carried, and by the odd and unexpected turns of fancy which run through it. When it is at its worst, the observation has sunk into the indolent selection of one single trait, which is brought in at every third line in order to keep up the remembrance of what is being talked about, and the fancy becomes mere exaggeration of expression. When, for instance, in the chapter on Refreshment Rooms, we are told that the waiter came in bringing 'a small landed estate of celery and water-cresses,' this is only unmeaning exaggeration, and whatever fun it has can only be in the exaggeration. But in a description of an unemployed waiter who stands by looking at the traveller, there is not only nice observation but lively fancy, although they are so blended that it is hard to say where the one ends and the other begins. 'All this time the other waiter looks at you with an air of mental comparison and curiosity, as if it had occurred to him that you are rather like his brother.' A few lines lower down we read—'The other waiter changes his leg and takes a new view of you—doubtfully now, as if he had rejected the resemblance to his brother, and had begun to think you more like his aunt or grandmother.' An excellent instance of the way in which Mr Dickens lets his fancy play round an unpromising subject is furnished by a long description of a dusty locker outside a solicitor's chamber in Gray's-inn. The description ends by saying that the clerk used to tap his key on the locker, to shake out the dust; 'and so exceedingly subject to dust is his key, and so very retentive of that superfluity, that in exceptional summer weather, when a ray of sunlight has fallen on the locker in my presence, I have noticed its inexpressive countenance to be deeply marked by a kind of Bramah erysipelas or small-pox.' Sometimes these products of observation and fancy are much more condensed. One of the happiest in the volume seems to us to be the description of a woman in a baker's shop—'a hard little old woman, with flaxen hair, of an undeveloped farinaceous aspect, as if she had been fed on seeds.' But this is a style of writing which it is not difficult to imitate. Every one who pleases can go and add up all the points of a thing, let his fancy run on, and then condense the result into smart writing. This is the process adopted by the numerous writers who imitate Mr Dickens. The difference is merely that his observation is much truer and juster, and his fancy is original and endless. The wording is the least thing with him, but it is everything with them. . . .

114. From an unsigned review of *Mrs Lirriper's Lodgings*, *Saturday Review*

12 December 1863, xvi, 759–60

This was the Extra Christmas Number of *All the Year Round*, 1863. Mrs Lirriper was vastly popular, and Dickens revived her the following year, in *Mrs Lirriper's Legacy*. Noticing this the *Saturday Review* wrote: 'The twelve pages in which, last Christmas, Mr Dickens made her a familiar friend to so many thousands of people are perhaps the most inimitable of his performances', but regrettably Dickens had now sentimentalized her—'The last half of Mr Dickens's contribution to the present number might almost have been written by the authors of the stories which make up the rest, and anything less flattering could scarcely be said' (10 December 1864, xviii, 724–5). Probably by James Fitzjames Stephen.

Mr Dickens, to the delight of hundreds of thousands, is himself again in *Mrs. Lirriper's Lodgings*. The public can have the satisfaction of renewing its old pleasure, and reading something new which Mr Dickens has scarcely, if ever, surpassed. Mrs Lirriper is entitled to rank with Mrs Nickleby and Mrs Gamp. And when Mr Dickens writes at his best, it is surprising how very unlike him are all his imitators, and how subtle and numerous are the touches by which he maintains his superiority. There are one or two faults in Mrs Lirriper, as it seems to us—more especially her turn for verbal epigrams and little smartnesses of language, which appears inconsistent with the simple ungrammatical shrewdness and volubility of her utterances. The general impression she produces is not that of a woman who would say of the opposition lodgings in her street that the bedrooms advertised as airy are 'stuffy,' and that the advertised night-porter is 'stuff.' Nor would she be likely, we should have thought, to say of teeth, 'that they are nuisances from the time we cut them to the time they cut us.' But even if this criticism

413

is right—and we must acknowledge that the enormous observation of lodgings which could alone have revealed to Mr Dickens so many secrets of the life led in them may have introduced him to epigrammatic landladies—this is a very small blot in a great performance. There are only twelve pages of Mrs Lirriper, and yet she is so drawn in that short space that we can scarcely believe that there really is no such person, and that a fortnight ago no one had ever heard of her. She is one of those creations which show how genius is separated from mere clever analysis. She stands before us like a living character, and not, as even in the works of Mr Dickens is so common, as a peg on which funny drolleries and references to some physical peculiarity are hung. She is quite the lodging-keeper; fills her house as well as she can; hates Miss Wozenham, her rival, with a true professional hatred; and yet she has a goodness, an overflow of humour and sense, and a benevolence quite her own. The abundance of by-remarks that proceed from her is inexhaustible, and although, by the characteristic oddity of expression, they are tolerably well connected with her, they are often instances of the drollest and happiest fancies that have come from Mr Dickens. What, for example, can be more far-fetched and yet more true than Mrs Lirriper's view of photographs, as 'wanting in mellowness as a general rule, and making you look like a new-ploughed field'; or the description of a boy with a parcel, as 'a most impertinent young sparrow of a monkey whistling with dirty shoes on the clean steps and playing the harp on the airy railings with a hoopstick'; or her confession, as to Norfolk Street, Strand, that 'of a summer evening, when the dust and waste paper lie in it, and stray children play in it, and a kind of a gritty calm and bake settles in it, and a peal of churchbells is practising in the neighbourhood, it is a trifle dull.' At the same time, it must be owned that any single detached oddity, however happy, cannot give any idea of the successful whole. For in those of Mr Dickens's works which, in comparison with *Martin Chuzzlewit* or *David Copperfield*, are utter failures, there were never wanting some scattered happinesses of this sort, and it might be possible to pick a sparkling sentence or two even out of the vast waste of *Little Dorrit*. Things become amusing, when said by Mrs Lirriper or Mrs Gamp, which would scarcely raise a smile if they came from one of the sham funny people who in themselves are mere blanks. . . .

115. [E. S. Dallas], from a review of *Doctor Marigold's Prescriptions, The Times*

6 December 1865, 6

Dallas (see No. 121) had reviewed the *Mrs Lirriper* stories enthusi-astically in *The Times* (3 December 1863, 12; 2 December 1864, 12). *Doctor Marigold* was immediately turned into a public reading. First performed on 10 April 1866 (after over 200 rehearsals), it proved very popular, and the episode of the Cheap Jack at work with his daughter dying in his arms was one of the most celebrated moments of pathos in Dickens's repertoire.

Mr Dickens has this Christmas earned our admiration by the freshness with which he tells his annual story. The Christmas number of *All the Year Round* is, it is well known, a batch of stories connected together by an editorial narrative which professes to account for the collection of so many separate tales. Of the separate tales now published we do not propose to speak, although one of them is by Mr Dickens himself. They are a well-selected batch of short stories, which, however, call for no special remark. The interest of the critic and of the reader will rest upon Mr Dickens's introductory narrative, which is even better in its way than the introduction to *Mrs Lirriper's Lodgings*. Mrs Lirriper was one of our author's most characteristic sketches. . . . But this year Mr Dickens has come forward with a character destined to be more popular than even Mrs Lirriper. Dr Marigold is only a sketch, but it is a masterly sketch, and one that deserves a place in our memories beside the best picture ever drawn by Dickens. Doctor Marigold is the name of a Cheap Jack who delights us with his eloquence, with his cleverness, and with his goodness. Mr Dickens is particularly happy when he can get an eloquent character, and all his more memorable personages, as Sam Weller, Mrs Gamp, and the rest, are chiefly memorable for the peculiar eloquence with which they assert themselves. Dr Marigold has all the eloquence of a Cheap Jack, asserts himself with vigour, and is very amusing.

[Quotes from his opening monologue.]

This is the style of the man who is exhibited before us in many such amusing attitudes, and Mr Dickens, displaying his characteristics, has the opportunity of indulging in his broadest humour. At the same time, however, he shows the more serious aspect of the man's character. We all know the story of the clown who had to crack his jokes in the sawdust while his wife was dying in the room hard by. Cheap Jack in his fashion has to amuse the crowd that come to buy his wares while his child is dying in his arms. The situation here is an old one, but Mr Dickens has touched it with new feeling, and set it before us in the tenderest light.

116. From an unsigned review of *Doctor Marigold's Prescriptions*, *Saturday Review*

16 December 1865, xx, 763–4

To this Extra Christmas Number (price 4*d.*) of *All the Year Round* Dickens contributed the opening and closing stories (about the Cheap Jack) and ch. vi (about a murdered man's ghost). The others mentioned by the reviewer were by Rosa Mulholland (the Irish legend), Charles Collins (ch. iii), Hesba Stratton (about the Quakeress), and Walter Thornbury (about the detective). Mrs Gascoyne contributed 'To be taken and tried', not mentioned here.

. . . It is not certainly by these lighter efforts that [Dickens] ought to be judged. The two characteristics to which he owes his reputation are beyond all doubt his sentiment, and his share of that humour which really forms a part of sentiment, though it is often considered as independent of it. As a sentimentalist, Mr Dickens in his best moments has not often been surpassed in English literature. His bizarre and grotesque literary taste, and the curious light under which he sees almost all the common things and the common events of life, drag him down, in his intervals of weakness, into the mire. But, with all his failings and vulgarities, Mr Dickens at his best is a very great author, and a consummate sentimentalist. His attempts to portray or to caricature or to satirize the upper classes of society have always been ludicrous failures. When Mr Dickens enters a drawing-room his genius deserts him, and hurries down the kitchen stairs into more congenial company. One is in danger, accordingly, of forgetting the astonishing power with which he draws life in its less polished but equally healthy and vigorous forms. His sympathy for poor people is real and unaffected, and helps to make him the great writer he is; and when we look through all the romantic literature of the day, and see how little genuine feeling there is that comes up in power and pathos to Mr Dickens's feeling for the poor, we cannot but acknowledge the charm that this trait lends to most of what he produces. This makes him the very writer for Christmas. There is a warmth and a cheeriness in his stories that reminds one of the mistletoe and the holly. Nor is Mr Dickens satisfied with being himself full of warmheartedness and sentiment. Whatever he is describing, whether it be animate or inanimate nature, must fall in with and follow in his train. Orpheus, as the legend goes, made the trees come dancing after him, and Mr Dickens is not above performing the same feat with the chairs and tables, and the rest of the furniture of the rooms upon which his fancy descends. He has only to strike the right key-note, and immediately a concert begins about him, in which the kettles on the hearth begin to sing, and the fire to talk, and the fire-irons and the fender to smile, and all together to chime in with the lyrical poem which forms the chief subject-matter of the chapter. Nobody expects to find in his Christmas number the sentiment and the humour which might be looked for in larger works, but it is not difficult to discover something of the same tone. Doctor Marigold's description of little Sophy's death, for example, is not meant to compete with twenty similar pictures that Mr Dickens has drawn already; but there are little pathetic touches in it which no one in our day, except Mr Thackeray and Mr Dickens, is in the habit of producing. Little Nell is a far more finished portrait than little Sophy, but little Sophy bears quite the same relation to little Nell that a Christmas number of *All the Year Round* does to a two-volume novel. ...

The pity is that he does not turn his attention annually to something a little better, and on a larger scale. A Christmas book by Mr Dickens used to be one of the entertainments of the season. It has been succeeded by a witty and pleasing chapter in which Mr Dickens attempts to carry off the absurdity and the dead weight of the chapters which his joint-stock company have added to his. The Irish legend which comes second in *Dr Marigold's Prescriptions*, and which is 'not to be taken at bedtime,' might, we believe, be taken with perfect impunity at that or any other hour, even in the most haunted house. The narrative of the composer of popular conundrums, like popular conundrums in general, is very deadly; and if any man is capable of spending his life in producing rebuses, it is possibly the gentleman who has devoted so much of his valuable time to composing Chapter III in *Dr Marigold's Prescriptions*. Stories of a Quakeress, of a detective policeman, and of a murdered man's ghost follow. They are very poor and very stupid, and are only fit for perusal in a railway train at that critical period when all the daily papers have been exhausted, and no book or periodical of any kind is to be had within a hundred miles. *Dr Marigold's Prescriptions* are to be had for a moderate sum. Mr Dickens is doubtless worth it all; but we very much doubt whether his assistants are worth the paper on which their efforts of genius have been printed.

117. [Charles Kent], from an unsigned review of *Mugby Junction*, *Sun*

7 December 1866

'It delighted me to find you so taken by the Xmas No.', Dickens wrote to Kent (14 December 1866)—adding that 'Yesterday Evening *Mugby Junction* was 11,000 past the 200,000 and it was 40,000 and odd ahead of *Doctor Marigold* [the 1865 Christmas Number of *All the Year Round*] at the same date after publication'. The date Kent cites (1845) should of course be 1843. Dickens devised three public readings from this Christmas Number, but they did not repeat the success of *Doctor Marigold*.

As seasonably welcome as either plum-pudding let us say, or as mince-pies—and, happily, just as inevitable for many years past, on the annual coming round of December—have been the successive Christmas Numbers of Mr Dickens's periodical. He has so far spoilt us in their regard, that we have long since come to look forward to them every succeeding twelvemonth almost as mere matters of course. We would as soon think, somehow, of celebrating Christmas without, for example, dangling a pendant bunch of mistletoe overhead, or without wreathing green branches and red berries about the pannellings of our home-rooms, as without according once more a welcome, not merely upon our hearths, but within our hearts, to some new tale or series of tales more or less appropriate to the season—to the holy-days and the holly-nights of Christmas-tide—tales told by our Great Novelist at regular intervals now during a goodly span of one whole score of years—between 1845, the first memorable year thus celebrated by Mr Dickens with the best of all his Christmas Books, the *Christmas Carol*, and the last year, 1865, hardly less noticeable in its turn as the year within which he produced about the finest of all his Christmas Numbers, *Doctor Marigold*. Happily his inventiveness as a Christmas story-teller appears to be fairly inexhaustible. He never seems to lack, year after

419

year, some ingenious device—some device perfectly new and original in itself, and never previously thought of as a medium for the relation of a series or cluster of narratives—upon which, as upon a connecting thread, he can string together the priceless pearls, blown eggshells, winter daisies, or what not, making up the miscellaneous assortment of each successive Christmas Number. Here, in *Mugby Junction*, is the last, and certainly not the least surprising evidence of this extraordinary ingenuity of his in the way of imaginative contrivance. It is as different from *Doctor Marigold*, in the root idea of it, and in the whole manner and treatment of it, as *Doctor Marigold* was, in each of those particulars, different from *Mrs Lirriper*. Each as a Christmas Number stands absolutely *per se*—must be regarded as distinctly *sui generis*—'none but itself can be its parallel.' It was the same one year with the *Poor Traveller*—another with the *Wreck of the Golden Mary*—another with the *Holly-Tree Inn*. Mr Dickens never repeats himself. One while a Lodging Housekeeper—another a Cheap Jack—now a Boots—now a Railway Porter—his identity is swallowed up, as one may say (and say, too, without one atom of extravagance) in the last of his great realistic idealizations. As well might you strive to detect the voice of the Globe Theatre Manager and Dramatist speaking variously through Malvolio and Touchstone, through Gobbo and Autolychus, as endeavour to detect that of the Conductor of *All the Year Round*, and as previously of *Household Words* through Major Jackman, let us say, or Master Walmers Junior, through the weak-minded and feeble-voiced Giant Pickleson—or, as in the present instance, through such perfectly new creations as Lamps, and Polly, as the Boy Ezekiel, or as the nameless Signalman. . . .

. . . The main excellence, value, and attraction, however, of the number all lie as a matter of course in the four opening papers from the hand of our great novelist. Foremost among them, to our thinking, being beyond all comparison the best of the four—the story of 'The Signalman.' Brief though it is, it is perfect as a work of art. It shows again, and in a remarkable manner, Mr Dickens's power in his mastery of the terrible. The pathetic force of it, is truly admirable. It is, surely, the finest Tale of Presentiment that has ever yet been told. . . . Immediately after 'The Signalman' in excellence—and thoroughly delightful, if only by way of contrast—commend us to 'The Boy at Mugby'—own brother to Trabb's boy in *Great Expectations*—friend of the heart to Tom Scott, in the *Old Curiosity Shop*—worthy of being comrade and associate of Bailey Junior in *Martin Chuzzlewit*. . . .

A TALE OF TWO CITIES

All the Year Round,

30 April–26 November 1859

This later became one of the most popular of Dickens's novels, partly no doubt because it has been dramatized with notable success, and partly because it is short; but it has been little discussed by the critics. At the time, it was reviewed coolly and without much acumen. Indeed, for no other novel have I filed fewer reprintable discussions. The *Athenaeum*, which usually gave three or four columns to a Dickens novel, despatched the *Tale* ('exciting . . .') in ten lines and a quotation in 'Our Library Table' (26 November 1859, 774). It 'pleased nobody,' according to the *Eclectic Review* (October 1861, n.s. i, 458); for Adolphus Ward (1870) it was 'one of the very few of Mr Dickens's works which require an effort in the perusal' (No. 149). E. P. Whipple, who wrote appreciatively about it, deplored the fact that it was 'hardly known by thousands who have *Pickwick* or *Nickleby* almost by heart; and among their thousands are many intelligent as well as unintelligent readers of Dickens' (*Dickens, the Man and his Work* (Boston, 1912), ii, 185). It had some other defenders, of course: Carlyle declared that it was 'wonderful!' and Wilkie Collins called it Dickens's 'most perfect work of constructive art' (Preface, *The Woman in White*). Dickens himself, on completing it, wrote: 'I hope it is the best story I have written' (*To* F. J. Régnier, 15 October 1859).

Two reasons may be suggested for its indifferent reception. Its predecessor, *Little Dorrit*, was widely considered a failure (see headnote, above), and *Hard Times*, just before that, had excited little enthusiasm. 'I don't attempt', wrote 'Christopher Grim' in the *Dublin University Magazine*, 'to conceal the fact that I have a great dislike to this writer's works, especially of late years', and he regretted 'having been such a fool' as to try reading the *Tale* (February 1860, lv, 238–9). By 1859, many critics had written Dickens off as having entered a gloomy dotage. The *Tale* did not charm them out of this verdict, as *Great Expectations* was to do, by offering more of the 'Dickensian humour' for which many of them pined. On the contrary (and here is the second reason): the *Tale* was an experiment. As Forster puts it:

There is no instance in his novels, excepting this, of a deliberate and planned departure from the method of treatment which had been preeminently the source of his popularity as novelist. To rely less upon character than upon incident, and to resolve that his actors should be expressed by the story more than they should express themselves by dialogue, was for him a hazardous, and can hardly be called an entirely successful experiment. With singular dramatic vivacity, much constructive art, and with descriptive passages of a high order everywhere, . . . there was probably never a book by a great humourist, and an artist so prolific in the conception of character, with so little humour and so few rememberable figures. Its merits lie elsewhere . . . (*Life*, 731).

In his review at the time, Forster loyally explored the merits, rather than dwelling on the hazards and failures.

One notable review was James Fitzjames Stephen's in the *Saturday Review* (17 December 1859), not reprinted here because it has been made easily available in *The Dickens Critics*, ed. Ford and Lane, 38–46. Stephen was predictably scathing. See Arthur B. Maurice's survey of criticism, in *The Bookman* (New York), April 1903, 130–8; Heinz Reinhold, 'Dickens' *Tale of Two Cities* und das Publikum', *Germanisch-romanische-Monatsschrift*, xxxvi (1955), 319–37; and, on reviews of this and other books in 1859, Michael Wolff's essay (see Bibliography).

118. Dickens on *A Tale of Two Cities*

1859–60

(*a*) gives Dickens's fuller account, to Forster, of his 'experiment'. The nature of Wilkie Collins's suggestion to Dickens about Dr Manette may be inferred from his reply in (*b*), but (*c*) is added, in which Dickens further distinguishes his 'manner' from Collins's. In (*c*), Dickens has been praising Collins's *Woman in White* (1859–60), before he expresses some reservations.

(*a*) Extract from a letter to Forster, 25 August 1859:

'I have written and begged the *All the Year Round* publisher to send you directly four weeks' proofs beyond the current number, that are in type.

I hope you will like them. Nothing but the interest of the subject, and the pleasure of striving with the difficulty of the forms of treatment, nothing in the mere way of money, I mean, could also repay the time and trouble of the incessant condensation. But I set myself the little task of making a *picturesque* story, rising in every chapter with characters true to nature, but whom the story itself should express, more than they should express themselves, by dialogue. I mean, in other words, that I fancied a story of incident might be written, in place of the odious stuff that *is* written under that pretence, pounding the characters out in its own mortar, and beating their own interests out of them. If you could have read the story all at once, I hope you wouldn't have stopped halfway.'

(*b*) Extract from a letter to Collins, 6 October 1859:

'I do not positively say that the point you put might not have been done in your manner; but I have a very strong conviction that it would have been overdone in that manner—too elaborately trapped, baited, and prepared—in the main anticipated, and its interest wasted. This is quite apart from the peculiarity of the Doctor's character, as affected by his imprisonment; which of itself would, to my thinking, render it quite out of the question to put the reader inside of him before the proper time, in respect of matters that were dim to himself through being, in a diseased way, morbidly shunned by him. I think the business of art is to lay all that ground carefully, not with the care that conceals itself—to show, by a backward light, what everything has been working to—but only to *suggest*, until the fulfilment comes. These are the ways of Providence, of which ways all art is but a little imitation.

"Could it have been done at all, in the way I suggest, to advantage?" is your question. I don't see the way, and I never have seen the way, is my answer. I cannot imagine it that way, without imagining the reader wearied and the expectation Wire-drawn.

I am very glad you like it so much. It has greatly moved and excited me in the doing, and Heaven knows I have done my best and believed in it.'

(*c*) Extract from a letter to Collins, 7 July 1860:

'I seem to have noticed, here and there, that the great pains you take express themselves a trifle too much, and you know that I always contest your disposition to give an audience credit for nothing, which necessarily involves the forcing of points on their attention, and which

I have always observed them to resent when they find it out—as they always will and do. But on turning to the book again, I find it difficult to take out an instance of this. It rather belongs to your habit of thought and manner of going about the work. Perhaps I express my meaning best when I say that the three people who write the narratives in these proofs have a DISSECTIVE property in common, which is essentially not theirs but yours; and that my own effort would be to strike more of what is got *that way* out of them by collision with one another, and by the working of the story.'

119. [John Forster], from an unsigned review, *Examiner*

10 December 1859, 788–9

This novel is remarkable for the rare skill with which all the powers of the author's genius are employed upon the conduct of the story. In this respect it is unequalled by any other work from the same hand, and is not excelled by any English work of fiction. The subtlety with which a private history is associated with a most vivid expression of the spirit of the days of the great French Revolution is but a part of its strength in this respect. If the whole purpose of the author had been to show how the tempest of those days of terror gathered and broke, he could not have filled our hearts more truly than he has done with a sense of its wild pitiless fury. But in his broadest colouring of revolutionary scenes, while he gives life to large truths in the story of a nation, he is working out closely and thoroughly the skilfully designed tale of a household. The story is all in all, yet there is nothing sacrificed to it. It is as truly the *Tale of Two Cities* as it is the touching history of Doctor Manette and Lucie his daughter. The pleasure will be great to any thoughtful man who reads the book a second time for the distinct purpose of studying its exquisite construction. Except Mr Stryver, who is necessary to the full expression of the character of Sydney Carton, and the slightly sketched family of Jerry Cruncher by the help of which Jerry himself is cunningly defined, there is not a person in the book who is not an essential portion of the story, there is not a scene that does not carry the tale onward, not even a paragraph that is not spent on urging forward the strong purpose of the book.

Mr Dickens has obtained his hold upon the public by the energy of an original genius, that penetrates with a quick instinct through the outer coverings of life to much of its essential truth. Even when he has succeeded least, the living force of a mind rarely gifted has been strongly felt. In this book all his natural powers seem to have been concentrated and directed steadily with a consummate art towards the purpose and the end it had in view. There are worse books with plots more highly wrought and exciting, deep as is the interest awakened by the *Tale of Two Cities*. In most of Mr Dickens's works there is more of the quaint humour by which his reputation was first won. Here we especially admire the energy of genius, the concentration of innumerable subtleties of thought upon a single purpose, the abiding force of the impression that is made.

The skill spent upon the depiction of the mind of Doctor Manette during the life following his release from a long burial in the Bastille it is hardly necessary to illustrate. The detail is original in its conception, yet it carries with it the conviction of deep truth. We may recal as one example of the manner of the book, the art with which the echoes of the future are suggested by the echoes in Doctor Manette's quiet street corner, near Soho square. A little group sits under the plane tree in the garden, on a sultry summer afternoon. Darnay, the future husband of Lucie, the inheritor, as it will appear, of the curse upon those by whom the Doctor had been buried alive, has by chance struck heavily upon the hidden chord that yields the key-note of the story. The Doctor starts, but refers this to one of the slight surprises against which he is not yet proof, and shows on the back of his hand that the first large drops of rain are falling. The slow coming of the storm, the hurrying of the echoes, the bursting of the tempest, blend with the innocent fancy of a girl to suggest the greater storm of which the first drops had then fallen. This is artifice, but it is the artifice of a poet, and by like touches that often are flashed suddenly into a word or through a single line, the force of poetry is added to the book. We are inevitably strengthened by a work like this, in the conviction that Mr Dickens's place hereafter in our literature will be in the first rank of the poets who have not expressed themselves in verse. . . .

A few touches here and there may be in excess; we are hardly content, for example, that it should occur to Miss Pross, at a critical moment, to compare Madame Defarge's eyes to bed winches; but these faults, natural to an active fancy, are very few and very slight in the work now before us. It is written throughout with an energy that never wanders from its aim, a strength that uses with the subtlety of genius the resources of a studied art.

GREAT EXPECTATIONS

All the Year Round,

1 December 1860 – 3 August 1861

'You will not have to complain of the want of humor as in the *Tale of Two Cities*,' Dickens wrote to Forster in October 1860. 'I have made the opening, I hope, in its general effect exceedingly droll.' From many recent discussions of this famous opening, one would certainly not imagine that anything so low as drollery was being offered, but at the time of publication this element was much noticed and welcomed with vociferous relief, after the decade of grimness since *David Copperfield*. Even the *Saturday Review* began to relent: 'Mr Dickens may be reasonably proud of these volumes. After a long series of his varied works— after passing under the cloud of *Little Dorrit* and *Bleak House*—he has written a story that is new, original, powerful, and very entertaining. . . . *Great Expectations* restores Mr Dickens and his readers to the old level. It is in his best vein, . . . quite worthy to stand beside *Martin Chuzzlewit* and *David Copperfield*' (20 July 1861, xii, 69). This was generally felt, even if put in such grudging tones as Mrs Oliphant's ('a gleam of departing energy': see No. 124).

Other interesting reviews include those in the *Athenaeum* (13 July 1861, 43–5, by H. F. Chorley), *British Quarterly Review* (January 1862, xxxv, 135–59), *Examiner* (20 July 1861, 452–3, by Forster), *Atlantic Monthly* (September 1877, xl, 327–33, by E. P. Whipple). For a fuller list, and a reprint of Whipple's 1877 essay, see *Assessing Great Expectations*, ed. Richard Lettis and William E. Morris (San Francisco, 1960).

120. [Edwin P. Whipple], from a review, *Atlantic Monthly*

September 1861, viii, 380–2

. . . We have read it, as we have read all Mr Dickens's previous works, as it appeared in instalments, and can testify to the felicity with which expectation was excited and prolonged, and to the series of surprises which accompanied the unfolding of the plot of the story. In no other of his romances has the author succeeded so perfectly in at once stimulating and baffling the curiosity of his readers. He stirred the dullest minds to guess the secret of his mystery; but, so far as we have learned, the guesses of his most intelligent readers have been almost as wide of the mark as those of the least apprehensive. It has been all the more provoking to the former class, that each surprise was the result of art, and not of trick; for a rapid review of previous chapters has shown that the materials of a strictly logical development of the story were freely given. Even after the first, second, third, and even fourth of these surprises gave their pleasing electric shocks to intelligent curiosity, the *dénouement* was still hidden, though confidentially foretold. The plot of the romance is therefore universally admitted to be the best that Dickens has ever invented. Its leading events are, as we read the story consecutively, artistically necessary, yet, at the same time, the processes are artistically concealed. We follow the movement of a logic of passion and character, the real premises of which we detect only when we are startled by the conclusions.

The plot of *Great Expectations* is also noticeable as indicating, better than any of his previous stories, the individuality of Dickens's genius. Everybody must have discerned in the action of his mind two diverging tendencies, which, in this novel, are harmonized. He possesses a singularly wide, clear, and minute power of accurate observation, both of things and of persons; but his observation, keen and true to actualities as it independently is, is not a dominant faculty, and is opposed or controlled by the strong tendency of his disposition to pathetic or humorous idealization. . . .

In *Great Expectations* . . . Dickens seems to have attained the mastery of powers which formerly more or less mastered him. He has fairly discovered that he cannot, like Thackeray, narrate a story as if he were a mere looker-on, a mere 'knowing' observer of what he describes and represents; and he has therefore taken observation simply as the basis of his plot and his characterization. As we read *Vanity Fair* and *The Newcomes*, we are impressed with the actuality of the persons and incidents. There is an absence both of directing ideas and disturbing idealizations. Everything drifts to its end, as in real life. In *Great Expectations* there is shown a power of external observation finer and deeper even than Thackeray's; and yet, owing to the presence of other qualities, the general impression is not one of objective reality. The author palpably uses his observations as materials for his creative faculties to work upon; he does not record, but invents; and he produces something which is natural only under conditions prescribed by his own mind. He shapes, disposes, penetrates, colors, and contrives everything, and the whole action is a series of events which could have occurred only in his own brain, and which it is difficult to conceive of as actually 'happening.' And yet in none of his other works does he evince a shrewder insight into real life, and a clearer perception and knowledge of what is called 'the world.' The book is, indeed, an artistic creation, and not a mere succession of humorous and pathetic scenes, and demonstrates that Dickens is now in the prime, and not in the decline of his great powers.

The characters of the novel also show how deeply it has been meditated; for, though none of them may excite the personal interest which clings to Sam Weller or little Dombey, they are better fitted to each other and to the story in which they appear than is usual with Dickens. They all combine to produce that unity of impression which the work leaves on the mind. Individually they will rank among the most original of the author's creations. . . .

The style of the romance is rigorously close to things. The author is so engrossed with the objects before his mind, is so thoroughly in earnest, that he has fewer of those humorous caprices of expression in which formerly he was wont to wanton. Some of the old hilarity and play of fancy is gone, but we hardly miss it in our admiration of the effects produced by his almost stern devotion to the main idea of his work. There are passages of description and narrative in which we are hardly conscious of the words, in our clear apprehension of the objects and incidents they convey. The quotable epithets and phrases are less numerous than in *Dombey and Son* and *David Copperfield*; but the scenes and events impressed on the imagination are perhaps greater in number and more vivid in representation. The poetical element of the writer's genius, his modification of the forms, hues, and sounds of Nature by viewing them through the medium of an imagined mind, is especially prominent throughout the descriptions with which the work abounds. Nature is not only described, but individualized and humanized.

Altogether we take great joy in recording our conviction that *Great Expectations* is a masterpiece. We have never sympathized in the mean delight which some critics seem to experience in detecting the signs which subtly indicate the decay of power in creative intellects. We sympathize still less in the stupid and ungenerous judgments of those who find a still meaner delight in wilfully asserting that the last book of a popular writer is unworthy of the genius which produced his first. In our opinion, *Great Expectations* is a work which proves that we may expect from Dickens a series of romances far exceeding in power and artistic skill the productions which have already given him such a preëminence among the novelists of the age.

121. [E. S. Dallas], from an unsigned review, *The Times*

17 October 1861, 6

Dallas (1828–79), author of *The Gay Science* and other notable critical books and reviews, was certainly acquainted with Dickens in 1862, and in August 1865 Dickens supported his application for the Chair of Rhetoric and Belles-lettres at Edinburgh. He reviewed the *All the Year Round* Christmas Numbers very warmly in *The Times* (3 December 1863, 12; 2 December 1864, 12; 6 December 1865, 6: see No. 115): also *Our Mutual Friend* (No. 130).

Mr Dickens has good-naturedly granted to his hosts of readers the desire of their hearts. They have been complaining that in his later works he has adopted a new style, to the neglect of that old manner which first won our admiration. Give us back the old *Pickwick* style, they cried, with its contempt of art, its loose story, its jumbled characters, and all its jesting that made us laugh so lustily; give us back Sam Weller and Mrs Gamp and Bob Sawyer, and Mrs Nickleby, Pecksniff, Bumble, and the rest, and we are willing to sacrifice serious purpose, consistent plot, finished writing, and all else. Without calling upon his readers for any alarming sacrifices, Mr Dickens has in the present work given us more of his earlier fancies than we have had for years. *Great Expectations* is not, indeed, his best work, but it is to be ranked among his happiest. There is that flowing humour in it which disarms criticism, and which is all the more enjoyable because it defies criticism. Faults there are in abundance, but who is going to find fault when the very essence of the fun is to commit faults? . . .

The method of publishing an important work of fiction in monthly instalments was considered a hazardous experiment, which could not fail to set its mark upon the novel as a whole. Mr Dickens led the way in making the experiment, and his enterprise was crowned with such success that most of the good novels now find their way to the public in the form of a monthly dole. We cannot say that we have ever met with a man who would confess to having read a tale regularly month by month, and who, if asked how he liked Dickens's or Thackeray's last number, did not instantly insist upon the impossibility of his getting through a story piecemeal. Nevertheless, the monthly publication succeeds, and thousands of a novel are sold in minute doses, where only hundreds would have been disposed of in the lump. . . . On the whole, perhaps, the periodical publication of the novel has been of use to it, and has forced English writers to develop a plot and work up the incidents. Lingering over the delineation of character and of manners, our novelists began to lose sight of the story and to avoid action. Periodical publication compelled them to a different course. They could not afford, like Scheherazade, to let the devourers of their tales go to sleep at the end of a chapter. As modern stories are intended not to set people to sleep, but to keep them awake, instead of the narrative breaking down into a soporific dulness, it was necessary that it should rise at the close into startling incident. Hence a disposition to wind up every month with a melodramatic surprise that awakens curiosity in the succeeding number. Even the least melodramatic novelist of the day, Mr Thackeray, who, so far from feasting us with surprises, goes to the other extreme, and is at particular pains to assure us that the conduct and the character of his personages are not in the least surprising, falls into the way of finishing off his monthly work with a flourish of some sort to sustain the interest.

But what are we to say to the new experiment which is now being tried of publishing good novels week by week? Hitherto the weekly issue of fiction has been connected with publications of the lowest class—small penny and halfpenny serials that found in the multitude some compensation for the degradation of their readers. The sale of these journals extended to hundreds of thousands, and so largely did this circulation depend on the weekly tale, that on the conclusion of a good story it has been known to suffer a fall of 40,000 or 50,000. The favourite authors were Mr J. F. Smith, Mr Pierce Egan, and Mr G. W. Reynolds, and the favourite subjects were stories from high life, in which the vices of an aristocracy were portrayed, now with withering sarcasm, and now with fascinating allurements. Lust was the *alpha* and murder the *omega* of these tales. When the attempt was made to introduce the readers of the penny journals to better authors and to a more wholesome species of fiction, it was an ignominious failure. ... Mr Dickens has tried another experiment. The periodical which he conducts is addressed to a much higher class of readers than any which the penny journals would reach, and he has spread before them novel after novel specially adapted to their tastes. The first of these fictions which achieved a decided success was that of Mr Wilkie Collins—*The Woman in White*. ... After Mr Wilkie Collins's tale, the next great hit was this story of Mr Dickens's to which we invite the attention of our readers. It is quite equal to *The Woman in White* in the management of the plot, but, perhaps, this is not saying much when we have to add that the story, though not impossible like Mr Wilkie Collins's, is very improbable. If Mr Dickens, however, chose to keep the common herd of readers together by the marvels of an improbable story, he attracted the better class of readers by his fancy, his fun, and his sentiment. Altogether, his success was so great as to warrant the conclusion, which four goodly editions already justify, that the weekly form of publication is not incompatible with a very high order of fiction. And now there is being published, in the same periodical another novel, which promises still more. It is by one who of all our novelists is the greatest master of construction, and who knows how to keep an exciting story within the bounds of probability. The *Strange Story* which Sir Edward Lytton is now relating week by week, is not only interesting as an experiment in hebdomadal publication, it is doubly interesting as a scientific novel. Scientific novels are generally dull, dead things. Sir

Edward Lytton undertakes the most difficult of all tasks—to write a scientific novel in weekly parts. It appears to be the greatest of all the successes achieved by *All the Year Round*. Hundreds of thousands of readers rush to read 'the fairy tales of science and the long results of time' as recorded by Sir E. B. Lytton.

Great Expectations is republished as a three-volume novel. Mr Dickens, we believe, only once before published a three-volume tale—*Oliver Twist*. We mention the fact because the resemblance between the two tales is not merely the superficial one that they are both in the same number of volumes, but is also one of subject very much and of treatment. The hero of the present tale, Pip, is a sort of Oliver. He is low-born, fatherless and motherless, and he rises out of the cheerless degradation of his childhood into quite another sphere. The thieves got a hold of Oliver, tried to make him a pickpocket, and were succeeded in their friendly intentions by Mr Brownlow, who thought that he could manage better for the lad. Pip's life is not less mixed up with the ways of convicts. He befriends a convict in his need, and henceforth his destiny is involved in that of the prisoner. The convict in the new story takes the place of Mr Brownlow in the old, and supplies Master Pip with every luxury. In either tale, through some unaccountable caprice of fortune, the puny son of poverty suddenly finds himself the child of affluence. If we are asked which of the tales we like best, the reply must be that the earlier one is the more fresh in style, and rich in detail, but that the later one is the more free in handling, and the more powerful in effect. It is so, even though we have to acknowledge in the work some of Mr Dickens's worst mannerisms. For example, it is a mere mannerism that in all his tales there should be introduced some one—generally a woman—who has been confined indoors for years, and who, either from compulsion or from settled purpose, should live in dirt and gloom, never breathing the fresh air and enjoying the sunshine. A lady who has a whim of this sort is here, as in most of Mr Dickens's tales, the blind of the story. Making every allowance, however, for repetitions, the tale is really worthy of its author's reputation, and is well worth reading. . . .

[Dallas offers some samples.]

These few quotations are taken from the first two volumes. When Mr Dickens gets into the third he is driven along by the exigencies of the story, and he can no longer afford to play with his subject. The interest is still sustained, but it is of a different kind. We might quote whole pages of eloquent writing and passionate dialogue, but readers, we dare say, will be better pleased with the sort of extracts we have given. The public insist upon seeing in Mr Dickens chiefly the humourist; and, however great he may be in other directions, they count all as nothing beside his rare faculty of humour. To those who may not be satisfied with a work of this author's unless humour superabounds most, we can heartily commend *Great Expectations*.

122. From an unsigned review, *Dublin University Magazine*

December 1861, lviii, 685–93

If the title of Mr Dickens's last novel could fairly be taken to mean more than a slight foreshadowing of the plot therein developed, we could not easily bring ourselves to congratulate the author on a hit so curiously unhappy as that which a playful fancy will be prone to lay to his account. Of those who may have had the boldness to expect great things, even in these latter days, from the growing weakness of a once mighty genius, there can be few who have not already chewed the cud of a disappointment bitter in proportion to the sweetness of their former hopes. Doubtless there were some good easy souls who saw in *Hard Times* and *Little Dorrit* either the fitting outcome or the momentary eclipse of bygone triumphs won by the pen of 'Boz.' In *A Tale of Two Cities*, friendly critics of the latter class seemed to discover flashes of something that might, by courtesy, be taken for the well known brilliance of other days. But, after all, how many of those who have helped to carry *Great Expectations* into a fourth or even fifth edition, entered on the reading of it with any serious hope of finding in Pip's adventures a worthy pendant to those of Pickwick or Martin Chuzzlewit? Would it not be far nearer the truth to say, that nine persons out of ten have approached these volumes with no other feeling than one of kindly regard for the most trivial utterances of an old favourite, or of curiosity, half painful, half careless, to see what further ravages time might have yet in store for the mental frame of a novelist already past his prime?

To ourselves, indeed, the title of the book suggested something utterly at variance with the mood of mind in which we sat down to read the book itself. Expecting little, we gained on the whole a rather agreeable surprise. Our last effort at reading a new novel by the author of *Pickwick*, had left us stranded high and dry among the midmost chapters of *Little Dorrit*. Thenceforth nothing could tempt us into renewing our olden intercourse with a writer whose pen had lost so large a share of its olden cunning, until the perusal of some half dozen conflicting criticisms on his latest performance aroused within us an amused desire to ascertain for ourselves, how far the more flattering opinions had overshot the bounds of literal truth. After a careful reading of *Great Expectations*, we must own to having found the book in most ways better than our very small expectations could have foreboded. But, in saying this much, we are very far from endorsing the notion that it comes in any way near those earlier works which made and which alone are likely hereafter to keep alive their author's fame. The favourite of our youth still stands before us, in outline but little changed, the old voice still sounding pleasantly in our ears, the old humour still peeping playfully from lip and eye; but time, flattery, and self-indulgence have robbed his phrases of half their whilom happiness; the old rich humour shines wan and watery through an ever-deepening film of fancies farfetched or utterly absurd; while all the old manner-isms and deformities that once seemed to impart a kind of picturesque quaintness to so many neighbour beauties, have been growing more and more irredeemably ungraceful and pitilessly obtrusive. . . .

To a reader ignorant of his earlier works and tolerant of all extrava-gances, if only they can tickle his fancy or keep his interest in full play, *Great Expectations* would offer a plenteous stock of enjoyable or exciting passages. Take for granted the truthlikeness of his portraiture, and you cannot but admire the clearness with which he conceives, and the consistency with which he works it up. After a little, the most critical reader resigns himself to the passing witchery, and begins to believe in Magwitch, Gargery, Miss Havisham, almost as heartily as their creator himself might be supposed to do. Each character speaks a language of its own, and behaves, however farcically, in its own peculiar fashion. Round each there circles a distinctive atmosphere made up of the humorous, dashed, more or less largely, with the sentimental or the frightful. Of food for laughter, for compassion, for eager curiosity, there is here no lack, if once you can lay aside your own ideas of what is fit and probable, and enter without reserve into the spirit—wild, whimsical, outrageous though it often be—of an entertainment got up by the oldest, yet still the first of our living humorists. . . .

. . .[The characters] in his present work are for the most part not more distinct from each other than from any to be found in former works. His plot, like his characters however improbable, has a kind of artistic unity and clear purpose, enhanced in this case by the absence of much fine-drawn sentiment and the scarcity of surplus details. If the author must keep on writing novels to the last, we shall be quite content to gauge the worth of his future essays by the standard furnished to us in *Great Expectations*.

123. [John Moore Capes and J. E. E. D. Acton], from a review in the *Rambler*

January 1862, n.s. vi, 274–6

Capes (1812–89), a convert to Roman Catholicism, had founded the *Rambler* in 1848, had edited it, and was now its proprietor. Richard Simpson, who was now editor, sent some of Capes's book-reviews to Acton (the great historian, 1834–1902) who, on 3 December 1861, returned them with approval, but added some comments, e.g., that *Pickwick* was 'not so decidedly his best book as to deserve to be always referred to as such'. In a further letter to Simpson, Acton discussed Dickens further: 'Certain Germans of the last century remind me of him as to religion . . . He . . . knows nothing of sin when it is not crime . . .' (*Lord Acton and his Circle*, ed. Abbot Gasquet (ND: 1906), 238–42). Simpson incorporated all of Acton's comments, almost *verbatim*, into Capes's review. See R. J. Schoeck, 'Acton and Dickens', *Dickensian*, lii, (1956), 77–80.

... The thorough youthfulness, fun, and animal spirits of *Pickwick* will always make it the characteristic work of the author; but it is not so decidedly his best book as to deserve to be always referred to as such. Nancy refusing to be delivered from Sikes, when her love for the child had brought her a chance of redemption, and Charley Bates turning against the murderer, are in a higher style than any thing in *Pickwick*.

But both the fun of *Pickwick* and the genuine pathos of *Oliver Twist* soon degenerated into a tedious reiteration of some superficial absurdity that does duty for humour, and into the pathos of a melodrama at a minor theatre. We trace this fall partly to Mr Dickens's views about religion; he reminds us of certain Germans of the last century, of whom we may take Herder as the type: they saw no divine element in Christianity, but they made humanity their God, and so made their religion simply human, and taught that man was perfectible, but childhood perfect. ... They professed a kind of natural religion, adorned with poetry and enthusiasm, quite superior to the narrowness and lowness of Christianity.

Mr Dickens is very like these men. Nothing can be more indefinite or more human than his religion. He loves his neighbour for his neighbour's sake, and knows nothing of sin when it is not crime. Thus one whole lobe of the human soul is dark to him; he cannot see a whole character, or perhaps has disabled himself from seeing it by his persevering purpose to write up his own particular views. This partly explains his defects of humour—his giving us so few characters and so many caricatures. And these caricatures have been the winding-sheet and the leaden coffin of his humour. For what fun can any one person find in describing a man by an ever-recurring absurdity, by his ever sucking his thumb, by his having a mouth like a letter-box, or by his firing a gun at sundown? It is the mere poverty of an imagination self-restrained to one narrow field of human nature, that makes him search curiously for such follies, and ransack newspapers for incidents to put into his books. A novelist of a more creative genius describes not a particular individual, but a general character, summed up in one, but fitting many, like Major Pendennis.

It is the determination to make every thing subservient to this fetishism of sentimental civilisation that spoils not only the humour of Mr Dickens, but the temper of his intelligent readers. They do not choose to be insulted with the negative sermons of those pathetic death-beds which are made so much happier by the want of all spiritual assistance, and where the 'babbling of green fields' is the all-sufficient substitute for the sterner truths of which dying Christians naturally think.

Yet, with all his faults, we should be puzzled to name Mr Dickens's equal in the perception of the purely farcical, ludicrous, and preposterously funny, though not so much now, perhaps, as in the days when he had not adopted the stage-trick of putting some queer saying into his characters' mouths, and making them utter it on every possible occasion. It is by a partial flickering up of this bright gift that *Great Expectations* has proved an agreeable surprise to so many of his readers. The story is as exaggerated and impossible as any he ever perpetrated; it is uncomfortable, too, and abounds with those tedious repetitions to which he has become so grievously addicted. Mr Jaggers is always biting his forefinger; Provis begins his speeches with a stereotyped phrase. But there is some very good fun in the story, nevertheless; not jovial, not hearty, not Pickwickian indeed, but really comic, and sufficient to excite a pleasant quiet laugh on a dull winter-day. Wemmick, the lawyer's clerk, who lives in a cockney castle at Walworth, and fires off his gun at sundown every night, is a conception, barring the last characteristic, worthy of Dickens's happiest days. The walk to the wedding is delicious. And, on the whole, then, we may rejoice that even in Mr Dickens's ashes still live his wonted fires. Perhaps, if he would but lie fallow for a year or two, and let his thoughts range at will, and eschew every thing that is tragic, sentimental, or improving, especially in his particular line of improvement, we need not despair of seeing a still more lively reproduction of the delightful absurdities with which he charmed his readers a quarter of a century ago.

124. [Mrs Margaret Oliphant], from 'Sensational Novels', *Blackwood's Magazine*

May 1862, xci, 574–80

'Dickens is not a favourite of mine,' Mrs Oliphant told Blackwood
at this time; 'I think it would go against the grain to applaud him
highly in his present phase.' She felt, on the other hand, a strong
'technical admiration' for Collins's *Woman in White*, discussed
along with other novels in the same review (*Autobiography and
Letters*, ed. Mrs H. Coghill [1899], 186).

So far as *Great Expectations* is a sensation novel, it occupies itself with
incidents all but impossible, and in themselves strange, dangerous, and
exciting; but so far as it is one of the series of Mr Dickens's works, it is
feeble, fatigued, and colourless. One feels that he must have got tired
of it as the work went on, and that the creatures he had called into being,
but who are no longer the lively men and women they used to be, must
have bored him unspeakably before it was time to cut short their
career, and throw a hasty and impatient hint of their future to stop the
tiresome public appetite. Joe Gargery the blacksmith alone represents
the ancient mood of the author. He is as good, as true, patient, and
affectionate, as ungrammatical and confused in his faculty of speech, as
could be desired; and shields the poor little Pip when he is a child on
his hands, and forgives him when he is a man too grand for the blacksmith, with all that affecting tenderness and refinement of affection
with which Mr Dickens has the faculty of making his poor blacksmiths
and fishermen much more interesting than anything he has ever produced in the condition of gentleman. Near Joe's abode, however,
dwells a lady who is intended to have much more influence upon the
fortunes of the hero than his humble protector. Here is the first sight of
Miss Havisham and her surroundings, as they are disclosed to little
Pip and to the reader.

[Quotes from ch. viii.]

This is fancy run mad. As the story progresses, we learn that this poor lady, who is perfectly sane, much as appearances are against her, has lived in this miraculous condition for five-and-twenty years. Not very long ago we heard an eminent Scotch divine pause in the middle of his exposition to assure his hearers that it was not necessary to believe that the garments of the children of Israel were literally preserved from the wear and tear of the forty years in the wilderness, but simply that God provided them with clothing as well as food. We should like to know what the reverend gentleman would say to that wedding-dress of Miss Havisham's, which, in five-and-twenty years, had only grown yellow and faded, but was still, it appears, extant in all its integrity, no tatters being so much as inferred, except on the shoeless foot, the silk stocking on which 'had been trodden ragged.' In this ghastly company lived a pretty young girl called Estella, whom Miss Havisham had reared with the avowed intention of avenging her own wrongs against men in general by breaking as many hearts as possible. The unlucky little Pip is the first victim selected. He is brought there to be operated upon in the special hope that he may learn to love Estella, and by her means have his heart broken—though the unfortunate little individual in question has no connection whatever with the breaking of Miss Havisham's heart, nor any other title to be considered as a representative of male humanity. If startling effects were to be produced by any, combination of circumstances or arrangement of still life, here, surely was the very scene for a sensation. But somehow the sensation does not come. The wretched old heroine of this masquerade is, after all, notwithstanding her dire intentions of revenge upon the world, a very harmless and rather amiable old woman, totally incapable of any such determined folly. Estella grows up everything she ought not to grow up, but breaks nobody's heart but Pip's, so far as there is any evidence, and instead of carrying out the benevolent intentions of her benefactress, only fulfils a vulgar fate by marrying a man without any heart to be broken, and being miserable herself instead. Here there is the most perfect contrast to the subtle successes of the *Woman in White*. Mr Dickens's indifference or languor has left the field open to his disciple. With the most fantastic exaggeration of means, here is no result at all achieved, and no sensation produced upon the composed intelligence of the reader. The shut-up house does not deceive that wary and experienced observer: he waits to see what comes of the bridal dress of twenty-five years' standing, and its poor old occupant; and as nothing in the least startling comes of either the one or the other, declines to be excited on the subject. The whole of this scene, and of the other scenes

which follow in this house, and the entire connection between Miss
Havisham, Pip, and Estella, is a failure. It is a mere piece of masquer-
ading which deceives nobody, and carries to the utmost bounds of
uninteresting extravagance that love of the odd and eccentric which
has already brought Mr Dickens to occasional misfortune in his long
and well-deserved round of success.

Very different, however, is the darker side of the story. The appearance of the escaped convict in the squalid and dismal solitude of the
marsh—the melancholy landscape with that one wretched figure
embodying the forlorn and desolate sentiment of the scene—is perhaps
as vivid and effective a sketch as Mr Dickens ever drew. It is made in
fewer words than usual, done at a breath, as if the author felt what he
was saying this time, and saw the scene too vividly himself to think a
full development of every detail necessary to enable his reader to see it
also. Here is the apparition and the scene:—[quotes from ch. i.]

After another very vivid picture of the same marshes under the wild
torchlight of a convict-hunt, this horrible figure disappears out of the
book, and only comes to life again at the end of the second volume,
when, as Pip's unknown benefactor, the mysterious secret friend who
has made the young blacksmith a gentleman, he re-emerges, humanised
and horribly affectionate, out of the darkness. The young fellow's utter
despair when he finds himself held fast in the clutches of this man's
gratitude and bounty—compelled to be grateful in his turn while
loathing the very thought of the obligation which he has been unwittingly incurring—is very powerfully drawn, and the predicament
perhaps as strange and frightful as could be conceived. . . .

The secondary persons of this book, however—almost entirely
separated as they are from the main action, which is connected only in
the very slightest way with the rest of the story—are, so far as they
possess any individual character at all, specimens of oddity run mad.
The incredible ghost, in the wedding-dress which has lasted for five-
and-twenty years, is scarcely more *outré* than the ridiculous Mrs
Pocket. . . . Of the same description is the ingenious Mr Wemmick, the
lawyer's clerk, who lives in a little castle at Walworth, and calls his
old father the Aged, and exclaims, 'Hulloa! here's a church—let's go
in!' when he is going to be married. Is this fun? Mr Dickens ought to
be an authority in that respect, seeing he has made more honest
laughter in his day than any man living, and called forth as many
honest tears; but we confess it looks exceedingly dull pleasantry to us,
and that we are slow to accept Mr Wemmick's carpentry as a substitute

for all the homely wit and wisdom in which Mr Dickens's privileged humorists used to abound. Besides all this heavy sport, there is a sensation episode of a still heavier description, for the introduction of which we are totally unable to discover any motive, except that of filling a few additional pages—unless, perhaps, it might be a desperate expedient on the part of the author to rouse his own languid interest in the conduct of the piece. Otherwise, why Pip should be seduced into the clutches of the senseless brute Orlick, and made to endure all the agonies of death for nothing, is a mystery quite beyond our powers of guessing. And again Mr Dickens misses fire—he rouses himself up, indeed, and bethinks himself of his old arts of word and composition, and does his best to galvanise his figures into momentary life. But it is plain to see all along that he means nothing by it; we are as sure that help will come at the right moment, as if we saw it approaching all the time; and the whole affair is the most arbitrary and causeless stoppage in the story—perhaps acceptable to weekly readers, as a prick of meretricious excitement on the languid road, perhaps a little stimulant to the mind of the writer, who was bored with his own production—but as a part of a narrative totally uncalled for, an interruption and encumbrance, interfering with the legitimate interest of the story, which is never so strong as to bear much trifling with. In every way, Mr Dickens's performance must yield precedence to the companion work of his disciple and assistant. The elder writer, rich in genius and natural power, has, from indolence or caprice, or the confidence of established popularity, produced, with all his unquestionable advantages, and with a subject admirably qualified to afford the most striking and picturesque effects, a very ineffective and colourless work; the younger, with no such gifts, has employed the common action of life so as to call forth the most original and startling impressions upon the mind of the reader. The lesson to be read therefrom is one so profoundly improving that it might form the moral of any Good-child story. Mr Dickens is the careless, clever boy who could do it twice as well, but won't take pains. Mr Wilkie Collins is the steady fellow, who pegs at his lesson like a hero, and wins the prize over the other's head. Let the big children and the little perpend and profit by the lesson. The most popular of writers would do well to pause before he yawns and flings his careless essay at the public, and to consider that the reputation which makes everything he produces externally successful is itself mortal, and requires a sustenance more substantial than a languid owner can be expected to give.

125. John Ruskin on Dickens

1863, 1870, 1886

For earlier comments by Ruskin (1819–1900) see Nos. 27, 88, 93, and, for more of his numerous discussions of Dickens, consult the Index to the *Works*, ed. E. T. Cook and Alexander Wedderburn, 39 vols., 1902–12. Ruskin particularly admired his descriptive powers, and often specially commended the storm in *Copperfield*: 'there is nothing in sea-description, detailed,' to compare with it (*Frondes Agrestes*, §31, 1875, *Works*, iii, 570n; and cf. (*a*) below).

(*a*) Extract from letter to his father, 18 January 1863:

'I quite agree in your estimate of Dickens. I know no writer so voluminous and unceasingly entertaining, or with such a store of laughter—legitimate, open-hearted, good-natured laughter; not at things merely accidentally ridiculous or at mere indecency—as often even in Molière and Le Sage, and constantly in Aristophanes and Smollett—but at things inherently grotesque and purely humorous; if he is ever severe—as on Heep, Stiggins, Squeers, etc.—it is always true baseness and vice, never mere foibles, which he holds up for scorn. And as you most rightly say of his caricature, the fun is always equal to the extravagance.

'His powers of description have never been enough esteemed. The storm in which Steerforth is wrecked, in *Copperfield*; the sunset before Tigg is murdered by Jonas Chuzzelwit; and the French road from Dijon in *Dombey and Son*, and numbers of other such bits, are quite unrivalled in their way.' (*Works*, xxxvi, 431–2)

(*b*) Extract from letter to Charles Eliot Norton, 19 June 1870, on Dickens's death:

'The literary loss is infinite —the political one I care less for than you do. Dickens was a pure modernist—a leader of the steam-whistle party *par excellence*—and he had no understanding of any power of antiquity except a sort of jackdaw sentiment for cathedral towers. He knew nothing of nobler power of superstition—was essentially a stage manager, and used everything for effect on the pit. His Christmas meant mistletoe and pudding—neither resurrection from dead, nor rising of new stars, nor teaching of wise men, nor shepherds. His hero is essentially the ironmaster; in spite of *Hard Times*, he has advanced by his influence every principle that makes them harder—the love of excitement, in all classes, and the fury of business competition, and the distrust both of nobility and clergy which, wide enough and fatal enough, and too justly founded, needed no apostle to the mob, but a grave teacher of priests and nobles themselves, for whom Dickens had essentially no word.' (*Works*, xxxvii, 7)

(*c*) Extract from letter to Charles Eliot Norton, 8 July 1870:

'I quite feel all that you say of Dickens; and of his genius, or benevolence, no one, I believe, ever has spoken, or will speak, more strongly than I. You will acquit me, I know, of jealousy; you will not agree with me in my acknowledgment of his entire superiority to me in every mental quality but one—the desire of truth without exaggeration. It is my stern desire to get at the pure fact and nothing less or more, which gives me whatever power I have; it is Dickens's delight in grotesque and rich exaggeration which has made him, I think, nearly useless in the present day. I do not believe he has made *any* one more good-natured; I think all his finest touches of sympathy are absolutely undiscovered by the British public; but his mere caricature, his liberalism, and his calling the Crystal Palace 'Fairyland'[1] have had fatal effect—and profound.' (*ibid*, 10)

(*d*) Extract from letter to W. H. Harrison, 17 July 1870:

'I note what you say of poor Dickens—no death could have surprised or saddened me more. I suppose no man was ever, not only more popular, but more truly beloved by his friends. Mr Norton is never weary of speaking of him, and I have made him almost angry with me by maintaining that precious as Dickens's books have been, they have on the whole done harm to the country. I wish he had lived to do us more mischief, however.' (*ibid*, 11)

(*e*) Extract from *Praeterita*, vol. ii (1886). Ruskin has been discussing his childhood and youth.

---

[1] Referring to 'Fairyland in Fifty-four', *Household Words*, 3 December 1854, viii, 313 (by W. H. Wills and G. A. Sala, not Dickens). Ruskin often alluded to this essay.

'I remorsefully bethink me that no word has been said of the dawn and sunrise of Dickens on us; from the first syllable of him in the *Sketches*, altogether precious and admirable to my father and me; and the new number of *Pickwick* and following *Nickleby* looked to, through whatever laborious or tragic realities might be upon us, as unmixed bliss, for the next day. But Dickens taught us nothing with which we were not familiar,—only painted it perfectly for us. We knew quite as much about coachmen and hostlers as he did; and rather more about Yorkshire. As a caricaturist, both in the studied development of his own manner, and that of the illustrative etchings, he put himself out of the pale of great authors; so that he never became an educational element of my life, but only one of its chief comforts and restoratives.' (*Works*, xxv, 303)

126. [Justin McCarthy], from 'Modern Novelists: Charles Dickens', *Westminster Review*

October 1864, n.s. xxvi, 414–41

Reprinted in McCarthy's *Con Amore* (1868).

McCarthy (1830–1912), Irish journalist, historian, and novelist; later an M.P. for Irish constituencies, 1879–1900. In his *Reminiscences* (1899) he recalls his arrival in London in 1852:

England was under the sway of a great literary triumvirate: Dickens, Thackeray, and Tennyson ... Dickens, of course, was by far the most popular of the three; no one since his time has had anything like the same degree of popularity. No one born in the younger generation can easily understand, from any illustration that later years can give him, the immensity of the popular homage that Dickens then enjoyed (i, 32).

McCarthy met him many times:

To say the truth, Dickens rather frightened me ... His manner was full of energy; there was something physically overpowering about it, as it then seemed to me; the very vehemence of his cheery good-humour rather bore one down (i, 34).

In the 1864 article, he is reviewing the Library Edition (22 vols. 1858–62).

... His genius is entirely original. It is scarcely an exaggeration to say that the light literature of the present generation has been created and moulded under the influence of his style. *Pickwick* has been to us very much what the *Rape of the Lock* was to the poets of the last century. It has revolutionized comic writing, and introduced a new standard of humour.

Nor is it only or chiefly in the field of letters that the power of Mr Dickens is felt. He has entered into our every-day life in a manner which no other living author has done. Much of his phraseology has become common property. Allusions to his works and quotations from them are made by everybody, and in all places. If Sir Edward Bulwer had never written a line there would be a blank on our shelves, and perhaps in some of our thoughts; but assuredly there would be no perceptible difference in our conversation. But take away *Pickwick* or *Martin Chuzzlewit*, and the change would be noticed any day in Cheapside.

... Novels are now some thing more than the means of passing away an idle hour. They supply thousands of readers with a philosophy of life, and are at this moment almost the only form of poetry which is really popular. Time was, when seriously disposed people would have nothing to do with them. The model governess of that period always locked them up; the wicked pupil always read them. The current of opinion now sets in an exactly opposite direction. The novelist has taken rank as a recognised public instructor. Important questions of social policy, law reform, the latest invention, the most recent heresy, are formally discussed in his pages, in the most attractive manner too, with a maximum of argument and a minimum of facts.

This change is in a great measure owing to Mr. Dickens himself. . . . [When he began writing, the] stir of the Reform movement was at its height. Everywhere questions were being asked, changes advocated, abuses swept away. Even the novel-reading public caught the enthusiasm, for they saw an opening to a new kind of excitement. The diffusion of common knowledge had brought social questions within the ken of a large class who, fifteen years before, were, and were contented to be, perfectly ignorant of them. Clearly, all the conditions requisite for a highly popular treatment of politics were there—an interested public and unlimited means of communicating with them. Still, we doubt whether any one less gifted than Mr Dickens, or with qualifications different to his, would have succeeded in inducing half England to read books which had anything to do with the Poor Laws or Chancery reform. He has certainly effected thus much, and we believe him to have been the main instrument in the change which has perverted the novel from a work of art to a platform for discussion and argument.

But this is only part of his originality. When he began to write, the life of the middle and lower classes had found no chronicler. The vagabonds of our London streets, the cabmen, the thieves, the lodging-house keepers, the hospital-nurses and waiters, with whom we are now so familiar, passed away unhonoured and unmourned for want of a poet. Here was a mine of life and character which might have been profitably worked by a less skilful hand than Mr Dickens'. He entered into indisputed possession of it, and made it his own. This happy choice of subject has had much to do with his success. In his later works he has always mixed up with his unrivalled descriptions a serious element, or, to speak more strictly, he has made the descriptions themselves subservient to a moral or political purpose. It is but fair to say that this habit seems to have been gradually forced upon him by the character of his genius. There is no trace of it in his earliest work, the *Sketches by Boz*. There is only a faint trace of it in *Pickwick*. It appears more decidedly in *Oliver Twist* and *Martin Chuzzlewit*, and it arrives at maturity in *Bleak House* and *Little Dorrit*. In attempting to write with an object, Mr Dickens has committed the very common error of mistaking the nature of his own powers. He possesses in high perfection many rare and valuable gifts. But he is in no sense, either as a writer or a thinker, qualified to cope with complicated interests. . . .

The want of analytical power with which we are disposed to charge, Mr Dickens is in certain directions compensated by his extraordinary delicacy of observation. Outward peculiarities—the details of manner, speech, and appearance, are at best but an imperfect index of character. But they are always worth something, and there are cases in which they tell us all that we care about, or indeed, are able to know.[1] The moral and intellectual peculiarities of animals, for example, are sufficiently described, when we are told how they look and behave. Mad, half-witted, weak, and simple people, again, are adequately represented by their obvious and external qualities; for, as regards the former class, inasmuch as we cannot rely on inferences from the ordinary laws of mind, there is nothing but manner to look to; and as regards the latter class, there is a tolerably constant relation between what they think and what they say and do. In noting these surface attributes, Mr Dickens has shown an exquisite tact. Accordingly in his sketches of animal life, in his description of madness, and in the working out of such characters

[1] Pages of analysis would not give us more insight into Doctor Blimber's character than the following short description of his manner of walking: 'The doctor's walk was stately, and calculated to impress the juvenile mind with solemn feelings. It was a sort of march. But when the doctor put out his right foot, he gravely turned upon his axis with a semicircular sweep towards the left; and when he put out his left foot, he turned in the same manner towards the right. So that he seemed, at every stride he took, to look about him as though he were saying, "Can anybody have the goodness to indicate any subject, in any direction, on which I am uniformed? I rather think not."'—*Dombey and Son* [ch. xii; McCarthy's footnote].

as Tom Pinch, Dora Spenlow, Esther Summerson, Toots, Smike, and Joe Gargery he is perfectly satisfactory. . . .

For the same reason Mr Dickens describes children singularly well. But he always appears anxious to make too much of them, giving them a prominence in the story which throws an air of unreality over it. Prodigies like Paul Dombey, or girls with the sagacity and heroism of Eleanor Trench, are not children at all; they are formed characters who talk philosophy and happen accidentally to be small and young. But Pip, and David Copperfield (when he is not too conscious in his simplicity), and Sissy Jupe, and little Jacob, are what they profess to be, and are created and carried out with unusual skill. Oliver Twist is merely a lay figure, like one of those in Mrs Jarley's Waxworks, who are so well described as 'standing more or less unsteadily upon their legs, with their eyes very wide open, and their nostrils very much inflated, and the muscles of their legs and arms very much developed, and all their countenances expressing great surprise.' Up to a certain point Paul Dombey himself is natural and delightful. Abstraction made of what the waves were always saying—there is a duet about these waves of which it is impossible to think without a shudder—his thoughts are such as might well occur to a child under peculiar circumstances. The episode of Doctor Blimber's Academy—the solemn politeness, pretension, and weariness of that establishment—is nearly as good as anything in the whole of these volumes. . . . His minor characters are generally good.

[McCarthy instances Mr Littimer, Mr Crummles, young Bailey, Mrs Skewton, and Mr Bucket.]

But when Mr Dickens writes on principle, with an object before him, and, above all, when he tries to enlist our sympathy or dislike, he signally fails. We search in vain throughout these sixteen novels for any one man or woman whom we really admire, really fear, or whom we should at all desire to imitate. If the figures in a tailor's shop were to become suddenly animated they would be exceedingly like Mr Dickens' heroes. . . .

[McCarthy contrasts the variety of Charlotte Brontë's heroes with the dull sameness of Dickens's.]

There is just one exception to the triviality of his heroes. David Copperfield has some marks of life about him. And it is generally believed that in this novel Mr Dickens has drawn largely from actual experience.

After all, Mr Dickens the artist is only subsidiary to Mr Dickens the philosopher, the moralist, and the politician. We should not have ventured to regard him in this threefold capacity were it not that he expressly claims to have views in some of his prefaces[1] and that he insists on those views in his books.

Most people who affect to think have some kind of notion about the world in general. It commonly resolves itself into one of these two propositions: (1), that things are right; (2), that they are not right. The philosophy of Mr Dickens is contained in the former statement.

. . . His theory of life is very complete and comfortable. He believes the world we live in to be, in the main, a happy world, where virtue is rewarded and vice punished on the strictest principles of poetic justice. There is, of course, a great deal of want, and wretchedness, and crime; but the poor people are compensated for their poverty by being more cheerful and virtuous than the rich; and the wretchedness and crime are chiefly owing to the absurdity of our government and laws, to our neglect of sanitary improvements, and to the selfishness of the great. A few obvious reforms, such as putting all the right men in the right places, and seeing that the labouring population lived in airy, clean, and well-ventilated houses, would soon put things to rights. This is his theory, and his practice accords with it. The deserving people are rewarded with a uniformity which is exceedingly gratifying. Those who are young enough are married happily—some of the very good ones twice; those who, like Miss Trotwood, the brothers Cheeryble, Mr Pickwick, and Tom Pinch, could scarcely be married without destroying the romance of the thing, become accessories, before or after the fact, to the marriage of somebody else, and live a quasi-domestic life surrounded by their friend's children. No mercy is shown to the Fagins, the Quilps, the Pecksniffs, the Squeers, the Heaps. The rewards of virtue are, it is true, somewhat commonplace, and the highest good of which any example is found in these volumes does not rise much above the level of material comfort. We believe that if Mr Dickens were king he would first of all take care that in England seven half-penny loaves should be sold for a penny, and he would make it felony to drink small beer.[2]

As a mere matter of political expediency, we are not at all disposed to quarrel with this view. It is what would be called 'healthy,' and it

---

[1] See particularly the Prefaces to *Martin Chuzzlewit*, *Little Dorrit*, and *Bleak House*. [McCarthy's footnote]

[2] Jack Cade's proclamation, *2 Henry VI*, iv, ii, 72–7.

supplies a motive to that large class of people who insist on taking a commercial view of moral obligations. But it is by no means the last word on the subject. When an author steps forward and says, 'I propose to write a funny book;' very well; no one troubles himself to examine his theories. But Mr Dickens claims to represent large phases of modern thought and life. Therefore we think it a pity that he should have set out with so trivial a belief as that virtue is usually rewarded and vice usually punished.

His moral and political speculations take their colour from the opinions of the public for whom he works. Like many other novelists, he has two classes of readers. There are those (including, we should think, everybody who has sense to understand a joke,) who admire him greatly for certain special qualities. Then there are those who thoroughly understand and believe in him, and whom he may be said to represent—just as Cambridge men are represented by Mr Kingsley. This class is not easily defined. It is chiefly made up of the impulsive people who write letters to *The Times*; of practical, well-to-do men who understand their own business, and see no difficulties elsewhere; and of those to whom it is a pleasure to have their feelings strongly acted upon. That Mr Dickens must keep constantly before him the requirements of some such class as this, is plain from his manner of dealing with the pathetic, as well as from the freedom with which he constantly expresses himself on subjects which he cannot possibly be supposed to understand. . . .

. . . His views, both of life and morals, are imperfect and of the first impression; being, in fact, just what would occur offhand to any ordinary warm-hearted person who had not reflected on the subject. With these characteristics it is particularly unfortunate that he should have attempted to express himself on questions of State. Mr Tupper's poetry, Dr Cumming's theology, Mr Samuel Warren's sentiment, are not worse than Mr Dickens' politics. And this is saying a good deal. He seems, however, to have thought otherwise. It is difficult to name any important subject which has arisen within the last quarter of a century on which he has not written something. Imprisonment for Debt, the Poor Laws, the Court of Chancery, the Ten Hours' Bill and the relations of Workman and Employer, Administrative Reform, the Ecclesiastical Courts, the Civil Service Examinations, and National Education, have all been illustrated, criticized, and adjudicated upon. We should be sorry to say that he has not pointed out many defects in the working of these institutions; it was not difficult to do so; but he has uniformly overstated the case, he has often not understood it, and never has he pointed out any remedy. It may be added that his criticism has generally come too late. The account of the Fleet Prison in *Pickwick* was published in the year in which the Act for the amendment of the Insolvent Laws was passed. The Poor Laws had just been improved when *Oliver Twist* exposed the horrors of the workhouse system. The description of Mr Bounderby and the hands of Coketown closely followed the last of a series of statutes regulating the management of factories. Jarndyce and Jarndyce might or might not have been true in the time of Lord Eldon, but it bears about as much relation to the present practice of the Court of Chancery as to that of the Star Chamber. It is all very well meant, but very ignorant. . . .

It is hard to be obliged to find fault with Mr Dickens. We owe him too much. He is a man of genius; in many respects rarely gifted. He has exceptional powers of observation and description, great imagination, and an intuitive tact in appreciating many of the more delicate shades of passion. On the other hand, his intellect is, we will not say ruled, but crushed and dwarfed by his emotional faculties. Partly from a defective education, and partly from a constitutional bias, he seems unable to take either an extensive or an intensive view of any subject; neither grasping it as a whole, nor thoroughly exhausting any single part. His writings show the same union of strength and weakness; his plots inartificial, his genesis of character rude and unphilosophic, his literary execution oscillating with tolerable evenness between the intensely vulgar and commonplace, and passages of the most striking beauty.

We cannot think that he will live as an English classic. He deals too much in accidental manifestations and too little in universal principles. Before long his language will have passed away, and the manners he depicts will only be found in a Dictionary of Antiquities. And we do not at all anticipate that he will be rescued from oblivion either by his artistic powers or by his political sagacity.

OUR MUTUAL FRIEND
May 1864–November 1865

'*Our Mutual Friend*, like all these later books of Dickens, is more interesting to us today than it was to Dickens's public,' writes Edmund Wilson (*The Wound and the Bow* (1952 edn.), 66). Certainly the subtleties and profundities that are now discovered in it were not noticed by the reviewers, and it never became a general favourite: but its original reception was fairly cordial, and its sales—as the first Dickens novel for several years—were good. The *Annual Register* forgave Dickens for not being always able to muster his highest inventive powers, though it did not doubt that he 'still possesses the qualities which enabled him to write the *Pickwick Papers*, the *Old Curiosity Shop*, and *Martin Chuzzlewit*' (1865, 323). It was doubtless because Dallas, in *The Times* review, refrained from thus harking for the early style, that Dickens gratefully presented him with the manuscript of the novel (see No. 130). He was also much moved by Chorley's review in the *Athenaeum* which, though ranking *Our Mutual Friend* below *Copperfield* and other earlier novels, declared that it was 'one of Mr Dickens's richest and most carefully-wrought books . . . an accumulation of fine, exact, characteristic detail, such as would suffice to set up in trade for life a score of novel-spinners . . .' (28 October 1865, 570; cf. *To* Chorley, same date). Forster, aware of Dickens's unaccustomed difficulties in composing the novel (*Life* 740–3), concentrated his rather brief review in the *Examiner* on demonstrating the 'deep-seated unity' of this and other Dickens novels, despite what was alleged by 'Latinized races', i.e. Taine, whose history of English literature had just been published (28 October 1865, 681–2; cf. No. 97). In the *Life*, however, Forster expressed his reservations about this novel: 'it wants freshness and natural development', 'has not the creative power which crowded his earlier page', and 'will never rank with his higher efforts' (pp. 743–4).

As my selections will show, some reviewers were severe on *Our Mutal Friend*, finding it laboured, and hard reading. Dickens's renewed attack upon the Poor Law was generally approved, though the propriety of his using fiction as the medium for his political ideas was disputed (see Nos. 129 and 132). This Betty Higden part of the novel, and Dickens's combative remarks in the Postscript, attracted all the more attention because this was his first direct comment on social institutions, in fiction, since the Circumlocution Office in *Little Dorrit* eight years ago. Some new types of character were noted, and generally approved: the Veneerings and Podsnaps, Headstone, and Bella Wilfer. Lizzie Hexam was liked: Thomas Love Peacock, a recent convert to Dickens, declared her to be 'his ideal of womanhood' (Carl Van Doran, *Life of Peacock* (1911), 255).

127. From an unsigned review, *London Review*

28 October 1865, 467–8

Mr Dickens has now been so long before the public, and his name is associated with so many triumphs, some of which were achieved before the present generation of young men and women was born, that he has already obtained the position of a classic, and we judge him by the standard of names consecrated by time. He has exhibited a degree of productiveness rarely seen except in combination with a marked and melancholy falling off from the freshness and power of early manhood. The collected editions of his works now spread over many volumes; the characters he has invented would almost people a town; and we might well excuse an author who has done so much, if we found in him some slackening of the creative force which has been at work for such a length of time. But Mr Dickens stands in need of no allowance on the score of having out-written himself. His fancy, his pathos, his humour, his wonderful powers of observation, his picturesqueness, and his versatility, are as remarkable now as they were twenty years ago. In some respects, they are seen to still greater advantage. The energy of youth yet remains, but it is united with the deeper insight of maturer years. Not that we mean to say Mr Dickens has outgrown his faults. They are as obvious as ever—sometimes even trying our patience rather hard. A certain extravagance in particular scenes and persons—a tendency to caricature and grotesqueness—and a something here and there which savours of the melodramatic, as if the author had been considering how the thing would 'tell' on the stage—are to be found in *Our Mutual Friend*, as in all this great novelist's productions. But when a writer of genius has fully settled his style, and maintained it through a course of many years—when his mind has passed beyond the period of pliability and growth, and can only deepen without essentially changing—it is the merest vanity on the part of a critic to dwell at any great length on general faults of manner. There they are, and there they will remain, say what we will. The tender rind wherein they were cut in youth has become hard bark long since, and the incisions are fixed for ever. To rail at them is simple waste of time, besides implying a great deal of ingratitude on the part of the railer. We shall therefore make but brief allusion here to the characters of Wegg and Venus, who appear to us in the highest degree unnatural— the one being a mere phantasm, and the other a nonentity—and shall pass on to a consideration of the more solid parts of the book, in which Mr Dickens's old mastery over human nature is once more made splendidly apparent.

As in its author's previous fictions, we are almost oppressed by the fulness of life which pervades the pages of this novel. Mr Dickens has one of the most mysterious attributes of genius—the power of creating characters which have, so to speak, an overplus of vitality, passing beyond the limits of the tale, and making itself felt like an actual, external fact. . . . The creations of authors such as Mr Dickens have a life of their own. We perceive them to be full of potential capacities— of undeveloped action. They have the substance and the freedom of actual existences; we think of what they would do under other conditions; they are possessed of a principle of growth. Certainly, the most amazing manifestation of this amazing gift is that which is to be found in the plays of Shakespeare; but all men of genius have it in a greater or less degree, and that strange and even awful power is, perhaps, the surest test for distinguishing between genius and talent. That Mr Dickens possesses it to a remarkable extent, we believe few will be found to dispute. The chief characters even of his earlier books dwell in the mind with extraordinary tenacity, sometimes quite apart from the plot wherein they figure, which may be utterly forgotten; and no writer of our time has furnished contemporary literature and conversation with so many illustrative allusions. This imaginative fecundity is seen in *Our Mutual Friend* in undiminished strength. The book teems with characters, and throbs with action; but it may perhaps be objected that there is a want of some one conspicuous figure, dominating over the rest, and affording a fixed centre to all this moving wealth of life. John Rokesmith must, we suppose, be regarded as the hero; but he is certainly not the chief character, nor the most interesting. Though in many respects well-drawn, he does not greatly enlist our sympathies— perhaps because his motives of action are strange and improbable. Indeed, the whole story of old Harmon's bequest, and what arises out of it, strikes us as being faulty. This, we are aware, is to proclaim a serious defect in the novel, as such, since we have here the basis of the whole fiction. But Mr Dickens's collateral conceptions are often better than his main purpose. We must confess that in reading *Our Mutual Friend* from month to month, we cared very little as to what became of old Harmon's property, excepting in as far as the ultimate disposal of that sordid aggregation of wealth affected the development of two or three of the chief characters. The final explanation is a disappointment. The whole plot in which the deceased Harmon, Boffin, Wegg, and John Rokesmith, are concerned, is wild and fantastic, wanting in reality, and leading to a degree of confusion which is not compensated by any additional interest in the story. . . .

The termination of Mr Dickens's novels is often hurried, and such is the case in the present instance. The complication of events does not work itself clear by a slow and natural process, but is, so to speak, roughly torn open. And, even before we are half through the book, the mystery concerning John Rokesmith is explained in an equally objectionable manner. Young Rokesmith, or Harmon, *tells himself* his own previous history, in a sort of mental soliloquy (in which a long series of events is minutely narrated), evidently for no other purpose than to inform the reader. It is surprising that so experienced a romance-writer as Mr Dickens could not have devised some more artful means of revealing that portion of his design. Yet, notwithstanding these defects (which we have pointed out with the greater freedom, because such a writer demands the utmost candour from his critic), the story of *Our Mutual Friend* is interesting for its own sake, even apart from its treatment; which, we need not say, is that of a master, if we except those points already objected to. We repeat what we said at the commencement—that, in conception and evolution of character, and in power of writing, this latest work of the pen that has so often delighted and astonished us shows not the slightest symptom of exhaustion or decline

Perhaps the most admirable of the *dramatis personæ*, considered on artistic grounds, are Eugene Wrayburn, Lizzie Hexam, Bradley Headstone, and Bella Wilfer. The first of these characters is a consummate representation of a nature, originally noble, degenerating, under the effects of a bad education and of subsequent idleness, into a laughing indifference to all things worthy—into a gay and sportive disbelief in itself, in manhood, in womanhood, and in the world. From first to last, the conception is wonderfully developed, and the change that is afterwards wrought in Eugene's disposition is worked out without the smallest violence. In strong contrast with the good-natured levity of Wrayburn is the stern, self-contained, narrow, yet (within its contracted and mechanical limits) earnest, nature of Bradley Headstone, the self-educated schoolmaster. Lizzie Hexam is the cause of bringing these two men into dangerous contact. . . .

Bradley Headstone also is in love with Lizzie; and the way in which his impassive, artificially-restrained nature breaks up into raging fury under the combined influences of hopeless love, jealousy, and some pungent taunts which Wrayburn gaily flings at him, is exhibited by Mr Dickens with marvellous power and truthfulness. The transformation of this pattern of all the decencies into a dark, haggard, self-tormenting evil genius, perpetually dogging the steps of Eugene Wrayburn, and at length making a murderous attack on him in a lonely place up the river, is one of the finest things in fiction. Bradley Headstone is a psychological study of the deepest interest, and, we are persuaded, of the profoundest truth. Natures like his, originally cold, and still further repressed by the routine of a dry and formal education, are no doubt especially liable to outbreaks of ungovernable passion when some great emotion at length sweeps away the old habits of self-control. Mr Dickens has traced this with a singularly close and analytical eye, and nothing can be more tragic and impressive than the culmination of Bradley Headstone's wrath in the attempted murder of Eugene. All the preparations for that act, and all the accessories in the way of scenery and atmospherical conditions, are managed in Mr Dickens's highest style; and the mental state of a man about to commit the greatest of crimes has seldom been depicted with such elaboration and apparent truthfulness. We are prepared to hear from a certain class of critics who can tolerate nothing beyond the civilities of everyday life, and who seem to think that great passions are among those vulgar mistakes of nature to which novelists should be superior; that this character is 'sensational;' but the genius that could conceive it has nothing to fear from such objectors. Very touching and beautiful is the character of Lizzie Hexam; but probably the greatest favourite in the book will be—or rather is already—Bella Wilfer. She is evidently a pet of the author's, and she will long remain the darling of half the households of England and America.

... Of the less important characters of the book it is impossible to speak, they are so numerous; but reference should be made to the pathetic sketch of Betty Higden and little Johnny, her great-grandchild....

We must also instance among the creations of this book the little deformed dolls' dressmaker (fantastic and semi-poetical, yet with a deep instinct of truth); her drunken father—a sketch in which tragedy and comedy are mingled in a way wherein Mr Dickens is quite unrivalled; Bella's father, a beautiful specimen of a truly lovable nature; the Podsnaps and Veneerings, and the crew of rapscallions and adventurers, male and female, by whom they are surrounded—portraits admirable for the social satire they embody; Rogue Riderhood, and some of the other hangers-on about the river. We might almost mention the river itself as a character. It plays a most important part in the story, and always with great picturesqueness....

128. From an unsigned review, 'Mr Dickens's Romance of a Dust-heap', *Eclectic and Congregational Review*

November 1865, n.s. ix, 455–76

... Mr Dickens has now, to our knowledge, for sixteen years been haunted by a great Dust-heap. In the *Household Words* for 1850 first appeared the account of that amazing mound. All his life long, at any rate in all that portion of it with which the public is acquainted, our writer has been industriously engaged in attempting to ferret out the bright things in dirty places; he has been like a very Parisian chiffonnier, industriously searching, with intense eye, among the sweepings, the odds and ends, and puddles of society, if haply some overlooked and undiscovered loveliness might not be found there. . . .

[The reviewer makes a long quotation from 'Dust; or Ugliness Redeemed', *Household Words*, 13 July 1850, i, 380 (not by Dickens but by R. H. Horne), about the valuable dust-heaps of London.]

Since the publication of this paragraph, of course many of these heaps have been compelled to yield to that great Macadamizing spirit of change and progress, the railway line and station. The North London line now probably cuts right through that very region where stood Mr Boffin's Bower, and the vast heap of miserly old John Harmon. Thus, it is only like Mr Dickens to attempt to construct his fairy palace upon such an unsightly mound. A romance from a Dust-heap is so far from impossible that it is not even improbable. Following Mr Dickens's observant eye and rapid foot, other visitors have traversed and circumambulated these extraordinary mounds. In that excellent and arousing little book, *The Missing Link*, there is a chapter entitled 'The Bible Woman among the Dustheaps;' and many facts recited in that interesting little chapter go to confirm the more romantic and imaginative settings of the great social novelist. . . .

Needless work, we presume, it would be to attempt to tell the outline of Mr Dickens's story. Most of our readers have either read, or will read it; those who have not read will, perhaps, not thank us for attempting to tell it. We have already said, however, that, as in all Mr Dickens's books, so in this, the story is only a part of the work. Yet, perhaps, as a story, it is quite equal to any Mr Dickens has told; it is sustained throughout; there is nothing in the plot too strained or unnatural. Mr Dickens has not always been thought happy in this, for a writer with so much of nature; he has sometimes and often devised most unnatural positions and situations. . . . Yet there is less that offends in this way than in many other works of the writer, as even in *Great Expectations*, where the reader is startled by the half grotesque and half horrible episodical thread of Miss Haversham. Perhaps the first thing which will strike the reader in the work will be its severe, although good-natured satire upon, we will not say our social foibles, but our great social sins; the Veneerings, Podsnaps, the Lady Tippinses, the invisible Lord Snigsworth, the Brewers, Boots, and Buffers, expressing in their persons the voice of 'society.'

[The reviewer praises Dickens for the accuracy and justice of his satire;

then commends his attack on the Poor-Law administration, and his pictures of London, as 'fresh as if he had never written upon London before'.]

. . . Fond of conducting some character through a hunt or a flight, Mr Dickens often tells some such story: our readers recollect the wanderings of the old man with little Nell, the terrible and pitiful tragedy of Lady Dedlock's long rushing from place to place, and night to night; the reader feels the same impression of interest through those chapters to which we have referred, in which the bird of prey is brought down; but Betty Higden and her flight is in our author's sweetest style of sympathy with the proud but holy poor. Critics of the hard-headed school will call this mere sentiment. Such critics have been fond of charging upon Mr Dickens the spreading upon his palate certain colours, and sketching out upon his canvas certain patchwork forms intended to produce the mingled effects of the grotesque and the pathetic; but very different is our impression. There are many things in the writings of Mr Dickens, perhaps in these volumes, which we regret, and from which we are free to dissent; but, true in these, his last essays, to the spirit of his earliest works, the poor—the poor, lowly, unknown outcasts and offcasts, seem to be the objects of intensest interest to him. 'Mr Dickens,' say many of his critics, 'always fails when he attempts to draw the habits of good society. . .' . . . But we could very well conceive Mr Dickens replying, were he to condescend to reply, to such critics, 'Well, I know what you call "good society," but it is not so interesting to me; it is monotonous; it wants variety, it wants earnestness. Even Rogue Riderhood, the villain, is a more entertaining character to me than your Podsnaps. There is a character all alive, no make-up there; neither whitewash, veneer, nor lacquer; an utter rascal, but a most interesting one, always up to dodges, which are not merely a shuffling of shares about, but dodges having all the interesting intensity of a real rascal in them'. . . .

129. From an unsigned review, *Saturday Review*

11 November 1865, xx, 612-3

... After securing a central incident sufficiently extraordinary, the author crowds into his pages a parcel of puppets as uncommon as the business which they are made to transact. Nobody is admitted to the distinction of a place in *Our Mutual Friend* who is at all like the beings who have a place in the universe. The characters may be divided into two sets of people—those whom the author intended to be faithful copies of ordinary persons or classes of persons, and those whom even the author must in his inner consciousness know to be immeasurably remote from the common experience of human life. But, in one set of people as much as in the other, the writer seems to notice nothing which is not odd and surprising and absurd. The people whom he does, equally with those whom he does not, intend to be curious and abnormal, are caricatured in the most reckless way. Mr Venus, who is meant for an oddity, is in reality not a bit more odd, and does not act or talk more inconsistently with the common modes of men, than does Mr Eugene Wrayburn, who is not meant for an oddity at all. Silas Wegg, the sort of man whom Mr Dickens does not expect us to be familiar with, and Lady Tippins, the sort of woman with whom he does expect us to be familiar, are strange and unknown just in the same degree. The majestic Mrs Wilfer, avowedly an exceptional person, does not strike one as being at all more exaggerated and uncommon than Betty Higden, expressly designed to exemplify the feelings of a very common class. In this respect *Our Mutual Friend* is like all the novels that have come from the same mint. Mr Dickens has always been, and always will be, essentially a caricaturist. He always either discovers people who are grotesque enough in themselves and their surroundings to bear reproducing without caricature, or else he takes plain people and brings them into harmony with the rest of his picture by investing them in caricature. And it is just to notice two things. First, as a caricaturist, Mr Dickens, in humour, in inexhaustible fertility of fancy, in quickness of eye for detecting the right points, when he is at his best, stands altogether unrivalled. And, in the next place, as is the case in all good caricature, Mr Dickens, in those books in which he has been most himself, is substantially truthful. He exaggerates, but he adheres to the original outline, and conveys a virtually correct impression. Chadband, Jefferson Brick, Elijah Pogram, Gradgrind, and a long gallery of others, the very recollection of whom makes one look into *Our Mutual Friend* with blank amazement, are all caricatures, many of them broad caricatures; still they do not convey a single untrue impression of the originals, and they do convey the truth which is most striking about the people caricatured. In *Our Mutual Friend* we still find only caricatures, but they are caricatures without either of Mr Dickens's characteristic excellences. They are not very witty or humorous, and we are unable to recognise their truth and purpose. Nothing, for instance, can be more dismal in the way of parody or satire than the episode of the Veneerings and their friends. Where is either the humour or the truth of the caricature? The execution is coarse and clumsy, and the whole picture is redolent of ill-temper and fractiousness. This spoils it. A good caricaturist enjoys his work, however angry he may be against the object of it. Mr Dickens, in this case, seems to screech with ill-will and bitterness. Yet he could caricature Chadband and Bumble, whom he had much more reason to detest, without raising his voice into a scream of anger....

The odious vulgarity and malevolence which Mr Dickens has put into the mouth of Society are mere moonshine, and not creditable to the author's insight or shrewdness. We do not venture to deny that Mr Dickens knows 'what is best in his vocation.' Only, 'in the interests of art,' as he would say, we cannot but think the vocation of making spiteful and clumsy attacks on Society is an uncommonly poor one. And, unfortunately, we cannot help wondering whether the artist would consider equally good in its way the genial and witty picture of the Eatanswill Election for instance, and what strikes us as the sour and pithless account of the election of Mr Veneering for the ancient borough of Pocket Breeches. Angry, screaming caricature such as this is not caricature at all, and we frankly confess ourselves ignorant of the 'denomination of art' to which it may be considered to belong. It was not always Mr Dickens's vocation.

In the character of Mr Podsnap, blunt as is a good deal of what is designed for cutting humour, there is still, it must be admitted, a large amount of underlying truthfulness. Most of Mr Dickens's readers were quick to recognise what he means by Podsnappery. After all, Podsnap is only a very roughly executed representation of what the Germans call a Philistine and the French a grocer. Many persons who would perhaps have failed either to create from their own observation this ogre of society, or to acquire from the light touches of a more refined and a deeper satirist a proper idea of the hateful traits of the ogre, may have their minds opened by the telling, if broad and coarse, sketch in the present story. And this is connected with one of Mr Dickens's most conspicuous merits. In spite of the lurid and melodramatic air which he loves to throw over parts at least of nearly all his novels, in spite of his exaggeration and frequent affectations of all sorts, he has always shown a sincere hatred of that form of cant which implies that all English habits and institutions are the highest product of which civilization is capable. He has a most wholesome conviction that the abuses of the world are more or less improvable, and were not ordained and permanently fixed by the Almighty. This is patent enough, no doubt, but it is the most patent truths which are most habitually overlooked. Mr Dickens has always been more or less in earnest about things, and has not contented himself with looking out on the world from the dilettante point. For example, in *Our Mutual Friend*, the character of Betty Higden, the old woman to whom the prospect of coming on the parish is the most appalling thought of her life, and whose only wish is that she may die in a ditch—this character is to our minds thoroughly sentimental and over-done. The reflections to which her terror gives rise are, from the point of view of 'the interests of art,' thoroughly out of place in a novel. But, for all this, one cannot help feeling that Mr Dickens is both sincere and justified in his abhorrence of much in the administration of the Poor Law. We demur altogether to an 'artist' writing a story to show or prove a position of this sort. But it is impossible for those who watch the subject not to feel that Mr Dickens is not wrong in his emphatic assertion that 'there has been in England, since the days of the Stuarts, no law so often infamously administered, no law so often openly violated, no law habitually so ill supervised.' His outspoken disgust at cant and red-tape and Bumbledom has perhaps won him almost as many admirers as his fancy and wit. Admirers of this sort will certainly not be diminished by Mr Podsnap. . . .

. . . On the whole, this makes a very tedious performance, and the general verdict will probably be that *Our Mutual Friend* is rather hard reading. . . .

130. [E. S. Dallas], from
an unsigned review, *The Times*

29 November 1865, 6

On Dallas, see No. 121. This review so pleased Dickens that he made a gesture unique in his responses to his reviewers—he presented Dallas with the manuscript of the novel. See K. J. Fielding, *Charles Dickens: a Critical Introduction* (1958), 186–7.

Novels published in parts have the advantage and disadvantage that their fortunes are often made or marred by the first few numbers; and this last novel of Mr Charles Dickens, really one of his finest works, and one in which on occasion he even surpasses himself, labours under the disadvantage of a beginning that drags. Any one reading the earlier numbers of the new tale might see that the author meant to put forth all his strength and do his very best; and those who have an eye for literary workmanship could discover that never before had Mr Dickens's workmanship been so elaborate. On the whole, however, at that early stage the reader was more perplexed than pleased. There was an appearance of great effort without corresponding result. We were introduced to a set of people in whom it is impossible to take an interest, and were made familiar with transactions that suggested horror. The great master of fiction exhibited all his skill, performed the most wonderful feats of language, loaded his page with wit and many a fine touch peculiar to himself. The agility of his pen was amazing, but still at first we were not much amused. We were more impressed with the exceeding cleverness of the author's manner than with the charm of his story; and when one thinks more of an artist's manner than of his matter woe to the artist. Very soon, however, Mr Dickens got into his story; the interest of it grew; the reader, busied with the facts of the tale, learned to forget all about the skilfulness of the artist, and found himself rushing on eagerly through number after number of one of the best of even Dickens's tales. Still, upon some minds the first impression prevails, and Mr Dickens's publishers have been obliged to announce that complaints are made of the difficulty of procuring his work at some of the London libraries, and that this difficulty is caused entirely by the librarians who have contented themselves with a short supply....

That *Our Mutual Friend* has defects we not only allow, but shall ruthlessly point out. The weak part of the work is to be found in what may be called 'The Social Chorus.' This is the title which Mr Dickens gives one of his chapters; but it is the proper name not only for that chapter, but also for every chapter in which the same personages figure. We can divide the tale distinctly into two parts, like a Greek drama— one part truly dramatic and given to the evolution of the story which Mr Dickens has to tell; the other, a sort of social chorus, having no real connexion with the tale in which we are interested, and of importance only as representing the views of society on the incidents of the story as it comes before them. Now, the idea here is a great one, but it has not been worked out with details of sufficient interest. Of Mr Dickens's main story—the line of action into which he has thrown his whole heart, we cannot speak too highly; it is a masterpiece. We see life in all its strength and seriousness and tenderness; the fierce passion that drives it into action, and the gentle passion that stirs it into play. But in contrast to this fine story Mr Dickens has thought fit to present to us in a parallel line of action—the spectator—the chorus of the Greek play....

Here is a great mistake—the mistake of the author in naming his work from the least interesting portion of it, the mistake of the too superficial reader in not finding out the author's mistake. The Social Chorus who do the 'mutual friendship' business first of all provide the story with a false name, and then to the world of readers they give it a bad name. The reader is not happy in their company, and, looking for the story in their movements, he finds none. The story is elsewhere. We cannot, however, dismiss 'The Social Chorus' from further notice without remarking on the cleverness with which they are delineated by Mr Dickens. It must be remembered that if they somewhat bore the reader, it is because they are bores by nature. ... The people to whom Mr Dickens introduces us in 'The Social Chorus' are, properly speaking, not people at all, but sticks; and his business is to show as well as he can the wooden character of their mind. In the passage above quoted [from Book I, ch. ii] in which Mr Dickens introduces them to our notice, Twemlow is described as a piece of furniture that went upon easy castors; and all through the novel we have to think of him and his associates not as men with the hearts of men, but as a species of knick-knacks. The carefulness of the writing, however, in that passage contains sufficient evidence that Mr Dickens has spared no pains in the exhibition of such knick-knacks. With great zest he exposes the solemn twaddle of stiff dinner parties and the hollow friendships of which they are the religious rites. Some of his portraits, too, of the Veneering lot are, with a few swift touches, given with great effect, as that of Lady Tippins, the aged flirt and again those of the Lammles, who married each other for money, and discovered amid the joys of the honeymoon that they were deceived.

So far we have dealt with the mere onlookers of the story, not with the story itself; and we say deliberately that we have read nothing of Mr Dickens's which has given us a higher idea of his power than this last tale. It would not be wonderful if so voluminous an author should now show some signs of exhaustion. On the contrary, here he is in greater force than ever, astonishing us with a fertility in which we can trace no signs of repetition. We hear people say, 'He has never surpassed *Pickwick*.' They talk of *Pickwick* as if it were his masterpiece. We do not yield to any one in our enjoyment of that extraordinary work. We never tire of it. We are of those who can read it again and again, and can take it up at any page with the certainty of finding in it the most merry-making humour. But we refuse to measure a work of art by the amount of visible effect which it produces; and we are not going to quarrel with tragedy because it is less mirthful than comedy. What if we allow that *Our Mutual Friend* is not nearly so funny as *Pickwick*? It is infinitely better than *Pickwick* in all the higher qualities of a novel, and, in spite of the dead weight of 'The Social Chorus,' we class it with Mr Dickens' best works.

One thing is very remarkable about it,—the immense amount of thought which it contains. We scarcely like to speak of the labour bestowed upon it, lest a careless reader should carry away a notion that the work is laboured. What labour Mr Dickens has given to it is a labour of love, and the point which strikes us is that he, who of all our living novelists has the most extraordinary genius, is also of all our living novelists the most careful and painstaking in his work. In all these 600 pages there is not a careless line. There are lines and pages we object to as wrong in execution, or not quite happy in idea; but there is not a page nor a line which is not the product of a full mind bursting with what it has to say, and determined to say it well. Right or wrong, the work is always thoroughgoing and conscientious. There is nothing slurred over—no negligence, no working up to what are called in stage language 'points'—to the detriment of the more level passages. And then see what a mass of matter he lays before his readers. There is a gallery of portraits in the present novel which might set up half a dozen novelists for life: Bella Wilfer, the most charming of all, her father, her mother, her sister; then Boffin and Mrs Boffin, and Silas Wegg, and Venus, the practical anatomist; then, again, Riderhood, and Lizzie Hexam, and Bradley Headstone; once more, Mortimer Lightwood, Wrayburn, the dolls' dressmaker, and her father. There are many more, and among these we must not forget poor old Betty Higden, because without such a character as hers Mr Dickens's tales would be unlike themselves. Mr Dickens cannot write a tale without in some way bringing it to bear upon a social grievance, with regard to which he has a strong feeling. He has a strong feeling as to the manner in which the Poor Law is administered in this country, and he devotes one of his most powerful chapters to showing with what horror poor Betty Higden shrinks from parochial charity.

[Dallas quotes from Book 3, ch. viii.]

We quote that passage, because when such a man as Mr Dickens has a practical object in view, it is more in his mind than all the triumphs of his art. It would please him more to do good to the thousands of poor people who never read novels than to entertain all the novel readers in the world. Still, it is not with these practical questions that we are now concerned, but with the question of the writer's art, and we return to the point on which we were insisting, as to the fulness of matter that appears in the pages of *Our Mutual Friend*. We have referred to one of Mr Dickens's peculiarities, that he generally makes his novels bear on some practical grievance to which he desires to call attention. Another of his characteristics is, that he likes to introduce us to people engaged in some special business. In one little tale he will tell us all about the man who draws the picture of salmon on the pavement; in another story we shall have the man-milliner; in yet another, Mrs Gamp and her congeners. Here we are introduced to two great curiosities—the dolls' dressmaker, and the man who makes it his business to find dead bodies in the Thames. In the occupation of the latter there is something too horrible to permit of our being thoroughly entertained by Mr Dickens's revelations of the secrets that belong to such a calling; but the dolls' dressmaker is one of his most charming pictures, and Mr Dickens tells her strange story with a mixture of humour and pathos which it is impossible to resist. The picture is one of those in which he delights, in which he can give the reins to his fancy; and as he displays all the sorrow and all the pleasantry of the little dressmaker we are driven to the dilemma of not knowing whether to laugh or to be sad.

But the finest picture in the novel is that of Bella Wilfer. Mr Dickens has never done anything in the portraiture of women so pretty and so perfect. . . . [Bella in love] is without exception the prettiest picture of the kind he has drawn—one of the prettiest pictures in prose fiction. The little dialogues in which Mr Dickens has exhibited first her love for her father, then her love for her lover, and then the two combined, are full of a liveliness and a grace and a humour that seem to us to surpass any attempt of the same description which he has ever before made. There is an enchanting airiness and a winning charm about the lady which mark her out as one of his most brilliant portraits—and that, too, in a species of portraiture peculiarly difficult of attainment. Everybody knows and admires the odd sort of characters for which Mr Dickens is famous, such as Mrs Gamp; but to paint Bella Wilfer seems to be a higher reach of art. The strong hard lines of Mrs Gamp's character it is comparatively easy to draw. In drawing Bella Wilfer, Mr Dickens has to touch most delicately a beautiful woman, and render with the utmost tenderness the soft contour of her character. He has perfectly succeeded, and we shall be greatly surprised if the portraiture of this wayward girl does not rank among his highest performances.

The story, of course, we are not going to tell. It is very ingenious, and the plot is put together with an elaboration which we scarcely expect to find in a novel published in parts. All we shall say of it is, that those readers who pant for what is called 'sensation' may feast in it to their heart's content on sensation; and that those who care more for quiet pictures and studies of character will also find that the author has provided for them. Mr Dickens's range is wide, and none of our living novelists can adapt himself, or herself, to so wide a circle of readers.

131. [Henry James], review in *The Nation*, (New York)

21 December 1865, 786–7

Reprinted in James's *Views and Reviews* (Boston, 1908), 153–61.
'The Dickens review is perhaps the most acute of all of Henry's
early writings; he is freeing himself of an early idol and at the same
time giving free play to his critical faculties' (Leon Edel, *Henry
James: the Untried Years 1843–1870* (1953), 216). James (1843–1916)
had published in 1864 his first story and his first critical essay. See
headnote to No. 168.

Our Mutual Friend is, to our perception, the poorest of Mr Dickens's
works. And it is poor with the poverty not of momentary embarrassment, but of permanent exhaustion. It is wanting in inspiration. For
the last ten years it has seemed to us that Mr Dickens has been un-
mistakably forcing himself. *Bleak House* was forced; *Little Dorrit* was
labored; the present work is dug out as with a spade and pickaxe. Of
course—to anticipate the usual argument—who but Dickens could
have written it? Who, indeed? Who else would have established a lady
in business in a novel on the admirably solid basis of her always putting
on gloves and tieing a handkerchief round her head in moments of
grief, and of her habitually addressing her family with 'Peace! hold!'
It is needless to say that Mrs Reginald Wilfer is first and last the occasion of considerable true humor. When, after conducting her daughter
to Mrs Boffin's carriage, in sight of all the envious neighbors, she is
described as enjoying her triumph during the next quarter of an hour
by airing herself on the door-step 'in a kind of splendidly serene
trance,' we laugh with as uncritical a laugh as could be desired of us.
We pay the same tribute to her assertions, as she narrates the glories of
the society she enjoyed at her father's table, that she has known as many
as three copper-plate engravers exchanging the most exquisite sallies
and retorts there at one time. But when to these we have added a dozen
more happy examples of the humor which was exhaled from every

line of Mr Dickens's earlier writings, we shall have closed the list of the merits of the work before us. To say that the conduct of the story, with all its complications, betrays a long-practised hand, is to pay no compliment worthy the author. If this were, indeed, a compliment, we should be inclined to carry it further, and congratulate him on his success in what we should call the manufacture of fiction; for in so doing we should express a feeling that has attended us throughout the book. Seldom, we reflected, had we read a book so intensely *written*, so little seen, known, or felt.

In all Mr Dickens's works the fantastic has been his great resource; and while his fancy was lively and vigorous it accomplished great things. But the fantastic, when the fancy is dead, is a very poor business. The movement of Mr Dickens's fancy in Mrs Wilfer and Mr Boffin and Lady Tippins, and the Lammles and Miss Wren, and even in Eugene Wrayburn, is, to our mind, a movement lifeless, forced, mechanical. It is the letter of his old humor without the spirit. It is hardly too much to say that every character here put before us is a mere bundle of eccentricities, animated by no principle of nature whatever. In former days there reigned in Mr Dickens's extravagances a comparative consistency; they were exaggerated statements of types that really existed. We had, perhaps, never known a Newman Noggs, nor a Pecksniff, nor a Micawber; but we had known persons of whom these figures were but the strictly logical consummation. But among the grotesque creatures who occupy the pages before us, there is not one whom we can refer to as an existing type. In all Mr Dickens's stories, indeed, the reader has been called upon, and has willingly consented, to accept a certain number of figures or creatures of pure fancy, for this was the author's poetry. He was, moreover, always repaid for his concession by a peculiar beauty or power in these exceptional characters. But he is now expected to make the same concession with a very inadequate reward. What do we get in return for accepting Miss Jenny Wren as a possible person? This young lady is the type of a certain class of characters of which Mr Dickens has made a speciality, and with which he has been accustomed to draw alternate smiles and tears, according as he pressed one spring or another. But this is very cheap merriment and very cheap pathos. Miss Jenny Wren is a poor little dwarf, afflicted, as she constantly reiterates, with a 'bad back' and 'queer legs,' who makes dolls' dresses, and is for ever pricking at those with whom she converses, in the air, with her needle, and assuring them that she knows their 'tricks and their manners.' Like all Mr

Dickens's pathetic characters, she is a little monster; she is deformed, unhealthy, unnatural; she belongs to the troop of hunchbacks, imbeciles, and precocious children who have carried on the sentimental business in all Mr Dickens's novels; the little Nells, the Smikes, the Paul Dombeys.

Mr Dickens goes as far out of the way for his wicked people as he does for his good ones. Rogue Riderhood, indeed, in the present story, is villanous with a sufficiently natural villany; he belongs to that quarter of society in which the author is most at his ease. But was there ever such wickedness as that of the Lammles and Mr Fledgeby? Not that people have not been as mischievous as they; but was any one ever mischievous in that singular fashion? Did a couple of elegant swindlers ever take such particular pains to be aggressively inhuman?—for we can find no other word for the gratuitous distortions to which they are subjected. The word *humanity* strikes us as strangely discordant, in the midst of these pages; for, let us boldly declare it, there is no humanity here. Humanity is nearer home than the Boffins, and the Lammles, and the Wilfers, and the Veneerings. It is in what men have in common with each other, and not in what they have in distinction. The people just named have nothing in common with each other, except the fact that they have nothing in common with mankind at large. What a world were this world if the world of *Our Mutual Friend* were an honest reflection of it! But a community of eccentrics is impossible. Rules alone are consistent with each other; exceptions are inconsistent. Society is maintained by natural sense and natural feeling. We cannot conceive a society in which these principles are not in some manner represented. Where in these pages are the depositaries of that intelligence without which the movement of life would cease? Who represents nature? Accepting half of Mr Dickens's persons as intentionally grotesque, where are those exemplars of sound humanity who should afford us the proper measure of their companions' variations? We ought not, in justice to the author, to seek them among his weaker— that is, his mere conventional—characters; in John Harmon, Lizzie Hexam, or Mortimer Lightwood; but we assuredly cannot find them among his stronger—that is, his artificial creations. Suppose we take Eugene Wrayburn and Bradley Headstone. They occupy a half-way position between the habitual probable of nature and the habitual impossible of Mr Dickens. A large portion of the story rests upon the enmity borne by Headstone to Wrayburn, both being in love with the same woman. Wrayburn is a gentleman, and Headstone is one of

the people. Wrayburn is well-bred, careless, elegant, sceptical, and idle:
Headstone is a high-tempered, hard-working, ambitious young schoolmaster. There lay in the opposition of these two characters a very good
story. But the prime requisite was that they should *be* characters: Mr
Dickens, according to his usual plan, has made them simply figures, and
between them the story that was to be, the story that should have been,
has evaporated. Wrayburn lounges about with his hands in his pockets,
smoking a cigar, and talking nonsense. Headstone strides about,
clenching his fists and biting his lips and grasping his stick. There is one
scene in which Wrayburn chaffs the schoolmaster with easy insolence,
while the latter writhes impotently under his well-bred sarcasm. This
scene is very clever, but it is very insufficient. If the majority of readers
were not so very timid in the use of words we should call it vulgar. By
this we do not mean to indicate the conventional impropriety of two
gentlemen exchanging lively personalities; we mean to emphasize the
essentially small character of these personalities. In other words, the
moment, dramatically, is great, while the author's conception is weak.
The friction of two *men*, of two characters, of two passions, produces
stronger sparks than Wrayburn's boyish repartees and Headstone's
melodramatic commonplaces. Such scenes as this are useful in fixing
the limits of Mr Dickens's insight. Insight is, perhaps, too strong a
word; for we are convinced that it is one of the chief conditions of his
genius not to see beneath the surface of things. If we might hazard a
definition of his literary character, we should, accordingly, call him the
greatest of superficial novelists. We are aware that this definition con-
fines him to an inferior rank in the department of letters which he
adorns; but we accept this consequence of our proposition. It were, in
our opinion, an offence against humanity to place Mr Dickens among
the greatest novelists. For, to repeat what we have already intimated,
he has created nothing but figure. He has added nothing to our understanding of human character. He is master of but two alternatives: he
reconciles us to what is commonplace, and he reconciles us to what is
odd. The value of the former service is questionable; and the manner in
which Mr Dickens performs it sometimes conveys a certain impression
of charlatanism. The value of the latter service is incontestable, and
here Mr Dickens is an honest, an admirable artist. But what is the
condition of the truly great novelist? For him there are no alternatives,
for him there are no oddities, for him there is nothing outside of
humanity. He cannot shirk it; it imposes itself upon him. For him
alone, therefore, there is a true and a false; for him alone it is possible

to be right, because it is possible to be wrong. Mr Dickens is a great observer and a great humorist, but he is nothing of a philosopher. Some people may hereupon say, so much the better; we say, so much the worse. For a novelist very soon has need of a little philosophy. In treating of Micawber, and Boffin, and Pickwick, *et hoc genus omne*,[1] he can, indeed, dispense with it, for this—we say it with all deference—is not serious writing. But when he comes to tell the story of a passion, a story like that of Headstone and Wrayburn, he becomes a moralist as well as an artist. He must know *man* as well as *men*, and to know man is to be a philosopher. The writer who knows men alone, if he have Mr Dickens's humor and fancy, will give us figures and pictures for which we cannot be too grateful, for he will enlarge our knowledge of the world. But when he introduces men and women whose interest is pre-conceived to lie not in the poverty, the weakness, the drollery of their natures, but in their complete and unconscious subjection to ordinary and healthy human emotions, all his humor, all his fancy, will avail him nothing, if, out of the fulness of his sympathy, he is unable to prosecute those generalizations in which alone consists the real greatness of a work of art. This may sound like very subtle talk about a very simple matter; it is rather very simple talk about a very subtle matter. A story based upon those elementary passions in which alone we seek the true and final manifestation of character must be told in a spirit of intellectual superiority to those passions. That is, the author must understand what he is talking about. The perusal of a story so told is one of the most elevating experiences within the reach of the human mind. The perusal of a story which is not so told is infinitely depressing and unprofitable.

[1] 'And all their kindred' (Horace, *Satires*, I, ii, 2).

132. From an unsigned review, *Westminster Review*

April 1866, n.s. xxix, 582–5

... The more we study Falstaff, Gulliver, and Sancho Panza, the more we perceive the art of the artist and thinker, but the closer we look at Mr Dickens's characters, the more we detect the trickery of an artificer. The more we analyse Mr Dickens, the more we perceive that his humour runs into riotous extravagance, whilst his pathos degenerates into sentimentality. His characters, in fact, are a bundle of deformities. And he appears, too, to value them because they are deformed, as some minds value a crooked sixpence more than a sound coin. He has made the fatal mistake against which Goethe warned the artist. Everything with him is not *supra naturam*, but *extra naturam*.[1] His whole art, as we shall presently show, is founded upon false principles. When we put down a work of his, we are tempted to ask, *Quid hinc abest nisi res et veritas?*[2] And if this criticism may be pronounced upon his master-pieces, what can be said of his later works? Our answer must be found in our remarks upon *Our Mutual Friend*. As it is impossible for us here to analyse the whole work, we must content ourselves with a chapter. To do this in most cases would be as absurd as to exhibit a man's tooth as a specimen of his eloquence. But Mr Dickens does not suffer by the process. He is seen to the best advantage in detached pieces. And we shall take the chapter on Podsnappery, both because it has been so much praised by Mr Dickens's admirers, and because, too, we think it is most characteristic of his mind. A more suitable character then Podsnap could not have fallen into Mr Dickens's hands. We fully sympathize with him in his hatred of Podsnappery. ... And Podsnap, if well conceived and well carried out, might have been the pendant to Pecksniff. But when we open the chapter, we find it an explosion of dulness. A number of automatons are moving about, who are all, so to speak, tattooed with various characteristics. There is the great automaton Podsnap, who is tattooed with a flourish of the right arm and a flush

[1] Not 'above nature' but 'outside nature'.
[2] 'What is lacking here, except matter and truth?'

of the face, and the minor automaton Mr Lammle, who is tattooed with ginger eyebrows. Dancers are called 'bathers,' and one of them is distinguished by his ambling. In fact Mr Dickens here seems to regard his characters as Du Fresne says the English did their dogs, *quanto deformiores eo meliores æstimant.*[1] The conversation is still more wonderful. Mr Dickens here alternates between melodrama and burlesque. If he is not upon stilts, he goes upon crutches. For instance, take the following—

> Said Mr Podsnap to Mrs Podsnap, 'Georgiana is almost eighteen.'
> Said Mrs Podsnap to Mr Podsnap, assenting, 'Almost eighteen.'
> Said Mr Podsnap then to Mrs Podsnap, 'Really I think we should have some people on Georgiana's birthday.'
> Said Mrs Podsnap then to Mr Podsnap, 'which will enable us to clear off all those people who are due.'

The only thing we can compare with this wonderful passage is 'Peter Piper picking pepper.' Let us now turn to the satire. Here are Mr Podsnap's views upon art—

> Literature; large print, respectfully descriptive of getting up at eight; shaving close at a quarter past, breakfasting at nine, going to the City at ten, coming home at half-past five, and dining at seven.

Now as these exact words are repeated under Painting and Music and again under Dancing, we must conclude that Mr Dickens thinks he has written something very effective. Our comment is that sham wit, like a sham diamond, can cut nothing. But then whilst some jokes are dull, others are old. Thus we read of an epergne 'blotched all over as if it had broken out in an eruption'. This poor old joke has broken out year after year amongst Mr Dickens's followers ever since Leech's woodcut of the page 'who had broken out into buttons and stripes.' The chapter [Book I, ch. xi] also contains a specimen of Mr Dickens's bad grammar. We are told that a certain meek young man 'eliminated Mr Podsnap's flush and flourish', whereas the context shows that he produced them. Such a blunder implies that Mr Dickens knows neither the meaning of the French *éliminer* nor the Latin *elimino*. He appears to confuse 'eliminate' with 'elicit'. . . .

Much of the caricature in the second volume is simply like trying to frighten a man by making faces at him; whilst in the chapter on 'The Voice of Society,' Mr Dickens becomes as angry as a woman, and as inconsistent as *The Times*. But more extraordinary than any chapter

---

[1] 'The uglier they are, the higher they value them.'

is the preface, or postscript, or apology, for we don't know what to call it, which closes the work. . . . His object in *The Mutual Friend*, he says, is to 'turn a leading incident to a pleasant and useful account,' that is to say, if we rightly understand him, to set forth the wrongs of Betty Higden and the Poor Law. Now, true art has nothing to do with such ephemeral and local affairs as Poor Laws and Poor Law Boards; and whenever art tries to serve such a double purpose, it is like an egg with two yolks, neither is ever hatched. This clause also contains the further fallacy that a work of art is best produced in a serial form. As Mr Dickens gives no reasons whatever for this opinion, we cannot possibly examine them . . . a novel is not the place for discussions on the Poor Law. If Mr Dickens has anything to say about the Poor Law, let him say it in a pamphlet, or go into Parliament. Who is to separate in a novel fiction from fact, romance from reality? If Mr Dickens knows anything of human nature, he must know that the practical English mind is, as a rule, repelled by any advocacy in the shape of fiction. And to attempt to alter the Poor Law by a novel is about as absurd as it would be to call out the militia to stop the cattle disease. . . .

133. James Hannay, from his *Course of English Literature*

1866, 321–3

Hannay (1827–73), journalist and novelist, was a friend of Thackeray, about whom he wrote biographical and critical studies.

Dickens has surpassed every contemporary in popularity—always an interesting thing about a man, and illustrative of his period. He typifies and represents, in our literary history, the middle class ascendancy prepared for by the Reform Bill; since Sir Walter Scott, with all his fame and his audience, represented mainly the tastes and ideas of the upper class and of the old world. This, which is Dickens's strength, is also his weakness; for his faults, such as they are, are the faults belonging to a too zealous and narrow worship of modern social ideas, and a too great neglect of established, classical, and ancient literature.

Dickens's forte is not his literal fidelity to life, as clumsy observers fancy, but the vividness of his imagination and sentiment. He is more true to *general* than to *individual* human nature: for while the power of the heart is felt all *through* his pages, many of his *portraits* are exaggerations and caricatures. Indeed, he depicts what used to be called 'humours' rather than persons, for the most part. If we turn over in our memories the figures in his fictions that most strike us, we shall find them more or less odd and irregular specimens of humanity. Each of them is an individual, and not (what Johnson observed of Shakspeare's characters) a *species*. The Wellers, Skimpoles, Cuttles, Dombeys, Pecksniffs are not unnatural at heart, but neither are they 'representative men,' such as occur in a few of the leading fictions of the world. Fielding's landlords and landladies might be found in the average inns of his time; a similar character in Dickens would be dressed in *his* livery and inseparable from the locality where *he* placed him, and yet human enough to be interesting too.

This fact marks the peculiar section of novelists to which Dickens belongs—the school of Sterne and Goldsmith, rather than the school of Fielding and Smollett. And hence, if he is read by a distant posterity, it will be for his own sake, rather than from their curiosity to know exactly what kind of men their ancestors were.

Imagination, then, is Dickens's real master-faculty. His descriptions, characters, humour, and pathos are equally marked with it; and it is always in the ascendant in his books. To be employed with most effect, however, Dickens's imagination requires to be employed on the real and material world, and to have a variety of stuff to work upon. He could not make an Ariel out of the mere air, though he could put wings on a very homely (in the eyes of other men) ballet-fairy, and raise *it* into the regions of imagination. . . .

134. [Edwin P. Whipple], from
'The Genius of Dickens',
Atlantic Monthly

May 1867, xix, 546–54

Reprinted in Whipple's *Success and its Conditions* (Boston, 1877).

... The nature of a writer determines the character of his creations. Though the terms 'subjective' and 'objective' now play a prominent part in criticism, and are good to indicate loose distinctions between classes of minds, it is important to remember that all creative minds are subjective,—that the subjective includes everything in nature and human life, which such minds vitally perceive, absorb into their own being, and literally make their own. In the case of Dickens, gifted though he be with wonderfully acute powers of external observation, this is obviously the fact, for no writer stamps the character of his genius on everything he writes more plainly than he. It is impossible to mistake his style, his method, his sentiment, his humor, his characters. His observing power, when extended beyond the range of his sympathies, becomes 'objective,' it is true, but ceases to be creative. In his genuine productions he not only embodies all that he knows, but communicates all that he is. The reality of his personages comes from the vividness of his conceptions, and not from any photographic quality in his method of representation. Observation affords him materials; but he always modifies these materials, and often works them up into the most fantastic shapes. Individuals, incidents, scenery, the very pavement of his streets, the very bricks of his houses, the very furniture of his apartments, are all haunted by Dickens's spirit. To read one of his romances is to see everything through the author's eyes; the most familiar objects take an air of strangeness when surveyed through such a medium; and the interest excited by the view has always in it a kind of fascination. We may dissent, criticise, protest, but still his clutch on our attention is never relaxed.

The weird imagination which thus penetrates his books is, however,

THE CRITICAL HERITAGE

but a single element of his nature, and indeed would not exercise so
great a charm over so many classes of readers, were it not connected
with such warmth of heart, keenness of observation, richness of humor,
and controlling common-sense. In the foundation of his character,
Dickens agrees with the majority of well-meaning mankind. He has no
paradoxes in morality to push, no scientific view of human nature to
sustain, no philosophy of society to illustrate, no mission to accomplish.
His general opinions are those of a man of sound sense and wholesome
sensibility; his general attitude towards the world is that of one who
sympathizes and enjoys; his test of worth is amiability; his cure for
every form of mental and moral disease is the old one of work. Nobody
ever thinks of going to his writings for light on such moral problems as
are opened in Hamlet and Faust. Intellectually, he seems incapable of
generalization. Judged by his feelings and perceptions, no writer of his
time seems so broad; judged by his philosophical comprehension of
laws, few seem so narrow. The whole system of English jurisprudence,
the whole machinery of civil administration, the most clearly demonstrated principles of political economy, appear worthless or mischievous
to his eyes, when his attention is concentrated on cases where they bear
hard on individuals. He looks on such matters as humane men of un-
generalizing minds ordinarily do, though he gives to their complaints
a voice which is heard wherever the English language penetrates. It
would be in vain to search his writings for a single example in which he
views a subject affecting the welfare of society in all its relations. The
moment his sense is shocked and his sensibilities stirred, his reflective
reason almost ceases to act, but his humor, his imagination, his conscience are all in motion. The systematic study of anything appears
abhorrent to his feelings; and even in such a matter as the training of
youth in the grammar of languages he has some of Susan Nipper's own
indignation at 'them Blimbers.' So entirely is he absorbed by the perception of the moment, that often in the same book we have characters
exhibiting exactly opposite traits, who are equally satirized. Thus in
Bleak House, Mrs Jellaby is a philanthropist who subordinates the care
of her family to the welfare of Borrioboola-Gha; but in that romance
we also have Mr Vholes, who is not less ridiculed and contemned for
subordinating the welfare of the public to the support of 'his three
daughters at home, and his venerable father in the Vale of Taunton';
and there is just as much reason why reformers should laugh at Mr
Vholes, as that conservatives should shake their sides over Mrs Jellaby.
The truth is, that no organizations and no persons can stand this method

479

of judging of them by their weak points, and the detection of weak points is of the very life of humorous perception.

And this limitation of Dickens's intellect is also a limitation of his power of characterization. Because his genius personifies everything it touches, we must not, on that account, accept all its products as persons. There are scores of people in his novels who are 'hit off,' rather than delineated, and are discriminated from the mere names of persons in didactic satire only by that strong individualizing tendency in his mind which makes him give consciousness even to inanimate things, and which one critic goes so far as to call 'literary Fetichism.' The professional guests at Mr Merdle's dinner-parties, in *Little Dorrit*, the Veneerings and their associates, in *Our Mutual Friend*, the company that gathers in Sir Leicester Dedlock's country-seat, in *Bleak House*, are three among twenty instances which must readily occur to every reader. In these he individualizes the tone of the society he satirizes, rather than attempts to portray its individual members. This habit of sketchy characterization, in which the character is only shown by some external peculiarity or vice of opinion, and his interior life is entirely overlooked, is the ordinary mode in which Dickens's satirical talent is displayed, and it overloads his books with impersonated sarcasms. All these, however, may be deducted from his stories, and still leave him richer in solid characterizations than any half-dozen of his contemporaries combined.

Indeed, when Dickens resolutely sets to work to embody an imagined nature, he ever makes it self-subsistent and inwardly as well as outwardly known. His joy in some of these creations is so great, he floods them with such an abounding wealth of life, he makes them so intensely real to his own mind, and treats them so much like companions of his heart's hilarious hours, that the very excess of his characterizing power has led some critics to deny to him its possession. He so surcharges his characters with vitality that they seem like persons who have taken something to drink; and, as they burst into the more decorous society delineated by other English novelists, there is a cry raised for the critical police. This exaggeration, however, is not caricature, for caricature never gives the impression of reality; and even in our age of historic doubts we have yet to learn of the sceptical Betsey Prig who had the audacity to doubt the existence and reality of Tony Weller, of John Willet, of Mr Squeers, of Richard Swiveller, of Edward Cuttle, of Sarah Gamp, of Wilkins Micawber, of Mr Boffin, or any other of Dickens's quaint specimens of human nature which he has overcharged with humorous vitality. Dickens caricatures only when his special object is to satirize; and the characters which illustrate his satirical genius we have already admitted to have no real natures. In his true province of characterization, he is certainly peculiar, for his personages are not only original but originals. As a general thing, he does not develop his characters, but conceives them in their entirety at once, and the situations and incidents in which they successively appear simply furnish occasions for their expression. Their appearance, opinions, manners, and even their phrases, he makes identical with their natures. He gives a queer application to the transcendental principle that 'the soul does the body make,' and supplies an external peculiarity for every inward trait. Beings which have no existence out of his own mind, he yet sees them in their bodily shape and motions as clearly as he sees his familiar acquaintances. Their unconscious actions are recorded with the accuracy of a witness who testifies under oath. He was evidently near Miss Brass when that grim spinster was questioned as to the plot in which she and her brother had been engaged, and noticed that, before she answered, she 'took two or three pinches of snuff, and, having by this time very little left, travelled round and round the box with her forefinger and thumb, scraping up another.' Most observers of Mr Squeers's habits when drunk would have been satisfied with stating that he went to bed with his boots on; but Dickens adds,—'and with his umbrella under his arm.' When Uriah Heep is present, we are not only constantly reminded that he is "umble,' but we are forced to note 'the snaky undulation pervading his frame from his chin to his boots,' 'his shadowless red eyes, which look as if they had scorched their lashes off,' and the frequency with which he grinds 'the palms of his hands against each other, as if to squeeze them warm and dry, besides often wiping them, in a stealthy way, with a pocket-handker-chief.' Indeed, so close and minute, as well as vivid, is Dickens's method of delineation, that it is impossible *not* to perceive and realize his creations. The critic who decries them as caricatures must be conscious, all the time, that they are more real to him than the carefully drawn characters he praises in other novelists of the time. Besides, they have a strange attraction to the mind, and are objects of love or hatred, like actual men and women. A large number of excellently drawn persons in modern fiction are uninteresting or commonplace in themselves, and hardly reward the labor expended on their delineation. In reading Anthony Trollope, for instance, one feels that here is an author who will never fail for subjects as long as the kingdom of Great Britain and

Ireland contains thirty millions of people, 'mostly bores,' and as long as he has his mental daguerreotype machine in order. But the poetical, the humorous, the tragic, or the pathetic element is never absent in Dickens's characterization, to make his delineations captivating to the heart and imagination, and give the reader a sense of having escaped from whatever in the actual world is dull and wearisome. A free abounding life also animates his pages; and the subtle scepticism as to the worth of existence itself, which infects Thackeray's narratives, and makes us close his most entertaining novels with a jaded feeling, is entirely absent from those of Dickens.

The plots of his romances, though frequently improbable in themselves, always seem probable in relation to the characters they are devised to bring vividly out. In the *Pickwick Papers*, the work which excels all its successors in riotous animal spirits, and in the power to communicate the sense of enjoyment, there is no plot, properly speaking, but only a succession of incidents. In *Oliver Twist* and *Barnaby Rudge* there is a strong infusion of the melodramatic element, which also appears less prominently in *The Old Curiosity Shop*, *Nicholas Nickleby* and *Martin Chuzzlewit*. The height of his power as story-teller was reached in *David Copperfield*, which is perhaps the best of his works in all respects, though *Dombey and Son* is written with more sustained *verve*. The plot of *Great Expectations* is the most cunningly devised of all, to stimulate and to baffle curiosity; while that of *A Tale of Two Cities* is the most tragically impressive; but neither equals *David Copperfield* in both interest and charm. *Hard Times* is essentially a satire, and the stories of *Bleak House*, *Little Dorrit*, and *Our Mutual Friend*, though they give occasion for the display of brilliant powers of narrative, description, and characterization, are somewhat lumberingly constructed. In all these successive books we observe a constantly increasing disposition to combine seriousness, both of moral and artistic purpose, with his whimsical, or comical, or pathetic incidents; his style grows more and more elaborate, more and more strewn with curious felicities of phrase, without losing much of its elasticity and ease; and if we miss something of the intoxicating animal spirits which gladden us in the *Pickwick Papers*, the loss is more than made up by the superior solidity and depth which thought and experience have given even to his humorous vein. The impression left by all his books is not only humane but humanizing. He is a philanthropist, both positively and negatively. He makes us interested in the most ignorant, credulous, foolish, or grotesque personages, simply by the goodness of heart he puts into them; and he makes us dislike the proudest, highest, most cultivated, and most beautiful, provided they are tainted with selfish indifference to their kind. His imagination so delights in lovely embodiments of disinterestedness, that we are sometimes tempted to class him with philanthropic sentimentalists, idly fondling images of excellence impossible of realization; but we read a few pages on, and find him the intrepid practical assailant of everything in life which he considers mean, base, exclusive, illiberal, unjust, and inhuman.

The humor, the pathos, the power of weird description, the power of tragic representation, in Dickens, seem but the efforts of one faculty of imagination, as it is directed by different sentiments, and acts on different materials. His superabundant humor, though quotable in sentences, depends for its full appreciation on a knowledge of the personages whence it comes and the incidents which call it forth. But it also has something odd, droll, unexpected, and incalculable in itself, which always marks it as the product of one peculiar and creative mind. When Mrs Crupp, David Copperfield's laundress, is asked by that young gentleman how she knows that love is the cause of his restlessness and bad spirits, she, slightly boozy with David's brandy, solemnly replies, 'Mr Copperfull, I'm a mother myself.' Venus, the artist in bones and amateur in skeletons, who lends such ghastly drollery to so many scenes in *Our Mutual Friend*, says to the impertinent boy who chaffs him: 'Don't sauce *me* in the wicious pride of your youth; don't hit *me*, because you see I'm down. You've no idea how small you'd come out, if I had the *articulating* of you.' When Jerry Cruncher, suspected by Mr Lorry of having passed his nights in digging up bodies for the doctors, is asked by his employer what he has been besides a messenger, he conceives the luminous idea of replying, 'Agricultooral character.' Mr Swiveller, informed by the Marchioness that Miss Brass calls him a funny fellow, does not consider the description derogatory to his dignity, because, he says, 'Old King Cole was himself a merry old soul, if we may put any faith in the pages of history.' Mr Vincent Crummles, wishing to do justice to the dramatic powers of Miss Henrietta Petowker, of the Theatre Royal, Drury Lane, closes his eulogy with the climax, 'She's the only sylph *I* ever saw who could stand upon one leg, and play the tambourine on her knee, *like* a sylph.' Mr Wemmick, when he invites Pip to dine with him, remarks: 'You don't object to an aged parent, I hope. Because I have got an aged parent at my place.' Mr Wegg charges Mr Boffin more for reading poetry to him than he does prose, for 'when a person comes to grind off poetry, night after night, it is but right he should expect to be paid for its weakening effect on his mind.' The 'young man of the name of Guppy,' in his memorable proposal of marriage to Esther Summerson, mentions as one of the advantages she would receive from the alliance, that his mother 'is eminently calculated to be a mother-in-law.' Mr Dennis, the hangman, when desirous of propitiating the sentimental and scraggy Miss Miggs, addresses her by the endearing appellation of 'My sugar stick.' The Augustus of Miss Pecksniff runs off on the morning of his intended marriage with that meek maiden, and, as soon as he is safe on board ship, writes to her: 'Ere this reaches you, the undersigned will be—if not a corpse—on the way to Van Diemen's Land. Send not in pursuit! I never will be taken alive!' And the immense humor of bringing a man of Mr Boffin's mind and experience into contact with such a book as Gibbon's *Decline and Fall* could only have occurred to Dickens. The blank wonder of such a guileless soul in listening to the recital of the crimes of the Roman Emperors is delicious. 'Wegg takes it easy,' he says, contemplatively, 'but, upon my soul, to an old bird like myself, these are scarers!' . . .

In regard to Dickens's serious characterization, and his dealings with the deeper passions, a distinguished French critic, M. Taine, has sneered at his respect for the proprieties, and contrasted his timidity with the boldness of Balzac and George Sand, especially in the analysis and representation of the passion of love. It is true that Dickens is excluded, like other English novelists, from the full exhibition of the allurements which lead to the aberrations of this passion; but what critic but a French one could have emphasized this deference for decorum, as if it shut him out altogether from the field of strong emotions? It does not exclude him from the minutest internal scrutiny and complete representation of the great body of the generous and the malignant passions. No Frenchman, even, could say that he was not sufficiently frank, exact, particular, and thorough in his exhibitions of pride, envy, fear, vanity, malice, hatred, duplicity, jealousy, avarice, revenge, wrath, and remorse. He has threaded the intricacies of these, with the penetration of a psychologist, while he has combined their action and varied their expression according to the modifications they receive from individual character. He has not won the reputation of being the most genial, pathetic, and humane of contemporary novelists by declining to describe some of the most tragic scenes that romancer ever imagined, and to represent some of the most hateful forms of humanity which romancer ever drew. Fagin, Noah Claypole, Ralph Nickleby, Arthur Gride,

Quilp, Dombey, Carker, Pecksniff, Jonas Chuzzlewit, Uriah Heep, Grandfather Smallweed, Rigaud, Rogue Riderhood, Bradley Head-stone, the ghastly and gushing Mrs Skewton, the weird and relentless Miss Havisham, could never have been shaped by a man who had not closely studied the fiercest, harshest, meanest, and basest passions of human nature, or who hesitated to follow intrepidly out their full logical effects on character and conduct. Often grotesque in his tragedy, he is never wanting in intensity and vividness. The chapter in *Oliver Twist* entitled 'The Jew's last Night alive', the description of Jonas Chuzzlewit's flight and arrest after his murder of Tigg, and the account of Bradley Headstone's feelings and reflections after his murderous assault on Eugene, are a few among many specimens of that minute and exact inspection of criminal spirits with which he so frequently both appalls and fascinates his reader. His antipathy to malignant natures contrasts strangely with the air of scientific indifference with which Balzac regards them; but it seems to give him even more power to penetrate into their souls. He is there as a biassed observer, detesting what he depicts; but his insight seems to be sharpened by his abhor-rence. They are altogether out of the pale of his instinctive sympathies, but yet he is drawn to them by a kind of attraction like that which sustains the detective on the track of the felon. If he errs at all, he errs in making them sometimes too repulsive for the purposes of art.

In the representation of love, Dickens is masterly only in exhibiting its affectionate side, and in this no contemporary, English or French, approaches him. His favorite heroines, Agnes Wickfield, Lucie Manette, Florence Dombey, Esther Summerson, Little Dorrit, Lizzie Hexam, are models of self-devoted, all-enduring, all-sacrificing affec-tion, in respect both to sentiment and principle. Illustrating as they do the heroism of tenderness, the most beautiful and pathetic scenes in his works draw from them their inspiration. It may be that they are too perfect to be altogether real; it may be that, as specimens of genuine characterization, they are inferior to Dora Spenlow, or little Miss Wren, or Bella Wilfer, in whom affection is connected with some kind of infirmity; but still, so intensely are they conceived, so unbounded is their wealth of love, that their reality, if questioned by the head, is accepted undoubtingly by the heart. Every home they enter is made the better for such ideal visitants, and the fact that they are domesticated by so many thousands of firesides shows that they are not the mere airy nothings of sentimentalizing benevolence, but have in them the sub-stance of humanity, and the attractive force of individual life. . . .

[Whipple refers to] many instances of that searching pathos of Dickens which irresistibly affects the great body of his readers, and even forces unwilling tears from hostile critics.

Why, then, it may be asked, is Dickens not to be ranked with the greatest masters of characterization? The objection as to his exaggerated manner in representing, we have found to be superficial, as his exaggeration rather increases than diminishes our sense of the reality of his personages; the real objection is to his matter. Great characterization consists in the creation and representation of great natures; and the natures which Dickens creates may be original, strange, wild, criminal, humorous, lovable, pathetic, or good, but they are never great. The material of which they are composed is the common stuff of humanity, even when it is worked up into uncommon forms. His individualizing imagination can give personality to everything coming within the range of his thoughts, sentiments, and perceptions; but that range does not include the realm of ideas, or the conflict and complication of passions in persons of large intellects as well as strong sensibility. The element of thought is comparatively lacking in his creations. Captain Cuttle is as vividly depicted as Falstaff, but the Captain would be a bore as a constant companion, while we can conceive of Falstaff as everlastingly fertile in new mental combinations, and as never losing his power to stimulate and amuse. Esther Summerson is, like Imogen, an individualized ideal of womanhood; but Esther's mind never passes beyond a certain homely sense, while Imogen is the perfection of imagination and intelligence as well as of tenderness, and we feel that, though she should live a thousand years, she would never exhaust her capacity of thinking, any more than her capacity of loving. But if Dickens's genius never goes beyond a certain limit of observation, nor rises above a certain level of thought, it has still peopled the imagination, and touched and gladdened the hearts, of so many thousands of readers, that it seems ungenerous to subject him to tests he does not court, and ungrateful to note the shortcomings of a power which in itself is so joyous, humane, and beneficent.

135. George Augustus Sala, from 'On the "Sensational" in Literature and Art', *Belgravia*

February 1868, iv, 449–58

Sala (1828–96), journalist and novelist, had been one of 'Mr Dickens's young men' on *Household Words*, and later wrote a biographical sketch and sundry reminiscences of him. *Belgravia* was edited by Miss M. E. Braddon, the leading 'Sensation Novelist', and Sala's article was one in a series on 'The Sensational in ...' this and that.

May I whisper in the reader's ear that the agitation against 'Romanticism' in literature and art in France was an exactly analogous outcry to that with which we are now deafened in England against 'Sensationalism'? But ere I take up that Cry of cries, and strive to show what a hollow, windy, worthless ululation it is, I wish to say a few words concerning a Cry as worthless, which immediately preceded it.

Mr Charles Dickens has enjoyed European, world-wide fame for thirty years. I have watched his career as narrowly as I have watched it admiringly; and I think I have read every line he has written, and have been enabled to trace with sufficient accuracy the successive phases of development through which his genius has passed, the mellowing of his faculties, the chastening of his style, and their gradual culmination into a splendid but sober afternoon of intellect. He is probably, at this moment, the best-known and the most deservedly popular author in the world; and in the very first number of the very next serial in the familiar old green cover which he might publish, we should probably be constrained to admit that there was something—in the way of character or of description—as good as, if not better than, Charles Dickens had ever done before. Yet, having a pretty retentive memory, and having been all my life more or less intimately connected with what are called 'literary circles,' I can perfectly well recollect that, in the year 1842—and we are now, I take it, in 1868—there was no commoner cry in 'polite society' than that 'Dickens had written him-self out.' ... 'Boz' wrote the *Old Curiosity Shop*, and pending the appearance of his next book the charitable souls reported that he had gone raving mad. He went to America, and the charitable souls put it about that he was dead. He wrote *Martin Chuzzlewit*, and the charitable souls declared that there was 'a great falling off in his style.' He went to Italy, and the charitable souls hinted that he had pawned his plate to raise funds for the voyage. There was no end to the malice of the charitable souls [who were so fond of repeating that 'Boz' had 'written himself out']. *Dombey, Copperfield, Bleak House, Hard Times*, the *Two Cities, Great Expectations, Our Mutual Friend*, were all asserted to be infinitely inferior to their predecessors; but somehow the man went on writing, and enlisting fresh tens of thousands of readers with every new book he wrote. ...

The only wonder is that the charitable souls have failed to discover that among modern 'sensational' writers Mr Charles Dickens is perhaps the most thoroughly, and has been from the very outset of his career the most persistently, 'sensational' writer of the age. There is sensation even in *Pickwick*: the 'Madman' and the 'Stroller's' story, the death of the 'Chancery Prisoner,' and the episode of the 'Queer Client,' for example. The *Old Curiosity Shop* is replete with sensation, from the extravagant pilgrimage of Nell and the old man to the death of Quilp. *Barnaby Rudge* begins with the sensation of an undiscovered murder, and ends with the sensation of a triple hanging and a duel *à mort*. In *Nicholas Nickleby* the end of Mr Ralph Nickleby and the shooting of Lord Frederick Verisopht by Sir Mulberry Hawk are sensational enough to suit the strongest appetite. And the murder of Tigg Monta-gue by Jonas Chuzzelwit; and the mysterious husband of Miss Betsy Trotwood in *David Copperfield*; and the convict millionaire in *Great Expectations*; and the grinding of the 'National Razor' in the *Tale of Two Cities*; and Monks's confession, and the murder of Nancy, and the death of Sykes, in *Oliver Twist*; and finally, the spontaneous combustion in *Bleak House*; and the tumbling down of the house in *Little Dorrit*; and Mr Carker's death in *Dombey and Son*. Are not all these pure 'sensation'?

When the charitable souls had found out that the rocket-and-stick cry was growing stale, they discovered that Mr Dickens, being a young man with a thoroughly new style, had become the founder of a new school, and that he had for his disciples many young men whose intellects were growing with his growth and strengthening with his strength; although at that necessary distance which should always in the subordination of mind, separate Master from Scholar . . . so, when Mr Dickens started *Household Words*, and successively gathered round him as contributors such young men as James Hannay, Blanchard Jerrold, Robert Brough, Walter Thornbury, and, later, John Hollings-head, the cry was raised against these gentlemen that they were each and all 'slavish imitators of Dickens'—mere clients and convenient men of the great patron. This Cry died out as these young gentlemen grew middle-aged, and found that they could do something for themselves. For a while there was rather a cessation in literary Cries. . . .

136. R. H. Hutton,
'Mr Dickens's Moral Services to Literature',
Spectator

17 April 1869, xlii, 474–5

Clearly by R. H. Hutton, editor of the *Spectator* (see No. 144). Some phrases are repeated in essays known to be his.

. . . We doubt if there ever were so great a humourist in the world before, Aristophanes and Shakespeare not excepted. But . . . it is singular how very little of passion there is in him. There is more passion in Charles Lamb, there is infinitely more passion in Dr Johnson, than in Dickens. It is true that his melodramatic efforts are often very effectively worked up,—that the murder of Mr Tigg in *Martin Chuzzlewit*, for instance, and the craven panic of Jonas Chuzzlewit, show considerable power, but it is anything but the power of true passion; it is the power of melodrama consciously adding stroke after stroke to the desired effect.

That Dickens's moral influence has been, on the whole, healthy and good we heartily believe. It has been certainly profoundly humane. The hatred of cruelty diffused through the wonderful picture of Dotheboys'

Hall is alone sufficient to earn him the gratitude of all English-speaking peoples. The feeling expressed towards a different kind of cruelty, that of Steerforth the seducer, in *David Copperfield*, is equally sincere, though less effective. And the hatred of cruelty is not more keen than the contempt for hypocrisy in the narrower sense,—such hypocrisy as Pecksniff's, or even mere pompous humbug like Podsnap's,—but here the humourist not unfrequently swallows up the moralist, and his delight in the grand incoherency of human nature often overpowers his scorn for falsehood. Still, the last moral service we should think of ascribing to Dickens's literary influence would be the diffusion of a genuine reverence for absolute sincerity and realism. The great writer himself falls into the most mawkish and unreal sentimentalism. Half the geniality which is supposed to be Mr Dickens's great merit is the most vulgar good-humour of temperament,—a strong disposition to approve the distribution of punch and plum-pudding, slap men heartily on the back, and kiss pretty women behind doors. . . . But the gospel of geniality is better than the caressing sort of praise lavished on spoony young men and women simply because they are spoony, in those multitudinous passages tending to excite nausea, of which the type is the blessing pronounced over Ruth Pinch because she frequents the fountain in the Temple, is in love with John Westlake, and makes a rumpsteak pie with some deftness. Mr Dickens has brought people to think that there is a sort of piety in being gushing and maudlin,—and this is anything but a useful contribution to the morality of the age. His picture of the domestic affections . . . seems to us very defective in simplicity and reserve. It is not really English, and tends to modify English family feeling in the direction of theatric tenderness and an impulsiveness wholly wanting in self-control.

In one word, it seems to us that Mr Dickens's highest and lowest moral influences arise from the same cause, his wonderful genius for caricature. All vices arising from *simple* motives he makes contemptible and hideous,—avarice, cruelty, selfishness, hypocrisy, especially religious hypocrisy. But then he has a great tendency to make the corresponding virtues ludicrous too, by his over-coloured sentiment. The brothers Cheeryble always seem to be rubbing their hands from intense brotherly love; the self-abandonment of Tom Pinch is grotesque; the elaborate self-disguise of Mr Boffin as a miser in order to warn Bella Wilfer of her danger, is an insult to both the reason and conscience of the reader; and Mr Dickens's saints, like that Agnes in *David Copperfield* who insists on pointing upwards, are invariably detestable. His morality concentrates itself on the two strong points we have named, a profound horror of cruelty and a profound contempt for humbug; but Mr Dickens has no fine perception for the inward shades of humbug,— relaxed and cosseted emotions.

His greatest service to English literature will, after all, be not his high morality, which is altogether wanting in delicacy of insight, but in the complete harmlessness and purity of the immeasurable humour into which he moulds his enormous stores of acute observation. Almost all creative humourists tend to the impure—like Swift and Smollett, even Fielding. On the other hand, there are plenty of pure humourists who are not creative, who take the humour out of themselves and only apply it to what passes, like Charles Lamb and Sydney Smith. But Dickens uses his unlimited powers of observation to create for himself original fields of humour, and crowds grotesque and elaborate detail around the most happy conceptions, without ever being attracted for a moment towards any prurient or unhealthy field of laughter. Thus, as by far the most popular and amusing of all English writers, he provides almost unlimited food for a great people without infusing any really dangerous poison into it. In this way, doubtless, he has done us a service which can scarcely be over-estimated. . . .

137. George Stott, from 'Charles Dickens', *Contemporary Review*

January 1869, x, 203–25

The *Wellesley Index* (i, 1105) suggests that this George Stott is probably the clergyman, born 1814–15 and educated at Oxford, where he became a Fellow of Worcester College in 1839.

Whether or not Mr Dickens will be popular a century hence is a question quite impossible to decide, and therefore very unprofitable to discuss. Very few books of one age are really *popular* in the next—read, that is, by the many, and not merely cherished by the few; nor is it often easy to fix on the particular quality which has kept them afloat, when so many other, and not unfrequently, to a critical taste, worthier craft have, as far as general appreciation goes, sunk hopelessly beneath the waves of time. But whether our great-grandchildren do or do not read Mr Dickens, they will all the same have to recognise that their great-grandfathers certainly did. Let them form what judgment they please on the fact, there it will be, distinct and undeniable. On the annals of English literature, during at least half of this nineteenth century, he has written his name in broad and ineffaceable characters. ... One who had never opened a book of Mr Dickens's would still, if he kept *au courant* with what was going on around, have to recognise him as one of the great literary facts of the age. As such he is worthy of careful investigation. To have laid hold of the mind of his time as he has done is, limit it and qualify it as we may, no slight achievement. On *a priori* grounds we should say that it necessarily implies the presence in him of something original, and striking, and his own—in a word, of genius. Nor, in our judgment, does experience contradict this natural presumption. In spite of all his imperfections and faults, his manifold sins of commission as well as of omission, we still hold him to be

emphatically a man of genius. He is not thereby excused; far otherwise. . . .

There is a preliminary question that may be asked of Mr Dickens,
as of all artists whatever their degree. Is he artist only, or moralist as
well? . . . He has a Theory of Life; he has strong though vague and
uninstructed notions upon what he considers certain abuses and wants
in our political and social system; he is, in his own way, an ardent
reformer. And his convictions have, from the first, impressed themselves as motive principles on his books. Nearly every one has even
partaken of the nature of the political essay. Witness the attacks on the
law and lawyers in *Pickwick* and *Bleak House*; on workhouse administration in *Oliver Twist* and *Our Mutual Friend*; and on the management
of public business in *Little Dorrit*. Whether he is right or wrong in these
is not to our present purpose; what we maintain is, that in all his novels
Mr Dickens has a distinct and conscious moral aim which inspires and
dominates over the narrative. Of course we have not to deal with a
hand that will drive home the lessons it wishes to convey by violent and
clumsy *tours de force*. The bad boy will not casually meet a lion and be
eaten up alive; and the good boy will not light upon an old pot full of
guineas whilst virtuously cultivating his garden. But while George
Eliot weaves her stories without seeming anxiety as to their moral
effect—the lesson lies ready to hand if we care to draw it, but is not
sought after; with Mr Dickens the doctrines are not only latent in the
stories, they are their formative principle—the stories are built up so as
to body them forth to best advantage. It is no more than justice to say
that this is generally done with the hand of a master—so well done that
it can hardly be seen to be done at all. Mr Dickens's skill in construction
is so great that he blinds all eyes not on the watch to the trick and artifices to which he has recourse to bring about the desired results, the
unnaturalness of the atmosphere in which he habitually makes us
dwell.

That Mr Dickens, having a doctrine to preach as well as a story to
tell, should, as an artist, be, as we certainly consider him, an Idealist,
not a Realist, is no more than natural. Nevertheless, the assertion may
well sound startling. The bulk of his characters, it may be said, are
invariably ordinary, common-place people—trades-people, clerks, and
artizans, and their wives and families; his scenes are laid in places familiar to every one; and his plots turn on incidents of every-day life. If he
does not paint reality, then who does? But the difference lies not in the
subject-matter of the representation, but in style of treatment. Here,

again, it is a question of more and less. All art is, and must be, idealization. A mere copy of the facts of nature or of human life, in so far as
it was possible, which it would be only to a very limited extent, would
seem unlike them. . . .

Now the similarity which presents itself on the surface between Mr
Dickens's methods of treatment and those of the realists is so striking,
that it is no wonder that he should usually be numbered among them.
His minuteness and elaborateness of detail; the pains he takes to make us
form some sort of picture of his characters; and the prominence with
this view given to Mr Dombey's cravat, Captain Cuttle's glazed hat,
Mrs Gamp's umbrella, and Mr Wilfer's curly hair; the tricks, and
mannerisms, and oddities of phrase he is so fond of assigning to them—
all seem to stamp him as of the class who seek to reproduce that which
is as nearly *as* it is as possible, rather than of those who would show
some element of human nature at its most complete development, freed
from the incongruities and hindrances which in actual life would be so
likely to hang about it and cramp its action. Nevertheless we are
persuaded that an idealist he is. For, if looked into, this carefulness about
details, and accessories, and colouring, will be found to have the form
of realism without the power thereof. It seems at first sight to spring
from that anxious endeavour after *vraisemblance*, which is the mark of
realism. But further investigation shows that the realism is illusory;
that we are introduced to a state of things quite inconsistent with fact—
a world peopled by grotesque impossibilities. . . .

. . . All honour to Mr Dickens's great constructive power. Merely as
stories, his novels are generally excellent; and when content to rely for
his effects on his *vis comica*, he is at no loss for incidents and situations
exquisitely amusing, and adapted to bring out just those features of the
actors he wishes us to look at. But for pictures of life!—why *Box and
Cox*[1] itself, with its two heroes habitually occupying the same room,
and only by the merest accident discovering one another's existence, is
hardly more ludicrously extravagant. What do we meet with in
Pickwick but a funny fairyland? And we believe that it is just because
this is so, and that here Mr Dickens has given his genius the fullest
scope, that the general verdict, with which we altogether agree, places
it at the head of his works. That it is utterly unlike any actual state of
things is of course obvious; so is a pantomime, and none the worse for
that. From a realistic point of view it is a tissue of absurdities and impossibilities, but as a certain kind of idealism it is very nearly perfect.

[1] One-act farce by John Maddison Morton, 1847.

494

All that the ingenuity of man can get out of puppets, Mr Dickens succeeds in getting; but then comes the limit. When he abandons the field of farce for loftier aims, where its methods are inapplicable, he at once makes us sensible of his deficiencies. Success requires the employment of tools over which he has a most imperfect mastery, or none at all, and the result naturally is failure—failure often so absolute and unequivocal, as to tempt one in moments of uncontrollable irritation to ignore his many excellences, and pronounce him—how unjustly, we are well aware—as, after all, nothing more than a consummate literary charlatan.

The causes of this curious mixture of success and failure—of striking merit and glaring imperfection, in Mr Dickens's productions, are not far to seek. We have already partly indicated them in characterizing his genius as akin to that of the caricaturist and the farce-writer, but the point requires a fuller elucidation. We have said that his realism is illusory; we may now add that his idealism is arbitrary. He seeks to produce the effects of idealistic art by idealizing that which is not legitimately susceptible of idealization at all, or, at any rate, to more than a very limited extent. Mr Dickens works from the eye, not the imagination. He creates, to borrow a phrase of Mr Carlyle's, 'from the clothes inwards,' not 'from the heart outwards.' In power of observation he is a giant: one would say that every scene he has witnessed, every company he has mixed in, has stamped its characteristics on his mind as available artistic material. In this sense he certainly knows men: he can 'reckon them up,' like his own Mr Bucket; but this is rather the knowledge of a sharp detective than of a philosopher. But mere observation, however quick a sense it may give for the peculiarities of individual men, affords no general imaginative insight into human nature; and this is Mr Dickens's stumbling-block, inasmuch as such insight is indispensable to all idealism other than grotesque. . . .

The general drift, then, of our previous remarks is, that Mr Dickens, though he can succeed in idealizing the grotesque, fails in higher efforts, through the limitation both of his knowledge of, and imaginative sympathy with, human nature, and the insufficiency and unsuitableness of his methods in an unfamiliar field. An illustration may, perhaps, best show our meaning. We will take one of his most ambitious attempts—Mrs Dombey. She is neither comic, nor, like the general run of his women, a mere unmeaning angel of beauty and goodness. The subject required to be treated after the manner of the higher school of art: with all the pains which Mr Dickens has evidently bestowed upon it, how has he succeeded? Is Edith Dombey as impressive and effective as he meant her to be? Do we get any clear idea of her? ... Mrs Dombey is a mere enigma; her action inexplicable and arbitrary, dependent wholly on the *sic volo, sic jubeo*[1] of Mr Dickens. . . . He fails here because he is on unknown ground. He has not really seized the meaning of his own creation. He has endowed her with qualities that could hardly coexist, and he does not understand their action—does not feel, for instance, that *no* consideration for herself or any one else would lead such a woman to submit to the degradation of holding confidential intercourse with a man like Carker, when she saw through him and what he was driving at. And he knows no better way of expressing the passions that were boiling and surging within her, than by putting into her mouth declamation painfully suggestive of the heroine of a transpontine melodrama. The passions are a sealed book to Mr Dickens; to get the effect of them, he can only exaggerate language.

This indifference to motive—this want of sense of its importance on which we have just been commenting, so characteristic as it is of the manner of farce—is a very marked feature in Mr Dickens. He does not feel it incumbent on him to *account* for his characters. As long as the scene is shifted often enough, and the 'business' of the piece does not flag, he seems to think his audience should be satisfied. He requires to be read with well-nigh as complete a submission to his guidance as the *Arabian Nights*. . . . [Stott analyses old Martin Chuzzlewit, to demonstrate this point further.] There is a wide field from which we might cull further examples to the same effect, but *ex uno disce omnes*.[2] *Bleak House*, however, is too striking an instance to be passed over without a word. Why should Mr Tulkinghorn, whose time was valuable, give himself so much trouble to find out Lady Dedlock's secret? Why should she fear his divulging it, when he could gain nothing, and might lose much by so doing; and when, if it had been divulged, it need not have affected her position unless she had chosen? Her excessive alarm is unintelligible; as unintelligible as her walking—she, a delicately-nurtured woman—in bad weather the greater part of the way to St Albans and back, without any particular rest or refreshment, one day, and spending the next wandering about the streets of London.[3] Why did Hortense,

---

[1] 'I will this, I insist upon it' (Juvenal, *Satires*, vi, 223).

[2] 'From one, learn all the rest' (Virgil, *Aeneid*, ii, 65–6).

[3] Mr Dickens apparently entertains very curious notions about the walking powers of ordinary people. Thus in *Pickwick*, the male guests at the wedding at Dingley Dell are

the French waiting-maid, take off her shoes, and walk home barefoot through the wet grass? Why did she murder Mr Tulkinghorn? Why — but to what purpose multiply questions which no man may answer? We have said enough, we think, to justify our estimate of Mr Dickens as no psychologist; and without psychology, success in the higher walks of idealization is unattainable.

It is pleasant to turn to the brighter side of the picture, and express some of the admiration which Mr Dickens, with all his shortcomings, cannot fail to inspire. It seems to us that hardly sufficient justice has been done to the great constructive power displayed in his stories considered merely *as* stories—as novels of incident, without regard either to their *vraisemblance* or to the methods to which he has recourse to bring about his effects. It has been rather the fashion to treat them as merely pegs to hang characters on. . . .

Now there is none of this looseness of construction in Mr Dickens. As well framed stories, perhaps there are no better models than some of his earlier and greater novels—*David Copperfield, Martin Chuzzlewit,* or *Dombey and Son.* This part of the work shows the conscientious labour characteristic of the true artist. There is no hurry, and no bungling. If the fulness and careful workmanship of his plots is contrasted with the poverty of incident, the sketchiness and slovenliness which disfigure the works of so many who yet are strong where he so signally fails, the critic may well say, *Cum talis es, utinam noster esses!*[1] What might not Mr Dickens have been if to his many natural gifts he had added culture; if he had spurned popularity, and resolve to aim at nothing short of perfection! . . .

Mr Dickens's pathos we can only regard as a complete and absolute failure. It is unnatural and unlovely. He attempts to make a stilted phraseology, and weak and sickly sentimentality do duty for genuine emotion. The result is that when he would move us most deeply he is apt to become rather a bore. Hard-hearted as it may sound, we must confess to having found little Paul Dombey and little Nell and Tiny Tim exceedingly tiresome, and to have been glad to be rid of them on any terms. The subject is too insignificant for the treatment it receives.

---

made to take a five-and-twenty mile walk, between breakfast and dinner, *to get rid of the effects of the wine.* Has he any definite idea of what a five-and-twenty mile walk means, to men not in training? or the kind of preparation for it afforded by an over-dose of champagne? See also the pedestrian exploits of Eugene Wrayburn, when engaged in tormenting the schoolmaster, Bradley Headstone, in *Our Mutual Friend.* [Stott's footnote.]

[1] 'When you are thus, would that you were ours!'

Even as sentimentalism the art is a failure from being so much over-done. Mr Dickens sets himself to work to makes us cry just as openly and deliberately as to make us laugh, but his resources for producing the two effects are anything but equal. The pathos is 'stagey;' it lacks simplicity, grace, dignity. Mr Dickens cannot make sorrow beautiful, and does not seem to have realised that if he failed in doing this he ran a great risk of making it vulgar. Not all the 'damnable iteration' with which he dwells on the woes of his Florence Dombey, and Esther Summerson, and the like, saves them from appearing utterly silly and common-place young women. In truth, we should doubt if he has more than a faint understanding and appreciation of the beautiful. To art, for anything that he shows, one would say he was insensible. He can see nothing more in pictures than the subject represented, and clearly regards music only as 'tunes.' Nor does he seem to have much love for scenery: when he introduces it, it is generally transformed and coloured by some grotesque fancies as a means of adding to the effect of the situation he is evolving. Mere *prettiness* he can appreciate, and such charm as lies in the sight of order and plenty and comfort, but not beauty. His few attempts in this direction sound affected and conventional. Hence he is much more successful when painting emotion as shown by comic characters. There is something touching, we are quite ready to grant, in the almost dog-like fidelity and devotion of Sam Weller to his master. The reason is plain enough: pathos in comic characters need not be beautiful, and a few blots and incongruities rather add to the effect. But when he tries higher flights, he misses his mark. Mr Dickens is no doubt entitled to the credit of making weak people, women, and children, cry copiously; but we do not think there is a single passage in his writings which a pure and cultivated taste would pronounce beautiful.

But if Mr Dickens is insensible to beauty, he is no less so to intellectual excellence, and the aims and pursuits of intellectual men. We can hardly fail to be struck by the marked absence in him of anything like loftiness of thought. Not only has he no reverence for abstract speculation, or learning, or statesmanship, he does not seem to believe that there *are* such things, or that they are more than shams, disguised with fine names. He has, as was said of him long ago, just that smattering of law which a clever attorney's clerk might pick up,—an acquaintance with common forms and technicalities,—but no insight into its spirit. To him it is simply a system of chicanery and 'Wiglomeration' devised for the ruin of mankind. Politics, again, are but a struggle for place, pay, and the means of providing for poor relations at the expense of the country, between Doodle on the one side and Coodle on the other—an affair with which no man of sense and honesty can have any possible concern. This ridiculous travesty does not spring from any cynical contempt for political differences on Mr Dickens's part. It is due, as it seems to us, partly to an almost feminine incapacity for grasping abstract notions; partly to sheer ignorance. Mr Dickens's range of thought and experience has manifestly been limited, and he has been very little indebted to the wisdom of others. This is, no doubt, the cause in no small measure of his striking originality. It is no more than natural that he should show no signs of having imitated or been influenced by writers whom he had never read. In all his works there is hardly a quotation or an allusion except occasionally from Shakespeare and the best known parts of the Bible. And, as we before had occasion to remark, imagination does not help him where observation fails. What lies beyond the limits of his own experience he neither understands nor cares for. Theology, philosophy, science, history, seem all closed books to him; he is quite content that they should be, and, to all appearance, thinks his ignorance of such unmeaning rubbish very much to his credit. That his instincts are generous and kindly, and revolt from baseness and cruelty, this of course we grant most readily; but we can think of no writer of mark who shows a more uninstructed mind, or on whose judgment on any question involving mastery of facts, or breadth of view, or critical acumen, we should set less store. For good breeding and refinement he exhibits a very decided contempt, nor, we are bound to admit, if the specimens he has given of these qualities really express his idea of them, without just cause. He seems incapable of creating a gentleman. . . .

With all this ignorance, and prejudice, and narrowness of mind, it is plain how little qualified Mr Dickens is for that *rôle* of social reformer which he is so ambitious of filling. We are sorry to remark that his later novels show a growing tendency in this direction, and suffer much thereby. Surely Mr Dickens's claims to distinction in his own line are quite enough to allow him to forbear from meddling with what he does not understand, and darkening counsel by words without knowledge.

Mr Dickens, however, does not confine himself to ignoring most of the leading influences which have made the world what it is. He has something to give us in their stead. Though he has not expressed his views in any connected form, and we have to piece them together as best we may, still a sort of theory of life as it should be may be found in his writings without much difficulty, by any one who will take the trouble to look for it. We shall, perhaps, best define it by saying it is an expansion of the idea of Christmas—of Christmas as seen in vision by Mr Dickens, and described as follows:— [Quotes from *Pickwick*, ch. xxviii.] It is a gospel of geniality that Mr Dickens sets himself to preach; the feelings and sympathies supposed to be evoked by the annual holiday are to be the ruling principles of life, the model keeper of Christmas, our guide and example. Joviality and high living; benevolence, good humour, and good fellowship—*sic itur ad astra*.[1] There should also be a sprinkling of tender regrets for the dead and the absent—just enough to subdue part of the picture with a pleasing shade of darker colouring. Such is Mr Dickens's Utopia. It is easy to see then why learning, and culture, and sagacity, and subtlety of understanding, and wit and eloquence meet with such slender recognition at his hands. What have these to do with an ideal social system, where every man best fulfils his end by a general readiness to shake hands and clink glasses with every one else? Intellect is only admissible as represented by medical men, engineers, and skilled artizans, in whom it shows itself directly concerned in ministering to the relief of man's estate. Schoolmasters too, we suppose, must have a place in the system; for Mr Dickens would certainly have every one possess the rudiments of education, and he seems rather to approve of a knowledge of foreign languages. But beyond purposes of immediate practical utility he would appear to consider learning rather a waste of time. It does not make us happier or kinder-hearted; it may even lead to fastidiousness as to our company, and an indisposition to that hearty, instinctive way of getting at the right and the wrong of everything, which is so much the safest guide in settling great questions. So political economists, scholars, statesmen, lawyers, *et hoc genus omne*,[2] may make up their minds to burn their books, and be abolished as pretentious nuisances. We really do not think we have been exaggerating. Mr Dickens has very possibly not fully grasped the bearing of the doctrines he has laid down in one part of his works and another; but if he had the power to reform the world according to his own principles, the result would be to turn it into the vulgar Arcadia we have been depicting—fit habitation only for those benevolent but eccentric elderly gentlemen, virtuous artizans, and gushing young ladies on whom his warmest admirations are lavished.

---

[1] 'That is the way to the heavens' (Virgil, *Aeneid*, ix, 641).
[2] 'And all their kindred' (Horace, *Satires*, I, ii, 2).

All that gives interest to life, and makes it worth the living, would be gone. Can Mr Dickens really think that the ideal of humanity is attained in his Tom Pinches, and Esther Summersons, and Millies, and Dots? Though wearisome by reason of much silliness, they are estimable people in their way; but a world in which they, and their like, were the presiding influences! It would, indeed, require nothing short of that new birth unto imbecility which Mr Dickens is so fond of bestowing on his penitents, as Mr Dombey and Mr Gradgrind, to fit one for admission into such a paradise of fools. . . .

OBITUARY TRIBUTES, 1870

Under the heading 'A Household Tribute to Charles Dickens', *The Times* of 16 June 1870 printed a letter from Elihu Burritt: 'I propose to collect as many of the newspaper notices of his death . . . as I may be able to obtain; also as many allusions to his life and character made in the pulpits of different denominations on the following Sunday as can be procured from their authors.' Such a collection, from all over the world, would 'prove, by new evidence, that Charles Dickens's name is a household word to all the great families of mankind.' Burritt seems not to have published his collection, but it (or another such compilation) is happily preserved in the Henry E. Huntington Library, San Marino (MS 32410–11), and provides impressive evidence of the affection and respect in which he was internationally held. The 'household', 'family' and 'friend' notes recur in dozens of them: 'Men seemed to have lost, not a great writer only, but one whom they had personally known; who was the friend of them and of their families' (Benjamin Jowett, sermon in Westminster Abbey, 19 June 1870, in his *Sermons, Biographical and Miscellaneous* (1899), 275). The lamentation was general, at all ages and many levels of literacy, as well as all over the world. Shortly after Dickens's death, one of his sons was recognised by a cabbie. 'Ah! Mr Dickens', he said, 'your father's death was a great loss to all of us—and we cabbies were in hopes that he would soon be doing something to help us' (Henry Fielding Dickens, *Recollections* (1934), 61). Elsewhere this son recalled that to walk with him in the streets of London had been 'a revelation; a royal progress; people of all degrees and classes taking off their hats and greeting him as he passed' (*Memories of my Father* (1928), 17). 'Dickens dead?' a coster-monger's girl in Drury Lane was heard to exclaim. 'Then will Father Christmas die too?' (epigraph to 'Dickens returns on Christmas Day', in Theodore Watts-Dunton's *The Coming of Love, and other Poems* (1899), 191). At the other end of the social scale, Queen Victoria, who had very recently met him, recorded in her diary: 'He is a very great loss. He had a large loving mind and the strongest sympathy with the poorer classes. He felt sure that a better feeling, and much greater union of classes, would take place in time. And I pray earnestly it may' (11 June 1870, *Letters, 1862–78*, ed. G. E. Buckle (1906), ii, 21).

Obituary tributes inevitably commented upon this universal appeal, and tried again to explain it. The peaks of his achievement were again identified (usually *Pickwick* and *Copperfield*), and his social and political influence was assessed. The moral decency of his sentiments, situations, and vocabulary was often mentioned again, as a cause for rejoicing and a reason for his being read by everyone in the family. A recurring critical question was the quality of his pathos. 'Essayists of a *Saturday-Review* type of mind' had charged him with mock-sentimentality; but, asserted William Mackay, this reflected badly upon them: 'That man must, indeed, have a mind either thoroughly bedimmed with conceit, or entirely degraded with more enormous vices, who can see nothing tender and touching in the narrative of the deaths of Paul Dombey or Little Nell, and who rises unaffected from their perusal' (*New Monthly Magazine*, July 1870, cxlvii, 91).

For other comments on Dickens's death, see above: Carlyle (No. 59), Trollope (No. 95), Ruskin (No. 125).

138. Unsigned article, 'The Death of Mr Charles Dickens', *Daily News*

10 June 1870, 5

... It is not easy to realise at this moment how Mr Dickens will be missed. He was without any exception or any chance of approach the most popular author of the time. He was emphatically the novelist of the age. In his pictures of contemporary life posterity will read, more clearly than in any contemporary records the character of our nineteenth century life. They will see us as we are, in our strength and our weakness, with all our social sores, and all the healing influences exerted to cure them. But Mr Dickens has not merely shown us to posterity, he has shown us to ourselves. His genial satire, his kindly and gentle humour, his hearty love of human nature, and his reverence for everything that is good and true, have all been exerted to make us think better of our neighbours, and more humbly of ourselves. In all his works there is a high moral aim, and we may surely add, a high moral teaching. There are few men who have written so much as Mr Dickens, and there can be none who, having written so much, could so truly look back upon their writings and feel that there was no line they would wish to blot. Mr Dickens was the one writer everybody read and everybody liked. His writings had become classics even during his lifetime. They are suited alike to all classes, and have been as welcome in the cottage as in the country house, in the Far West of America, and in the Australian bush as in our English homes. More than any other writer he has been the home favourite. People who never read any other novels, read Mr Dickens's; many of his favourite characters are household words among us. Who has not laughed at Mr Pickwick and Sam Weller; or cried over little Little Nell or Paul Dombey; or formed good resolutions in company with Old Scrooge or Tony Veck? Even for the innocent pleasure, the genuine enjoyment, Mr Dickens has given to the generation which has had the privilege of reading his works as they have appeared, he would deserve to be reckoned among the benefactors of mankind. But the enjoyment Mr Dickens has given us has left no dissatisfaction behind it. A high and pure moral tone breathes through all his writings, his scorn is only for meanness, his contempt only for pretence, his denunciation and hatred only for the wrongs which oppress us and the evils which scourge us. For everything which tends to elevate the low or enlighten the ignorant, or rescue the outcasts of society, he not only had an enthusiastic admiration, but could communicate it to his readers. There were thousands to whom the reading of the *Christmas Carol* made a new era, or on whom the picture of the Brothers Cheeryble exerted the influence of a good example, or who learned in Mr Dombey or Mr Skimpole to see the undesirable features of their own characters. Mr Dickens was in fact a moralist; his novels were the parables of a teacher, and all that he taught was so taught that the youngest might learn. And now, alas! the pleasant, happy, genial teacher is no more. . . . His eloquent tongue and more eloquent pen will no longer rebuke our vices, or commend to us the charities of life; his satire will no longer shed its vivid light upon our favourite follies to make us ashamed of our littleness, and ashamed of ourselves; nor his broad and widening sympathy fall like gentle rain upon the dusty arena of our social conflict to cool the heat and purify the air. . . .

[A biographical sketch follows. The writer refers to Dickens's being founder editor of the *Daily News*.]

It was his desire to make this journal what it has ever since endeavoured to be—the unswerving and consistent advocate of Liberal measures at home and abroad. . . .

Mr Dickens was, however, not only a successful author. No hearer of his readings could doubt that he had faculties which would have led to similar success in other pursuits. As an amateur actor he was, perhaps, almost without an equal, and even his reading of his own writings gave evidence of his wonderful power of impersonation. He was also an admirable and effective speaker, excelling in that peculiarly difficult form of eloquence which is appropriate to festive occasions. He was probably the best after dinner speaker in England. . . . His capacity for business was as great as his power of speech and of writing; in fact, he was a clear-headed, prompt, vigorous man, of pure feelings and lively sympathies, who used his great powers under a sense of responsibility for the public good. He leaves a literary example which will be of lasting value to the morals and literature of his country. . . .

139. From an unsigned leading-article, *The Times*

10 June 1870, 9

Reprinted in *Eminent Persons: Biographies reprinted from The Times*, Vol. I, 1870–1875 (1892), 8–11. The obituary notice (*The Times*, 11 June, 9) is reprinted also, pp. 12–15. 'The death of Charles Dickens found *The Times* quite unready with a biographical sketch. Mr Edward Walford, author of *The County Families*, wrote the notice for *The Times* between midnight and four in the morning, with messengers at his elbow all the time to carry the MS. to the printer. Mr Walford has written the majority of the long obituary articles for *The Times* since 1868' (Joseph Hatton, *Journalistic London* (1882), 80–1). Whether Walford also wrote this leading-article is doubtful. For Walford (1823–97), see *D.N.B.*

... The loss of such a man is an event which makes ordinary expressions of regret seem cold and conventional. It will be felt by millions as nothing less than a personal bereavement. Statesmen, men of science, philanthropists, the acknowledged benefactors of their race might pass away, and yet not leave the void which will be caused by the death of DICKENS. They may have earned the esteem of mankind; their days may have been passed in power, honour, and prosperity; they may have been surrounded by troops of friends, but, however pre-eminent in station, ability, or public services, they will not have been, like our great and genial novelist, the intimate of every household. Indeed, such a position is attained not even by one man in an age. It needs an extraordinary combination of intellectual and moral qualities to gain the hearts of the public as DICKENS has gained them. Extraordinary and very original genius must be united with good sense, consummate skill, a well-balanced mind, and the proofs of a noble and affectionate disposition before the world will consent to enthrone a man as their unassailable and enduring favourite. This is the position which Mr DICKENS has occupied with the English and also with the American public for the third of a century. If we compare his reputation with that of the number of eminent men and women who have been his contemporaries, we have irresistible evidence of his surpassing merits. His is a department of literature in which ability in our time has been abundant to overflowing. As the genius of the Elizabethan age turned to the drama, so that of the reign of VICTORIA seeks expression in the novel. There is no more extraordinary phenomenon than the number, the variety, and the generally high excellence of the works of fiction in our own day. Their inspirations are as many as the phases of thought and social life. They treat not only of love and marriage, but of things political and ecclesiastical, of social yearnings and sceptical disquietudes; they give us revelations from the empyrean of fashion and from the abysses of crime. Their authors have their admirers, their party, their public, but not the public of DICKENS. It has been his peculiar fortune to appeal to that which is common to all sorts and conditions of men, to excite the interest of the young and the uninstructed, without shocking the more refined taste of a higher class and a more mature age. Thus the news of his death will hardly meet the eye of an educated man or woman who has not read his works and who has not been accustomed to think of him with admiration and friendly regard. . . .

We are inclined to think that [*Pickwick*], the first considerable work of the author, is his masterpiece; but, whatever may be the world's decision on this point, it can hardly be doubted that the prize must be given to one of the group of fictions which he produced within the first ten or twelve years of his literary life. *Nicholas Nickleby* teems with wit, and the characters, with one or two exceptions, are life-like in the extreme. *Oliver Twist* everybody knows; *Martin Chuzzlewit* is excellent, and the American portions are not only the most amusing satire that has been published in the present age, but fill us with wonder that the peculiarities of thought, manner, and diction of a people should be so surely seized and so inimitably expressed by a young writer who had been only a few months in the country.

. . . When young in years he showed the mental balance of an experienced writer. And yet what freshness and vigour there was in those wonderful serials which, about the time the present QUEEN came to the throne, changed the popular literature of the day! When that young unknown author appeared on the field he was at once hailed as the new chief of popular fiction. It is a long time ago, but our older readers will remember the excitement caused by the *Pickwick Papers*. . . . This popularity they fully deserved. They are among the few books of the kind that one can return to again and again; or having opened at any page can read straight on, carried forward by a sense of real enjoyment. The best characters stand out in real flesh and blood, and in this respect are superior to those of THACKERAY, which, though excellently designed, show too much the art of an able sketcher from artificial types. For this reason, THACKERAY, though he has always maintained his hold on the London world in which his personages figure, has never come near to DICKENS in popularity with the great mass of the people. The characters of DICKENS have been accepted by all men's discernment as the true reflection of human nature; not merely of manners or costume. . . . Perhaps a more signal proof of the genius of DICKENS is the manner in which his style and diction have penetrated into the ordinary literature of the country. So much has become naturalized and is used quite unconsciously that it is only by re-reading those earlier works which most impressed his contemporaries that one becomes aware how great has been their influence.

We cannot conclude these remarks without paying a tribute to the moral influence of the writings of which we have spoken. Mr DICKENS was a man of an eminently kindly nature, and full of sympathy for all around him. This, without being paraded, makes itself manifest in his works, and we have no doubt whatever that much of the active benevolence of the present day, the interest in humble persons and humble things, and the desire to seek out and relieve every form of misery is due to the influence of his works. We feel that we have lost one of the foremost Englishmen of the age. There are clever writers enough, but no one who will take the place, literary and social, that belonged to him. It was but the other day that at the Royal Academy Banquet he made the best speech of the evening, in matter, language, and manner. His powers as an actor are well known, though, of late years, they have been only exhibited in the narrower field of public readings. He was made to be popular, and, even irrespective of his literary genius, was an able and strong-minded man, who would have succeeded in almost any profession to which he devoted himself. We can but condole with the public on his sudden and premature loss.

140. From an unsigned article, 'The Death of Mr Dickens', *Saturday Review*

11 June 1870, xxix, 760–1

Wilhelm Dibelius (*Charles Dickens* (Leipzig, 1916), 493) attributes both this, and the article on Dickens in the *London Quarterly Review*, January 1871 (see No. 154), to G. Fraser. Two George Frasers are known to have been active in literary journalism around this time: which, if either, of these wrote which, if either, of the 1870–1 items cannot be ascertained.

. . . The characters of Mr DICKENS are a portion of our contemporaries. It seems scarcely possible to believe that there never were any such persons as Mr PICKWICK and Mrs NICKLEBY and Mrs GAMP. They are to us not only types of English life, but types actually existing. They at once revealed the existence of such people, and made them thoroughly comprehensible. They were not studies of persons, but persons. And yet they were idealized in the sense that the reader did not think that they were drawn from the life. They were alive; they were themselves. And then the atmosphere in which they lived was one of such boundless fun, humour, and geniality. No book ever was or will be like *Pickwick* in this respect, and Mr DICKENS wrote it when he was twenty-four. Age did not certainly improve Mr DICKENS's powers, for, as must necessarily happen, his works were very unequal, and some of his later works were his worst. But it is astonishing to think what an extraordinary wealth of creations of character of the first order of excellence he has left behind him. With the single exception of *Little Dorrit* there is not one of his numerous stories that has not touches of the master-hand and strokes of indisputable genius. To a degree unequalled by any other novelist except perhaps SCOTT, he had the power of making the reader feel thoroughly at home in an imaginary world, and of being and living and moving in it naturally. No club of a benevolent old gentleman and a few friends ever went on as the Pickwick Club is represented to have gone on, just as no knights and barons and Jews and foresters ever went on as their representatives go on in *Ivanhoe*. But the world of the Pickwick Club and the world of *Ivanhoe* seem not merely entertaining and natural, but actually existing to the reader. And of all great novelists Mr DICKENS was far the easiest to read and re-read. *Pickwick* and *Martin Chuzzlewit* are exactly as entertaining the fortieth time they are read as the first. The goodness of the fun, the delightfulness of passages we know thoroughly well in them, takes us continually by surprise, just as FALSTAFF is always better if we open the book than we recollect him to be. And then the characters of DICKENS are drawn from such a wonderful variety of sources. Without vulgarity they give a body to what we may imagine to be the varieties and habits of character in sets of persons with whom we are unacquainted. SAM WELLER and his MARY are the expressions of all that a boots and a housemaid are capable of being; and as to the United States, all that can be said or thought of that portion of the life led there which comes within the sphere of a novelist is to be found in *Martin Chuzzlewit*. The characters of Mr DICKENS exist almost entirely in what they say, and this is the highest and rarest form of the art of the novelist. BALZAC, for example, who on the whole has no superior and few equals in the composition of fictions, scarcely depends on the dialogue at all for giving a clue to the character; whereas SAM WELLER, DICK SWIVELLER, and Mrs NICKLEBY are scarcely known to us at all except by what they say. It is this peculiarity which perhaps has made the writings of Mr DICKENS so popular with persons of all classes, and all types and degrees of education. The sayings of the characters in them are recollected, but these sayings are themselves the constituent elements of the characters, and thus the characters of themselves become to the public a part of the public itself.

. . . It is useless to pretend that the later writings of Mr DICKENS are equal to his earlier writings. After he was thirty-five he published nothing of first-rate excellence except *David Copperfield*. . . . But even if it is admitted that his range of creation was proved to be exhaustible, yet it is equally true that of characters neither sublime nor vulgar he had a greater range than any other novelist ever had. It is scarcely an exaggeration to say that twice as many of such characters can be named from the writings of Mr DICKENS as can be named from the writings of any one of even the first writers of fiction. And then in all the best of his works the story is so good throughout. There is so little that is dreary or dull or poor, and the aspect of things presented to us is so pleasant and cheerful. The workhouse of OLIVER TWIST, the den of FAGIN, the school of Mr SQUEERS, are all lighted up with the drollery and oddity and rapid touches of quaint vitality that enter into the description. In his later works, Mr DICKENS became too minute in his descriptions, and he was often minute in describing what had no power to interest the reader. But in his best novels the amount of life and movement that is put into each chapter is wonderful. . . .

Mr DICKENS, however, was to himself always something more than an artist. . . . Much of the liberalism of the present day in England, and of its peculiar type, is due to Mr DICKENS. So far as the exclusiveness of religious sects has died away in England, its decay may fairly be in a large measure attributed to the circulation of Mr DICKENS's works in the families even of the most exclusively religious people. That there is fun and goodness in all sorts of persons, high and low, and even very low, was a theme on which he loved to dwell, and which he brought home to all his readers by the example of the characters he delineated. There was also in all his works an unvarying respect for the sanctity of home and the goodness of women. To be liberal, to be fond of fun, and to like a happy, innocent home, was the type of excellence he has set before the generation which he has largely influenced; and possibly his sentimentalism, while it wearied some of his more fastidious readers, may have helped to produce a good moral effect on the wider world which he attracted and enlightened. He was also a just man, a hater of petty tyranny, of the despotism of beadles, and the recklessness of the lower herd of schoolmasters. His evident sincerity of purpose gave a kind of dignity to his writings, and took away from them all air of coming from a man who was merely making merry to get money from the public. On one or two occasions he set himself to attack abuses of a larger kind, the existence of which filled him with real pain and grief; and even if he exaggerated the slowness of Chancery and the ineptitude of the Circumlocution Office, it was clear that he was attacking real abuses, which practical men since he wrote have striven hard to remedy, and satisfactory remedies for which are being only slowly and with great difficulty discovered. Lastly, he was an artist who was not only fond of his art and proud of his success in it, but who looked on art as imposing duties and responsibilities on those who devote themselves to it. . . .

141. From an unsigned leading-article, *Sunday Times*

12 June 1870

. . . What need can there be to tell the history of CHARLES DICKENS? His life is a part—intimate, affectionate, vital—of the experience—we might almost say the consciousness of his generation. His thoughts, sympathies, aims, have become graciously and grandly intermingled with its thoughts, sympathies, and aims. He lived not only before our eyes, but in our very hearts. He not only had a place there, but a home —a home, too, which he continually occupied, and which his presence made too glad and happy for memory to lose or eloquence explain. And now he is dead, and the home is darkened, and there reigns solemn stillness, broken only by sobs of unavailing woe. The gladness is turned to grief, and all the household mourns. For CHARLES DICKENS was the dear friend of men and women and children, even as he was the strong warm friend of humanity. The creations of his genius were our companions, and by them he told us how rich he was in the knowledge of human nature, how genuine was his humour, how kindly and universal his sympathies, how patient and noble his art. Those creations have an actual life of their own. They, too, have warm breath and radiant vitality. They have been our sweet familiar companions—dear to our hearts themselves, and making their parent dearer for the elevated pleasures they have afforded us. The CHEERYBLE Brothers, LITTLE NELL, TOM PINCH, DORA, PEGGOTTY, PICKWICK, and a crowd of other most human creatures, the product of a most human genius, seem now to gather about the soul, stricken with the mystery of the death of our friend their father, as though they were sensible of the dark shadow and participated in the solemn lamentation. They are as animated and as actual as he ever was; and now he is as incorporeal as they ever were. . . CHARLES DICKENS—the power, the teacher, the good friend, the great creator of more than a hundred beings who cannot die—is not dead. In those living beings he lives. By them he continues, and will through uncounted generations continue to influence mankind, softening the asperities of caste and class, redeeming poverty from shame, giving tenderness to compassion, suffusing justice with mercy, gently making the pietist ashamed of his hypocrisies, and stimulating all to broader charities, to more genuine nobleness, and more genial dignity.

And his power in the long future will be, even as in the past it has been, a power for good alone. We confess that we are old-fashioned enough to cherish a distinct veneration for that quality of moral elevation which marks all the productions of the great man whose removal from the world is now so universally and so bitterly deplored, and the absence of which from much of the fiction of our age, is one of its most melancholy phenomena. Even if it be granted that CHARLES DICKENS sometimes allowed his sentimentalism to become extravagant, not to say affected or morbid, and that his moral mannerism, if we may be permitted the use of such a phrase, occasionally became artificial, he never left on one of his pages the slur of corruption, or the blot of vicious impulse. His inspiration was ever pure. His thoughts and aims and sympathies were delicate, refined, *clean*. The tears and the laughter he drew from his readers were alike honest. He never made an apology for a bad passion, any more than he pursued its victim with unrelenting reproaches. As has been well said, he never wrote a line which his daughter would blush to read aloud in miscellaneous company—a fact which should teach the novelist and the dramatist that the nasty and the infamous are never necessary as elements either of interest or effect. . . .

142. Unsigned notice, 'Charles Dickens', *British Medical Journal*

18 June 1870, i, 636

How true to Nature, even to their most trivial details, almost every character and every incident in the works of the great novelist whose dust has just been laid to rest, really were, is best known to those whose tastes or whose duties led them to frequent the paths of life from which Dickens delighted to draw. But none, except medical men, can judge of the rare fidelity with which he followed the great Mother through the devious paths of disease and death. In reading *Oliver Twist* and *Dombey and Son*, or *The Chimes*, or even *No Thoroughfare*, the physician often felt tempted to say, 'What a gain it would have been to physic if one so keen to observe and so facile to describe had devoted his powers to the medical art.' It must not be forgotten that his description of hectic (in *Oliver Twist*) has found its way into more than one standard work, in both medicine and surgery (Miller's *Principles of Surgery*, second edition, p. 46; also, Dr Aitken's *Practice of Medicine*, third edition, vol. i, p. III; also several American and French books); that he anticipated the clinical researches of M. Dax, Broca, and Hughlings Jackson, on the connection of right hemiplegia with aphasia (*vide Dombey and Son*, for the last illness of Mrs Skewton); and that his descriptions of epilepsy in Walter Wilding, and of moral and mental insanity in characters too numerous to mention, show the hand of a master. It is feeble praise to add that he was always just, and generally generous, to our profession. Even his descriptions of our Bob Sawyers, and their less reputable friends, always wanted the coarseness, and, let us add, the *unreality*, of Albert Smith's; so that we ourselves could well afford to laugh with the man who sometimes laughed at us, but laughed only as one who loved us. One of the later efforts of his pen was to advance the interests of the East London Hospital for Children; and his sympathies were never absent from the sick and suffering of every age.

143. From an unsigned article, 'The late Charles Dickens', *Illustrated London News*

18 June 1870, lvi, 639

[Dickens was] one of those who had been thought of, by the most distant lovers of his writing, as an ever-welcome friend and companion of their leisure, amusing and soothing, delighting if not exalting, the mind in its most weary or languid mood; and one who seemed capable of adding without limit to its store of novel and original conceptions. For their novelty was a great part of their charm; and the readers of Dickens, who have read him up to this time, will henceforth lack that element of gratification, though it may be enjoyed by their children in the next age, to whom these books and the whole world will be new. Not only so; but we are deprived of the agreeable sense of being directly addressed by this man of genius, this man of feeling and intelligence. He used to invite us to sympathise with him, to see what he was seeing, and to share his present ideas and emotions; to put ourselves in his place as he put himself in the place of imaginary persons, and to laugh or to sorrow with them, as he was wont to do. He has done with us now, though we have not yet done with him.

His method of composing and publishing his tales in monthly parts, or sometimes in weekly parts, aided the experience of this immediate personal companionship between the writer and the reader. It was just as if we received a letter or a visit, at regular intervals, from a kindly observant gossip, who was in the habit of watching the domestic life of the Nicklebys or the Chuzzlewits, and who would let us know from time to time how they were going on. There was no assumption in general, of having a complete and finished history to deliver; he came at fixed periods merely to report what he had perceived since his last budget was opened for us. The course of his narrative seemed to run on, somehow, almost simultaneously with the real progress of events; only keeping a little behind, so that he might have time to write down whatever happened, and to tell us. This periodical and piecemeal form of publication, being attended by a fragmentary manner of composition, was not at all favourable to the artistic harmony of his work as a whole. But few persons ever read any of Dickens's stories as a whole for the first time; because every one was eager to enjoy the parts as they were printed, going on a twelvemonth or twenty months in due succession, and growing in popularity as the pile of them increased. The obvious effect was to inspire all his constant readers—say, a million or two—with a sense of habitual dependence on their contemporary, the man Charles Dickens, for a continued supply of the entertainment which he alone could furnish. He was personally indispensable to them, as a favourite actor might be to the inveterate playgoers of a former age, who lived upon their Garrick or their Kemble. If each of his stories had appeared complete in three octavo volumes, with the lapse of a couple of years between one work and another, the feeling of continual dependence on the living author would have been less prevalent among us.

... Dickens is always a great writer; but he is a most successful creator in the department of quaint figures and odd habits, curious bits of human life picked up in corners of the world, often torn and trampled into fantastic shapes, and soiled with the mire and soot of London streets. In this department he excels Balzac and Victor Hugo, while he resembles the latter, and differs from the former, in his respect for the humanity clothed in such a ragged garb, of such uncomely aspect and ungainly demeanour. The peculiarities of certain classes in the lower regions of London society, where the outward life, the facial expression, the gestures, the speech, and the manners of many people, as well as their dress and dwellings, betray the effects of habit in their peculiar occupations, were studied by Dickens, as those of Paris by Balzac. In the description of the inferior commercial boarding-house, its landlady, and its lodgers, which opens *Le Père Goriot*, we find the counterpart of Mrs Todgers's frowzy and greasy establishment behind Monument-yard. In the bar-room of a small public-house, in the back shop of a petty tradesman; in vulgar places of amusement—the gallery of a theatre or a free-and-easy concert-saloon, where smoking and drinking go on with the singing and dancing; in the police court, among the crowd of defendants or complainants, their loquacious witnesses or sympathising comrades, through whom the attorney's clerk and the official constable elbow their way to find the person they want; in the swarm of a parasitical population, honest and dishonest, some respectably and usefully industrious, some pretentious impostors or vicious mendicants, some downright swindlers or thieves, all clinging to the body of a rich old city and sucking it for their daily food, or teasing it with their inveterate tricks; here it was that the lively curiosity of Dickens and his keen enjoyment of the ridiculous delighted to revel. He loved to exhibit the warts and wens, the distorted toes and fingers, the bald or scrubby patches of hair, the broken teeth, the crooked back, the voice cracked or hoarse, the bleared and blinking eyes, the pimple on the nose, the halting awkwardness in the deportment, the sordid stains on the apparel of our hard-living race; but he did this in the spirit of compassion. He did with the pen what some of the old Dutch painters—Ostade, and Teniers, and Jan Steen—had done with the pencil, revealing not only the picturesque effects, but the interesting moral characteristics, that lie in the commonest and even the basest forms of plebeian life. This was a reaction, about thirty-four years ago, as many of us can well remember, against the high-flown affectation of classic and aristocratic elegance which pervaded the romances of Sir Edward Bulwer-Lytton. Just when Ernest Maltravers had posed himself in a sublime attitude of transcendental nobility, Mr Pickwick, of Goswell-street, in his gaiters and spectacles, with Sam Weller at his heels, toddled forward and took possession of the stage. The school of refined æsthetic idealism was broken up at once, having originated in the example and poetry of Byron, which had so much influence on the last generation. It has never since revived in England; for the ablest authors of our day—Charles Dickens, Thackeray, Antony Trollope, masters of the knowledge of English life; George Eliot and Kingsley, artists of romance; and the sensation story-tellers, who are clever and popular too—have kept within the realistic lines. By-and-by the fashion of our literature will, perhaps, undergo another change, which none of us can yet foresee. The humorous appreciation of vulgarity and eccentricity in our social world has been carried to its highest pitch. The supreme performer in this style was Dickens. In other styles he never equalled one or two of his contemporaries above named. He was inferior to Bulwer-Lytton, George Eliot, and Charles Kingsley, in the art of composing a narrative plot, and of preserving and enhancing its dramatic interest; while his perception of the delicate shades of character, the refined touches of sentiment, which belong to the comedy of polite life, to the intercourse of ladies and gentlemen with each other, was far below that of Bulwer-Lytton, Thackeray, or Trollope. . . . Dickens possessed as full command of all the resources of our language as Ruskin; and he could, when it suited his purpose, write with as much force and precision as Macaulay. A volume of 'elegant extracts' might be gathered from his works to exemplify the rules of idiomatic English prose composition. . . .

The very highest type of manly or womanly virtue, not mere good-humour, frankness, and generosity, but self-sacrificing devotion to duty, is often commended in his stories. It is ascribed to some of his characters; their actions are made to correspond with this description. But they have not the substantial reality of the persons animated by lower motives. Has he created one such character as that of Jeanie Deans, or Colonel Newcome, or Lily Dale, or Romola? for we need not go to the poets, to Tennyson, Browning, and Shakspeare, for pure specimens of the moral ideal in fiction; the novelists of our time have supplied them. Tom Pinch and his sister Ruth are represented as being very good indeed, and laughably simple; but where are the persons in these novels who are wholly deserving of our respectful esteem; who command the full measure of our reverent affection? Where is the prose Arthur, the blameless and fearless knight? Where is the knight, that is, the perfect gentleman, whose presence among us, diffusing around him the spirit of Christian chivalry, 'truth and honour, freedom and courtesy,' as old Chaucer has put it, is a prophecy of the happier future, and not only a want and wish of the present, or a romantic dream of some past age, when saints and heroes trod the earth? And where is the lady, worthy to be mated with his ideal perfection, the moral flower of womanhood, as he of manhood, lovely in her own nature, attired with all graceful accomplishments, as in the casket of beauty is inclosed the jewel of virtue? It is surely worth while for the writer of popular stories to create now and then a character of ideal moral excellence in a warm and breathing body of flesh and blood, and to set it handsomely upright, with no ugly stoop, or squint, or spot, but standing free from all ludicrous or pitiable associations, to win the homage of his readers to that which is eternally good, and true, and fair. This is what Dickens has not done to such an extent as he might. The satirist and burlesque humourist were stronger in him than the reflecting moralist. . . .

144. [R. H. Hutton], from
'The Genius of Dickens', the *Spectator*

18 June 1870, xliii, 749–51

Reprinted in Hutton's *Brief Literary Criticisms*, ed. Elizabeth M. Roscoe (1906), 48–58.

Hutton (1826–97), prolific writer on literary and religious topics, had edited the *National Review* with Walter Bagehot, 1855–64, and was joint-editor and part-proprietor of the *Spectator*, 1861–97. He wrote again about Dickens in the *Spectator*: 'The Dispute about the Genius of Dickens', 7 February 1874 (xlvii, 169–70, reprinted in *Criticisms on Contemporary Thought and Thinkers* (1894), i, 87–93), and in 'What is Humour?' (25 June 1870, xliii, 776–8) and 'Pathos' (13 August 1887, lx, 1082–3), both reprinted in *Brief Literary Criticisms*, 59–68, 75–80. See also Nos. 136, 152, 162, 164.

. . . What was the secret,—if it be possible in any brief way to describe the secret,—of a genius so rich to overflowing in the creation of English types of humour? Mainly it was, we think, due to three great literary gifts combined,—a sense of humour as delicate as Charles Lamb's, and much more inventive and active, which was at the basis of Dickens's genius, and by which he *sorted* his conceptions; a power of observation so enormous that he could photograph almost everything he saw; and, perhaps partly as the result of these two powers in combination, but partly, it may be, of some others, a marvellous faculty of multiplying at will, and yet with an infinity of minute variety, new illustrations of any trait, the type of which he had once well mastered. Indeed, just as the great mystery of physiology is said to be how a single living cell multiplies itself into a tissue composed of an indefinite number of similar cells, so the great intellectual mystery of Dickens's fertile genius was his power of reduplicating a single humorous conception of character into an elaborate structure of strictly analogous conceptions. His greatest successes have always been gained on types of some complexity, such as that smart, impudent, cockney, be it serving boy, or serving man, or adventurer, which is the basis of such characters as Bailey Junior's, Sam Weller's, Jingle's, and several others,—and his greatest failures have been made on attempts to convert individual peculiarities, like Mr Jaggers's habit of biting his thumb, or Mr Carker's of showing his teeth, into the key-note of a character. But take which of his books you will, from the first to the one of which the publication had only just reached its third number at his death, and you will find the same secret of success and failure,—the former, the secret of success, inexhaustible power of illustrating an adequately-conceived physical type of character, such as Mrs Gamp, or Mr Pecksniff, or Mr Squeers, or either of the Wellers, or Mr Winkle, or the Marchioness, or Miss Miggs, or Mr Toots, or Mrs Pipchin, or Noah Claypole, or Bradley Headstone, or Mr Venus,—the latter, the secret of failure, a monotonous repetition of some trait too individual to admit of any adequate variety, and which consequently becomes the mere incarnation of a bodily habit or trick, such as the Fat Boy, and Joe Willett, and the brothers Cheeryble, and Cousin Feenix, and Mr Jaggers, and 'the Analytical Chemist,' and a number of others. But whether a success or a failure, Mr Dickens's characters are invariably structures raised by his humour on a single physical aspect.

[Sam Weller, Mrs Gamp and others cited.]

... The great and unfailing wonder is how any novel-writer who gives so absolutely identical a tone to all the characters he conceives, manages to make them so full to overflowing of fresh vitality and infinite humour. No one ever gets tired of Dick Swiveller or Bailey Junior, or Mr Pecksniff, or Mrs Gamp, or old Mr Weller, or Fanny Squeers, or Mr Lillyvick, or Sawyer late Knockemorf, or Barnaby Rudge and his raven, or Simon Tappertit, or even of Jenny Wren. And it is marvellous that it should be so, for all these are always precisely consistent with the first glimpse we get of them; and with any genius less rich in variations on the same air than Dickens's we should be sick of them in no time.

But then no writer ever had the power which Dickens had of developing the same fundamental conception in so infinitely humorous a variety of form. Hunt through all Mrs Gamp's monthly-nurse disquisition, and you will never find there a repetition,—excepting always in those great landmarks of the conception, the vast selfishness and self-admiration, the permanent desire to have the bottle left on 'the chimley piece' for use 'when so dispoged,' and the mutual confidence between her and her mythical friend Mrs Harris. With these necessary exceptions there is not one single repetition of a speech or a maxim. The central cell, as we may call it, of the character has multiplied itself a thousandfold without a single echo of an old idea. The marvel of Dickens is the exquisite ease, perfect physical consistency, and yet wonderful variety of paths by which he always makes his characters glide back into their leading trait. His greater characters are perfect labyrinths of novel autobiographical experience, all leading back to the same central cell. Mrs Gamp, for instance, is barely introduced before she introduces also to the reader her great and original contrivance for praising herself and intimating decently to all the world the various stipulations on which alone she agrees to 'sick or monthly,'—that intimate friend whose sayings cannot be verified by direct reference to herself, because she is in reality only the reflex form of No. 1,—Mrs Harris. 'Mrs Gamp,' says this imaginary lady, as reported by Mrs Gamp herself, 'if ever there was a sober creetur to be got at eighteen-pence a day for working people and three-and-six for gentlefolks,—nightwatching,' said Mrs Gamp, with emphasis, 'being a extra charge, —you are that inwalable person.' 'Mrs Harris,' I says to her, 'don't name the charge, *for if I could afford to lay all my feller creeturs out for nothink*, I would gladly do it, sech is the love I bears 'em.' [*Chuzzlewit*, ch. xix]. But this, we need hardly say, is a great humourist's creation *on a hint* from human life, and not human life itself. Any actual Mrs Gamp no doubt might have invented sayings for actual friends of her own, but would never have indulged in the intellectual audacity of reproducing herself as her own best friend, and investing her with another name and a great variety of imaginary babies. And so, too, it is the great humorist, and not Mrs Gamp, who answers so generously for her willingness 'to lay all my fellow-creeturs out for nothink, sech is the love I bears 'em.' . . . The infinite number of avenues by which Mr Dickens makes Mrs Gamp, as Hegel would say, *return into herself*, and the absolutely inexhaustible number of physical illustrations all of the monthly-nurse kind by which she effects it, are the key-notes to his genius. . . . His power is like that of a moral kaleidoscope, all the various fragments of colour being supplied by actual experience, so that when you turn and turn it and get ever new combinations, you never seem to get away from actual life, but always to be concerned with the most common-place of common-place realities. All the while, however, you are really running the changes on a single conception, but with so vast a power of illustration from the minutest experience, that you are deceived into thinking that you are dealing with a real being. Of course, no man ever really pretended to be so scrupulously candid as Mr Pecksniff when he complained, 'I have been struck this day with a walking-stick, *which I have every reason to believe* has knobs on it, on that delicate and exquisite portion of the human anatomy, the brain;' [*Chuzzlewit*, ch. lii] nor was there ever any one so persistently desirous of finding disagreeable circumstances under which it would be a credit to be jolly, as Mark Tapley. This is the idealism of the author, idealism only disguised by the infinite resource of common physical detail with which he illustrates it. How little of a realist Dickens actually was in his creations of character, may be seen whenever he attempts to deal with an ordinary man or woman, like Nicholas or Kate Nickleby, or again David Copperfield, who is to us quite as little real as Nicholas Nickleby, even though intended, as has always been said, for the author himself. Mortimer Lightwood and Eugene Wrayburn, in *Our Mutual Friend*, are deplorable failures, and the worthy minor Canon in *The Mystery of Edwin Drood* promised to be so too. The infinite multiplication of detailed illustrations of a single humorous type has always been Mr Dickens's real secret of power. A realist as regards *human* nature, he never was at all.

... we do not believe that Dickens's pathos is by any means his strong side. He spoils his best touches by his heavy hand in harping on them. Even in the death of little Paul, a great deal too much is made of a very natural touch in itself,—the child's languid interest in the return of the golden ripple to the wall at sunset, and his fancy that he was floating with the river to the sea. Dickens is so obviously delighted with himself for this picturesque piece of sentiment, that he quite fondles his own conception. He used to give it even more of the same effect of high-strung sentimental melodrama, in reading or reciting it, than the written story itself contains.[1] We well remember the mode in which he used to read, 'The golden ripple on the wall came back again, and nothing else stirred in the room. The old, old fashion!...' [*Dombey*, end of ch. xvi]. It was precisely the pathos of the Adelphi Theatre, and made the most painful impression of pathos feasting on itself. We more than doubt, then, whether Dickens can be called a great master of pathos at all. There is no true lyrical, no poetic touch, about his pathos; it is, in the main, the overstrained pathos of melodrama. And that precisely agrees with our estimate of what he was greatest in. He could

[1] *The Story of Little Dombey*, one of Dickens's public readings, ended with the passage Hutton quotes.

always abstract any single trait of human life, and collect round it all sorts of natural physical details. Just so, he describes the pity excited by little Paul's death, and frames his death-bed, as it were, in those gradual changes from light to shade, and shade to light, which take up so much of the perceptive power of a dying child. Of course, however, in all Dickens's attempts to describe, he describes with the intensity of genius. No one can fail to feel horror at the description of Sikes's feelings as he wanders about with his dog after the murder of Nancy. In the delineation of remorse he is, too, much nearer the truth of nature than in the delineation of grief. True grief needs the most delicate hand to delineate truly. A touch too much, and you perceive an affectation, and, therefore, miss the whole effect of bereavement. But remorse when it is genuine is one of the simplest passions, and the most difficult to over-paint. Dickens, with his singular power of lavishing himself on one mood, has given some vivid pictures of this passion which deserve to live. Still this is the exception which proves the rule. He can delineate remorse for murder because there is so little limit to the feeling, so little danger of passing from the true to the falsetto tone. In general there is no delicate painting of emotion in Dickens. His love-passages are simply detestable. . . .

145. A. P. Stanley, from a sermon in Westminster Abbey

19 June 1870 (*Sermons on Special Occasions* (1882) 127–37)

Also printed as a pamphlet (1870), and in *Speeches, Letters and Sayings of Dickens*, ed. G. A. Sala [1870].
Stanley (1815–81), Dean of St Paul's, biographer of Dr Arnold, and prominent Broad-churchman, first met Dickens shortly before his death: see A. A. Adrian, 'Dickens and Dean Stanley', *Dickensian*, lii (1956), 152–6. Stanley was preaching from *Luke* xv, 3; xvi, 19–21 (the parable of Dives and Lazarus). Forster quotes further from this sermon (*Life*, 842): also from a sermon by the Bishop of Manchester (Dr Peter Frazer), *Life*, 762–3.

... By him that veil was rent asunder which parts the various classes of society. Through his genius the rich man, faring sumptuously every day, was made to see and feel the presence of the Lazarus at his gate. The unhappy inmates of the workhouse, the neglected children in the dens and caves of our great cities, the starved and ill-used boys in remote schools, far from the observation of men, felt that a new ray of sunshine was poured on their dark existence, a new interest awakened in their forlorn and desolate lot. It was because an unknown friend had pleaded their cause with a voice which ran through the palaces of the great, as well as through the cottages of the poor. It was because, as by a magician's wand, those gaunt figures and strange faces had been, it may be sometimes, in exaggerated forms, made to stand and speak before those who hardly dreamed of their existence.

Nor was it mere compassion that was thus evoked. As the same Parable which delineates the miseries of the outcast Lazarus tells us also how, under that external degradation, was nursed a spirit fit for converse with the noble-minded and the gentle-hearted in the bosom of the Father of the Faithful, so the same master hand which drew the sorrows of the English poor, drew also the picture of the unselfish kindness, the courageous patience, the tender thoughtfulness, that lie concealed behind many a coarse exterior, in many a rough heart, in many a degraded home. When the little workhouse boy wins his way, pure and undefiled, through the mass of wickedness in the midst of which he passes—when the little orphan girl brings thoughts of heaven into the hearts of all around her, and is as the very gift of God to the old man whose desolate life she cheers—when the little cripple not only blesses his father's needy home, but softens the rude stranger's hardened conscience—there is a lesson taught which touches every heart, which no human being can feel without being the better for it, which makes that grave seem to those who crowd around it as though it were the very grave of those little innocents whom he had thus created for our companionship, for our instruction, for our delight and solace. He laboured to tell us all, in new, very new, words, the old, old story, that there is, even in the worst a capacity for goodness, a soul worth redeeming, worth reclaiming, worth regenerating. He laboured to tell the rich, the educated, how this better side was to be found and respected even in the most neglected Lazarus. He laboured to tell the poor no less to respect this better part in themselves, to remember that they also have a call to be good and just, if they will but hear it. If by any such means he has brought rich and poor together, and made Englishmen feel more nearly as one family, he will not assuredly have lived in vain, nor will his bones in vain have been laid in this home and hearth of the English nation. . . .

146. From an unsigned notice, 'Charles Dickens', *Fraser's Magazine*

July 1870, n.s. ii, 130-4

... When the sad news was made public it fell with the shock of a personal loss on the hearts of countless millions, to whom the name of the famous author was like that of an intimate and dear friend.

For five-and-thirty years his keen observation and his exuberant and vivacious fancy had issued in an incessant bright stream of story-telling —a series of books readable beyond rivalry, describing his own time to itself in a new and striking style; heightening the familiar so as to give it an artistic impressiveness, enriching it with humour, softening it with sympathies, mingling shrewd sense with a fanciful picturesqueness so as to produce the most unexpected effects out of commonplace materials, and discovering many quaint and strange things lurking in the midst of everyday life.

A mere list of his fictitious personages would be testimony enough to his copiousness and variety, ... Perhaps of the many qualities that combined to produce his unrivalled success, not the highest but the most unmistakable and most telling is his constant flow of animal spirits—his vivacity, his clearness and *grip*. He excels in gay, voluble people; rejoicing to speak for Sam Weller, for the lively rogues Jingle, Montague Tigg, Smangle, or for the good-humoured insolvents, Mr Slum the poet, Dick Swiveller, or Wilkins Micawber. He delights to put his persons in active motion, walking, cricketing, skating, dancing, playing blindman's buff, and what not, and he revels in a stage-coach journey. There is abundance of eating and drinking, especially at Christmas, which figures itself as it were a smoking mountain of roast turkeys and plum puddings, irrigated with rivers of punch.

In fact—while impatient of time-honoured abuses and worn-out formulas, and pelting them with unmerciful ridicule—his tastes and modes of thought were essentially middle-class English. He was a Radical, it is true, but never obtrusively or wildly, and the reforms which he most desired were of a practical sort, aimed especially at the improvement of the condition of the working poor and their families....

In the ordinary intercourse of life his bright look, cheery grasp of hand, active and lively bearing, his tact and readiness in conversation, his hearty laugh, and ready sympathy, and his general *savoir faire*, made him, as will be easily conceived, widely popular. His intimate circle was, all things considered, perhaps a small one, and he seems to have taken pains to limit it, as a shrewd man who worked hard and liked his work, and who not only in his working but in his leisure hours pursued with determination and consistency his own natural bent.

His fondness for all matters theatrical was well known. He was himself the very prince of amateur actors, and in his readings his remarkable mimetic powers enchanted countless audiences on both sides of the Atlantic. In fact, a story of his is like a drama for the fireside, furnished not only with situations and dialogue, but with appropriate scenery, gestures, action, by-play; the author, scene-painter, stage-manager, and moreover the whole company, tragic and comic, male and female, from 'stars' to 'supers,' being one and the same skilful individual.

The figures impress one rather as impersonations than as persons. But how telling they are, and what a list of dramatis personae is that of the *Theatre National Charles Dickens!* . . . His way is to catch a type (and he has caught a wonderful number of distinct ones), grip it fast, put it into a number of appropriate situations, and illustrate by means of an endless play of fancies. His characters are all *humoristic*, so to speak. He has no developed tragic character, and no pathetic, but he often places his personages in tragic and pathetic situations, and makes a strong impression mainly by his own conviction and earnestness, and his thorough working-out of his intention. . . .

In landscape and still life description he excelled, seizing with firm grasp the characteristics of a room, a house, a village, a city, a wide prospect, any locality he selected for his scene. Many out-of-the-way nooks of London and bits of the rural scenery of England appear on his canvas with distinct outlines and effective colouring. In fact, he was an artist. He decided on the *effect* to be produced, chose his point of view, and worked on steadily in his own way. Keen observation of facts, humorous seizure and often grotesque exaggeration of the salient points, brilliant *quasi*-theatric expression of these; such was his method, instilled by nature, matured by steady practice. He studied the world around him—first and mainly the English world—at once as his repertory of characters and situations, and as furnishing the audience whom he desired to please.

As to his literary style, that was his own—striking, brilliant, not seldom odd, sometimes awkward, yet even then with its own sort of tact. He was artful and skilful, but never attained, and never seems to have sought to attain, the kind of art which conceals itself; a certain care and elaboration were never absent; he took his aim carefully (he was in dress and in every other respect the opposite of a negligent man) and usually hit the mark.

His tastes, as we have said, were strongly, though not blindly, middle-class British, and he was no wise ashamed of them. He made no pre-tence of caring for old pictures, or classic music, or poetry as a special thing. He enjoyed a brisk dance-tune, a simple song, and admired cheerful pictures like those of Frith, Stanfield, and Maclise. In literature he liked what most people like, in scientific matters he knew what most people know. He spent no thought on religious doctrines or religious reforms, but regarded the Sermon on the Mount as good teaching, had a regard for the village church and churchyard, and quarrelled with nothing but intolerance. In politics he took no side, but perhaps might be described as a practical, not at all a speculative, Radical, who desired to get rid of humbug and inefficiency in all departments, and to extend —not patronage, which he loathed, but—national justice and brotherly help to all honest working people, to secure them fair wages, fit leisure, good shelter, good diet, good drainage, good amusement, and good education for their children.

He had a deep pity, a deep sympathy (and no idle or barren one) for the poor, and especially the hardworking poor. He could indicate and emphasise the absurdities of their manner and speech, their awkward gestures, bad grammar, inelegant pronunciation, without one touch to feed the contempt of the most cynical or the most ill-natured hearer; and he inculcated at every moment, directly or indirectly, the lesson of brotherly kindness. We have spoken of his high and unflagging animal spirits—a nature ever brisk, cheerful, and animated; yet withal, he is from first to last thoroughly innocent, and addresses himself at the gayest, without effort, *virginibus puerisque*.[1] Neither has any satirist ever laughed at mankind so entirely without bitterness or ill nature.

The last seventy years in English literature form a period in which novel-writing has attained an unprecedented growth and influence. Now the most popular and most personally regarded novel-writer that ever handled pen is gone for ever, leaving no man like him in the world. . . .

[1] To maidens and boys (Horace, *Odes*, III, i, 4.)

147. Arthur Helps, from 'In Memoriam', *Macmillan's Magazine*

July 1870, xxii, 236–40

Helps (1813–75), Clerk to the Privy Council since 1860, knighted 1875, was a warm friend of Dickens during his later years. John Forster particularly commended this obituary appreciation (*Life*, 832) and silently stole or adapted some passages from it.

... There will be few households that will not desire to possess some portrait of Mr Dickens; but alas, how little can any portrait tell of such a man! His was one of those faces which require to be seen with the light of life. What portrait can do justice to the frankness, kindness, and power of his eyes? They seemed to look through you, and yet only to take notice of what was best in you and most worthy of notice. And then his smile, which was most charming! And then his laughter—not poor, thin, arid, ambiguous laughter, that is ashamed of itself, that moves one feature only of the face—but the largest and heartiest kind, irradiating his whole countenance, and compelling you to participate in his immense enjoyment of it. ...

It need hardly be said that his powers of observation were almost unrivalled; and therein, though it is a strange comparison to make, he used to remind me of those modern magicians whose wondrous skill has been attained by their being taught from their infancy to see more things in less time than any other men. Indeed, I have said to myself, when I have been with him, he sees and observes nine facts for any two that I see and observe.

As is generally the case with imaginative men, I believe that he lived a great deal with the creatures of his imagination, and that they surrounded him at all times. Such men live in two worlds, the actual and the imaginative; and he lived intensely in both.

I am strongly confirmed in this opinion by a reply he once made to me. I jestingly remarked to him that I was very superior to him, as I had read my *Pickwick* and my *David Copperfield*, whereas he only wrote them. To which he replied that I did not know the pleasure he had received from what he had written, and added words, which I do not recollect, but which impressed me at the time with the conviction that he lived a good deal with the people of his brain, and found them very amusing society.

He was of a commanding and organizing nature—a good man of business—frank, clear, decisive, imperative—a man to confide in, and look up to, as a leader, in the midst of any great peril.

This brings me to another part of his character which was very remarkable. He was one of the most precise and accurate men in the world; and he grudged no labour in his work. Those who have seen his MSS. will recollect what elaborate notes, and comments, and plans (some adopted, many rejected), went to form the basis of his works. To see those manuscripts would cure anybody of the idle and presumptuous notion that men of genius require no forethought or preparation for their greatest efforts, but that these are dashed off by the aid of a mysterious something which is comprehended in the word 'genius.' It was one of Mr Dickens's theories, and I believe a true one, that men differ hardly in anything so much as in their power of attention; and certainly, whatever he did, he attended to it with all his might. . . .

His love of order and neatness was almost painful. Unpunctuality made him unhappy. I am afraid, though, some people would hardly have called him punctual, for he was so anxious to be in time that he was invariably before time. . . .

He had the largest toleration. I had not intended to say anything about this works; but I must do so now, as I see that they afford a singular instance of this toleration. Think of this precise, accurate, orderly, methodical man depicting so lovingly such a disorderly, feckless, reckless, unmethodical character as that of Dick Swiveller, and growing more enamoured of it as he went on depicting! I rather think that in this he was superior to Sir Walter Scott, for in almost all Scott's characters there appear one or the other, or both combined, of Scott's principal characteristics, namely, nobility of nature and shrewdness. . . .

Mr Dickens's own kindness of nature is visible in most of his characters. He could not well get rid of that, as a general rule, by any force of fiction. Still there are a few characters, such as that of Jonas Chuzzlewit, in which he has succeeded in denuding the character of any trait belonging to himself.

We doubt whether there has ever been a writer of fiction who took such a real and living interest in the actual world about him. Its many sorrows, its terrible injustice, its sufferings, its calamities, went to his heart. Care for the living people about him—for his 'neighbour,' if I may so express it—sometimes even diminished his power as an artist; a diminution of power for which, considering the cause, we ought to love his memory all the more.

I have sometimes regretted, perhaps unwisely, that he did not take a larger part—or shall I say a more prominent part!—in public affairs. Not for our own sakes, but for his. Like all men who see social evils very strongly and clearly, and also see their way to remedies (to be, as they think, swiftly applied), he did not give enough weight, I think, to the inevitable difficulties which must exist in a free State to prevent the rapid and complete adoption of these remedies. 'Circumlocution' is everywhere—in the Senate, at the Bar, in the Field, in ordinary business, as well as in official life; and men of Mr Dickens's temperament, full of ardour for the public good and somewhat despotic in their habits of thought, find it difficult to put up with the tiresome aberrations of a freedom which will not behave itself at once in a proper way, and set to work to provide immediate remedies for that which ought to be remedied. When you come close to any great man, you generally find that he has somewhat of a despotic nature in this respect. . . .

He ardently desired, and confidently looked forward to, a time when there would be a more intimate union than exists at present between the different classes in the State—a union embracing alike the highest and the lowest.

It always seemed to me that he had a power of narration which was beyond anything even which his books show forth. How he would narrate to you, sitting on a gate or on a fallen tree, some rustic story of the people he had known in his neighbourhood! It was the very perfection of narrative. Not a word was thrown away, not an adjective misused; and I think all those who have had the good fortune to hear him recount one of these stories will agree with me, that it was a triumph—an unconscious triumph—of art. . . .

Everybody has heard of Mr Dickens's pre-eminence as an actor, but perhaps it is not so generally known what an admirable speaker he was. The last speech, I believe, that he ever made was at the Academy dinner; and I think it would be admitted by every one, including those who also made excellent speeches on that occasion, that Mr Dickens's was the speech of the evening. He was herein greatly aided by nature, having that presence, conveying the idea of courage and honesty, which gives much effect to public speaking, and also possessing a sweet, deep-toned, audible voice, that had exceeding pathos in it. Moreover, he had most expressive hands—not beautiful, according to the ordinary notions of beauty, but nervous and powerful hands. He did not indulge in gesticulation; but the slight movements of these expressive hands helped wonderfully in giving additional force and meaning to what he said, as all those who have been present at his readings will testify. Indeed, when he read, or when he spoke, the whole man read, or spoke. . . .

148. Alfred Austin, 'Charles Dickens', *Temple Bar*

July 1870, xxix, 554–62

Austin (1835–1913), poet, miscellaneous writer, and journalist, became Poet Laureate in 1896. His striking re-assessment of Tennyson (*Temple Bar*, May 1869) is reprinted in *Tennyson: the Critical Heritage*, ed. John D. Jump, (1967), 294–311.

Once when a bad man died, a savage wit, being apprised of the event, observed that the average value of mankind was sensibly raised. Who does not feel that, by the death of Charles Dickens, the average value of ourselves, as Englishmen of the nineteenth century, is incalculably lowered? Our really great men we love, not only because they are great, but because we, in a sense, share their greatness. ... We can exult no more over the possession of Charles Dickens. He is dead, and forthwith we dwindle. We live a lesser life, and if we measure our importance in just balances, we find it sadly diminished. Dickens has joined the Immortals, and their glorious company is grandly strengthened by his presence. But in the ranks of us poor mortals there is a horrible gap, and who, or how many whos, shall fill it? ...

With a Thackeray, a Lytton, an Eliot, on the course, we cannot say that Dickens was first and the rest nowhere; but though, ever and anon, men might momentarily think that these would overtake and even outstrip him, they never did so. They made great spurts, and slackened; but he, though he sometimes amazed us by accelerating the pace, rarely diminished it, and never halted. If the meditation of novels may, in one sense, be said to be the meditation of trifles, of Dickens it may be affirmed that he was *totus in illis*.[1] His whole heart, indeed his whole nature, was in them. And he is the only English novelist of real genius of whom this can truly be said. ... The writer of these lines need not conceal that he is one of those who think that the later works of this great master are not equal to those with which he first delighted the world, but he is glad that the minority to which he belongs should have

[1] 'Wholly absorbed in these things' (Horace, *Satires*, Book I, ix, 2).

been a minority as long as Charles Dickens lived. Dickens was first favourite to the last, and he deserved to be. Both by genius and hard work he maintained to the end the position he reached quite in early manhood. . . .

And still more happy was the genius of Dickens, being such as it was, in that he reached his majority at the precise time he did. The hour and the man arrived together. A change had come over the national dream. The world had pledged itself to a new gospel. Rightly or wrongly, public opinion had veered, as the phrase is, 'slap round,' and laws, some of which may be called Draconian, and others of which Draco would certainly have approved, had received their condemnation. . . . Almost simultaneously, a host of freshly-enfranchised electors were to give us a new Parliament, and the foundations were laid, as many knew at the time, for household and, ultimately, for universal suffrage. These, however, were but the political phenomena of a revolution which had deeper roots and more solid aims. When the world began thus practically to assert in its rough-and-ready way that every man ought to have a chance, there naturally were not wanting advocates to plead that many men ought to have more chances than one. That the gallows then groaned with victims, and that the prisons swarmed with debtors, sufficiently demonstrate that such had not been the old doctrine. But the old doctrine was to be doctrine no more, and Justice without Mercy was to be for ever proscribed.

Now Justice without Mercy—a doctrine that has much to say for itself, but that said it in vain forty years ago, says it almost in vain even now, yet may possibly say it again, unless Humanity mends, and may again find a hearing—was the one thing on earth repugnant to the soul of Charles Dickens. He was the very son of his time. He was all for giving the worst men a chance, and giving it them many times over. Moreover, he was for giving Man generally a chance, and many chances. In a word, he was an ardent believer in the perfectibility of the human species,—in a creed which is certainly generous and, let us devoutly hope, true, though it is not easy for every impartial person to hold it. It is a matter that may still be disputed, and can never be demonstrated either way, and which men therefore accept or reject according to their disposition, and not according to the bluntness or acuteness of their dialectical faculties. To Charles Dickens, no doubt, a belief in human perfectibility was probably so strong that he was unable even to conceive its negation. In that, he was the man of his epoch, and had the spirit-time throbbing within him. Here again was his good fortune; here again do we have him as the Happy Author—always and for ever in harmony with his conditions. Let no one underrate this circumstance. The names of the authors of whom it can be predicated could be counted almost on one's fingers; and those of whom it can be predicated, generally had miserable compensation of unhappiness in other respects. To name Jean-Jacques Rousseau is to point my meaning. But Dickens had no penalty of any sort to pay for being in full harmony with the disposition of his time. . . .

. . . Yet, whilst speaking of this English character of Charles Dickens's humour, let us say that we scarce know where it came from. England at once accepted it as the best humour ever offered it; and since the nation was thus obviously prepared to appreciate it, the nation must in some way have contributed towards its production. But we fail to see what prior events or authors led up to Charles Dickens. He is, without any exception, the most original writer in the language. The sources of his genius, and of the form his genius assumed, are as hidden, from our eyes at least, as were once from all eyes the sources of the Nile. We see the great fertilising stream; but only in some dim Mountains of the Moon can we dream of its fount or origin. This gives to Dickens an exceptional and solitary position. He is the only great English writer of whom it cannot be said that he is a classic. Once more he was the 'Happy Author,' for surely we no longer live in classic times!

Of his pathos we cannot candidly speak in such glowing terms as of his humour—not, however, because his pathos was not good, but because his humour was so matchless. He was humoristic by nature, and because he could not help himself. He was pathetic by art, and because pathos is indispensable to the writer of fiction. . . .

In respect of those qualities of Charles Dickens's genius of which we have spoken, we imagine there is but little difference of opinion. There is one point, however, on which it would appear that there are conflicting judgments. We have constantly seen Charles Dickens spoken of as eminently a realistic writer, and in his portrayal of character as an humble and accurate imitator of actual life; and this view has been recently reproduced, and notably in *The Times* newspaper, in notices intended to be highly eulogistic of the great novelist. From the view in question we totally dissent, and hold it to be the very reverse of the real truth. Had Dickens been pre-eminently a realistic writer, we at least should not be speaking of him here as great, as we now do with all the sincerity of deep conviction. No realistic writer can by any possibility be a great writer. He may be amazingly clever, remarkably entertaining, and even overwhelmingly popular; but the gods know him not. He is at best and highest 'a literary mechanic, doing good work for excellent pay. No doubt Dickens had abundance of realistic machinery at his command, and right well he used it; but he used it for the accessories, not for the substance of his art—prodigally for the *mise en scène*, little or not at all for his *dramatis personae*. . . . For Dickens was a man of visions, and hence his greatness. Hence the height he attained, to which the realistic novelist cannot even look up. It is for this reason that, were the possibilities of prose equal to the possibilities of verse, Dickens would be as great as Shakespeare. Of course he is not—he is unspeakably below him; but he is unquestionably as far above all other English novelists, as Shakespeare is above all other English dramatists. And this he is by virtue of his imagination, not by virtue of his realism, in respect of which he has many equals and some superiors. But it is a small matter to be inferior or superior in, when we are talking of an artist's realms.

. . . He is perhaps, the very last—or the last for many generations to come—of our great unscientific writers. He saw men and things with his own eyes, and glorified them. He was true to nature in the sense that Shakespeare was, but in no other. He has had a host of imitators, but it is not they who really understood, and appreciated him, or they would not have travestied him so deplorably. Other writers have, by dint of imagination, exalted soldiers, statesmen, and great nobles, and by taking thought have added many cubits to the stature of kings. It was the privilege of Dickens, by dint of that same inestimable gift of imagination, to raise and transfigure the lowly. Indeed, we know of no words that could be more fittingly inscribed on his tomb than two simple ones from Holy Writ—*Exaltavit humiles*.[1]

[1] 'He hath exalted them of low degree' (Luke, i, 52).

149. A. W. Ward, from
Charles Dickens: a Lecture

30 November 1870

Science Lectures for the People, 2nd Series (Manchester [1871]), 238–59. Also published separately (Manchester, 1870).
Ward (1837–1924), Professor of History and English at Owens College, Manchester at this time, had a distinguished academic career, ending as Master of Peterhouse and Vice-Chancellor of Cambridge University, and editor of both the *Cambridge Modern History* and the *Cambridge History of English Literature*. His lecture was commended by Forster as 'the best criticism of Dickens I have seen since his death' (*Life*, 727n). In 1882, he contributed the *Dickens* volume to the 'English Men of Letters' series.

... Compared with his other powers, his power of *construction*, however, remained his weak point to the last, though he endeavoured to make good a natural defect by unabated and unwearying labour. As a constructor of plots, he grew more elaborate and artificial as he went on, but not, I think, more effective and artistic. *Oliver Twist*, the first of his novels, is simply and powerfully put together; in *Nicholas Nickleby*, the interest in the story is already fainter; in the *Old Curiosity Shop* the original thread is flung aside altogether, and the story itself totters to its end almost as feebly as the old man whom Little Nell led through the country lanes. *Martin Chuzzlewit* is quite improbable; and the visit to America, an inimitable episode in itself, is simply foisted into the general action; *David Copperfield*, poor boy, gets into his troubles for no particular reason, and gets out of them as easily as he gets into them. In his later works, Mr Dickens, perhaps under the influence of Mr Wilkie Collins's example, attempted plots of extreme intricacy. Indeed, he seems almost to hint as much in the preface to his *Tale of Two Cities*, of which he informs us he first conceived the main idea when he was acting with his friends and children in Mr Wilkie Collins's drama of the *Frozen Deep*; yet the tale itself is one of the very few of Mr Dickens's works which require an effort in the perusal. The master of humour and pathos, the magician whose potent wand, if ever so gently moved, exercises effects which no one is able to resist, seems to be toiling in the mechanician's workshop, and yet never attains to a success beyond that of a more or less promising apprentice. To take only his last two works, is there any man not blessed with the experience of a detective policeman, who could furnish an intelligible account of the plot of *Our Mutual Friend*? And if he is at times obscure when in the end he of course means to be clear, he is elsewhere transparent where he intends to be secret. Have you read the *Mystery of Edwin Drood*, which, alas! its author was not himself to unravel? We have lost much by its sudden interruption; but not the key to the mystery. I certainly do not flatter myself with being more than ordinarily acute in penetrating such problems; but after reading the very first number of that work I told a lady who was beginning it that it would be no mystery to her, and she found it out at once.

If Dickens was never destined to attain to high distinction as a constructor of plots, the wonderful fertility of his imagination, and the marvellous dramatic sense which he in so many ways displayed, could hardly fail to make him eminent as an inventor of *situations*. I need hardly point out the distinction; it is in a word, the distinction between the devising of effective scenes, and the combining of effective scenes into a harmonious whole. Nor need I from the wealth of instances which at once crowd into the memory, select more than one or two instances in illustration. . . .

[Ward cites the storm in *Copperfield*, and the death of Little Nell.]

In his works we . . . find an extraordinary, but not an absolutely exhaustive, variety of character-studies. I wish to speak rather of what we find, than of what we do not find there; and I will not therefore dwell on the absence of certain types which it is strange to find all but unrepresented in the works of the most popular of modern English writers. A simple reference will suffice to the fact, that he never gives us the character which to the minds of most modern Englishmen is the most acceptable type of human worth—the man of public spirit; that he never draws the positive to the negative which he so constantly satirises, the Bounderbies who burlesque civic virtue and the people 'with a small p,' who in the Circumlocution Office, and elsewhere, condescend to misgovern us. Again, it is remarkable that he who beyond all question was conscious of the infinite value of a single-minded devotion to the claims of art, who was ready to recognise its elevating influence in others, and to sacrifice to it all secondary views in his own career, should never have essayed the portrait of an artist devoted to art for its own sake alone.

The reason of this seems to be, that Mr Dickens's artistic sympathy was limited to other types of virtue—types which I may possibly allow myself to call those of the private or domestic kind. His sympathy with the affections of the hearth and the home knows no bounds, and it is within this sphere that I confess I know of no other writer—in poetry or prose, amongst ourselves or other nations—to compare to him. Where shall I begin and where end in speaking of this side of his genius? Who ever understood children better than he? Other writers have wondered at them; he understands them,—the romance of their fun, the fun of their romance, the nonsense in their ideas, and the ideas in their nonsense. It was only the other day that I heard him read, in the Free Trade Hall, a portion of one of his best Christmas serials— *Boots at the Holly Tree Inn*—it is called—a story of baby love which would have drawn smiles and tears from Mr Gradgrind, and which, as I am here to testify, was recognised on the spot as absolutely true to nature by a mother in the gallery, whose sympathy I thought at the time would be too much for Mr Dickens himself. Who could picture better than he that curious animal, the British boy? Why, he understood him in every phase and under every aspect of his existence, whether he was the pupil of Dr Blimber's classical academy or of Mr Fagin's establishment of technical education. Who, again, fathomed more profoundly that sea whose dimples so often deceive us as to its depth, the mind of a young girl?. . . .

But society, we know, is not made up of boys and girls; and in Mr Dickens's characters of men and women we must seek for his most sustained efforts. Here again he moves within certain bounds. The effects of passion upon character he has very generally preferred to depict on the background of domestic life. . . .

As a novelist of *manners* Dickens is, in his own sphere, without an equal. In this direction he had his earliest successes; and in this direction his hand never lost its cunning. Even before *Pickwick* was written, the *Sketches by Boz* had shown that the life of our middle and lower classes, and more especially the middle and lower classes of that great city where it displays itself in the most multitudinous variety, of London, was the chosen sphere for his inimitably faithful observation and inimitably faithful reproduction. In *Pickwick* he never left this ground;

in *Oliver Twist* he explored some of its darkest passages, and was able to represent them at once with truth and with good taste. In *Nicholas Nickleby* he for the first time ventured upon sketching the manners and customs of what were intended not of course as types of the aristocracy, but *in manners and customs* were supposed to be faithful portraitures. This attempt he afterwards repeated in *Dombey and Son*, in *Bleak House*, in *Our Mutual Friend*, and elsewhere; but he never succeeded in producing anything but caricatures. Why this should have been so, I will not pretend to determine; that it was so, is my deliberate opinion. Even in the *Mystery of Edwin Drood* he seems, accidentally no doubt, to enter into competition with a very popular novelist of the present day, Mr Anthony Trollope, as a describer of clerical life. I don't pretend to know in what way Deans and Canons talk when they are at home; but I will venture to say they don't talk in the way Mr Dickens seems to suppose. The truth is that there were limits which Dickens could not pass with safety: there is nothing to be said on the subject except that those limits in his case included a variety which is in one sense infinite....

... Of his studies of life I have already spoken. There never was a writer less ostentatious of his reading; but I can see in his works many traces of the fact that he read much, and chiefly good books; and we have it on undoubted testimony that in writing he worked conscientiously and hard. He owed it to the style which he perfected—I say perfected, for if in his later works he was sometimes artificial in manner, in his earliest he was comparatively rough. But primarily, and above all, he owed it to that gift of genius which no toil can secure, though neglect may fritter it away, or abuse pervert. For Dickens possessed an imagination unsurpassed, not only in vividness, but in swiftness. I have intentionally avoided all needless comparisons of his works with those of other writers of his time, some of whom have gone before him to their rest, while others survive to gladden the dulness and relieve the monotony of our daily life. But in the power of his imagination—of this I am convinced—he surpassed them, one and all. That imagination could call up at will those associations which, could we but summon them in their full number, would bind together the human family, and make that expression no longer a name, but a living reality. ...

This is the power wielded by an imagination like that of the great genius of whom we have spoken to-night. Do we then owe him nothing beyond many pleasant hours which have refreshed us after our day's toil, and the memory of those hours which makes us long to return to the spell of the kindly enchanter? We owe him much more than this;

for he who has made human nature and its surroundings speak to us, and claim our sympathy for that to which we should have otherwise remained half deaf and half blind, has multiplied the richness of our existence, and has enabled us to hear with his ears and see with his eyes what our own were too dull to hear and to see.

EDWIN DROOD

April – September 1870

On 2 April 1870 both *The Times* and the *Athenaeum* critics welcomed No. 1 of what was to prove Dickens's last novel with almost the same words: 'As he delighted the fathers, so he delights the children, and this his latest effort promises to be received with interest and pleasure as widespread as that which greeted those glorious *Papers* which built at once the whole edifice of his fame' (*The Times*, 2 April 1870, 4: by Frederick Napier Broome); 'Mr Dickens . . . has had the privilege of delighting two generations; and it is not often that one writer can turn the privilege to such graceful account as Mr Dickens has done. . . . Mr Dickens has begun his new story in excellent vein' (*Athenaeum*, 2 April 1870, 443–4). 'What other story-teller, English or foreign, ever maintained so great and increasing a popularity for six and thirty years!' exclaimed the *Graphic* (26 March 1870, 388). This particular welcome—felicitous, in view of Dickens's death two months later—was occasioned by the general gratitude at finding 'a favourite author in a shape and fashion in which he has not been seen for many a weary day' (*Athenaeum, loc. cit.*); the four-and-a-half-year gap since the completion of his previous novel was quite unprecedented in his career. The reviews when its last completed part, No. VI, was published were similarly affected by a special sense of occasion: this was the last of the monthly 'green numbers' which had been a recurrent delight for over a third of a century. Some reviews were affected by a *de mortuis* . . . hushfulness: more, I think, by a feeling of exhaustion, as if most critics had shot all their best bolts in obituary appreciations two or three months back. Attempts to surmise how the story would have ended—a major preoccupation of dedicated Dickensians later—were disappointingly few and unadventurous.

'Dickens's last laboured effort, the melancholy work of a worn-out brain', was Wilkie Collins's surprisingly asperous comment on a novel manifestly akin to his own (No. 163). Few verdicts were as unfavourable, though Mrs Oliphant was scathing (No. 155, June 1871). The novelist with whose works *Drood* was most often compared was not Collins but Trollope. *The Times*'s reviewer approved of this invasion of the Barchester territory: Dickens's Deans were as real as Trollope's, 'delighting us as much but delighting us for other reasons' (*loc. cit.*). Others felt otherwise (e.g., *Guardian*, 28 September 1870, 1152; A. W. Ward, No. 149). Few noticed, as did the *Dublin Review*, that *Drood* was 'in some respects, a singular repetition of its immediate predecessor' (April 1871, n.s. xvi, 329). Much of the praise *Drood* received took the form often employed in these later years of Dickens's career—hailing it as a happy return to his old manner, with touches of the old Bozzian humour. So Durdles proved a general favourite. (See bibliographies of *Edwin Drood* in *Dickensian*, i (1905), 240–320 *passim*; vii (1911), 130–3; xxiv (1928), 236, 301–2; xxv (1929), 42–4, 185–7.)

150. From an unsigned review, *Saturday Review*

17 September 1870, xxx, 369

… Mr Honeythunder is a mere wooden figure, as lifeless as that which Mr Quilp was in the habit of belabouring, pretty much in the same spirit as that in which Mr Dickens belabours sham philanthropists, though from less amiable motives. The worst of it is that Honeythunder, whilst fully as grotesque as any of Mr Dickens's earlier creations, is far less amusing, simply because a man when he is over fifty cannot design grotesques with the spirit which he possessed when he was under thirty. The oddity, as we have said, remains, but oddity requires to be carried off by a certain reckless audacity which is only to be expected from a youthful writer. Honeythunder, it is to be added, is only a subsidiary character, as he is one of the least satisfactory in the book; but the same taint of mannerism and forced humour is more or less evident in most of the other actors.

To make a more serious criticism, the pathetic and passionate parts of the book are, as usual with the author, the least satisfactory. There is some love-making which reminds us of Dora in *David Copperfield*, and there is a murderer (so at least we infer, though the mystery is not fully revealed) of the melodramatic type. This person endeavours to recommend himself to a young lady, whom, after the fashion of his kind, he regards with a certain wolfish admiration, by insinuating that if she marries him he will not procure the execution of another young man for a crime which he has himself committed. The general situation of the brutal villain threatening the amiable heroine into compliance with his wishes by revealing part of his diabolical character is familiar enough. We quote a fragment of his address as a specimen of the more high-flown passages:—

'Rosa,' says the villain, 'even when my dear boy was affianced to you, I loved you madly; even when I thought his happiness in having you for wife was certain, I loved you madly; even when I strove to make him more ardently devoted to you, I loved you madly; even when he gave me the picture of your lovely face, so carelessly traduced by him, which I feigned to hang always in my sight for his sake, but worshipped in torment for years, I loved you madly; in the distasteful work of the day, in the wakeful misery of the night, girded by sordid realities, or wandering through Paradises and Hells of visions into which I rushed, carrying your vision in my arms, I loved you madly.' [ch. xix]

In this precious oration we recognise the worst style of Mr Dickens, 'ticking off' each point (as Mr Grewgious expresses it on a similar occasion) by the burden of 'I loved you madly.' But do we recognise anything like the language of a passionate and blackhearted villain trying to bully a timid girl? It is the sort of oration which a silly boy, nourished on bad novels, might prepare for such an occasion; but it is stiff and artificial and jerky to a degree which excludes any belief in real passion. It is rounded off prettily enough for a peroration in a debating society; or it might be a fair piece of acting for a romantic young tradesman who fancies himself doing his love-making in the high poetic style; but it has an air of affectation and mock-heroics which is palpably inappropriate to the place. It is really curious that so keen an observer should diverge into such poor and stilted bombast whenever he tries the note of intense emotion.

In spite, however, of this and more which might be fairly said, there is much in *Edwin Drood* to remind us more pleasantly of the author's best days. There are a good many passages of genuine and easy humour; and, if the manner is apt to be rather cramped and deficient in the old flow and vivacity, there is yet abundant fertility in inventing really telling characters. There is nothing indeed to set beside our old familiar friends, such as Sam Weller and Mrs Gamp, but there is something which nobody but Mr Dickens himself could have written. The story, too, so far as we can judge from a fragment, is more skilfully put together than was usually the case, and may be read with interest in spite of the absence of a conclusion. We may guess pretty safely how the schemes of the bad characters would have been defeated, and all the good people portioned off with comfortable incomes and abundance of olive-branches....

151. 'H. Lawrenny' [Edith Simcox], from a review in the *Academy*

22 October 1870, ii, 1–3

Edith Simcox (1844–1901), the devoted admirer of George Eliot, was author of *Natural Law* and other books, and a prolific reviewer in the *Academy* from its inception in 1869 until the 1890s. The *Academy* was a scholarly periodical, established by a group of young Liberals; see D. Roll-Hansen, '*The Academy*' *1869–79* (Copenhagen, 1957). Most of its reviewers were distinguished Oxford men: hence Edith Simcox's writing under a pseudonym. In a brief notice of No. 1 of *Edwin Drood*, the *Academy* reviewer had commented (14 April 1870, i, 201) that the opening scene 'looks very like a reminiscence of Bracebridge Hemyng's *Visit to Bluegate Fields*, in Mayhew's *London Labour and the London Poor*, extra vol. pp. 231–2 (1862).'

... *The Mystery of Edwin Drood* may either be the subject of speculation as a novel, or of study as the last fragment from his fertile pen. In the first respect there are signs of a more carefully-designed intrigue than in most of his earlier works. John Jasper, opium-eater, music-master and murderer, is a villain of the melodramatic type, who is in love with his nephew's betrothed, and arranges, months in advance, how his nephew shall disappear and another young man be suspected of the deed. He has strange mesmeric power, and a remarkable gift of rehearsing in his visions, before and after the event, the crime which we are given to understand he has committed. As in Wilkie Collins's *Moonstone*, the mystery is evidently to be explained by the principal actor in a trance, and a mysterious woman who keeps an opium-shop for Chinamen and Lascars, lies vindictively in wait to betray him. It would be in vain to speculate whether Edwin Drood would have turned out somehow or other not to have been murdered, in spite of such omens as a heap of quicklime to consume his bones (p. 90), a black scarf of strong close-woven silk to throttle him (p. 112), and all the dreadful things that were evidently done while Durdles slumbered, and perhaps Deputy watched, on page 94. The solution of this problem was evidently reserved for the sagacity of Mr Datchery, agent doubtless of Mr Grewgious, seconded by the still unexplained animosity of the opium-seller. But Dickens was never very particular as to the possibility of the means by which his characters were made happy towards the last number, and for aught we can tell to the contrary, half-a-dozen principal contributors to the dénouement may have remained uninvented when the work was cut short in the middle. . . .

On the whole *The Mystery of Edwin Drood*, viewed as a fragment, shews little falling off from the writer's second-best works; the unfortunate cause of its fragmentary form lends it a peculiar interest, and we welcome these new actors the more because they are the last who will join the company. But after assigning them their places, there is room for a word on the moral and intellectual atmosphere which pervades and surrounds them. The first thing that strikes a reader of Dickens is the absence of all familiar boundaries and landmarks: class distinctions are ignored or obliterated; different ages and sexes assume the prerogatives of their opposites; people transact incongruous business in impossible places; and with it all there is no apparent consciousness that the social order is confused and inverted. It is still more curious to watch this levelling tendency applied to matters of intellect. Dickens has a positive affection for lunatics, and with the exception of the favourites to whom he lends touches of his own imagination, a vast majority of his characters are born fools. In his queer world they fare none the worse for this; they cluster round one delusion or another, and defend it with just as much formality as if they were reasoning beings, and it almost seems as if, *caeteris paribus*, he preferred the thought that travelled by a crooked lane. The only light in this chaos is what falls from a few moral axioms concerning the duty to our neighbour, and these are of such universal application as to be rather indefinite. In such books as *Dombey* and *Martin Chuzzlewit* we seem lost in a millennium of illogical goodwill, in imagining which, no doubt, Dickens was principally influenced by his natural humour. But the only approach to an opinion on things in general that can be gathered from his works, is derived by implication from his moral system. The world, we are given to understand, would be more amiable than it is, and could not be more absurd, if the virtues of Mr Toots were universally practised. This is by no means a bad position for a humourist to occupy, for though we may have our doubts as to what makes Dickens's characters so much more laughable than life, it is something to have extracted the maximum of amusement out of innocent and even admirable eccentricities.

152. An unsigned review in the *Spectator*

1 October 1870, xliii, 1176–7

Probably by R. H. Hutton. The cover-design mentioned was in fact the work of Charles Collins, not of Luke Fildes, who provided the illustrations.

In the notice prefixed to this volume it is stated that no notes of the conclusion of the story have been found, and that therefore the publishers have done 'what it is believed that the author would himself have most desired,' in placing the fragment of *Edwin Drood* without further note or suggestion before the public. But in point of fact the publishers have hardly given to the future readers of Mr Dickens's latest fragment even as much clue as to the past readers. We think that under the circumstances of a story so carefully and apparently so skilfully plotted and so remarkably broken off, they were bound to have given a facsimile of the vignetted cover in which the course of the story is evidently prefigured. And to this might surely have been added any

instructions received by the artist who prepared that vignetted cover,—
for some such instructions there must clearly have been. Several of the
scenes in the actually completed parts are distinctly represented on the
cover, and the drift of those which are not must have been more or less
explained by Mr Dickens to the artist who designed them for him. For
instance, by whom was the lamplight discovery of a standing figure
apparently meant for Edwin Drood in the vignette at the bottom of the
page intended to be made? Is the man entering with the lanthorn his
uncle John Jasper? and what were the directions given by Mr Dickens as
to the ascents of the winding stair-case depicted on the right hand of the
cover? Though we quite agree with the publishers that any attempt to
complete the tale by a different hand would have been an insult to Mr
Dickens, and altogether unwelcome to the public, we do think that any
authentic indications which may exist of the turn he intended to give to
the story, ought to have been furnished to the readers of the fragment,—
as even adding to the materials for judging of the skill the author had
displayed in the first half of his tale. Nor can we see how it can be
possible that no such indications exist, with this prefiguring cover to
prove that he had not only anticipated, but disclosed to some one or
other, many of the situations he intended to paint. In any case a fac-
simile of the sketches on the cover should clearly have been given in the
finished volume. If Mr Fildes, as we suppose, designed the cover as well
as the very clever illustrations to *Edwin Drood*, Mr Fildes must have had
instructions which should, we think, have been communicated in the
'advertizement' to the reader.

We have seen it asserted by the critics that Mr Dickens had lost, long
before he wrote *Edwin Drood*, the power of giving to his grotesque
conceptions that youthful *élan* which is essential to their perfection after
their kind, and consequently to their fascination. But may not a great
part of the explanation be that the critics, before they read *Edwin
Drood*, had lost that youthful *élan* which was essential to enjoying it,—
and that they continue to enjoy even Mr Dickens's younger works
more by the force of memory and tradition, than by virtue of any vivid
and present appreciation of their humour? At least, so far as we can
judge by close observation of those who now read *Edwin Drood* at the
same age at which most of us first learnt to enjoy the *Old Curiosity Shop*
and *Martin Chuzzlewit*, there does not seem to be any deficiency in the
capacity of the rising generation to enter heartily into its still fresh
humour. We sincerely believe that the picture of Durdles, the Cathedral stonemason, and of the young imp who stones him home at night,

would have been welcomed twenty-five years ago with as much delight as was at that time the picture of Poll Sweedlepipes, barber and bird-fancier, and his distinguished customer, Bailey Junior. We do not, of course, mean that *Edwin Drood* is nearly as brimful of humour as *Martin Chuzzlewit*. Few men ever reach a second time the standard of their most characteristic works, and the American tour of Mr Dickens evidently gave a stimulus to his sense of humour which brought it all at once into its fullest flower. But *Edwin Drood* does seem to us nearer the standard of his first few works than anything he had written for many years back. It shows his peculiar power of grasping the local colour and detail of all characteristic *physical* life, in the exceedingly powerful sketch of the den of the East-End opium-smoker; it shows a different side of the same faculty in the abundant and marvellous detail as to the precincts and interior of the Cathedral; while all his old humour comes out in the picture of Miss Twinkleton's girls'-school, of Billickin the lodging-house keeper, and in the figures to which we have before referred, of the Cathedral stone mason and his attendant imp. No doubt there are all Mr Dickens's faults in this story quite unchanged. He never learned to draw a human being as distinct from an oddity, and all his characters which are not oddities are false. Again he never learned the distinguishing signs of genuine sentiment; and just as nothing can be vulgarer than the sentimental passages of *Nicholas Nickleby* and *Martin Chuzzlewit*, so nothing can, at any rate, be much falser or in worse taste than the sentimental scenes in *Edwin Drood*. Mr Dickens could not get over the notion that a love scene was a rich and luscious sort of juice, to be sucked up in the sort of way in which a bowl of punch and a Christmas dinner are so often enjoyed in his tales; and not only so, but all beauty, all that he thinks lovable, is apt to be treated by him as if it were a pot of raspberry jam, something luscious to the palate, instead of something fascinating to the imagination and those finer powers by which harmony of expression is perceived. All these faults, which have appeared in every tale of Mr Dickens from the very first, have not, of course, in any way disappeared from this. But they are certainly not more obtrusive than usual, while the very unusual phenomenon of a story constructed with great care and ingenuity, relieves the ill-drawn and over-coloured characters of much of their ordinary tedium. As mere incidental evidence how little his greatest and most characteristic power of close humorous observation had decayed, take this perfect sketch of the two waiters from Furnival's Inn who attend the little dinner which Mr Grewgious gives in his chambers.

[Quotes from ch. xi.]

Did Dickens in his best book ever write a passage of more closely observing humour than that, or finish it off with a finer stroke than that touch about the flying waiter's leg preceding himself and tray into the room 'with something of an angling air about it?' Any critic who holds that Dickens had lost the youthful *élan* of his humour in writing that passage, must clearly have himself lost all the youthful *élan* essential to the full appreciation of humour. Or take another very different touch, in which 'the Billickin' rises almost to the imaginative level of Wordsworth himself, while recalling the fatal influence which the poor diet at her boarding-school has exercised on her life:—'I was put in life,' she says to Miss Twinkleton, 'to a very genteel boarding school, the mistress being no less a lady than yourself, of about your own age, or it may be, some years younger, *and a poorness of blood flowed from the table which has run through my life.*' Is it possible to miss the analogy to Wordsworth's fine passage in the *Prelude?*—

> Was it for this
> That one, the fairest of all rivers, loved
> To blend his murmurs with my nurse's song,
> And from his alder shades and rocky falls
> And from his fords and shallows, *sent a voice*
> *That flowed along my dreams?*   [i, 269–74]

We think it will be admitted that the Billickin's metaphor, though not exactly the grander of the two, is, at least, the bolder imaginative flight.

However characteristic the faults of the fragment which embodies Mr Dickens's last literary effort, we feel no doubt that it will be read, admired, and remembered for the display of his equally characteristic powers, long after such performances as *Little Dorrit* and *Bleak House* are utterly neglected and forgotten.

153. From an unsigned article, 'Two English Novelists: Dickens and Thackeray', *Dublin Review*

April 1871, n.s. xvi, 315–50

Possibly by Mrs Frances Cashel Hoey (1830–1908), writer of fashionable novels, translator, etc. The *Dublin Review* was a Roman Catholic journal, published in London.

[The writer foretells that, with the advance of education, Thackeray will overtake Dickens in popular esteem.] We have only to ask ourselves, what books must any person who proposes to enjoy the perusal of Mr Dickens's works have previously read? What amount and manner of acquaintance with the world of men, cities, or letters, with politics, art, or philosophy, must he possess? Surely little or none. As far as the greater number of his works are concerned, they might be the only books in existence, and be just as intelligible and delightful; and in the case of those which form the exceptions to this rule, *Hard Times* and *A Tale of Two Cities*, we do not think the political and social views of the former, or the historical appreciation of the latter, sufficiently sound or profound to merit the attention of educated minds, though they are striking and picturesque enough to interest the uneducated . . .

In the early days of Mr Dickens's fame his style of sentiment had many hearty admirers among his young readers. They were enraptured with Little Nell; they copied whole pages about her and her death into their albums; and Smike was also a great favourite. Nothing more opposed to truth was ever written than the apostrophe to that 'dread disease,' consumption, in *Nicholas Nickleby*, but, twenty-five years ago young ladies learned it by heart, and inscribed it on those many-coloured pages which were innocent and pretty enough records of their passing tastes and fancies. We suspect there are very few young people of the present day so 'exceedingly young,' as Mr Littimer would say, as to be attracted by Mr Dickens's pathos. We do not affirm this as an improvement, but only as a fact. It is sufficient for his fame that he has made one generation cry in his and their time. He will make a few generations to come laugh. Not as the great and terrible wits make the men and women of the ages which come after them laugh,—by the sparkling result of their deep proficiency in the 'noblest study,' whose subject, 'man,' is ever the same;—but because his humour is so rich, so thorough, so varied, and so original that it must always appeal to the liking for oddities and eccentricities inherent in human nature, which increases with the pace of life, and is felt more and more as a relief to its growing weariness. There is humour which does not exactly amuse, though it receive the utmost recognition. There is humour which simply amuses, which is merely quite delightful. Mr Dickens had extraordinary humour of the latter sort. He may have intended sometimes to be savagely satirical, but could not keep from caricature, and with exaggeration savageness, even severity, is done away. He was infinitely droll and various in his mirthful moods, and the animal spirits which overflow through all his earlier writings abounded up to the latest of them.

That the sentimental creations of Mr Dickens, the impossible children, the preposterous mechanics, the jovial landladies, the charming youths of the David Copperfield and Edwin Drood school, will be entirely repudiated by future generations (they are barely tolerated now) we make no doubt, but we believe that the delightful absurdities, of whom the chief are Dick Swiveller and Mark Tapley, Miggs and Mrs Gamp (who has been flattered by imitation more extensively than any personage in the history of fiction) will be delightful to reading humanity for a long time to come.

Mr Thackeray was a humorist in the other category. There is profound intellectual satisfaction in our helpless involuntary recognition of the truth of his delineations of the smallnesses, the weaknesses, the follies, and the absurdities of ourselves and our fellows,—but especially ourselves. His insight is only equalled by the dexterity with which he exposes his discoveries. But it does so much more than amuse that it does less. It occupies so entirely; it is so suggestive; it comes so thoroughly home to the reader; it is so sad, with all its good humour; so depressing, with all its sparkle and finish; so savagely satirical, with its contemptuous admission that no one is much less of a fool, or a snob, or a swindler, pretender, ass, or coquette, of a hero, saint, exemplary person, bore, or Philistine than his neighbour; it has, for all its power and extent, such a monotonous *refrain*, that it does not rest or refresh.

It taxes the mind, and while we recognize the great gift, and its cultivated and lavish use, it no more cheers one's spirits or turns one's
thoughts out of a work-a-day groove than a comedy of Molière
does. By general consent all novels are classed as 'light reading.' Mr
Thackeray's ought to be excepted. They are amazingly clever, and in
parts incomparably entertaining, but they are serious reading. . . .

There is also among Mr Dickens's works one which it would be
well for his future fame if he had not written. It is to be supposed that
the world, which is to be so much better educated immediately, will
not henceforth tolerate books made up of flimsy, intolerant, and
ignorant remarks upon a number of subjects of which the writers
know nothing; and therefore we anticipate that *Pictures from Italy* will
modify the estimate of the next generation of its author's powers and
place in literature. The complacency of his ignorance, when he treats
of subjects which need information for their correct appreciation, is
provoking to educated people. His mind was distinctly objective, and
his descriptions, when he kept clear of his characteristic affectations,
were reliable and delightfully fresh. Not so his observations and deductions. His writings give us reason to believe that he had very little
knowledge of art, literature, and politics, no reverence for them, and
scant sympathy with the minds to which they are interesting, important
and precious. The social questions which he illustrates are treated with
more zeal than knowledge; and though his good faith and good feeling
are evident, he is much too vehement, and deals too largely in the
picturesque to be regarded as a public instructor on all or any of his
topics. *Hard Times* is amusing and clever, but while he exaggerates out
of all practical utility as an example the Gradgrind system, we regard
that which Mr Dickens would have substituted for it with little more
favour. We do not think he had any of the elements of a social reformer
in him, except that of a keen perception of evil, and a happy facility for
pooh-poohing difficulties which he was not called upon to combat or
expected to overcome. Only the cheerfulness of an uneducated mind
could inspire the complacent self-glorification of his tone when he
ridicules and reproves the institutions of his own country, institutions
which grave, educated, and gifted men are content to pass their lives in
the effort to improve, day by day, here a little and there a little—those
among them who are God-fearing and God-loving, with an awful
sense of insufficiency and responsibility. This is still more remarkable,
and is reinforced by an exuberant sense of the absurdity naturally and
inevitably inherent in anything which he does not admire or like when

his subject is a foreign country and a foreign race. It does not readily occur to uneducated people, unless they have the grace of humility, that more exists in what they are looking at than they can see, and that things which puzzle them may possibly be above their comprehension, instead of being beneath their notice. . . .

. . . No writer gets such a hold of our feelings at the expense of our common sense, or fails more completely to secure sympathy where he claims it most eagerly and ostentatiously. Who cares about his young lady heroines? Though Sydney Carton,—one of the finest of Mr Dickens's creations,—died for her, Lucie Manette is not really interesting, in spite of the use made of her expressive forehead and her golden hair. Emma Haredale is the most noble and attractive of the series of girl heroines, but we see little of her, and she is always in an exceptional position. Dolly Varden is charming, chiefly because she is *not* a young lady, and her coquetries and affectations are of an original sort. Mary Graham is the most shadowy of heroines. Ada, the 'darling' of Miss Esther Summerson, is rather more sly and deceitful than is quite consonant with our idea of an 'angel girl.' Estella is an impossibility, happily of a kind which not the most impressionable of Mr Dickens's young readers will try to imitate. Little Dorrit is the dreariest of heroines, a Mrs Gummidge without the drollery of that doleful relict of the 'old 'un.' Florence Dombey, whose grim and exclusive bringing up leads to such incongruous consequences, is the most interesting, though not the least improbable in the long list. Rosa Bud, the last of the young lady heroines, is a *resumé* of the silliness of all her predecessors, with the addition of a special silliness peculiar to herself.

Mr Thackeray's young ladies have been much derided and decried, and, with the exception of Ethel Newcome, we have nothing to say for them; but we suspect Amelia Sedley or Charlotte Baynes would be a more endurable companion for a rational man through life than Dora or Rosa, and Miss Laura Bell or Theo Leigh, though they are both, in their several ways, wearisome, are incomparably less so than those dreadful specimens of the 'household angel' class, Ruth Pinch and Esther Summerson. In the first place, they are ladies, while Miss Pinch and Miss Summerson are as fussy and vulgar as they are vapid and tiresome. . . .

154. From an unsigned article, 'Dickens', London Quarterly Review

January 1871, xxxv, 265–86

A review of the 'Charles Dickens' edition of the *Works*. The *London Quarterly Review* was a learned Methodist journal. For possible authorship of this item, see No. 140.

... The genuine success of Dickens ... is an unquestionable fact, demanding to be faced, not in the spirit of noisy detraction or of stupid wonder, but in an attitude of inquiry and calm appreciation ... [The reviewer attempts to explain his popularity.] The facts and reasons of the situation seem, then, to shape themselves thus:—Starting with a lucky hit, which placed him in a position of temporary influence, Charles Dickens put in force an almost unparalleled energy in applying with tact the literary qualities we have glanced at. First of all, the British public must have amusement pure and simple, of an easy and straight-forward class; and that he could provide in bulk. Next, the proverbial taste of the Englishman for what is melancholy and sombre must be met; and that was a task which he could accomplish with the requisite spice of vulgarity. Thirdly, there was a popular move in favour of instructive books; so conspicuous morals must at all hazards be brought into his fictions. Fourthly, the passion for reform was still strong upon the middle-class mind; and well for the author who could show the middle-class mind real or imaginary fields for reform! Fifthly (and this point is perhaps the most important item in the qualification for popular authorship), it is so nice to see the foibles of one's fellows placed in an amusing light, and to have the laugh in one's sleeve at all one's neigh-bours, so to speak, and yet never to be able to recognise in any figure of the amusing picture *one's own portrait*: and in this Dickens is the most successful writer the world has ever seen.

This last point seems to us to be so preponderant among the causes of Dickens's popularity, that we must dwell on it a moment before

passing to consider the nature and quality of the influence he was
enabled to exert through the medium of that so great popularity. It is,
perhaps, uncharitable to the world at large to say so; but there is no
doubt that man's mind is, and ever has been, as far as we can trace it,
so constructed as to find a vast satisfaction in the half-compassionate,
half-contemptuous contemplation of persons rendered by situation
either ludicrous or objects of pity. The psychology of this phenomenon
has been over and over again discussed, nor is there any need to discuss
it here; but we may take it for granted that the explanation lies in the
individual man's indomitable vanity and self-love—the pleasure he has
in feeling that he is superior to other people. No works more than
Dickens's pander to this self-love and vanity. Looked at superficially,
his characters are all possible characters in the main; but they are dis-
severed from the rank of characters that reflect oneself to oneself by the
fact that every one of them is marked by peculiarities more pronounced
than the faults or eccentricities a person sees or deplores in himself. We
are lenient to our own faults and idiosyncrasies, and by habit scarcely
know them very often; but we are severe on the faults of others, and
acute to see their idiosyncrasies; and Dickens is severe on the faults and
idiosyncrasies of all his characters,—sufficiently so to bring them, in the
mind of each individual, up to the level of *other people's* peculiarities.
His works want that deep truth and earnestness that carries a fictitious
life-lesson home to the man or woman to whom it is most appropriate,
and thus they steer clear of a great quicksand of offence. . . .

We are aware that we are laying ourselves open to a torrent of
censure, and provoking the ready question, 'How is it that, if things are
as you represent, Dickens has managed to make people all over the
English-speaking world,—ay, and elsewhere,—think him the greatest
fictionist of this or any other age? Is he not the greatest fictionist the
human race has yet produced, and is not this fact the undescribed *something* about him that has seized the whole world?' But we are prepared
for the torrents of censure, while to the question our reply is—that,
though Dickens's works are still by far the most popular of the age, we
have never met a single man of high cultivation who regarded Dickens
in the light of an artist at all, or looked upon his books as greatly worth
the attention of persons capable of appreciating better things: the undescribed *something* we have above attempted to analyse into its component parts; but however important any of those parts may be as
elements in the question, we hold that the culminating and indispensable part is the enabling of everyone to have, when so disposed, a 'jolly

good laugh at people and things in general,' as the treat may with apposite inelegance be termed. . . .

[The reviewer then discusses the nature and quality of Dickens's influence.]

. . . He takes a place very different, and probably much more power-ful, than that taken by the ablest pamphleteer or press-man in the growth of these detailed reforms for which he seems to have had so honest a love; but the place must always remain impossible to fix. We faithfully believe that the reforms would each and all have come duly about without him; but with equal faith do we believe that they have been hastened by him, without any counterbalancing result of evil from the caricaturing of the various subjects, and undue odium thrown on classes in some instances. . . . We need but to instance one or two cases in point. Let any person of frankness and intelligence examine the scene in the drawing-room of Mr Dombey with the family doctor and consulting physician. The whole thing is thoroughly unlifelike: any one who has had to do with doctors such as would be called in by a man of Mr Dombey's wealth and position knows them not to be the mean-souled mountebanks there portrayed; knows that their language, their deportment, their subject-matter of conversation, are one and all absurdly distorted. No doubt there are mean mountebanks to be found among the members of this profession as in others, but they lurk in the by-places of the class, and do not represent it. The caricature in such an instance as this is thoroughly misplaced, but we conceive that although numerous silly people might deem their oracle to be bestowing deserved castigation on a gang of impostors, still the general status of medical practitioners could not be materially injured by such a trivial and transparent piece of buffoonery.

Again, in *Bleak House*, there is a noteworthy instance of an analogous kind—the caricaturing of certain nonconformist clergy, under the disgusting figure of the Rev Mr Chadband, whose conversation and behaviour are outrageous beyond all bounds of any art, except that which we presume Dickens's admirers call *his* 'art.' This is a far worse case than the other, for while Dr Parker Pepps is a mere occasional figure playing no considerable part in the book, the Rev Mr Chadband embodies an elaborate calumny, asserted and reasserted throughout the volume. Without any wish to repudiate on account of the clerical faculty, more than of any other class, the weaknesses inseparable from flesh and blood, we protest that Dickens committed a flagrant and unpardonable offence in putting forth such a creation as the one in question, under the well-known *hazard* of its being taken as an attack on a set of men, even if such were not the *intention*. Let any man search the dismal outskirts of Christianity for the foundation of this personage, and where will he find it? Go whither he will among those who are or seem to be set apart to the ministry, whether in the Established Church or in the many Dissenting communities, he will find perhaps some proportion of weak preachers and persons who are mere men of no special qualification for the work they have assumed. But the low sensuality dressed in a sanctimonious garb, the absurd unmeaning rigmarole of comparisons and illustrations that have nothing to do with each other or with any thread of discourse, the fetid vulgarity oozing, so to speak, from every pore of the man's dirty skin,—where did Dickens get these things, or the gaping idiotcy of adult persons ready to accept the satyr [*sic*] as a very embodiment of greatness and nobility?. . .

155. [Mrs Oliphant], from 'Charles Dickens', *Blackwood's Magazine*

June 1871, cix, 673-95

... There is something half affecting, half ridiculous—and which shows in the very best light the grateful docility of the common mind—in the eagerness with which the public tried to convince itself that it was charmed by the opening of the fragment called *Edwin Drood*. We all said to each other that this was going to be a powerful story—one of his best, perhaps; we were on the outlook for the familiar delights, the true Dickens vein, which we knew so well. The effect was flat, no doubt, and the effort severe; but perhaps we thought that was our own, the reader's, fault. Thus faithfully does the British public, much-maligned and sorely-tried audience, uphold the minstrel who has once got possession of its ear. It stood by him with a piteous fidelity to the last....

... He who has always preached the most amiable of sentiments—he who was the first to find out the immense spiritual power of the Christmas turkey—he who has given us so many wonderful instances of sudden conversion from cruelty and unkindness to the most beaming, not to say maudlin, amiability,—shall we venture to say of him that his influence has not been of an elevating order? We shrink from the undertaking. But still we venture to repeat, it is a curious fact that this most influential writer has brought his readers into a great deal of very indifferent company, and has not left to us to neutralise it a single potential image of the elevated or the great—nay, has left us nothing but the weakest, sloppiest, maudlin exhibitions of goodness, big in complacency, but poor in every other point.

... His instinct leads him to keep on the surface. There is more true insight in half-a-dozen lines which we could select here and there from other writers as to the effects of street education than in all Sam Weller.

Nevertheless, Sam Weller is not only true, but original. There is no tragic side to him. There is no real tragic side, indeed, to any of the Dickens characters. And Dickens, perhaps, is the only great artist of whom this can be said; for to most creative minds there is a charm indescribable in the contact of human character with the profounder difficulties of life. An instinctive sense of his own weakness, however, keeps him as far as possible from these problems. And his Sam is the most light-hearted hero, perhaps, that has ever been put upon canvas. He is the very impersonation of easy conscious skill and cleverness. He has never met with anything in his career that he could not give a good account of. Life is all above-board with him, straightforward, jovial, on the surface. He stands in the midst of the confusion of the picture in very much the same position which the author himself assumes. He is the *Deus ex machina*, the spectator of everybody's mistakes and failures —a kind of laughing providence to set everything right. Sam's position in the *Pickwick Papers* is one of the great marvels in English art. It is the first act of the revolution which Mr Dickens accomplished in his literary sphere—the new system which has brought those uppermost who were subordinate according to the old canons. This ostler from the City, this groom picked up from the pavement, is, without doubt or controversy, everybody's master in the story of which he is the centre. When the whole little community in the book is puzzled, Sam's cleverness cuts the knot. It is he who always sees what to do, who keeps everybody else in order. He even combines with his *role* of all-accomplished serving-man the other *role* of *jeune premier*, and retains his superiority all through the book, at once in philosophy and practical insight, in love and war.

The *Pickwick Papers* stands by itself among its author's works; and as the first work of a young man, it is, we think, unique in literature. Other writers have professed to write novels without a hero: Dickens, so far as we are aware, is the only one who, without making any profession, has accomplished that same. To be sure, *Pickwick* is not, in the ordinary sense of the word, a novel, and yet it would be hard to classify it in any other list. Strangest of books! which introduces us to a set of people, young men and old, women and girls, figures intended to represent the usual strain of flesh and blood—in order that we may laugh at them all! There is a horrible impartiality, a good-humoured universal malice, running through the whole. The author stands in the midst, half himself, half revealed in the person of his favourite Sam, and looks at the world he has created, and holds his sides. He does not even feel contempt, to speak of—he feels nothing but what fun it is to see so many fools disporting themselves according to their folly. There is, as we have said, a horrible impartiality in it. Other writers have preserved a little respect, a little sympathy, for the lovers, at least—a little feeling that youth must have something fine in it, and that the gallant and the maiden have a right to their pedestal. But not to Dickens: the delight with which in this book he displays all the ridiculousness and inherent absurdity which he finds in life, is like the indiscriminate fun of a schoolboy who shouts with mirth at everything which can by any means be made an occasion of laughter, without acknowledging any restraint of natural reverence or decorum. In *Pickwick*, the work is that of a man of genius, but the spirit is almost always that of a mischievous innocent schoolboy. When the great contemporary and rival of Dickens produced his first great work, all the virtuous world rose up and condemned the cynicism of *Vanity Fair*; but nobody has ever said a word about the cynicism of *Pickwick*; and yet, to our thinking, the one is a hundred times more apparent than the other. *Vanity Fair* is a book full of deep and tragic meaning, of profound feeling and sentiment, which crop up through the fun, and are ever present, though so seldom expressed. The historian, story-teller, social philosopher, laughs, it is true, but he has a great mind to weep: he sneers sometimes, but it is because his heart grows hot as he watches the pranks that men play before high heaven. But the author of *Pickwick* cares not a straw what fools his puppets make of themselves; the more foolish they are, the more he laughs at their absurdity. He is too good-humoured, too full of cheerful levity and the sense of mischief, to think of their lies and brags and vanity as anything vile and blameable; they are so funny, that he forgets everything else. His characters go tumbling about the world as the clown and pantaloon do in the midst of those immemorial immoralities of the pantomine—the ever-successful tricks and cheats in which we all find once-a-year an unsophisticated pleasure. In short, the atmosphere of *Pickwick* is more like that of a pantomime than of any other region we know. . . Never was there such a big, full, crowded pantomime stage—never so many lively changes of scene and character. There is scarcely more art or skill in the situations than is necessary to please the most indulgent holiday audience. . . . It is of its nature delightful to the very young—to the schoolboy mind yet unawakened to anything beyond the fun of existence; and at the very other end of the social scale, it is full of amusement to the wearied man, who has enough of serious life, and to whom it is a relief to escape into this curious world, where all is fun, and nothing serious. But of all the revelations of mind made by the first works of great artists, *Pickwick* is perhaps the most incomprehensible. With all its charming gaiety and good-humour, with its bits of fine moral reflection and demonstrative worship of benevolence, it is without heart and without sympathy—superficial and profane.

We do not use the latter word, however, in a religious sense; for Dickens has always persistently and most benevolently countenanced and patronised religion. He is humanly, not sacredly, profane in the first great effort of his genius—not bitterly sceptical of, but light-heartedly indifferent to, human excellence. This will, we fear, be considered strange doctrine by those who have taken for granted all his subsequent moralities on the subject, and the very great use he has made of moral transformations. But in *Pickwick* there is absolutely no moral sense. It either does not exist, or has not been awakened; and there is the deepest profanity—a profanity which scorns all the traditions of poetry and romance, as well as all the higher necessities of nature—in the total absence of any sentiment or grace in the heroes and heroines, the lovers, the one class of humanity on whose behalf there exists a lingering universal prejudice. . . .

[A lengthy survey of Dickens's career follows. '*Pickwick* was full of the most genial, natural, easy indifference to the higher morality; but every subsequent work is heavy with meaning and has an almost polemical moral.' The later novels present an almost continuous decline: '*Little Dorrit* is, again, a step lower down in the scale than *Bleak House*. . . . There is a gleam, however, of departing energy in the curious book called *Great Expectations*, which is worth noticing' (see Mrs Oliphant's review of it, No. 124).]

To *Our Mutual Friend* and *The Tale of Two Cities* we can give no place at all. The latter might have been written by any new author, so little of Dickens there is in it. In short, we believe there are at least half-a-dozen writers extant who could have produced a piece a great deal more like the master, and with much more credible marks of authenticity. *Edwin Drood* has been supposed by many a kind of resurrection, or at least the forerunner of a resurrection, of his characteristic force. But we cannot say that such is the impression produced upon our own mind. Of all undesirable things to be deprecated by an admirer of Dickens, we should say that the resurrection of his peculiar style of tragedy would be about the greatest—and this is all which could be hoped from the opening of *Edwin Drood*. . . . .

And when we look back upon the works of Dickens, they divide themselves at once into these two classes—the works of his heyday and prime, and the works of his decadence. The natural vigour of the one contrasts in the most singular manner with the strain and effort of the other; and yet, if we examine into the matter, the change is very natural and explainable. The great source of his popularity is the immense flow of spirits, the abundant tide of life, which runs through his early works. He never spares himself in this respect, but pours forth crowds of super-numeraries upon his stage, like an enterprising manager at Christmas time, sparing no expense, as it were, and giving himself infinite trouble merely to provide a rich and varied background for his principal figures. He leaves upon our minds an impression of unbounded wealth and illimitable resources. We know that it will be no trouble to him to fill up any vacant corner with a group; and even while the thought crosses our mind, his eye has caught the vacancy, and a half-dozen of living creatures are tossed into the gap in the twinkling of an eye. This overflowing abundance has a wonderful effect upon the public mind. A sense of something like infinity grows upon us as we see the new forms appear out of the void without even a word, at a glance from the painter's eye. And then his creative energy was such that a stream of fun passed into the dulness along with this strain of life. These new people amused their author. He dressed them in the first fantastic garb that might come to his hand, and set them free to dance through their eccentric circle as they chose. This immense energy, fertility, and plentifulness is, however, one of the gifts that can least be warranted to last. It belongs to the first half of life, and could scarcely be expected to survive beyond that period. When the intellectual pulse began to beat slower, and the tide of existence to run less full, this power abated, as was natural. Though there were still as many people on the canvas, these people were but the ghosts of the lusty crowds of old; and even the numbers got reduced; the supers began to be dismissed; and economy stole in where prodigality had once ruled the day. If the reader will look at the later works, he will perceive at once this lessened fulness. When the author himself became aware of it, the knowledge roused him to preternatural exertions. The absurder oddities of Dickens are crowded into these later books in a forlorn attempt to make extrav-agance do the work of energy. . . . This extreme strain and effort to prolong the prodigality of early work is at the same time, no doubt, one of the reasons why he never attains in any solitary instance to the vigour and originality of his beginning. It might have been supposed that the very narrowing of the sphere would intensify the individual conceptions; but Dickens would not consent to narrow his sphere, and did not give his powers fair-play. Thus the tide of his genius fell, as the tide of life falls. That elaboration which experience and study make natural to the mature mind, struck at the very roots of his success, for his success had never been due to art. It had been the spontaneity, the ease and freedom, the mirrored life, versatile and rich and ever-moving as life itself, though seldom more profound than the surface picture which a glass reflects and brightens, which had been his grand charm. The 'thoughts which sometimes lie too deep for tears;' the 'richer colouring' given by the deep glance of those eyes 'which have kept watch o'er man's mortality,' did not lie within his range. Therefore, as he grew older, he waned, and his power went from his hands. . . .

Yet with all his limitations and deficiencies the genius of Dickens was one of which England has reason to be proud. When he held the mirror up to Nature, he never showed, it is true, anything heroic, or of the highest strain of virtue and nobleness: but he showed such a picture of the teeming animated world as few men have been able to do—he expounded and cleared to us some unseen corners of the soul, so as to make them great in the perfectness of the revelation; and here and there he cleared away the rubbish from some genial sunshiny spots where the flowers can grow. We may apply to him, without doubt, the surest test to which the Maker can be subject; were all his books swept by some intellectual catastrophe out of the world, there would still exist in the world some score at least of people, with all whose ways and sayings we are more intimately acquainted than with those of our brothers and sisters, who would owe to him their being. While we live, and while our children live, Sam Weller and Dick Swiveller, Mr Pecksniff and Mrs Gamp, the Micawbers and the Squeerses, can never die. They are not lofty personages, perhaps, nor can they do us much good now that they are here. But here they are, and nothing can destroy them. They are more real than we are ourselves, and will out-live and outlast us as they have outlived their creator. This is the one proof of genius which no critic, not the most carping or dissatisfied, can gainsay. Would there had been among them even one soul of higher pretensions to give dignity to the group! but such as they are, they are indestructible and beyond the power of decay. . . .

FORSTER'S *LIFE OF DICKENS*

1871-3

The first volume of the *Life*, published in November 1871, was in its ninth edition before the year ended: some sign of the interest Dickens commanded, for, while Forster was generally credited with some degree of competence, few critics expressed much warmth for his art as a biographer. A. W. Ward sensibly remarked, however, that 'the shortcomings of the *Life* have ... been more often proclaimed than defined; ... its merits are those of its author as well as of its subject' (*Charles Dickens* (1882), v). The jibe that it was 'The Life of Forster, with notices of Dickens' (attributed to G. H. Lewes and Wilkie Collins) is often quoted, but stupid. Other friends of Dickens found that it brought 'his dear presence back to us again with intense vividness' (*James T. Fields: Biographical Notes* (1881), 196).

Reviewers were surprised, and moved, by the blacking-warehouse revelations, but almost universally shocked to learn that Dickens had depicted his father as Micawber, and distressed by the concern for money apparent in the Readings phase. Many critics took the opportunity to survey Dickens's achievement and critical reputation, as well as to explore his personality. The defects of his education were noted again, as was his not being a complete gentleman in manners or outlook (e.g. *The Times*, 26 December 1871, 4, in a review of over five columns). One phrase of Forster's was quoted and discussed by many reviewers (e.g, R. H. Hutton in No. 162): 'There was for him no "city of the mind" against outward ills for inner consolation and shelter' (*Life*, 641). In later editions, and in Volumes 2 and 3 (published in November 1872 and December 1873), Forster accommodated some of the corrections and criticisms made by reviewers and other readers, and also replied to criticisms made of Dickens in reviews of previous volumes; notably, he took issue with G. H. Lewes (see No. 158), whose assessment of Dickens manifestly struck him as the act of a false friend and an interested party. See an account of his correspondence with readers, W. J. Carlton, 'Postscripts to Forster', *Dickensian*, lviii (1962), 87-94; also Sylvère Monod, 'Forster's *Life of Dickens* and literary criticism', *English Studies Today*, 4th series (Rome, 1966), 357–73. F. G. Kitton has useful lists of and selections from critiques of the *Life*, and the *Letters*, in *Dickensiana* (1886), 314–39.

156. Thomas Carlyle on the *Life*

1871, 1874

(*a*) (Letter to Duffy, 12 December 1871) 'The whole world is, in these very days and weeks, full of Forster and his *Life of Dickens*, for which there is a perfect rage or public famine (copies not to be supplied fast enough). . . . It is curious, and in part surprising; yields a true view of Dickens (great part of it being even of his own writing). . . . Me nothing in it so surprised as these two American explosions around poor Dickens, *all* Yankee-doodle-dom blazing up like one universal soda water bottle round so very measurable a phenomenon, this and the way the phenomenon takes it, was curiously and even genially interesting to me, and significant of Yankee-doodle-dom.' (Charles Gavan Duffy, *Conversations with Carlyle* (1892), 245).

(*b*) (Letter to John Forster, 16 February 1874) 'This Third Volume throws a new light and character to me over the Work at large. I incline to consider this Biography as taking rank, in essential respects, parallel to Boswell himself, though on widely different grounds. Boswell, by those genial abridgments and vivid face to face pictures of Johnson's thoughts, conversational ways and modes of appearance among his fellow-creatures, has given, as you often hear me say, such a delineation of a man's existence as was never given by another man. By quite different resources, by those sparkling, clear and sunny utterances of Dickens's own (bits of *auto*-biography unrivalled in clearness and credibility) which were at your disposal and have been intercalated every now and then, you have given to every intelligent eye the power of looking down to the very bottom of Dickens's mode of existing in this world; and I say have performed a feat which, except

THE CRITICAL HERITAGE

in Boswell, the unique, I know not where to parallel. So long as Dickens is interesting to his fellow-men, here will be seen, face to face, what Dickens's manner of existing was; his steady practicality, withal; the singularly solid business talent he continually had; and deeper than all, if one had the eye to see deep enough, dark, fateful silent elements, tragical to look upon, and hiding amid dazzling radiances as of the sun, the elements of death itself. Those two American Journies especially transcend in tragic interest to a thinking reader most things one has seen in writing.

On the whole, therefore, I declare you to have done right well, my Friend; and my first and last word about the Book is, *Euge, euge.*' (Charles Richard Saunders, 'Carlyle's Letters', *Bulletin of the John Rylands Library*, xxx (1955–6), 223)

157. Lord Shaftesbury on Dickens

1871

Journal 20 December 1871 (Edwin Hodder, *Life and Work of the Seventh Earl of Shaftesbury* (1886), iii, 298).

Shaftesbury (1801–85), philanthropist and politician, had been acquainted with Dickens, who in earlier years had worked in some of the same charitable fields as he, though Dickens disliked many of the implications of his Evangelical beliefs. Shaftesbury's letter to Forster, quoted in the journal entry, continued: 'He felt what he wrote, and he wrote what he felt; and, as a result, he obtained, and I am sure to his heart's joy, a mighty alleviation of tyranny and sorrow. And yet, strange to say, he never gave me a helping hand —at least, I never heard of it' (quoted by W. J. Carlton, *Dickensian*, lviii (1962), 91).

Forster has sent me his *Life of Dickens*. The man was a phenomenon, an exception, a special production. Nothing like him ever preceded.

567

Nature isn't such a tautologist as to make another to follow him. He was se[n]t, I doubt not, to rouse attention to many evils and many woes; and though not putting it on Christian principle (which would have rendered it unacceptable), he may have been, in God's singular and unfathomable goodness as much a servant of the Most High as the pagan Naaman, 'by whom the Lord had given deliverance to Syria'! God gave him, as I wrote to Forster, a general retainer against all suffering and oppression.

158. G. H. Lewes, from a review of Vol. I of Forster's *Life*, *Fortnightly Review*

February 1872, xvii, 141–54

Reprinted in full in *The Dickens Critics*, 54–74.

On Lewes (1817–78), see headnote to No. 80; he had been founder-editor of the *Fortnightly Review*. This important essay shares with Taine's assessment of Dickens in 1856 (No. 97) the role of critical Villain, in Forster's *Life*: 'the pretentious airs of [Lewes's] performance, with its prodigious professions of candour, . . . the trick of studied depreciation was never carried so far or made so odious as in this case . . .' (*Life*, 716). Forster's sneer at these 'professions of candour' is doubtless meant to imply that Lewes was not disinterested, but was trying to down Dickens as a way of increasing the stature of his consort, George Eliot. G. H. Ford offers a useful assessment of Lewes, in the history of Dickens-criticism (*Dickens and his Readers*, 149–54). See also Morris Grunhut, 'Lewes as a Critic of the Novel', *Studies in Philology*, xlv (1948), 491–511; Alice R. Kaminsky, ed., *Literary Criticism of G. H. Lewes* (Lincoln, Nebraska, 1964); and above, Nos. 17, 80.

. . . One thing is certain: [Forster's] admiration was expressed long before all the world had acknowledged Dickens's genius, and was continued through the long years when the majority of writers had ceased to express much fervour of admiration, preferring rather to dwell on his shortcomings and exaggerations.

And this brings me to the noticeable fact that there probably never was a writer of so vast a popularity whose genius was so little *appreciated* by the critics. The very splendour of his successes so deepened the shadow of his failures that to many eyes the shadows supplanted the splendour. Fastidious readers were loath to admit that a writer could be justly called great whose defects were so glaring. They admitted, because it was indisputable, that Dickens delighted thousands, that his admirers were found in all classes, and in all countries; that he stirred the sympathy of masses not easily reached through Literature, and always stirred healthy, generous emotions; that he impressed a new direction on popular writing, and modified the Literature of his age, in its spirit no less than in its form; but they nevertheless insisted on his defects as if these outweighed all positive qualities; and spoke of him either with condescending patronage, or with sneering irritation. Surely this is a fact worthy of investigation? Were the critics wrong, and if so, in what consisted their error? How are we to reconcile this immense popularity with this critical contempt? The private readers and the public critics who were eager to take up each successive number of his works as it appeared, whose very talk was seasoned with quotations from and allusions to these works, who, to my knowledge, were wont to lay aside books of which they could only speak in terms of eulogy, in order to bury themselves in the 'new number' when the well-known green cover made its appearance—were nevertheless at this very time niggard in their praise, and lavish in their scorn of the popular humorist. It is not long since I heard a very distinguished man express measureless contempt for Dickens, and a few minutes afterwards, in reply to some representations on the other side, admit that Dickens had 'entered into his life.'

Dickens has proved his power by a popularity almost unexampled, embracing all classes. Surely it is a task for criticism to exhibit the sources of that power? If everything that has ever been alleged against the works be admitted, there still remains an immense success to be accounted for. It was not by their defects that these works were carried over Europe and America. It was not their defects which made them the delight of grey heads on the bench, and the study of youngsters in the counting-house and school-room. Other writers have been exaggerated, untrue, fantastic, and melodramatic; but they have gained so little notice that no one thinks of pointing out their defects. It is clear, therefore, that Dickens had powers which enabled him to triumph in spite of the weaknesses which clogged them; and it is worth inquiring what those powers were, and their relation to his undeniable defects.

I am not about to attempt such an inquiry, but simply to indicate two or three general points of view. It will be enough merely to mention in passing the primary cause of his success, his overflowing fun, because even uncompromising opponents admit it. They may be ashamed of their laughter, but they laugh. A revulsion of feeling at the preposterousness or extravagance of the image, may follow the burst of laughter, but the laughter is irresistible, whether rational or not, and there is no arguing away such a fact.

Great as Dickens is in fun, so great that Fielding and Smollett are small in comparison, he would have been only a passing amusement for the world had he not been gifted with an imagination of marvellous vividness, and an emotional, sympathetic nature capable of furnishing that imagination with elements of universal power. Of him it may be said with less exaggeration than of most poets, that he was of 'imagination all compact;' if the other higher faculties were singularly deficient in him, this faculty was imperial. He was a seer of visions; and his visions were of objects at once familiar and potent. Psychologists will understand both the extent and the limitation of the remark, when I say that in no other perfectly sane mind (Blake, I believe, was not perfectly sane) have I observed vividness of imagination approaching so closely to hallucination. . . .

Returning from this digression, let me say that I am very far indeed from wishing to imply any agreement in the common notion that 'great wits to madness nearly are allied;' on the contrary, my studies have led to the conviction that nothing is less like genius than insanity, although some men of genius have had occasional attacks; and further, that I have never observed any trace of the insane temperament in Dickens's works, or life, they being indeed singularly free even from the eccentricities which often accompany exceptional powers; nevertheless, with all due limitations, it is true that there is considerable light shed upon his works by the action of the imagination in hallucination. To him also *revived* images have the vividness of sensations; to him also *created* images have the coercive force of realities, excluding all control, all contradiction. What seems preposterous, impossible to us, seemed to him simple fact of observation. When he imagined a street, a house, a room, a figure, he saw it not in the vague schematic way of ordinary imagination, but in the sharp definition of actual perception, all the salient details obtruding themselves on his attention. He, seeing it thus vividly, made us also see it; and believing in its reality however fantastic, he communicated something of his belief to us. He presented it in such relief that we ceased to think of it as a picture. So definite and insistent was the image, that even while knowing it was false we could not help, for a moment, being affected, as it were, by his hallucination.

This glorious energy of imagination is that which Dickens had in common with all great writers. It was this which made him a creator, and made his creations universally intelligible, no matter how fantastic and unreal. His types established themselves in the public mind like personal experiences. Their falsity was unnoticed in the blaze of their illumination. Every humbug seemed a Pecksniff, every nurse a Gamp, every jovial improvident a Micawber, every stinted serving-wench a Marchioness. Universal experiences became individualised in these types; an image and a name were given, and the image was so suggestive that it seemed to *express* all that it was found to *recall*, and Dickens was held to have depicted what his readers supplied. Against such power criticism was almost idle. In vain critical reflection showed these figures to be merely masks—not characters, but personified characteristics, caricatures and distortions of human nature,—the vividness of their presentation triumphed over reflection: their creator managed to communicate to the public his own unhesitating belief. Unreal and impossible as these types were, speaking a language never heard in life, moving like pieces of simple mechanism always in one way (instead of moving with the infinite fluctuations of organisms, incalculable yet intelligible, surprising yet familiar), these unreal figures affected the uncritical reader with the force of reality; and they did so in virtue of their embodiment of some real characteristic vividly presented. The imagination of the author laid hold of some well-marked physical trait, some peculiarity of aspect, speech, or manner which every one recognised at once; and the force with which this was presented made it occupy the mind to the exclusion of all critical doubts: only reflection could detect the incongruity. Think of what this implies! Think how little the mass of men are given to reflect on their impressions, and how their minds are for the most part occupied with sensations rather than ideas, and you will see why Dickens held an undisputed sway. Give a child a wooden horse, with hair for mane and tail, and wafer-spots for colouring, he will never be disturbed by the fact that this horse does not move its legs, but runs on wheels—the general suggestion suffices for his belief; and this wooden horse, which he can handle and draw, is believed in more than a pictured horse by a Wouvermanns or an Ansdell. It may be said of Dickens's human figures that they too are wooden, and run on wheels; but these are details which scarcely disturb the belief of admirers. Just as the wooden horse is brought within the range of the child's emotions, and dramatizing tendencies, when he can handle and draw it, so Dickens's figures are brought within the range of the reader's interests, and receive from these interests a sudden illumination, when they are the puppets of a drama every incident of which appeals to the sympathies. With a fine felicity of instinct he seized upon situations having an irresistible hold over the domestic affections and ordinary sympathies. He spoke in the mother-tongue of the heart, and was always sure of ready listeners. He painted the life he knew, the life every one knew; for if the scenes and manners were unlike those we were familiar with, the feelings and motives, the joys and griefs, the mistakes and efforts of the actors were universal, and therefore universally intelligible; so that even critical spectators who complained that these broadly painted pictures were artistic daubs, could not wholly resist their effective suggestiveness. He set in motion the secret springs of sympathy by touching the domestic affections. He painted nothing ideal, heroic; but all the resources of the bourgeois epic were in his grasp. The world of thought and passion lay beyond his horizon. But the joys and pains of childhood, the petty tyrannies of ignoble natures, the genial pleasantries of happy natures, the life of the poor, the struggles of the street and back parlour, the insolence of office, the sharp social contrasts, east-wind and Christmas jollity, hunger, misery, and hot punch—these he could deal with, so that we laughed and cried, were startled at the revelation of familiar facts hitherto unnoted, and felt our pulses quicken as we were hurried along with him in his fanciful flight.

Such were the sources of his power. To understand how it is that critics quite competent to recognise such power, and even so far amenable to it as to be moved and interested by the works in spite of all their drawbacks, should have forgotten this undenied power, and written or spoken of Dickens with mingled irritation and contempt, we must take into account two natural tendencies—the bias of opposition, and the bias of technical estimate. . . .

Something like this is the feeling produced by Dickens's works in many cultivated and critical readers. They see there human character and ordinary events pourtrayed with a mingled verisimilitude and falsity altogether unexampled. The drawing is so vivid yet so incorrect, or else is so blurred and formless, with such excess of *effort* (as of a showman beating on the drum) that the doubt arises how an observer so remarkably keen could make observations so remarkably false, and miss such very obvious facts; how the rapid glance which could swoop down on a peculiarity with hawk-like precision, could overlook all that accompanied and was organically related to that peculiarity; how the eye for characteristics could be so blind to character, and the ear for dramatic idiom be so deaf to dramatic language; finally, how the writer's exquisite susceptibility to the grotesque could be insensible to the occasional grotesqueness of his own attitude. Michael Angelo is intelligible, and Giotto is intelligible; but a critic is nonplussed at finding the invention of Angelo with the drawing of Giotto. It is indeed surprising that Dickens should have observed man, and not been impressed with the fact that man is, in the words of Montaigne, *un être ondoyant et diverse*. And the critic is distressed to observe the substitution of mechanisms for minds, puppets for characters. It is needless to dwell on such monstrous failures as Mantalini, Rosa Dartle, Lady Dedlock, Esther Summerson, Mr Dick, Arthur Gride, Edith Dombey, Mr Carker—needless, because if one studies the successful figures one finds even in them only touches of verisimilitude. When one thinks of Micawber always presenting himself in the same situation, moved with the same springs, and uttering the same sounds, always confident of something turning up, always crushed and rebounding, always making punch—and his wife always declaring she will never part from him, always referring to his talents and her family—when one thinks of the 'catchwords' personified as characters, one is reminded of the frogs whose brains have been taken out for physiological purposes, and whose actions henceforth want the distinctive peculiarity of organic action, that of fluctuating spontaneity. Place one of these brainless frogs on his back and he will at once recover the sitting posture; draw a leg from under him, and he will draw it back again; tickle or prick him and he will push away the object, or take *one* hop out of the way; stroke his back, and he will utter *one* croak. All these things resemble the actions of the unmutilated frog, but they differ in being *isolated* actions, and *always the same:* they are as uniform and calculable as the movements of a machine. The uninjured frog may or may not croak, may or may not hop away; the result is never calculable, and is rarely a single croak or a single hop. It is this complexity of the organism which Dickens wholly fails to conceive; his characters have nothing fluctuating and incalculable in them, even when they embody true observations; and very often they are creations so fantastic that one is at a loss to understand how he could, without hallucination, believe them to be like reality. There are dialogues bearing the traces of straining effort at effect, which in their incongruity painfully resemble the absurd and eager expositions which insane patients pour into the listener's ear when detailing their wrongs, or their schemes. Dickens once declared to me that every word said by his characters was distinctly *heard* by him; I was at first not a little puzzled to account for the fact that he could hear language so utterly unlike the language of real feeling, and not be aware of its preposterousness; but the surprise vanished when I thought of the phenomena of hallucination. . . .

How easily the critic falls into the mistake of overvaluing technical skill, and not allowing for the primary condition, how easily he misjudges works by applying to them technical rules derived from the works of others, need not here be dwelt on. What I wish to indicate is the bias of technical estimate which, acting with that bias of opposition just noted, has caused the critics to overlook in Dickens the great artistic powers which are proved by his immense success; and to dwell only on those great artistic deficiencies which exclude him from the class of exquisite writers. He worked in delft, not in porcelain. But his prodigal imagination created in delft forms which delighted thousands. He only touched common life, but he touched it to 'fine issues;' and since we are all susceptible of being moved by pictures of children in droll and pathetic situations, and by pictures of common suffering and common joy, any writer who can paint such pictures with sufficient skill to awaken these emotions is powerful in proportion to the emotion stirred. That Dickens had this skill is undisputed; and if critical reflection shows that the means he employs are not such as will satisfy the technical estimate, and consequently that the pictures will not move the cultivated mind, nor give it the deep content which perfect Art continues to create, making the work a 'joy for ever,' we must still remember that in the present state of Literature, with hundreds daily exerting their utmost efforts to paint such pictures, it requires prodigious force and rare skill to impress images that will stir the universal heart. Murders are perpetrated without stint, but the murder of Nancy is unforgettable. Children figure in numberless plays and novels, but the deaths of little Nell and little Paul were national griefs. Seduction is one of the commonest of tragedies, but the scene in Peggoty's boat-house burns itself into the memory. Captain Cuttle and Richard Swiveller, the Marchioness and Tilly Slowboy, Pecksniff and Micawber, Tiny Tim and Mrs Gamp, may be imperfect presentations of human character, but they are types which no one can forget. Dr Johnson explained the popularity of some writer by saying, 'Sir, *his* nonsense suited *their* nonsense;' let us add, 'and his sense suited their sense,' and it will explain the popularity of Dickens. Readers to whom all the refinements of Art and Literature are as meaningless hieroglyphs, were at once laid hold of by the reproduction of their own feelings, their own experiences, their own prejudices, in the irradiating splendour of his imagination; while readers whose cultivated sensibilities were alive to the

most delicate and evanescent touches were, by virtue of their common
nature, ready to be moved and delighted at his pictures and suggestions.
The cultivated and uncultivated were affected by his admirable *mise en
scène*, his fertile invention, his striking selection of incident, his intense
vision of physical details. Only the cultivated who are made fastidious
by cultivation paused to consider the pervading commonness of the
works, and remarked that they are wholly without glimpses of a
nobler life; and that the writer presents an almost unique example of a
mind of singular force in which, so to speak, sensations never passed
into ideas. Dickens sees and feels, but the logic of feeling seems the only
logic he can manage. Thought is strangely absent from his works. I do
not suppose a single thoughtful remark on life or character could be
found throughout the twenty volumes. Not only is there a marked
absence of the reflective tendency, but one sees no indication of the
past life of humanity having ever occupied him; keenly as he observes
the objects before him, he never connects his observations into a general
expression, never seems interested in general relations of things. Compared with that of Fielding or Thackeray, his was merely an *animal*
intelligence, *i.e.*, restricted to perceptions. On this ground his early
education was more fruitful and less injurious than it would have been
to a nature constructed on a more reflective and intellectual type. It
furnished him with rare and valuable experience, early developed his
sympathies with the lowly and struggling, and did not starve any intellectual ambition. He never was and never would have been a student...

[Lewes then recounts some personal reminiscences of Dickens.]

In bringing these detached observations to a close, let me resume
their drift by saying that while on the one hand the critics seem to me
to have been fully justified in denying him the possession of many
technical excellencies, they have been thrown into unwise antagonism
which has made them overlook or undervalue the great qualities which
distinguished him; and that even on technical grounds their criticism
has been so far defective that it failed to recognise the supreme powers
which ensured his triumph in spite of all defects. For the reader of
cultivated taste there is little in his works beyond the stirring of their
emotions—but what a large exception! We do not turn over the pages
in search of thought, delicate psychological observation, grace of style,
charm of composition; but we enjoy them like children at a play,
laughing and crying at the images which pass before us. And this illustration suggests the explanation of how learned and thoughtful men

can have been almost as much delighted with the works as ignorant and juvenile readers; how Lord Jeffrey could have been so affected by the presentation of Little Nell, which most critical readers pronounce maudlin and unreal. Persons unfamiliar with theatrical representations, consequently unable to criticise the acting, are stirred by the suggestions of the scenes presented; and hence a great philosopher, poet, or man of science, may be found applauding an actor whom every playgoing apprentice despises as stagey and inartistic.

159. Robert Buchanan, 'The "Good Genie" of Fiction: Thoughts while reading Forster's *Life of Charles Dickens*', St Paul's Magazine

February 1872, x, 130–48

Reprinted in Buchanan's *A Poet's Sketch Book* (1883), 119–40.

Buchanan (1841–1901), Scottish poet, novelist, and dramatist, is best remembered for his attack on the Pre-Raphaelites, 'The Fleshly School of Poetry' (*Contemporary Review*, October 1871), which occasioned one of the several prolonged squabbles in which he was involved.

... Mighty as was the charm of Dickens, there have been from the beginning a certain select few who have never felt it. Again and again has the great Genie been approached by some dapper *dilettante* of the superfine sort, and been informed that his manner was wrong altogether, not being by any means the manner of Aristophanes, or Swift, or Sterne, or Fielding, or Smollett, or Scott. This man has called him, with some contempt, a 'caricaturist.' That man has described his method of portrayal as 'sentimental.' MacStingo prefers the humour of Galt.[1] The gelid, heart-searching critic prefers Miss Austen. Even young ladies have been known to take refuge in Thackeray. All this time, perhaps, the real truth as regards Charles Dickens has been missed or perverted. He was not a satirist, in the sense that Aristophanes was a satirist. He was not a comic analyst, like Sterne; nor an intellectual force, like Swift; nor a sharp, police-magistrate sort of humorist, like Fielding; nor a practical-joke-playing tomboy, like Smollett. He was none of these things. Quite as little was he a dashing romancist or fanciful historian, like Walter Scott. Scott found the Past ready made to his hand, fascinating and fair. Dickens simply enchanted the Present. He was the creator of Human Fairyland. He was a magician, to be bound by none of your commonplace laws and regular notions: as well try to put Incubus in a glass case, and make Robin Goodfellow the monkey of a street hurdy-gurdy. He came to put Jane Austen and M. Balzac to rout, and to turn London into Queer Country. Yes, my Gigadibs[2], he was hotheaded as an Elf, untrustworthy as a Pixy, maudlin at times as a lovesick Giant, and he squinted like Puck himself. He was, in fact, anything but the sort of story-teller the dull old world had been accustomed to. He was most unpractical. His pictures distorted life and libelled society. He grimaced and he gambolled. He bewitched the solid pudding of practicality, and made it dance to aërial music, just as if Tom Thumb were inside of it. . . .

Only the first instalment of Mr Forster's biography has yet appeared, and already the subject eclipses even the Tichborne case[3] as a topic of after-dinner chat. It is not without a shock that we are admitted behind the curtain of the good Genie's private life. All is so different from what we had anticipated. The tree which bore fruit as golden as that of the Hesperides was rooted in a wretched soil, and watered with the bitterest possible tears of self-compassion.

We see it all now in one illuminating flash. We see the mightiness of the genius and its limitations. We see why, less than almost any great author, Dickens changed with advancing culture; how, more than ninety-nine out of a hundred men, he acquired the habit of instant observation, false or true; why he imparted to things animate and inanimate the qualities of each other; wherefore all life seemed so odd to him; why, in a word, instead of soaring at once into the empyrean of

[1] John Galt (1779–1839), Scottish novelist, author of *Annals of the Parish* (1821), etc.
[2] i.e., journalistic hack: from the character in Browning's 'Bishop Blougram's Apology' 1855).
[3] *Cause célèbre* about an inheritance, which led to a prolonged controversy, 1871–4.

the sweet English 'classics' (so faultless that you can't pick a speck in them), he remained on the solid pavement, and told elfin and goblin stories of common life. It may seem putting the case too strongly, but Charles Dickens, having crushed into his childish experience a whole world of sorrow and humorous insight, so loaded his soul that he never grew any older. He was a great, grown-up, dreamy, impulsive child, just as much a child as little Paul Dombey or little David Copperfield. He saw all from a child's point of view—strange, odd, queer, puzzling. He confused men and things, animated scenery and furniture with human souls, wondered at the stars and the sea, hated facts, loved good eating and sweetmeats, fun, and frolic,—all in the childish fashion. Child-like he commiserated himself, with sharp, agonising introspection. Child-like he rushed out into the world with his griefs and grievances, concealing nothing, wildly craving for sympathy. Child-like he had fits of cold reserve, stubborner and crueller than the reserve of any perfectly cultured man. And just as much as little Paul Dombey was out of place at Dr Blimber's, where they tried to cram him with knowledge, and ever pronounced him old-fashioned, was Charles Dickens out of place in the cold, worldly circle of literature, in the bald bare academy of English culture, where his queer stories and quaint ways were simply astonishing, until even that hard circle began to love the quaint, questioning, querulous, mysterious guest, who would *not* become a pupil. Like little Paul, he was 'old-fashioned.' 'What,' he might have asked himself with little Paul, 'what could that "old-fashion" be, that seemed to make the people sorry? What could it be?'

Never, perhaps, has a fragment of biography wakened more interest and amazement than the first chapters of Mr Forster's biography. . . .

160. [William Dean Howells], from an unsigned review of Vol. II, *Atlantic Monthly*

February 1873, xxxi, 238–9

Howells (1837–1920), American novelist and essayist, was editor of the *Atlantic Monthly* 1871–81. He wrote again about Dickens in his *Criticism and Fiction* (New York, 1890), *My Literary Passions* (New York, 1895) and *Heroines of Fiction*, vol. i (New York, 1901).

... Though the letters given are not easy reading, though their fun seems often pitilessly forced, and their seriousness of the blackest midnight hue, and their fervor of the very red hottest, they are extremely useful in possessing us fully with an idea of the pressure under which Dickens felt, joked, wept, wrote, lived. His whole existence was a prolonged storm and stress, and the wonder is, not that he died so young, but that he lived to be so old. This pressure told upon his quality. A man of unquestionable genius, his material, at its finest, was never of the finest. The melodramatic was his notion of the dramatic, the eloquent was his idea of the poetic; his humor was burlesque; his pathos was never too deep for tears. It seems that he could not like anything better, if we are to judge from his estimate of Hawthorne's matchless romance:

I finished the Scarlet Letter yesterday. It falls off sadly, after that fine opening scene. The psychological part of the story is very much overdone, and not truly done, I think. Their suddenness of meeting and agreeing to go away together, after all those years, is very poor. Mr Chillingworth ditto. The child out of nature altogether. And Mr Dimmesdale never could have begotten her.

This failure to understand the subtle perfection of art so far above his is all the more sadly amusing when one thinks, in connection with it, of the shapelessness of his own plots, the unnaturalness of his situations, the crudity of his treatment of characters similar to those he censures. Indeed, when you go back to the most popular of the Dickens romances, you marvel at the effect the earlier books had upon the generation in which they were written, and question whether there is not some witchery in the mere warmth and novelty of a young author's book that makes it captivating to his contemporaries. In this biography you read with amazement the letters of Lord Jeffrey, in which the old reviewer bewails himself over little Nell and Paul Dombey. Does any peer of the realm now shed tears for their fate? Dickens, full of his *Chimes*, came all the way from Italy in midwinter to read it to Carlyle, Forster, Jerrold, and other intimate friends, and made them cry; but he could hardly do that with any literary company now if he came back from the dead. And is it then all a fashion only?

The tireless industry of Dickens continued throughout the years recorded in this volume. . . . His literary history is very fully given, and amidst much that is not important there is a great deal that is very interesting. His method of publication was adverse to any exactness of plot; and as he wrote from month to month his romances took shape from the suggestions and exigencies of the passing time. It is easy to see how he padded when he could not otherwise fill out the due number of pages; in some of his books, as *The Old Curiosity Shop*, he wholly changed his plan, and in *Our Mutual Friend* it is hard to believe that he had any plan. . . .

161. From an unsigned review, *Temple Bar*

May 1873, xxxviii, 169–85

Probably by Mrs Frances Cashel Hoey (see No. 153).

. . . Mr Forster is emphatic in his blame of every one who was concerned in the matter—or indeed who was not, for 'friends' are taken to task—that Charles Dickens was not given a good education, and eloquent about the education which he afterwards gave himself. Here, again, the besetting temptation of the biographer to invest his subject with attributes which do not belong to him, as well as to exaggerate those which do, assails Mr Forster. There are no facts in his narrative to prove that Mr Dickens ever was an educated man, and all the testimony of his works is against the supposition. No trait of his genius is more salient than its entire self-dependence; no defects of it are more marked than his intolerance of subjects which he did not understand, and his high-handed dogmatic treatment of matters which he regarded with the facile contempt of ignorance. This unfortunate tendency was fostered by the atmosphere of flattery in which he lived; a life which, in the truly educational sense, was singularly narrow; and though he was not entirely to blame for the extent, it affected his later works very much to their disadvantage. As a novelist he is distinguished, as a humourist he is unrivalled in this age; but when he deals with the larger spheres of morals, with politics, and with the mechanism of state and official life, he is absurd. He announces truisms and tritenesses with an air of discovery impossible to a well-read man, and he propounds with an air of conviction, hardly provoking, it is so simply foolish, flourishing solutions of problems, which have long perplexed the gravest and ablest minds in the higher ranges of thought.

We hear of his extensive and varied reading. Where is the evidence that he ever read anything beyond fiction, and some of the essayists? Certainly not in his books, which might be the only books in the world, for any indication of study or book-knowledge in them. Not a little of their charm, not a little of their wide-spread miscellaneous popularity, is referable to that very thing. Every one can understand them; they are not for educated people only; they do not suggest comparisons or require explanations, or imply associations; they stand alone, self-existent, delightful facts. A slight reference to Fielding and Smollett, a fine rendering of one chapter in English history—the Gordon riots—very finely done, and a clever adaptation of Mr Carlyle's 'Scarecrows' to his own stage, in *A Tale of Two Cities*, are positively the only traces of books to be found in the long series of his works. His *Pictures from Italy* is specially curious as an illustration of the possibility of a man's living so long in a country with an old and famous history, without discovering that he might possibly understand the country better if he knew something about the history. He always caught the sentimental and humourous elements in everything; the traditional, spiritual, philosophic, or æsthetic not at all. His prejudices were the prejudices, not of one-sided opinion and conviction, but of ignorance 'all round.' His mind held no clue to the character of the peoples of foreign countries, and their tastes, arts, and creed were ludicrous mysteries to him. His vividness of mind, freshness and fun, constitute the chief charm of his stories, and their entire originality is the 'note' which pleases most; but when he writes 'pictures' of a land of the great past of poetry, art, and politics, with as much satisfied flippancy as when he describes the common objects of the London streets (for which he yearned in the midst of all the mediæval glories of Italy), he makes it evident that he had never been educated, and had not educated himself. If we are to accept Mr Forster's version of his friend's judgment and intellectual culture, apart from his own art as a novelist, we get a sorry notion of them from the following sentence, which has many fellows. At page 82 of the first volume, Mr Forster writes:

His (Mr Dickens') observations, during his career in the gallery, had not led him to form any high opinion of the House of Commons or its heroes; and of the Pickwickian sense, which so often takes the place of common sense, in our legislature, he omitted no opportunity of declaring his contempt at every part of his life. [*Life*, 64]

This is unkind. We do not like to believe that the famous novelist was so insolent and so arrogant as his biographer makes him out to have been, and it is only fair to remark that it is Mr Forster who represents his 'subject's' contempt for men and matters entirely out of his social and intellectual sphere as something serious for those men and those matters. That Mr Dickens was rather more than less unfortunate than other people when, like them, he talked of things he did not understand, is abundantly proved by his *Hard Times*, the silly Doodle business in *Bleak House*, the ridiculous picture of an M.P. in *Nickleby*, and the invariable association of rank with folly and power with incompetence in all his works. He knew nothing of official life; he had no comprehension of authority, of discipline, of any kind of hierarchical system, and his very humour itself is dull, pointless, laboured, and essentially vulgar, when directed against the larger order of politics; it becomes mere flippant buzzing, hardly worth notice or rebuke. . . .

162. [R. H. Hutton], from a review of Vol. III of Forster's *Life*, the *Spectator*

7 February 1874, xlvii, 174–6

Reprinted in Hutton's *Criticisms of Contemporary Thought and Thinkers* (1894), 94–102.

We have here a melancholy close to a book which, in spite of the many traits of astonishing perceptive power, and prodigal generosity, and unbounded humour, contained in it, will certainly not add to the personal fascination with which Dickens is regarded by so many of his countrymen. The closing volume contains more evidences than any of the others of the very great defect of character which seems to have grown from the very roots of Dickens's genius. Mr Forster himself admits it fully enough, though he hardly seems to be aware what an admission it is. 'There was for him,' says his biographer, 'no "city of the mind" against outward ills for inner consolation and shelter.' In other words, Dickens depended more than most men on the stimulus which outer things provided for him; first, on the excitement caused by the popularity of his books, and on that which he drew from his own personal friends' private appreciation; then on the applause which attended his actings and readings, the intensity of the eagerness to hear him and the emotion he excited; and lastly, on the triumph excited by the counting-up of the almost fabulous sums which the readings produced. These were evidently the moral drams without security for which his life would have lost all its spring and interest, and it is clear that as his productiveness as an author began to fail, he grasped eagerly at the quasi-theatrical powers displayed in his readings to fill up the blank he was beginning to feel, and to compensate him for the restlessness and almost despair which the consciousness that his genius was on the wane began to produce in him. . . .

The volume before us, so far as it illustrates Dickens's moral qualities at all, may be said to be one long chronicle of his craving for these delights of popular applause,—sometimes outweighing, as in the case to which we have alluded, what the least modicum of magnanimity would have enforced upon him,—at other times, extinguishing all the sense of personal dignity which might have been expected in an author of so much genius,—and finally overpowering the commonest prudence, and leading directly, no doubt, to his premature death. Mr Forster, by giving so much prominence to the certainly extraordinary and marvellous popularity of the public readings, and recording, at excessive length, Dickens's unbounded triumph in the enthusiasm and numbers and reckless prodigality of his audiences, has given to this craving of his hero's a somewhat needless emphasis, and has, more-over, extended his already very big book beyond reasonable limits. Nobody wants to hear how the people at Tynemouth did exactly what the people at Dover did; how Cambridge and Edinburgh behaved in exactly the same manner as Dublin and Manchester, and so forth. There is something a little ignoble in this extravagant relish of a man of genius for the evidence of the popularity of his own writings. Dickens must have known that theatrical effects are by no means the best gauge of the highest literary fame. He must have been well aware that no one could have produced with scenes from Shakspeare or from Scott anything like the intensity of superficial excitement which he himself produced with the death of little Paul Dombey or the pathetic life of Tiny Tim; and whether the difference were due to something of melo-drama in him or something of deficiency in the greater masters, must, at least, have been a question on which his mind could hardly have been definitely made up in his own favour. We by no means deny the value of the test to which his readings subjected the literary power of his writings. Undoubtedly it demonstrated very great qualities. We believe that it also demonstrated some great defects; and certainly the passion with which he gave away his very life to producing these popular emotions, pointed to a grave want of that higher life in himself which could not have been compatible with such constant superficial strains on his nervous energy. It would have added to the literary worth of the book, and certainly not have diminished the reader's admiration, if Mr Forster had curtailed greatly the tiresome redundancy of Dickens's own gratitude for the popular enthusiasm with which he was received.

Mr Forster notes another quality besides this absence in Dickens of any inner life in which he could take refuge from the craving for external excitement,—a quality which, while it very much increased the danger of this dependence on the stimulus of bursts of popular favour, was also inseparable from his greatest qualities. There was 'something of the despot, seldom separable from genius,' says Mr Forster, in Dickens. No doubt there was, but we should say that genius is quite as often found without it as with it; that it was the peculiarity of Dickens's own genius, and closely connected with his highly-strung nerves, rather than the token of genius in general. There are many types of genius which are too largely tolerant, like Scott's or Thackeray's, for this kind of disposition; many, too, which are too purely receptive, too sensitive to external influences, for anything like despotism. But Dickens's genius was of neither kind; he hardly enjoyed his visions at all merely as intellectual perceptions, as food for his own reflection. He enjoyed them solely as materials for sensation, as the means of producing an intense effect on the world without. 'I wish,' said Landseer of him, 'he looked less eager and busy, and not so much out of himself or beyond himself. I should like to catch him asleep and quiet now and then.' But that was not in him. Never was there a genius so little contemplative. Never had a man of such wonderful powers so little of—

> The harvest of a quiet eye,
> That broods and sleeps on his own heart.

His mind was always trying to 'work up' even the most idle and worthless fancies and situations into pictorial effects. Mr Forster's chapter called 'Hints for Books Written and Unwritten' seems to us much more of an evidence of weakness in this respect than of power. The forced and extravagant suggestions which Dickens sets down for himself as possible hints for future works are far more numerous than those of real power or promise. In fact, what even his marvellous humour lacks is repose. Often he cannot leave even his most humorous things alone, but must tug and strain at them to bring out their full effects, till the reader is nauseated with what was, in its first conception, of the richest and most original kind. Dickens was too intensely practical, had *too much* eye to the effect to be produced by all he did, for the highest imagination. He makes you feel that it is not the intrinsic insight that delights him half so much as the power it gives him of moving the world. The visible word of command must go forth from himself in connection with all his creations. His imagination is not of the ruminating kind. He uses his experience before it is mellow, in the impatience of his nervous haste. . . .

163. Wilkie Collins, marginalia in the *Life*

Pall Mall Gazette, 20 January 1890, 3

From 'Wilkie Collins about Charles Dickens'.

Collins (1824–89), though a close friend, colleague and collaborator of Dickens's, has left only meagre comments upon him. Their personal and literary relationships, including the question how much each influenced the other, have been much discussed recently: see essays by R. P. Ashley, K. J. Fielding, and A. A. Adrian in *Nineteenth-Century Fiction*, iv (1950) 265–73; *Dickensian*, xlix (1953), 59–65, 130–6; *Huntington Library Quarterly*, xvi (1953), 211–13; also Earle Davis, *The Flint and the Flame: the Artistry of Dickens* (1964), ch. x. Collins was certainly impressed by Dickens's earning-power: 'This is indeed a great age for authors,' he wrote in January 1849, several years before turning novelist himself. 'Dickens told a friend of mine, that he had made *four thousand guineas* by his last year's Christmas book—(The Battle of Life)—a five shilling publication, (!) which everybody abused and nevertheless, everybody read' (Nuel Pharr Davis, *Life of Wilkie Collins* (Urbana, 1956), 60).

... discussing *Oliver Twist*, Mr Forster remarks, 'Here was the interest of a story simply but well constructed' [*Life*, 106]. 'Nonsense', writes Wilkie Collins, 'the one defect of that wonderful book is the helplessly bad construction of the story. The character of "Nancy" is the finest thing he ever did. He never afterwards saw all the sides of a woman's character—saw all round her. That the same man who could create "Nancy" created the second Mrs Dombey is the most incomprehensible anomaly that I know of in literature.'

The next note ... relates to *Barnaby Rudge*. [Forster notes that Dickens had a 'fancy' to make the leaders of the Gordon riots 'three splendid fellows ... who should turn out, when all was over, to have broken out of Bedlam'. With some difficulty, Forster made him see 'the un-soundness of this' (*Life*, 168).] Concerning this Wilkie Collins writes, 'Where is the unsoundness of it? I call it a fine idea. New, powerful, highly dramatic, and well within the limits of truth to nature. It would have greatly improved the weakest book that Dickens ever wrote'. . .

. . . Mr Forster compares the description in *Edwin Drood* with the dialogue in *Oliver Twist* (*Life*, 809). On which Mr Wilkie Collins remarks: 'He would have pointed out the contrast more fairly if he had compared dialogue with dialogue or description with description in both cases. A novelist knows what Forster does not know—that dialogue is more easily written than description. To my mind it was cruel to compare Dickens in the radiant prime of his genius with Dickens's last laboured effort, the melancholy work of a worn-out brain.'

'I do feel we ought to produce a wonderful Book—like a new one from the dear dead Hand!' wrote Georgina Hogarth in 1878, when she and Mamie Dickens were preparing the *Letters* for publication (A. A. Adrian, *Georgina Hogarth and the Dickens Circle* (1957), 208; see ch. xiii on the editing and reception of the three volumes). The letters were found vivid and entertaining, if sometimes trivial and repetitive. They contained relatively little about his creative life, so reviewers concentrated on the relation between his personality and his art, and on the range of his interests and the nature of his convictions. Several reviewers noted how few of the letters referred to politics: 'We doubt if as many letters of any of the men worthy to be ranked as his compeers could be collected which would show such a limited concern for the world in which he personally played no part' (*Nation* (New York), 4 December 1879, 389; cf. No. 166, and *Westminster Review*, April 1880, n.s. lvii, 438). The sincerity of his religious beliefs gave widespread satisfaction, though his theology was seen to be tenuous. Reviewers mainly found in the letters confirmation of their existing opinion of Dickens, the artist, the man, and the social critic. Those who had always found him lovable and lively had a renewed sense of his amiable qualities, vivacity, and common sense; those who were already conscious of intellectual and artistic shortcomings pointed to corresponding limitations in his letters, and were less tolerant of the egotism that most readers noted in them. One point disputed among critics was how revealing the letters were: whether, as William Minto put it, 'In this book, which was never intended to be a book, we come nearer to the man as he was than any biographer could have brought us' (*Fortnightly Review*, December 1879, n.s. xxvi, 845), or, as W. B. Rands asserted (No. 165), the letters failed to provide any key to his emotional life.

164. From an unsigned review, *Spectator*

29 November 1879, lii, 1506–8

This is the 'First Notice'; the review continued the following week (pp. 1539–40) with a very intelligent discussion of Dickens's politics, as seen in his letters. Almost certainly by R. H. Hutton.

... About half these letters,—certainly not more,—are delightful additions to the rich materials we already have for forming a picture of Dickens. The other half should have been suppressed, and by their suppression would have given much additional effect to those which remained.

With this exception, it is hard to say too much in praise of the letters. Their nonsense is, not quite always, but almost always, delightful; the vividness and vivacity of their descriptiveness are unique, and their *pace* is something marvellous. One seldom reads any of these letters without the feeling that the stream of Dickens's life, mental and physical, was more nearly what seafaring men call a 'race,' than even a current. One's head grows giddy sometimes with the dash and tension at which he lived. As a natural consequence, there is hardly any reflectiveness in his letters, and when a touch of reflectiveness comes—as, for instance, in the following, written when he had just returned from a most successful tour of private theatricals—one appreciates it all the more.

[Quotes from *To* Mrs Watson, 27 July 1848: '... I don't know how it is, but the ideal world in which my lot is cast has an odd effect on the real one, and makes it chiefly precious for such remembrances' as those of Switzerland, which he has just been describing.]

But even such brief reflectiveness as this is rare. For the most part, these letters represent a life always much too eager for the next interest in view, to pause for any longer period than was necessary just to photograph the interest that was passing. But this Dickens did, apparently, all the more, instead of the less, effectually, that he did it at such high speed. People sometimes talk of writing so large that 'he who runs may read.' Dickens seems to teach us that there are some things so small that only he who runs *can* read them,—that it is only one whose life drives on at a great rate who can really catch, and then only by a sort of sympathy, some of the most transient features of the life around him. Whatever wanted a meditative kind of observation, Dickens did not describe well. What he saw,—and he saw much,—that nobody could have described at all without a throng of appropriate sensations rushing through his mind, he described as no one else could have described it. Take, for instance, this description of the anxiety displayed by his son and some other Eton companions as to the possible effect of the weather on the proposed festivity which Dickens was to give them on the river, and of their subsequent demeanour. No man could have caught the details of that description as Dickens catches them, who had not had in his own experience all the 'cues' for interpreting what he saw, so that a small compendium of the Eton boy's anxiety and hopes passed rapidly through his mind as he stopped at the Slough station.

[Quotes from *To* Mrs Watson, 11 July 1851.]

It was the rapidity and vividness of Dickens's own life which enabled him to catch and read off all those minute shades of expression in the boys' faces with so much brilliance. . . . With regard to the nonsense of these letters, it is good or bad,—generally very good,—almost in direct proportion to the tendency to extravagance which it contains. When Dickens is extravagant, he is always good. It is hardly possible for him to fail when he is in an extravagant humour. On the other hand, when he attempts anything in the vein of subdued humour—the vein of Charles Lamb—he sometimes fails sadly. . . . When Dickens once began to rattle, he was always delightful. But in the more twilight moods, he was not even up to a high mark. His genius revelled in high lights, strong colours, rapid movement, and intense effects.

. . . Hardly anything that had a 'purpose' in it which Dickens ever did, was done well. His astonishing genius, his unfathomable stores of humour, his quaint and wild power of caricature, were all apt to go terribly astray directly they were put in harness by that—in his case— most destructive agency, a moral purpose; and even in these letters we never feel his want of a reflective mind so keenly as when he is planting what he calls heavy blows in the face of 'Cant', or even when he is assailing a real injustice, like the piracy of copyright. In such cases, he never seems to ask himself what is the position of the foe whom he has to meet. He only strikes out wildly, like a man who disdains even to look at that which he feels it a solemn duty to detest.

165. 'Matthew Browne' [W. B. Rands], from a review in *Contemporary Review*

January 1880, xxxvii, 77–85

William Brighty Rands (1823–82), journalist and miscellaneous writer, wrote many poems and fairy stories for children, and was named 'the laureate of the nursery.' 'Matthew Browne' was one of his pseudonyms. His essay 'From Faust to Mr Pickwick' appeared in the *Contemporary Review*, July 1880, xxxviii, 162–76.

... One thing is exceedingly obvious on the face of these letters, as, indeed, it is obvious in the books, and was obvious in the life of Dickens. He had but little secretiveness. That is undoubtedly a disadvantage to a man, when the question is once raised whether he is an egotist or not. This want caused his books to be destitute of whatever charm 'the retarding art' can give; and, as a rule, even the best effects of even his most homely writing leap into your eyes, as the French phase goes, when you would rather they stole upon you.

This, however, is not solely the result of lack of secretive power, for we sometimes find 'the retarding art' practised by writers who have less of that power than he had. There was something else. The truth must be spoken—Dickens lacked reverence. There is an amusing reply of his to a Mr David Dickson, who had expostulated with him about some point in the Chadband business, and a very clever reply it is—but totally inapprehensive, unless we may take it to be evasive. There are a few other things of a similar order in the letters; but it is not upon these that we found the remark that Dickens had but little capacity of reverence. It is shown in his 'accost;' as it appears in his face. It was not necessary to crouch to anybody on earth, much less to play the 'snuffling hound' (his own phrase); but his whole manner, to men and women alike, is that of marching down upon them. The eyelid never droops; there is but little obeisance; it is hail-fellow-well-met, right on. Even the praise is usually too direct; as the criticism generally is too firm of hand. It is usually very good, when it is directed to questions composed of business and literary quality, and nearly always it contains fine strokes. But, on the whole, we might maintain of his treatment of great topics that it is like his treatment of persons—it is too often rash, and wanting in self-suspicion.

The process by which Dickens reached the most positive and the most controlling of his opinions in matters of politics, and social philosophy generally, is never disclosed to you. Perhaps there hardly ever *was* a process, such as takes place in the minds of thoughtful students of life, history, and biography. It is difficult to conceive how there could have been; for he never read much, and he passed at one bound from undistinguished striplinghood to what might be called the mature manhood of life-absorbing fame. The wonder is that his brain did not turn round; it says much, very much, for his natural goodness and strong common sense that he kept his head as he did. There is nowhere a trace of pride (in any vulgar sense) about the man; you can see in his portraits, especially the later ones, that he was entirely simple. A little dignity of the soft and reticent order would have done him good. But to return to the point we have for a moment left, there is no case on record like his—a man who must be called great as a humorist, and ranked, after all deductions, with the foremost men, living entirely the life of the brain, and yet being so utterly destitute of the pure think-ing faculty, and the tendency to resort to artistic and scientific checks. His common sense had all the force of genius; and there the matter stood. His morality—considered as a system—was altogether second-hand, and he displayed no leaning towards any great, any leading idea, that he had to do more than open his hand to receive. He was always ready to take the part of the poor, and he was the friend of 'the working man.' He hated humbug and cant, not only because they were things at war with his natural directness, but because they were in an especial manner hindrances in the way of good-fellowship, and his off-hand, earnest good-fellow's view of life. That view had nothing in common with the outlook of the mere *bon vivant*; the nature of Dickens was stringent; he set metes and bounds everywhere, to himself as well as to others; there was not a lax-drawn stitch in his scheme of life.

But it cannot be denied that *commonplace* was at the bottom of much of his work, and that sometimes you feel this in a very irritating manner. Strong opinions on political or social questions do not always come with the *best* grace (though all sincerity is good) from a man who, you feel afraid, would have been a Mohammedan all his life if he had been born one, and who never showed the slightest disposition to attack any evil at its tap-roots. It would be interesting to know how he got at his religious opinions. In one of his letters he shows that he had a fairly good understanding of the drift of such a book, for example, as the *Essays and Reviews*[1]; but that is not saying much, for the noise made by that work proved nothing so much as the dense ignorance of the religious public: since there was scarcely one idea in it from cover to cover which was not familiar to intelligent and thoughtful people who had made anything like a study of such matters. However, Dickens did understand it, and abstracts it very well. His letters to his boys, when he starts them in life, are also good from the 'serious' point of view; but never for a moment, never by the turn of a phrase, do you see the bottom of his mind in matters of moral and religious speculation. It has been very unjustly said that his writings are mainly a glorification of the spirit of the English Christmas. They are much more than that—they are, apart from the attractive force of their humour, mighty lessons in the first humanities, they have the immense merit of never lowering your faith and hope. When we consider how many villains Dickens has drawn; how he has groped and grubbed—we were going to say—in the lowest kennels of human baseness and squalor, it is a fine thing to say, it is a noble feather in his cap, that he never gives you a heart-ache in the bad sense. This suffices to give him high rank. It places him by the side of men like Goldsmith and Scott, whose great glory it is that they are always ready to reconcile us to human nature when we have fallen out with it. It is, indeed, true that Dickens is never in advance of his time, and seldom in advance of his theme. He is thoroughly at home in the world as it is, willing and often eager to change the machinery of civilization, but never intent on questioning accepted principles, either as to their history or their relevancy; but if his want of apprehensive intelligence on certain great questions compels us now and then to feel as if we should like a little more sense of solid foundation for so much very decisive writing about this or that, he makes us amends by putting us on the heights which we should be only too glad to keep in our most restless and most revolutionary moods.

It does not follow that the master is never sad, or never overwhelms you with pictures of human misery, or suggestions of the devil that lurks in too many of us. It appears from these letters that it was only after an effort, which made him ill, that he could bring himself to read

---

[1] A controversial book on theology and religious history, published in 1860. See Dickens's letter to W. F. de Cerjat, 21 May 1863.

the Death of Nancy in public. And who can wonder? that scene may be criticized, but who can forget it, or who, remembering it after the lapse of years, can help feeling the old creepiness come over him? If it were not for the sudden outbursts of humour, the picture of Dotheboys Hall, and of the early troubles of Oliver Twist, would be cruel reading. But there is something better than that. Now and then, there is a touch that thrills you to the roots of your being with the sense of brotherhood, of the oneness of the whole human story. . . .

It is hard not to deplore the immense popularity of this man, and (cruel as it sounds) the manner in which he was followed up by troops of friends all his life. To lie fallow was what was wanted, both for his genius as a writer, and his better nature as a man. There is something startling in the frequent recurrence of illness and exhaustion from literary labour which these letters record. He had a very powerful physique, and yet the breakdowns are painful to read about. Let those who fancy literature, as a profession, is an easy one, be warned! He died of downright wear and tear—mainly the wear and tear of inventing and writing.

166. From an unsigned review, *Dublin Review*

April 1880, 3rd. series, iii, 409–38

... there was never a writer privileged with so wide a personal popularity. One reason may be, because its character was identical with his
own, and he reflected his own self in his imaginations. His personality,
once revealed, is the counterpart of the reader's conception of him from
impersonal knowledge. There is hardly in the history of literature such
another case of likeness between an author and his work; unless it be
the case of one of that brilliant cluster of poets with whom the century
opened, and there the likeness was England's loss and his; while, on the
contrary, the similarity between the novelist in, and out of, his works, is
a pleasure to his readers and an honour to himself. The second reason
why his memory is linked with his fancies, is simply because it is a
memory well known, and now wonderfully perpetuated in one of the
most graphic biographies ever written. If Dickens had not been one of
the most remarkable men of his time, his life would still have been
worth placing on record; for it was as great a romance, and as full of
silent suggestion, as anything he ever wrote. ...

Turning to Charles Dickens seen in [another] aspect—as a reformer—
we find him working out a mission to his discharge of which he attributed the greatest importance. Others flattered him, and he flattered
himself; there was exaggeration on all sides. But for all that he worked
a certain amount of good, which would be much more deserving of
note, if it had not been magnified too much already. ... The triple
weapons he held were his power in fiction, his weekly magazine, with
its serious social articles, and lastly, his personal influence. With these
three he assailed a numberless host of abuses, from slavery, 'that
accursed and detested system,' down to Chancery, 'that den of iniquity;'
from public executions to ill-managed prisons; from pauperism and
ignorance down to the window tax, which kept out health and instruction by keeping out light; and in one letter (given in his biography) he
was as strongly in favour of temperance through improved and orderly
homes for the poor, as he was against it unconsciously and unfortu-

nately in his first book. The education of the working classes was seldom in his mind confounded with the unsuitable learning, false ambitions, and consequent social restlessness and political speechifying which is sometimes supposed to be implied in the education of the people. . . .

. . . In most published letters of eminent men, there is reason to look for some political opinions worth reflection, or some impression of the events that change the surface of the world, some faithful copy of at least a few details of a stirring time. But there are few who will seek any of these in the letters of Dickens, and the few who may seek have but little to find. . . .

Of public political life he knew nothing, having no nearer practical acquaintance with it than the part he took once in an Administrative Reform meeting. One of his most fixed habits of mind was to have a supreme self-opinionated contempt for the House of Commons. But had he accepted any one of the chances of public life that he was offered, he would have learned there, in seeing every possible side of any one measure, that every reform must needs be a far slower and more patient business than the preaching of its theories. He was all energy and impetuosity; he was as sanguine as no one could be who had not judged all things by the experience of such a triumph as his. He took no meaning from the fact that it has been the toil of lives, and it has taken the judgment of years of trial, for men to make for the multitude one law that can lift them up without causing worse confusion, one system of lightening their burdens without disturbing the balance of a whole community. Again, in his novels the same too-sanguine spirit shows itself in many merely domestic characters; though in truth, we own to a weakness for preferring to be deluded with the brighter view of mankind rather than deceived in the other direction by sweeping satires upon all the world's hollowness. Whatever was bright and hopeful had a special attraction for Dickens. In the short narrative that finishes the Letters with a sketch of his life's close, we are told that his love of fresh air, light, and flowers amounted almost to a passion. It is a counterpart of his being drawn to dwell upon the pleasant and sunny side of life. 'The comfort is,' he wrote once, on hearing painful news, 'that all the strange and terrible things come uppermost, and that the good and pleasant things are mixed up with every moment of our existence so plentifully that we scarcely heed them.' The chance expression covers much of his philosophy of the world, and it holds a great deal of comforting truth. But when he went so far as to work with hot impulse in the confidence that human things were righting themselves easily, swiftly, through mere human wisdom and cheery good-nature, then it was that his philosophy failed him. Witness the sanguine view he took of the work that was to be done by his weekly magazine, with its gospel of good-fellowship and its campaign of reforms, to be worked by means of unearthing and denouncing all abuses, and recommending a cheerful hand-in-hand system of providing for the people. His object, he wrote, was 'the raising up of those that are down, and the general improvement of our social condition.' This sounds very well, if there had not been added in another letter the avowal of the self-reliant system:—'We hope to do some solid good, and we mean to be as cheery and pleasant as we can.' The magazine was a pecuniary success and nothing else, and the proposed motive has sunk out of sight years ago. The first hopefulness was much the same as that which prompted him to say to Lord Lytton, regarding the Guild of Literature and Art, that they held in hand 'the peace and honour of men of letters for centuries to come;' and yet it ended only in a bitter disappointment. He carried the same too-rash confidence into the philosophy advocated by his novels. It is far too often of the earth, earthy; of endowing attractive characters with a liking for showing generosity in convivial pleasures, or making them work out noble ends by means and from motives utterly human. We have before now dwelt on the almost total want of any recognition there of the doctrine of grace. . . .

167. Mowbray Morris, from 'Charles Dickens', *Fortnightly Review*

1 December 1882, n.s. xxxii, 762–79

The author of this signed article is doubtless Mowbray Walter Morris (1847–1911), son of Mowbray Morris (manager of *The Times*). He was dramatic critic on *The Times*, 1873–1885, and then succeeded John Morley as editor of *Macmillan's Magazine*.

It is stated, and on the very best authority, that within the twelve years that have passed since Dickens's death no less than 4,239,000 volumes of his works have been sold in England alone! A long way the first on this astonishing list stands *Pickwick*, while *David Copperfield*, the second, is almost equally far in front of *Dombey and Son*; *Little Dorrit* has found nearly as many readers as *Martin Chuzzlewit*, while, with the exception of *Edwin Drood*, *The Tale of Two Cities* and *Great Expectations* take the lowest place. Nor has his popularity been confined to England or to English-speaking people. French, German, and Italian, Russian and Swedish translations of his works appeared during his lifetime; when he was still but a young man the pages of 'Boz' were devoured, we have been told, with enthusiasm in Silesian villages; *Pickwick*, it is said, and on no less circumstantial authority, was found equal, when all else failed, to the task of soothing the sleepless nights of Mehemet Ali; Mr Forster has published a story of a strange half-human recluse who had built his cell amid the eternal snows of the Sierra Nevada, and who found in *Pickwick* and in *Nicholas Nickleby* the only intercourse with humanity that he desired. If it were true, as has been said by one who has certainly managed to refute his own words [Lord Jeffrey], if it were true that present popularity is the only safe presage of future glory, what an eternity of glory should await Charles Dickens!

And yet present popularity, a vogue, how brilliant and irresistible soever it may be, or what manner of prologue it may furnish to future glory, is quite another matter from that glory itself, from the real definitive glory, the one thing, as M. Renan tells us, which has the best chance of not being altogether vanity. That posterity will regard Dickens as he was regarded in his lifetime, or even as we now regard him, is of course out of the question. 'To the public,' said Professor Ward, in a lecture delivered at Manchester in the year of Dickens's death, 'to the public his faults were often inseparable from his merits; and when our critical consciences told us that he was astray in one of his favourite directions, the severest censure we had for him was that he was growing "more like himself" than ever.' That the critical conscience of posterity will have far severer censure for Dickens than this one cannot doubt, nor indeed can any one thoughtful for the fame of English literature desire that it should not.

. . . Not, indeed, that Dickens rested from criticism during his lifetime. So sudden and universal a popularity as his, so original, so self-contained and self-reliant a genius, could not but attract criticism, or what often passes by the name of criticism among contemporaries, both kindly and otherwise. He found, indeed, plenty of both, but all or almost all the criticism he encountered in his lifetime took a bias of one kind or other, the bias of enthusiasm or the bias of opposition, the one perhaps an irresistible consequence of the other—the enthusiasm seeing all things in him because of his marvellous popularity, the opposition seeing nothing in him but that popularity, which, according to its wont, it made every effort to explain away. Neither bias is, of course, so strong now, and particularly the bias of opposition, which is in most cases the soonest counteracted by death. Nevertheless, to form a just estimate of his work, to weigh its merits and its defects and to strike a balance between them, is still perhaps impossible, must certainly, even for us of a later generation, be very difficult. Brought up, as most of us have been, in the faith of Dickens, whose earliest laughter has been stirred by Sam Weller and Dick Swiveller and Mr Micawber, whose earliest tears have flowed for the sordid wretchedness of David Copperfield's forlorn childhood, or for Florence Dombey toiling up the 'great wide vacant stairs,' with her brother in her arms, and singing as she goes—who have stolen trembling after Jonas Chuzzlewit through that awful wood, or stared with face as pale as Pip himself at that grim midnight visitor in the lonely Temple chambers; to such it must surely seem little short of profanity to consider too curiously the old familiar pages, to stand afar off, contemplating with cold impartial scrutiny the old familiar figures, as though, like Trabb's boy, we did not know them.

And besides such sentimental hindrances, the temporary and, as one may say, local hindrances to all criticism, there are others which must always render more than commonly difficult, if indeed possible at all, an absolute judgment on works of fiction which deal so primarily, if not wholly, with the emotions as do the works of Dickens. . . . There are no doubt some passages in imaginative writing which one may fairly say *should* stir the heart of every man.

[Morris cites examples from the *Iliad* and *King Lear*.]

Nevertheless, with works of a lower class, with works rather of the fancy than the imagination, we cannot in reason quarrel either with those who indulge in the 'luxury of woe' over passages which leave ourselves unmoved, or with those who can read dry-eyed the words which unlock for us 'the sacred source of sympathetic tears.' And so with Dickens's humour. It is conceivable that human souls exist who do not laugh at Dick Swiveller or Mrs Gamp. We should not, some of us, perhaps care greatly for travelling in far countries with such, or for passing many hours in commune with them anywhere; but it would be vain to attempt to demonstrate to them that they should laugh, or to insist upon regarding them as lost to all sense of literary or artistic decency because they did not. Wordsworth could find Voltaire dull; and what Carlyle thought of Charles Lamb we all know.

Of course, with the other qualities or characteristics of Dickens's work, as of all work—his powers of description, for example, of observation, his powers of narration and composition, his style and his literary workmanship generally—the case will be different. But these two, the qualities of humour and of pathos, so largely predominate all his work, that it seems to me almost impossible for any judgment to be *absolute*, to use Lewes' phrase; it must, I think, be *individual*. Still, from many individual judgments a deduction may perhaps be made which, though not in itself absolute, nor even tending to the absolute, may yet be of avail in promoting a sounder estimate, in counteracting the bias both of enthusiasm and opposition.

Merely personal considerations, that 'soul of good nature and kindness,' which Mr Matthew Arnold has found so irresistible in *David Copperfield*, and which his friends loved so wisely and so well in the man, largely as such influences must always inform contemporary judgment, will not avail with posterity, nor is it right that they should. . . . Nevertheless, a clear knowledge of Dickens's life and character, of his age and his position with regard to his age—to which knowledge Mr Forster's very full biography, ardent admirer and affectionate friend as he was, must always largely contribute—will go far to explain and to account for many things in his writings which may puzzle posterity, which would certainly puzzle a posterity which had derived its knowledge only from that other friend of his [Sala] who has described him as 'followed, admired, courted, lionised, almost idolised, by almost all that was wealthy and dignified and beautiful in society.' It will go far, for instance, to account for the extraordinary one-sidedness and the consequent ineffectualness of so much of his satire, and especially of his satire on the governing classes and the upper classes of society generally. It will go far to explain whence it happens that, despite his own disclaimer of 'placing in opposition those two words, Aristocracy and People,' he yet seems so often unable to resist the temptation of the contrast, and always, or nearly always, to the disadvantage of the former; to explain whence it comes, though he has avowed that he 'would not on any account deprive either of a single just right belonging to it,' that the rights of the one seem to him so much more just, so much more certain than the rights of the other. 'I believe,' he said, speaking at Boston during his first visit to America, 'I believe that virtue dwells rather oftener in alleys and byways than she does in courts and palaces.' A judicious use of the historical method will no doubt help to explain the grounds for this belief, to explain the lack of firmness in the step, of keenness in the eye, of sureness in the touch, as he gets farther away from the alleys and byways, and nearer to the courts and palaces; but to say that this method will be necessary to enable the reader to *detect* the faults which arise from the prevalence of these sentiments, and their too aggressive advocacy, is surely to attribute to him an incapacity for judging which no method of criticism hitherto revealed to man could really hope to counteract. ... [For instance] to know how deep the admiration Dickens felt for Carlyle, and his readiness always to accept the latter's teachings, will no doubt help the future student to *account* for much of Dickens's work, but will hardly help him to judge it.

Again, the historical method, to keep it with us a while longer, may undoubtedly avail to enable the reader to account for that note of extravagance which is too rarely absent from Dickens's work, and which, it seems to me, is likely to tell most strongly against it in the future—the want of a capacity of self-judgment and restraint. . . . Every one who has read Mr Forster's biography will remember the exuberant delight with which Dickens recounts the increasing sale of each successive work, without any apparent thought of their respective deserts. That his bad work should sell as well as his good suggested nothing to him, because to him there seemed no difference between the two; the work he was for the moment engaged on was to him the best. '*Little Dorrit,*' he writes, 'has beaten even *Bleak House* out of the field. It is a most tremendous start, and I am overjoyed at it;' and 'you know,' he adds, 'that they sold 35,000 of number two on New Year's Day.' He can see no reason why this should not be; he sees no distinction, or he does not care to see any, between perhaps the worst book he ever wrote and one which is certainly among his best. . . . We may detect the same note, too, in what Mr Ward calls his 'innocent ecstasies' over the success of his readings, ecstasies which, as Mr Ward so truly says, would in any other man have furnished him with inexhaustible subjects for parody. And still more clearly do we find it in his feverish descriptions to Forster of the manner in which he flung himself into his characters, and of the reality which their counterfeit emotions aroused in him. I will not instance his well-known letter about little Nell, for with that was interwoven the recollection of a real sorrow which removes it without the pale of criticism. But the death of little Paul affected him in an equal manner, and he seems to have regarded it as an equal masterpiece of pathetic writing. . . . As far as the little girl is concerned, perhaps the balance of opinion leans towards Dickens; but certainly nowadays the majority of readers experience a sense mostly of relief at the premature blighting of the other of these two 'opening buds.' . . .

All that we know of Dickens forbids us to doubt that he wrote such things in perfect sincerity, and not merely with a view to effect, as so many distinguished men have written to a sympathetic friend in whom they foresaw a future biographer: to doubt that he really was, or— which is practically the same—really believed himself to be, in the mental and bodily condition he has described, whether in sober earnest he was so or not. And with this assurance do we not come at once to the secret of that want of proportion, of the artistic sense of limitation and restraint, which, now showing itself in this phase and now in that, is the one capital defect of Dickens's work? A man who could write about himself as he has so often written to Forster, and write in perfect honesty, could not, one feels, have the shaping power, the control of the true artist so important in all works of the imagination, so vital to an imagination of such astonishing fertility and vividness working without a basis of training and education—an imagination which many, by no means inclined to accept Dickens without reservation, have thought is not to be surpassed outside the works of Shakspeare. And just as Mr Arnold has shown us how we do not conceive, or should not at least conceive, of Shakspeare as pre-eminently the *great artist* in that sense, which is the real sense, of the word, the sense of 'pure and flawless workmanship,' so, it seems to me, we cannot properly conceive of Dickens, often as the word has been applied to him, often, no doubt, as it will be. It is not necessary to compare him with Thackeray in the sense in which such comparisons may be said to be odious, to affect to decide which is the greater of two so great writers. Hereafter, of course, such a comparison will have to be made, as it must inevitably be made in the case of all fellow-workers of importance in any field; but for us now, standing so close to them as we do, it were better, perhaps, to remember the saying of Goethe: 'For twenty years the public has been disputing which is the greatest, Schiller or I; and it ought to be glad that it has got a couple of fellows about whom it *can* dispute.' Nevertheless, that unthinking partisanship which we so often meet with among the admirers of Dickens, and which 'stares tremendous with a threatening eye' at the very name of Thackeray, is surely no less idle. To compare these two men—friends, contemporaries, each working in the same field of letters, to examine their different modes of handling similar, or nearly similar, subjects—to compare them, in short, in the sense of illustrating the one by the other, must surely be as inevitable as it should be fruitful. And so, in thinking of Dickens's position as the *artist*, of the quality of his workmanship, in considering him, if I may coin the word, *architectonically*, there inevitably rises also in one's thoughts the predominance of this quality in Thackeray. Profound as is my admiration for Thackeray, and ever fresh the pleasure with which I go back again and again to his writings, it seems to me impossible to deny that Dickens was the more abundantly gifted of the two; he had, I mean, a larger proportion of the gifts which go to make the writer of fiction, and those he had in which the other was wanting, or possessed, at least, in a less degree, are precisely those which commend themselves most immediately and vividly to the majority of readers, which take soonest hold of the popular imagination and sympathy, and keep them longest. But the true artist's touch, the sense of limitation, of symmetry, the self-control, the sure perception, in a word, of the exact moment when 'the rest *should be* silence,' which so powerfully impresses us in Thackeray's best work—in such work as *Vanity Fair*, and *Esmond*, and *Barry Lyndon*—we never, or hardly ever, find in Dickens. And is it not by this quality, in this secret of consummate workmanship, that the novelist has, after all, the best chance of surviving; that the works which show this pre-eminently, or even conspicuously, are likely to keep sweet the longest? The fictions which paint the manners and humours of contemporary life, which deal with portraits rather than with types of humanity, with the individualities of nature rather, and not with her universal and eternal properties, must inevitably lose, for an age which cannot recognise the fidelity of the painting, cannot, perhaps, comprehend the possibility of fidelity, much of that which once constituted its chiefest charm. But the charm of perfect workmanship can never die. . . .

Scott, when he describes a scene or an incident, does so in a few broad strokes; Dickens with an extraordinary number of minute touches, each one of astonishing accuracy and fineness, such as would have occurred probably to no other man. In reading Scott we are not at the moment struck with the felicity or the power of any particular touch, but the general impression left upon our imagination is singularly precise and luminous. On the other hand, in reading Dickens, we are continually pausing to wonder at the quickness, the accuracy, the range of his vision, but the general impression is often vague and confusing from this very many-sidedness. He seems, as it were, to see too many things, and to see them all too instantaneously, to allow his reader to get a clear recollection of any one. He catalogues rather than describes. Admirable in their way as are the pictures of the French Revolution in *The Tale of Two Cities*, or of the Gordon Riots in *Barnaby Rudge*, the impression of them we keep with us as we lay the book down is hardly so clear and strong as the impression left on us, for example, by the description of the death of Porteus in the opening chapter of *The Heart of Midlothian*. The most profuse and elaborate embellishments of Dickens's fancy cannot vie with the stern and grand straightforwardness of the incomparable scene in Wandering Willie's tale, where Steenie Piper goes down into hell to win the receipt back from his old master [*Redgauntlet*, letter xi]. Hazlitt says somewhere of Crabbe's poetry, that he 'describes the interior of a cottage like a person sent there to distrain for rent.' The illustration is not inapplicable sometimes to the method of Dickens.

And yet at other times how large and free that method can be in painting scene or incident! Here, as elsewhere, Dickens can himself supply the antidote no less surely than the bane. He himself can show us how differently he works when he is describing, as M. Taine says, like Scott, 'to give his reader a map, and to lay down the locality of his drama;' and when 'struck with a certain spectacle, he is transported, and breaks out into unforeseen figures.' If any one will turn to *Great Expectations* and read the description of that fruitless journey down the river from Mill-Pond Stairs to the Nore [ch. liv], or to almost any of the descriptive passages in *Oliver Twist*,[1] and then to *Dombey and Son* and read the description of Carker's return to England [ch. lv], he can make the contrast for himself.

It is only natural that this want of proportion and control, this riot of fancy, should be most conspicuous on the romantic and sentimental side of Dickens's work. But we may trace it with more or less distinctness everywhere. We find it even in his own particular domain, in the scenes where he walks supreme, the mighty master of a humour incomparable and his own. There we are so completely in his power that he has but to wave his wand and we are prostrate. Yet it is impossible not to feel even here that he uses this power too indiscriminately, intemperately sometimes, and unreasonably. It is so rich and so wonderful, that humour of his, that we cannot but welcome it whenever and wherever it greets us. Yet when the 'burst of joyful greetings' is over, reflection will sometimes obtrude. There is an instance in *David Copperfield*—in which delightful book, by the way, instances of this or of any other of the writer's defects are few and far between. It is in the scene where that 'HEEP of villany' has forced his suspicions on the old Doctor, and has dragged David in as his unwilling witness. David, it will be remembered, concentrating years of distrust and loathing into one moment, has struck the scoundrel in the face, and the singularly calm reception of the insult has not improved his temper. Then he leaves him: 'merely telling him that I should expect from him what I always had expected, and had never yet been disappointed in. I opened the door upon him, *as if he had been a great walnut put there to be cracked*, and went out of the house' [ch. xlii]. One cannot but smile at the quaintness of the fancy here, and one cannot but feel how sadly out of place it is in so serious, so pitiful a scene. In *Martin Chuzzlewit* there is a still more painful instance in the description of the poor old clerk's grief for his dead master, where he mixes up recollections of the counting-house with his sorrow in the strangest and most incongruous manner. 'Take him from me, and what remains?' [ch. xix]. Every one must be conscious what a terribly false note is struck here. It is in such writing as

[1] The journey of Sikes and Oliver to Chertsey, for example, in chap. XXI, or the description of Jacob's Island in chap. L, and, indeed, the whole of that wonderful scene. [Morris's footnote.]

this that Dickens's vulgarity lies. He is not vulgar because he deals with common subjects—subjects which are called vulgar by his genteel depreciators, the Mr and Mrs Wititterleys of our day—but because he too often deals with great subjects in a vulgar, an ignoble manner. There is extraordinary humour, and wit too, in the old clerk's wail of despair—'Take him from me, and what remains?' but in the circumstance how cruel it is! how brutal, one feels inclined almost to say! It is, to use Joubert's phrase, a monstrosity of literature. Professor Ward talks of Dickens's characters being as true to nature as the 'most elaborated productions of Addison's art.' But there is a production of Addison's art in which an old servant bewails his master's death in a very different fashion to this—I mean the letter in the 517th number of the *Spectator*.

But who would speak harshly of Dickens, of that 'soul of good-nature and kindness!' There are instances in plenty of this want of perception and proportion, where it exists only, and does not shock; where, too, it not seldom has an effect, though an inharmonious, an isolated effect of its own. Take, for example, that so common trick of his, of pointing, of underlining, as it were, his character's comical sayings with an explanation of his own—comical, too, in itself often enough—as though he were so delighted with the fun (and who can blame him for it!) that he could not leave it. The immortal Mrs Gamp supplies an instance of it, in her magnificent apostrophe to the 'Ank-works package.' 'And I wish it was in Jonadge's belly, I do,' cried Mrs Gamp, *appearing to confound the prophet with the whale in this miraculous aspiration* [*Martin Chuzzlewit*, ch. xl]. If this were our first introduction to Mrs Gamp, possibly some explanation might be due. But already, when we meet her among the steam-boats, we know her well, her marvellous phraseology, her quaint illustrations, her irrelevant turns of thought. Nothing could be happier than the explanation, but it is a mistake. 'I wish it was in Jonadge's belly, I do;' this ends it. Thackeray, let me say, is singularly free from this fault, which is of course by no means common to Dickens. Thackeray never explains. He will talk often enough in his own person, too often, perhaps, some may think; but while his characters are talking he stands aside and lets them speak for themselves. . . .

How far a regular education would have supplied the one thing wanting to Dickens, or whether it would not rather have tended to restrict and weaken his native gifts without any counterbalancing advantages, has always been, and probably always will be, a disputed

point. Mr Bagehot was root and branch opposed to the notion. . . .
And Dickens, as he is, is so wonderful, so delightful, that it is, perhaps,
no more than natural to distrust any proposition which might have
tended to make him other than he is. Nevertheless his defects exist, and
are what they are; and, remembering what they are, it is surely impossible to doubt that some stricter intellectual and æsthetical discipline than fell to his share would not have greatly lessened, if not altogether removed them. This prime defect, the defect from which all his
others spring, the want of artistic perception and control, is precisely
such as a larger and deeper acquaintance with 'the best that has been
said and thought in the world' would have been most instrumental in
removing. It would have tempered his fancy and strengthened his
imagination; it would have fertilised a soil naturally rich and productive, but inevitably weakened by a system which drained without
renewing the gifts of nature. When those splendid and untiring spirits
which count so eminently in his earlier work died, as in the course of
nature they could not but die away, it would have given him in their
stead a second harvest, less easy to gather perhaps, and less alluring to
the eye, but of larger grain and mellower growth. . . . That Dickens's
acquaintance with any kind of literature was extremely superficial even
Mr Forster is obliged to confess; and though that thorough-going
friend has sought to show that Dickens's judgments on such literature
as he had read were sound, he does not really prove much more than
that he had read very little. No doubt the influence of his great fore-
runners, Fielding and Smollett, may be detected in his writings—of
Goldsmith, the traces that Professor Ward discovers are hardly so
clear—but it seems to me that it was less the way in which they worked
that had influenced him than the material with which they worked. . . .

I have said that in *David Copperfield* Dickens is freer from defect than
in any other of his works. It is rarely that public opinion has ratified
an author's judgment so completely as it has here. As we all know, this
was Dickens's favourite, and the reason we all know. . . . But not in the
charm of autobiography alone lies the fascination which this delightful
book has exercised on every class of readers. It is not only Dickens's
most attractive work, but it is his best work. And it is his best for this
reason, that whereas in all his others he is continually striving to realise
the conception of his fancy, in this alone his business is to idealise the
reality; in this alone, as it seems to me, his imagination prevails over his
fancy. In this alone he is never grotesque, or for him so rarely that we
hardly care to qualify the adverb. Nowhere else is his pathos so tender

and so sure; nowhere else is his humour, though often more boisterous and more abundant, so easy and so fine; nowhere else is his observation so vivid and so deep; nowhere else has he held with so sure a hand the balance between the classes. If in the character of Daniel Pegotty more eloquently and more reasonably than he has ever done elsewhere, even in honest Joe Gargery, he has enlarged on his favourite abiding-place for virtue, he has also nowhere else been so ready and so glad to welcome her in those more seemly places wherein for the most part he can find no resting-place for her feet. Weak-minded as Doctor Strong is, fatuous, if the reader pleases, we are never asked to laugh at the kindly, chivalrous old scholar, as we are at Sir Leicester Dedlock; Clara Pegotty is no better woman than Agnes Wickfield. And even in smaller matters, and in the characters of second-rate importance, we may find the same sureness of touch. It has been made a reproach against him that his characters are too apt to be forgotten in the externals of their callings, that they never speak without some allusion to their occupations, and cannot be separated from them. In the extraordinary number and variety of characters that he has drawn, no doubt one can find instances of this. For so many of these characters, nearly all, indeed, of the comic ones, real as he has made them to us, are not, when we come to examine them, realities, but rather conceptions of his fancy, which he has to shape into realities by the use of certain traits and peculiarities of humanity with which his extraordinary observation has supplied him. Major Pendennis, and Costigan, and Becky Sharp *are* realities whom Thackeray idealises, makes characters of fiction out of. But Sam Weller and Mrs Gamp are the children of fancy whom Dickens makes real, partly by the addition of sundry human attributes, but even more so by the marvellous skill and distinctness with which he brings them and keeps them before us. But in order to do this he is obliged never to lose sight, or to suffer us to lose sight, of those peculiarities, whether of speech, or manner, or condition, which make them for us the realities that they are. And in so doing it cannot but happen that he seems to thrust those peculiarities at times somewhat too persistently upon us. In *David Copperfield* this is not so, or much less so that anywhere else, except, of course, in *The Tale of Two Cities*, Dickens's only essay at the romance proper, where the characters are subordinate to the story. We may see this, for example, by comparing Omer, the undertaker, in *David Copperfield*, with Mould, the undertaker, in *Martin Chuzzlewit*. Mould and all his family live in a perpetual atmosphere of funerals; his children are represented as solacing their young existences by 'playing at buryin's down in the shop, and follerin' the order-book to its long home in the iron safe;' and Mr Mould's own idea of fellowship is of a person 'one would almost feel disposed to bury for nothing, and do it neatly, too!' On his first introduction, after old Anthony's death, he sets the seal on his personality by the remark that Jonas's liberal orders for the funeral prove 'what was so forcibly observed by the lamented theatrical poet—*buried at Stratford*—that there is good in everything' [ch. xix]. That touch is very comical, but also very grotesque; it is a touch of fancy, not of nature. But when David Copperfield, as a man, recalls himself to the recollection of the good-hearted Omer, who had known him as a boy, the undertaker is revealed in a very different fashion. 'To be sure,' said Mr Omer, touching my waistcoat with his forefinger; 'and there was a little child too! *There was two parties. The little party was laid along with the other party.* Over at Blunderstone it was, of course. Dear me! And how have you been since?' [ch. xxi]. Every one must be conscious of the difference here.

'*Coragio*! and think of 2850,' wrote Macaulay in his diary, to console himself for some bitter pill of American criticism he had been forced to swallow. We need not cast our thoughts quite so far into the future to see that much of what gave Dickens his popularity, and still keeps it with so many of us, will avail him nothing then. Those qualities which so endeared his writings to the great mass of his contemporaries, and won the respect even of those who could not always admire the method and direction of their employment, will have for posterity no more attraction than will many of the subjects on which he so lavishly and dauntlessly expended them. Our descendants will have, we may be very sure, too frequent and too real claims upon their compassion to let them spare many tears for those rather theatrical personages which Dickens too often employed to point his moral. Harsh as it may seem to say, whatever his writings may actually have done to reduce the sum of human suffering will tell against rather than for them. It will always be so with those who employ fiction for the purpose of some particular social or political reformation; for the wrongs they help to remove, and the evils they help to redress, will seem slight and unreal in the pages of fiction, because they have so long ceased to form a part of actual existence. A soul of good-nature and kindness is a quality we are right to recognise in contemporary work, and for that work it consti- tutes a special and a noble title to our praise; but posterity will judge the writings of one whom their forefathers called a great writer by the sheer value of the writing, and such praise, if it be found to rest on no more practical foundation, will seem to them, to use the words of one of Dickens's own characters, pious, but not to the purpose. It is inevitable that much of his serious and sentimental work will have for future generations neither the attraction nor the solidity that it had for his own. For the tears he sought to draw, the graver feelings he sought to move, he went too often, if I may use the word, to local sources, too often to artificial. What Lamb said of comedy is surely true to a certain extent of all fiction: our 'fire-side concerns,' attractive as they are to us, cannot in reason have the same attraction for those who have never warmed themselves at our hearth. Each age has its own fireside; each age provides its own tears. The 'familiar matter of to-day' will not be the familiar matter of to-morrow. It is the splendid sorrows of a Priam or a Lear that touch the heart of Time. . . .

But the quality of a humour founded in the roots of our common humanity can never wax old nor die, and it seems impossible to imagine a day when the world will refuse to laugh with Dickens. The careless glance of curiosity, or the student's all-ranging eye, may turn a century hence upon the little Nells and Pauls, the Joes and the Trotty Vecks; but the Wellers and the Pecksniffs, the Swivellers and the Micawbers must surely abide for ever, unchanging and immortal—immortals of lesser note, and with more of mortal mixture, but still of the same lineage with Falstaff. And then with the laughter that they stir will be remembered and confessed the real worth of the noble praise Dean Stanley gave to their creator's memory, praise whose significance our own age has in truth too ample means for judging:

Remember, if there be any who think you cannot be witty without being wicked; who think that in order to amuse the world, and to awaken the interest of hearers or readers, you must descend to filthy jests, and unclean suggestions, and debasing scenes, so wrote not the genial loving humorist we now mourn. However deep his imagination led him to descend into the dregs of society, he still breathed an untainted atmosphere around him; he was still able to show by his own example that, even in dealing with the darkest scenes and most degraded characters, genius could be clean and mirth decent.

168. Henry James on Dickens: 'no other debt in our time has been piled so high'

1913, 1914

These passages from James (1843–1916) were written later than the period to which this anthology has been confined. My excuse for including them—apart from the eminence of his name, the charm of his writing, and the felicity (as an *envoi* to this book) of the final sentence quoted here—must be that they come from his auto-biographies, and recall responses from the 1850s and 1860s. Notable in (*a*) is the admixture, in James's (as in other readers') imaginative apprehension of Dickens, of memories of dramati-zations and the original illustrations; elsewhere, for instance, he recalls one of his teachers as 'remaining with me a picture of somebody in Dickens, one of the Phiz if not the Cruikshank pictures' (*Autobiographies*, ed. Frederick W. Dupee (1956), 117). (*b*) is a useful reminder of the effect that serialization had, in sophis-ticated circles as well as among more common readers ('I . . . could take the general civilized participation in the process for a sort of basking in the light of distinction', *ibid.*, 252, referring to 'the prolonged "coming-out" of *The Newcomes*', 1853–5). Inevitably, when establishing his own stand as a fiction-writer, James reacted strongly against Dickens's methods (see No. 131), but his later criticism has many generous references to him. In 1880, he declined to write the 'English Men of Letters' volume on Dickens, preferring to cherish his memories rather than to overhaul them critically (see (*a*)). See Ford, ch. xi, and H. Blair Rouse, 'Dickens and Henry James,' *Nineteenth-Century Fiction*, v (1950), 151–7.

(*a*) [James is recalling his childhood years in New York]

It was the age of the arrangements of Dickens for the stage, vamped-up promptly on every scene and which must have been the roughest theatrical tinkers' work, but at two or three of which we certainly assisted ... Isn't it [William Evans Burton, the actor and comedian] whom I remember as a monstrous Micawber, the coarse parody of a charming creation, with the entire baldness of an Easter egg and collar-points like the sails of Mediterranean feluccas? Dire of course for all temperance in these connections was the need to conform to the illustrations of Phiz, himself already an improvising parodist and happy only so long as not imitated, not literally reproduced. ...

The second definite matter in the Dickens connection is the Smike of Miss Weston ... in a version of *Nicholas Nickleby* that gracelessly managed to be all tearful melodrama, long-lost foundlings, wicked Ralph Nicklebys and scowling Arthur Grides, with other baffled villains, and scarcely at all Crummleses and Kenwigses, much less Squeerses, though there must have been something of Dotheboys Hall for the proper tragedy of Smike and for the broad Yorkshire dialect, a precious theatrical value, of John Browdie. The ineffaceability was the anguish, to my tender sense, of Nicholas's starved and tattered and fawning and whining protégé; in face of my sharp retention of which through all the years who shall deny the immense authority of the theatre, or that the stage is the mightiest of modern engines? Such at least was to be the force of the Dickens imprint, however applied, in the soft clay of our generation; it was to resist so serenely the wash of the waves of time. To be brought up thus against the author of it, or to speak at all of the dawn of one's early consciousness of it and of his presence and power, is to begin to tread ground at once sacred and boundless, the associations of which, looming large, warn us off even while they hold. He did too much for us surely ever to leave us free— free of judgment, free of reaction, even should we care to be, which heaven forbid: he laid his hand on us in a way to undermine as in no other case the power of detached appraisement. We react against other productions of the general kind without 'liking' them the less, but we somehow liked Dickens the more for having forfeited half the claim to appreciation. That process belongs to the fact that criticism, round-about him, is somehow futile and tasteless. His own taste is easily impugned, but he entered so early into the blood and bone of our intelligence that it always remained better than the taste of overhauling him. When I take him up to-day and find myself holding off, I simply stop: not holding off, that is, but holding on, and from the very fear to do so; which sounds, I recognise, like perusal, like renewal, of the scantest. I don't renew, I wouldn't renew for the world; wouldn't, that is, with one's treasure so hoarded in the dusty chamber of youth, let in the intellectual air. Happy the house of life in which such chambers still hold out, even with the draught of the intellect whistling through the passages. We were practically contemporary, contemporary with the issues, the fluttering monthly numbers—that was the point; it made for us a good fortune, constituted for us in itself romance, on which nothing, to the end, succeeds in laying its hands.

The whole question dwells for me in a single small reminiscence, though there are others still: that of my having been sent to bed one evening, in Fourteenth Street, as a very small boy, at an hour when, in the library and under the lamp, one of [my] elder cousins ... had begun to read aloud to my mother the new, which must have been the first, instalment of *David Copperfield*. I had feigned to withdraw, but had only retreated to cover close at hand, the friendly shade of some screen or drooping table-cloth, folded up behind which and glued to the carpet, I held my breath and listened. I listened long and drank deep while the wondrous picture grew, but the tense cord at last snapped under the strain of the Murdstones and I broke into the sobs of sympathy that disclosed my subterfuge. I was this time effectively banished, but the ply then taken was ineffaceable. I remember indeed just afterwards finding the sequel, in especial the vast extrusion of the Micawbers, beyond my actual capacity; which took a few years to grow adequate—years in which the general contagious consciousness, and our own household response not least, breathed heavily through *Hard Times*, *Bleak House* and *Little Dorrit*; the seeds of acquaintance with *Chuzzlewit* and *Dombey and Son*, these coming thickly on, I had found already sown. I was to feel that I had been born, born to a rich awareness, under the very meridian; there sprouted in those years no such other crop of ready references as the golden harvest of *Copperfield*.

... [*Oliver Twist*] perhaps even seemed to me more Cruikshank's than Dickens's; it was a thing of such vividly terrible images, and all marked with that peculiarity of Cruikshank that the offered flowers or goodnesses, the scenes and figures intended to comfort and cheer, present themselves under his hand as but more subtly sinister, or more suggestively queer, than the frank badnesses and horrors. The nice people and the happy moments, in the plates, frightened me almost as much as the low and the awkward ... The Dickens of those years was ... the great actuality of the current imagination. ... (*A Small Boy and Others* (New York, 1913), in *Autobiographies* (1956), 65–70)

(b) [James is recalling the thrilling monthly arrival of the opening numbers of the *Cornhill* (established 1860), and of the serial parts of novels.]

To speak of these things, in truth, . . . is to feel the advantage of being able to live back into the time of the more sovereign periodical appearances much of a compensation for any reduced prospect of living forward. For these appearances, these strong time-marks in such stretches of production as that of Dickens, that of Thackeray, that of George Eliot, had in the first place simply a genial weight and force, a direct importance, and in the second a command of the permeable air and the collective sensibility, with which nothing since has begun to deserve comparison. (*Notes of a Son and Brother* (New York, 1914), in *Autobiographies*, 251)

(c) [James recalls meeting Dickens in Boston, in 1867. In a 1905 note-book, too, he records 'the reminiscences of that night with Dickens, and the *emotion*, abiding, that it left with me. How it *did* something for my thought of him and his work . . .' (*Notebooks*, ed. F. O. Matthiessen and Kenneth B. Murdoch (New York, 1947), 319).]

As a young person of twenty-four, I took part, restrictively yet exaltedly, in that occasion—and an immense privilege I held it to slip in at all—from after dinner on; at which stage of the evening I presented myself . . . for the honour of introduction to the tremendous guest. How tremendously it had been laid upon young persons of our generation to feel Dickens, down to the soles of our shoes, no more modern instance that I might try to muster would give, I think, the least measure of; I can imagine no actual young person of my then age, and however like myself, so ineffably agitated, so mystically moved, in the presence of any exhibited idol of the mind who should be in that character at all conceivably 'like' the author of *Pickwick* and of *Copperfield*. There has been since his extinction no corresponding case—as to the relation between benefactor and beneficiary, or debtor and creditor; no other debt in our time has been piled so high, for those carrying it, as the long, the purely 'Victorian' pressure of that obligation. (*Notes of a Son* . . ., in *Autobiographies*, 388)

APPENDIX I

The Sales of Dickens's Works
by Robert L. Patten

Sales of Dickens's writings varied considerably throughout his career. *Pickwick* (1836–37) began with a printing of 1000 copies, 400 of which were bound up for sale; and the initial impression of Part II was reduced to 500.[1] Charles Tilt, the publisher, advised Chapman and Hall to send out 1500 copies of each of the early numbers to provincial booksellers on sale or return, but the returns averaged 1450.[2] However, after the introduction of Sam Weller in Part IV, sales sky-rocketed, reaching 14 000 by Part XII,[3] 20 000 by Part XIV, 26 000 by Part XVII, 29 000 by Part XVIII,[4] and nearing 40 000 by the end of its run.[5] Its popularity extended far afield: *Pickwick* was published in Philadelphia, New York, Paris, Leipzig, Calcutta, and Van Diemen's Land by 1838, and parodied in Mauritius by 1839. And the demand multiplied in succeeding years: above 31 000 copies of the Cheap Edition (1847) were sold in the first year;[6] by 1863, 140 000 copies in all had been sold;[7] and by the end of 1878, 1 600 000 in England and America combined.[8] When the copyright expired, eleven new English publishers rushed into the market with versions, yet Chapman and Hall, who themselves printed eleven separate editions, managed to sell 521 750 of them between 1872 and 1892.[9]

Bentley's Miscellany, in which *Oliver Twist* appeared (1837–39), sold over 6000 per month,[10] rising to 7500 in January 1838.[11] Before its completion in the magazine *Oliver* was issued in three volumes at the reduced price of 25s, selling out its first printing of perhaps 2000 copies within a month.[12] As the initial title in the Household Edition (1871–79), divided into weekly numbers and monthly parts, it sold 150 000 penny numbers in three weeks.[13] The purchase of 50 000 copies of the first Part of *Nicholas Nickleby* (1838–39) 'was the supreme and striking confirmation of *Pickwick*'s triumph';[14] the novel yielded profits of £14 000, equal to those from *Pickwick*, '*upon the numbers and without the sale in books*.'[15] By 1863 Chapman and Hall had distributed a hundred thousand *Nicklebys*.[16] The first impression (60 000) of the weekly *Master Humphrey's Clock* (1840–41) was entirely subscribed before publication day, 4 April, and orders for 10 000 more were in hand.[17] Sales of the second number slumped, perhaps by as much as 20 000,[18] and fell still further with the third, prompting Dickens to abandon its miscellaneous contents in favour of a continued story, *The Old Curiosity Shop* (1840–41), which proved so popular that the circulation rebounded to 100 000 during its final instalments.[19] The novel that followed, *Barnaby Rudge* (1841), failed to sustain this readership, plunging sales to around 30 000.[20]

Economic depression, social turbulence, political instability, and a flood of cheap publications hurt most publishers during the early 1840s: in 1839 John Murray II, 'The Emperor of the West', 'found it absolutely necessary to withdraw from the Printers every work' that he had in the press.[21] Nonetheless, *American Notes* (1842), helped by enraged reviews and several cheap editions priced at six cents a copy, sold briskly in America—50 000 in two days, 3000 in half an hour[22]—while in England 3000 copies were subscribed by the trade a week before publication, orders 'much larger than have ever been known since Scott's time', Dickens told his sister Fanny,[23] and four editions were required within two months.[24] *Martin Chuzzlewit* (1843–44) could scarcely have come out at a worse time: in 1843 Richard Bentley saw the circulation of his *Miscellany* drop by two-thirds, and one of his literary advisers, R. H. Barham, reported that only one novel in three was paying its way.[25] Though *Chuzzlewit* did that, its sales, beginning at a little over 20 000, and rising 2000 more on the announcement that Martin would go to America,[26] netted too little to repay money Chapman and Hall had advanced Dickens in 1841–42 on security of its profits. William Hall's mere suggestion that £50 might have to be deducted from Dickens's £200 monthly stipend and applied to reducing the debt so infuriated him that he determined to ask Bradbury and Evans to act as his publishers as well as printers. This resolution was confirmed when the first edition of *A Christmas Carol* (1843)—begun, Forster says, 'with but the special design of adding something to the *Chuzzlewit* balance',[27] and published by Chapman and Hall on commission—yielded a net profit of only £186 on 6000 copies, and but £726 on 14 930 copies to 31 December 1844.[28] Bradbury and Evans's Christmas books fared somewhat better: *The Chimes* (1844) sold at least 20 000 yielding £1400 to £1500 profits;[29] *The Cricket on the Hearth* (1845) 'at the outset doubled [the sales] of both its predecessors';[30] *The*

APPENDIX I

Battle of Life (1846), sold 24 450 by the end of the year, £1281 15s 4d as Dickens's share; *The Haunted Man* (1848), 17 776 to 31 December, £793 5s 11d profits to Dickens.

The new publishers, 'very anxious to know what [Dickens] thought of their management' of the *Chimes*, were relieved to hear that he 'was greatly pleased', and thought them 'the men for me to work with'.[31] For the next fourteen years (1844–58) they published all of Dickens's new work, starting with the successful and profitable *Dombey and Son* (1846–48), which was 'out of print on the first night',[32] and sustained a circulation of nearly 33 000. The expectation of an equally large sale of *David Copperfield* (1849–50) was disappointed, however, the later numbers barely reaching 20 000. As '*Chuzzlewit* with its small sale sent me up,' Dickens told Forster, '*Dombey's* [*sic*] large sale has tumbled me down.'[33] Sales of *Copperfield's* back numbers were the strongest of any of Dickens's work, however, and later editions did very well: better than 83 000 of the Household Edition (1872) were taken.[34] *Bleak House* (1852–53), which Dickens believed was sent up again by *Copperfield's* high reputation,[35] repeated *Dombey's* success, attaining an average circulation in excess of 34 000; and in America it was estimated that before the end of 1853 not less than a quarter of a million copies had been supplied in magazines, newspapers, and books.[36] Of *Little Dorrit* I (1855–57) over 36 000 were sold, but by the end only about 29 000 parts were being stitched into wrappers. *Household Words* (1850–59) had at best an average weekly sale of 40 000, but this declined steeply in the autumn of 1853.[37] Dickens countered with *Hard Times* (1854), which at least doubled its circulation;[38] the Christmas number sold 80 000 by 3 January 1855.[39]

Sales of *All the Year Round* (1859–70), opened by *A Tale of Two Cities* (1859), 'treble[d] that now relinquished in *Household Words*'.[40] The novel appeared simultaneously in eight as seven monthly parts at 1s, but this experiment was so unpopular that Chapman and Hall, to whom Dickens returned in 1858, printed only 5000 copies each of the last five numbers. A year later *Great Expectations* (1860–61) stopped the flight of subscribers bored by the journal's serialization of Charles Lever's *A Day's Ride*. The 1866 Christmas number, containing *Mugby Junction*, evidently exhausted its printing of 265 000;[41] and sales of the magazine approached 300 000 by Dickens's death.[42]

The last twenty-monthly-number novel, *Our Mutual Friend* (1864–65), though it started bravely with a press run of 40 000, lost half its buyers. But *Edwin Drood* (1870), designed for twelve monthly parts, '*very, very far outstripped every one of its predecessors*',[43] reaching 50 000 of Part I.[44]

During his lifetime, Dickens also authorized and supervised four collected editions of his works. The early volumes of the Cheap Edition (first series, 1847–52) also came out in $1\frac{1}{2}d$ weekly numbers, and in $7d$ monthly parts, composed of four numbers sewn in wrappers.[45] About 8 500 000 numbers, over 40 000 complete sets, of the works from *Sketches by Boz* through the Christmas books were sold in this series by 1870. The second series, the novels from *Dombey* to *Dorrit*, appeared, in volumes only, between 1858 and 1861; and a third series in volumes began in the 1860s; approximately 80 000 of these volumes were distributed by Dickens's death. The Library Edition (1858–63) was not at first profitable, but when in 1861 illustrations were added, sales soared, converting Chapman and Hall's deficit balance to a net profit in six months. The People's Edition, launched in 1865 for distribution through railway bookstalls, sold above 380 000 volumes, better than 15 000 sets, in five years. Of the Charles Dickens Edition (begun in 1867) over half a million volumes, nearly 30 000 sets, were bought by June 1870. In the twelve years after Dickens's death, 4 239 000 volumes had been bought in England alone.[46] Between 1846 and 1870, his annual earnings from his writings, exclusive of the two journals, averaged just over £2900, substantial receipts, but hardly entitling him to the nickname bestowed by one journal of 'a literary Croesus.'[47]

APPENDIX I

REFERENCES

[1] Thomas Hatton and Arthur H. Cleaver, *A Bibliography of the Periodical Works of Charles Dickens* (1933), 6.

[2] Frederic G. Kitton, *The Novels of Charles Dickens* (1897), 9.

[3] *Pilgrim*, i, 238 and n. 2.

[4] Taken from the headings of '*The Pickwick Advertiser*'.

[5] *Life*, 302.

[6] Edward Chapman to Charles Dickens, 23 March 1848, bound in with MS Account Books, Forster Collection, Victoria and Albert Museum, quoted by permission, and printed in Gerald G. Grubb, 'Some Unpublished Correspondence of Dickens and Chapman and Hall', *Boston University Studies in English*, i (1955), 106. Unless otherwise stated, all subsequent figures derive from these accounts.

[7] 'The Circulation of Modern Literature', Supplement to *Spectator*, 3 January 1863, 17.

[8] Anthony Trollope, 'Novel-Reading', *Nineteenth Century*, January 1879, v. 33.

[9] *Publishers' Circular*, 2 July 1892, 6; 13 August 1892, 161.

[10] Edgar Johnson, *Charles Dickens: His Tragedy and Triumph* (1953), i, 188.

[11] *Pilgrim*, i, 402 n. 3.

[12] Kathleen Tillotson, 'Introduction', *Oliver Twist* (Oxford, 1966), xxiv–xxvi.

[13] *P.C.*, 15 July 1871, 426; cf. Anthony Trollope, *Letters*, ed. Bradford A. Booth (1951), No. 485, showing that a sale of 200 000 was anticipated.

[14] Sylvère Monod, *Dickens the Novelist* (Norman, Oklahoma, 1967), 141.

[15] *Pilgrim*, i, 570.

[16] 'The Circulation of Modern Literature', 17.

[17] *Life*, 158.

[18] William M. Thackeray, *The Letters and Private Papers*, ed. Gordon N. Ray (1945–6), i, 444 and n. 65. The letter, No. 162 to Mrs Carmichael-Smyth, was written during the first week in May 1840, so the reference to the *Clock*'s selling 50 000 may, despite Professor Ray's note, be to a later number.

[19] Kitton, *op. cit.*, 64.

[20] Johnson, *op. cit.*, i, 345.

[21] George Paston, *At John Murray's 1843–1892* (1932), 25.

[22] Meade Minnigerode, *The Fabulous Forties* (New York, 1924), 284.

[23] To Mrs Henry Burnett, [October 1842] (*Nonesuch*, i, 482.)

[24] Johnson, i, 443.

[25] Royal A. Gettmann, *A Victorian Publisher* (Cambridge, 1960), 23.

[26] *Life*, 302.

[27] *Life*, 299.

[28] *Life*, 315.

[29] To Thomas Mitton, 14 April 1845 (*Nonesuch*, i, 671).

[30] *Life*, 380.

[31] To Mitton, 14 April 1845 (*Nonesuch*, i, 671).

[32] *Coutts*, 88.

[33] *Life*, 509.

[34] *P.C.*, 9 December 1872, 807.

[35] To W. F. de Cerjat, 8 May 1852 (*Nonesuch*, ii, 394).

[36] H[enry] C. Carey, *Letters on International Copyright* (Philadelphia, 1853), 59.

[37] Johnson, ii, 946, and William E. Buckler, 'Dickens's Success with *Household Words*', *Dickensian*, xlvi (1950), 198–9.

[38] *Life*, 565, and Buckler, *loc. cit.*, 200 n. 6.

[39] *To* de Cerjat, 3 January 1855 (*Nonesuch*, ii, 615).
[40] *Household Words*, 28 May 1859, xix, 601.
[41] *To* W. H. Wills, 24 January 1867 (*Nonesuch*, iii, 504).
[42] *Life*, 674.
[43] *To* James T. Fields, 18 April 1870 (*Nonesuch*, iii, 771).
[44] *Life*, 807 n., and Arthur Waugh, *A Hundred Years of Publishing* (1930), 134–5.
[45] Simon Nowell-Smith, 'The "Cheap Edition" of Dickens's Works [First Series] 1847–52', *The Library*, 5th ser., xxii (1967), 245–51.
[46] See above, opening of Mowbray Morris's essay (No. 167).
[47] Quoted in Carey, *op. cit.*, 37.

APPENDIX II

Authorship of Anonymous Items: Evidence for Attributions

Much the most important source has of course been *The Wellesley Index to Victorian Periodicals 1824–1900*. Only Volume I has so far appeared (1966), which covers these journals: *Blackwood's, Contemporary Review, Cornhill Magazine, Edinburgh Review, Home and Foreign Review, Macmillan's Magazine, North British Review, Quarterly Review.*

The Editor, Professor Walter E. Houghton, and his colleagues have, however, kindly given me the authorship of items from the following journals too, when they know it: *Dublin Review, Dublin University Magazine, Fraser's Magazine, Monthly Chronicle, New Monthly Magazine, Rambler, Tait's Edinburgh Magazine, Temple Bar, [London and] Westminster Review.*

The Wellesley Index will also cover some other monthly and quarterly journals, but the editorial staff has not yet begun to work on these, so could not answer enquiries about them.

Other sources of evidence were, for the following journals:

Athenaeum: Leslie A. Marchand, '*The Athenaeum*' (Chapel Hill, 1940).

Examiner: except for one item, John Forster's authorship of the reviews of Dickens can be established only by internal evidence. I have argued that this is conclusive, in 'Dickens's Self-estimate: some new Evidence' (see Bibliography).

Household Words: unpublished office 'Contributors' Book', now in the Parrish Collection, Princeton University Library; typescript copy at Dickens House, 48 Doughty Street, London WC1.

Saturday Review: Merle Mowbray Bevington, '*The Saturday Review*' *1855–1868* (New York, 1941).

Times: The History of '*The Times*', vol. ii (1939).

The present staffs of the following journals kindly answered my enquiries, though usually unable to find any evidence: *Atlantic Monthly, British Medical Journal, Economist, Illustrated London News, Punch, Spectator,* and *Sunday Times.* I mention this, not only to thank the archivists and librarians who answered my letters, but also to save them from further fruitless enquires about the same items.

Evidence for attributions not covered by the sources named above is given in the headnote to the item.

Bibliography

Place of publication London, unless otherwise stated. This list does not include items already cited in the headnotes (about individual novels or reviewers), nor items about periodicals cited in Appendix II.

ANDERSON, JOHN P., Bibliography, appended to Frank T. Marzials, *Charles Dickens* (1887), pp. i–xxxii.

BARWICK, G. F., 'The Magazines of the Nineteenth Century', *Transactions of the Bibliographical Society*, ix (1909–11), 237–49.

BOEGE, FRED W., 'Recent Criticism of Dickens', *Nineteenth-Century Fiction*, viii (1953), 171–87.

CALHOUN, PHILO and HOWELL J. HEANEY, 'Dickensiana in the Rough', *Papers of the Bibliographical Society of America*, xli (1947), 293–320. Also reprinted separately (New York, 1947). A criticism of Miller's *Dickens Student* (*below*). Includes a bibliography of sources.

COCKSHUT, A. O. J., 'Dickens Criticism', *Critical Survey*, iv (1964), 229–31.

COLBY, ROBERT A., '"How it strikes a Contemporary": the *Spectator* as Critic', *Nineteenth-Century Fiction*, ii (1956), 182–206.

COLLINS, PHILIP. 'Charles Dickens', *New Cambridge Bibliography of English Literature*, ed. George Watson, vol. iii (Cambridge, 1969), cols. 779–850. Reprinted separately, as *A Dickens Bibliography* (1970).

—— 'Dickens's Self-estimate: some new Evidence', in *Dickens the Craftsman: Strategies of Presentation*, ed. Robert B. Partlow (Carbondale, Illinois, 1970), 21–43. Forster's reviews of Dickens in the *Examiner*.

CROTCH, W. WALTER, 'The Decline [in Dickens's reputation] and After', *Dickensian*, xv (1919), 121–7.

CRUSE, AMY, *The Victorians and their Books* (1935), ch. viii.

DELATTRE, FLORIS, *Dickens et la France* (Paris, 1927).

DEVONSHIRE, M. S., *The English Novel in France 1830–1870* (1929).

DIBELIUS, WILHELM, *Charles Dickens* (Leipzig, 1916). Extensive bibliography appended.

Dickensian, 1905– (continuing). Numerous contemporary reviews, tributes, etc., reprinted. Index, 1905–34 (1935), 1935–60 (1961).

DYSON, A. E., ed., *Dickens: Modern Judgments* (1968). Useful Introduction, surveying Dickens-criticism, past and present.

ELLEGÅRD, ALVAR, *The Readership of the Periodical Press in mid-Victorian Britain* (Göteborg, 1957).

FIELDING, K. J., *Charles Dickens: a Survey* (1953, revised 1960, 1963).

—— 'Dickens and the Critics', *Dickensian*, lviii (1962), 150–1.

FINLAY, IAN F., 'Dickens's influence on Dutch Literature', *Dickensian*, liii (1957), 40–2.

FLAMM, DUDLEY, *Thackeray's Critics: an Annotated Bibliography of British and American Criticism 1836–1891* (Chapel Hill, 1967). The Index refers to over 70 comparisons between Dickens and Thackeray.

FORD, GEORGE H., *Dickens and his Readers: Aspects of Novel-criticism since 1836* (Princeton, 1955).

—— and LAURIAT LANE, Jr., eds., *The Dickens Critics* (Ithaca, 1961). Contains 'A Checklist of Dickens Criticism (1840–1960)'.

FORSTER, JOHN, *Life of Charles Dickens* (1872–4), ed. J. W. T. Ley (1928).

FRIDLENDER, Y. V. and I. M. KATARSKY, *Charles Dikkens: Bibliografya russkikh . . . 1838–1960* (Moscow, 1962). Summary in English, pp. 25–7.

GARIS, ROBERT, 'Dickens criticism', *Victorian Studies*, vii (1964), 375–86.

GIBSON, FRANK A., 'Dickens and Germany', *Dickensian*, xlii (1947), 69–74.

GIFFORD, HENRY, 'Dickens in Russia: the initial phase', *Forum for Modern Language Studies*, iv (1968), 45–52.

GILENSON, BORIS, 'Dickens in Russia', *Dickensian*, lvii (1961), 56–8.

GRAHAM, KENNETH, *English Criticism of the Novel 1865–1900* (Oxford, 1965).

GRAHAM, WALTER, *English Literary Periodicals* (New York, 1930).

GROSS, JOHN, 'Dickens: some recent approaches', in *Dickens and the Twentieth Century*, ed. John Gross and Gabriel Pearson (1962). Also, in the same volume, Gabriel Pearson, 'Dickens: the present position'.

GUMMER, ELLIS M., 'Dickens and Germany', *Modern Language Review*, xxxiii (1938), 240–7.

—— *Dickens's Works in Germany 1837–1937* (Oxford, 1940).

HAMMERTON, J. A., ed., *The Dickens Companion* (1910). Vol. xviii of the 'Charles Dickens Library' edition of the *Works*. Extracts from many contemporary reviews, etc.

HOLLINGSWORTH, KEITH, *The Newgate Novel 1830–1847: Bulwer, Ainsworth, Dickens and Thackeray* (Detroit, 1963).

HOUTCHENS, CAROLYN W. and LAURENCE H., 'Contributions of early American journals to the study of Dickens', *Modern Language Quarterly*, vi (1945), 211–17.

JAMES, LOUIS, *Fiction for the Working Man 1830–1850* (1963). Ch. iv, 'Plagiarisms of Dickens'.

JOHNSON, EDGAR, *Charles Dickens: his Tragedy and Triumph* (2 vols., 1953). The standard biography.

JUMP, J. D., 'Weekly Reviewing in the Eighteen-Fifties' and 'in the Eighteen-Sixties', *Review of English Studies*, xxiv (1948), 42–57; n.s. iii (1952), 244–62.

KATARSKY, I. M., *Dikkens v Rossii: seredina xix veka* [Dickens in Russia: middle of the 19th century] (Moscow, 1966). See account by Henry Gifford, *Dickensian*, lxiii (1967), 120–2.

KITTON, FREDERIC G., *Dickensiana: a Bibliography of the Literature relating to Charles Dickens and his Writings* (1886). Many extracts reprinted. See addenda, by Charles F. Carty, *The Literary Collector*, v (1902–3), 12–14, 43–6.

——, ed., *Dickens by Pen and Pencil* (with Supplement, 1890).

LANE, LAURIAT, Jr., 'Dickens Studies 1958–1968: an Overview', *Studies in the Novel*, i (1969), 240–54. See also J. Van Dann, 'A Checklist of Dickens Criticism, 1963–1967', *ibid.*, 255–78.

MAURICE, ARTHUR B., 'Famous Novels and their Contemporary Critics', *Bookman* (New York), xvii (1903), 130–8. Discusses *American Notes, Chuzzlewit, Tale of Two Cities*.

MILLER, WILLIAM, *The Dickens Student and Collector: a List of Writings relating to Charles Dickens and his Works 1836–1945* (1946; supplements, privately printed, Brighton 1947, Hove 1953). See *above*, Calhoun and Heaney.

NISBET, ADA C., 'Charles Dickens', in *Victorian Fiction: a Guide to Research*, ed. Lionel Stevenson (Cambridge, Mass., 1964).

NOLIN, JOSEPH, 'The Appreciation of Dickens by his French Contemporaries', *Dickensian*, xxiii (1927), 235–9.

PEYROUTON, NOEL C., ed., *Dickens Criticism: Past, Present, and Future Directions: a Symposium* (Boston, 1962). See K. J. Fielding, *Dickensian*, lix (1963), 73–7.

PHILLIPS, WALTER C., *Dickens, Reade, and Collins: Sensation Novelists* (New York, 1919).

PIERSON, WILLIAM C., 'The Reaction against Dickens', in his *English Novel in Transition 1885–1940* (Norman, Oklahoma, 1942).

RANTAVAARA, IRMA, *Dickens in the Light of English Criticism* (Helsinki, 1944).

SENELICK, LAURENCE, 'Charl'z Dikkens and the Russian Encyclopædias', *Dickens Studies*, i (1965), 129–44.

SLATER, MICHAEL, ed., *Dickens and Fame 1870–1970: Essays on the Author's Reputation* (Centenary Number of the *Dickensian*, lxvi (1970), 73–200). Essays by K. J. Fielding, Sylvère Monod, Michael Slater, Philip Collins and George Ford.

SMITH, MABELL S. C., ed., *Studies in Dickens* (New York, 1910). Reprints contemporary reviews, etc.

STANG, RICHARD, *The Theory of the Novel in England 1850–1870* (1959).

SUMMERS, MONTAGUE, 'Dickens and the Decadent', *Dickensian*, xliii (1967), 61–4.

TILLOTSON, GEOFFREY and DONALD HAWES, eds., *Thackeray: the Critical Heritage* (1968). Numerous comparisons with Dickens.

TOMLIN, E. W. F., 'Dickens's Reputation: a Reassessment', in *Charles Dickens 1812–1870: a Centenary Volume*, ed. E. W. F. Tomlin (1969), 237–63.

TRILLING, LIONEL, 'The Dickens of our day', in his *A Gathering of Fugitives* (1957).

VERKOREN, L., 'Dickens in Holland', *Dickensian*, lv (1959), 44–6.

WILSON, R. A., 'Translations of the works of Dickens', *British Museum Quarterly*, xiv (1940), 59–60.

WOLFF, MICHAEL, 'Victorian Reviewers and Cultural Responsibility', in *1859: Entering an Age of Crisis*, ed. Philip Appleman *et al* (Bloomington, 1959).

ZABEL, MORTON D., 'Dickens: the Reputation revised', in his *Craft and Character in Modern Fiction* (1957).

Index

The Index is divided into three sections: I. Charles Dickens: writings; II. Charles Dickens: characteristics of his work, his personality, and his reception; III. General (includes authors, periodicals, etc.). Characters, etc., in C.D.'s novels are indexed under the story in which they appear. Works by other authors are indexed under the authors' names.

I. CHARLES DICKENS: WRITINGS

All the Year Round, 402, 408–20, 421, 427, 430, 432–3, 596, 598, 619

American Notes, 11, 13, 118–39, 140, 169, 171, 618, 627

Barnaby Rudge, 91, 92, 101–11, 169, 229, 254, 258, 262, 332, 334, 482, 484, 488, 554, 582, 587–8, 605, 618

Battle of Life, The, 145, 147, 154, 176, 178–9, 219, 265, 587, 619

Bleak House, 14, 15, 272–99, 303, 333, 359, 362, 386, 409, 469, 479, 480, 482, 484, 496–7, 550, 554, 562, 583, 603, 619; Bucket, 273, 279, 286, 288, 292, 323; Chadband, 272, 297, 333–4, 462, 557–8, 592; Chancery, 196, 272, 273, 283–4, 291, 319, 346–7, 349, 369, 452, 511; Lady Dedlock, 278, 279, 286, 296, 496–7, 574; Esther, 273, 276–7, 285, 289, 291–2, 295, 334, 485–6, 498, 501, 554, 574; Jo, 273, 279, 286, 288, 291, 377, 611; Skimpole, 272, 274, 278, 287, 386, 505; spontaneous combustion, 272, 274–5, 277, 285, 296, 488

'Boots at the Holly-Tree Inn', 539

Child's History of England, A, 118, 402

Chimes, The, 11, 144–5, 146, 147, 150, 153–67, 168, 169, 172, 176, 211, 514, 581, 611, 618; Alderman Cute, 145, 156, 160, 169; Will Fern, 155, 158, 167

Christmas Carol, A, 2, 11, 144, 146, 147–50, 152–3, 155, 157, 162, 164, 169, 171, 176, 202, 354, 361, 505, 618; Tiny Tim, 145, 147, 150, 229, 377, 497, 525, 575, 585

Cricket on the Hearth, The, 12, 140, 145, 146, 147, 148, 154, 159, 174–6, 205, 210, 230, 501, 575, 618

David Copperfield, 212–13, 237, 242–69, 288, 333, 334, 359, 382, 481, 483, 488, 489, 490, 512, 537, 574, 575, 599, 606, 608–10, 614, 615, 619; C.D.'s masterpiece? 242, 319, 332, 337–8, 427, 482, 503, 510, 608; autobiographical origins, 242, 246, 333, 449, 522, 608; David, 327–8, 333, 449, 522, 579, 600; Micawber, 246–7, 260, 350, 386, 470, 565, 574, 575, 613; storm scene, 242, 247, 443, 538

Doctor Marigold's Prescriptions, 415–18, 419, 420

Dombey and Son, xvi, 120, 184, 212–34, 248, 261, 265, 332, 351, 359, 386, 443, 448n., 482, 486, 514, 547, 554, 599, 600, 606, 619; Carker,

II. CHARLES DICKENS: CHARACTERISTICS

exaggeration, extravagance, 50, 230,
239–40, 247, 257, 260, 276–8, 284–
6, 287, 308, 314, 338, 348, 351, 441,
444, 455, 480, 486, 591, 602. *See
also* caricature

fairytale elements, 84, 204, 235, 494,
578–9
foreigners, C.D. as a guide for, 30,
210–11, 236
French novelists, C.D. contrasted
with, 320–1, 339–42, 484–5. *See
also names of authors*
friend, C.D. seen as a, 1, 3–4, 114, 116,
228, 232, 244, 302, 335, 502, 506,
511, 515, 526

gentlemen: *see* aristocracy

heroes, 50–1, 88, 194, 199, 323, 327–8,
331, 449, 522, 552
heroines, 75, 83, 194, 263, 265, 332–3,
334, 396, 485, 490, 495, 501, 554,
580
humour, comedy, fun, 3, 18–19, 21,
30–2, 33–5, 52, 57, 111, 139–1,
193–4, 240, 288, 340, 358, 395,
400–1, 410, 427, 434, 438, 441, 443,
469–70, 474, 479, 483–4, 489, 491,
509, 519, 521, 535, 549–50, 552,
570–1, 580, 586, 590–1, 595, 601,
606–7, 610. *See also* wit

illustrations of his works, 9, 37, 59,
70, 71–2, 86, 87, 95, 96–7, 111, 141,
159, 161, 190, 227, 445, 612. *See
also names of illustrators*
imagination, fancy, 7, 21, 192, 240,
255–6, 337–8, 410–12, 429, 439, 470,
477, 478–83, 486, 493–4, 535–6, 540,
550, 571, 578–9, 586, 603, 606,
608–9. *See also* reality

influence, literary, 23–4, 34, 81–2, 93,
154, 177, 193, 326, 385, 399, 405–7,
410, 412, 431, 446–7, 475, 488–9,
507–8, 570
influence, moral and social: reformism, sense of purpose, 2, 3, 11–12,
24, 37, 73, 78, 80, 84, 93–4, 98, 99,
114, 132, 133, 153, 154, 156, 157–8,
162–3, 164–7, 180, 191, 199, 202,
205–6, 226, 229, 231, 235, 245, 248,
253–4, 257–8, 263, 275, 281, 301,
304, 323, 326, 343, 346–7, 357, 359,
378, 379–82, 385, 444–5, 467, 482,
489–91, 504–5, 508, 511, 512–13,
518, 524–5, 553, 555–7, 559, 567–8,
581, 596–7
influences, literary, upon C.D., 5–7,
32, 57, 59, 65, 72, 132–3, 201, 535,
608. *See also names of authors*
institutional status, 2, 15, 243–4, 329,
506
intellectual qualities and limitations,
118, 122, 125–7, 134, 149, 151, 180,
208, 214, 237, 251–4, 303–4, 315–18,
348–9, 391–2, 400, 409–10, 444, 448,
451–2, 472–3, 475, 479–80, 486,
498–501, 565, 576, 579, 582–3, 593,
607–8. *See also* philosophy, *and* range

law, presentation of the, 31–2, 54,
60–1, 74, 84, 346–7, 386, 369, 498
London, depiction of, 42, 49, 52, 60,
70, 75, 81, 90, 98, 100, 126, 152, 214,
343, 384, 393–4, 447, 460, 516,
539–40, 578
love, presentation of, 178, 194, 341,
367, 396, 468, 484–5, 490, 523,
543–4, 549

naming of characters, 180, 210–11,
407
narrative art, plots, 42, 50, 76, 84,
105–11, 278, 281, 351, 396, 424, 428,

narrative art, plots—*cont.*
456, 459, 465, 482, 494, 497, 510,
517, 531, 537–8, 545. *See also* unity,
artistic

painters, C.D. compared with, 5–6,
527. *See also names of painters, and*
Dutch painters
Parliament, presentation of, 121, 325,
346, 349, 583, 597
pastoral scenes, countryside, 52, 53,
60, 82, 92, 100, 103, 255, 339, 393
pathos, 14, 21, 42, 93, 131, 147, 155,
176, 198, 211, 212, 215, 216–18, 288,
296, 300, 302, 307, 321, 327, 335,
339, 344, 361, 383–4, 397, 415, 417,
471, 486, 497–8, 503, 522–3, 535,
551–2, 580–1, 601, 603, 610–11
period, C.D. belongs to his, 53, 201,
294, 340–1, 504, 512, 534–5, 594,
601–2. *See also* Reform era, *and*
topicality
philosophy, outlook, 65, 204, 235,
341–2, 384, 450, 473, 479, 493, 500–
1, 511, 526, 528, 546–7, 590, 593,
597–8. *See also* intellectual qualities
photographic qualities, 6, 190, 255,
284, 343, 350, 519
plots: *see* narrative art
poetical qualities, 131, 135, 149, 174–
5, 193, 218, 233–4, 252, 262, 265,
290, 362–3, 365, 425, 430, 482, 580
political economy, 163, 237, 301, 315–
16, 318, 376, 479
politics, 13, 78, 84, 116–17, 121, 122,
125n., 134, 146, 155–6, 158, 159,
172, 174, 205, 207, 210, 214, 273,
300, 318, 325, 327, 329, 344–9, 358,
361, 368–74, 375–7, 397–9, 411,
444, 447–8, 450–2, 462–3, 479, 493,
499, 505, 511, 526, 528, 531, 538,
553, 557, 582, 583, 589, 590, 593,
594, 596–7, 602

poor, the, concern for, presentation
of, 6, 29, 30, 35, 46, 60, 73, 81, 83,
85, 93, 98, 113–14, 117, 136, 145–6,
151, 153–67 *passim*, 173, 191, 207,
208, 235–6, 239, 279, 286, 291, 304,
305, 306–7, 317–18, 323, 335–6,
341–2, 343, 359, 393, 447–8, 450,
460, 516–17, 524, 528, 552, 602
popularity, 4–5, 15, 17–18, 48, 52,
56–7, 64–5, 69–70, 71–3, 81, 133–4,
136, 144, 150–1, 168, 173, 190, 205,
236, 243–4, 270, 275, 322, 323–4,
326, 383–4, 463, 492, 528, 533, 540,
555–6, 559, 563, 569–70, 575–6, 582,
595, 596, 599–600, 614–15; class-
less, universal, 18, 48, 64, 70, 244,
289, 290, 318, 324, 353, 382, 390,
502–3, 504, 506–7; international,
xvi, 4, 202, 203, 245, 382, 487, 502,
504, 599, 617, 625–8 (*and see also
under individual nations*)
posterity, its attitude to C.D. sur-
mised, 70, 173, 177, 202, 290, 303,
308, 384–5, 394, 452, 454, 492, 512,
552, 600, 601–2, 610; reputation
since 1880s, 17–21

range, 30, 52, 60, 72, 82–3, 100, 121,
125, 136n., 140, 169, 173, 174, 191,
214, 255, 286, 307, 367–8, 391–4,
409–10, 499, 518, 538–9, 564, 573
reality, 28, 30, 34, 37, 43, 48, 72, 128,
165, 232, 235, 236, 260, 276–7,
392–4, 417, 428–9, 461, 471, 477,
478, 493–4, 522, 535–6, 578–9. *See
also* imagination
Reform era, C.D. belongs to, 117,
132, 165–6, 239, 344–5, 380, 397–9,
447, 476–7, 534, 555
religion, depiction of, belief in, 12, 102,
119, 159, 160–1, 171, 191, 205, 254,
259, 294, 296–7, 333–6, 363, 411,
436–8, 511, 562, 568, 589, 594, 598

sales, 2, 4, 16–17, 36, 47, 70, 144, 145, 176, 182, 212, 324, 326, 402, 419, 432, 453, 465, 516, 587, 599, 602–3, 617–20

satire, 67, 72–4, 126, 195–6, 270–1, 285, 316–17, 348, 351, 374, 462–3, 475–6, 479–81, 507, 528, 602

sentiment, sentimentality, 43, 51, 73, 192–3, 265, 359, 417, 463, 490, 498, 511, 513. *See also* pathos

serialization: effects on C.D.'s art, 14, 76, 182, 264–5, 364, 423, 431, 468, 476, 516, 581; effects on his sales and readers, xvi, 2, 43, 47–8, 70, 101–2, 136–7, 227, 228, 233, 274, 280, 329, 362, 428, 431–3, 464, 515–16, 612, 614, 617–20

slang, 35, 39, 60, 70, 83, 187–9, 201, 244, 383

style, 3, 11, 18, 21, 26 (n. 36), 42, 48–9, 51, 54, 67–8, 72, 102, 122–3, 130–3, 135, 140–1, 142–3, 168, 170, 174–6, 181, 187–90, 193, 200–1, 209–10, 221, 226, 240–1, 245, 250–2, 262, 265–6, 295–6, 308, 324–5, 326, 350–2, 359, 364–5, 385, 391, 399–400, 406–7, 429, 464, 466, 482–4,

507, 517–18, 527–8, 540, 606. *See also* animism

symbolism, 21, 213, 222, 234

theatrical qualities, 30, 35, 94, 143, 284–5, 295, 308, 314, 362, 437, 444, 455, 496, 522, 527, 580, 585

topicality, ephemerality, 42, 43, 70, 72, 213, 215, 290, 368, 372–3, 404, 476. *See also* period

tragic qualities, 92, 163–4, 198, 225, 263, 330, 343, 361, 438, 485, 527, 559–60, 562, 567

unity, artistic, 7, 42, 50, 76–7, 95, 171, 182, 183, 187, 231, 264, 283–4, 288, 291, 302, 341, 394, 425, 429, 436, 538, 556, 603

visual qualities, descriptions, observation, 75–6, 77, 82, 131, 151, 185–6, 189–90, 228–9, 255, 273, 274, 293, 307, 330, 337–9, 359, 378, 380–1, 393–4, 443, 448, 478, 498, 511, 527, 571–2, 605–6. *See also* photographic qualities

wit, 31, 52, 82, 130, 173, 175–6, 294, 367, 395

III. GENERAL

Academy, 545–7

Acton, J. E. E. D. (1st Baron Acton), 2–3, 436–8

Addison, Joseph, 6, 57, 607

Administrative Reform Association, 357

Ainsworth, William Harrison, 8, 43, 45, 57, 93–4, 220, 350

Ainsworth's Magazine, 91, 118, 144, 183

Altick, Richard D., 17

America, United States of, C.D.'s reception in, xvi, 4, 16, 112–18, 130, 133–4, 206, 319, 506, 617, 619, 627

Annual Register, 453

Arnold, Matthew, 15, 16, 267–9

Athenaeum, 6, 10 (n. 25), 32–3, 94–8, 103–5, 145, 276–9, 300, 356, 421, 427, 453, 540, 623

Atlantic Monthly, 238, 315–21, 427, 428–30, 478–86, 580–1, 623

Austen, Jane, 19, 578